MUIRHEAD LIBRARY OF PHILOSOPHY

AN admirable statement of the aims of the Library of Philosophy was provided by the first editor, the late Professor H. J. Muirhead, in his desscription of the original programme printed in Erdmann's *History of Philosophy* under the date 1890. This was slightly modified in subsequent volumes to take the form of the following statement:

The Muirhead Library of Philosophy was designed as a contribution to the History of Modern Philosophy under the heads: first of different Schools of Thought—Sensationalist, Realist, Idealist, Intuitivist; secondly of different Subjects—Psychology, Ethics, Aesthetics, Political Philosophy, Theology. While much had been done in England in tracing the course of evolution in nature, history, economics, morals and religion, little had been done in tracing the development of thought on these subjects. Yet 'the evolution of opinion is part of the whole evolution'.

By the co-operation of different writers in carrying out this plan it was hoped that a thoroughness and completeness of treatment, otherwise unattainable, might be secured. It was believed also that from writers mainly British and American fuller consideration of English Philosophy than it had hitherto received might be looked for. In the earlier series of books containing, among others, Bosanquet's *History of Aesthetics*, Pfleiderer's *Rational Theology since Kant*. Albee's *History of English Utilitarianism*, Bonar's *Philosophy and Political Economy*, Brett's *History of Psychology*, Ritchie's *Natural Rights*, these objects were to a large extent effected.

In the meantime original work of a high order was being produced both in England and America by such writers as Bradley, Stout, Bertrand Russell, Baldwin, Urban, Montague and others, and a new interest in foreign works, German, French and Italian, which had either become classical or were attracting public attention, had developed. The scope of the Library thus became extended into something more international, and it is entering on the fifth decade of its existence in the hope that it may contribute to that mutual understanding between countries which is so pressing a need of the present time.

The need which Professor Muirhead stressed is no less pressing today, and few will deny that philosophy has much to do with enabling us to meet it, although no one, least of all Muirhead himself, would regard that as the sole, or even the main, object of philosophy. As Professor Muirhead continues to lend the distinction of his name to the Library of Philosophy, it seemed not inappropriate to allow him to recall us to these aims in his own words. The emphasis on the history of thought seemed to me also very timely; and the number of important works promised for the Library in the near future augur well for the continued fulfilment, in this and in other ways, of the expectations of the original editor.

H. D. LEWIS

THE MUIRHEAD LIBRARY OF PHILOSOPHY

General Editor: H. D. Lewis

Professor of History and Philosophy of Religion in the University of London

THE MUIRHEAD LIBRARY OF PHILOSOPHY—*contd.*

The Muirhead Library of Philosophy

EDITED BY H. D. LEWIS

THE NATURE OF THOUGHT

THE NATURE OF THOUGHT

By

BRAND BLANSHARD

Professor of Philosophy, Yale University

In Two Volumes

VOLUME ONE

LONDON: GEORGE ALLEN & UNWIN LTD
NEW YORK: HUMANITIES PRESS INC

FIRST PUBLISHED IN 1939
SECOND IMPRESSION 1948
THIRD IMPRESSION 1955
FOURTH IMPRESSION 1964
FIFTH IMPRESSION 1969

BRITISH SBN 04 153002 0

PRINTED IN GREAT BRITAIN
by Photolithography
BY JARROLD AND SONS LIMITED
NORWICH

To

Two Oxford Teachers

The late HAROLD HENRY JOACHIM

and

EDGAR FREDERICK CARRITT

This Book is Dedicated

in

Gratitude and Friendship

PREFACE

WHAT I have attempted in this book is an analysis of thought that will neither be instantly repudiated by the psychologist nor indignantly disowned by the metaphysician. That is a higher aspiration than some may think. Between the account of ideas and inference supplied by the psychologists, eager to construe their study as a natural science, and that of the epistemologist and logician, there has gradually appeared a chasm that is now all but impassable. This chasm, nevertheless, I have set myself to bridge. I have sought to show that for any adequate theory of ideas and the thought process, psychology and philosophy must supplement each other. On the one hand, to treat ideas as images, or reflexes, or acts, or mere psychical events, is to miss what is most essential in them; to treat the movement of inference as explicable by the laws of psychology, regarded as a natural science, is to be blind to the very springs of the movement. On the other hand, to treat thought in complete abstraction from its psychical setting, as is done so often in logic and the theory of knowledge, is also to miss something essential, namely that every achievement of thought, the best like the worst, is a matter of level and degree. In reading psychological accounts of ideas and their succession, one wonders at times how these odds and ends of imagery, motor set, and the like, ever yield us *knowledge* of anything. In reading philosophical accounts of universals, abstract and concrete, of pure necessities in inference, of coherent systems of 'thought', one wonders what the connection is between these Olympian forms and anything that seems to occur in one's own mind. This book attempts to work out the connection. I have tried to study the facts about ideas and reflective processes without forgetting that by far the most significant of these facts is that they are means to the end of knowledge.

The book has a curious history. In 1923, a public-spirited citizen of Detroit, Henry G. Stevens, asked the writer, then

on the staff of the University of Michigan, to make a study
and compendium for him of those results of recent psychology
which would be of most value to social workers. It soon
appeared that this had been repeatedly and well done already.
What had been much less adequately done was a study of
the interactions between intelligence and the other functions
of human nature; and with Mr. Stevens's encouragement and
assistance, I set to work in this field. Substantial progress had
been made when the award of a Guggenheim fellowship led
me once more to recast the project, limiting rather than
extending it. I was to find in the end that to examine very
imperfectly the single function of thought had taken two
volumes and the leisure of twelve years. Perhaps, in consequence of the delay, the result may be viewed with a somewhat
greater satisfaction. But it has cost me dear in another kind of
satisfaction, since three friends who helped in various ways
to make the book such as it is, and whom I should most wish
to have seen it, can do so no longer. One of these is Mr. Stevens
himself. A second is Professor Robert M. Wenley, who gave
me invaluable aid and friendship over a period of many years.
To the third, Professor H. H. Joachim, I have made acknowledgement in the dedication of this book. He was a teacher
whose fastidiousness of thought and scholarship, first felt
in my undergraduate days, has remained with me always as
an inward monitor, approving when I took due care, and
reproaching me gently, as his way was, when I thought or
wrote carelessly.

In a book produced piece by piece over a long period, it is
not unnatural that there should be differences in emphasis and
style. The emphasis of the earlier chapters on empirical psychology is gradually replaced by a more metaphysical interest,
which in the end becomes quite dominating. This change is due
in part to the demands of the subject-matter. But I think it is
also due in part to a certain advance in insight; the end toward
which the argument tended became steadily clearer to me as I
went on. I therefore attach a somewhat higher value to the later
and more speculative parts of the book than to the earlier. In

every part, however, the reader will find the course of the argument plainer if he makes free use of the detailed analysis in the table of contents. This may serve to make more evident what I hope is not obscure in the text, that the work is a sustained defence of a single conception of thought.

There are further debts that it is a pleasure to acknowledge. I hope it is generally known how much the Guggenheim Foundation is doing for younger American scholars in its capacity of nurse and midwife for their multifarious projects; I can only say that without its aid this work could not have been born. I owe a special debt to Frank Aydelotte, president of Swarthmore College, both for his unflagging personal interest in what I was doing, and for his wise and far-seeing efforts to create for his faculty the conditions of productive scholarship. Acknowledgement is due to the Warden and Fellows of Merton College, Oxford, for allowing me to work for some months in the seclusion of the Bradley Library. My colleague, Professor R. B. MacLeod, has rendered generous assistance by reading some of the earlier chapters in manuscript. The editors of the Library of Philosophy, Dr. J. H. Muirhead and Dr. J. E. Turner, have by their criticisms improved the work both in its proportions and in its details. Of my personal debts, however, the greatest is to my wife who, called upon to bear with my long preoccupation, has borne it not only unmurmuringly, but with encouragement unfailingly renewed.

B. B.

ACKNOWLEDGEMENTS

CITATIONS have been made from F. H. Bradley, *Principles of Logic* and *Essays on Truth and Reality*, from H. W. B. Joseph, *Introduction to Logic* and *The Concept of Evolution*, and from J. Cook Wilson, *Statement and Inference*, by permission of the Clarendon Press, Oxford; from W. James, *Principles of Psychology*, and W. Temple, *Nature, Man and God*, by permission of Macmillan & Co.; from C. D. Broad, *The Mind and Its Place in Nature*, K. Koffka, *Principles of Gestalt Psychology*, and H. Hankin, *Common Sense and Its Cultivation*, by permission of Kegan Paul, Trench, Trubner & Co.; from A. C. Ewing, *Idealism*, by permission of Methuen & Co., Ltd.; from Herbert Spencer, *Autobiography*, by permission of The Rationalist Press Association; from J. Ward, *Psychological Principles*, and J. M. E. McTaggart, *The Nature of Existence*, by permission of the Cambridge University Press; from Graham Wallas, *The Art of Thought*, by permission of Messrs. Jonathan Cape; from F. W. H. Myers, *Human Personality* by permission of the author's executors and of Longmans, Green & Co.; from J. L. Lowes, *The Road to Xanadu*, by permission of Constable & Co.; from C. I. Lewis, *Mind and the World Order*, by permission of Charles Scribner's Sons; from Lewis and Langford, *Symbolic Logic*, by permission of Appleton-Century; from B. Bosanquet, *Implication and Linear Inference*, W. K. Clifford, *Lectures and Essays*, and E. B. Titchener, *Experimental Psychology of the Thought Processes*, from Macmillan & Co. The author acknowledges the courtesy of these publishers with thanks.

ANALYTICAL TABLE OF CONTENTS

BOOK I

THOUGHT IN PERCEPTION

CHAPTER I

THE GENESIS OF PERCEPTION

CHAPTER II

THE INFERENTIAL ELEMENT IN PERCEPTION

CHAPTER III

THE THING AND ITS ARCHITECTURE

CHAPTER IV

THE NATURE OF PERCEPTUAL MEANING

CHAPTER V

THE OFFICES OF PERCEPTUAL MEANING

CHAPTER VI

THE STRUCTURE OF PERCEPTUAL MEANING

BOOK II

THE THEORY OF THE IDEA

CHAPTER VII

THE IDEA AS IMAGE

CHAPTER VIII

MR. RUSSELL ON IDEAS

CHAPTER IX

BEHAVIOURISM AND THOUGHT

CHAPTER XI

REALISM: ACTS REPLACE IDEAS

CHAPTER XII

CRITICAL REALISM: ESSENCES REPLACE IDEAS

CHAPTER XIII

BRADLEY ON IDEAS IN LOGIC AND IN PSYCHOLOGY

CHAPTER XIV

A THEORY OF THE IDEA

CHAPTER XV

THE ELEMENTARY TYPES OF IDEA

CHAPTER XVI

THE FALSE OR ABSTRACT UNIVERSAL

CHAPTER XVII

UNIVERSALS, GENERIC AND SPECIFIC

CONTENTS OF VOLUME TWO

BOOK III

THE MOVEMENT OF REFLECTION

CHAPTER XVIII

THE GENERAL NATURE OF UNDERSTANDING

CHAPTER XXIII

THE NATURE OF INVENTION

CHAPTER XXIV

THE SUBCONSCIOUS IN INVENTION

CHAPTER XXV

THE TESTS OF TRUTH

CHAPTER XXVI

COHERENCE AS THE NATURE OF TRUTH

CHAPTER XXVII

COHERENCE AND DEGREES OF TRUTH

BOOK IV

THE GOAL OF THOUGHT

CHAPTER XXVIII

EMPIRICISM AND NECESSITY

CHAPTER XXXII

CONCRETE NECESSITY AND INTERNAL RELATIONS

BOOK ONE

THOUGHT IN PERCEPTION

CHAPTER I

THE GENESIS OF PERCEPTION

1. Thought is that activity of mind which aims directly at truth. There are many activities of mind that aim at truth indirectly, such as learning to read, or to use instruments of research. There are many others that do not aim at it at all, such as sleeping, chopping wood, and playing tennis. But when and so far as we are seeking truth directly, we are thinking. The meaning and defence of this statement will cost us a great many pages, but if the reader can accept it provisionally, we shall save time in getting under way. Activities that lack this aim may be ruled out; further, if a process is such by nature that it could not conceivably yield truth, it too may perhaps be ruled out.

2. Assuming that it would be well to begin with the most elementary form of thought and that our search for it should be made with the above restrictions in mind, our question will now be, What is the simplest activity of mind that aims at truth directly and may conceivably yield it? And to this the answer is clearly Perception. The simplest form of thought is, by general admission, judgement; and perception in turn is the simplest form of this. The reasons for these propositions are easy to see. First, judgement is thought at its simplest because nothing simpler could yield either truth or falsity. For example, while the judgement A is B, 'snow is white', may be either true or false, this would plainly not hold of either component singly; it would be meaningless to say that 'snow' is true when nothing is true *of* it, or that 'white' is true when it is true *of* nothing. Hence anything simpler than judgement will fall outside the sphere of thought. But secondly, perception is judgement at its simplest. For with the barest and vaguest apprehension of anything given in sense *as* anything, perception is already present.

Now the theory of perception is one of the chief traditional battle-grounds of philosophy, and to give an adequate account of it we should have to raise, and, what is worse, to settle, some of the oldest and knottiest problems of metaphysics and epistemology. We shall not avoid such problems where they are forced upon us, but happily most of them we can leave untouched. For our study is not of perception generally, but of the emergence in and through it of thought. Now in essence thought is the same from first to last. Still, between its first appearance in rudimentary perception and that achievement of systematic insight which is its end and aim there are so many intermediate stages, and these stages are to all appearance so deeply different, that we may seem not seldom to be wandering from the track. And no doubt the wandering will at times be more than an appearance. But, partly as a pledge of good intentions, partly to provide sign-posts for the reader, we shall enumerate at once those questions from among the many that might be asked about perception which we propose to treat particularly. They are four: First, how does that simplest form of thought which we find in perception come into being? Second, what is the structure of perception at the level of everyday life? Third, considered as a stage in the effort of thought after understanding, how far can perception go? Fourth, what leads it in the end to break down and give place to free ideas? The first of these will occupy us in the present chapter: the others will be dealt with successively in the chapters that follow.

3. First, then, as to the beginning of perception. And for the sake of clearness, let us work with a definition in mind. Perception is that experience. in which, on the warrant of something given in sensation at the time, we unreflectingly take some object to be before us. The terms 'object', 'unreflectingly', and 'sensation' call for comment. 'Object' is a wide term here; it may mean a certain *thing*, a certain *kind* of thing, or what is not properly a thing at all, but a quality or relation. We are obviously perceiving, for example, when we happen to recognize our typewriter or our dog. We are also perceiving when we take something to be *a* typewriter or *a* dog. But we are no less perceiving when we listen to music or conversation, when we relish the taste of a plum pudding, when we observe one car to be going faster than another, or when we stop before a shop window to admire the blue in a new dress. In all these cases we are perceiving, because, with what is given in sense as our cue, we go on without reflection to take some object as presented. And it is evident that perception in this sense is an experience we have every hour of our waking lives. Unfortunately such extreme familiarity does not make it easier to analyse. It is so completely automatic and effortless that we seldom have occasion to think of it, and its parts are so cemented by habit that we are hardly able, even ideally, to take them apart.

It is the more satisfactory, therefore, to find that the comments naturally called for on 'sensation' and 'unreflectingly' serve to define perception for us in a new way. They mark its limits in a course of evolution, so that we may see it as a segment or stage in a continuous growth. Perception is not perception unless it supplies us a ground in sensation for something that goes beyond this. But if sensation is present alone, we are below the perceptual level; judgement, or something like judgement, must be present also. If, for example, when we looked at the dress we were aware of nothing but blue, we should not in strictness be perceiving; perceiving proper would appear when we took the blue *as* something—as the colour of the dress, or as one of the series of colours, or even merely as blue. Sensation is the nether limit of perception. Explicit judgement is the upper limit. We are clearly beyond mere perceiving when judgement is made reflectively, when what we assert is no longer taken as simply presented, but is recognized as a venture of our own that may be mistaken. For example, if the light raised doubts about the colour and we said 'That is a darker blue than it looks', we should have passed beyond mere perception into the region of explicit judgement. Thus the territory we are first to explore lies between two well-marked boundaries, pure sensation on the one hand and explicit judgement on the other. But while differing from both of its neighbours, perception has something in common with each. It plainly involves sensation, though sensation moulded and 'interpreted'; it involves judgement, but judgement that is still in the implicit stage.

4. How does perception arise? Does an infant enjoy it from the first moment he opens his eyes, or is there, as we have implied, some earlier form of experience from which it grows?

None of us has any memory of a stage before perception; our earliest recollections are of persons or objects or events. And however dimly these things came to us, if they came *as* anything at all, we were already perceiving. But what is beyond reach of memory can often be reached by inference, and in the present case we may argue as follows: We have not always been able to perceive as we do now. There was a time in the life of each of us, when the most familiar things about us were not known for what they were. Bottles and toys were presumably there awaiting our recognition, but this was as yet beyond us; and to perceive father and mother for what they were was perhaps still farther in the future. But even if we grant that we were perceiving nothing, does it follow that our minds were blank? Are we to say that between birth and the first triumphant recognition of bottle or rattle, we lived the life of a cocoon, and then burst out suddenly one day with the wings of cognition? This certainly will not do. If we agree that perception is not there at the start and yet that our mind, even at birth, has somehow bettered the cabbage, we shall no doubt agree that we were having some sort of experience. And as students of the growth of the mind, we must try to conceive what this is.

Now this task is enormously difficult. Indeed the problem

of initial experience stands as a melancholy reminder of the rash things that may be said by great men. We are almost certain to go wrong unless we hold before our eyes conspicuously and from the beginning certain elementary warnings whose violation has caused most of the trouble.

5. (1) *We must not confuse first reactions with first experiences.* Many skilful observations have been made to settle such questions as these: How does an infant first react to a loud noise? How does it react to a bright light? to a furry surface? to a shiny surface? Such observations undoubtedly help to reveal what the infant mind is like. But they are of little use for our present purpose, for they convey far less about how the child feels than about how his body behaves. It is true of course that the behaviour of his body may furnish valuable clues to what goes on in his mind. If on touching a hot object, his hand starts back abruptly, we may infer that he feels a burn; and if when dosed with Fletcher's Castoria he proceeds to cry, we may even say, as the advertisements do, that he is crying for more. But for us the bodily reaction is only a sign, and unless it is capped by an inference as to the nature of the accompanying experience it has no place in the study of mind. The withdrawal of a hand is one thing, the feeling of pain is another, and it is this second kind of thing, experience, that we shall be concerned with altogether. One hesitates to call attention to a distinction so elementary or a confusion so incredibly gross, but the confusion has actually been made, even by psychologists of some name.

6. (2) *We must not confuse what is analytically simplest with what is historically first.* If we take our present field of consciousness and break it up into elements which cannot be analysed further, we shall have on our list such qualities as 'this shade of green' and 'this peculiar sound'. When we try to break these up into something simpler, we find we cannot do it. They seem to be ultimate constituents of consciousness. And then when we try to show how our consciousness came to be what it is, we are tempted to start with these elements and to show how, in course of time, they might have been combined or aggregated into the patterns we now find. We are confronted with a Chinese puzzle; we ideally take it to pieces; then to show how the whole may have grown we build it up again, part by part, until it is complete as we now know it. But this process, as applied to the mind, is radically vicious. It assumes that the mind is an aggregate of pieces, in which parts may be added or subtracted without any effect on the rest, and this assumption we shall find to be false. It assumes further that the simples gained by such analysis are the elements the mind starts with, whereas a very little reflection will show that to single out such a quality and attend to it in isolation requires a considerable power of abstraction, and that what is first in the order of nature may be last in the order of knowledge. Nevertheless, this movable block view of the mind, or something like it, has imposed on eminent thinkers, and is still so seductive as to be worth a warning.

7. (3) *We must avoid reading acquired meanings into the experiences we start with.* When we display a puppy or a toy to a baby, and say he sees it, it is hard to keep from supposing that he sees something like what we do. But it is pretty certain that he does not. For, as we shall discover in a few moments, adult perception is a stage Falstaff, so padded and puffed out with stuff that has been gathered elsewhere that the original figure is lost. This padding from past experience the baby's perception lacks. But since the only Falstaff we know is the familiar portly figure, we are apt to think of him so, even off stage and in his native state. We know of course that the child sees something, but what this is will appear, if at all, only to a careful study of how experience moulds perceiving. This warning has been so dinned into people's ears, as 'the psychologist's fallacy' and otherwise, that there is perhaps no need to enlarge upon it. But its counterpart error, which comes next, is less noticed, though perhaps equally dangerous, and we shall have to say more about it.

8. (4) *We must so construe the world we first live in as to make escape from it conceivable.* It is true that we must not read into the earlier what comes later, but it is also true that we must see it in the light of the later, if our account is ever to reach the later at all. Herbert Spencer once suggested that the qualities of sensation could be explained as rapid tattoos of 'nervous shocks' differing in their frequency.[1] If such shocks are taken as units of consciousness, the theory is instructive and interesting; if they are taken as nervous impulses we should be placing the beginning of thought in something from which its escape *in aliud genus* would be unintelligible. Dr. Edgell has argued, effectively I think, that Mr. Russell's 'knowledge of acquaintance' could not be an initial stage in knowledge 'for the reason that from it there could be no advance', that 'any conception of cognition as originating in discrete, insulated items of knowledge' could never lead on to 'knowledge about'.[2] Because the rule before us is an important one, because it is often violated unwittingly, and because it has been violated instructively by writers of great competence, we shall go on to illustrate it in two cases of particular interest.

9. The first example is from Lotze. Experience in each of us begins, he would say, in a 'sensation' or 'feeling' which 'is in itself nothing but a state of our consciousness, a mood of ourselves'.[3] Now the instant the reader sees this there looms up the obvious difficulty: if we start with mere 'moods of ourselves', how do we ever reach that independent and common

---

[1] *Principles of Psychology,* Sec. 60.
[2] *Arist. Soc. Proc.,* Supp. Vol. II. 196; cf. *Mind,* XXVII (1918), 174–187.   [3] *Logic,* Sec. 2.

world in which, apparently, we now live? If we are closed up at the beginning in states of our own consciousness, how do we manage to get out of them and lay hold, in common with others, on stars and atoms? Lotze feels the difficulty and attempts to meet it. What really happens, he says, is that by a series of acts of thought, not perhaps necessarily successive, we convert these states of ours into objects. By the first of these acts we take such states 'no longer as a condition which we undergo, but as a something which has its being and its meaning in itself, and which continues to be what it is and to mean what it means whether we are conscious of it or not';[1] by the second, we distinguish this object from others;[2] by the third we compare it with others, and so arrive at common features or universals.[3] But such an account implies nothing short of this, that our present world is one vast illusion; we are all engaged in the extraordinary business of taking 'moods' of ourselves for things. Of course Lotze does not fail to see this either. But his way of meeting it is peculiar; he inserts in the interstices of his account a series of *caveats* which, if taken seriously, supply another account, at odds with the first. According to the first account, the objectivity of things, the character they possess for thought, all relations and universals, are manufactured by mind out of states of itself. According to the second account, these are not made, but found, and if they were not there to be found, would never have been reached at all. The red and blue that we compare are there waiting before we compare them;[4] it is the relations themselves already subsisting between impressions when we become conscious of them, by which the action of thought, which is never anything but reaction, is attracted;[5] the earliest universals are 'no product of thought, but something which thought finds already in existence'.[6] In one account intelligence fashions its world very nearly out of whole cloth; in the other it only follows a webwork of things and relations supplied by

---

[1] *Logic*, Sec. 2.   [2] Sec. 9–11.   [3] Sec. 12–14.
[4] Sec. 11.   [5] Sec. 9.
[6] Sec. 14. See also Jones, *The Philosophy of Lotze*, Chap. III.

nature. Lotze could not to the end make a firm choice between these doctrines, and as a result, there runs through his close-knit theory of knowledge a vein of inconsistency, like a crack in a marble block. Perhaps this makes him the more instructive. Indeed, men who, like Mill and Lotze, are victims of an extraordinary power of seeing both sides of a question are very often more instructive than those who purchase consistency by averting their eyes.

10. The second example concerns space. The attempt has often been made to show how our conception of space grew out of perceiving something else. Berkeley thought that the notion of our 'seeing' a third dimension sprang from our perceiving things in two dimensions and combining with this perception the thought of the amount of muscular effort required to touch the things. Others have explained the perception of space as arising out of an earlier apprehension of 'extensity' supplemented by that 'of local signs'. The argument runs as follows. A child cannot distinguish at the start positions, distances, or directions, but his sensations do have a characteristic 'which everybody knows who knows the difference between the ache of a big bruise and the ache of a little one, between total and partial immersion in a bath',[1] to whom there is a difference between 'the bare "feel" of a penny and that of a pinpoint or the mere sight of a glow-worm in the darkness and that of a forest on fire'.[2] This characteristic is 'massiveness' or 'voluminousness', or, as it is most commonly called, 'extensity'. It is not yet space; 'extensity and extension are not to be confounded'.[3] And yet it is something so much like space that we may believe that out of our perception of the one there grew our perception of the other.

Now we may press against such a theory the dilemma which Mr. Joseph has pressed against it as defended by Professor

---

[1] Ward, *Psychological Principles*, 78.   [2] *Ibid.*, 116.
[3] *Ibid.*, 79. Ward would in the same way distinguish 'protensity' from time: pp. 107, 213.

Stout. If extensity is a name for 'something which we apprehend at first confusedly and afterwards clearly' then extensity and space are the same thing. If it is different from space, 'as would also seem to be implied by the pains taken to explain to us what the word indicates, it must for ever remain different; one could no more become the other than heat can become cold'.[1] We do not *explain* how one thing arises by saying that it was preceded by something radically different. Nor are we in principle better off if we fall back on 'local signs'. The doctrine of local signs is roughly this, that each of the sensations 'coming from' different points on the body, has a quality of its own, distinct from its chief one of warmth, pain, etc., and when these special qualities are arranged in series we have space. When a fly walks across my nose, the sensation at each instant has a quality which I may connect with that of the sensation at the next, and by so connecting these qualities, I perceive position and direction in space.[2] Will this help? Unfortunately not, for the same dilemma holds. If local signs are positions in space, or something which we manage to correlate with these, they explain nothing, for we have already what they seek to explain. If they are not positions but qualities, no non-spatial way of connecting them will explain how we arrive at *space*. Thus in the growth of spatial perception we have another important example to show that we must construe the start of experience in such a way that advance from it is possible.

11. We must now try to describe the experience out of which perception arises. Our tools must be imagination and inference. We cannot fall back on experiment, for there is no experiment that will show how it feels to be an infant; we must beware of filling the mind of innocence with logical simples and

---

[1] *Mind*, XIX (1910), 311. Mr. Joseph has written four articles on 'The Psychological Explanation of the Development of the Perception of External Objects' (*Mind*, 1910, 1911, 1928), to which I owe much. On this point, Bradley's criticism would be similar. See *Mind*, IV (1895), 232, 233.   [2] The example is Stout's.

acquired meanings; we must beware, finally, of making it a prison from which the child could never escape. With these warnings in mind, we proceed.

'The baby', says James in a well-known passage, 'assailed by eyes, ears, nose, skin, and entrails at once, feels it all as one great blooming, buzzing confusion.'[1] Probably all the major types of sensation—sights and sounds, smells and tastes, hots, colds, pains and the rest—form ingredients in the brew. And probably within any of these the range is considerable. The baby who cries at a loud noise but not at a low one, or cries harder at a bad than at a mild digestive attack, is feeling various intensities of sound and pain. But does he perceive the loud sound *as* loud, or as a sound, or even as distinct from the pain? These questions raise a different issue, and they must all, I think, be met with a No. You cannot perceive loud as loud without placing it in a scale where it is opposed to the less loud, and at the beginning there are no less louds. Not that the mere experience of loudness depends on experiencing other loudnesses, for then the first sound could have had no loudness at all; but rather that loudness is not perceived *as* loudness till it is set off against something else. Indeed, at the start, no sound is perceived as a sound, nor anything as what it is. This is not merely because materials for distinction are absent; the required differences may be there in plenty if only we knew how to use them. It is because there is absent a root condition on which depend alike our power to perceive these differences and the power to perceive anything as itself, a condition, therefore, which lies at the root of intelligence generally. This is the power to see in things the embodiment of universals. To perceive a sound *as* a sound, you must perceive it as *a* sound, as an example of what might be embodied in other sounds. And at the start this perception must be supposed absent. Why? Because it is only as other sounds are given that it could dawn on us that they are cases of one kind, only then that each could be seen in the light of the common nature of all. One could hardly ask that upon hearing the first sound,

[1] *Principles of Psychology*, I. 488.

the mind should at once seize it as a revelation of what might be embodied otherwise. The approach to sound is through sounds, the road to the universal, through particulars.[1] So far, the empiricists are right. If our first sound is a sound at all, it must be so in virtue of a nature that is realized also in other sounds, though not in smells or colours, and we must suppose this nature present whether it is apprehended as such or not. The history of perception is a history of the gradually improving grasp of the universal.

12. 'Do you mean to say', we may be asked, 'that from the moment of his first perception, a child has dealings with universals? Is he not to be allowed to perceive a sound without getting involved with timeless logical essences? If any such doctrine is true, why should it not carry on down to dogs and cats? And shall we not be compelled next to hear of barn-yard fowls who are in commerce with Platonic εἰδή?' Now it is easier to satirize this view than to produce another that will work. Any theory that is to work must, as we have seen, provide a passage to later experience. This later experience involves perceiving things *as* things of a kind, and it leads on continuously to the judgement of recognition, 'this is what I have seen before'. Now what would critics have? If they start with sensations of the purely particular, or transient 'moods of the self', they will either end where they began, or, like Lotze, retrace their steps and insert, from later necessity, the universals omitted at first. For if we are really confined to transient particulars, then every judgement of recognition, every identification of anything, and in the last resort every perception, is a snare and a delusion. For the claim of all these experiences is to take us beyond the moment's impression, not merely to give us a 'this' but to tell us something about it. And this they cannot do if impressions are the whole

---

[1] When we refer to 'particulars', as we shall occasionally, the reference should be taken subject to the discussion of Chap. XVII, where the traditional view of particulars is considered and rejected.

story. But if impressions are not the whole story, and we do in perceiving go beyond bare sensation, what is it that we first reach? It is clearly a universal. And when we begin to realize its presence on coming to our second sound or perhaps our hundredth, there is no reason to think that it only then began to exist. What has a history is not *it* but our perceiving of it. And if this implies that dogs and cats in perceiving are grasping universals, our answer is not, So much the worse for universals but, So much the better for dogs and cats.

Indeed we may say confidently that there is no stage in experience, not even pure sensation, if such a stage exists, in which universals are not present. Much depends here, of course, on what is meant by universals. It would be absurd to say that at the beginning a child has general ideas, such ideas as we employ ourselves when we use the word 'colour' or 'man'. It would be absurd also to credit him with abstract ideas, such as the thought of the redness of this ball in distinction from its other qualities. But this special shade of redness is not necessarily confined to this context; it may be given in various contexts; and if so, it is, in an important sense of the word, a universal. Now there is every reason to believe that from the very earliest moment when visual sensation is possible the child is apprehending this shade, and therefore that he is apprehending universals from the very inception of his sentient life. If it is intolerable to say that the child is *sensing* a universal, then we must deny that there has ever been a time when he was confined to mere sensation. What must not be done is to say that we begin with the sensing of bare particulars in which nothing is identical with anything else, and that we somehow find identities as we go on. Identities that are not there cannot be found. We shall not argue this matter, because one of the decisive battles of modern philosophy was fought over it. The reader who is interested will find an arsenal of what we believe to be unanswerable argument in Green's account of the British empiricists. In that classic criticism the old bridge from acquaintance with sense particulars to knowledge of actual things was damaged beyond repair.

But of course to say that we begin with universals does not mean that we begin by knowing them as universals. It is only very gradually and with the help of processes still to be examined that this knowledge is achieved. Much of the confusion here is due to the assumption that our only contact with universals is through general ideas, and hence that to say universals are apprehended from the beginning is equivalent to saying that general ideas are used from the beginning. But the assumption is a mistake.

13. To return now to describing. We saw that when we open our eyes on the world, we experience sights and smells, sounds and pains, though all in an undistinguished jumble. But we do not perceive the loudness of the sound *as* loudness, nor the sound *as* sound, nor therefore, by the same reasoning, anything for what it is. But it may be said that the mixture is at any rate not a blend. Even at the beginning a pain and a sound differ widely, and, as different, must be distinct. But this again is scarcely correct. It is true that sounds and pains, every shade of colour and every degree of heat that enter into experience has a character of its own which sets it off from everything else. But to be different and to be distinguished are not the same. We must believe that in the experience of the infant, however dim and undiscriminated its sensations may be, those sensations are still different. But they are certainly not distinct, in the sense of being distinguished. One cannot distinguish anything until one has perceived it *as* this rather than that (for otherwise *what* is distinct?) and in this first experience no whats have yet been recognized. Distinctness of characters from each other and the use of universals as universals have their beginning together. However, it would be still another error to suppose, in line with James's phrase about the 'blooming, buzzing confusion', that because our first experience is undifferentiated it is therefore confused. Confusion is not mere absence of distinction. It takes two things that are recognizably distinct to be confounded, and where differentiation has not begun, this twoness has not yet been arrived at. Some sophistication is necessary before one can be really confused.

When we spoke a moment ago of perceiving a character as such, the phrase we used was 'perceive it as this rather than that'. This is the natural form of expression, and it is significant. It suggests that the recognition of the universal and the placing it in relation to other universals are aspects of the same process. To *be* for thought at all is to be distinct, and to be distinct is to be related to something else through space, time, degree, or otherwise. And this something else in turn receives and maintains its character for thought only through distinction from the first thing. Here is the first intimation of a truth which, as it recurs over and over again in the study that follows, will gain an increasing significance, namely that to think involves the relating of the object thought of to something else within a system. Abstract thinking, in the sense of dealing with any character quite alone and apart is not only an impossibility; it is a self-contradiction.

14. The process of distinction could hardly get under weigh, as we have admitted, unless it had differences to start with, and such differences we must suppose to subsist even within the immediate experience from which we start. But now a doubt suggests itself. Is there any reason to suppose that the universals that emerge into explicitness through this joint recognition and distinction are the same as those present in the initial experience? There is no conceivable experiment that could settle this question, since anyone who could apply experiment would have left his first immediacy far behind, and the mind that was still immersed in this would be incapable of reports. It is a question that has to be settled by resort to some general principle, and unfortunately what this principle should be is one of the most disputed points in contemporary thought. The issue is whether or not the nature of a thing is affected by being placed in new relations. This very difficult question is more appropriately considered later,[1] but we may perhaps say at once that we believe the nature of a term *is* thus affected. And if so, the conclusion will follow that the emergence of the mind from immediacy is its emergence into a world in some degree new. How new we cannot tell. But if the above principle is accepted, we may be confident of two things, first that some change in the content of initial experience is made by its explicit ordering and, second, that this change is not a total transformation. Complete breaks in continuity are not the way of the mind. For example, while it seems reasonable to suppose that human pain is made different from animal pain by its relations to a remembered past and a foreseen future, still the man who should presume on such differences to the extent of denying, like certain Cartesians, that animals suffered at all would be absurd. In like manner we are entitled to speak of sensations, pleasures, etc., as components of initial experience, but if we spoke quite strictly, we should have to say, not that they are simply identical with those we are now familiar with, but rather that they are the same *sort* of thing.

15. To proceed, then, with our somewhat conjectural description: is our first experience simply a mass of undistinguished sensations? No, it is undoubtedly more; there is no reason to exclude other elements. It certainly includes both varieties of affection, pleasure and displeasure; and it would be hard to deny that emotion also is there. Again, if these different elements are present, they are not present as unconnected fragments, but are united by relations, spatial, temporal, and other. Such relations must be there from the start, though they are no more perceived *as* relations than qualities as qualities. The child's mind has its bony framework as truly as his body, and it is interesting to note that growth follows similar lines in both. As the fleshy volume increases, the bony framework extends and strengthens. Similarly, as

[1] See Chaps. XXXI and XXXII.

the mass of experience widens, the framework of inner relations gains greater explicitness and gives greater definition to the parts. Indeed, we shall see that the ordering of the mass of experience into a special kind of structure or system is at once the principal aim of thought and the measure of its advance. In the experience with which we start, then, sensation is present, and relations, and pleasure, and displeasure, and emotion. On the other hand, there is no proper perception, no memory, nor even recognition. There are no ideas of any kind, no images, no judgements, no desires, no anticipations, nothing that we should now call hopes or fears, no wishes or regrets, no sense of right or wrong, beautiful or ugly, true or false. Nor is there yet any sense of self and not-self, for it is only gradually that experience comes to be split up and apportioned, part to me and part to the world of external things.

Is it possible to go beyond such summaries and get a notion through example of what this primitive state is like? It does seem that, in some present states of mind and in certain areas of our conscious field, we even now approach it. In the drowsiness that precedes full waking and in the dullness of extreme fatigue, the meanings that we usually attach to things may almost vanish, and we may be sunk in a state that is not far from mere sensation. Indeed, something like such a state we carry about with us always. On the margins of our field of vision there is a region where we can neither quite deny that we are sensing something nor be sure that we perceive. And then there is what the psychologists call coenaesthesia, or what Bradley called the 'felt surplus in our undistinguished core'.[1] At any moment of our waking life, one part of our experience is a mass of obscure sensation connected with breathing and digestion, the pressure of clothes, vague hungers and fatigues, our bodily fitness or unfitness. We seldom think of these feelings, but they are there undoubtedly; if they are disordered, as they often are in illness, we may become painfully conscious of them, while if, as apparently happens in some extreme cases, they vanish wholly, the foundations of

[1] *Appearance and Reality*[2], 293.

sanity are threatened. It is true that if we were asked to furnish
proof that these states exist, we might find the question awkward.
The reply that we can introspect them directly will hardly
pass, for once such feelings are dragged into the limelight of
attention they are no longer the twilight creatures we wanted.
But we need not discuss the technique of our knowledge of
immediacy, since our interest is less in the state itself than in
our way of escaping from it. It is enough if the reader agrees
that it exists or has existed, and that from its morass of indistinctness our thought does in fact arise.

16. How do we make our way out? It is by finding in the
bog piers or stepping-stones that will give footholds for our
escape. The level waste is, after all, not quite level. There are
minor mounds in it, pushed up by subterranean forces that
are very imperfectly understood. These come to stand out for
our notice, to attain some clearness of outline, and at last to
set themselves before us as objects. How do they do this?
There are three chief factors involved.

(1) Even in the primitive state of indistinctness there is a
great difference in the *force* or *intensity* with which sensations
come to us. It would be absurd to say that because a child
cannot identify lights or pains they are all felt on the same
level of vividness. The range of intensity of some sensations,
particularly pains, in minds in which perception has scarcely
begun is probably enormous. There are few persons who can
have known the minds of lowly animals better than Darwin
did, and he tells us how, convinced that even earthworms
have reached the dignity of pain, he used to administer a home-
made anaesthetic before he used them in his fishing.[1] He was
certainly nearer the truth than the Cartesians above mentioned.
Sensations may be very intense before there is any power to
say, or even to think, what they are sensations of. To be sure
we must beware of a fallacy here. The intensity of a sensation
is not the same thing as the perception of it, and in theory

---

[1] *Life and Letters*, I. 30.

the intensity could be increased to infinity without producing the smallest recognition, or even what we now call notice. When we notice anything we always invest it with significance drawn from past experience, and it is usually in virtue of this significance that we come to single it out. And such significance at the first is wanting. Nevertheless, just as in later life it is the vivid experiences that remain in memory and not the faint ones, so here at the beginning it is the vivid sensations that are most likely to leave the traces needed in identifying them later on.

17. (2) Again, some sensations from the beginning have an *interest* that others lack. This is what is meant when it is said that we 'instinctively notice' some things rather than others. It obviously holds of both animal and human infants. An early observer, Douglas Spalding, hooded some chicks the instant they left their shell and kept them hooded for periods of one to three days, but on taking the hoods off, found them, sometimes within two minutes, following clearly with their eyes the movements of crawling insects.[1] The same inquirer, immediately after working with puppies, put his hands into a basket of three-day-old kittens, still with their eyes unopened, and produced a storm of spitting and puffing, owing, he thought, to the puppy smell.[2] Through practically the whole animal scale we find this instinctive favouritism, a curious and unlearned selection of certain qualities for special attention. Strings and straws that have hitherto been beneath notice become interesting to the bird at mating time; the fresh meat to which the young horse or cow is indifferent sends the young cat or dog into transports of excitement; the dog seems to live as much in a world of smells as we do in a world of sights. The dog's 'system of logic', if he had one,

[1] Romanes, *Mental Evolution in Animals*, 161.
[2] *Ibid.*, 164. If the kittens would have behaved in this way, even without the puppy smell, as I suspect they would, the force of the example is still not wholly destroyed.

says Bradley, 'would be simple, for it would begin, I am sure, and end with this axiom, "What is smells, and what does not smell is nothing".'[1] So exclusive is this preference among animals for some sensations rather than others that a major difficulty in training them is to get them to notice any but the familiar cues. Now such instinctive favouritism appears from the beginning in man also. The nipple of a bottle at an infant's lips is to him the most interesting thing in the world.[2] From the very beginning a loud sound will arouse his fear. As his growth goes on and his instincts ripen, things that were before indifferent—toys, mechanical devices, games, members of the other sex—take on a special interest, not because he has learned from experience that it pays to attend to them, but because his nature dictates that at this stage he should find them appealing.

The proposal has been made by Professor Drever that this original and instinctive interest should be taken as the first form of meaning.[3] Now 'meaning' usually refers to something in the way of thought. 'Strictly', says Professor Broad, 'a thing has meaning when acquaintance with or knowledge about it either enables one to infer or causes one by association to think of something else.'[4] Now when a sensation comes to us clothed in a special interest, is our thought being carried to something else? Clearly this is not necessary. Meaning as feeling is a different thing from meaning as thought, wherever it appears in the scale. How far apart they are may be seen from the fact that the very simplest thought-meaning that can enter into perception may in principle be mistaken, while the most developed of feeling-meanings could not possibly be mistaken. In sensation invested with such feeling-meanings

---

[1] *Logic*, I. 31.
[2] 'The hungry child is indifferent to everything else until his hunger is appeased. During his greedy feeding, all attempts to divert his attention—it is not until late that we can even direct his attention at all—from the gratifying of his demand for food are at first almost absolute failures.'—Preyer, *Mental Development in the Child*, 18.
[3] *Instinct in Man*, Chap. VI and App. I.
[4] *Perception, Physics and Reality*, 97.

we are not taking anything *for* anything; and hence we are strictly below the level of perceiving, thinking, or knowing. But Professor Drever's suggestion stresses a fact of the greatest importance in understanding the rise of perception, namely that there is no democracy among the sensations with which we start, that some from the very beginning are weighted with 'affective meaning'. It is these that get the preference when explicit noticing arises.

18. But *why* this favouritism among sensations? Why should we find some interesting from the outset and others not? No answer need be expected in these pages; indeed it is more than possible that no answer will ever be found. Certain suggestions have been made that have often been taken for answers, but they will hardly bear examining. It has been suggested, for example, that we may look for the origin of the species of sensation where scientists commonly look for the origin of animal species, in natural selection. The animal or human child that was loftily indifferent to the sensations connected with eating, but found insistently attractive the sensations of falling or getting burned, would soon join the great majority who tell no tales. We find those sensations interesting which are useful to us in getting food, in avoiding danger, in preparing us through playful experiment for the exigencies of later life. This at first sounds plausible. But natural selection in the mind has precisely the defect of natural selection in biology. That theory, as has been pointedly said, explains the survival but not the arrival of the fittest. Given certain powers of dealing with nature, certain animals will survive, while those lacking them will not. True enough. But where is there anything in this to show how those that have them got them, and why those that lack them did not get them? This is the essential point, and natural selection does not touch it. There is a very simple fallacy in supposing that because possession of these powers explains survival, you can turn the argument round and say that survival explains their possession. To say this is like saying that a hole in a target accounts for a gun being fired.

When it is seen that natural selection will not serve, many inquirers turn to physiology. The explanation, they say, for our preferring some sensations to others, as indeed for our having sensations at all, is to be found in our brains and nervous systems. Some forms of stimulus, e.g. heat or friction, our nerves will respond to; to others, e.g. magnetism, they will not. When we do respond nervously we have the corresponding kind of sensation, and if some sensations are more interesting than others, that is because of the pre-formed nervous connections in our brains. Now that there is some causal connection between nervous change and sensation seems indubitable. But before anyone accepts this as an explanation of our sensing and feeling as we do, he may well reflect on the following points. (a) There is no connection in the range of our knowledge that has proved more utterly opaque than the connection of body and mind. We have not the faintest notion how a change in a nerve could give rise to a pain. It is a complete mistake to suppose that such brilliant recent work as that of Adrian on the nervous impulse improves our understanding of how this impulse could generate experience. And if it is said that this is mere passing ignorance, that though we do not know as yet how one thing could produce another so very different, we may be sure of a point-for-point correspondence between changes in brain and mind, the answer is (b) that even so much is unwarranted. We shall see in Chap. XXII that in a course of reflection the fact that A is seen to necessitate B may play a vital part in causing the thought of B to arise, that logical connection helps to determine psychological succession. But in the movements of physical particles it is generally supposed that logical necessity plays no part. And when the laws of succession in the two series are thus so widely different it is hard to believe that point-for-point correspondence is more than a provisional working assumption. It is true that in reflective thought we find the divergence at its widest, and that there is not *prima facie* an equal divergence if we choose from the psychical series a train of sensations. But even here we must be sceptical. For the content of sensation enters as an integral fact into the same mind that does the reasoning and may figure in the reasoning itself. So far as it subjects itself to the laws that govern such reasoning it shares the divergence of that reasoning from the type of law that governs physical process. And thus even that modest form of explanation which consists in exhibiting detailed correspondence must, we suspect, be denied in the end to the physiological psychologist.

With aid from these sources so restricted, the question why some sensations come clothed from the first with interest is likely to remain long unanswered. But so, for that matter, are the questions why we have sensations at all, and why, having them, we should have these rather than others, and why we should not have a hundred senses instead of the paltry few that we have. There are probably minds in the animal world whose sensations are totally different from anything we can imagine. The antennae of the ant, for example, appear to be sense organs by which it finds its way about, discovers food, and distinguishes between companions, friends, and foes.[1] To all appearance it has many kinds of sensation. But what kinds? It is as improbable that they are like ours as it is that we shall ever know precisely what they are like. Compare our sense of direction with the sense that enables a bee to make a 'bee-line' home; or our vision or touch with that of a mosquito exploring a pore. And when we think of the entities with which the speculations of modern physics have acquainted us, invisible protons and electrons which may themselves turn out to be complicated, and the indefinitely varying wave-lengths in air and 'ether', to only a fraction of which we can make any sensory response, our senses seem poor and crude in the extreme. For all we know, the world is full of things to which we are blind and deaf. We may have lost many senses along

[1] One is reminded of Darwin's remark, 'the brain of an ant is one of the most marvellous atoms of matter in the world, perhaps more so than the brain of a man'.

the evolutionary road, and it is not unlikely that in course of time we may gain others. Meanwhile, the world we live in must be built of the limited materials supplied us. In our present state of knowledge it is idle to ask, Why these and not others? They are given us; that is all we know; and we must make of them what we can.

19. (3) Two factors have been mentioned that tend to break up the initial continuum and bring qualities into relief, the *intensity* of certain sensations and their *interest*. One other factor must be named. When a sensed quality appears in company with another, then, upon the reappearance of the first the second also tends to recur. Now suppose that quality A appears successively with a number of other qualities B, C, D; that a shade of red presents itself first in a ball, then in a toy, and then in a dress. If the rule just laid down is correct, the red on its second appearance will tend to recall the *shape* that first came along with it. But this tendency is checked by the fact that there is now given a very different shape. The outcome is that the repeated quality gets an emphasis that makes it stand out, while its conflicting associates cancel each other. Similes are dangerous, but the process is rather like that of compound photographs in which, after many exposures to different faces, a film registers prominently the common features and shows only a blur for the differences. Since retention and association work from the beginning, this process also may be presumed at work. And it is an extremely important aid in making distinctions. For as a rule we can distinguish more completely sensations that come one after the other than sensations which we can hold before us both at once. If we are in doubt which of two tones is the higher, we shall not, if we are well advised, strike both at once; we shall sound first one and then the other. And so in most cases of touches, tastes and odours.

We have now seen the general character of the experience in which we start and the chief factors which bring some elements

rather than others into prominence. We do not suggest that
these are the only factors. There are others of great importance;
but since their effect is to bring into prominence things rather
than sensations, they are more conveniently dealt with later.
Nor is it suggested that sensed qualities are discriminated
before things; the two kinds of discrimination grow up
together. It is clear on the one hand that a thing can be discriminated before all its qualities are; but it is clear on the
other hand that when we perceive a thing we seldom sense
it as a whole; we take it to be there on the warrant of certain
of its qualities that are sensed while others are not. The
discrimination of qualities and the perception of things advance
together and support each other.

20. With the discernment of things and qualities we are
launched on a form of experience that everyone would call
perception. Nothing below this, we have held, can properly
be so named. But there are those who would hold that perception begins far earlier, and in a certain sense they are right.
It is worth while to see in what sense.

Many psychologists would say, with James, that 'every
perception is an acquired perception'.[1] If sensations which
now occur come with a fringe or context of 'meaning', it is
held that this is because of past association; we have experienced
the colour of an orange along with its juiciness, taste and weight,
and hence when now we catch sight of a round patch of its
special colour we piece this out with expectations about the
rest of it which could derive only from past experience. This
is a very plausible doctrine for the sort of perception that is
in mind. It is the sort in which, on the warrant of sensing
certain qualities, we go on to expect or take for granted certain
others. And it seems pretty clear, as Locke maintained, that if we
expect one quality to be found together with another, it is
because we have found them together in the past; such expectations are not innate. But it is not so clear that this is the only

[1] *Psychology*, II. 78.

process deserving the name of perception; what, for example, of a quality and its major relations? Whenever we see a patch of colour, we not only find it occupying space, but take for granted that it is connected spatially with everything else we might see. We place it in one space with all other seen colours. Is this an acquired association? The answer may come, Why not? we have always experienced colour and space together; we naturally expect them to continue together. But this will hardly do. The togetherness of colour and space is not like the togetherness of colour and softness; colour can be disjoined from softness; it cannot from space. There is something like an abuse of language in describing merely as an 'associate' something that makes possible the very existence of what goes with it. Space is not the same as colour, and yet every colour from the beginning is so necessarily seen as spatial that if it were not, it would not be seen at all. As Kant pointed out, we do not start below the categories in a region where there is nothing at all but sensation. What we sense invariably comes to us as belonging to a wider order; it carries in its nature a reference beyond itself; and this holds from the very beginning. But if so, we have from the beginning what some persons, Kant himself for example, would unhesitatingly call perception. This, it should be noted, is not the sense in which we have preferred to use the term. But the fact it points to, that what comes to us through sensation always comes invested with relations that carry us beyond itself, is not only a fact we admit, but one we should like to emphasize.

21. To summarize: Perception is an experience in which, on the warrant of what is given in sensation, we take some object to be before us. It is the sort of experience we have in the apprehension of red as red, or of an orange as an orange. Such experience is an achievement, since in the unbroken continuum with which we start, nothing is grasped *as* what it is. This primitive state we cannot now reconstruct with accuracy, but if we avoid certain errors of method, we may at least gain some helpful clues to it. From the very first, universals are present. The growth of perception is a process in which these gradually come to explicitness, and the main factors that force certain points into prominence are (1) the intensity of some sensations, (2) their interest, and (3) their repetition in varying contexts.

CHAPTER II

THE INFERENTIAL ELEMENT IN PERCEPTION

1. In the first sentence of our first chapter we pointed out that thought is an activity with an end or aim. Its end is truth. Now if we are to understand any purposive activity, some knowledge of its end is required. To a person who had no knowledge of what wealth and its attractions were like, most of the activities of commerce would be so much 'busy-work'; and if one had no experience of beauty, the activity of artists would be unintelligible. Similarly, if we are to make anything of the activity of thought, we must know what sort of satisfaction the thinker is seeking. But thought at the level of perception is still in its infancy, and when an activity is at this stage, it is usually very difficult to know what its end is; the school-boy who is taking his first lessons in arithmetic or music would give a very sorry account of the musical or mathematical ideal. The end we are seeking reveals itself only as the seeking goes on. Thus to insert a study of the goal of thought into an account of perception would be an anachronism. Yet it is only with reference to this goal that we can select the functions within perception that are relevant to our study. The best course, perhaps, is to compromise, to indicate in a few sentences what we take the end to be, and to leave the justification to later chapters.[1]

If the end of thought is truth, what is truth? It lies, we shall hold, in system, and above all in that perfect type of system in which each component implies and is implied by every other. We shall speak sometimes as if the aim of thought were understanding, and this also is true; the two aims are equivalent to each other. To know the truth about anything is, so far, to apprehend it in a system of relations that makes it intelligible, and this is what we mean by understanding it. These positions will be defended in detail later on; here they

[1] See Chaps. XXVII and XXXII.

are mentioned in anticipatory justification of our studying some elements in perception rather than others. If it is true that the special end of thought is to attain the sort of system we have mentioned, then all those types and levels of organization within perception which illustrate the path to this end will be of interest to us.

2. Viewing perception, then, as the first stage in a long journey, the first halting endeavour to introduce into experience, or discover in it, a system that will satisfy intelligence, we shall ask first what organization is to be found in perception in its most characteristic form, viz., the perception of things. Or perhaps we should say what varieties of organization. For with a very little scrutiny we can discover within it a great many fragmentary systems, whose parts are connected by the most diverse relations. Most of Kant's *Critique* is occupied with exhibiting and analysing the various relations to be found in the apprehension of a thing as a thing. And the mention of his analysis reminds us of a distinction which will serve to narrow our study further. The relations within perception that he was concerned to examine were all of them a priori relations, which he conceived to be absolutely necessary, and thus to have the highest intelligibility that the understanding could aspire to. But here again, if we were to ask what perfect intelligibility means and how far these relations conform to the ideal, we should be ahead of our story; such relations are not peculiar to perception and they are more effectively studied as they appear in explicit reflection. So instead of dealing now with the types of arrangement involving necessity, we shall defer these to the end, and take up now those forms of organization that belong to perception specially. Those that call for most particular treatment may be named at once.

First, some parts of a perceived thing appear to be given in sensation, others not. How does perceptual consciousness get from the one to the other? Secondly, to the constitution of the ordinary thing go many different kinds of qualities, such

as shape, colour, size and weight. On what principle or principles are such groupings carried out? Thirdly, our perception
of a thing has a history consisting of successive perceptual
events. How are the objects of the successive perceptions
combined into a thing conceived as enduring? Fourthly, a
thing commonly presents appearances within the same kind
that seem incompatible with each other; for example it may
present many different shapes. How are these all combined in
the perceptual thought of one thing? Fifthly, all these perceived
characters are taken as *belonging* to a thing. What sort of relation
is belonging? Sixthly, the perceived thing as a whole is set
over against the perceiver as external, substantial, and independent. Here are three further relations that call for examining.
There are others still that might be examined, but these are
the most important ones that belong typically to the perceptual
level. The first mentioned, which is also from our point of view
the most interesting, will be examined in the present chapter,
the others more briefly in the chapter that follows.

3. To this procedure there is a general objection that should
be met at once. Why say that in studying such relations we
are studying the organization of *thought*? Surely most of
these connections hold in things rather than in thought.
Perhaps it will be granted that the way we pass from what is
given to what falls beyond it is of interest to the student of
thought, but the relations between the qualities of an object
would seem to be far from thought-relations. The answer
lies partly in theories we are to develop later, in which the
existence of mental acts of sensing and perceiving is called in
question,[1] and the difference between idea and object is conceived as a difference in degree.[2] But it is difficult to see how
even those who would reject such theories could manage a
study of thought except through a study of its object. Does
logical necessity, for example, hold in thought or in the things
thought about? Obviously in both. As Mr. Joseph says of

[1] Chap. XI.   [2] Chap. XIV.

the 'laws of thought', *we cannot think* contradictory propositions, because we see that *a thing cannot have* at once and not
have the same character; and the so-called necessity of thought
is really the apprehension of a necessity in the being of things'.[1]
The attempt to study apprehension apart from the objects
of that apprehension is at every cognitive level a pursuit of
shadows,[2] and the only possible way to study the organization
of thought is to study the organization it finds or introduces
among its objects. The greater part of what follows would
perhaps be admitted, even by those critical on this score, to
be in the proper sense a study of perceptual thought, since
in it we shall be concerned for the most part with those elements
that are not presented but taken for granted; but it need not
be assumed that we are simply wandering from the track
when we turn, as we shall, to scrutinize the relations of the
presented elements themselves.

We turn now to examine the first of the above relations,
the relation between what is given in sense and what is not.

4. That there really is in the perception of things something
that goes beyond sensation it is easy to show. Suppose that,
glancing up at the sky, I see a tiny cross-shaped object and
hear a certain pervasive hum. I at once recognize an aeroplane,
and if questioned, I should say I 'perceived' it. But how much
have I actually seen or heard? I have seen little more than a
speck, and have heard nothing but a peculiar hum. Now to
say that a speck plus a hum *is* an aeroplane would of course be
absurd, as absurd as to say that the tip of a cat's tail which I
see vanishing through a door *is* the cat complete. Yet if the
speck and hum are the only elements in the experience, how
could I say I perceive an *aeroplane*? It is obvious that in perception something besides what is given in sensation is involved,
and that in many cases this something else includes nearly
everything of importance. In the actual work of perceiving,

---

[1] *Introduction to Logic*[2], 13; italics in original.
[2] Cf. the strictures on Titchener's psychology of thought, Chap. VII.

the relative parts of sensation and of this supplementary process vary greatly. When we perceive a slip of paper a few feet from our eyes, a large part of the perceived object is sensed, and the supplementary process has comparatively little to do; when we perceive a dot in the sky as an aeroplane, the role of sensation is relatively small and of the supplementary process large. Sir William Hamilton even laid it down as a precise law that 'these elements are always found to exist in an inverse proportion',[1] and, as one might expect from Sir William, called in aid Joannes Secundus, 'his learned commentator Bosscha', Cicero, and Shakespeare. We cannot follow him in his quantitative precision, but we can say at least that in all perception of things both processes are present. This may be proved by the ideal experiment of removing either one. Remove sensation and what is left? Some sort of reference or acceptance, no doubt, but nothing that anyone would call perception. Remove the supplementary process and what is left? Either pure sensation or, if it is doubted whether there is such a process, something which approaches it as a limit, and in any case falls short of the perception of things. In all such perception both processes are essential.

To one who has never reflected on the matter, the realization that perceiving involves this leap beyond the given comes as a surprise. But that it should come thus as a surprise is not itself a matter to be wondered at. In the business of making distinctions, the mind is capable of vast inertia; it is not accustomed to dissecting things except in the service of some practical end. And there is seldom any practical point in distinguishing the sensible from the non-sensible in perception, since the assumption that we see things whole and without any guess-work generally carries us through. But occasionally it does not, and nothing shows more clearly how we normally and without knowing it go beyond what is given than the way in which perception at times plays us false. A man 'perceives a hundred-pound weight', braces himself to lift it, and finds that it is only paper. Certainly his perceiving the weight here

[1] *Lectures on Metaphysics*, II. 99.

is no process of sensation. A man 'sees a ghost' in a moon-lit hallway, takes his courage in his hands, runs to seize it, and finds himself in the embrace of the window curtain. Did he *see* the ghost at all? These cases may be unimportant and out-of-the-way, but it often happens, and particularly in studying perception, that the abnormal cases are the most enlightening ones. When we reflect on these instances it is plain that if we do not literally see and hear physical things when we perceive wrongly, neither do we see or hear them when we perceive rightly; all perception, true or false, involves a leap in the dark.

None of the writers who have dealt with perception has brought out these points more clearly perhaps than Mill, though his terms would to-day require revision. He wrote in his *Logic*:

> 'The universality of the confusion between perceptions and the inferences drawn from them, and the rarity of the power to discriminate the one from the other, ceases to surprise us when we consider that in the far greater number of instances, the actual perceptions of our senses are of no importance or interest to us except as marks from which we infer something beyond them. It is not the colour and superficial extension perceived by the eye that are important to us, but the object of which those visible appearances testify the presence; and when the sensation itself is indifferent, as it generally is, we have no motive to attend particularly to it, but acquire a habit of passing it over without distinct consciousness, and going on at once to the inference. So that to know what the sensation actually was, is a study in itself, to which the painter, for example, has to train himself by special and long-continued discipline and application.'[1]

5. What is it precisely that happens when, on the warrant of certain sensations, we pass to the perception of a thing? Various interesting suggestions have been made.

(1) Perhaps the least plausible suggestion has been offered by the behaviourists. What happens, they say, is a 'conditioned reflex'. To the members of this school, a sensation is nothing

---

[1] *System of Logic*, Bk. V, Chap. IV, Sec. 5.

but a nervous reaction. When two reactions have accompanied each other for a time, the stimulus that arouses one of them will arouse the other too. In my past experience of aeroplanes, the present visual and auditory reactions have been accompanied by many others to details of the machine, with the result that the latter have become 'conditioned' by the former; that is, when the visual and auditory reactions are aroused again, they arouse also, in an incipient form, their old companions. These companion reflexes are then the supplementary process in perception. Now we shall pay our respects to behaviourism later. It must suffice here to say that from our point of view this account is simply irrelevant. That the process it describes does go on in the nervous system may very well be the fact. But it is at any rate not what we are talking about. What we are talking about is not a reflex, nor anything made up of reflexes, but a kind of experience. When the behaviourist speaks (he dislikes such language) of my sensations of a sound he means a change in the nervous system, which, if the conditions and instruments were right, could actually be *seen* taking place. When we speak of the sensation of sound, or of the process of taking for granted, we mean something that could not possibly be seen. The two of us are therefore concerned with different things. His contention that we have no right to take perception in the non-physical sense is dealt with below.[1]

6. (2) A theory less wide of the mark has been popular since the time of Hume. It was uncompromisingly put by Sully:[2] 'perception is that process by which the mind, after discriminating and classing a sensation or sensation-complex,

---

[1] Chap. IX.

[2] *The Human Mind*, 212. Cf. the following from Binet, who seems to have swallowed associationism whole. 'Percevoir un corps qui se trouve actuellement dans le champ de la vision . . . c'est réunir dans un même acte de conscience des éléments actuels—c'est-à-dire les sensations optiques de l'œil—et des éléments passés—c'est-à-dire une foule d'images.'—*Psychologie du Raisonnement*, 66.

supplements it by an accompaniment or escort of revived sensations. . .' At some time in the past, and perhaps repeatedly, I have sensed the colour and shape of an orange along with its weight, its taste and its juiciness; if now the colour and shape appear to me, I supplement them in my mind with *images* of the qualities missing. This sounds fairly plausible at first. Indeed it was probably the belief that the mind ought to act in this way that led people to suppose it does so act, for the most casual glance at the facts shows that its behaviour is nothing of the sort. Let the reader try an experiment. Let him look at any object in the room and identify it as a book, table, chair, or flower-pot, and let him then introspect. Did he, or does he, in perceiving the flower-pot, have in his mind *images* of its unseen side and its weight and coldness? 'A painter might possibly recall one or two—but, if so, his state would be more than merely perceptual.' As for the rest of us, 'we simply do *not* recall a vast and various multitude of past sense-data which have accompanied this sense-datum in the past'.[1] We may find that we *can* form such images with perfect ease, that we can imagine with great vividness the weight of the flower-pot as we lift it, the rough texture of the edge, and the rest; but knowing so clearly what these images are like when they are present only makes us the more certain that they are not present now.

And the mistake of this doctrine is more than a mistake in fact. There is a failure to understand the sort of supplement required by theory, since even if the images were there, they would not suffice. Perception involves not merely the presence of something, but also the taking of something as present which is not actually sensed, and an image of juiciness is not a taking of juiciness as present. The depth of difference between the two is shown by the fact that in perception we sometimes err, whereas an image can no more be erroneous than can a sensation. A judgement *about* the sensation or *that* the image is like something can of course be erroneous, but that is another matter. Images themselves are neither true nor false,

[1] H. H. Price, *Perception*, 154.

a ruinous fact for Hume's theories of belief and perception. Since, then, perception can err, and neither a sensation, an image, nor a flock of images, can possibly be in error, perception is not a process of tacking images to sensations.

7. (3) Does it then involve a process of inference? Do we *reason* from what is given to something else that is not? Professor Price is as certain on this point as he is about images: 'When we have perceptual consciousness of a house we simply do *not* infer from the sense-datum to the front surface of the material thing, nor from the front surface to the other surfaces, nor from these to the insides. We must not allow philosophers to bully us into saying that we are "thinking" when we are not.'[1] It is not philosophers only who have done the bullying, however; one of them, indeed, has implicated 'all psychologists' in the gross business. This philosopher may as well be the spokesman for the group. Spencer wrote:

'All psychologists concur in the doctrine that most of the elements contained in the cognition of an observed object, are not known immediately through the senses, but are mediately known by instantaneous ratiocination. Before a visual impression can beco..ae a perception of the thing causing it, there must be added in thought those attributes of trinal extension, size, solidity, quality of surface, etc., which, when united, constitute the nature of the thing as it is known to us. Though these seem to be given in the visual impression, it is demonstrable that they are not so, but have to be reached by inference.' This inference is a classing of appearances 'with like appearances before known, and an assumption that they stand toward certain other phenomena in relations parallel to the before-known relations.'[2]

This doctrine, once so popular, has now gone out of fashion, owing largely perhaps to the onslaughts of Stumpf and James. The attack has been renewed of late by Professors Broad and Price, and by the *Gestalt* psychologists. But I am inclined to

[1] *Perception*, 154.
[2] *Principles of Psychology*, II. 133–4.

think that Spencer was right, and that with a little qualification his doctrine will hold. Let us look at the objections to it.

8. (i) It is said that inference takes time, while the functions of perception are simultaneous. When I look at a house the sensation does not come first, and the awareness of a house come trundling after it; sensation and awareness come together. But in inference there is a *passage* from grounds to conclusion. Hence the process of perception cannot be a process of inference. Now this objection is pretty clearly worthless. The essential thing in inference is the insight into the connection of ground and consequent, and this insight is not a whit the less inference because it happens to occur in a flash. The truth is that though it commonly does take time to work out what the premises imply, the amount of time consumed and whether any is consumed at all are really irrelevant to inference, which consists properly in nothing whatever but the insight into connection. The objection that perception is not inference because it is instantaneous is therefore without weight.

9. (ii) It is sometimes said that the passage within perception is rather association than inference, and assumed that if it is the one, it cannot be the other. Stumpf wrote that where there seem to be two judgements and a passage between them, 'one judgement may be joined mechanically to another in consequence of habit, and be merely called up by it . . . The first judgement is by no means a premise in the logical sense; there is no sort of reflection and no rational insight . . . to assume a process of *unconscious reasoning*, a clearly formed conclusion with an unconscious premise, is wholly gratuitous. What we actually have is an association and reproduction . . .'[1] The point of interest here is the contention that the perceptual process is not inference because it is merely association, thus failing of rational insight. Now that these last are distinct we

[1] *Tonpsychologie*, I. 89–90. A useful bibliographical note is added.

agree, and indeed we shall later contend that nothing is in the full sense inference except the insight into necessity. But this purist conception of inference is certainly not the one commonly held by psychologists, or commonly meant when perception is denied to be inference; James indeed finds the very essence of reasoning in 'similar association in an extreme degree';[1] to exclude from inference all processes not logically necessary would exclude most of the reasoning in science. Induction is surely reasoning in the ordinary sense, yet it is not strictly necessary reasoning. And if reasoning may still be reasoning when it falls short of rational insight, there is no force in an argument that would deny perception to be reasoning merely because such insight is lacking to it.

10. (iii) An argument of a different type is offered by James. To holders of the inference theory he attributes the view that when, for example, we perceive an orange, 'some process like the following runs through the mind: "This" is M; but M is A; therefore "this" is A. Now there seem no good grounds', he says 'for supposing this additional wheel-work in the mind. The classification of *this* as M is itself an act of perception, and should, if all perception were inference, require a still earlier syllogism for its performance, and so backwards *in infinitum*.'[2] Professor Price argues similarly. Of both image and inference theories he says that they could 'only apply to what we call acquired perceptual consciousness, when the thing whose existence we take for granted is familiar. And of course the familiarity arises from other perceptual acts, so that either view if put forward as an explanation of *all* perceptual acts would lead to an infinite regress'.[3] Now with the highest regard for Professor Price's discernment in these matters, I can see no reason whatever for this confining of the inference theory to 'acquired perceptual consciousness'. It may very well be true that all such consciousness *is* acquired,

[1] For a discussion of his theory of reasoning see Chap. XXIII.
[2] *Principles*, II. 112.   *Perception*, 154-55.

THE INFERENTIAL ELEMENT IN PERCEPTION 89

but if it is not, why should that weigh against the inference theory, unless indeed inference is *defined* as a rehearsing of learned connections, a definition one can hardly suppose Mr. Price would accept? Likewise of James's argument; it bears, not against the inference theory as such, but against a special view of what perceptual inference is like, namely that it is always a syllogism. If one conceives inference more generally as a process of arriving at judgement from grounds, the infinite regress is needless, since the inference may then be conceived as a passing directly from the datum given in sense to the accepted presence of a thing, or of the unsensed parts of the thing. Why it should be objectionable to call this inference I do not know, nor can I see that the question whether the connection is a priori or acquired has anything to do with the matter.

I would go farther. I even think that the hue and cry against the old theory that perceptual process is quasi-syllogistic has been more vigorous than convincing. Of course the view that every time I pick up a pencil I am formulating a full-blown syllogism is absurd enough if it means that premises and conclusion are distinctly and explicitly present. But have the holders of the inference theory ever believed that? What they have held, I take it, is this, that one can see on later reflection that three terms must have been implicitly present even though not singled out, and that the passage between them was effected in a way which, if the process *had* been explicit, we should have called syllogistic. I confess that this seems to me innocent. When I perceive the pencil now lying before me, a yellow colour is given in sense. Is it this determinate colour that carries me on to the acceptance of a pencil? No, or at least not necessarily; for I might go on to this acceptance even if I had never seen this determinate shade in a pencil before. What works is (in part) the universal of which this shade is but one embodiment. That universal in certain embodiments has been associated in the past with the other features in pencils, and when it is now presented, these associates tend to arise. The three 'terms' are sensed content, universal, associated universals. One may object that the minor term here is not in the logical sense a term at all; it is not a concept. That is true. But if one reflects on any good formulation of the principle of syllogism, e.g. what satisfies the condition of a rule falls under the rule, I do not see how it can be denied that we have here a movement in essence syllogistic.

What line will critics take? They may remind us that James's infinite-regress argument is not yet answered. The minor term of our syllogism, they will point out, is (in part) a determinate shade of yellow, but if this is perceived *as* yellow, there is required another syllogism, and so on without end. The answer is that the perception of things and the perception of qualities are not to be confused, and that the contention we are putting forward, namely that the perception of *things* involves quasi-syllogistic reasoning, does not at all commit us to the view that the perception of *qualities* involves this. We quite admit that a claim to implicit syllogizing put forward for this latter process would be untenable. But unless such a claim is made, which it certainly is not here, this difficulty about the infinite series does not arise.

11. (iv) A further objection sometimes made is that in perceptual inference there could be no universal middle. The objection is of course without point unless such inference is taken as mediate: but even so it is unconvincing. The reply is this: that between the perceptual acceptance[1] of an object, say a man, and its basis in sensation, there is something else that leads on to this acceptance and, so to speak, carries the conclusion. It is not this particular shape, behaviour, etc., that the character *man* is connected with, but this *kind* of shape and behaviour, and within the range of this kind many different specializations would give the cue. When we speak of a universal here we mean a kind or genus which can be exemplified in various ways, and when we say that this is used as a middle we mean that the passage from the sensed content

[1] I borrow this useful term from Professor Price.

to the perceptual acceptance or judgement is made through this generic term.

It is not suggested, of course, that this universal is apprehended as such and explicitly. 'We must remember', as Professor Broad warns us, 'that ignorant men, and presumably animals, perceive as well as philosophers.'[1] But there is every reason to think that ignorant men and even animals do use such terms, and it is hard to see how they could perceive at all if they did not. What carries them to the acceptance of, say, a man as present is certainly not the moment's sensation, regarded as a psychological event, since that could never have been associated with anything. Nor is this determinate content essential, since the acceptance would still have occurred if a somewhat different content had been offered. One may take refuge in a doctrine of 'traces' and say that what actually happens is the revival of such traces by a present stimulus; but this is too vague to help. If the traces are taken as physical, the problem is dealt with by dodging it, after the fashion of the behaviourists. If the traces are taken as mental, the problem recurs what aroused them, and for this problem the only plausible answer seems to be the one here defended, that there is at work in the perceiving mind an implicit universal.

12. There are readers who will still feel that such universals are out of place in the primitive mind. But the position will seem less fantastic if we pause for a moment and consider some illustrations. Animals are sometimes supposed to be moved only by sensible details while man alone is moved by general identities. But when one reflects on this, does it not appear clearly as a mistake? The books on animal intelligence, and indeed our ordinary experience, are full of facts to the contrary. F. H. Bradley, who gave much thought to the beginnings of judgement and inference, illustrates the point in his *Logic*. Suppose one goes walking with one's dog to-day and he has a fight at a certain place with a 'black retriever with a large

[1] *The Mind and Its Place in Nature*, 153.

brass collar'; what will he ordinarily do if, on a walk to-morrow, he finds a dog of rather different cast in the same place? Will he ignore him because what is given is sensibly different? Not he:

> 'he will certainly attack him, and the less intelligent he is the more catholic is his action. . . . He may turn from a small dog, or a white dog, or a smooth-coated dog, but size, blackness and roughness, are the typical ideas which will certainly operate.'

Bradley concludes that

> 'from the outset universals are used. . . . From the first beginnings of intelligence it is the type that operates and not the image. . . . The lower we descend in the growth of our own functions, or in the scale of animate nature, the more typical, the less individual, the less distinct, the more vaguely universal and widely symbolic is the deposit of experience. . . . It is not universal in the sense that analysis has distinguished the relevant from the irrelevant detail. . . . But in the sense of not using the particular as particular, and of taking the meaning while leaving the existence, in the sense of invariably transcending the given, and of holding true always and valid everywhere what has ever and anywhere once been experienced, the earliest and the latest intelligence are the same from one end to the other of the scale of life.'[1]

The fact that the use of universals is coextensive with the perception of things might be illustrated by many interesting minor points. Among them would be the facts that as perception fails the use of the universal is the last thing to go, and that as it recovers from a temporary suspension, as by hypnosis, this is the first thing to return. As the faculties begin to fail, the power to identify a particular man is lost before the power to perceive him as a friend, and the power to perceive him as a friend before the power to perceive him as a man. The story of Emerson at Longfellow's funeral, gazing at his friend of many years and being able to say only, 'That was a good man', is a familiar and touching example. The case seems to be the same if we turn to such curious discoveries as those

---

[1] *Logic*, I. 36–8.

of Binet and Féré, about the recovery of the power to perceive after it has been hypnotized away. They suspended so completely the power of a certain subject to perceive M. Féré that nothing he could do would attract her attention, and a hat and cloak put upon him seemed to be suspended in air; his very name and existence seemed to be blotted from her memory. The hardy experimenters left her in this state for days, whereupon, reports M. Binet, 'we had some difficulty in making M. Féré visible to her again. She at last saw his person, but oddly enough, did not recognize him and took him for a stranger, and it was most comic to see her anger when M. Féré addressed her as "tu".' Binet goes on to say that it is the most general properties of things that are the last to be lost to view under anaesthesia and the first to be recovered as it goes; and this, he thinks, is only an example of a wider law that perception develops not from the special to the general but from the general to the special.[1] We shall have something to say about this later when we consider the growth of general ideas.

13. (v) But there are careful writers who think that in talking of inference in perception, 'we express the position far too intellectually'.

> 'It would be false psychologically', says Professor Broad, 'to say that we *infer* from the nature of the objective constituent and from any other knowledge that we may have that it is part of a larger spatio-temporal whole of a certain specific kind. It is perfectly evident that we do nothing of the sort. Of course we can talk of "unconscious inferences" if we like; but at most this means that we in fact reach without inference the sort of conclusion that could be defended by inference if it were challenged. It would be nearer the truth to say that, at the purely perceptual level, people do not have the special experience called "belief" or "judgment." To believe so and so at this level really means to act as it would be reasonable to act *if* one believed so and so, and to be surprised if the action turns out to be a failure.'[2]

[1] *Psychologie du Raisonnement*, 71–3.
[2] *The Mind and Its Place in Nature*, 151, 153.

I think that Professor Broad here falls into the opposite error from the one he deprecates and *under*-intellectualizes perception. The reason for saying this is that on the view he expresses perception could not be mistaken, whereas it may be and sometimes is. If perceptual belief 'really means to act' in a certain way, it would be meaningless to say that we had ever perceived correctly; no mere act is true or false. Professor Broad in the same discussion suggests another view which seems equally hard to accept, namely that belief is 'represented at this stage by the bodily feelings' that go with automatic adjustment. But I do not see how feelings can be mistaken any more than acts. It may of course be denied that we ever do make mistakes in perception. It may be said that when I approach a weight marked '100 lb.', brace myself, and find the weight to be made of paper, no mistake was involved; my body adjusted itself, with certain accompanying feelings, and I was surprised at the event. But it certainly accords better with ordinary usage and thought, and I think also with critical reflection, to say that I *was* mistaken, and that if I adjusted my muscles as I did, it was *because* I took the weight to be heavy. This is not to deny that a process of adjustment may become unperceptive and quasi-mechanical, but to maintain that in ordinary perception we have placed our feet on the bottom rung of the ladder of thought. Nor is it suggested that perceptual judgement is fully explicit. It is not, but this means little. For, as we shall see in a moment, there is no reason whatever to deny that implicit thinking exists. The criterion of the presence of thought, whether explicit or implicit, is the possibility of error; and in perception there is clearly a process capable of error. And Professor Broad makes use of language that implies this. In every perceptual situation there is 'the *conviction* that this particular something is not isolated and self-subsistent . . .';[1] we may 'feel our *expectations* frustrated, though', he adds, 'these expectations were not really present at the time as distinct beliefs about the future'.[2] Now convictions and

[1] *The Mind and Its Place in Nature*, 151.
[2] *Ibid.*, 153; my italics in both cases.

expectations are very far indeed from either acts or bodily feelings; and it is as difficult to see how they could be 'frustrated' if they were *not* beliefs about something as if they *were* acts or feelings.[1]

14. (vi) It is often said that unconscious inference is worse than mythology; it is downright contradiction. Now we are holding no brief for unconscious inference, though we shall see in a later chapter that reasoning of much complexity may go on below the level of explicit consciousness.[2] Whatever difficulties there may be, however, in the notion of unconscious inference, the description of the process as implicit is quite legitimate. And it is time to say what we mean by this ambiguous word 'implicit'. Of the four senses that are probably commonest we mean to use it in one only.

(*a*) It is sometimes said of a scholar that he carries around a vast store of knowledge, and this would be considered true of him even while he was at breakfast or nodding at the theatre. If it is asked in what form he carries this store during the times when he is not using it, the answer comes that he owns it 'implicitly'. This does not mean that he is conscious continuously of all the facts that make up his knowledge; it means *that, if he cared to, he could recall them*; he is learned because they are at his beck and call. In this sense implicit knowledge may be completely unconscious. It is *not* our present sense of the word. (*b*) The oak is said sometimes to be implicit in the acorn, and a 'soul of goodness in things evil'. Such phrases *may* mean only this, that there is something in the acorn that will in time give rise to the oak, and that the apparently evil event will lead on to good. In this sense, the effect is implicit

---

[1] Professor Price, who also thinks that to find judgement or inference in perception is to over-intellectualize it, nevertheless writes as follows: 'What is taken for granted is, after all, *that* so and so is the case—that a material thing exists here and now, that it has a surface of such and such a sort, that it is grass, etc.—in short, what is taken for granted is a set of propositions.' *Perception*, 166. Between this and our 'implicit judgement' I see no essential difference.

[2] Chap. XXIV.

in the cause. Again, this is not our meaning. (c) It is sometimes said that in an argument there is an implicit contradiction or an 'implicit denial of free trade'. Here 'implicit' means 'implied'. We do not mean this either. (d) It is sometimes said that an old sailor knows implicitly when a storm is approaching, or that one has implicit grounds for thinking so-and-so untrustworthy. In such cases there is pretty clearly something present in experience which serves as ground, even though it may be very difficult for the judger to say what it is. One may be aware of something and use it as a ground without singling it out for full and specific attention. This is our sense of the term.

15. It will now, perhaps, be clear what is meant when we say that perception is implicit inference. It means that when, for example, I perceive a house, both the grounds on which I take it as a house and my grasp of the connection between those grounds and their consequent are implicit in the above sense. (a) To deal briefly with the latter first: perceptual inference is of course not a movement along a row of conspicuous stepping-stones in the form of explicit judgements. But the essential thing about inference is not the conspicuousness of the stepping-stones but the fact of the passage, and if the passage is actually made, though on stones that are submerged, it is better called inference through implicit steps than not inference at all. This passage need not be a temporal one in which first there is the appearance of the ground and *then* of the conclusion. It may, for all we can see, be instantaneous. When we perceive an orange, we do not first catch the sensory cue and *then* pass to the conclusion that an orange is there; cue and conclusion seem to present themselves together and blend in a single percept. It may be said that if the process is not a process in time, it is not a process at all, and so not inference. But that would imply that no instant apprehension that p implies q is ever inference; and this is absurd. However, we have dealt with this mistake already.[1]

---

[1] Above, Sec. 8.

It may be said further that even granting an 'instant apprehension', there is no grasp of implication. If this means 'no grasp of full or abstract necessity', it is true; the process, as we have admitted, is largely associative. But while it is important to distinguish implication from connections that are associative, it is important also to see that the line between them is not a hard and fast one. Necessity may be already at work within processes that seem merely associative; indeed, as we shall see later, no process is *barely* associative.

(*b*) Just as a connection may be apprehended, though not explicitly grasped or formulated, so grounds are often employed that are all but inaccessible. As Sir William Mitchell says,

'we have all sorts of beliefs for which we cannot give a reason. The suspicions and the hopes that we call groundless are so in the sense only that the ground cannot be given, or that it is a bad one, for there always is one. We may dislike Dr. Fell with reason, though we cannot give it; even a judge was advised to decide without stating his grounds; a woman may always make the same claim for her intuitions; in all the arts taste goes before analysis; and a man of genius may leave it to others to discover how reasonable he has been.'[1]

If perception did not carry implicitly the relation of ground and consequent, much of the reflection that comes later would be wasted, since that is engaged, in no small measure, in dragging to light and explicitly formulating the connections found in perception. This bringing to light of the grounds of our perceptual beliefs is commonly easy enough. There is a characteristic colour, shape and size about the orange, a characteristic posture and gait about my friend, which not only make recognition effortless, but make evident why it is so. But since the grounds we use in perceiving may have all degrees of explicitness, they may at times be exceedingly obscure. Bosanquet somewhere remarks that he has been repeatedly baffled in his attempt to find the datum by which he has fixed the direction of a sound. A person practised in

---

[1] *Structure and Growth of the Mind*, 248-9. I should like to express here a large obligation to this admirable book.

introspection will sometimes succeed where another will fail. But it would be a mistake in principle to make the presence of grounds depend merely on their conspicuousness or one's skill in eliciting them. The best course is to recognize that, at least from the earliest perception of things, an inferential movement is present which may be explicit in all degrees.

16. (vii) We turn to a further criticism of the doctrine of perceptual inference. Professor Price says of those who hold it that

'they have confused the *conditions* of perceptual consciousness with perceptual consciousness itself. No doubt it is true that if we had not performed certain intellectual acts in the past (acts rather of synthesis than of reasoning) as we went from the front of a house to the back and from one room to another, we could not *now* have perceptual consciousness of a house at all. . . . But it does not follow that we are at this moment performing any intellectual acts. All that follows is that the mental disposition which these past acts formed in us is a necessary condition of our present perceptual acceptance.'[1]

The confusion imputed here to defenders of the inference theory I understand to be this: they have seen that our present perception of houses would be impossible without past experience of them. They then argue that if this past experience is necessary, it must be necessary as a component in present perception, to recall and apply which is an 'intellectual act'. And this is confused because they are passing unwittingly from one sense to another of 'necessary', from 'necessary as a past condition' to 'necessary as a present part'. Now this is to my mind a curious criticism. I should have thought it is precisely those, or some of those, who have believed in implicit inference—Bradley, for example—who have made *most* of the distinction between present perception and the conditioning past particulars. They do hold, to be sure, that something is used now which has also been used in the past, namely a

[1] *Op. cit.*, 154-5.

universal connection between terms themselves universal, but the confusion of universals now employed with past particular experiences, a confusion they are continually charging upon the associationists, is something they have guarded against specifically and even loudly. If they hold that there is a present 'intellectual act', it is not because they have confused what are so obviously different, but because they have seen clearly the crucial fact that perception may be true or false, and have sought a theory that will comport with it.

17. (viii) We must deal with one more criticism of the theory, which is recent, determined, and competent. It is made on psychological grounds and comes from a group of psychologists with whom, as will appear, we have much in common, the school of *Gestalt*. Köhler and Koffka have both offered vigorous criticisms of the inference theory. Professor Köhler, in the third chapter of his *Gestalt Psychology*, examines it as held by Titchener, who used it in interesting fashion to defend his own view of the province of psychology. According to this view, psychology should be confined to a narrow territory which lies between the field of physiology on the one hand and of general philosophy on the other, the field of sensory experience. It is true that experience contains much besides this; our sensations normally carry *meanings* which, from the point of view of knowledge, are the most important things about them; but Titchener insists that unless psychology can exclude these meanings, its field will be the world and it will have no special province at all. It is true again that these sensations depend directly on certain changes in the body; but such changes are the concern of physiology, and should be handed over to it. We can thus recognize a threefold hierarchy: at the bottom, physical changes; resting on them, sensations; and resting on these again, meanings. According to Titchener, psychology should resolutely cut off both extremes and confine itself to the middle. To do so, particularly to amputate the last term, is difficult; in ordinary perception meaning so dominates sensation, making us perceive squares when we really sense rhomboids, and circles where we sense ellipses, and stable sizes where sensa vary, that only with the greatest care and patience can we learn to isolate what is actually given in sense. It is against the meaning theory in this context that Professor Köhler's criticism is directed. He argues (1) that the dominance of meaning has been overstressed, that in many cases like that of apparent constancy in brightness or size more is due to sensation and less to the influence of meaning than is here supposed; (2) that to assume a sensum to depend on nothing but a single localized stimulus is unfounded; and (3) that if sense data are taken as elements sharply distinguishable from, and uninfluenced by, their context of meaning and attitude, they are myths. Now we think it very likely that Professor Köhler is right on all these points. They contain nothing that conflicts with the meaning theory as here advocated, except more scepticism as to its adequacy in special cases; Professor Köhler himself writes, 'I do not deny that objective experience is imbued with acquired meaning in many respects'; 'probably no experience escapes from the influence of meaning';[1] and he insists, in a manner which we shall cordially underline later,[2] on the necessity of retaining such meaning within any sane psychology.

Koffka is more unsparing. He considers the theory at length in the light of many experiments and concludes with a 'radical rejection of it'. To do full justice to his discussion would require more space and more knowledge in detail of the experiments than we have at our disposal. But we can at least indicate the sort of argument he relies on.

The theory that perception involves inference or interpretation attained its vogue, he says, because of the aid it seemed to offer in answering the question, Why do things look as they do? It is queer, on reflection, that things do look as they do. When a man walks away from us down the street, the image of him on our retina gets smaller and smaller, and also—it

---

[1] *Gestalt Psychology*, 79–80; 61.   [2] Chap. VII, Secs. 10–14.

was natural to say—our sense datum gets smaller and smaller; yet *he* does not seem to shrink; we perceive him as a full-sized man, not as some miraculous dwarf or homunculus who shrivels away before our eyes. Yet that is just what he ought to do if it is really sensation only that presents him to us. Since no such apparent shrinkage occurs, there must be some element in perception that counteracts the diminishing size of the sense datum. And what could this be but the judgement or inference that the actual man does not shrink, though the datum does? We have learned this fact from experience, and in the present case we simply draw on that experience and compensate the diminishing sense-datum with a corrective judgement.

Now Professor Koffka will have none of this. Experimental facts, he thinks, have been brought to light that are 'utterly incompatible with a meaning theory'. He believes that what is supposed to be gained indirectly by inference or 'interpretation' is really gained by direct apprehension, and considers that this has been proved by excluding all possibility of interpretation and discovering that the same facts may be apprehended without it. Let us look at an experiment or two of the kind he relies on.

You look with one eye through a round hole, through which you can see nothing but an illuminated white wall. Just beyond the hole, and stretched up and down across the centre of the field is a thread, with its points of attachment out of sight. Suppose this thread is moved gradually away from the eye; what will the observer see? Will it seem to move? Yes, in point of fact it does seem to move away. How are we able to perceive this movement? The 'meaning-theory' has its explanation pat. As the thread moves away, our sensum of it grows narrower, and the appearance of increasing distance is an inference from this. But there is one fact that destroys the theory; our sensum of the thread does *not* grow narrower; its thickness seems to remain the same. There is thus no basis for the inference whatever. Hence no inference could have occurred. Hence the movement must have been apprehended directly.[1]

___
[1] Koffka, *Principles of Gestalt Psychology*, 82 ff.

The theory becomes less plausible still, says Koffka, as you eliminate the chances of drawing on past experience. So he turns to similar experiments on infants and young animals.

> 'An infant of eleven months, e.g., who had been trained to select the larger of two boxes standing side by side, continued in her choice when the larger box had been removed to a distance at which its retinal image was less than $\frac{1}{15}$ of the area of the retinal image of the smaller, nearer box. . . .'[1]

Since it is unreasonable, Koffka argues, to suppose that the child could have *learned* to interpret the sensum from the smaller image as meaning a more distant box, she must have grasped the distance directly. Still more impressive are the performances of chicks:

> 'Götz has proved that chicks only three months old show constancy of size in their behaviour. Since chicks choose spontaneously the larger grains first, it was not difficult to train them consistently to peck first at the larger of two simultaneously presented grains. For the purpose of the experiment it was necessary to go beyond this and train them to peck at the bigger grains *only*, a result that was safely though not quite so easily accomplished. Then in critical experiments the two grains were so deposited that the smaller was 15 cm. distant from the chick emerging from the door of an antechamber to the food box, whereas the bigger grain was at a greater distance. The chicks chose consistently the bigger grain up to a distance of 73 cm. between the two grains . . . the results of the critical experiments are truly astounding, for in them the animals selected as the bigger a grain whose retinal image was but about $\frac{1}{30}$ of the area of the smaller, corresponding to a linear proportion of $1 : 5 \cdot 5 !$'[2]

The argument is, as before, that since the chicks could not have learned to interpret one sense datum as *meaning* greater distance than another, the distance must have been grasped directly. Koffka regards these experiments as decisive, and we may fairly take them as typical.

[1] *Op. cit.*, 88.   [2] *Ibid.*, 88–9.

18. We would venture the following comments upon them: (a) Assume that Koffka is quite correct in his reading of them; do they disprove the inference theory? It seems to us that at most they could only limit the range within which it holds. The experiments we have mentioned, on which he places much stress, are all concerned with a single point, the estimation of distance. To be sure he cites further experiments designed to show that size and brightness may also be estimated on occasion without resort to judgement. And undoubtedly if judgement plays no part in such estimates, its presence in perception is a less sweepingly useful hypothesis than was supposed. But that this calls for a 'radical rejection' of the theory, in the sense of a general rejection, I do not see, nor can I believe that in the end that is Koffka's intention. For he gives full assent to the above discussion of Köhler's in which it is said expressly that 'objective experience is imbued with acquired meaning in many respects' and that 'probably no experience escapes from the influence of meaning'. This, I think, is the evident truth. Suppose these experiments prove their point, it still remains that every time we perceptually recognize a tree by its leaf, or a soldier by his uniform, or a + as a sign of addition, or indeed any *thing* as what it is; whenever in driving a car we stop at a red light, or in tennis adjust our stroke to the prospective flight of the ball, whenever we choose or avoid anything because we have found it good or bad, whenever indeed we make any use whatever of past experience in identification or new adjustment—which would cover, surely, a large part of our perceptual life—we are employing what would here be described as implicit inference. Perhaps Koffka would agree with much of this. What he attacks particularly is the application of the inference theory to explain 'why things look as they do'. It is not clear how much is to be included in the 'look' of things; but if something before us *looks like* an orange, or like something with another side, or like something juicy or moderately soft or easy to roll or a first-rate missile, can any of these ascriptions, or a hundred others named as easily, be plausibly accounted for on any but the 'meaning theory'? We do not see how they can. And if not, the success of these experiments would affect the theory in a fraction only of its field.

19. (*b*) Even within this fraction the experiments seem less than conclusive. In the cases just cited the results depend on excluding any possibility that past experience has been used in determining what is now perceived. The belief that this has been excluded rests on two grounds: (*a*) that there is nothing in present sensation from which inference could leap, (β) (an additional ground in the last two examples) that there was nothing in past experience for it to use. Both these grounds seem questionable.

(*a*) It is surely hard to be confident that there is *no* basis in present sensation for the judgement of distance. In the thread experiment the argument is that though the thread was seen to move away, its apparent thickness remained the same, and hence that a judgement of motion could have no possible ground. Now I should have supposed that when one was looking at a thread with one eye, it would be far from easy to be sure whether the thread as sensed grew thinner or not, and that if it did, nothing would be easier than to overlook it.[1] This indeed is the interpretation of the experiment offered by Jaensch and others; there *was* a sensory difference that passed unnoticed. Koffka replies that 'this removes the last vestige of plausibility from this theory. . . Since I cannot judge about something I am not aware of, the term judgement must have a different meaning from the ordinary one';[2] and it seems to him incredible that a judgement should be based on what is 'unnoticed, i.e. unexperienced'. But (*a*) why identify the unnoticed with the unexperienced? There are many sensations connected with breathing, for example, that we do not ordinarily *notice*, but it would be difficult to say that we

---

[1] To argue from changes in the retinal image would beg an important question, as Koffka rightly points out.   [2] *Ibid.*, 86–7.

are not experiencing them at all.[1] (*b*) Nor is it clear why, on the theory, I should be supposed to judge 'about something I am not aware of', or why 'the term judgement must have a different meaning from the ordinary one', or why the process of so judging should be thought in any way exceptional. To use something I am not explicitly aware of as a *ground* of judgement is not to say that I am judging *about* this ground; when I form an impression of someone's untrustworthiness on some ground that I cannot specify, I am judging about the person, not about my own elusive data. And far from being uncommon or untypical, we should have thought judgement on grounds of this sort was one of the most familiar kinds of judgement, that we are daily and hourly judging upon the basis of sensory data not explicitly singled out, and difficult to recover. Of course, to fabricate data in order to bolster up a theory otherwise implausible would be absurd, but it is not absurd to suppose the existence of a kind of data often found if that will extend the range of a theory known to be widely applicable. And if we turn to the other two experiments above, the likelihood of such undistinguished data becomes greater, for both are cases of binocular vision. The argument here seems to assume that the *only* respect in which the sense data presenting two grains or two boxes can differ is *size*, so that when the datum of the farther box or grain becomes smaller than that of the nearer one, there is nothing left in it on which a judgement of greater distance could be founded. But we should have supposed it beyond question that the image of a remoter box seen by binocular vision, even if it is exactly the same in size as that of a smaller but nearer box, *does* differ in other ways, and hence that some basis for a differential judgement of distance *is* present. And whether it is or not, the method used in these experiments for deciding that it is not is illegitimate on Koffka's own showing. He insists, and we think rightly, that you cannot, following the 'constancy hypothesis', assume any close correlation between the retinal image and the experienced datum. Yet it will be observed that in both these

[1] Cf. Chap. IV, Sec. 8 ff.

instances he states carefully the comparative size of the retinal image and argues directly from this size to the experienced datum itself. But how can he have it both ways? If one can argue in this manner from retinal image to datum, there is more in the constancy theory than he admits; if one cannot, the datum is admitted to be imperfectly known to us, and then how can one be so confident that it can supply *no* basis for judgement?

(β) The dismissal of judgement, then, for the reason that in these experiments there is no possible ground for it seems hasty. But in the last two cases a further reason is suggested, namely that chick and child were too young to have learned how to interpret data of distance even if they were there. The child was eleven months old; the chicks were three months old; the distances involved ranged from a few inches to a few feet or yards. 'Chicks must be geniuses', Professor Koffka writes, 'if they can discover in the first three months of their lives that something that looks smaller is really bigger.'[1] On reading this, I am torn between my respect for Professor Koffka's great knowledge in these matters, and a conviction which still lingers that if this is brilliance, then the chick is a master mind. With recollections of Lloyd Morgan's old experiments, showing how very quickly a chick could learn to avoid a piece of orange-peel or an unsavoury caterpillar, I am surprised at the disesteem into which the chick mentality has fallen, and still cling to the belief that in three months (surely no mean period in the *Lehrjahre* of a chick) animals that, by express statement, had already been taught other things, could also achieve the insight 'that something that looks smaller is really bigger'. Knowing human stupidity, perhaps one should be less confident about the child; but even here, one would have supposed eleven months gave time and to spare for the learning of anything that these experiments tested.

20. (*c*) We suspect that the Gestaltists, in their account of the inference theory, inadvertently do less than justice both

[1] Koffka, *Principles*, 89.

to the motives of those who hold the theory and to their own in rejecting it. They do not place high enough among the former the value of this view for the theory of knowledge; we suspect they do not place high enough among the latter their own loyalty to the phenomenological method. Both miscalculations are dangerous.

(a) When Gestaltists attack the inference theory, the villain of the piece is usually the 'constancy hypothesis'. If one starts, they say, by assuming a constant correlation between datum and local stimulus, then when the stimulus changes without change in the presented object, judgement or inference must be called in to account for this strange stability. And no doubt the constancy hypothesis has played its part. But there is another conviction also that has played an important part, and not, as we conceive, a mistaken one, namely that unless perception involves judgement, it cannot intelligibly be true or false; the fact that perception may obviously be either has made the presence in it of judgement an inevitable conclusion. Indeed, what judgement means to epistemologist and logician is the assertion of something as true, and the possibility of error is taken as the best test of its presence. This way of using the term is useful and well established. Suppose we refuse to apply it to perception; what is the alternative? Apparently direct apprehension in sense. Let us assume, then, that the apprehension of a tree as a hundred yards away or a weight as a hundred-pound one is taken as a case of direct sensation. It will then be necessary to say that some sensations are in error. But obviously not *all* sensations are in error; it would be absurd to say that a bare sound could be false or a bare pain true. A division would hence be necessary between those sensations that could, and those that could not be true or false. But as soon as one examined the class of true-or-false sensations, one would find in them the other traits that logic has found implied in assertions of truth or falsity; e.g., there would always be discernible in them, however vaguely distinguished and in however rudimentary a form, something asserted, i.e. a predicate, and something asserted about, a subject. Even in what is expressed by an exclamation like 'how hot!' these features, as Bosanquet points out, are already dimly present. Now the contention of those who hold the judgement or inference theory is here simple enough. They say that if a process has all the logical features of judgement, then judgement it should be called.

21. (β) If Gestaltists would not accept this, we suspect it is because the other neglected motive above referred to is coming upon the scene, their own loyalty to the phenomenological method. This method lays down the admirable rule that before you try to analyse or explain an experience you should describe accurately what is there. The instant this seemingly simple requirement is taken seriously, it shows that such attempts as that of the behaviourists to reduce experience to reactions, and that of some introspectionists to reduce it to sensations and affections, are elaborate ways of missing the point; and the Gestaltists have done an immensely valuable work in helping to clear the ground of these psychologies of 'nothing but'.[1] The first thing to do, they have insisted, if one is to analyse the experience of an object, is to find what the object *seems like* to the person experiencing it, since that *is* the experience to be dealt with. And an object does not normally seem like a mosaic or collection of sense data. 'A face, for example, certainly does not appear to a baby as hair *and* eyes *and* nose and so on, but as something friendly or nasty'; 'heaps or even groups of colour-sensations do not make a chair'.[2] Now when we perceive teacups or colonels as what they are, our experience certainly does not *seem like* the experience of a sense datum plus an inferred obverse side or military rank; no such patchwork appears; there is just a teacup or a colonel, all of a piece. And when Gestaltists show so much resistance

[1] See Köhler's *The Place of Value in a World of Facts* (1938), and Koffka's *Principles*, Chap. I.
[2] Koffka, 'Introspection and the Method of Psychology', *Brit. Jour. of Psych.*, XV. 158. 153.

to our inference theory, we suspect they are inwardly stiffened
by this doctrine that, as experienced contents, things are what
they seem to be.

22. But there is a dilemma here. Push the phenomenological
method through, and you wholly destroy psychological analysis;
let in the thin edge of analysis, and there is nothing in principle
to exclude the sort of analysis we have proposed. Consider
the teacup again. When I see it in the ordinary course of things,
it is an unanalysed whole, and is part of a larger unanalysed
whole which is perhaps suffused with a certain emotion and
unified by certain attitudes or ends. The Gestaltists urge with
much force that each part of this experienced whole is so
dependent on the other parts that it would not be itself if you
cut it off from the rest. But you must, in a measure, do that
whenever you analyse at all. The change to the analytic
attitude is itself enough to destroy the old whole, and hence
every component part of it. Indeed this is admitted by Professor
Koffka; the new method, he says, 'leads to the abolition of
psychological analysis in the sense hitherto generally understood'.[1] In what sense, then, is analysis still possible? Koffka's
reply is in substance this, that the attitude of analysis may be
remote by *more or less* from that of the state to be analysed,
that its destructiveness of the original state will hence be a
matter of degree, and that we can tell by the 'feel' of it how
destructive it is. There is a great deal of sense in this. But the
question for us must be, will the admission of analysis to this
extent admit also the distinction within perception of sense

[1] *Ibid.*, 155, though he says in the same context: 'The original
reactions are to be studied just as they are and not merely under the
aspect of what they will become when analysis is applied to them.
Only in this way shall we be able to find their proper laws.' Our difficulty is as to how the original reactions *can* be studied if the attitude
of study is itself enough to make them into something else. It should
be added that in an important sense we agree with the Gestaltists'
distrust of analysis (see Chap. XXXI, Secs. 21, 25). But we are freer
than they are to accept the implied criticism of science as such.

data and judgement? To this is is not quite easy to get an answer from the Gestaltists. They concede readily enough that when they take the analytic attitude, they find sense data present; 'I do not feel justified', writes Professor Köhler, 'in calling those artefacts *unreal*. When I apply the introspectionist's methods I myself can get those special experiences which corroborate his findings.'[1] He would agree in like manner that the meaning can, at least on occasion, be singled out; the sound represented by 'eagle' stands in German for a hedgehog (*Igel*) and in English for a bird; 'here it is obvious that we have to discriminate between a genuine sensory experience which is the same in both languages, and two different meanings. . . .'[2] Professor Köhler would say, I suppose, that neither the sensory element nor the meaning thus dissected out is quite the same as that which entered into pre-analytic experience. But he would agree, I imagine, that the identity as compared with the difference is very great; and this, combined with his statement that sensory element and meaning *can* be discriminated introspectively, supplies sufficient ground, we suggest, for our analysis into datum and judged accompaniment. In sum, if the Gestaltists apply the phenomenological method in root-and-branch fashion, analysis goes altogether. But then psychology goes with it. Compromise with the analytic method is therefore inevitable. But if this method is admitted at all, it is bound to light upon the broad distinction on which we have been insisting. Hence in spite of their recurrent criticism, we cannot regard the Gestalists as really enemies. They do admit, though reluctantly, and with a salutary warning, that the line we have sought to draw runs through most, and possibly all, perceptual experience.

23. (*d*) There is another way in which the Gestaltists provide material for the theory they seem so reluctant to admit. They have shown by many neat and, we think, con-

---

[1] *Gestalt Psychology*, 66.   [2] *Ibid.*, 55.

clusive experiments that the mind is no *tabula rasa*, that from the beginning it has preferences for certain kinds of lines and figures, that if supplied with a line capable of being completed into various figures, it will, through an internal organizing force, complete it into one figure rather than another, that if given a set of dots capable of being construed in various patterns, it will commonly construe the dots into some pattern natively determined.[1] What is given is taken as not complete in itself but as a fragment of some whole. Nor is it a matter of learning; the mind does this sort of thing quite independently of tuition. Some at least of the forms or structures so used the Gestaltists, following Wertheimer, are quite willing to call 'intelligible', implying that they give 'understanding' of the subject-matter arranged in accordance with them. Now we not only accept this argument of theirs; in dealing with inference in our later books we carry their principle, or something like it, far beyond any point to which we should be confident they would go with us. But whether they would go so far or not, we would point out that in their 'laws of organization' of the perceptual field they have in any case granted us what we are now contending for. The taking of a given datum *as* part of a larger structured whole, the completion of a given fragment in accordance with 'intelligible' form or necessity, is indeed a peculiarly fine example of what we mean by perceptual inference.[2] When the Gestaltists criticize the inference theory, they commonly assume that it *must* mean the supplementation of the given by the deposit of past experience, and that it is therefore what they call an 'empiristic' theory. I see no ground whatever for limiting the inference theory in this way. The material used in the inference may be drawn from past experience or it may not; or again, there may be empirical matter with an a priori nerve of necessity; inference as such is confined to no one of these forms. Indeed, if argument were wanted that it may be

[1] See Koffka, *Principles*, Chap. IV, Köhler, *Gest. Psych.*, Chap. V.

[2] 'Even among the simplest objects', says Koffka, 'each part points beyond itself and implies a larger whole. Facts and significance cease to be two concepts belonging to different realms, since a fact is always a fact in an intrinsically coherent whole.'—*Op. cit.*, 176.

genuinely a priori, it is to the Gestaltists that we should go for some of our most telling evidence.

24. The reader will now have had enough of perceptual inference. But there is a closely associated point that cannot well be passed over. If there exists in perception an inferential passage at all, it will lead to something like a judgement or belief, and we have in fact made use of both these terms. It is now time to examine perceptual belief more closely. Let us look briefly at (i) its definition, then at (ii) its variation in explicitness and definiteness, and finally at (iii) the line that marks it off from its ground.

(i) In examining any implicit process it is a help to be familiar first with its explicit form. What is ordinarily meant when we say we *believe* something? One may reply that it is the acceptance or conviction or adoption or affirmation or mental assertion of some proposition, but these are all synonyms, not definitions. The fact is that belief, central as it is in the life of thought, and perhaps because it *is* so central, is indefinable and probably indescribable. The reader may more readily admit this if he is apprised of the results of some of the most competent attempts to describe it. We will devote a paragraph each to the results of two such investigations.

25. Much of Professor Titchener's *Experimental Psychology of the Thought Processes* was devoted to precisely this attempt; and the work is the more to our purpose because it reviews the results of perhaps the most patient and persistent introspective attack yet made on the nature of belief, that of the Würzburg school in Germany. According to one set of observers, what we ultimately reach is indescribable *Bewusstseinslagen*, 'certain conscious processes which obviously refused description either as determinate ideas or as volitions'.[1] According to another, the ultimate fact is 'a content image-

[1] *Experimental Psychology, etc.*, 100 (Mayer and Orth).

lessly present as knowledge'; to the reader of a term, 'the meaning is present simply as an awareness'.[1] According to a third, the final fact appears as an 'intellectual attitude' which 'may be just a glow or halo of indescribable consciousness'.[2] A fourth group, seeking to find what 'must supervene upon conscious processes' to make them judgements, 'much to their own astonishment', could find, in eight series of observations, nothing at all.[3] A fifth reports that at the heart of judgement lies 'something that shows no trace of sensible quality or sensible intensity', which 'is determined quite differently from anything that in the last resort may be reduced to sensation', something described as 'awareness, or sometimes knowledge, or simply "the consciousness that", but most frequently and most correctly, thoughts'.[4] We read such results, the product of skilled and exhaustive search, and we are exactly where we were before. They look like descriptions of the indescribable.

There are writers, however, who believe that much more than this can be said by psychology about the nature of belief, and from one of them, who has been described as the 'least confused of all analysers of confused happenings',[5] we should naturally expect much light. 'The content of a belief', says Mr. Russell, 'may consist of words only, or of images only, or of a mixture of the two, or of either or both together with one or more sensations. It must contain at least one constituent which is a word or an image . . . For example, you hear a noise, and you say to yourself "tram". Here the noise and the word "tram" are both constituents of your belief . . . The same noise may bring into your mind the visual image of a tram, instead of the word "tram". In this case your belief consists of a sensation and an image suitably related. Beliefs of this class are what are called "judgments of perception". '[6] Now a

---

[1] *Experimental Psychology*, 104–5 (Ach).   [2] *Ibid.*, 112 (Messer).
[3] *Ibid.*, 118 (Marbe).
[4] *Ibid.*, 143–4 (Bühler). For Titchener's own view of thought see below, Chap. VII.
[5] Vernon Lee, in Introduction to Semon's *Mnemic Psychology*, 44.
[6] *Analysis of Mind*, 236–7.

rough count discloses in this passage some fifteen distinguishable propositions about such judgements of perception, of
which one seems to me true, one doubtful, and thirteen
false. This of course is a sweeping statement, and the
support that it calls for will be attempted later,[1] but even
the less critical reader, in search of some clear picture of
belief, is sorely puzzled when he learns on one page that
'objective reference is of the essence of belief',[2] and on the
next that a belief may consist 'wholly of words or of images';
when he finds that belief is an image or set of words accompanied by a 'belief-feeling',[3] though this 'feeling' is also
described as an 'act', an 'attitude' and 'a complex of sensations,
attached to the content believed';[4] when he reflects that if
beliefs may be 'added to sensation to make perception',[5]
this would mean, if put together with what has just been quoted,
that the perception of a tea-pot is (*a*) a sensation, plus (*b*) a
set of words or images, plus (*c*) a complex of other sensations.
The reader may feel unable to give a clear account of what
he does mean by belief, perceptual or other, but one may be
pretty certain that he does not mean this.

26. These are the attempts of unusually competent re-
searchers to describe belief. But we may perhaps be forgiven
for saying that the sum of the first is nothing and of the second
nonsense. Reflection on them tends to support the view of
James that belief is 'perfectly distinct, but perfectly indescribable in words', that 'it feels like itself—and that is about
as much as we can say'.[6] However, this is not quite all we
can say. We can say that belief is *not* sensation, that it is *not*
the use of words or images, though these may accompany it,
and that it is *not* the same as desire or feeling, though it is
most intimately connected with both. James, to be sure,
thinks it *is* a feeling, and speaks of those states of intoxication
'in which a man's very soul will sweat with conviction, and

---

[1] Chap. VIII.   [2] *Analysis*, 238.   [3] *Ibid.*, 242.
[4] *Ibid.*, 250.   [5] *Ibid.*, 242.   [6] *Psychology*, II. 284, 286.

he be all the while unable to tell what he is convinced of at all'.[1] But one questions here whether the belief and the 'emotion of belief' are rightly called the same; whether, when a man asserts passionately that his country is right, he really believes it more than that he has five fingers on his hand, which he accepts quite unexcitedly. And if these two do not vary together, to take something as true or false is not the same as to have an 'emotion of conviction' about it. Bain sought to equate belief with the influence of an idea on conduct;[2] Descartes[3] and Newman[4] sought in different ways to make it an act of will. The common difficulty of all such views is that they make judgement or belief too specific a function, whereas the fact is that it is virtually identical with mind on its intellectual side. Its distinctive character is such, Mill said, that 'when we arrive at it, we seem to have reached, as it were, the central point of our intellectual nature' which all other mental functions presuppose.[5] It is present, and indispensably present, in perception and reflection, in desire and will, in memory and expectation, even in imagination and doubt. In the eyes of some philosophers who have remained very close to the facts of mental process, it is a tenable view 'to take judgement as present whenever we have an object at all before the mind'[6]: indeed 'the whole of consciousness, in as far as it is the consciousness of a single world that shares the reality of our waking self, may be regarded as a continuous judgment. . . . '[7]

Such statements may appear vague, but they are less vague than general; and any view of belief or judgement that is to be true *must* be so general as to apply to what we are doing at every instant of our waking lives. When we attempt defining

---

[1] *Psychology*, II. 284.

[2] See his note to James Mill's chapter on belief in the latter's *Analysis of the Human Mind*, II. 392–402; also the comments of J. S. Mill, immediately following, and of Bradley, *Logic*, II. 17–20.

[3] *Meditation* IV (Works, Haldane and Ross, I. 174–7).

[4] *Grammar of Assent*, Chap. VI.

[5] In a note to James Mill's *Analysis*, II. 423.

[6] Bradley, *Logic* I. 39.   [7] Bosanquet, *Logic*[2], I. 84.

anything as general as this, we find that what is most common and familiar is just what is indefinable. But indefinableness is neither vagueness nor mysteriousness, and in spite of our inability to define belief, we can see pretty clearly what is meant by it, can distinguish it from words, images and feelings, and can recognize its presence in different forms of experience. In the perception of 'things' we can see its presence plainly. Here that taking of something *to be*, a process which is always present in belief, appears as the taking of certain qualities to 'belong to' an object which has other qualities besides them. It is not quite correct to call this an 'expectation', for the belief is rather a judgement as to what now is than a prediction of what I shall find later, though the judgement regarding what is may be made for the sake of some practical end. How important belief is for perception may be made clear by considering (1) that if in perceiving an orange our thought were confined to what we see, we should remain penned in a coloured patch and never arrive at an orange at all, and (2) that to say, as some writers do, that we should even see a coloured patch is, strictly, wrong. One can no doubt see a colour, but at the level at which one apprehends a coloured patch, rudimentary judgement is present. To talk of 'sensing *patches* of colour', except by way of metonymy, is to talk loosely; no patch could possibly be sensed.

We have not hesitated to speak of the implicit judgement or belief within perception. But it needs to be remembered that some of the conditions ordinarily present in belief are here absent. When we say we believe something, we are usually aware that this belief must be justified by evidence, and that since our evidence may possibly be insufficient, our belief may possibly be wrong. If we are wholly confident in our belief, that is not because it has never been questioned but because we are sure it could stand up under questioning; whether we can produce the evidence or not, we accept the belief because we think the evidence is there. Now in perception, this consciousness that belief must go back to evidence is quite absent.

'This state of mind much more resembles what Cook Wilson calls *being under an impression that* than what he calls belief. In "being under an impression" we simply jump straight from the awareness of A to the thought of B, without any preliminary wondering or considering of evidence, indeed without any rational process whatever; for instance, we jump from hearing a knock on the door to the thought that our friend Jones has arrived. And as there has been no consideration of evidence, so there is no consciousness that we may be wrong: one has just not raised the question whether one is liable to be wrong or not.'[1]

27. (ii) Professor Price gives the name 'acceptance' to this process; Sir William Mitchell calls it 'taking for granted'. The latter term has perhaps the merit of suggesting that such belief is not always explicit. In perceiving an orange, we give no express attention to its weight and juiciness, though if it turned out a paper shell, we should say 'it is quite different from what we thought'. We have seen already that belief is not explicit always; we have now to emphasize that its degree of explicitness may vary from a concentration which neglects the given altogether down to a point where thought has nearly or wholly vanished. In this matter introspection is not a trustworthy guide. When I introspect my perception of a tea-kettle to see if it contains any thought of another side, I may find nothing to report. But if perception were really confined to the side I see, I could not take what I see to belong to a *tea-kettle*, which is just what I do.

As perceptual belief varies in explicitness, so also it varies in definiteness. The two, of course, are different. When I look nervously at a fire-cracker which is about to explode in some novel way, my thought is explicit, but indefinite; when later, I pick up the shell almost mechanically, what thought I have is definite enough, but it is implicit almost to vanishing. And definiteness may have many degrees.

Does belief itself have degrees? I think we must say No. We may believe that x is y or that it is not y, but more or less to take it as y seems meaningless. If I take what is before me as

---

[1] Price, *op. cit.*, 140–1.

a tea-kettle, it is hard to see how I could increase my doing so, or reduce it. I may, of course, think it more or less probable that I am perceiving a tea-kettle, but that is another matter. And if, with a profound 'emotion of conviction', I swear that yonder object is a tea-kettle and that, Heaven helping me, I can no other, I am still judging neither less nor more than that is a tea-kettle; what has changed is only the feeling with which I assert it.

28. (iii) Can we draw any line within perception between what is given and what is thought? Bosanquet thinks we cannot; 'it is vain to attempt to lay down boundaries between the given and its extension. The moment we try to do this we are on the wrong track'; 'the so-called "given" is no less artificial than that by which it is extended'.[1] If this means that we never in practice succeed in reaching a datum unaffected by thought —for example a pure sensation—it is not improbably true. If it is taken to mean that there is no distinction at all between sensation and thought, and that the world of material things can accordingly be resolved away into thoughts, we cannot accept it. This is not to say that the world may not be resoluble into *experience*; nor is it even to deny that the objects of sensation are exclusively universals. It is merely to say that from what we have called the inferential element in perception another can be distinguished which, if we never quite capture it in its own character, we can at least approach asymptotically.

But while presumably there is some line between the given and its extension, we may almost as well assume that there is not. For any line that we actually draw proves arbitrary and inconstant. The inference in perception was not, so far as we could see, a process in which the ground first appears by itself, and then the belief that rests on it; the two present themselves together; the ground comes clothed or invested with the belief. And the influence between these two sides of perception does not work one way only, but both ways. The

---

[1] *Logic²*, I. 72.

'solid facts' on which theories are built turn out, to an astonishing extent, to be the product of the theories supposedly based on them, and the line between fact and theory to be elusive and vanishing.[1] When a fact has been seen in the light of a theory, does it remain the same fact as before? We shall see that on the answers to this question depend different views of the nature of analysis, and so of the nature of understanding itself. But all we are concerned to show at present is that thought does seem to react on its grounds at the perceptual level.

29. We cannot do this more effectively than by taking examples from various senses. First, sound:

> '*Pas de lieu Rhône que nous:* one may read this again and again without recognizing the sounds to be identical with those of the words *paddle your own canoe.* As we seize the English meaning the sound itself appears to change. . . . Our own language would sound very different to us if we heard it without understanding, as we hear a foreign tongue. . . . All of us are conscious of the strong inflections of voice and explosives and gutturals of German speech in a way no German can be conscious of them.'[2]

Next, sight:

> 'according to the calculations of Helmholtz, a picture representing a Bedouin's white raiment in blinding sunshine, will, when seen in a fairly lit gallery, have a degree of luminosity reaching only to about one-thirtieth of that of the actual object. On the other hand, a painting representing marble ruins illuminated by moonlight, will under the same conditions of illumination, have a luminosity amounting to as much as from ten to twenty thousand times that of the object. Yet the spectator does not notice these stupendous discrepancies.'[3]

Then touch and pain:

> 'Gratiolet relates that when two medical students were engaged in dissection, one playfully passed the handle of his

---

[1] See also below, Chap. XXV. Sec. 17 ff.
[2] James, *Psychology*, II. 80. [3] Sully, *Illusions*, 88–9.

scalpel across the fingers of his friend, who started, shrieked, and then, laughing at his error, confessed that he felt the pain of the blade cutting through to the bone.'[1]

Such illustrations could be continued indefinitely; everybody could parallel them from his own experience; and if one were to draw on the region of the abnormal, much more striking examples could of course be found. They all tend to show that 'sense data', instead of being hard little pellets offered us by nature, are so plastic to thought that to catch them in an untouched state is really a vain attempt.

30. We may now summarize as follows: Our second problem about perception concerned its structure in the leading case of the perception of things. Such perception involves a relation between what is actually given in sense and what is only thought or judged. The passage from one of these to the other is not, we saw, the supervening of one reflex upon another, or the addition of images to sensation, but a movement that may be described as implicit inference, in which neither what is sensed nor what is taken for granted is singled out for express attention. Taking for granted is a species of belief, and hence, though itself indefinable and without degrees, it has attributes of explicitness and definiteness that vary widely. Further, it so reacts upon its ground that in practice no sharp line can be drawn between them.

[1] Lewes, *Problems of Life and Mind*, 3rd series, Vol. II. 279.

CHAPTER III

THE THING AND ITS ARCHITECTURE

1. In studying perceptual intelligence we decided to select the chief relations involved in the perception of things and centre attention upon them, omitting for the time those fundamental categories that are used at every level of thought. We have now dealt with the first of these relations, the relation between the sensory element in perception and what we have called the inferential. In the present chapter we shall review the chief remaining relations. What does this study have to do with the nature of thought? We may repeat what was said in the last chapter, that thought is a seeking for truth, that truth is here conceived (the argument to come later) as a single intelligible system, and that a study of thought in perception will thus naturally fix attention on the sort of structure or organization that is found in the perception of things. The organization achieved in perception is of immense importance because all animal experience and much of human experience takes place upon this level. Nevertheless the general thesis of this chapter is that so far as thought is concerned that achievement is a very poor one. Those solid everyday things which seem constructed in a fashion so firm and so inevitable are really thrown together in a most hit-or-miss way, and if thought for a time comes to rest among them, this is only because it has ceased to press its own interest and has surrendered to the competing claims of convenience and practical necessity.

2. (1) Our first question[1] is as to the sort of unity things possess. Why do we group these particular qualities into a whole as belonging to one thing?

Reflection on this matter is likely to pass through several stages. Our first response is perhaps that the whole problem is

[1] The series of questions we are considering is listed on pp. 79–80.

artificial. '*Why* should I take a certain shape and taste and colour to belong together in an orange! But how could I do anything else? Is it suggested that I might have assigned them instead to the bookcase or the clock? If I assign them as a group to the orange, it is surely because I find them there, because I see that it has them and nothing else has.' But with a little reflection this easy confidence begins to fade. What do we mean by saying 'it has them'? What is the 'it' of this orange which holds its qualities together? Is it something distinct from the qualities themselves? It is certainly not something we can think of as *apart* from the qualities, for if we try the experiment of ideally stripping these off we have nothing left. This does not prove, to be sure, that a thing is not a 'substance' which is actually distinct from its qualities though non-existent apart from them; and philosophers of note have believed in such substance.[1] But since many other philosophers have found it not only hard to accept, but hard to conceive, it is not likely that animals and primitive men started with it and grouped qualities at its dictation. Yet if it goes, what have we left to provide the inner bond among the qualities of one thing?

We may next surmise that the bond is a common cause. We take the yellowish colour, the roughish surface, the peculiar taste, as the qualities of one orange because one thing has caused them all, or at least caused us to sense them all. Now if this means that we group them together because we *recognize* a common cause, it puts the cart before the horse, for we group the qualities of one thing together long before we are able to conceive them as the effects of a single cause. On the other hand, if it means that the grouping is forced on us willy-nilly by the common cause, once again it will not serve. For in any moment of perception a great many different qualities are being forced on us from a great many different sources. If we do not know as yet which qualities come from which source, countless groupings are theoretically possible. And the question still remains why, from among these countless possibilities,

[1] *E.g.* McTaggart, *Nature of Existence*, Sec. 68.

this particular grouping is arrived at? Appeals to physical causation will not explain this.

We may try another shift. Perhaps there is something. in the qualities themselves that makes them cluster into these particular combinations. But this also seems to lead nowhere. What is there in the colour of an orange to condemn it to marriage with a round shape, or in a round shape that it should unite with this weight, or in a weight that it should come mated with this taste? Such matches are *mariages de convenance*, in which mutual suitability of character can hardly have been considered. The qualities might as well have been grouped in any number of other ways. We cannot see in the least why an orange should not be purple and weigh tons, and combine six-sidedness with the habit of speaking when spoken to. Such pairings would at least be more interesting than the relatively dull groupings we have; and, so far as we can see, there are no incompatibilities of temper that would prevent any bulk or shape from finding its affinity in any colour or odour or taste. When we think of what might have been, the present unions seem not only irrational but often perverse.

Still, it is incredible that such combinations should represent nothing but chance, and a little further reflection does reveal some traces of necessity floating about among them. When we say the orange is round, for example, we are using a relation, that of substance and attribute, which, however difficult to interpret exactly, is commonly taken as a category, and is so central in our thinking that if it were really to prove irrational all intelligence would be shaken. And there are other relations also that go beyond chance conjunction. Though, so far as we can see, the colour of the orange need not appear with this particular shape, could it appear without extension at all? There is plainly more than chance here; and the same may be said of other connections. What moves *must* occupy space; what has size *must* have some shape; what is hard *must* be in some degree solid or impenetrable. Still, such relations hold less between the particular qualities of a given thing than between types of quality or attribute; motion *as such* must be spatial; *any* size implies shape. For the reasons why particular colours, tastes, etc., flock together as they do, we must turn to considerations of a different kind, which have nothing to do with necessity and very little to do with each other. The chief factors appear to be five.

3. (i) First, joint prominence. In our early experience, there are many cases in which a group of qualities stand out in such joint conspicuousness from an unappealing background that we can hardly fail to notice them, as when the bright disc of the moon appears in the dark sky.[1] There the colour and the shape, exactly coextensive, stand out against a background contrasting with both; the brightness and the sharp contour support each other and leap jointly into prominence. Such prominence has various conditions. It depends in part on our native capacity for some sensations rather than others, a capacity we cannot explain; in part on the strength of sensations; in part on their interest, native or acquired; in part on contrast. The coldness, the shape, the smoothness, the glint, of a block of ice stand out together conspicuously at one place in space; it is only natural that we should group them together. So of the shape, colour, and size of some peak that stands out against the sky, or of the sun at any time of day, or of a pine tree on a hill. In all of them diverse qualities rise into prominence jointly.

The word 'jointly', however, conceals a problem. Part of its meaning is 'at the same time', but only part; if a flash of light and a pain in my eyes occur at the same time, I do not take them as attributes of one thing. 'Jointly' may also mean 'at the same place'. But here there is a well-known and much-canvassed difficulty which we cannot quite avoid, though we can hardly treat it as it deserves. When I see and feel the block of ice, how do I manage to locate in one spot the shape that I see and the hardness that I feel? The two qualities are in different orders. One of them belongs to the order of sight,

[1] Cf. Stout, *Manual of Psychology*, fourth edition, 429; also 416–20 on 'unity of attributes in the same subject'.

where everything has extension, but where there are no 'feels', weights, sounds or tastes. The other is in the order of tactile sensations which is so different from the other that some philosophers have thought that the two have nothing in common. How do members of these different orders get unified in one place?

The process is a gradual one. This is illustrated by the helplessness of the young baby to resist what is done to him when, for example, vaccination is necessary.[1] He has not the faintest notion *where* the operation is going on. He has never gazed at that spot on his arm while at the same time exploring it with his fingers and feeling the pain, so he has not established it as a point of intersection between his different kinds of experience. Little by little, in the course of his restless movements, he does this. And his way of grouping qualities at a point outside his body is essentially the same as his way of grouping them at some locality on his skin. If we take as typical the perception of the ice as having shape and hardness, what happens is something like this: A person perceives in the middle of his visual field a coloured expanse of a certain shape and size. He moves in such a way as to experience simultaneously two series of changes, one a continuous increase in size of the coloured expanse, its shape remaining nearly the same, the other a series of 'muscle-joint-tendon' sensations. If he continues his movement, he finds that the two series end abruptly at about the same time. The tactile series (if we may group as tactile somewhat different kinds of sensation) ends abruptly in a sensation of hardness, and at about the same time the visual series ends in a size which no attempt at continued movement will make larger. This size and this degree of hardness appear repeatedly together, thus welding an association between them. And when they do so appear together a new series may be started which further cements the association. For while the visual size remains the same, the tactile series may be extended; one may run one's finger over the various parts of the visual expanse and find that when it reaches the

<hr/>

[1] Cf. James, *Psychology*, I. 186–7.

limit of that expanse, the series of hardness-sensations ends too. And since the joint experience of the hardness and the visual extent is often repeated and can be secured at will, the two become so intimately connected that we no longer think of them as inhabiting separate orders. We say that the hardness is extended and that it occupies the same space as the colour.

4. Our location of visual and tactual qualities in the same space seems, then, to be a matter of association. To guard this statement against ambiguity certain comments must be added. (a) It may be protested that such an account implies that visual and tactual space are two different spaces, and that the supposed single space we live in is an illusion patched up for convenience. I do not for a moment mean to suggest this. The proposal that we begin with a different space for every sense, combine them into one, and then combine the space so formed with other people's spaces to make one public space, seems clearly untenable. How could a mind that was really confined to private space ever correlate that space with others? If he could, he would have a leg in both worlds, and would no longer be confined to one. There is nothing inconsistent in itself about spatial solipsism, but, as Bradley remarks, we can hardly enjoy the delights of solitude together.

(b) If such criticism is sound, are we not speaking inaccurately when we speak of correlating sight space with touch space? I am inclined to think we are. I am inclined to think that the only space we know is that of sight, and that when we speak of space that is touched we are falling into confusion or metaphor. This involves, indeed, the consequence that for the man who has always been blind the sort of space that the rest of us apprehend by sight does not exist at all; and it will at once be pointed out that for him things are still outside of each other and movement through space still possible. That he does order his tactual data in some ways and does speak of them as outside each other are beyond dispute, but can he mean by 'outside' what we do? I cannot profess confidence here, but

in examining my own experience of space I find that if I carefully exclude all reference to visual extension, what I ordinarily
mean by space has disappeared with it. This does not imply,
of course, that if I were to go blind now, I should cease to
live in a spatial world. The tactual relations between objects
have become so intimately associated with the spatial relations
of sight that I should no doubt go on translating them in spatial
terms. But if I had never known sight at all, should I mean by
'distance', 'outside', etc., what I now mean by them? I cannot
persuade myself that I should.[1]

(c) Even movement is probably not spatial to the man
congenitally blind in the sense that it is to us. Muscle-joint-
tendon sensations are sometimes called sensations of movement, and for practical purposes, correctly enough. Their
connection with visible movement has been so long and
intimate that they are instantly read with their visual meanings,
and we say we *feel* our arm moving. And therefore when we
spoke as we did above about a kinaesthetic series at whose
'intersection' with a visual series we place the qualities of a
thing, we were speaking of a virtual movement-series; the
muscular sensation is so impregnated with suggestions of
visual movement, that it cannot be had alone. Thus in grouping
in one place the colour and the feel of an orange, we are using
two visual series, one being directly visual, namely the series
of increasing sizes, and another indirectly visual, namely the
series of muscular sensations read in terms of visual distance.

[1] Contrast the following from Professor Price: 'We may deal in a
similar way with the spatial relations of tactual sense-data to visual
ones. This is a famous problem, and very strange views have been
held on it; but I cannot see that it deserves its reputation. It has been
thought that a tactual datum is never even similar to a visual one, and
that the relation between them is simply the being associated by
temporal contiguity. . . . It is plain that this doctrine is just untrue.
When I lay my hand on a penny I sense a cold circular expanse; and
when I look at a penny from directly above I sense a brown circular
expanse. It is just obvious that these two shapes are exactly alike', etc.
(*Perception*, 244). I confess it is not 'just obvious' to me that I can
touch the same 'circular expanse' that I see, or any circular expanse
at all; I even doubt whether, strictly speaking, one can *see* such an
expanse, though no doubt one can see the colour.

But in kinaesthetic sensation itself there would seem to be nothing spatial.

(d) Nor is it clear that the space we are said to see is present in any touch sensation. I suspect that we are speaking in metaphor when we say either that hardness or smoothness extends over the whole of a surface, or that something is hard at a particular point. Sensed hardness is not itself extended. We commonly think it is because we so habitually see what we touch, and read it in terms of sight; and when the blind man calls it extended, the succession or peculiar compresence of tactual data that he presumably means is not to be confused with the visual spreadoutness that we mean. If this is true, then in correlating visual with tactual characters at one place we are not correlating two spaces at all, but forming an association between a tactual character that is not spatial and one or more visual qualities that are. Hence when we speak, as we sometimes do, of the tactual size of anything being the real size, we are again speaking intelligibly but in metaphor. We mean, or rather ought to mean, not that the true size is revealed through our hands, but that the aspect of it when we are so placed as to handle it, and the clear visual experiences that are afforded us in the handling supply us our standard spatial impressions.

The reader need not be deterred from accepting our main point here by disagreement on the extension of tactual qualities. Our main point is that joint prominence in one place is a factor in our coming to group qualities as we do, and this indeed is more plainly true if tactual qualities *are* extended than if they are not.

5. (ii) Another important condition of the prominence of qualities, whether singly or in groups, is movement. What moves has a native fascination for every level of mind. Let an object that lay motionless against its background begin to move at a moderate speed and the likelihood of its being noticed is at once multiplied indefinitely. 'Schneider found that a shadow, with distinct outline, and directly fixated, could still be perceived when moving, although its objective strength might be but half as great as that of a stationary shadow so faint as just to disappear.'[1] Consider the bird in a tree and the man beneath it, and how likely he will be to stay unnoticed if he suddenly leaps up and swings his arms; or the case of the kitten and the rolling spool; or the case of the infant who ignores one wholly until one begins to dance about, then crows for more. Qualities which move together gain the joint prominence of which we were speaking; their common motion sets them off against the duller unchanging background, and they become united in the thought of one thing.

6. (iii) Joint *change* has the same effect, whether motion is observed or not. 'Changes which affect a group of qualities together, either as regards their spatial relations or otherwise, tend to be regarded as changes in the qualities of the same thing. When a piece of paper comes in contact with a flame and burns, the resulting change affects permanently its appearances to all our senses.'[2] When the Ancient Mariner was scanning the horizon, he beheld

> 'A something in the sky.
> At first it seemed a little speck
> And then it seemed a mist;
> It moved and moved, and took at last
> A certain shape, I wist.'

This pregnant speck turned out, of course, to be a sail, and sails may turn to specks again on the horizon, but there is no hesitation, for all that, in taking speck and sail as the same thing since the change in qualities from one to the other is joint and continuous.

7. (iv) But more important, probably, than joint prominence, joint movement, or joint change, is joint utility. We group

---

[1] James, *Psychology*, II. 174.   [2] Stout, *Ibid.*, 445.

together in one thing qualities that serve one purpose. Chairs are continuous with floors and walls, but without the least hesitation we discriminate parts of the chair from the floor with which it is continuous and group them into one thing. It is in such man-made articles that we find the most perfect examples of things, for they possess all the types of unity in high degree. Objects in brute nature are of course regarded as things, such as boulders, brooks, and clouds, but if they cannot be *used* as wholes they lack that best title to the name which makes even humble knives and forks aristocrats in the world of things. Indeed, there are writers who would say that utility is the sole ground for selecting any set of qualities as essential to any object. 'The only meaning of essence is teleological', James wrote.

> 'The properties which are important vary from man to man and from hour to hour. Hence divers appellations and conceptions for the same thing. But many objects of daily use—as paper, ink, butter, horse-car—have properties of such constant unwavering importance, and have such stereotyped names, that we end by believing that to conceive them in those ways is to conceive them in the only true way. Those are no truer ways of conceiving them than any others; they are only more important ways, more frequently serviceable ways.'[1]

This overshoots the truth. That utility is not the only ground for our grouping qualities as we do, James would probably agree; but it is also not the only ground for our regarding some as more essential than others. Some qualities have a priority in nature which they owe to no man's preference; they are more essential to the thing because, logically or causally, they determine a larger range of the other qualities than these other qualities themselves. It may be true that the biologist thinks of man as a large-brained animal, and that the seller of ribbons thinks of him as a creature whose powers of ribbon-buying are the most interesting thing about him. But neither would say that these characters could be dropped with equal ease from our idea of man. Both would agree that

---

[1] *Op. cit.*, II. 335–6.

if man were not a large-brained animal he would probably buy no ribbons at all, while his dealings in ribbons might vanish utterly without jeopardizing his place as a large-brained animal. If, therefore, we cling to some characters as more indispensable than others in the constitution of a given thing, this is dictated at least partly by nature and not solely by our own interests.

Nevertheless, so great is the extent to which the world of things is marked out by our practical ends that, once we realize it, the order of common sense disintegrates in our hands. Much that appeared fixed and final is seen to be at bottom arbitrary. There may be readers who remember how as children they watched a cook roll out a sheet of dough and then stamp out the shapes of cookies ready for the oven. The process of perceiving is like this. What parts of the vast continuum of nature shall be fixed upon and marked off as 'things' depends to an astonishing extent on the bent of our interests.[1] A knife and a violin are taken unhesitatingly as things; their qualities co-operate to obvious ends of ours. A stretch of stone in a cliff is hardly a thing, though if a fragment detaches itself, and particularly a fragment with which we can do something or which can do something to us, it becomes a thing at once. But no one would describe as a thing an acre of desert on the moon, a gallon of water in mid-Pacific or a cubic mile of sky; these are not usable units. Again, a grain of sugar, although for us undoubtedly a thing, approaches the lower limits of observable thinghood; to an ant it is probably a big and complex boulder; and to the parasite on the ant it may, as a thing, have wholly vanished through exceeding the *upper* limits of perceivable size. To us a mountain is so large that it is only by placing ourselves at a distance that we can manage to view it as one thing; but it is conceivable that there should be minds

---

[1] 'We have learned the meaning-for-life of appearances so well that we understand them, as it were, in shorthand. The subtlest differences of appearance that have a utility value still continue to be appreciated, while large and important visual characters, provided they are useless for life, will pass unnoticed.'—Roger Fry, *Vision and Design*, 47.

to which a mountain was invisible, and that nothing less than a solar system would catch their notice. Our practical dealings, and therefore our perceptions, move in the intermediate range, among things that bear manageable proportion to our own bodies; if our body were the size of an ant's, tables and houses and mountains could hardly figure. Is there any reason, then, to regard our own markings on the face of nature as *the* right ones? None whatever. They are the arbitrary products of narrow powers and circumscribed interests.

Such reflections have been fortified by recent advances in physics. Though speculative physics has passed far beyond the range of observable things, we could follow it for a while in fair comfort, for though it talked of invisible entities like molecules and atoms, it conceived these as small-scale models of the things we see. But once it had reached electrons, which are not really things at all, we began to feel uneasy. In this world of electric charges, our familiar 'thingy' world is an 'unsubstantial pageant', a baseless cloud-castle. Not that the stuff of which it is made can be intelligibly called unreal, but that the pattern it now wears for us is plainly a dissolving view, necessary at this stage of the mind's advance by reason of its present powers and interests, but so largely a temporary make-shift that in time it may disappear and that even now it turns to a mirage when a reflective eye is cast upon it.

8. If this book had been written twenty years ago, the account we have so far given of the grouping of qualities into things would have been regarded as fairly adequate. We tend to take qualities as belonging to one thing when they are jointly prominent, when they move together, when they change together, when they serve a single purpose. The reason why such an account was considered adequate was that these factors were themselves assigned to further agencies, two in number, which were supposed to exhaust between them all the possible agencies that might affect the grouping. The first three factors—prominence, movement, and change—were to be attributed to the stimulation of particular sensory nerve ends; when the moon was singled out as one thing, that was because the retina was stimulated in such a way as to make brightness and shape stand out; the prominence of the data rested on the relative strength of stimuli. The influence of joint utility had another source; it represented the control over present groupings of past association. And when these two agencies, native nervous connection and experience, had been appealed to, it seemed fairly certain than no further agency remained. This confidence has been rudely shattered of late by the Gestalt psychologists. Fascinated as they are by the problems of form or structure in experience, they never find a new Gestalt or configuration without pouncing upon it and trying to find by speculation or experiment how it came to be there. And they argue that there are groupings of sensory elements which are due to neither of the types of agency earlier regarded as exhaustive, but to such a response of the organism as a whole to its stimuli as a whole as leads to the ordering of sensory elements in certain preferred patterns. They even hold that without this ordering tendency neither of the other agencies could do its work. Agreeing that we do tend to group together qualities that are jointly prominent, they would reject the explanation of this in terms of jointly prominent stimuli; 'on the retina we have the indifferent mosaic of millions of local stimuli and nothing else . . . we may imaginatively impose all possible forms upon the retina . . . We must not forget, however . . . that the form of these objects is at this moment not more really there physiologically than that of an angel or of an Arabic letter'.[1] Similarly of the factor that was to explain the working of joint utility; this helps, but the mind is not passive *until* meanings develop; it does not so much group qualities because they have a joint use as find a joint use for them because they are grouped already; it shows from the very beginning a powerful disposition to order its data in accordance with forms of its own.

It may be that these psychologists, in their enthusiasm for

[1] Köhler, *Gestalt Psychology*, 150.

such *Gestalten*, try to explain too much by them. But there can be no reasonable doubt that these forms exist, or that the organization of things in accordance with them reveals a deep, original, and significant bias of the mind. The Gestaltists have shown the workings of this bias in numerous ways, and in spite of much experimentation have not yet exhausted them. What kinds of *Gestalt* seem to be preferred? Probably the best summary answer is given in a law suggested by Wertheimer; and we shall take the satisfaction of this law as a fifth condition of the grouping of sensory elements into things.[1]

9. (v) This is the so-called 'law of *prägnanz*'. As applied to the field of sense qualities, it means roughly that the field will organize itself as economically as the conditions will allow. What does 'economically' mean? The meaning is complex and not yet completely developed, but its most important elements appear to be simplicity, regularity, and symmetry. Let us illustrate these.

'If we look up at the sky on a clear night, some constellations of stars are seen immediately as belonging together and as detached from their environment. Cassiopeia is an example, the Dipper is another. In past ages people saw the same groups as belonging together and at the present time children do not need instruction in order to perceive them as units.'[2] Now there is nothing in these stars themselves, or, abstractly taken, in the points of light we see, to make them hang together; they could equally well be kept apart, and each be considered as belonging to a different figure; indeed the sky is an invitation to the forming of millions of figures of enormous complexity. Yet only certain ones emerge. Why? Surely, say the Gestaltists, mere simplicity of pattern has something to do with it. Where

---

[1] In distinguishing these conditions, we do not intend to suggest that any one of them is enough alone to account for the demarcation of a thing, though this does not seem impossible. For example, what we have called joint prominence may not be enough unless the 'law of *prägnanz*' is working also, while possibly the working of this law will on occasion serve by itself.   [2] Köhler, *ibid.*, 117.

alternative groupings are possible, we are far more likely to isolate a figure with a few straight sides than a figure with numerous and meandering sides. This illustrates the bias for *simplicity*. It is also illustrated in what Wertheimer calls the law of good continuation, viz., that a line tends to be completed in accordance with its own rule, a straight line continuing straight, the arc of a circle developing into a true circle, not into some figure which would complicate the pattern. This tendency has been prettily demonstrated in persons who, through brain injury, have lost half of their field of vision. When asked to fixate the centre of a circle, briefly exposed, they saw the circle; but they saw it also when only half of it was exposed; that is, they automatically completed the arc into the simplest closed figure its law would allow.[1]

There is a like bias for *regularity*. Make an inkspot shaped like a polygon of twelve or more sides, with the sides very slightly uneven, and present it to an observer. His first impression will probably be that the spot is circular, a circle being a simpler figure than a polygon; his next will be that it is a *regular* polygon; the tendency to see a regular shape will override the inequalities of length.[2] Empiricists have often been troubled by the fact that though the physical things about us seldom if ever present figures that by actual measurement are perfect squares or circles, we are far more familiar with such figures than with those that are slightly less regular. The Gestaltists have pressed this difficulty home. They have presented complicated patterns in which the influence of experience made for the detection of one figure and that of simplicity and regularity for another, and found that, within limits, the latter won out. They contend that unless there is a predisposition for such patterns the results are inexplicable.

Once more, there is a bias for *symmetry*. If two figures, say two triangles or diamonds, intersect each other in such manner as to form a symmetrical whole, for example a star, they will be seen as one, not two. If they intersect at some rakish angle

---

[1] Fuchs and Poppelreuter, reported by Koffka, *Principles*, 146.
[2] Koffka, *ibid.*, 140.

so that the whole is without any symmetry, they will normally be seen as two figures, each symmetrical in itself. The question has been asked why, when we look at a balustrade, we see the figures of the banisters or uprights rather than the figures of the holes between them. Part of the answer has been given by experiment. A researcher presented to a great many observers a sheet on which there were alternate black and white stripes, the black being figured somewhat like banisters, the white having no symmetrical figure. Practically all the observers reported that what they saw was the figured black stripes on a white ground. He then reversed the arrangement, giving the white stripes a figure and not the blacks. The obervers then reported that they saw *white* symmetrical stripes on a black ground.[1] In both cases, what had symmetry stood out.

These are typical Gestaltist results. In the light of them, and of a great mass of similar results produced in recent years, it is difficult to avoid the conclusion of this school: sense elements are not grouped into things by chance or by mechanical stimuli or by deliberate plan; throughout the work of construction we can see the evidences of a fixed urge or disposition to certain types of pattern to the exclusion of others. The Gestaltists are not unaware that such results have philosophical significance, and they have themselves begun to develop this significance in effective fashion.[2] Is it possible that from the very beginning, and even in the organization of sense qualities into things, there is a pressure toward intelligible order? This school has had the insight and courage to say that there is. To be sure, such order appears only brokenly upon the perceptual level, and in our treatment of the construction of things we shall place small stress upon it, reserving its discussion till later. But we hold the Gestaltists entirely right in their suggestion of an immanent pressure toward intelligible order even on the lower perceptual levels. The nature of that pressure and the character of its end will be studied in detail when we come to higher levels of experience.

[1] Bahnsen, reported by Koffka, *op. cit.*, 195.
[2] See Köhler's *The Place of Value in a World of Facts.*

10. (2) Things, then, are selectively constituted. To fashion them we bring together a variety of qualities on a strange variety of principles. And these principles gain still more variety when we turn to our second general problem about the perception of things,[1] namely, how we come to combine in a single thing groups of qualities that come *successively*.

It is obvious that a thing is not a mere complicated flash. It always *lasts*, not necessarily a long time, but long enough to give it some history. And what it is at one stage may be so different from what it is at a later stage that if the two were placed side by side, we should scout the idea that anyone could take them for the same. The hardened gangster is somehow bodily the same as the charming, pink-fleshed infant that he grew from. How do we come to regard as one such diversities as these?

Here Hume can give us aid. It is true that his famous account of identity[2] leaves out the most important things. He speaks in one breath of ideas as perishing existences, and in the next of our having memories of the past, and seems to have supposed that such an account contained no difficulty. He describes experience in such a way that we could not even '*mistake* the succession of our interrupted perceptions for an identical object', as he thinks we do. For such blunders and many others he paid his penalty at the hands of Green and others. And this penalty is an effective object-lesson to anyone who may try to construct an account of thought in which intelligence —the grasp of systematic necessity—is left out. But Hume was an acute psychologist, and in those regions where the mind is working below the level of necessity, his insights are always worth regarding. Now our method of assigning to one thing groups of qualities presented successively and perhaps diverging widely is, as we should agree with Hume, below this level, and his account of it has much force.

The principles used, he thinks, are resemblance and continuity. When I look at a moving picture, I am seeing thousands

---

[1] The third in the list above, pp. 79–80.
[2] *Treatise of Human Nature* (Green and Grose), 489–94, 533–43.

of different snapshots, but while engrossed in the action, this never occurs to me; what I seem to be seeing is the same person moving on from scene to scene. The pictures are different, the apparent places are different, the postures are different, and yet without the least hesitation I take the persons as the same. Why? If Hume were still alive, and were disposed to attend the 'movies' (a less incredible hypothesis in his case than in that of some other philosophers), I suspect he would use them as an excellent example of the way we arrive at enduring things, and would say that we consider the same person to be before us (1) because the resemblance is so great between one picture and the next that we find it easier to contemplate one person with a few small variations than many persons with many resemblances, and (2) because one picture comes so rapidly on the heels of another that to blend them is infinitely easier than to keep them distinct. 'The passage between related ideas is so smooth and easy that it produces little alteration on the mind and seems like the continuation of the same action. . . The thought slides along the succession with equal facility as if it considered only one object, and therefore confounds the succession with the identity.'[1] This last remark is characteristic; for Hume, the identity is a mere illusion, whereas if it really were so, the illusion itself could not have arisen. Still, his twin factors of resemblance and continuity are the factors we are looking for. Of these he most stresses resemblance, since the continuity of our impressions in time and space is being constantly broken, and to bridge the gaps we must fall back on the resemblance of what is present to what is past.

The resemblance may lie almost anywhere. Sometimes it is general and overwhelming, as when, after seeing an orange, I look again a moment later and find similar qualities combined in a similar form and similarly related to similar surroundings. Sometimes the principal resemblance is in a purpose, as when a patched and remodelled ship goes out under the same name. Sometimes it is remoter still, as when a church built first of

---

[1] *Treatise of Human Nature* (Green and Grose), 492-3.

brick is destroyed, and rebuilt of stone in another design, but is still considered the same church because of its similar relations to the parish (or, as Hume should but does not say, to a similar parish). In this case we see the importance of the other principle, continuity in space and time, for the further the church was removed from the former site and the greater the time before rebuilding, the more we should hesitate to call it the same. But the fact is that our groupings of the successive, like our groupings of the simultaneous, proceed according to shifting interests, and on no consistent principle. Sometimes we count things the same where there is continuity but little resemblance, as in the case of the caterpillar that turns to a butterfly; sometimes where there is resemblance but no continuity, as in the case of the rising sun. And since our principles would admit in practice contradictory views, we are at times considerably embarrassed. Sir John Cutler's classic silk stockings, for example, which Lady Cutler darned away until all the silk was replaced by worsted—were they the same or not? That depends. If our principle is continuity, yes. If it is resemblance, yes or no, according to the qualities in which we are interested. But no answer is *the* right one.

11. (3) We come now to another relation[1] involved in perception which is very familiar and yet puzzling in the extreme. We have pointed out that a thing is a composite product comprising qualities of various kinds. And so long as the qualities retain this difference in kind they keep the peace with each other; we are committing no breach of consistency if we think of the same thing as heavy, white and cold. But there is a proverb to the effect that antipathies are most intense among near relations, and if we look at the various characters of the same thing that come to us through a single sense, we shall find them squabbling scandalously as to which have the right of membership.

These quarrels are most conspicuous in the families of

[1] This raises our fourth question about perception, pp. 79–80 above.

shapes and sizes. Suppose that, while holding in the middle of my visual field the shape of a distant tree, I walk steadily towards it. Does the visible size remain constant? On the contrary, it remains the same for no two instants, but enlarges continuously as I go. We must note carefully what this means. (i) It does not mean that I perceive the tree as larger, for plainly I may not; when the visible size was yet tiny, I took the tree as of about the height of a house, and though the visible size has enlarged many times, that estimate may remain unchanged. And (ii) the term 'visible size' is itself dangerous, like the even more questionable 'sensed patches' of which we hear so much in contemporary writing. Such terms are likely to suggest that the visual sensum in perceiving a tree is as sharply and clearly defined as the coloured country I see on a map, and that to apprehend an area as being of a particular shape and size is a matter of mere sensing. Neither suggestion is true. My interest when I perceive is generally so fixed upon the object and so careless of the sensory cue, that 'the meaning tyrannizes over the image'[1] and buries it, sometimes too deep for recovery. The 'patch' I use in perceiving a tree is very difficult to describe, and to think of it as standing out quite definitely and explicitly, like a patch on a patch-work quilt, is certainly an error. And in just the degree to which it does gain describable features, it is not the object of mere sensing; the classifying and relating intelligence has begun to get in its work. Unless we bear in mind these warnings, we shall find ourselves using such phrases as 'acquaintance with sense data' and supposing them free from difficulty when they are full of difficulties of their own.

What is it, then, that we mean when we say that the visible size varies? We may put it as follows: the whole of our visual field consists of variously coloured extents or expanses, which bear very different ratios to the whole they compose. One coloured expanse, or set of such expanses, is accepted by us as presenting one thing, another as presenting another thing. And when we say that the visible size of something varies, we mean not that the absolute size of the coloured extent

[1] Bosanquet's phrase.

presenting it varies (for absolute size is unmeaning); we mean that the size of this extent relatively to the whole field varies. When, for example, a pencil first held at arm's length is brought close to my eye, its perceived size does not necessarily change, but what we have called the visible size does change enormously; it usurps most of the visual field. We read sometimes that this visible size is a datum with which we are directly acquainted through sensation. But this cannot be strictly true, since what is actually used in perceiving is, as we have seen, *relative* size, and relative size cannot be sensed.

Now our difficulty is that the visible size of the coloured extents we take as presenting a single thing varies indefinitely, and that the two most obvious ways of relating this variation to the supposedly stable thing appear to break down utterly. One of these ways is implied in the common belief that the coloured extents are the actual surfaces of the things perceived. This seems plausible enough until one reflects that if it is true, then the variation in visible size is also a variation in actual size, that as I approach the tree, the tree itself gets larger, and as I retreat from it, it dwindles away to a speck. And that is intolerable. But then comes the second suggestion, which runs as follows: The tree itself does not change in size, but as I move toward it the laws of perspective come into play and affect the size of my image. Now it would be absurd to take this image as part of the physical tree; it is only a sign or cue by which the size of the physical thing may be discerned. And if I do not take my varying images as *being* the same thing but only as *meaning* the same thing, there is no inconsistency whatever. But our difficulty is unremoved. The various visible sizes are cues or signs of the physical size. Very well, what *is* this size? Presumably that which is seen from a point near enough to command the 'best' survey of the tree. But is it not obvious that this size too belongs to the series of visible sizes, that it is, like them, a mere sign or cue, and that if it is taken as the real or physical size, this is for no more cogent reason than convenience, which is no *reason* at all? We are thus faced with a dilemma: if we take all the visual sizes as those of the physical tree our doctrine is self-contradictory, while if we take them as merely cues or signs of this, the physical tree forever eludes us.

Exactly the same difficulty breaks out in the family of shapes. As we walk round a 'square' card-table, we may perceive it as square from every position, but among the shapes we actually see is a wild profusion of rhomboids and lozenges. If we are asked why, from all this diversity, we select the square shape as the real one, we find it by no means easy to answer. If we say that it is the shape that presents itself when we are in such and such a position, we have to explain why this position should be preferred. If we say that square is the *tangible* shape, we shall still have to explain how a shape that is really square can be presented through so many shapes that are not, and why, apart from its greater *convenience* in supplying a standard, tangible shape should be supposed the real shape.

12. That these are genuine difficulties in the theory of perception is seen in the efforts to meet them by present-day thinkers; and for the sake of the non-technical reader we may summarize the chief ways of dealing with them. (i) At one extreme is a heroic realism. It would say that the whole riot of sizes and shapes exists out there in space exactly as we see them, whether we do see them or not.[1] The chief problem for this way of thinking is how to deal with illusions, and with the apparently contradictory properties that have to be assigned to one thing. (ii) There is a theory lying close to common sense, which holds with the first theory that when we perceive a tree we may be directly aware of the surface of the physical thing, that this can have but one shape and size, but that these may *appear* different from different points.[2] The main objection

[1] Alexander, *Space Time and Deity*, Vol. II, Chap. 7. In the references that follow only leading representatives of the various views are named.

[2] Dawes Hicks, *Arist. Soc. Proc.*, 1913–14, 1–48; 1916–17, 300–59; G. E. Moore, *Philosophical Studies*, 243–6. It is not implied that these two authors' theories are in other respects the same, or that the view of either has remained unchanged.

to this theory is that it 'is not merely to deny that we perceive physical objects as they are, but to take the much more serious step of asserting that our immediate experience is itself illusory, that we have been quite wrong in the majority of the judgments which we have made as to the data immediately given us. . . .'[1] (iii) A third theory, called the theory of multiple location, holds that sensible shape and size do not belong to things in as simple a way as we have thought, and that 'belonging' involves three terms instead of two. We should say not 'that pine tree is conical', but 'that pine tree is conical from point P'. And then if it happens to have another shape from point P', there is no inconsistency whatever.[2] One difficulty with this theory is that it requires the instantaneous projection of qualities into far-away places in a fashion that shocks our notions of causality; another is that it has no plausible way of dealing with hallucinations, and illusions of doubling. (iv) A fourth theory holds that when we see the various sizes and shapes, we are not aware of anything physical or even existent, but only of logical 'essences', and that every perception is an act of judgement by which we affirm these essences of some existing thing.[3] Its chief difficulty is that the relations of these essences to the physical thing on the one hand and the perceiving mind on the other are never made clear.[4] (v) A fifth theory would agree that the shapes and sizes are neither physical nor mental, but would hold that they are particular existents (sensa) which flourish in the private space of the mind that sees them. But while they are not the same as physical things, they give us a clue to those things, since they depend on them as part-causes and in some cases are also like them.[5] But it is not easy to make out how, if we are really confined to sensa, we also manage to go beyond them and gain real knowledge of physical things. (vi) A sixth theory, describing itself as the 'Collective Delimitation Theory', would define

---

[1] Ewing, *Idealism*, 281.   [2] Whitehead, *The Concept of Nature*.
[3] *Essays in Critical Realism*.
[4] For the detailed development of this criticism, see Chap. XII.
[5] Broad, *Scientific Thought*, Pt. II: *The Mind and Its Place in Nature*, Chap. IV, esp. 180–3.

a material thing as a combination of two factors, a family of sense data (roughly the entire set of shapes, sizes, odours, etc., that may be imagined as radiating from a common centre) plus a 'physical occupant' to account for the causal properties of things.[1] The notion of a family becomes paradoxical, however, when one learns that most of its members are '*facts or truths* of the form "if any observer were at such and such a point of view such and such a sense-datum would exist" '[2]; and the notion of the 'physical occupant' remains vague. (vii) A theory somewhat similar but more extreme would *identify* a thing outright with 'the class of its appearances'; it is a collection of *sensibilia*, some actually sensed and some not.[3] Among many other paradoxical consequences of this theory, however, it would follow that nothing has a place of its own, and that from the place where it is commonly supposed to be, it is completely absent, since at that point no appearances of it are to be seen.[4] Finally (viii) there is the theory that every perception is a judgement in which the entire content, both what is given and what is not, is asserted of reality. In this theory the object has its being in the judgement, and the only way in which an object more real than this can be attained is to develop the present judgement into a complete and coherent system.[5] The commonest criticism of this view is that it makes everything perceived or known inseparable from the knowing.

Of these views the fifth and sixth have gained an advantage that they do not, perhaps, wholly deserve through being worked out in masterly fashion by Broad and Price. To weigh the merits and defects of all these theories would be an interesting but immense undertaking. Fortunately, it is no part of our programme. Our question is not What right have we to assign all these appearances to one thing? but How do we actually come to do so? This question is far more manageable, and we

---

[1] Price, *Perception*, Chap. IX, esp. p. 303.   [2] *Ibid.*, 284.

[3] Russell, *Our Knowledge of the External World*, Chap. III.

[4] Cf. Lovejoy, *The Revolt Against Dualism*, 208.

[5] This, I take it, is the view of Bradley and Bosanquet.

may still hope to agree about it even though we differ widely as to how the appearances are *really* related to the object.

13. Again the principle that has been at work is convenience. To identify the thing, in Mr. Russell's fashion, with the entire family of shapes and sizes that we count as appearances of it would be too complicated for an ease-loving mind; on the other hand to accept none of these appearances as genuine parts of the thing would be too sophisticated and sceptical; what common sense actually does is to adopt a working compromise. It accepts some of the shapes and sizes as the real ones and rejects the others. *Which* are the real ones? They are those that appear to us when we place ourselves at the point where there is the fullest and clearest vision, which, in the case of most small objects, means the point from which we see them in handling them, and in the case of large objects like trees, that more roughly defined point from which we can grasp the most detail while still surveying them as wholes. Now, of course, there is no one point from which the size and shape of a three-dimensional thing can be wholly seen at once. It is therefore necessary, if we are to grasp these, to piece together various different sizes and shapes, which are seen from different points. But how can this be done? For if, remaining at the same distance, I walk round the object, the shapes I see are extremely different, and how can they all belong to one thing? The answer lies in this, that some of the shapes admit of combination into one continuous solid while others do not, and that our conception of the real shape is reached by grouping those that can be so combined and leaving out the others.[1] If I look at a cube at right angles to one face, the shape I see is square; if now I look in the same way at the other five sides, the shapes I see are also square. And these six sides can be fitted consistently together as bounding a single region. But if I look cornerwise at the cube, I see a bevy of rhomboidal shapes which could not possibly be those of the cube if the nuclear ones are also.

[1] In Price's language, the 'standard figure' of the family.

Those shapes that will not cohabit with the others we put down as appearances. They are not irrelevant to the thing; they are not altogether unlike it; they must be accounted as its appearances because they form a continuous series of distortions of the shapes and sizes that stand at the nucleus. But it is these latter and not the distortions that are parts of the real object. We deal in similar fashion with the troops of shapes and sizes seen from greater or nearer distances. When we see a bacillus through a microscope, we say we see it fifty times larger than 'the real size'. When we are dealing with such portentous distances as those of the fixed stars, common sense gets lost in them and its convention supplies no guide. It would probably say that the telescope reveals the size more nearly than the naked eye; but where should we have to stand to see this size as it really is? We get no answer from common sense. Its convention was framed for practice, not for astronomy.

In this same uncritical but practical fashion it deals with other conflicting qualities. A dress looks yellow in daylight, cream-coloured in lamplight, and to the eye that lacks the blue-yellow substance, a lightish grey. What is the 'real' colour? This is a matter of some practical moment, so common sense has contrived an answer. It accepts the yellow, and rejects the others as deceptive appearances. It considers that there is a normal eye and such things as standard conditions, and it sets these up as its umpire. Similarly of the orange that is sweet to the person who is well and sour to the person who is ill. The well man's verdict is accepted even by the person who is ill, who says that his illness has upset him and that he hopes to be able soon to enjoy the 'real flavour' of things again. These devices for selecting 'real' qualities as a rule work admirably. There is such very general agreement as to what constitutes standard conditions that when anyone talks of the taste of an orange or the size of an egg we know what he means. But if we regard the convention from the standpoint of theory, it will seem far less adequate. The distortionate and 'wild' appearances that we reject are, as sense data, just as real as those we elect to serve as constituents of the thing.

For the most part our method of grouping works, and it would be absurd to deny the importance of such working. But to say that the structure we thus give to things really satisfies intelligence, that there is anything logically necessary about it would also be indefensible. Convenience is here dictator.

14. (4) On our fourth question about perception, viz. How do we construe the relation between what is given and the physical thing we perceive? little further need here be said. If the question were how we *ought* to conceive this, it would of course be extremely difficult. Any answer would have to cover some very odd exceptional cases, and in the theory of perception it is the exceptional cases that are at once most treacherous and most significant. It is easy enough to stand boldly for common sense against all metaphysical nonsense if one glues one's attention to selected familiar cases. While we stay in their comfortable circle, the view that we need only open our eyes to see things as they are has some plausibility. But when we try to widen the circle so as to include the converging railway tracks and the bent spoon in the tumbler, mirror images and after-images and double-images and all the types of hallucination, then our formula begins to crumble, for if there is a single fact or case that does not comport with it, it is false. And once our naïve confidence is abandoned, we shall have to travel far to gain any firm foothold again. We shall have little credence, for example, for the compromise of traditional science, which would assign approximately half of the types of quality—the primary qualities—to the object, and keep the other half—the secondaries—within our minds. In short we should be fairly launched into the only science that on these matters has much weight, namely metaphysics.

But of all this common sense knows nothing. It fastens its eye on the normal cases, and notices others only to be amused, surprised, or inconvenienced, and then to forget. Again, within the normal cases it fastens its eye on the nuclear qualities and declines to consider the significance of the others. Hence its theory is of the simplest. What I see, it would say, is part of the physical thing; when I open my eyes and look at it, what I am primarily doing is not having private sensations, not drawing inferences, but simply seeing the thing as it is. The surfaces and corners out there before me are parts of the physical cube; the colour, smoothness, and hardness are actual constituents of it. Common sense is not given to considering the trapeziform and rhomboidal shapes through which some regular shapes are presented, and when they are pointed out, is content to say, as we have seen, that these are not the real shape of the thing, but appearances of it only, which could no doubt be explained by applying the laws of perspective. Touching but lightly on all these seemings, it would regard the mind as a sort of Kodak which records exactly what things are like; indeed even this is too sophisticated. The ordinary man does not conceive himself as going about making copies of outer objects; it is only when he sees ghosts or pink rats or is otherwise disturbed by the illusory, that he begins to distinguish between what is and what appears. There is the thing before him; he is simply seeing it as it is; and it does not occur to him that he may be copying the thing, or affirming, or interpreting, or allowing for distortions. The various processes involved in perception go on so implicitly, swiftly and easily that he never knows they are there. So effortless has it all become that every trace of the mind's labour in selecting and grouping qualities has disappeared. The thing simply stands there, apparently given as a whole, as solid and stolid and secure from private manipulations as a boulder on a plain.

15. (5) But fifthly and finally, the perceiving of things involves a set of relations that are so fundamental as to suggest at once a doubt whether they should not be placed among the categories. When we say, 'That orange yonder is round', there seems to be implied in our meaning (i) that it is external to us in space, (ii) that it is something distinct from its qualities,

(iii) that it is there not on our sufferance but in its own right. Can anything be said as to how we come to assign these traits of externality, substantiality and independence to the things we perceive? Yes, I think so. But the value of such an account as we are now interested in, a psychological as opposed to a metaphysical account, varies greatly in the three cases.

16. (i) Of most things, when we say they are external to us, or 'out there', what we mean is that they are external to our bodies; we consider that we are where our bodies are; and from this point of view, to say that anything is nearer to us than breathing, or closer than hands or feet, is mere rhetoric. But that this is not the only sense in which we regard things as external is shown by the fact that I can hold my hand 'out there' before my eyes and view the hand as itself external. Now, for every 'there' there must be a 'here', and where is 'here' in this case? It is no longer my body as a whole, but rather one place in my body, which can only be described as a place in my head behind my eyes, from which I vaguely conceive myself as looking out. It is this point which I seem to occupy when I see the other parts of my body; and since I cannot escape from it and look at it from without, as I can at other bodily parts, I take it as the innermost 'here'. This is the implicit standpoint of common sense when it thinks of things as external, or speaks of them as 'there'. And of the adoption of this standpoint psychology finds it possible, and even easy, to give an account. But if we take common sense at a somewhat more reflective level, we shall see that externality means more than this, and that an explanation of the deeper meaning is beyond the power of psychology to give. To say that my own brain gives a fixed 'here' is superficial. There is nothing inconceivable in my looking at my own brain just as I can look at my hands and feet. If I did look at it, I should regard every part of it as 'there', as an external object, and then what would become of my 'here'? It would be chased from the scene completely, and externality would have a new meaning. 'External' would then mean one or other of two things: (i) It might mean merely spatial; (ii) if the word were reserved for what fell outside my body or my head, this would be in virtue of some theory of how my mind could *be*, or at least be *in*, some part of my body. And neither of these meanings could well be dealt with by psychology. To explain the first we should have to explain the nature of space. To explain the second, we should have to explain how body is connected with mind. And these are matters for metaphysics, not for psychology.

17. (ii) If the question, then, is asked whether psychology can give an account of how we come to take things as external the answer is both yes and no, depending on the level of reflection from which the question is asked. It is the same with substantiality. When we say of an orange 'it is round', what do we mean by 'it', and how do we come by the notion? Again there are different levels of reflection from which the answer may be given.

To common sense, the 'it' that is round is a solid extended lump of matter. We have seen in discussing shapes and sizes that, though one thing may supply these in prodigal numbers, common sense has little trouble in singling out the 'real' ones. So it is with qualities generally. An orange possesses troops of them, but while some of these reside at headquarters, many are retained only on sufferance as more or less useful camp followers. We hold an orange in our hand, feeling its solidity and observing at the same time that it wears on its bosom the legend 'Sunkist'. Here are two attributes of the same orange. Do we regard them as equally essential to the orange's being? Obviously not. Things are in their manner potentates that may have armies of hangers-on, but exclude from the inner presence all but a favoured few. The superscription 'Sunkist' might vanish without being missed, but if solidity went too, we should feel that the very throne had been abdicated. From such facts we may gather that a thing has concentric rings of qualities, with all degrees of essentiality;

that at its heart lie some sturdy indispensables like solidity, 'real shape' and 'real size', the latter pair selected as shown earlier; and that if the choice were narrowed still further, it would fall upon solidity as being the orange's heart of hearts. Why solidity? Apparently the choice, as so often with common sense, has a pragmatic sanction merely; it is in virtue of their tangible qualities that objects can do things to us—hurt us, help us, be eaten by us; these qualities are therefore practically the most important, and we take them as lying at the core; convert a cobblestone into the ghost of a cobblestone, and we should feel that its 'substance' had gone. When, therefore, we speak of 'it' in referring to a physical thing, I think we usually mean a *solid* core, to which the other qualities are connected with varying degrees of closeness.

18. Common sense is very vague in these matters, and to condense mist into propositions is a hazardous business. But in this mist there is a metaphysic, however vaporous its state; and to precipitate out our naïve beliefs and discover the causes for them is a step toward beliefs that are better. Now if we look closely into the structure of things, we shall find not only this solid nucleus, whose manner of gaining the primacy is so dubious, but another element also, which has likewise got in by questionable methods. This is nothing less than a sort of self, modelled after our own self and, by a piece of uncritical mythologizing, injected into the physical thing. We have all, perhaps, seen a child collide with a chair, and then stop to chide it or even to give it a physical drubbing; he does really seem to think of the chair, however vaguely, as a self with a will of its own, which can at times be very perverse. So far he is a little animist, just as savages are animists when they fear a crooked tree or sacrifice to an angry ocean. Now it has been suggested that we are all animists, even in maturity. Not that the sane man thinks of his dining-room chairs as persons, but that in thinking of each as a subject uniting various powers, the power to offer sturdy resistance to whatever would dislodge it, the power to press down and hold up, etc., he is reading into the thing a centre of something like willing, a self somewhat like his own that may on occasion offer resistance to his own will. He conceives the 'it' of the object not merely as a group of nuclear qualities, but also, however vaguely, as a self that owns them. This I am inclined to think true. When the plain man says of the orange 'it is round', the meaning of 'it' is not exhausted by the set of nuclear qualities, for if he asked '*what* is solid', though he might well think the question trivial he would hardly take it as meaningless. And if he thought about it at all, he would be troubled. For he says as naturally 'it is solid' as 'it is round'; and this implies that however essential solidity is, there is something beyond that owns it. Yet if he tries to lay hold of this something, he finds himself always baffled. He is dismayed to find that there is really nothing there, and that he has disguised from himself the emptiness by taking the object vaguely as a self, controlling from its impalpable centre the powers and qualities of the thing.

This odd vestigial animism has often been noted and has been made to serve various ends. Martineau took it to be part of our idea of cause, and held that when we think of a thing exerting force upon another, we really think of it as exerting effort. In the writings of Ward and Stout, it plays an important role under the name of 'self-projection'. Professor Stout in particular has worked out an ingenious theory by which the very recognition of things as external is made to depend upon it.[1] The argument is that when I see parts of my body move, I also have, as a rule, the experience of willing them to move, that when this motion is stopped by contact, the sense of effort increases, and that by an easy analogy I read into moving and resisting things the same kind of will or effort that I find in myself. But Mr. Joseph has pointed out that in an argument from the analogy of my body, it is assumed that my body is already perceived; hence, some objects at least are perceived without self-projection, and this is not, after all, indispensable

[1] *The Groundwork of Psychology*, 96–8.

to the perceiving of things.[1] This seems to be valid criticism, and it cautions us to be careful as to the part we assign to self-projection. We must not attempt to explain by it the externality of objects; that, as we have seen, is beyond psychological explaining. We must not make it explain our taking some things as subjects or substances and others as attributes, for that, as we shall see in a moment, is also beyond such explaining. Still, the notion does, I think, throw light on our perceptual thought of things. 'Empathy' and 'the pathetic fallacy' would be less easy than they are if the mind had no natural bent to indulge itself in this fashion. The experience of our self as the source of various actions and the centre of various traits is the experience of a peculiarly intimate unity which we carry over into the thought of other persons and in less degree into the perception of inanimate things. The boulder does not really return our push; the kite does not really pull; but so naturally are they taken as centres of an impulse like our own that we escape this way of taking them only with effort. It is in persons that we find the distinctest individuality; and in the business of carving things out of the continuum of nature, we find it helpful to besoul those bodies that are unlike our own as well as those that are like. There is probably no one so sophisticated as to escape in his ordinary thinking this subtle, vestigial animism.

19. Psychology, then, can say something about our thought of things as substantial; it can point out our habit of making tangible qualities the core, and can describe that other habit, not perhaps quite consistent with it, of making things into individuals, vaguely patterned on selves. But neither of these habits represents anything fundamental and necessary in our thinking. The selection of a nucleus is governed by practical importance; self-projection springs from uncritical analogy. As we shall often have occasion to see, psychology is most illuminating precisely where the mind is least rational. But our

[1] *Mind*, N.S., XIX, 1910, 460–3.

thought of what we experience under the form of substance and attribute is not exhausted by devices like these. When both of them have broken down, and our thought has become highly self-critical, we still think in terms of substance and attribute; and this relation reflects itself in the subject-predicate form of our propositions. Even when the search for the 'it' of a physical thing has baffled us, and we can find nothing but qualities, we continue to use 'it' of the qualities. 'It (this orange colour) is redder than that (a yellow colour).' 'It (this difference in colour itself) is greater than that (another difference).' What the substance-attribute relation really is is a matter often disputed among philosophers, but this much would seem to be clear, that it is too fundamental to our ways of thinking to admit of psychological explanation. We cannot start with the thought of a state where things were *not* related in this manner and then show how we came to suppose they were so related, for we cannot conceive what such a state would be. Any explanation of how we came to think as we do is balked at the universal forms of thinking, for these forms determine the structure of any world we can think about, and thus to contemplate their emergence from a state in which they were not is beyond our powers.

20. (iii) Thus, regarding the more criticized form of our beliefs about the externality and substantiality of things psychology can say little. Is this true also of our belief in the independence of things? I think not.

There are philosophers who hold that the acceptance of things as independent is as much involved in our knowing them as the acceptance of their spatiality or the thought of substance and attribute. A distinguished realist philosopher writes: 'Knowledge unconditionally presupposes that the reality known exists independently of the knowledge of it, and that we know it as it exists in this independence.' To this Bosanquet replies: 'if we construe "independence" as "being apart from" I am quite sure that this statement is false.

Knowledge has no such presupposition. We have no such conviction.'[1] Where such doctors so disagree, it is difficult to be confident, but we must at least venture an opinion. And we must be clear as to the issue on which this opinion is called for. Is the issue this, whether in point of fact we assume, in typical cases of knowing, that what we know remains what it is apart from our knowing it? No; I think everyone would admit that we do assume this. Is the issue, then, a question of how knowing shall be defined? Suppose that I never did know anything independent, that my knowledge were, as the solipsist believes, only a transitory mental state with no significance beyond itself; is the question this, whether such a transitory state should be called knowledge? No; it would probably be agreed on all hands that nothing describable as knowledge is here present. Then is the question this, whether, when I examine the act or state in which I admittedly know something, I can find it in any *guarantee* that what I know is independent of the knowing? It is not this either; the question is not whether solipsism can be *disproved* from the nature of knowledge. Finally, is it this, whether in knowledge there is always the *claim* to know what exists independently, so that if anyone says 'I know', he is thereby committing himself to a belief in the independence of what he knows? Yes, this *is*, I take it, the issue; and if so, I incline to the answer of Bosanquet. Though we do undoubtedly take for granted that the objects we know exist independently of being known, I see nothing in the nature of knowledge to compel this belief; and I suspect that even realists would here for the most part agree.

Now if there is nothing in knowing as such to make us take objects as independent, and we do take them so nevertheless, what is it that makes us do so? Again we must guard against misunderstanding. Our question does not imply in the least that we start with our own sensations, either taken as such or not, and gradually come to delude ourselves into supposing groups of them independent. It *is* meant to imply that what we experience at the start is not taken as *either* dependent or

[1] *Logic²*, II. 305.

independent, and that its bifurcation into parts with these characters is what has to be explained. Our question is not as to the logical justification of the belief in independence, but as to its psychological origin. The former question is one of the most difficult and disputed issues of metaphysics, on which we have no desire to express a judgement in passing. But how in fact we arrive at this belief is a far more manageable matter.

21. The main factors are the following: (*a*) The defeat of expectation. An infant is repeatedly given a bottle from which he drinks warm milk. There is very good reason to think that long before he can perceive the bottle *as* a bottle, an association begins to form itself between his experiences of bottle and milk, so that on the appearance of the one he expects, however vaguely, the other. Suppose that the milk is now replaced by some bitter medicine. His expectation is flouted by fact; and when the bottle is next presented, it is suspect. The iron has entered his soul, and he is beginning to draw that distinction whose full mastery is a large business, between his own expectation or idea, and what fact forces upon him. And what thus flouts and collides with our expectation is naturally set down as not belonging to our own selves.

22. (*b*) Some groups of qualities, related in a certain way, maintain themselves apart from my will, while others fluctuate with it. I can hum a tune to myself, or picture Kubla Khan's 'pleasure dome', or gain whenever I please the sensations of turning my head. What can be conjured up or dismissed in this fashion seems clearly to depend on me. But suppose that, in turning my head, I see the fire on the hearth. Why do I not take this as dependent too? For this also I can experience or not, as I choose, by merely opening or shutting my eyes. The answer is in part that though I can will to look at the fire or not, *what* I see when I look is unaffected by my wishing or willing, while with the pleasure-dome it is otherwise; I can banish it if I please. But this is only a partial answer; for 'the sensations of moving my head' are likewise in character (though not in existence) independent of my will and still are regarded as dependent on me. So we must add another clause to the answer, namely that the fire maintains itself *the same*, regardless of my will, that when I open my eyes after shutting them, I find that the shutting has not affected the appearance before me. What thus maintains itself the same through my changing attitudes of will I naturally incline to take as not depending upon me.

23. (*c*) I also regard a group of qualities as independent if, instead of remaining the same, it seems to maintain, apart from my perceiving it, its ordinary rate of change. When, after an absence of some hours, I return and look at the fire, what I perceive may be only embers. But I do not assume that the two *percepta* are unconnected. I assume that I have seen two stages in an independent series, connected by intervening stages which occurred without my perceiving them. Why do I assume this? Because I have seen fires change while I watched them, and if I grant that this change owes nothing to my watching, I can readily explain why it is that whereas I saw a bright fire blazing, I now see nothing but embers. The argument is an example of the great stand-by of primitive thought, the argument from analogy. It is usually a dangerous argument, and if here soberly offered as proof, is not, I think, convincing. But that we actually do use it to arrive at the belief in independence seems clear.

24. (*d*) In some cases our senses confirm each other; in other cases they do not. Where they do, it is again natural that we should assign independence, for what has proved to be independent of one sense, may also be independent of the other, and of both. I seem to see a table in the middle of the room; does it depend upon my seeing it? No, for when not seeing it I can still touch it, just as when not touching it I can

still see it. If then the thing's existence depends neither on
seeing nor on touching, may it not be independent of both
together? On the other hand, when we expect one sense to
confirm another and it fails, our belief in independence is
shaken. My arm may seem, in hallucination, to be four feet
rather than three feet long, but when I try to touch the hand at
its end and find nothing there, I begin to doubt. Similarly,
after an amputation, one may continue to 'feel one's hand',
but if for sight there is nothing but vacant space, even the
strongest sensations are set down as illusory.

25. (*e*) We are here concerned with the perception of things,
not with the perception of other minds. But the suggestions
of such experiences as we have described are strengthened
enormously when communion with other minds is established.
It is chiefly on this that we must rely to clear up a difficulty
that has not always been noticed by writers on genetic
psychology. A toothache seems as heedless of my will as a fire
is, and it runs its course irrespective of desire; why then is
it not held, like the fire, to exist apart from me? I suspect
that the reason is mainly this, that my reports about the fire,
both of its existence and non-existence, are corroborated by
others, while I find that my report of a toothache cannot be
corroborated by anyone else. And this influence is so powerful
that if the circumstances were reversed, it is conceivable that
an opposite result should have emerged. If, whenever I reported
seeing a fire, I were met with a blank, uncomprehending stare,
it is not unlikely that I should come to regard it as a private
inspiration, of somewhat sinister augury. And if pain were
felt always and only at certain fixed points in space, which could
be occupied successively by the nerve-ends of different persons,
we should take it as residing there independently. Our beliefs
about independence have been worked out in co-operation.

26. We are now at the end of our discussion of the sort of
structure thought lays hold of in the perception of things.

However imperfectly we may have described this, our task would have been far greater if we had not confined ourselves deliberately to those relations within perception of which a psychological account can be given. Excluding categorial relations, those we thought most important were the relation of what is sensed to what is apprehended mediately, of qualities of different orders to each other, of the qualities of the *same* order to each other, of qualities of a later group to those of an earlier, of the qualities to the 'real thing' of common sense, and finally that trio of relations involved in setting things over against ourselves as external, substantial, and independent. These we have analysed as far as limited space would allow.

CHAPTER IV

THE NATURE OF PERCEPTUAL MEANING

1. The perception of physical things is the most familiar type of perception, and the discussion of it throws much light on perception generally, but of course it is not the only type. Nor is it, I think, the most interesting, since there are others in which we can study to better advantage the fascinating problem of the nature and range of perceptual meaning.

What we propose to study under the head of meaning, and what is meant by its varying range, will be clear from a few examples. Meaning is the element in the following cases which conspicuously expands as we go on. I perceive a sound *as* a sound. I perceive it as a human voice. I perceive it as the voice of a friend. I grasp what my friend is saying as a remark about the weather. I grasp it as a sagacious forecast of the results of a coming election. Or, finally, I grasp it as a statement that war has been declared, a war that by much reflection I have concluded would lead, by various and complicated routes, to the decay of civilization. None of these cases is the perception of a *thing*. In all of them there is something given, but what is interesting about them is their increasing volume of reference to that which lies beyond the given. The relative importance of the sensory element grows less; that of the non-sensory element grows greater; the perceptions are increasingly top-heavy with meaning. It is obvious that much of our thinking is done through perception of this kind, which indeed in its upper ranges is hardly to be distinguished from the free use of ideas. Of that use we shall speak later. Regarding the meaning used in perception, we must now inquire into its nature, its organization, and its range. In the present chapter we shall be concerned alone with the nature of this perceptual meaning.

To avoid needless confusions, we should do well to confine our attention to the middle range of the scale. In the series of instances just given it has been pointed out that at the end, where we seize the remote and complicated bearings of a remark, we are on the border of the region of free ideas; there are still sensory cues, to be sure, but we feel that the process is really nearer to reflection than it is to the mere sensation of a sound; what the mind is primarily engaged with is not a sound, but events suggested by the sound, events which are themselves complex and far removed. On the other hand, at the bottom of the scale there may be doubt whether meaning is present at all, and whether we have advanced beyond bare sensation. Both processes are called perception, and I think rightly; but both are borderline cases, and if we are to study perception in its typical form, we must take it in the middle of the series. It may be that at neither end is there any sharp limit, that there is no such thing as a wholly meaningless sensation or a wholly non-sensuous thought; but asymptotic limits are all we need. In the movement from one toward the other there is a gradual shift of cargo, and the clearest case of perception will fall in mid-voyage, when the two have reached a balance. Meaning will not be excluded by sensation, as in intolerable pain, nor sensation be a mere cue, as in my 'hearing the news' of war; they will have reached a sort of rough equipoise in which removal of either one would entail an equally radical change in the state of mind as a whole. It is perception of this level that we find in a critic's appreciation of a picture, or a motor mechanic's hearing of a defective engine. And our question is as to the form in which meaning exists in perception at this level.

Let us specify further and take a case. When I was learning to drive a motor-car, I was once proceeding down a main street when the machine began without warning to produce a hideous roar. It sounded as if the car were tearing itself in pieces and leaving its entrails along the road, though strangely enough the wheels continued to go round. I had not the faintest notion what the trouble could be, and there was nothing for it but to roar shamelessly on till I reached the nearest garage. There I hardened my heart for the verdict, and asked a mechanic what could have happened. 'That's simple enough', said he, 'your muffler's detached'; and with a moment's manipulation all was in order again. Once in a while the noise recurred; I was then able to identify it myself and take therapeutic measures; something went on in my mind which, however humble, was at least comparable to what went on in the mind of the mechanic. I began to see what it would mean to have that diagnostic mastery to which the purrs and roars of an engine would all speak an intelligible language.

Such mastery would mean, I suppose, the power to give the right significance to every sound and nuance of sound that engines, good and evil, emitted. It would mean the power to apply a special but extended experience to what is now presented in sense, and to apply this at once unreflectively and pertinently. But this, right enough in the large, is too general to be enlightening. What is meant by applying past experience? Literally, that is of course impossible. Again, what region does a meaning inhabit when it is neither a sensation nor an explicit idea? These are the questions we must now try to answer.

2. The meaning we are here concerned with is meaning acquired through past experience. There are senses, as we have seen, in which meaning may be innate; the order supplied by logical categories is an example; but for the present purpose such meaning is unimportant. It could supply at the utmost only the abstract framework of our perception, never its concrete filling. The meaning by which a mechanic diagnoses a difficulty and which he attaches to one sensation rather than another is in every case acquired. It is a result or deposit of past experience. It is an instance of that law of retention which is perhaps exemplified in all living things, a law that lies so near the heart of mind that, as Dr. Dawes Hicks has said, 'of retention in its essence we have no psychological account to offer; we have simply to accept the fact itself as lying at the very root of mental existence'.[1] Nevertheless the retention found in perceiving has at times been confused with retention of other

[1] *Proc. Arist. Soc.*, 1909–10, 241.

types, and we can at least guard against such confusions. It has been claimed, for example, that retention means the same thing in matter, both living and non-living, and in minds.

This is a peculiarly pernicious error, because it blurs distinctions that are vital. A little reflection will show that retention means different things on different levels.

(1) As an example from 'dead matter' take the case of an axle, newly greased. As the grease is more thoroughly 'worked in', i.e. more and more evenly distributed over the whole of the touching surfaces, the wheel runs more and more smoothly. Here what has occurred in the past affects what is occurring now, but there is no retention involved; it is a case of mere mechanical causality. Each turn of the wheel distributes the grease more evenly, and hence at the next there is less friction. To say that the wheel is improving or learning by experience would be nothing but a bad metaphor.

(2) But at the next stage it would be literal truth. Take the case of the acquisition of a habit, for example, the habit of working a typewriter. Here we may say as before, that past movements condition present ones, making them easier and more effective. But these phrases now have new meanings. For the point about learning by experience is not simply that one's behaviour is influenced by the past, but that it is influenced *selectively* by the past, that results tending to further the present activity tend to be retained while irrelevant results are dropped. My present working of a typewriter is not the equal result of all the clumsinesses, mistakes, and successes of past adventures on the machine; if mistakes and successes were registered equally, I should never have learned at all. The fact is that while the successes do tend to register themselves, the mistakes do not. It is as if the organism were seeking an end, and accepted what would help it while rejecting the rest. That such selection occurs seems undeniable. To the present writer it seems also necessary in the end to explain it purposively. My typewriting is now what it is because I am using the deposit from my past neither *in toto* nor indiscriminately, but in some sense selectively for an end. Probably no habit is ever merely mechanical.

The organism, it has been said, is a half-way house between inanimate matter and conscious mind.

(3) In the case of inorganic matter, the past influences the present through mere causation; in the case of organic habit through *selective* causation; in the case of full-blown perceiving through a selective causation whose results appear in consciousness. Suppose I recognize the voice of a friend. My present perception is, of course, conditioned by my past acquaintance. It is clear, further, that in interpreting the sound, I use the deposit of some parts of my past experience to the exclusion of others. But what makes perception so marked an achievement is that the past has left not simply a trace in my body but also a deposit in consciousness, and has left this in such fusion with what I am sensing that it is almost impossible to distinguish them. Further, what is contributed by the past may not only survive in present consciousness; in the upper ranges of perception, it may, as we have seen, form by far the more important element.

It will be noted that we have been saying the 'deposit' of the past, 'what is contributed by the past', not 'the past' itself. To apply the past in the present literally would be contradictory and impossible. Though the motor mechanic's perception is what it is because of a long experience of mufflers, this experience has been made up of successive events of seeing, touching, and hearing, and when an event is over, that is the end of it; it is dead. The past never survives. To say so would be to say that the past is present, which lacks sense. Yet we have been saying that perception involves retention, not mere causality; and we can hardly doubt that we see to-day some of the things we saw yesterday. Something *must* survive. This knot may be untied by a distinction. In every event the *occurrence* may be distinguished from *what* occurs. To say that the occurrence occurs again will then indeed be contradiction, since the second occurrence will be a new one; but to say that *what* occurs may occur again will make sense. The occurrence of a rainbow to-day is not the same as its occurrence yesterday, but the same semi-circular form may present itself repeatedly. And if yesterday it was explained to me how the physicist conceives a rainbow, and to-day I judge of it once more what I judged then, there is no more difficulty in supposing my thought to exhibit the same structure than in supposing the rainbow to do so. How the structure of thought is related to the structure of things is not at the moment our question, but if structure or content can reappear in the one, it may surely do so in the other.

We have seen that in the perception of things what is given in sense is taken as part of a larger whole. We have argued that such perception involves the implicit judgement that other parts of this whole exist; and we have described the process that leads to this judgement as implicit inference. But when we discussed some time ago the thought of what is not given, we were concerned rather with the process that led to it than with the nature of the thought itself. It is this last that now calls for comment. When the mechanic perceives the sound as indicating muffler-trouble, it seems clear enough at first sight that some thought of the muffler must be in his mind. What is such thought like? Is it even certain that there is any such thing?

3. That any such thing exists is of course denied by behaviourists. Their view of the thought process we shall examine later in detail, and shall not attempt to deal with it here. If anyone cares to believe that when the mechanic hears the sound nothing is happening but a change in his nervous system, that no sort of thought arises unless and until his larynx begins to move, and that when this does begin to move its movements *are* the thought, he shall meet with no protest here. This discussion is meant for others who have managed to persuade themselves that there is such a thing as consciousness. Among those who are so persuaded, two theories are current which, admitting that in perception we are conscious of what is given in sense, would still deny that in the 'thought' of what is not given there is anything conscious at all. Let us look at these theories first.

(1) One of them runs as follows. When the mechanic hears the sound, he is having a conscious experience in the same sense as when he feels a toothache or sees the moon. But the 'meaning' or 'thought of the muffler', supposedly aroused by hearing the sound, is not a thought, is not conscious, is not an experience of any kind. It is simply a 'motor set', or state of physical readiness; or, as it is sometimes described, a tendency to act in a certain way; or, again and perhaps more commonly, it is incipient action in a certain direction. In the mechanic's past experience, upon hearing this sort of sound, he has usually found the muffler detached and has proceeded to make certain movements by way of repairing it. Thus a connection has been set up between hearing this kind of sound and making these kinds of movement, and when the sound is heard again, the movements tend to come into play. And since 'tendency' is a treacherous term, it is often replaced by something more definite; a tendency to move is actually a beginning to move, not necessarily a visible play of arms and legs, but at least the occurrence of nervous discharges which, if intensified and extended, would lead to the same muscular adjustments as before. Perception, so far as meaning is concerned, is thus really a case of habit. It is not wholly and simply habit, since hearing a sound is a fresh conscious experience; but whatever goes beyond this can be dealt with as by the straitest sect of the behaviourists.

4. This theory will not serve. It is needless to deny the incipient action; it may be there. But there or not, it is not enough. For (i) a bodily change cannot be true or false; in perception there is something that can. In the present instance, the noise is *taken as* the noise of a detached muffler; if the mechanic found this in perfect repair, we should consider, and so would he, not that his body had been playing him a trick, but quite simply that he had made a mistake. It would be meaningless to say of an incipient movement that it was true or false, but we do say this, with obvious justification, of the judgement or acceptance by which the sound is *taken as* this or that. Since the process in question can give truth or falsity, while incipient movement cannot, to reduce perceptual meaning to movement will not suffice.

(ii) Again, the theory seems to be founded, not on the study of perceiving generally but on the study of a single branch of it, namely the perceiving that leads to action. In such cases it is more or less plausible. If I see a runaway horse bearing down on me, or hear a motor horn blow behind me, I unreflectingly leap aside, and it may be said that what the sound arouses in me is not an interpretation but a jump. According to this account, we must not say 'a jump for safety' or 'a jump out of danger', for that would suggest the conscious interpretation which it is desired to exclude. Now such an account is inapplicable, I think, even to this special sort of perception; but let us for the moment accept it and see where it leads. Some perceptions appear to be more closely connected than others with bodily reactions; for example, hearing a motor horn just behind one than hearing the Fifth Symphony, the perception of someone offering us a cup of tea than a glimpse of Betelgeuse through a telescope. Now if the theory is true that perceptual meaning consists in movement, overt or incipient, then as the connection of sensation with movement grows stronger and more varied, the meaning should increase, and with the decline of this connection, the meaning should diminish. It ought then to follow that the teacup means more than Betelgeuse and the motor horn (to borrow a good round phrase from E. M. Forster) than 'the most sublime noise that ever penetrated the ear of man'. It ought to follow that all those perceivings which, as done in an aesthetic or scientific interest, call for less bodily adjustment than the perception of knives and forks, should carry a narrower meaning. And this, I think, is not plausible. It seems clear, on the contrary, that the meaning a perception carries may be very great while any detectable impulse to movement is extremely small. Indeed, between the amount of *meaning* borne by an equation for a mathematician or an observation for an astronomer and the amount of *move-*

ment induced in him, it would be hard, I suspect, to find any sort of correlation. If so, meaning and incipient movement can hardly be the same.

5. (2) A somewhat similar theory would find the locus of meaning not in incipient bodily movement but in a certain condition of the brain. When, along with the hearing of the sound the mechanic thinks explicitly of the muffler, certain regions of the brain—let us say regions A and B—are undergoing certain degrees of excitation. The excitation of region A conditions the hearing of the sound; the excitation of region B conditions the thought of the muffler. Let us suppose now that region A is directly stimulated to a degree necessary to the hearing of the sound. Since the excitation of A has in the past been connected with the excitation of B, it will lead on to this again. But this latter excitation, being aroused indirectly through A and lacking such support as would be given by the sight of the muffler, will probably be pretty weak, too weak to give rise to consciousness. Thus if we are to describe the perception truly, we shall say that the region which conditions the hearing of the sound has been directly and fully excited, and that this excitement at once communicates itself to the region which conditions the meaning or thought of the muffler, but that this region is not strongly excited enough to generate consciousness. Does this improve on the previous theory?

6. No. It is less obviously wrong perhaps, since the presence of feeble brain processes is harder to deny than the presence of incipient movements. But (i) it is open to the same major objection, namely, that besides sensation, perception involves acceptance or judgement, something capable of truth or falsity, and that no physical change in the brain can supply such an element. Nor is this the only difficulty. (ii) The theory says that at the base of perception lie two purely physical processes, and these are assumed to be connected by some sort of mechanical causality. But we saw that perceiving involves *selection* among the results of past experience. The past hearing of a noisy engine may have been connected with all manner of other experiences; it may be that these experiences have been more vivid and more frequent than the experience of seeking its cause; nevertheless, on the present occasion, these experiences are kept in the background in favour of the thought of the cause; or, as the theory before us would put it, the only process excited is that which, if more intense, would condition such thought. But why is *this* process excited and the others not? It is futile to talk of 'openness of connection', 'lowered thresholds', 'synaptic resistances', and the like; these are metaphors, not observable facts. If we look at the facts directly, we can see that our perceiving of something as this rather than that—and hence presumably the conditioning cerebral process —varies with the interest of the moment. The mechanic's present interest is in finding the cause; if he were in a lovers' tryst at midnight and this noise were suddenly to begin, he would no doubt perceive it differently. For each of us, when mature, such a sensation has many possible associates. The theory before us would say that which of these is aroused depends on purely physical resistances in the brain. But this is not observable fact; it is a theory offered to account for the observable facts. And among these is the fact that the associates aroused by sensation often do vary with changing interest and purpose. To all appearances the perceptual reading of sensation is often determined purposively, while it is assumed that the brain connection is a matter of ordinary mechanical causation. *Now if the purposive determination is real, the mechanical determination will not by itself suffice.* And we shall see later in detail that to exclude purposive determination from a part in such events is to render mental process unintelligible.[1]

7. (3) In the theories that perceptual meaning is nothing but motor set or faint cerebration, we have found small plausibility.

[1] Chaps. XIV, XXII, XXIII.

The theory that most naturally comes next has escaped the identification of meaning with anything neural or muscular; it grants to meaning a character genuinely mental but below the level of explicit consciousness; it is the theory of meaning as *subconscious*. Those who hold this view have never, so far as I know, set it out in systematic fashion, but with their other expressions before us it is not difficult to see the outlines of their theory. This theory is important and persuasive; it must receive a more extended discussion than either of the proposals just dealt with. It runs about as follows:

In perception there is a nucleus of sensation; so much is agreed on all hands. But along with this nucleus goes a 'fringe' of meaning, and the question is as to the status, in consciousness or out of it, of this dubious fringe. Now to talk of *the* status at all is to use a misnomer, since this assumes that the fringe is a narrow band, of the same character throughout, whereas it is an enormously wide one which reaches out indefinitely in all directions and changes character as it recedes. When the mechanic hears the noisy engine, there lies near the focus of his attention, indeed occupying this jointly with sensation, the thought of the detached muffler. This thought has not the full explicitness it would have if it held the focus alone; attention is diffused; hence the thought lacks vividness and definition, and is on the road to becoming implicit. Still one can hardly deny that it is there. But is it *all* that is there? Most writers talk of perception as if it were, whereas reflection suggests that it is not. When a skilled mechanic listens to an engine or an accomplished critic looks at a picture, are the only factors at work those which could be singled out by introspection? Surely not. 'When an expert', says Mitchell, 'takes thought of anything in his province, he may bring pretty well the whole weight of his knowledge to bear on the single point in a single moment. And he uses his knowledge without having to ponder it, or attend to it by a process of reflection; he attends only to the point before him.'[1] In what form is this 'weight of knowledge' present? Mitchell's answer, that 'it is taken for

[1] *Structure and Growth of the Mind*, 268.

granted', leaves our question still open. But Ward presses the matter farther and concludes that it is there subconsciously; he thinks all other theories break down. The view that the 'weight of knowledge' is present as a mechanical arrangement of brain-cells or as mechanical nervous changes, he would rule out summarily. As for the theory that the body, as not a machine but an organism purposively governed and plastic to what acts on it, may serve as an active co-operator in thinking, he replies, as one would expect from his speculative writings, that this merely restates the problem; that plasticity and purpose already involve mind; that 'habit itself implies retention and is practically synonymous with disposition'.[1] There remains the theory of dispositions, mental but unconscious. Their unconsciousness, however, Ward declines to admit. They may be as faint and obscure as you like, but between extreme faintness and non-existence there is a wide difference. The memories that the past leaves with us are as truly present, affecting the focus of our perception, though themselves unattended to, as the moods that give to consciousness its atmosphere. 'Subconscious presentations may tell on conscious life—as sunshine or mist tells on a landscape, or the underlying writing on a palimpsest —although lacking either the intensity or the individual distinctness requisite to make them definite features.'[2] 'The sad memories of a great loss may continue as a chill substratum to check the springs of life like a wintry frost, long after the blight of it has disappeared from the surface.'[3]

According to Ward we are still actually remembering the loss, though only subconsciously. Is there any good reason to believe this? To marshal all the evidence for subconsciousness is here of course impossible, but the *kinds* of evidence offered for the type in question are not many, and we can ask what such-and-such kinds of argument could prove, without exhausting the particular facts on which they rest. Let us see what subconsciousness means here, and then the kinds of evidence advanced for it.

[1] *Psychological Principles*, 98.   [2] *Ibid.*, 94.
[3] *Ibid.*, 95.

8. This subconsciousness seems to differ from ordinary experience in two ways: its objects are less clear and vivid, and it is not itself anything that we can be clearly aware of. (i) When I look at the table I am writing on, its colour and grain have the highest vividness and clearness; the chair standing to its left has much less, and the wall at the side still less again. Clearness and vividness thus decrease as we recede from the centre, and subconscious experiences are those that lie on the margin and thus have these qualities only in low degree. (ii) Just as our consciousness of things has degrees of clearness and vividness, so has the *consciousness of our consciousness* of them. Suppose I am trying to introspect my awareness of the table; then the event of this awareness is as vivid and clear as can be. Suppose now that I am not introspecting, but merely looking at the table; have I ceased to be conscious that I am aware of it? Surely not. It is a curious and puzzling fact, which troubled Spinoza and perhaps should trouble more philosophers, that our focal experience is always double, or perhaps even treble or multiple; we are not ordinarily introspecting, and yet we know perfectly well, not only what we are conscious of but *that* we are conscious of it. And it would seem that this consciousness too is a matter of degree. From its height in introspection, it declines in ordinary perceiving until, when we reach our marginal experiences, we may be in doubt whether we are perceiving or not. Common sense would probably say that when we cease to be aware of our awareness, we are not aware at all. But the defenders of the subconscious would reply that *neither* awareness abruptly ceases, that not only our awareness but also our awareness of that awareness is a matter of degree, and that to talk roundly of 'not finding' something is pointless unless one remembers the gradations involved. Subconscious experience, then, is experience the objects of which are so faint and obscure, and the awareness of which is itself so dim, that we cannot, by direct evidence, say that it exists. Does such lack of evidence entitle us to say that it does not exist? The defender of the subconscious would say no; and for subconsciousness in perception he would offer three types of argument: (i) an argument from continuity, (ii) an argument from certain facts of common experience, and (iii) an argument *a fortiori*.

9. (i) For Professor Ward it was the need of continuity that supplied the principal argument.

> 'The hypothesis of subconsciousness is in the main nothing more than the application to the facts of presentation of the law of continuity,'[1] 'it is obvious that the continuity here implied (i.e. of degrees of consciousness), if strictly taken, logically commits us to a field of consciousness "extending" with ever diminishing intensity *ad indefinitum*.'[2] 'Even were there no facts to warrant this concept of an ultra-liminal presentation of impressions it might still claim *a priori* justification. For to assume that there are no presentations beyond those within the field of consciousness is as arbitrary and improbable as it would be to suppose—in the absence of direct evidence to the contrary—that there was no vision or audition save such as is mediated by human eyes and ears. Psychical magnification or diminution is not more absurd than physical, though neither is possible without limit. We cannot fix the limit at which the subconscious becomes the absolutely unconscious.'[3]

This line of argument seems (*a*) in its main contention to be a mistake, (*b*) to be implicitly self-contradictory, and (*c*) to make an arbitrary assumption. (*a*) That finding a series of degrees within the field of consciousness 'logically commits us' to extending this series *ad indefinitum*, is by no means 'obvious'. This would imply that every series can be extended indefinitely, which is not the case. (*b*) The point of the argument is destroyed when it is admitted of the mental and physical series that 'neither is possible without limit'. What we are told is apparently this: *principle* requires that the series of degrees of consciousness should go on indefinitely; experience suggests that it does not; and both must be believed. (*c*) If the series does not go on indefinitely, what more reason is there for thinking that it goes beyond the commonly accepted margin than for thinking

---

[1] *Psychological Principles*, 93.   [2] *Ibid.*, 90.   [2] *Ibid.*, 94.

that it stops there? Professor Ward admits that it stops some-where; must not our assumption, if we are to make one, be this, that it extends just as far as we can find evidence for this in our awareness, and that if it is held to continue farther, that must be on the strength of special evidence, not of a priori assumption? There is no 'law of continuity' which will enable us by itself to settle the issue.

10. (ii) It has been thought that certain familiar facts of perception lend countenance to the idea of a consciousness that extends indefinitely. There is the ancient case of the bushel of wheat, and the hardly less classical case of the ticking clock, and besides these a famous experiment of Stumpf's and certain facts of introspection which all point, or seem to point, in one direction. But I think we shall find on inspection that this evidence either proves nothing at all or else proves something other than what is required.

(*a*) First as to the argument about one's hearing of the bushel of wheat or the waves of the sea. A grain of wheat is dropped on the floor a certain distance away, and you hear nothing; a bushel of wheat is poured out, and you hear the sound distinctly. But the bushel is composed of single grains; each must have made its sound, for the noise of the bushel could not have been a sum of silences. Since the individual sounds must have been there, yet were not consciously heard, they must have been heard subconsciously. But the argument makes an assumption that is clearly false. It assumes that a complex stimulus never acts as a whole, that each part sets up its special awareness. In that case we ought to see every electron in a table and every separate wave of light. Obviously we do not, and hence the assumption must be mistaken.

11. (*b*) In the class of cases that prove something other than what is required fall Stumpf's experiment, the argument from ticking clocks and extinguished lights, the argument from the feeling of attending, and a number of others. They do, I think, show interesting things, but not an indefinitely large sub-consciousness.

Sound two notes, x and y, on a violin, and let their pitches be so near together that we cannot distinguish them. Then sound y and z, which also seem just alike. y has thus been a member of both pairs, and seems exactly equal in pitch to each of its fellows. These, therefore, should be alike, on the principle that things equal to the same thing are equal to each other. But the fact is that they may differ noticeably. 'We have thus', says Professor Ward, 'to recognize the existence of a difference between sensations, in cases where there is no so-called "sensation of difference". But if this much continuity be admitted we can hardly fail to admit more. If differences of presentation exist within the field of consciousness but beyond the utmost verge of the "threshold of *difference*", we cannot consistently deny the existence of any presentation at all beyond the threshold of *consciousness*.'[1] Now *is* it 'presentations beyond the threshold of consciousness' that Stumpf's experiment has revealed? That two sensations may be different without our being aware of their difference no doubt has been shown. What is undetected, then, is the difference; but need the difference between presentations be itself a presentation? There is no good reason to think so, and there is strong reason to think not. If every difference were presented, there could never be two shades of colour or degrees of brightness anywhere in the conscious field of a mouse or a man without an awareness *that* they are different, or—if this seems to require judgement—without an awareness of the relation of difference. And this seems clearly untenable. Thus the argument does show that differences may exist unattended to; but since differences need not be presentations, it does not show that presentations exist unattended to. And this is what it was supposed to prove.

12. (c) Then there are all the arguments that turn on the cessation of stimulus. I had not been explicitly attending to

[1] *Psychological Principles*, 92.

the light in the window next door, but I notice the change when it goes out, and hence must have been aware of it earlier. I had not known that I was aware of the clock's ticking, but when it stops I notice the difference, which shows I must have been hearing it subconsciously. The city dweller boasts that he no longer pays the slightest attention to the city's noises, and then goes into the country and is kept awake by their absence. Do not such facts force us to say that we can see and hear subconsciously?

Professor Broad thinks not.

> 'The fact that we notice a difference when the clock stops needs for its explanation no other assumption except that, while the clock is going, it produces *some* modification *somewhere* in our total sense-object, which ceases when the clock stops. This modification might not be auditory at all; it might be simply a vague toning of our general bodily feeling.' Supposing this toning to occur, it 'must often in the past have been accompanied by auditory fields in which ticking existed and was discriminated and ascribed to the clock. Hence this kind of modification will have come to suggest by association ticking and clocks. Its cessation would therefore tend to make us look at the clock and ascribe the change to it.'[1]

This appears to be a possible explanation. Still, we must doubt whether a 'vague toning of our general bodily feeling' is likely to carry anything as definite as a particular number of strokes of a clock. When we become aware at the same time that the clock is striking, and that it has arrived at the third or fourth stroke, it seems easier to believe that we heard the earlier strokes without explicitly noticing them than that we arrived at their number through association with a tone of feeling.[2]

---

[1] *The Mind and Its Place in Nature*, 405–6. In the context there is an admirable discussion of some of the points here raised.

[2] Cf. the following from Hans Gross: 'Since I was a child there had been in my bedroom a clock, the loud ticking of which habit of many years prevented my hearing. Once as I lay awake in bed, I heard it tick suddenly three times, then fall silent and stop. The occurrence interested me; I quickly got a light and examined the clock closely. The pendulum still swung, but without a sound; the time was right. . . . (He found the stopping to be due to a backward tilt of the clock

The more definite becomes the knowledge gained in this way, the harder it is to avoid saying that awareness has been present, and that subconsciousness exists. If one is to escape this conclusion, one must hold either that the facts are not correctly reported, or that what is not explicitly noticed cannot be recalled, or that in cases of this kind memory is mistaken. And there seems no sufficient reason to believe any of these things. Thus the view that some degree of subconsciousness exists is hardly to be escaped. But there is nothing in such cases as we have mentioned to justify the great extension of it which Ward would have desired.

13. (*d*) This would have been accepted by Bradley. While dissociating himself sharply from what he considered the extravagant developments of von Hartmann and Myers, he held that we have good, though not demonstrative, reasons for believing in subconsciousness. His main argument seems to me to involve a *petitio*, but his discussion singles out and holds firmly the critical point. That point is whether attention alters its object. Suppose that we did hear preceding strokes of the clock, or suppose that at the moment we are experiencing all sorts of marginal impressions and ideas; still, the instant we consciously attend to them they are *ipso facto* no longer subconscious, and if this making them conscious changes their nature, we have no right to say it was they that we experienced before. *Was* it they? Bradley argues as follows:

affecting the swing of the pendulum.) I immediately made an experiment. I set the clock going again, and again held the weight back. The last beats of the pendulum were neither quicker nor slower, nor louder nor softer than any others, before the sudden stoppage of the clock.' How could he have heard the three ticks if it were only their stopping that drew his attention to them? He suggests that the ticking produced a nervous stimulus without being perceived, and that at the stopping 'perception was intensified' and 'the latent stimulus' caused by the ticking worked backward. Here is still another theory. But he cites two further cases in which, apparently without realizing any change, he adopts the language of the subconscious theory.— *Criminal Psychology* (Eng. Trans.), 194.

'(a) We must first assume that anything remains the same except so far as I have reason to take it as altered. . . . (b) Next we must hold that apart from any attention we may be aware of a change in our condition. Without anything which could in the ordinary sense be called attending, we can experience a difference when a change takes place in our general or special felt state. (c) There is again an experienced change when attention (say to a feeling B) supervenes, and this particular experience is felt otherwise than as a mere change, say from A to B. Hence from the absence of this special feeling, as well as from the presence of the ordinary feeling of change to B, we infer that our sensation B does not depend upon attention, but was previously there.'[1]

This is a curious argument. The question before us is, can we be aware of anything without expressly attending to it? and Bradley lays down as second among the conditions of solving the problem the very point at issue. If it is accepted that 'apart from any attention we can be aware of a change in our condition', *cadit quaestio*; subconscious awareness is already taken as fact. Still, with a little restatement the argument will perhaps stand. Bradley was insisting that we can distinguish between feeling a change that is the effect of attention and feeling one that is not, between seeing a minute insect move, for example, and feeling the adjustments necessary to seeing it at all. Once this distinction is admitted, one can go on to make two points of some significance. Knowing what it feels like merely to fix attention, and finding more than this present in the change (e.g. the series of clock strokes) which seems now to be just ending, one concludes that this is no product of attention, but a change in the object of attention. A second point, also made by Bradley, is that the process of attention takes time; when I turn to a quite new object, it takes a moment to make the adjustment. But when I turn to an object which, on the theory, is in the conscious field but marginal, this time for adjustment is not needed; the object leaps at once into clearness. Hence, it is argued, some degree of awareness was given it already. These arguments, Bradley

[1] *Essays on Truth and Reality*, 163.

admits, do not amount to demonstration, for one can hold, if one wants to, that attention creates everything and you can hardly refute it. But he does think they afford ground for belief in a limited subconsciousness, and we agree.

We have now seen that the argument from continuity proves nothing, and that while these arguments from common experience tend to show a limited sub-consciousness, they give no sort of justification for holding that the whole volume of past experience that actually affects our present perception is there in subconscious form. Is there any other kind of evidence which would make this plausible?

14. (iii) Here we are met by the argument *a fortiori*. It consists in producing from abnormal psychology a staggering volume of evidence for subconscious thinking, and then asking why, if we swallow the camel of subconscious thinking, we should strain at the gnat of subconscious memories influencing present perception. Any good book on abnormal psychology— McDougall's for instance—will furnish masses of organized evidence for behaviour that is 'intelligent' and yet seems to have no connection with the consciousness of the moment. Nor are these cases necessarily pathological; they embrace such things as the writing down of mathematical solutions in sleep, the complicated performances of some sleep-walkers, and the extensive use of subconscious invention in scientific and literary work.[1] Cases that are more abnormal include the curious instances in which coherent prose and verse flow from a hand that writes automatically while the consciousness of the writer is engaged otherwise, and the strange feats carried out through post-hypnotic suggestion, such as the accurate but unconscious recording of time. And finally there is the great range of cases of extreme dissociation—'fugues', co-consciousness, alternating personality, etc.—which have only begun to be scientifically studied in the last few decades. These cases, including those investigated by the societies for psychical research,

[1] See Chap. XXIV below.

are of immense significance for the understanding of the mind, and Dr. Broad has set a good example in taking them seriously in a philosophical work. Our own concern with them must be slight. Do they point to a consciousness that is indefinitely extended, a consciousness that would explain how perception, in spite of its narrow limits, can yet be so expert and intelligent?

I do not think they do. It is true that to put such behaviour down to mechanical reactions of the body is impossible; 'to suggest that a person who speaks, solves problems,spontaneously shows likes and dislikes, chooses a course of his own, and often resists our orders, is no more conscious than a mechanical doll is to descend below even the famous theory of Descartes that animals are machines. For the consciousness of a somnambulist is far more evident than that of a dog, and that a dog is conscious no one doubts'.[1] And we shall see later that submerged but active processes have an essential part to play in the movement of reflection. But there are two considerations that make it doubtful whether the term subconscious, as used above, should be applied to them. One is that many of them are described more naturally as cases of dissociation. Dissociated consciousness, instead of being continuous with the dominant field, though less clear and vivid, is relatively independent and may maintain a life of its own. Frequently the two or more fields of consciousness are not contributory to each other, but opposed, so that when the normal field is in the ascendant, the soldier who has been 'shell-shocked' can remember nothing of the shock that brought on his trouble, or of the period immediately following, and it is only when this field is in abeyance, as in sleep or under hypnosis, that there seems to be any consciousness of the forgotten horrors. When physiologists attempt to deal with these things, it is commonly by supposing certain areas of the brain to have become functionally dissociated from each other. One may admit a dissociated consciousness without thereby committing onself to a subconsciousness continuous with the focus and extending indefinitely into the shadows.

Secondly, the very thing that makes these achievements so

[1] Janet, *L'Automatisme Psychologique*, 22.

remarkable is evidence against their being explicable by subconsciousness. We shall see later that much creative work of a high order both in science and in art has been done without explicit awareness of what was going on. Processes have been carried through which are so complex and so well-executed as to rival the best achievements of the most fully conscious moments. To suppose that these are either described or explained by calling them subconscious, in the sense of possessing only a marginal clearness and vividness, seems inept.

15. If all this is true, subconsciousness is not the answer we are seeking. But before we try again, let us summarize what has been said. The problem we set out to deal with was that of the nature of perceptual meaning. We saw that the ratio of meaning, so to speak, may vary greatly, so that at times the perception is very nearly pure sensation, while at the other extreme it is very nearly pure idea. We therefore selected as most typical, perception of an intermediate level, such as that of a mechanic who hears the noise of a defective motor, and asked as to the status of the non-sensible element in such perception. The first two theories suggested that this element was not conscious at all, but was a purely bodily change, either in the form of an incipient bodily motion, or of a physical-chemical change in the brain. But these theories were both wrecked on the fact that to perceive is to judge, and they were also defective otherwise. We turned next to the view that perceptual meaning consisted neither in physical change nor in explicit consciousness, but in less intense, or marginal, consciousness. But we were able to discover no arguments, either empirical or a priori, that proved the existence of a subconsciousness sufficiently extended to serve the purpose. So far, we are empty-handed. What is more, we seem to be cut off from all the natural suggestions. To say that everything the declaration of war means for the statesman, everything which, if laboriously put down in words, he would recognize that it had meant in the moment of hearing—to say that all this is actually present in consciousness seems absurd. To say on the other hand that the greater part of this meaning is merely a bodily reaction seems equally absurd. To say that it is psychical but unconscious seems to be using words with no clear sense. What *can* we say?

16. (4) Here there falls for consideration the theory of dispositions. These dispositions are accounted not physical but mental, though they are not necessarily either conscious or subconscious.

> 'It is impossible to formulate in words from the introspective standpoint the most ordinary facts of retentiveness and memory', Professor Stout once wrote, 'without implying that past experiences leave behind them after their disappearance persistent traces on which their revival depends. . . . it is very often necessary to separate unambiguously the purely psychological evidence concerning the inter-connection and mode of operation of residual traces, from corresponding physiological data and hypotheses. When and so far as this is the case, it is best simply to use the term "psychical disposition" without any physiological reference.'[1]

Such dispositions are 'something mental', though they fall 'outside the sphere of consciousness'.[1] They are the form in which we carry with us the results of past experience, the memories of events that are not at the moment being recalled, the meanings we hold in readiness to attach to words, the power to recognize things and faces. It is because they exist that we are able to perceive. In terms of this theory, when the mechanic heard the noise, it excited a 'pre-formed psychical disposition' left by his past experience, to take it in one way rather than another. Ordinarily the disposition lies in a state of unconscious dormancy, but it may be excited into various degrees of consciousness, up to the most vivid explicitness.

This view, it may be thought, is not quite relevant to what we are discussing, since it is a theory not of the state of meaning as actually used in perception, but of its state in the quiescent

---

[1] *Analytic Psychology*, I. 22–3.   [2] *Ibid.*, 64.

intervals when its only service is to stand and wait; and there is some point in this objection. Professor Stout would not suggest that meaning, as actually used in perceiving, is a mere unconscious disposition; it is an excited disposition, and thus may be as conscious as one pleases. Still the objection is not quite just, for it is a striking fact about perception that our reading of what is given seems to be controlled not merely by what introspection can bring to light as present in consciousness, but also by the results of a great range of past experience, results which are not in consciousness at all. Such results are in *some* sense present, for we read our sensations 'in the light of' them, but we cannot say that they are present consciously, for inner search fails to find them. According to the theory before us, these results are present as dispositions. Thus the theory has two uses; it fixes the status of meanings (*a*) when exerting no influence at all, (*b*) when exerting an influence from outside the sphere of consciousness.

17. I know of no more instructive criticism of this theory of dispositions than is to be found in scattered comments by Bradley, and it will repay us to review these. He kept returning to the problem at intervals for something like forty years, and while his central criticism is unvarying, the practical value he assigned to the theory seems to rise steadily. In 1883 he was looking at retention partly as a doctrine that the potential could exist actually, partly as the doctrine that particulars could persist. For both doctrines he had nothing but purple patches of scorn. 'We are accustomed to hear of "capacities" and "faculties", and to use such phrases as "potential energy", with but little regard for their actual meaning. The "potential" is regarded as something real, stored up outside existence, which hereafter may emerge in the world of fact. This deplorable piece of effete metaphysics takes a leading place in the popular versions of the truths of physics. Potential energy, of course, as such has no real existence.'[1] As for the survival

[1] *Principles of Logic*, I. 210.

of past experiences, 'there is no Hades where they wait in disconsolate exile, till Association announces resurrection and recall. . . . These touching beliefs of a pious legend may babble in the tradition of a senile psychology, or contort themselves in the metaphysics of some frantic dogma, but philosophy must register them and sigh and pass on.'[1] Four years later he is trying his own hand at psychology, and when confronted with 'the nature of "traces" or "residues" or "dispositions",' his damnation is a little more qualified. 'Associations are set up, and we say that these exist, but how can that be? Do the elements continue as psychical facts? . . .' Though the problem, he thinks, does not really belong to psychology, he goes on to suggest that there are 'four courses we may take, three bad and one good. We may follow the line laid down by Herbart and force out an explanation by audacious assumptions and complicated fictions'. Or we may 'deny that a disposition is really psychical, and leave psychology for a region which I assuredly would not venture to call physiology'. Or we may take 'a very common third course, and use phrases which may mean anything, to hide the fact that there is nothing distinct that we mean'. Or we may take the one 'scientific course, to say plainly that what a disposition really may be, we neither know nor care', that since 'we have in science to do solely with events and their laws', 'we mean by a disposition that, because something has happened, therefore something will happen, *suppose that* something else happens and nothing interferes'.[2] In 1893 he reiterates that 'we have no right to speak of dispositions at all, if we turn them into actual qualities of the soul', but emphasizes again 'that we have a right everywhere for the sake of convenience to use the "conditional" ', and that 'in saying that the soul has a disposition of a certain kind', we mean 'the soul at present is such that it is part of those conditions which, given the rest, would produce certain psychical events'.[3] In 1895 he is making free use himself of dispositions in explaining the intensity of psychical states, though

[1] *Principles of Logic*, I. 306.   [2] *Mind*, 1887, 362.
[3] *Appearance and Reality*, 312 (2nd ed.).

adding as before, 'to me a "disposition" is a convenient but clearly a mythological way of stating a general fact or law, a way of psychical happening which I do not pretend to understand'.[1] In 1900 though dispositions remain only legitimate fictions, their use in psychology is now not merely admitted, but is put forward as an absolute essential. 'For phenomenalism (i.e. for sound psychology) the soul is at any one time what is experienced at that time, but it is also more. For it is qualified also by the past which really belongs to it, and that past belongs to it not merely as what it has been but as what it now is. The soul, in other words, *is* the dispositions which it has acquired.'[2] Finally, in 1922, commenting on an early passage that we have quoted, he says 'I should certainly have used other language here with reference to "survival", if I had been better acquainted with the excellent work done in psychology by Herbartian writers. The doctrine that every mental state survives and is active below the conscious level, was, and is, as a working hypothesis, not to be treated with contempt'.[3] And instead of the first denunciation of dispositions as metaphysical impostures we have the rather more chastened pronouncement that 'if you ask for anything beyond an empirical Law or Laws', the problem of dispositions 'is in the end insoluble'.[4]

To sum up this criticism. As a metaphysician Bradley was clear from first to last that the question as to the real nature of unexcited dispositions or traces was a question beyond answering, and that we could not even, with certainty, say that there were such things. But when he turned from metaphysics to psychology, he found that what for the former was a gratuitous fiction was for the latter an indispensable working hypothesis. Whether dispositions exist or not, the mind operates as if they did. Does this practical success of the hypothesis justify us in taking it as true? Not in the least, he would say; we must continue to use dispositions, but also to regard them as one of the necessary fictions of science. When physicists became convinced that light travelled in undulations, they

[1] *Mind*, 1895, 25.
[2] *Mind*, 1900, 29.
[3] *Logic*, I. 346 (note 4).
[4] *Ibid.* (note 5).

found it helpful to postulate some medium to carry these, so
they invented the 'ether', and ascribed to it various properties.
It proved for a while a great success; were they therefore
justified in taking it as real? Bradley would certainly say no,
unless indeed they were willing ιo describe it, as did one eminent Victorian, merely as 'the substantive of the verb "to
undulate" '. For it was nothing but an unknown condition invented *ad hoc*, and to take it as anything more would be only
to deceive ourselves. Exactly the same was Bradley's view of
dispositions. To explain our present perceiving we must suppose that what we have experienced in some sense or other
continues, and regarding this as a total of unknown conditions,
we proceed to dump into the vacuum what present experience
seems causally to require. But to suppose that we know it as
it is, apart from this unverifiable inference, or can ever so know
it, would be to delude ourselves.

I think all this is very close to the truth. Of course it leaves
the real nature of dispositions in an extremely shadowy limbo,
for, not knowing what they are but only what they do, we can
hardly defend ourselves if someone denies their very existence.
It is true that there are things we may rightly believe in, even
if no one has experienced them, like the other side of the
moon; in such a case we can argue from analogy. But for dispositions there are no proper analogies, since mental retention
is unique. Professor Broad, at the end of his careful discussion
of traces and dispositions in *The Mind and Its Place in Nature*,
concludes, 'Whether traces and dispositions be purely mental,
or purely physiological, or both, or neither, we know absolutely
nothing about them in detail, and can predict nothing from
one hypothesis about their intrinsic nature which we could
not predict equally well from any other hypothesis'.[1] I am
not clear that he remains wholly consistent with this view,
since he proceeds to argue that construing them as mental

---

[1] 475–6; and cf. 'The plain fact is that we know nothing with
certainty about the intrinsic nature of traces, and we ought therefore
studiously to avoid all phrases which suggest some particular view of
their intrinsic nature.' 359.

enables us to explain certain abnormal phenomena which construing them as physical would not. But however that may be, he would say, as Bradley would, that 'we know what they *are* only from what they *do*'.[1]

This result may seem a very small mouse to have been produced by such mountainous labour. But if we set down explicitly the conclusions which our discussion has forced upon us, they will not, I think, seem trivial. They form the outline of a theory which, while admittedly incomplete, throws much light on perceptual meaning. Let us set out these conclusions in order.

18. (1) *All perception is a teleological affair.* We saw in an earlier chapter that it involves a process of implicit inference by which we pass from a sensation to the thought of something else; but then any sensation is a starting-point from which thought may leap, like a knight in chess, in many different directions; and the direction of the leap is determined by interest. The geologist draws on his experience differently when as a scientist he examines a stone and when he seizes it for a missile.

(2) *The mind is economical of consciousness:* in general it resists being more conscious than it needs to be for the purpose in hand. As applied to the evolutionary series this is a commonplace; it seems to be only when the smooth activity of habit or instinct is blocked that animal consciousness is fully roused. The same economy holds in man. When faced with problems of practice or theory, he confines his consciousness to the critical points and surrenders the others to a handling that is relatively unconscious. A tennis player makes in a flash a stroke which the bystander sees on reflection to involve elaborate and cunning strategy; did all that goes through the bystander's con-

---

[1] *The Mind and Its Place in Nature*, 476. In support of the view that there are psychical dispositions whose nature is beyond knowing one may add the name of Wundt.—*Physiologische Psychologie* (second edition), II. 203; (sixth edition, III. 304 ff.).

sciousness go also through the player's? Pretty certainly not. The player was concentrating on the ball, and both the minuter adjustments and what seems to the spectator a deep-laid strategy may well have taken care of themselves. So it is in perceiving and indeed all thinking. Conscious thought has been developed chiefly as an instrument for dealing with immediate practical difficulties; once we have used it to master a difficulty, we may go on dealing with this without it; and since it is expensive of effort and energy, we use, and can use, very little of it at one time. We are disposed sometimes to lament the narrowness of our small minds and to think of an intelligence like Newton's or Goethe's as if it commanded a comprehensive landscape in which all the details of a field of knowledge were simultaneously before its eyes. That is a mistake. Some minds do no doubt exceed others in the span of their grasp, in the number of considerations or details that can be held simultaneously in view, but it is not this that made Newton and Goethe what they were. They were certainly compelled to resort to our own somewhat pitiful device of shifting a narrow beam of consciousness and a small attacking force of ideas from one outpost to another, while the heavy battalions of their knowledge lay marshalled outside in the shadows. What makes them different from us is less the size of their conscious attacking force than the extent and organization of these outlying armies which they could mobilize in an instant in support of the conscious advance guard, and before whose silent thrust the resistance melted away. Of this we shall have more to say later. But so far as concerns breadth of the conscious field, the law of parsimony governs all intelligences alike.

(3) *We must suppose agencies that co-operate with consciousness from outside its field.* Unless these agencies exist, what are we to make of such cases as calculating prodigies, where elaborate purposive processes are carried out to a correct result, and yet there is nothing in consciousness to show how the result was reached? Indeed, what are we to say of more ordinary processes like an orator's making a speech or an accomplished writer's producing a sonnet, where the pertinent thoughts and words

are somehow supplied him as he goes along? In such cases dispositions are clearly called for; and if they seem uncalled for
in perception, that is only because they play a less active and
conspicuous role. The truth is that apart from dispositions
it would be as impossible for us to interpret a page of print as
it would be for the poet to write his sonnet. What is actually
there in our consciousness may be very little, but that little is
made what it is by being a constituent in a system of meaning
which, though present for the most part only in the form of
dispositions, is ready to be made conscious at need. And
however strange and perplexing it may be, we must admit and
stress the fact of co-operation between the conscious and non-
conscious sides of our nature. The fact about the mind's working
is never that we start with a clear-cut purpose, marked out by
consciousness alone, and that this conscious purpose, unaided,
drags relevant ideas to the light; our whole intellectual nature,
conscious and non-conscious, is at work, both in setting the
purpose and in producing the means to it. If either the poet or
ourselves can mobilize forces effectively, it is because these
forces are a citizen army who have voted the enterprise and are
throwing into it an active and independent energy.

(4) Hence, *the notion of such agencies is not, in the ordinary
sense, a scientific hypothesis.* The ideal of explanation in natural
science is to bring the event to be explained under causal law,
and such law is so far mechanical that all its requirements are
satisfied if the nexus it indicates shows neither necessity nor
purpose, but only correlation. The scientist who would explain
the tides considers that he has reached his explanation if he
can correlate their movement with the approach of sun and
moon, and when he formed his hypothesis about Neptune, he
was assuming that the movements of Uranus could be connected in the same way with a material body as yet unknown.
The hypothesis of a disposition is not of this type. For dispositions do not act like bodies but like constituents of a mind;
they supplement and co-operate with consciousness as if they
were continuous with it; their relation to it is not that of
common causality, or of spatial juxtaposition, or even of mental

association, but rather, if we are to choose an analogy, that of the members to their team when this team is in play, or of soldiers to their attacking regiment. In the absence of any of them, the whole and every other part would function differently. They are, if you will, so many x's whose precise nature is unknown to us but whose presence we are bound to infer from their activities in supplementing perception and in actualizing themselves as pertinent ideas in the course of reflection. But their status is not that of undiscovered mechanical factors in natural science, for they are factors in a purposive whole.

19. One can imagine how vague and futile this will seem to certain apostles of the empirically verifiable. They are compelled by their initial assumptions to rule out such agents as dispositions from the beginning. And we must own to a certain sympathy with them. From the point of view of science dispositions are extremely unsatisfactory things. I suppose that to the thoroughly empirical scientist Aristotle's talk of a potential that actualized itself would be mere nonsense. But are we to take this as decisive? May it not be the case that Aristotle was using a category which really does apply to nature, and that in refusing to use it empirical science is adopting a self-denying ordinance that is needless and crippling? Without pretending that dispositions as now known are entities with which we can rest satisfied, we should hold that the theories that dispense with them are even less able to cover the ground. Our later discussions of the teleological character of mind and of the processes of 'subconscious' thinking will make the necessity of some theory of dispositions clearer. But to the person who rejects such theories a priori, we would say: Try your hand at making a theory that will do better. Start from the selective use in present perception of past experience, *not* in the form of conscious memories, or from the emergence of timely and pertinent suggestions in the course of reflection. Remember the difficulties in saying that an aggregate of brain particles thinks, and in saying that the past is somehow 'stored up' in an actual consciousness. Remember that to talk of the body as a teleo-logical agent which co-operates actively with thought is to wear the wall between mind and body so thin that you are really talking our language. And then, with these facts and difficulties in mind, give us a theory that will meet them. Critics who seriously attempt this will be more ready to grant that if in a theory of dispositions there is vagueness, this is at any rate not gratuitous. It arises from the intrinsic difficulty of understanding a characteristic of mind that we shall have to struggle with later, a characteristic as undeniable as it is baffling. It is the charac-teristic in virtue of which something not yet actual is able to control and direct its own coming to be.

CHAPTER V

THE OFFICES OF PERCEPTUAL MEANING

1. From the nature of perceptual meaning we turn to its structure. In the discussion of this structure the conclusions of the last chapter will help to prevent misunderstanding. We have seen that a great range of knowledge is often brought to bear in perception, and it is tempting to say that knowledge which is effectively used is consciously present. But we have found that this need not hold. Much of the knowledge we use is present in the form of dispositions, and we can learn what these are only from what they do. However, such dispositional meaning, even if not conscious, acts precisely as if it were. Since it does so act, and since it can be converted on demand into conscious coin, we shall find it convenient, without being any longer misleading, to speak as if it were there consciously, all of it, and not continually to raise the question how much of it is redeemable paper and how much coin. In the last chapter we had to lay stress on the differing status of these two parts; in what follows we shall assume that for the business of either knowing or doing they are equally valid currency.

We may take our start from three striking facts about perception, of which the first two will be dealt with in the present chapter, and the third in the chapter that follows. An understanding of the first two will be an excellent introduction to the third and most important. (1) It often happens that with an object before our eyes we fail to perceive it at all. (2) When we do perceive it, we may each perceive it differently. (3) Even when we perceive it in the same way, we perceive it with different degrees of adequacy. Now the chief reason for both failure and variations lies in the mass of meaning with which we greet what is given us. Let us look at the working of this meaning-mass in these two cases.

It is probable that we never meet any sensation with a wholly blank mind. Locke, who thought that, at least to begin with, we do, was unable to maintain even this consistently; and whatever one may think about the beginnings of experience, it is plain that from an early age the mind is full of foreshadowings of what perception will offer it. Indeed, this follows from the fact of retention. Each perception of chair or table, dog or cat, is a particular event which is over in a moment and cannot itself be retained; but each contributes its mite to that general idea of furniture or of animal which our mind is gradually constructing, and which lives on in the expanding cloud of dispositions that everyone carries about with him If we figure what happens to the mind as the opposite of what Wordsworth imagined as happening to the soul, we shall have some suggestion of the truth. The soul, in the great Ode, is represented as 'trailing clouds of glory' when it first enters upon its course, and little by little losing them as 'the light of common day' prevails. The psychologist is more prosaic, but also more hopeful, since for him the cloud of significance that each mind trails along with it is cumulative, growing in volume hourly. Now in the character of this elusive cloud of meaning and its relations to present consciousness lies the secret of the richness and mobility of one's mind. It accounts for all manner of failures, variations, and successes in our thinking and perceiving. We are concerned for the moment with the failures. How can the presence of a mass of meaning cause an *absence* of perception?

2. We have seen that the field of actual consciousness is always narrow; not more than a tiny fraction of the ideas at our command can crowd into it at once. Yet the competition for a place in it is keen, since any organ or function that goes wrong, any appetite or interest that is restless, usually seeks relief through the office of consciousness. The field of consciousness is like the office of a Tammany politician after his election, with an ante-room full of applicants, and places for very few. By reason of limitations set by nature, to admit one group of ideas is, for the time, to exclude the rest.

Now it is always in groups that consciousness handles the

applicants. Of course it is often said that we can attend to only one thing at once, but in view of the fact that even a pin-head is complex and therefore in a sense is not one but many, such a statement is very loose; if 'one thing' means one distinguishable element, we can have a large number of things at the same instant in the very focus of consciousness. But when I say that what is ordinarily present is a group of ideas I mean more than this. I mean that at any one time, the mind confines itself, so far as it can, to one system of ideas, that it is willing to move about within the limits of that system, but that it resists breaking out of the circle and entering a new one. By a 'system of ideas' is meant here what logicians call a 'universe of discourse' or what is often called a 'single context'. What makes it single may be nothing as logical as the implication of its parts with each other; it may be only the fact that they serve in common a single interest. The examples of such systems are countless. The movements of the players when we are watching a game of football form parts of such a system. The science of botany, the life of Napoleon, the virtues of a new motor-car, cats, religious experience, spring fashions, this game of chess, the play of which we are now seeing the third act, are all examples. If the mind were a wholly logical instrument and grouped things into logical complexes only, these groups would never have been recognized. But the mind, as we shall see, is riotous with whimsies, and its groupings as a rule are queer compromises between the demands of reason and the demands of other competing interests.

3. Suppose that such a group has gained dominance in consciousness, that we are intent, for example, upon a game of chess; what will be the effect upon our perceiving? That depends upon the force and vigour with which the dominant group holds the field. What, then, does this vigour depend on? The degree of our interest. What is interest and what does *it* depend on? In the understanding of our actual thinking these are very important questions, and we must try to answer them later on. It must suffice for the moment to point as an example of interest to the familiar difference between being absorbed in something and being bored with it, and to remark the close connection between interest and purpose. Mind is purposive to its very roots; it is in its essence a set of wants cropping out into desires, and of desires pressing for their fulfilment. Now whatever satisfies a want has interest for us; whatever is interesting satisfies a want; and the strength of the want for anything is a measure of the interest in it. Witness the ripening interest of the adolescent in sex or the hungry man's interest in food. Suppose now that an idea group, supported by a powerful interest, holds the field of consciousness. Since it is sustained by an interest and therefore by a hunger of the mind, it maintains itself, develops in such fashion as to satisfy the hunger further, and excludes everything from the conscious field except what belongs to the group that dominates. To the engrossed chess player the universe has contracted to the dimensions of the game; his mind is a cloud of proposals and possibilities hovering anxiously over the pieces, responsive to the shift of a pawn, but dead perhaps to thunderstorms.

Freud has made it notorious how easily we forget what unwittingly we want to forget. In the same way we may fail to perceive what the dominant group of the moment forbids us to perceive. Not that sensations are as controllable as thoughts; of course they are not; but neither is it true that to open our eyes upon things is to see them. The mind excludes impertinent sensations much as it excludes impertinent ideas. The spectator intent on the game of football may have no eyes even for beauty three rows away, no ears for the vendor of chocolates, and not so much as a pang from the poisonous refreshment he has just made away with. A player may receive injuries that would ordinarily be painful and not even notice them until the idea-mass in control during the contest relaxes its hold at the close. It is said that in the old barbarous days when picking pockets was punished by hanging, pickpockets did a lucrative business among the very crowds assembled to witness the executions. They were relying on the principle that explains how a man can take out his watch, look at it, and put it back again, without getting the slightest notion what time it is. The same principle, again, explains how a prestidigitator does many of his tricks. If the spectators' minds can be filled with the importance of what he is doing with his right hand, the dark business his left hand is carrying on will have little chance of detection. And with regard to such blindness generally, we are in the position of neither knowing its extent nor even being able to know, for the same poverty of meaning that makes us blind prevents our discovering how large an area we are blind to. That this area is extensive is suggested by such incidents as the following, reported long ago by Edridge Green:

> 'The plane-tree is one of the commonest trees in London; most of the avenues contain large numbers of them, and nearly all the trees in the quadrangle of St. Bartholomew's Hospital are plane-trees; and yet I have taken a leaf and shown it to numbers of students and other persons, and asked them if they knew what it was. They have all said, "No: I have never seen anything like it before." . . . Now all these persons must have seen numbers of plane-trees *every* day. . . .' 'I was taking a walk with a relation who was very much interested in superficial botany, and anxious to know the names of the different trees and plants. So I went up an avenue (where nearly every second tree is a plane-tree), and pointed out various trees and shrubs, mentioning their names, of course taking no notice of the plane-trees. I then turned into a side avenue of a similar character, and having reached the centre of it, stopped in front of a plane-tree, and asked, "Have you ever seen a similar tree to that before?" and received the answer I expected. "No, I think that must be a very rare tree. I don't remember ever having seen one like it before." We were in sight of two or three dozen at the time, and the great surprise expressed at finding every other tree a plane was amusing.'[1]

The writer goes on to pile up evidence for our blindness and deafness. He notes it as a curious fact that when one is especially interested in some subject, 'everyone seems to be talking about it', whereas before nobody seems to have mentioned it. He

---

[1] *Memory*, 119–21. I owe notice of the passage to a reference of Stout's.

tries on the reader the familiar but effective experiment of asking him to draw the dial of his watch with the Roman numerals in their right places, than which nothing should be easier, since we have looked at our watches hundreds, perhaps thousands, of times; but if one's attention has not been specially drawn to the fact 'that the four is represented by IIII on time-pieces, and not by IV, he will almost certainly fail; and even if this be put correctly some other mistake will be made. I have tried this in numerous instances, and never received a correct answer'. His observation as a medical man was that when a new disease is described, apparently for the first time, similar cases begin to crop up all over the country.

This fact is significant, for it shows that even a special interest and knowledge are not enough to ensure perception unless they are concerned with a particular kind of thing. The word of some first-rate observer would be welcome here, and fortunately we have it. Darwin had been taking an early trip with the geologist Sedgwick. 'On this tour', he writes, 'I had a striking instance how easy it is to overlook phenomena, how-ever conspicuous, before they have been observed by anyone. We spent many hours in Cwm Idwal, examining all the rocks with extreme care, as Sedgwick was anxious to find fossils in them; but neither of us saw a trace of the wonderful glacial phenomena all around us; we did not notice the plainly scored rocks, the perched boulders, the lateral and terminal moraines. Yet these phenomena are so conspicuous that . . . a house burnt down by fire did not tell its story more plainly than did this valley.'[1] But this was in the dawn of geology; a few years later, when important theories turned on these things, they could hardly have been so overlooked.

Mr. Charles Fox has attempted to test the influence of 'preperception' experimentally. He exhibited to a large group of graduate students a lantern slide representing suits of armour, and had the spectators write down all the details they could remember. He then divided them into two groups, gave one of these a lecture on the structure of armour, and then,

[1] *Life and Letters*, I. 58.

reuniting them, exhibited a further slide. From among his results we may cite this, that the 'lance rest' though it forms 'a conspicuous feature' of a suit of armour, 'was hardly ever seen by a subject who did not know what it meant,' whereas 'in one slide where the lance rest was inconspicuous owing to ornamentation, it was never overlooked by those who knew what to look for'.[1] Blindness of the senses usually goes back to blindness in the mind's eye. 'Both passive observation and experimentation must be generally conducted by persons who know for what they are to look. It is only when excited and guided by a theory that the observer will notice many of the most important points; and when the work is not of a routine character no assistant can supersede the mind-directed observations of the philosopher.'[2]

4. Now so far as perception inclines one way rather than another through the influence of purpose, there is something like a paradox in its working. Suppose that I am a botanist, and have built up on this subject a large and well-ordered idea-mass, supported by a vigorous interest. It follows that when I walk abroad, I shall be far more likely to notice plants and mosses than if this idea-mass were absent. But how does this actually work? We say that it attaches meaning to some sensations and welcomes them for its own, while it excludes others from notice as irrelevant. Such statements are commonly repeated by writers on apperception as if they were free from difficulty. But observe the paradox: to some sensations no meaning is attached because they are irrelevant. But what makes them irrelevant? Not their character as sensations; mere sensations can be as little relevant or irrelevant as they can be true or false. What makes them relevant or not is the meaning placed upon them. Now if the only way they can be excluded as irrelevant is to have a meaning placed upon them, then they are not really excluded at all, since it is confessed in so many words

---

[1] *Educational Psychology*, 72.
[2] Jevons, *Principles of Science*, 404.

that the mind is construing them actively just as it is the other sensations. Hence a contradiction; the mind refuses to deal with them because they are irrelevant, but they could not be seen as irrelevant unless the mind *were* dealing with them. What shall we say to this?

There are some persons who would fall back here on what we know of the nervous system. They would point out that when a certain idea-mass is dominant, a corresponding region of the brain is in excitement, and that the strong functioning of one region inhibits the functioning of certain other regions. They would probably cite the work of Sherrington, which shows that a single stimulus may not only produce a reaction, but also inhibit other reactions that might conflict with it.[1] But Sherrington was working chiefly with fixed connections in the nervous system, such as that by which a stimulus produces at once a contraction of the muscles that flex a limb and a relaxation of those that extend it. And the striking fact about observation is that there are *no* such settled connections, that two perceptions—say of a flower and of its beauty—which are closely connected to-day, may to-morrow, when a new idea-mass is dominant, be mutually inhibitory. Where the interest may shift in any direction, and the line in the brain between the excited and inhibited areas follows the shift of interest, then limitation of interest may help in explaining neural inhibition, but neural inhibition will hardly explain limitation of interest. The idea that one is 'explaining' any thought process by stating it in terms of a bodily reaction, supposed itself to be mechanically explicable, is a superstition which appears the more clearly as superstition the more one reflects. Indeed we may suspect that it is superstition even in its dealings with so poor an integration as is shown by withdrawing a hand. It may be that 'the reflex action', as Sherrington himself has said, 'cannot be really intelligible to the physiologist until he knows its aim'.[2]

---

[1] *The Integrative Action of the Nervous System*, esp. 84–105.

[2] *Ibid.*, 236. For one ingenious hypothesis about the nervous correlates of apperception see McDougall, 'The Physical Factors of the Attention Process', *Mind*, N.S., XI, XII, esp. XI, 328–47.

Physiology, therefore, unless it is physiology impregnated with teleology, will do little to remove our paradox. It must be dealt with, if at all, by inferences from what we know of the working of consciousness. Now we know that when one idea-mass, say the botanical, is dominant, such things as rocks and clouds, which might otherwise be perceived, tend to be excluded from notice. We have every reason to think that interest and purpose have something to do with this exclusion. We know, again, that if they do have something to do with it, they must work by excluding those objects as irrelevant, and that they could not brand them as irrelevant except by attaching meaning to them. But does not 'attaching meaning to a sensation' here signify 'perceiving an object', and how can an object be perceived and excluded at the same time? The only solution, I think, is again to fall back on dispositions, however much we may dislike them. Of course, we may resort, if we please, to levels of consciousness, and say that the rocks and clouds to which our eyes are exposed are actually recorded through sense data and meaning at a subconscious level, and that as the meaning pushes for notice from the higher levels it is dismissed as an interloper. But there is a danger here of launching ourselves on that endless series of unverifiable consciousnesses which we have already found so unsatisfactory. Or we may say, if we like, that from the excluded objects the retina receives its usual impressions, which set up the usual central reactions, but that the nervous system, acting in pseudo-purposive fashion, isolates these from the major cortical concern. This may be perfectly true. It may be accepted so long as it does not delude us into supposing that we *know* how a physical body can behave intelligently. But if we are going to cover the facts, we must recognize here, as often, that there are agencies in us which somehow get rational results, although they can neither be shown to be conscious, nor, by one who thinks, be identified with mechanical reaction. These agencies we have called dispositions. It is to their activity that we must assign the spade-work preliminary to perceptual inhibition. If the perception of rocks and clouds, to be excluded by the dominant botanical

purpose, must carry meaning, and if this meaning is neither
conscious nor merely physical, we must suppose that both the
imposition of meaning and its exclusion as irrelevant to the
dominant end are due to the co-working of dispositions. If not
to them, then to what?

5. Of course lack of an appropriate idea-group is not the
only cause of failure to perceive, and for the sake of a more
balanced account, we may mention the chief other sources.
The trouble may lie in outside conditions, or in our nervous
system, or in some unaccountable blind spot in our mind. If
the cause is merely physical, it lies either in the medium through
which we perceive things or the special nature of the things
themselves. Through fogs we see dimly; through real darkness
no cat or owl can see anything at all. But if the difficulty lies in
the thing's own nature, it is less removable. No one has ever
seen an electron, and if it is argued that we conceivably might,
and therefore perhaps sometime shall, it seems fairly certain,
at least of such things as light rays, that even this possibility is
excluded, since the light sensation is not the function of one
wave alone, but of a series or succession of them. The new
world of physics is full of these imperceptibles. An immense
number of waves, of different types of radiation, are at this
moment beating a tattoo on the reader's ear-drum; the sky is
sprinkled with dark stars and invisible comets; each common
object is charged with electricity which we are too coarsely
constituted to feel. Sometimes outer events occur too rapidly
for our dull senses to keep them distinct, as when the series
of moving-pictures or the drops in a jet of water appear continuous. Sometimes, and much more commonly than we realize,
we fail to perceive because of some special defect in our sense
organs; about one man in twenty-five, we are told, suffers from
some type of colour-blindness, though frequently without
knowing it.

Sometimes, again, the difficulty affects more than the sense-
organs and there is a 'blind spot' in the mind for some special

type of relation, a blindness, furthermore, that may co-exist with exceptional alertness to other things. 'Johnson', says Macaulay, 'just knew the bell of St. Clement's Church from the organ.'[1] Of Macaulay himself, his biographer, in spite of a rare devotion, has to admit that there was only one occasion on which he was ever known to recognize a tune, namely when a certain band was blaring 'The Campbells are Coming'.[2] Charles Lamb, in his frank little 'Chapter on Ears', writes: '*organically* I am incapable of a tune. I have been practising "*God save the King*" all my life . . . and am not yet arrived, they tell me, within many quavers of it';[3] and Darwin admits 'I am so utterly destitute of an ear that I cannot perceive a discord'. . . .[4] When, as in all these cases, the subject knows his own deficiency, the loss is his alone, but cases are on record in which a man 'appeared not to be able to distinguish between the bass and the treble' and yet 'believed that he was a musical genius and that other people in general had not the right idea of music, and whenever he had an opportunity, volunteered to sing. . . . What accompaniment was played mattered not, and was varied according to the inclination of the pianist'.[5] On the modes of self-defence against such persons we are happily not called upon to comment; the point is the congenital and irremediable insensitiveness to relations of one special sort. It need hardly be remarked that this obtuseness may appear also in other senses.

Thus there are limits set to perception by congenital unresponsiveness to special qualities and forms. Within these limits, however, the failures are due for the most part to the absence of meanings supported by interest. And having seen the part played by such meanings in failures to observe, let us turn to their part in distorting what we do observe.

6. It is extremely unlikely that any two adult persons, supposedly seeing and hearing precisely the same thing, ever

[1] Essay on *Madame d'Arblay*.
[2] Trevelyan's *Life*, 549 (Silver edition).
[3] *Elia*, Ainger's edition, 53.
[4] *Life and Letters*, I. 49.   [5] Edridge-Green, *op. cit.*, 85.

have perceptions that are quite alike. How could they? Granting that their sensations are as much alike as different sensations can be, still perception always carries an element of meaning, and this meaning is a distillation from past experience. It will vary as this past varies, and since no two of us have the same past, no two of us give quite the same meaning to what is offered us in sense. Where the pasts have been extremely different this is even obvious. It is told that some American Indians were taken for the first time to see a great city in the expectation that they would view its elevated railways, its trams and motor-cars, with astonishment and delight. They did not. These things were so utterly outside the range of their experience as to be almost meaningless to them, and they could only stand and gape stupidly. But suddenly one of their number spied a repair man going up a telephone pole with the peculiar spurs used for this purpose, and before this phenomenon the group stopped and gazed in fascination. They had tried that sort of thing themselves; they knew there was point in it; they recognized the feat involved in doing it so well; the rest was all confusion. Darwin records that the Patagonians were entranced with the rowboat in which sailors from the *Beagle* rowed ashore, but that the big *Beagle* itself seemed a thing of no interest. In these cases the difference between the pasts was the difference of civilization from savagery, and the perceptions diverged correspondingly; but the difference must be quite as real, even if not so great, between two persons on the same level of culture. We shall never wholly understand each other, if only because we cannot exchange biographies; each man is like a nautilus who lives in a house of his own making, and carries it around on his back. We shall never know how our language sounds to a Frenchman, or precisely how a melody appeals to another person, or just how anything affects the opposite sex, or indeed exactly how anything strikes anybody but ourselves. We can guess and conjecture more or less successfully, but if we try to do more, we come to that 'salt estranging sea' which neither science nor romance has been able quite to bridge.

7. Now this control of perception by ideas is at once a great help and a great hindrance in the ordinary work of observing, and we shall understand it better if we study for a little how it works in practice. To point out first its advantages:

(1) It facilitates search. We are many times more likely to perceive something if we are expecting it or looking for it than if we are not. The reader may have attended a football match and later seen a photograph of that section of the crowded grandstand where he was sitting. If, when he looked at the photograph, he had no notion that his own face was in the crowd, how likely would he be to notice it? If he noticed it at all under such circumstances it would be by the merest chance. Everyone's experience will supply daily illustrations of the principle.

8. (2) Even where there is no active search, dwelling on something in thought makes us more likely to see it in fact. Savages may display the greatest keenness in detecting footprints, following trails, and hearing the sounds made by animals. But

> 'the results of tests made on savages in different parts of the world by scientific expeditions go to show that their senses are no more perfect than those of Europeans, in fact on the average are even less sensitive. It is merely that all their training during their lifetime has been concentrated upon recognizing and interpreting the particular objects and differences which have a meaning for the chase. . . . The acuteness of vision of the sailor is to be explained in the same way. For him every mark upon the horizon is correctly interpreted, and every small object is seen, because there are images in mind ready to be called out by any impression that is likely to appear there'.[1]

This effect of a prepared mind upon perceiving is prettily illustrated by an experiment of Helmholtz. He seated himself, in darkness, before a sheet of paper which had large printed letters scattered about on it. The only light visible came through

---

[1] Pillsbury, *Attention*, 41.

a pin-hole in the middle of the sheet, and on this pin-hole he fixed his eyes. The question he wanted to settle was whether, if he kept his eyes fixed on the pin-hole, the mere concentration of thought on one part of the sheet rather than another would enable him to see this part better when a light was flashed on. In order to be sure that it was the state of his mind that was at work and not an involuntary movement of his eyeballs, he arranged that the light should be turned on in so brief a flash as to give no time for such movement.

> 'Nevertheless', he says, 'I found it possible to fix beforehand on some part of the dark field, stretching out from the bright pin-point where my eyes remained fastened, which I cared to bring into indirect perception, and through the electric flash I could then recognize several groups of letters in that region of the field. . . . On the other hand, the letters of by far the largest part of the field did not come to perception at all, not even that which lay in the neighbourhood of the point of fixation. At a later flash I was able, while still fixating the pin-point, to direct my perception to another region and read a group of letters there.'[1]

So far as concerns physical effect on the eye, the perceived and unperceived regions must have acted in precisely the same way, yet because of the state of mind, one was seen and the others were not. 'This', says Helmholtz, after a similar experiment later, 'is one of the most significant of observations for a theory of attention.'[2]

9. (3) The presence of the appropriate ideas increases the power of the senses to discriminate. We may look directly at the region of the sky where a star is shining and see nothing. Even after our neighbour has pointed out that a star is there, we may still see nothing. Once we have caught it, however, it is much more easily seen again; the definite impression we have formed of it seems to sharpen our vision. 'Every artist knows how he can make a scene before his eyes appear warmer or colder in colour, according to the way he sets his attention.

---

[1] *Handbuch der Physiologischen Optik*, 605.   [2] *Ibid.*, 891.

If for warm, he soon begins to *see* the red colour start out of everything; if for cold, the blue.'[1] And he 'would never be able to analyse out the pervasive presence of the blue, unless he had previously made acquaintance with the colour blue by itself'.[2] The same holds of sensations of other kinds. We try to single out the sound of a 'cello in an orchestra and find it hard or impossible until the 'cello strikes into a solo passage; then with the sound in mind we can isolate later its thread of tone. Similarly of detecting the overtones of a note, and of discriminating one taste or odour from others. 'A highly cultured smoker may spend hours in describing the delicate variety of experiences which a single superb cigar gives him, while an ordinary mortal can only look on in amazement and wonder what he is talking about.'[3] Whatever the value of such discernment, it is something that attends only on wealth of one kind of experience.

10. (4) Again, the presence of a relevant meaning-mass quickens the speed of perception. Ever since Wundt's pioneer experiments on reaction-time, this has been a favourite subject for the laboratory, and the volume of data upon it has become too enormous even to review. In general, we seem to respond more quickly when we are expecting a stimulus than when we are not, when we know a particular sense is to be stimulated than when we are in doubt, when the nature of the stimulus is specifically rather than vaguely foreknown. From the present point of view, one of the most interesting results of reaction-time inquiries is that where the expectation is definite and strong, the time taken for the reaction is sometimes less than zero, which means that before the stimulus has actually arrived the subject thinks he perceives it. This is quite in line with what we are saying about the influence of ideas in perceiving. Of course, no measurement of the speed of reaction really measures the speed of perception, for the time taken to press a

---

[1] James, *Psychology*, I. 425. [2] *Ibid.*, 504.
[3] Stout, *Analytic Psychology*, I. 58.

key or withdraw a hand includes not only the time of perceiving but also that of the act which ensues upon it. Still one
can so arrange one's experiments that when, in some cases, the
reaction-time is reduced, one can be confident that the time
saved is in the afferent side of the process, and that the presence
of a preceding idea has made a notable difference in the speed
of perceiving.

11. (5) Again, the presence of such an idea helps us to hold
our attention on what is perceived by supplying from within
the necessary variations in the object. We have seen that from
the very beginning attention is attracted by change and movement. To the kitten, the puppy, or the child, an orange on the
table is little or nothing, while if it is rolled across the floor,
it becomes interesting at once. And we are so made that unless
things around us do change, we tend to withdraw express
notice from them. Here is another instance of the principle
of economy of consciousness; what consciousness is primarily
for is to deal with difficulties, and if there is nothing going on
around us to call for adjustments, or if what is going on is so
familiar that it can be handed over to habit, consciousness tends
to lapse. Change in what we attend to is therefore necessary if
attention is to be maintained. Now this necessary change may
be produced either outwardly or inwardly, and which of these
methods is employed depends on how far advanced the mind is,
on both the phylogenetic and ontogenetic scales. The farther
down we go upon the evolutionary ladder the more dependent
we find attention to be on changes happening to its object from
without, and if we go low enough even these may have to be
great and sudden if any effect is to be produced. The behaviour
of very low organisms would be similar, I believe, to that of
Preyer's decerebrated frog, which, though capable of many
reactions to sudden stimuli, died without making a movement
when the water in which it was living was heated by sufficiently
slow degrees. A cat, if nothing is happening around it and no
instinctive urges are troubling it from within, will go peacefully

to sleep. In the apes something more akin to theoretical interest begins to appear; the monkey will produce the changes that are needful to sustain his interest by turning an object round and round and cocking an eye at it from every angle. Now such change is still in man the condition of attention; he cannot hold his mind to a quite unchanging thing, say a dot on a page, for more than a few seconds at most. But he has the enormous advantage that the changes needed for his attention he can make for himself. He can force the dot to sprout fresh meanings in all directions, as if it were an amoeba gone on a spree and extruding pseudopodia hilariously. It can serve for him as the focus of many radiating interests; he can ask, How big is it? What colour is it? What is it made of? How long has it been there? and so on almost indefinitely. And each question invests the object with fresh meaning by connecting it with a new end. To put it formally, the attention depends on the relation between the thing and some farther end. Since this end is within our control, since we can raise new questions at will, we can dress out the stupid dot in continual changes of raiment; and such change is the chief condition for the maintenance of attention.[1]

Everyone knows how hard it is to train a pet dog to do a trick. He refuses to notice the hoop that is held for him, fails utterly to catch the meaning of a pointing hand, and can only bark in joyous stupidity at being the centre of a commotion. The lack, of course, is not in his senses but in his 'mind'. This same dog when sniffing a rabbit hole will show a truly remarkable concentration, since the hole is charged with dispositional meaning. But nothing can be more meaningless than the smell and look of an iron hoop, and no self-respecting dog will bother with it until it can be made to mean a biscuit or something else intrinsically worth while. Then there is no difficulty. In such matters the canine mind and the human work on precisely the same principles. There is no will strong enough to hold atten-

[1] 'The real development in an ideal form of the real object itself is in fact the positive end which against hindrance is pursued in attention. . . If we use in a wide sense the terms thought and idea, attention always, we must say, in this sense involves thinking.'—Bradley, 'On Active Attention,' *Mind*, N.S., XI. 5, 6.

tion on anything wholly without significance, and when the end is important and what is before us bears on it vitally, effort may be dispensed with. Could we, in ordinary circumstances, go on looking without distraction, say, at some wisp of smoke on the horizon? Could we do anything else if we were adrift in a boat on the open sea? Or consider two persons who are at a concert, side by side; one of them may give rapt attention to every bar, while the other suffers an almost insupportable boredom. There are many persons to whom an afternoon in a gallery of art is nothing but a weariness to the flesh, issuing often in revolt against all that would exact attention to things so barren. Against boredom of this type the only secure insurance is variety of internal resources. If these are present, external variety may be small, and experience rich and interesting none the less. If one is so made—and there have been such—as to find 'the earth and every common sight' invested with meanings drawn from old and multifarious reflection, one's existence may be far from thin, even if confined to some remote village where 'nothing ever happens'. For such persons their mind is their kingdom, and it is an ample one. It is immensely richer, for instance, than the experience of those persons one can always find on the busiest street-corners of large cities, drawn there because they must compensate for inner vacuity by the torrent and violence of sensation.

12. (6) Finally, preperception helps us to isolate the novel, and so to deploy our forces effectively in dealing with it. Houdin, the French juggler, did not think he was at his right level unless, while keeping four balls in the air, he could at the same time read a book; he considered that the simpler things in his art should become so far automatic as to leave his attention free for ulterior difficulties. Now assimilation by dispositional meaning is to the mind what habit is to the body. Most of the things we see are read off effortlessly through the aid of our existing meaning-mass, and there is no need to notice them explicitly. But of course this meaning-mass is built from the materials of a limited experience; the mind of the factory-hand or the farmer epitomizes a personal history. That history has supplied a meaning-system which may meet the exigencies of one kind of life as a cover fits a box. But if these exigencies change their pattern, the cover will fit no longer, and the point where it fails to fit will leap into instant prominence. The place where the shoe pinches, the furnace that in the course of a cold spell starts misbehaving, the unimportant but ridiculously conspicuous fact that a man has forgotten his tie—it is these departures from the round of normality that rivet our notice. Much of the tragedy in a disfigurement of face or limb lies in the fact that the thousand respects in which the sufferer is like other men are taken for granted while the one defect is singled out with an unconscious and hence inevitable cruelty as the prime distinguishing mark.

To be quite clear about all this we must note three points. First, the maxims that we see only what is familiar, that the traveller finds only what he brings with him, and so on, are both true and false. They are true in the sense that the only things we can rightly appreciate are things we are prepared for in idea, and that all beyond this calls for an effort in which we may very possibly fail. On the other hand, these maxims are false when they suggest unqualifiedly that it is the familiar we specially notice; we could say with equal truth that what we notice is the novel. But secondly, the novelty we do notice is not any and every kind of novelty, but only the novel within limits. For the Indians who were introduced to the centre of a city there was novelty around them in plenty, but they were incapable of special notice because the volume of novelty paralysed them; one cannot assimilate civilization at a stroke. What solicits notice, therefore, is novelty that is specific and limited —the man who is a foot taller than his fellows, the woman in Eastern dress. And thirdly, this suggests a normal condition for either perceiving or attending generally. This is a state of moderate tension at a particular point of the meaning-mass then in use. There must be *tension*, for if there is nothing novel to call for ideal readjustment, we shall deal with the given automatically. The tension must be *moderate*, for otherwise intelligence will fail under the strain of a too difficult adjustment. And it must be *specific*, for attention is confined to a narrow focus, and if diffused, is merely dissipated. Attention is at its best, therefore, when, in a scene familiar as a whole, there arises a particular point of challenge on which its powers may be mobilized, somewhat as the white corpuscles are mobilized about a bodily wound. One is continually tempted when discussing these things, to pause and point the educational moral, to show how the mastery of any matter requires a developed meaning-mass, the product of experience; how this grows through minor challenge and organic assimilation at one point after another of its periphery; how too strong a challenge may lead to stunting, and one too weak to flaccidity; and much else. But this is not a pedagogical manual; and, besides, for those who are interested the educational inferences are not difficult to draw.

13. Turning now to the *disadvantages* of the control of perception by idea, we may sum them all up by saying that it is the most fertile source of perceptual error and illusion. In many psychological books one finds drawings of simple figures which may be seen in quite different ways, as one looks at them with one idea or another uppermost in one's mind. The same figure appears now like a stairway, now like an overhanging cornice; now like a duck's head looking to the right, now like a rabbit's head looking to the left; the same set of dots will present now one figure, now another, as the ideal cue changes. These are relatively innocent examples; the dominion of meaning over perception may be far more despotic than anything they would suggest. It may not merely blind us to what we should perceive otherwise, and alter what we do perceive, but, at least to appearance, actually create the soil out of which it is supposed to grow. When a superstitious person visits a house, supposedly haunted, and sees strange things at midnight, we usually say that he has had some perfectly normal sensations of sight and hearing, but that an overwrought imagination has imposed on them an interpretation that does not fit. This is a thoroughly typical case of misperception; the error lies in supplying to given sensation an extension that it will not support. But what of the cases supplied in profusion by books on mental pathology, in which stigmata and other wounds are produced and healed, surgical operations performed painlessly, and a great variety of sensations apparently brought into being through hypnotic or other suggestion? Here meaning, instead of waiting upon the cue of sensation, seems to manufacture it for itself. It may be said that it does not really do this, but only seems to, that the person being operated on is really suffering though he thinks he is not, and the person suffering hypnotic pain is not really suffering, though he thinks he is. Nor can this reply be dismissed as in principle absurd, for it is clearly possible to be mistaken as to what one is experiencing. Still there is no reason to take it as true. If a man's words and actions comport with his experiencing intense pain, or with his feeling no pain at all, we must take his report as *prima facie* true, and throw the burden of proof on the negative; and it seems clear that the negative is not, in all these cases, made out. Are we to say, then, that meaning has such potency in perception that it can actually generate the sensory element? We must answer, I think, as follows: when it seems to do so, the sensations generated are always of a kind before experienced; but it is scarcely deniable that in occasional instances sense data *are* generated in such circumstances that the antedecent meaning-mass must be accounted a partial cause. And if true, this is significant. For if a mere expectation can not only determine how we shall read a sensation but can aid in generating sensation itself, then neither is meaning so passive an adjunct of sensation nor consciousness so passive an adjunct of the body as has been commonly supposed.

14. Now if the idea-group that is brought to bear in perception is so extremely potent an influence, if it may conceal

objects from our notice, cause perceptions of the same thing
to differ widely, even contribute to causing sensation itself,
it may be asked whether the world we find in perception is
not, as a whole, an arbitrary construct. When Hamlet pointed
out to Polonius that yonder cloud was very like a camel,
Polonius saw it that way; when Hamlet went on to suggest that
it also looked like a weasel and like a whale, Polonius saw these
with equal ease. Now are not all minds at bottom Poloniuses,
only a little more consistent in their caprice? Is there anything
in the nature of sensation to require that these particular con-
structions shall be imposed upon them? If the bent of our
interest were different, should we not build these into things
of a different nature and so into a different world? An answer
has already been suggested in dealing with Bosanquet's statement that in principle no line can be drawn between the given
and its extension. It is true that in any sensation which we
can actually examine thought is already at work; it is true
that from what is given, thought selects and synthesizes elements in a way that would be different were its purposes
otherwise. So far it is true that the kind of world we live in
depends on the activity of thought. But on two sides this
activity is limited by bounds it cannot hope to exceed. On the
side of what is presented, the qualitative character of sensations can only be accepted passively; we cannot create at will
new and other types of sensa; colours and sounds are not mere
whims. And again on the side of construction, though sensa
may be selected and grouped in various ways, there are limits
rigidly fixed; our construction always proceeds under the
charter and constitution laid down by the categories. Thus
perception may rightly be called arbitrary, if this means that it
varies widely with changing meaning-mass or purpose; but to
say that it is merely or wholly arbitrary would be to flout
plain fact.

15. We have now seen that perceptual meaning fills some
very important offices, both positive and negative, in the work

of perceiving. It may blind us altogether to what is before
our eyes. It may cause our perceptions, when we do perceive,
to vary immensely from person to person. Such influence has
many advantages. It facilitates the work of directed observation;
it widens the range of undirected observation; it refines the
power of the senses to discriminate; it renders perception more
swift and ready; through its kaleidoscopic function of making
the object change its aspect, it helps to maintain attention;
through its power to deal with the familiar by effortless automa-
tism it eases the task of attention in dealing with what is novel.
Against all these helpful offices must be placed one great dis-
service; it breeds continual error. The suggestion has even
been made that it breeds error exclusively, that the whole perceptual world is coloured and distorted by it. But its power,
as we have seen, is limited at both ends. In respect to its
material it is limited by the qualities of the given; in respect
to its structure, by the categories. The first of these limitations
was discussed in our opening chapter. To the more interesting
and complicated question of the structure of perceptual meaning we now turn.

CHAPTER VI

THE STRUCTURE OF PERCEPTUAL MEANING

1. Everyone knows that when an expert medical man observes the symptoms of a disease, or an accomplished critic listens to the reading of a poem, a very extended knowledge may be brought to bear. It may be used in a wholly effortless way; it may be so far from explicitness that no introspection can describe it; and yet, as we have seen in the last two chapters, it must be at work; the facts of perception are inexplicable without it; indeed its functions are both important and manifold. Does this meaning-mass have any discernible organization or structure? We shall see that it does, and that this may be highly complex. In the present chapter we are to examine this structure through looking successively at two properties which every developed meaning-mass possesses, namely depth and range.

What is meant by depth may be illustrated by a passage from James Ward.

> 'Suppose that in the course of a few minutes we take half a dozen glances at a strange and curious flower. We have not as many complex presentations, which we might symbolize as $F_1, F_2 \ldots F_6$. But rather, at first only the general outline is noted, next the disposition of petals, stamens, etc., then the attachment of the anthers, position of the ovary, and so on; that is to say, symbolizing the whole flower as $[p'(ab)s'(cd)\ o'(fg)]$, we first apprehend say $[p' \ldots s' \ldots o']$, then $[p'(ab)s' \ldots o']$, or $[p'(a \ldots) s'(c \ldots) o'(f \ldots)]$, and so forth. It is because the traits first attended to persist that those noticed later form an addition to them so that the complex at length may be complete.'[1]

It will be admitted that the perception is here improving at every step, and that it is improving because the advance is cumulative, each new glimpse retaining the result of the past ones and adding a deposit of its own. The last perception

---

[1] *Psychological Principles*, 81.

carries as strata in its own structure the deposits of all five of the preceding experiences. This is what is meant when we say that it carries more depth of meaning.

Some depth of meaning will thus belong to every perception after the first, since no perception merely repeats an earlier one. It might be supposed, therefore, that such depth is a mere matter of repeated experiences, so that we could fold our hands and look to the passing years to bring us the depth desired. This, of course, is untrue. We shall see in a moment that age does have advantages, though they are not to be measured by length of days. For one perception may be so like another, one day or year so like its predecessor, as to add virtually nothing to our funded capital; Peter Bell may see less in the primrose after a thousand glances than Ward's observer after half a dozen. If depth of meaning is to be acquired, therefore, it is necessary that the new perception should be not only another one but a fresh one, that it should make some deposit of its own in the bank of dispositional meaning.

2. Such meaning is always a hierarchy. At the top are elements that hold their places by the practically unanimous suffrage of all the perceptions of our past years—the ideas of time and space, of cause and number, of matter and thing. Every hour of our experience repeats them; they are so drummed and dinned into the substance of our minds that every expectation with which we greet experience includes them. If our expectation should be defeated with respect to any one of them, if the table we saw before us should offer no resistance to our hand as we touched it or to our body as we walked through it, if the familiar causal action of the floor on our feet, or of words on our friends, were to be suspended without notice, it is pretty certain that sanity too would be suspended, if indeed the word sanity had any longer a meaning. These elements are the bony framework of perceptual thought whose flesh and dress may change, but which itself is hardened into fixity. It must not be supposed, of course, that the presence of these

elements in all perceptions and expectations means a presence distinguished and explicit. As we shall see in treating of ideas, the very elements that are most universal, and therefore in a sense most familiar, are among the most difficult to isolate explicitly; what is first in order of nature tends, as Aristotle said, to be last in order of thought. But light may contribute to seeing even when unseen itself, and these elements are a 'master light of all our seeing'.

Below the highest levels in perceptual meaning lies a long series of others. There is a sense in which every man enters the world by climbing down the tree of Porphyry. If we were to name the character things possess for us at the start, we could hardly make it more definite than mere *being*, and it is only very slowly, within this frame of extreme generality, that the child goes on to distinguish the pleasant and the unpleasant, and later the living and not-living, self and not-self. The problem for the baby, Professor J. A. Smith once remarked, is less to find where the pain is within itself, than to find itself within the pain. When experience is also growth, it moves by a progressive definition of the general; its aim, where intelligently guided, is to become as specific and concrete as possible; the more a perceiver can take the general features for granted and confine himself to details, the better his perceiving becomes. Take the physician, for example. He starts with the same ill-defined impressions as the rest of us about the body in health and disease. Little by little these notions are specified; the vague notion of disease defines itself into this, that, and the other variety of it; and each of these into more specific forms. Each of these forms, again, has its special symptoms, and what may appear to an undiscerning practitioner as a single symptom—say an irregular pulse—may, to the expert diagnostician, be itself a feature within which many significant distinctions must be noted. Now part of what we mean by expert perceiving is just this depth of stratification in the meaning that is brought to bear. If the expert concentrates on minutiae that someone else would never notice, it is not because he is missing the most general features, but because he is beyond the need of noting them; the grasp of them is involved in the observation of those special features he does notice.

To speak of meaning as 'stratified' is, of course, to speak in metaphor, and this is dangerous. It is true, to be sure, that our present perceptual meaning contains characters of many levels of generality, and that acquaintance with these is acquired only gradually. But the metaphor may suggest that, as in a stratified river-bank, everything present may be placed in an order of layers corresponding to their formation in time, and this would be misleading. Advance in perception is not a triumphantly logical march from the big to the little end of a Goclenian sorites. When I perceive first the petals, then the stamens, then the anthers of a flower, each increment makes my perception more concrete and definite, but it is not an advance from genus to species; and in the structure of my perceptual meaning, all these elements are coexistent on the same level. Sometimes the order of experience reverses the order of scientific subordination, as when after a long familiarity with diamonds, I discover that they are to be classed with coal as carbon and inflammable. And partly because logic plays so small a part in the order of our experiences, it is possible that repeated exposure to something should do but little to improve our perception of it. It may only add one triviality to another, while everything of consequence is steadily missed. James has speculated on what would happen to the mind of a dog if it could live exclusively in a Vatican gallery, where every outlet to its vision was blocked by masterpieces. He concludes, of course, that to everything important in the work about it, it would come out as blind as it went in.

3. Length and repetition of experiences, then, are no guarantee of a significant depth of meaning. Indeed, so far as this depth implies ordering in a logical hierarchy, it is not to be explained without reference to a point soon to be considered, the integration of meaning. But apart from this, the chief factor in producing such depth is *continuity of interest*.

We have seen that to perceive is to judge, and to judge is to think. Now the right perceiving of what is new is a kind of thinking that may well take effort; and as a rule we avoid effort unless there is point in it. What gives point to it? Its serving an end or interest. Hence if observation is to be of the sort that enriches a mind, there must be a driving interest behind it; resolution helps, but less. And what does 'interest' here mean? We are not using the term in that broad sense in which 'it comprises pleasure, pain, and all emotions, including satisfactions and dissatisfactions, likes and dislikes of every kind, towards any kind of object'.[1] We are using it in the narrower sense of that kind of satisfaction in an object which impels us to keep the object before us, or that kind of satisfaction in an activity which impels us to maintain it. This satisfaction may be entirely non-rational, in the sense that it may not spring from any insight into the importance of its objects, but only from instinct or inexplicable liking. But if dwelling on a thing is satisfying, for whatever reason, we tend to go on dwelling on it, and since we can continue to dwell on it only if it changes before our attention, the result of interest is to make us develop and resolve it in our minds, and to put it through its perceptual paces. When the impulse to make a collection strikes a boy, whether it is of stamps, minerals, butterflies, or coins, his connoisseurship in these things may become extraordinary, and will go on refining itself while the interest lasts. When the instinct of sex ripens, he becomes intensely alive to details of face, figure, and dress in the other sex which before had scarcely existed for him, and the new interest invades his imagination also. Indeed if interest counts for as much in perceiving as we have suggested, then in an interest like that of sex, which is so powerful, general, and lasting, we should have a test case; its effect upon observing ought to be extraordinary. And it is. The average man has

[1] Mitchell, *Structure and Growth of the Mind*, 64. Professor Perry uses the term similarly to refer to 'instinct, desire, feeling, will, and all their family of states, acts and attitudes'.—*General Theory of Value*, 27.

more attentive eyes for women than for men; every newspaper editor knows that pictures or items dealing with sex situations will gain an attention out of all proportion to their intrinsic importance; the stage and screen, if deprived of the attention drawn from sex, would almost have to close their doors. Someone has said that the senses are themselves impulses, hungry for indulgence; and while this overshoots the mark, it is surprising how much of their activity is controlled and sustained by interest.

Now where an interest is strong and lasting, leading us to observe its objects alertly and revolve them in mind, we shall be adding continually to the depth of the mnemic mass (to use a convenient term of Semon's). Unhappily, in most of us, such interests are few. The result is that our minds, if we could look into them, would present a strange spectacle, a little like the skyline of New York. A horizon otherwise flat and un-interesting will be suddenly broken, in the region of our permanent interests, by isolated towering masses, the result of the ant-like building of many years. A man's mind may show mnemic masses that are nothing short of monumental in the region of his profession, health, and children, and show little else to break its monotony except, grotesquely enough, a colossal competence about right form in golf, or about the structure of radios. Nor is there anything hard to account for in this poverty of the outlying regions. To fulfil the dominant interests of most of us, it is needless to attend closely or often to such things as pictures or music, plants or machines or architectural effects. Such of their features as bear immediately on our ends are grasped quickly and easily; beyond these we need not go; hence, as a rule, those features only are seen; and hence, again, for these features there is a respectable meaning-mass always ready, while to the others there is nothing answering. If we are to take account of these others, a mnemic mass must be built for them in the same way as for the first, that is by an authentic and lasting interest.

4. How does this arise? Far too variously to discuss here in any detail. Sometimes it is pretty clearly congenital, as in a child of the writer's acquaintance, the daughter of gifted musicians, who displayed at the age of two an interest in melodies and some power of reproducing them, rather in the manner of the young Mozart. Sometimes it springs from seeing the connection between something hitherto unattractive and a further end that is ardently desired, as when an engineer gains an interest in geometrical matters from their bearing on problems of construction, or when Admiral Robley Evans, according to report, took a special interest in chess by reason of its supposed indication of a prowess for tactics. Sometimes— a most important case practically—it arises when, after long and tedious application by effort of will, we achieve a proficiency that is a source of pride; then our interest in the object receives the enormous reinforcement of our interest in being thought well of by others. Sometimes, again, it comes by the touching into life of a capacity for response which must have been lying latent, but required a special kind of stimulus to unlock it,

> A fancy from a flower bell, someone's death,
> A chorus-ending from Euripides,

or something equally unsuspected as the key to pent-up interests. This form of the birth of interest is illustrated by some of James's accounts of religious conversion, by Hobbes's discovery of Euclid at the age of forty, and by Malebranche's chance encounter of a treatise by Descartes, events which turned the currents of their lives. Such incidents throw a significant light on the connection of ideas and interest. It has often been said by writers on apperception that interest in an object is the *same thing* as having a meaning-mass which we may bring to bear upon it. But if, as in our musical instance, the congenital interest must be there already to account for the rapid accumulation of meaning; if, again, as in the case of those business men who gladly forsake and forget their business at the chance of retirement, the idea-system may remain when the interest has vanished, then however intimately they may be connected, the two things are not the same.

5. If the meaning, then, which we bring to bear in perception, is to have any considerable depth, it must spring from a *lasting* interest. It is plain, however, that for intelligent perceiving, the depth that comes from long experience and lasting interest is not enough. There are, perhaps, many persons who have been interested in insects as long as Fabre, in wasps as long as the Peckhams, in beetles and earthworms as long as Darwin; but it would be rash to say that these things possess for them generally the same fullness of meaning. What do such persons lack, that these remarkable observers had? The chief difference lies in the way in which meaning is integrated. Turning, then, to this important characteristic of *integration*, we shall try to say first, how it is produced, and then what it consists in.

6. The moving force in integrating is what we may call the reflective interest, that is, the desire to understand. This is quite distinct from the general interest we have been discussing. One's interest in something—in a friend or in listening to music —may be great when one's interest in understanding is small. The desire to understand is the desire to grasp the essential relations of things, to perceive A as a species of B, as the effect of C, as the cause of D, as the owner of properties E and F; and the natural result of this desire is that when something new presents itself, one not only notices it, but starts actively to reflect upon it, to place it in the context of things one already knows. For every first-rate observer, to observe means to assimilate, and not merely to recognize. There is a passage in Darwin's autobiography in which he seeks to analyse the qualities that brought him scientific success. After writing: 'Some of my critics have said "Oh, he is a good observer, but he has no power of reasoning!"' and answering with his astonishing but quite genuine modesty: the *Origin of Species* 'has convinced not a few able men. No one could have written it without having some power of reasoning', he goes on to place to his credit, and certainly with justice, precisely those two things we have named as necessary if depth and integration of meaning are to be achieved: 'On the favourable side of the balance, I think I am superior to the common run of men in noticing things which easily escape attention, and in observing them carefully . . . my love of rational science has been steady and ardent.' There is what we have called continuity of interest. He proceeds: 'From my early youth I have had the strongest desire to understand or explain whatever I observed,— that is, to group all facts under some general laws. These causes combined have given me the patience to reflect or ponder for any number of years over any unexplained problem.'[1] There is what we have called reflectiveness of interest. Both qualities could be paralleled in any first-rate observer.

7. This reflectiveness, however, is not so catholic an affair as Darwin appears to think. He did not really have 'the strongest desire to understand and explain *whatever* he observed'; his interests were notoriously concentrated on matters biological. And his case illustrates two facts which help us to define what we mean by reflectiveness: (1) it is catholic neither in its interest nor in its aim; it is never truly impartial; it is never willing to devote itself equally to everything cast up by experience, but always works on selected materials. One may bravely set out, like the young Bacon, to take all knowledge for one's province, but, to say nothing of the physical impossibilities, one is soon pulled up by realizing that not all things are equally worth knowing, and that one's interests are inevitably limited. The notion of a balanced intellectual development, if that means an equal interest in all the facts of the world around us and an equal acquaintance with them, is a vain dream. Our interests from the very beginning are warped by instincts im-

[1] *Life and Letters,* I. 103.

posed on us by the necessities of our race; by indulging these interests, we build up specialized mnemic masses, which in turn strengthen the interests that lead to them. Thus we may be even less capable at the end than at the beginning of an interest evenly diversified; witness Darwin's own famous confession, 'now for many years I cannot endure to read a line of poetry: I have tried lately to read Shakespeare and found it so intolerably dull that it nauseated me. I have also almost lost my taste for pictures or music'.[1] If we add to this a point to be explained later, that reflection in any field is hardly possible until one has gained some knowledge in it, we shall see that even the purest theoretical interest cannot move out in all directions into the universe at large, but must proceed along special roads. 'Nature has said it', and we may as well capitulate; if we cannot, as Emerson advised, adjust our aims mathematically to our powers, we must at least resign ourselves to be in some measure provincials or we shall end in general sciolism and futility.

8. (2) But reflective interest is limited in aim as well as material. Perception at its best is a process of asking silent questions. If a newly observed detail is to have full significance, it must bear upon some problem which the mind brings to the observation. One can no more reflect in general than observe in general; and the more definite the question that is put to observation the more effective as a rule will be its answer. The mere question, What is this? if competently asked, may be valuable, as anyone will attest who has taken a walk with an accomplished ornithologist or mineralogist. For this is really a question as to the place of something in a system of classification, and this is in turn a question as to the precise ways in which it is like other things or different. Hence to ask the question intelligently is to fix the mental eye on essential traits and to sharpen it for essential differences. Darwin's extraordinary eye for beetles[2] is a case in point. But the question

[1] *Life and Letters*, I 101.   [2] *Ibid.*, 50–1.

put to perception may be nothing so commonplace; it may be put in the interest of any kind of theory. To refer once more to one who should be 'observed of all observers', the vast mass of matter which is condensed into the *Origin of Species* could never have come to its author's notice if he had not gone about for many years bearding nature as Socrates bearded the philosophers, and putting his question tirelessly to every kind of organism, Is there anything about you that is not a modification of something else I have seen? In this respect perception is like experiment, which is only a means to observing better. Experiment is virtually useless except for settling some definite question formulated in advance: will silver dissolve in nitric acid? does a certain nervous arc pass through the cerebellum? The old idea possessed by the alchemists and strangely supported by Bacon that observation should be a passive recording, undirected by theory, is now everywhere abandoned. And the more perception generally can be vitalized by reflection, the greater will be its point and profit.

9. The immediate motive force, then, which integrates perceptual meaning is the desire to understand, a desire that, when effective, explores a specific region for a specific end. This may be questioned. It may be said that the desire to understand is in most men weak and rare, and that the motive for observing is usually practical. But the two positions are not inconsistent. We agree that observing is far more commonly done for a practical end than for any that is *merely* theoretical. But to say that because the dominant end is practical, there is no distinguishable interest in knowing, is an error of certain pragmatists which has been, I think, decisively exposed. The fact seems to be that knowing and acting are different functions of our nature; that for all forms of acting, beyond what is instinctive or impulsive, knowing is required as a guide; that though the interest in knowing may be present in many degrees, sometimes even dominating the interest in action, it is usually content with the subordinate place; but that even in subordination it remains distinct. A man who, in flight from a bear, arrives at a stream and perceives a log as something that will float, is obviously not a purely scientific observer; but in his recognition of a fact about the log, knowing is as distinct from acting as in the discovery of a planet. He wants to know *because* he wants to do, but that does not make the two wants the same. Now perceiving is a kind of knowing; and the interest in a fuller or better perceiving always involves the interest in knowing or understanding, however trivial may be the object, or however dominant may be the ulterior practical end. That the practical end is usually dominant we freely concede, while still insisting that the *immediate* motive to perception and to the increase and integration of its meaning is the impulse to understand.

10. Understanding takes various forms, and the way in which meaning is integrated turns on the kind of understanding attained. The understanding sought by the botanist may be a grasp of plant-affiliations; and if so, if his interest has been in placing rightly in the hierarchy of species, genus, class, family, variety, order, then his thought in perceiving will be hierarchically organized; in looking at a flower. his implicit thought will be not of its use or causes or beauty, but of its *kind*. On the other hand, understanding for the physician means for the most part a grasp of causes. His dominant interest when he meets a new patient is in diagnosing through symptoms, which means a reading of physical effects in the light of their origin. Hence, within this field his meaning-mass is organized causally, so that he perceives a physical state not as 'species of genus x' or 'useful for purpose y', but 'caused by z'. And the more expert he is, the less does he need explicit thought, and the more can he rely on organized perceptual meaning.[1] The

---

[1] The extent to which this perceptual diagnosis can be carried, without recourse to explicit reflection, is illustrated in the following:
'It frequently happens that doctors distinguished for their power of rapid and accurate diagnosis are unable to give reasons for the

mechanic, again, and the artist seek still different forms of understanding. Probably for the mechanic the dominant form is the relation of means to end; valves, levers, hammers, pistons, are in their very essence things with which to do something and are perceived in the light of their functions. In a sense things are read by the artist also in the light of their functions, as when a musician grasps a phrase in its relation to the whole piece. But words need not blind us to the fact that the relations between parts and whole in a machine and in a melody are very different relations, and therefore that the mechanical and the artistic mind, pursuing different satisfactions, are integrated in different ways.

No one's mind is integrated in one way only. Perhaps the nearest approach to this is made, at one extreme, by the uncivilized creature of a few animal impulses, and at the other by the man with an intense but narrow genius, who is a child outside his own field. Most of us are fairly normal, which means that our thought is organized on no one pattern, that various

opinions they form. For instance, a medical man gave me a detailed account of a doctor, at a hospital where my informant had been a student, who had a power of this kind that was little short of marvellous. A child arrived one day at the hospital very ill. Several members of the staff examined the child carefully, but were unable to discover what was the matter with it. Afterwards the doctor in question came to the hospital, and, not knowing of this failure in diagnosis, happened to walk past the child's bed, but without stopping, he remarked, "That child has pus in his abdomen". This rapid diagnosis was afterwards found to be correct. It is easy to say that this was a lucky guess. But the doctor in question so frequently made lucky guesses of this nature that it was impossible to ascribe them to chance. My informant, who was then at the head of a large hospital, had similar power. He told me that he is sometimes unable to tell the students the reasons for his diagnosis, despite his attempts to call his reasons to mind. The case of another physician has been related to me whose habit of intuitive diagnosis went so far that he was useless as a teacher. Frequently when asked why he had made a particular diagnosis he had to reply, "I am sure I don't know". This power of diagnosis without conscious reasoning seems to be by no means uncommon. Every doctor asked has been able to quote me instances, usually from amongst the staffs of large hospitals who include the picked men of the profession.'—Hanbury Hankin, *Common Sense and Its Cultivation*, 21–2.

ways of thinking are open to us, and that we can pass with some
facility from one to the other. It is, of course, rare to find a
mind possessing at once a rich and profound comprehension
of very different aspects of experience—say scientific, artistic,
and speculative—but such names as Leonardo's, Goethe's and
Lotze's show that this is not impossible. Most men are cut off
from such wealth, if only by lack of time; but when the time
is not wanting, the interest usually is, and where the interest
is not, the faculty. It is pretty clear that in some minds there
are specific deficiencies corresponding to certain of the categories; that some persons, for example, are natively unable to deal
with numbers, or with geometrical form; and there are at least
great variations in men's ability to work with the more important
frames of understanding we have just mentioned—genus and
species, causality, the teleologies of practice and art. And
experience cannot give richness and organization to one's mind
in the absence of initial capacity. There is no amount of experience that will make an observer like Watson into an observer like Sherlock Holmes, if he is unable to reason in causal
terms; nor was there any sort of effort that could have made
Lamb understand a symphony, if, as he claimed, he 'could not
distinguish a soprano from a tenor', and was 'organically
incapable of a tune'.

11. Still, the value of ability as opposed to experience is
often overrated. It is true that there are questions on which a
child with specific ability will do better than the most experienced man without it, because they are questions for which
'mnemic-mass' is relatively needless. Problems of calculation
are an example. Though numbers are many, their modes of
combination are few, and what is needed in dealing with them
is not experience, but a highly specialized gift of manipulation
which indicates little or nothing as to general capacity. When
Archbishop Whately was a boy of five, he could do vast
sums in his head, handling them much more quickly than any
one could on paper, and never, so far as he could remember,

committing an error. Experience had so little to do with this faculty that it actually grew worse, not better, with years, and 'when I went to school,' he says, 'at which time the passion wore off, I was a perfect dunce at ciphering, and have continued so ever since'.[1] In such matters, the gift is everything, and experience virtually nothing. But if we turn to concrete problems such as the judgement of character or the conduct of a business, where the elements are no longer bound by abstract necessity and are various in kind and value, there the situation is very different. With equal experience, the man of ability is still to be preferred, but here experience with small ability is better than transcendent ability without experience. The joint faculties of an Aristotle would go down to disastrous defeat before the problem of running a millinery shop without experience of what ladies like on their heads, because what ladies like on their heads is not perhaps deducible from anything which even Aristotle would be likely to have in possession. And an immense proportion of our decisions, in small matters and in great, require, as Burke used to insist, to be made on this same ground of experience, abstract principles confusing the issue more than clarifying it. What one wants in the Alps or the woods is an experienced guide, clever or not; what one wants at sea is a man who knows the ways of the sea with ships; and if there is anything in Carlyle's derisive comparison between settling public questions by counting heads and taking a ship around Cape Horn by passengers' committee meetings, then for political judgement too, the experience of men and affairs is indispensable. It is not without some reason that civilized peoples have repeatedly made their highest governing body a 'senate' from which, as the word implies, youth was excluded. And the more irrational is the behaviour of the things and people one has to deal with, the more necessary experience becomes. It would be unreasonable to refuse to listen, on grounds of youth merely, to one who professes logic or epistemology; the best work in these fields has been done at sur-

[1] Quoted by Myers, *Human Personality*, I. 82. For further comment on such cases, see below, Chap. XXIII, Sec. 6 ff.

prising ages—Spinoza's at about thirty, Hume's at about twenty-five, Schopenhauer's at twenty-six to thirty, Berkeley's at twenty-five and under; but is it prejudice to confess that one would listen with some suspicion to a fledgeling holding forth upon social ethics? In subjects of this kind, 'as years increase upon us, we are led to contrast the shallowness and rashness of youth with the depth and stability that age brings: "still waters run deep". The field of consciousness is different because of the greater volumes of subconscious experience on which it is superposed, and with which it is virtually continuous. There is less hopefulness, but also less fear, less sensitiveness, but more sagacity, in a word, more "presence of mind".'[1]

No doubt in the best equipped mind there are both the power of arranging things in an explicit and orderly whole, and a large circulating capital of experience. But the parts these play in perceptual thinking are often misunderstood. It is supposed (1) that such thinking is better in the degree to which it is a matter of explicit analysis, and (2) that if we cannot make it explicit, we are not really thinking at all. Both are mistakes, and bad ones. Let us try to see why.

12. Standing-room in consciousness is, as we saw, extremely limited, and the area of the brightly lighted focus still more limited. But the situations we are called upon to face are often complicated in the highest degree. Hence, to deal with them by explicit consciousness alone is impossible, and the attempt to do so may be disastrous. Let a football player try to thread his way through a broken field by a series of explicit calculations, and he will be considerably worse than useless; a baseball player who resorted to them in meeting a ball with the bat would probably not long survive to support his brand of philosophy. Dr. Hankin writes:

'Mr. A. E. Morgan, the Principal of Antioch College, O., has related to me that on one occasion in a lecture, he illustrated a point by saying that a person driving a motor would probably

[1] Ward, *Psychological Principles*, 95.

fail to get through a crowded street crossing if he depended on formal logical processes. Instead of doing this, he relies on complicated estimates of the speeds of other cars carried out subconsciously far more rapidly than could be done in consciousness. After the lecture a member of the audience came to him and told him that he had in his employ a mathematician who, in his subject, was of exceptional ability. But the bent of his mind was so strong towards formal logical processes that he had had to give up driving his motor. On reaching a crossing he would have to stop and calculate the probability of collisions with other motors. Even his rare mathematical ability was insufficient for such an occasion and he got into so much trouble in driving that he gave up the practice entirely.'[1]

It is more than motoring that would be abandoned if all our thinking had to be conscious. To take some examples at random, music would have to be abandoned, both heard and written. For it is only a tiny fraction of the melody that can enter the focus at once; and unless one could retain one's hold on matters beyond the focus, its place in the melody could not be grasped, nor indeed the fact that a melody was being played. And 'in reading music, the significance of the symbols, throughout the entire score, is determined by the clef which is prefixed to it', though 'certainly the thought of the clef does not persist through the entire process of reading';[2] it dominates from the background. Not only musical reading, however, but all reading would have to be abandoned. As the reader runs through this paragraph, what enters his perceptual focus is a little patch of print that stands out from the rest like the patch seen through a reading-glass, and runs rapidly down the page. But it is not merely this that he is engaged with; he is concerned in the large with the unexplicit thought, and it is such thought that controls the meaning of each fragmentary phrase that scurries into the focus and out again. Let him try to compass the paragraph's *details* in a single explicit idea and he will fail inevitably. So it is, to illustrate from what is more fundamental, with the apprehension of all change, in things or in ourselves. At any

---

[1] *Op. cit.*, 102.
[2] Stout, *Analytic Psychology*, II. 122, following von Kries.

instant, one position only of a moving body can present itself to us. But we must also in that instant retain and use the knowledge of some of its past positions, or we could not grasp the body as moving at all. Similarly of our own behaviour. Even when acting most self-consciously, we never catch all the thought that goes to the guiding of our action; indeed to try is often disastrous, as when the fluent pianist or typist begins to stumble when he 'stops to think' what he is doing, or when we become absurdly confused in trying to get clear how we tie our ties. To attempt to convert all routine adjustments into matters of explicit thought is to defy nature, and in these disputes, nature always wins.[1]

13. We have seen that the mnemic mass used in perceptual judgement is the deposit of numberless past experiences. But it would be a mistake to suppose that this deposit is present or usable only so far as the experiences are called up. The old treatment of memory as a selection from past experiences, to be sufficiently dealt with, like other associations, by laws of recency, frequency, vividness, etc., has long ceased to serve. It has become increasingly clear (a) that the part of unexplicit retention in our thinking is far greater than the part of memory proper; (b) that great tracts of our experience are not so much forgotten as repressed, and can again be called into consciousness when the repressions are removed; (c) that things which, in the first place, were not explicitly attended to can nevertheless, by special means, be explicitly recalled.[2] Such facts have

---

[1]   The centipede was happy quite
        Until the toad for fun
        Said: 'Pray which leg comes after which?'
        This wrought his mind to such a pitch,
        He lay distracted in the ditch
        Considering how to run.

[2] Morton Prince asked X for a description of how Y, who had just left the room, was dressed. X gave the best description he could. Dr. Prince then hypnotized him and asked again for the description. It

made some psychologists reluctant to set any limit whatever to the power of recall,[1] and they lend colour to the view accepted by Semon[2] and many others, that every experience, focal and marginal, contributes its quota to the mnemic capital that can now be drawn on. If this is true, if past experience can be used in present judgement whether it can be recalled or not, we should expect one's power to recall and apply it explicitly to have very little to do with one's soundness of judgement.

That, I think, is what we actually find. There is no need to cavil over what is meant by 'soundness of judgement', for it is easy to choose instances which unite such various types of distinction as to satisfy everyone. And from minds of this class we may easily draw instances of precisely opposite types, instances in which the power to adduce in explicit array the particulars on which a judgement rests has, on the one hand, been conspicuously absent, and on the other hand present in extremely high degree. In illustration of the former, consider the following note on Arthur Balfour, written by one who for fifty years had known him more or less intimately:

> 'With all his rapidity of brain, he had practically no memory for facts. He once told me that after he had finished a book he did not recollect a single fact in it—all that remained with him was the train of thought, or the state of mind, or conclusion arrived at from reading the book. This it was that made him unable to hold his own in a full-dress House of Commons debate of first-class importance, when the *facts* of the situation have to be marshalled. . . . He would forget figures, names, dates, details—facts of all kinds in short. . . . In ordinary or impromptu debate few could have approached him, and none

was given in far more minute detail.—Prince, *The Unconscious*, 53. Coleridge's case of the uneducated servant girl who, in delirium, spoke Greek, Latin, and Hebrew, has become a classic in this discussion.—*Biographia Literaria*, I. 78 (Shawcross edition).

[1] '. . . the phenomena of ordinary recall, of dreams, of hypnosis, and of psycho-analysis make it extremely difficult to subscribe to the common-sense view of a past in which certain things are really beyond recall.'—T. H. Pear, *Remembering and Forgetting*, 142.

[2] *Mnemic Psychology*, 154, 171.

could surely have surpassed him in dialectical skill and rapidity of thought and expression.'[1]

Contrast this with the account of another eminent writer and statesman:

> Macaulay, 'at one period of his life was known to say that, if by some miracle of vandalism all copies of *Paradise Lost* and the *Pilgrim's Progress* were destroyed off the face of the earth, he would undertake to reproduce them both from recollection whenever a revival of learning came. In 1813, while waiting in a Cambridge coffee-room for a postchaise which was to take him to his school, he picked up a county newspaper containing two such specimens of provincial poetical talent as in those days might be read in the corner of any weekly journal. . . . He looked them once through, and never gave them a thought for forty years, at the end of which time he repeated them both without missing—or, as far as he knew, changing—a single word.'[2]

Now if the use of past experience in present judgement needed explicit recall, the first of these persons would have been quite incapable of distinguished work in either letters or administration, which, of course, the facts belie on both counts. In case of a difference of judgement between two such minds, while the first was standing silent, the second would not improbably be delivering itself of a cataract of precedents and parallels. Does it follow that his judgement would spring more directly from his experience, or register its upshot with more point and accuracy? It does not. He would have a great advantage in articulateness and copiousness of speech;[3] but so far is this from corresponding to real advantage in judgement that

---

[1] Mrs. Drew (Mary Gladstone) London *Observer*, March 23, 1930. A memoir in *The Times* (March 20, 1930) bears similar testimony.

[2] Trevelyan's *Life*, I. 68.

[3] Cf. Carlyle's *Journal*, March 14, 1848: 'Friday last at Lord Mahon's to breakfast: Macaulay, Lord and Lady Ashley there, etc. Niagara of eloquent commonplace talk from Macaulay . . . stood my impatient fire-explosions with much patience, merely hissing a little steam up, and continued his Niagara . . . all that was in him now gone to the tongue; a squat, thickset, low-browed, short, grizzled little man of fifty. These be thy gods, oh Israel!'—Froude, *Life in London*, I. 432. One may of course accept the description of Macaulay's speech without the rest.

it may rise to great heights where judgement is conspicuously absent.[1]

14. It is clear, then, that the power to use our past experience has little connection with the power to recall it explicitly. But this has sometimes been confused with a different statement. It has been supposed that the type of mind that is capable of something like 'total recall' not only gains from this no advantage but is even handicapped in its thinking. A writer already quoted, Dr. Hankin, has written an ingenious and interesting book to prove that 'common sense and its cultivation' are wholly a matter of the subconscious self, and that the person who has been highly trained in explicit reasoning is usually a failure when faced with the situations of practical life. He thinks that 'for our past experiences to be at the disposal of our subconscious minds for the purpose of common-sense decisions, it is necessary for them to be forgotten';[2] and he marshals a great deal of evidence to show that experts who rely on processes of explicit reasoning generally lack practical judgement, while persons who distrust explicit reasoning and have trained themselves to rely rather on 'intuition'—he cites, for example, the Quakers—have been conspicuously successful. Now if this means only that the person will fail who refuses to act in complex matters before he has assembled all the grounds of his decisions in consciousness, we have agreed with the view already.[3] But if it implies, as it is evidently meant to, that the power to think explicitly and the training that leads to this are to be deprecated as hostile to common sense or practical

[1] 'The thought of Miss Bates in Jane Austen's *Emma* (Miss Bates has now been fittingly given a permanent emeritus appointment on the teaching staff of most psychology departments) and of Mrs. Nickleby deters us from encouraging any reader to try to fill his memory.'—Pear, *op. cit.*, 11.

[2] *Op. cit.*, 230.

[3] I have been told that Cook Wilson, professor of logic at Oxford, preferred not to serve on juries, feeling that his critical pre-occupation with the conditions of exact proof might actually lower his usefulness where the rough resultant of many probabilities had to be estimated.

judgement, I think a truth has been overstated. There is no reason why a person trained to analysis should therefore become its victim. There is no reason why the person who *can* adduce grounds for his decision should invariably try to do so, even when the occasion is inopportune, and should be unmoved by all but explicit and definite evidence. The very inability to decide where common sense is best and where not, which marked Dr. Hankin's experts, makes one suspect that their failure had a deeper root than any mere gift for explicit reasoning; and this suspicion would be amply confirmed if one reviewed, as Dr. Hankin does not, the cases in which eminent sense and judgement *have* been combined with a more than average power for analysis. It is true that the habit of analysis is dangerous, that at times it tends to wither feeling, as Mill holds it did for him;[1] that it may paralyse action, as it did for Hamlet; but one cannot argue from the fact that a habit has bad effects when overdeveloped and misapplied, to the conclusion either that it cannot be exercised seasonably, or that, when so exercised, it is anything but a blessing.

We have seen that the goodness or badness of thinking does not vary with its explicitness. We are only turning to the positive side of this when we say that thinking may be unexplicit, and still be (1) accurate, (2) complex, and (3) flexible.

15. (1) Mill speaks of an expert dyer who had a wide reputation for the remarkable effects he secured from mixing powdered dyes. A Scotch company tempted him north with very high wages to teach his methods to their workmen. He came, but completely failed. His method was to take up the dyes by handfuls, and judge by feeling when he had got the right amounts, but he never reduced these to explicit proportions, and had no rules that he could communicate. His thought on these matters was confined to the perceptual level. But, however dumb and unanalysed that thought may have been, one must at least concede its accuracy. And a large part of the

[1] *Autobiography*, Chap. V.

thinking that everyone allows to be expert belongs to this perceptual stage. Sometimes the accuracy is rather of sense than of thought, though of sense as refined by thought, as when the experienced wine-taster discriminates flavours, or the practised postman computes the postage on a letter by balancing it in his hand. Sometimes it is the accuracy of that curious sense-bound thought by which an old sailor tells the distance of a ship at sea. Sometimes, again, it is an accuracy in which thinking plays a clearer part, as in the perceptions of a good judge of character, or an art critic's instant recognition of a painter through his work.

16. (2) These last examples illustrate also the second point, that perceptual thinking may be very complex, that is, that it may render the sense of a great many factors without explicitly taking note of them. A better illustration is found in an often repeated quotation from Lord Mansfield. A young friend of his was appointed to a post in the West Indies, in which he would have to perform the functions of a judge, and he was much exercised as to whether he would prove equal to the task. He applied to the great jurist for advice, and received some startling counsel. He was told to give his decisions with confidence, for they would in all probability be right, but never to give his reasons, for they would almost certainly be wrong.[1] Herbert Spencer describes in his *Autobiography* how he went about it to make a decision on which his whole later life

[1] Mill tells the tale; Dr. Hankin, quoting from an out-of-the-way book on the curiosities of law, tells it with an odd sequel. 'Some years afterwards, Lord Mansfield, while sitting on Privy Council appeals, had a judgement of the Governor brought before his court, which seemed so absurd in its reasons that there was serious clamour for the recall of the Governor as incompetent. It was found, however, that the decision itself was perfectly right. It appeared that, at first, the Governor had acted on Lord Mansfield's advice by deciding without giving reasons; and, finding that he acquired a great reputation thereby, began to think himself a great lawyer, and then, at length, took to giving his reasons, with the above-mentioned result.'— *Op. cit.*, 45.

depended. It was proposed to him that he emigrate to New Zealand, and he was attracted strongly. 'Averse to unmethodic ways of judging', he took a sheet of paper and prepared two columns, listing against each other the advantages of England and those of New Zealand, and attaching to each item a number to denote its weight: excitement in literature, 20; music, 6; marriage, 100, etc. Then he added up his columns and found that England came out at 110 and New Zealand at 301. Where-upon he decided to stay in England![1] Everyone will feel that it is a little absurd to deal with an issue of this type in the manner of an adding-machine. We have all made complicated decisions, and made them successfully, in which such an explicit in-ventory would have been difficult and perhaps disastrous. Where great masses of relevant detail require to be considered, to get them before the mind's eye all at once is out of the question; and if we reduce them to anything as abstract and arbitrary as numerical weights, and add these up, we either survey our meagre result with an open scepticism or greet it with a furtive relief as falling in with inclinations that are already tending one way on other grounds. What we do is rather this: to turn up anxiously one point after another on both sides, and then after an interval, in which perhaps we 'sleep on the matter', find that the doubt has strangely vanished and we are ready to pass to a decision without effort. It is as if the factors in the decision had got together in conclave on their own motion and passed a vote which lay ready to our hand when we turned to the matter again.[2]

17. But it would be a mistake to dismiss Spencer's method as merely useless. Anyone so inclined would do well to recall an observation of Semon's that (to use his peculiar vocabulary) the ecphory of an engram leaves the engram itself altered,[3] which means that the deposit of a past experience is affected

---

[1] *Autobiography*, I. 370.
[2] For more detailed study of this process, see Chap. XXIV.
[3] *Mnemic Psychology*, Chap. XV.

every time the experience is called explicitly to mind. If it is wrong to say that Spencer could solve his complex problem in the same daylight fashion in which he would solve a simple equation, it is equally wrong to say that dwelling on the factors severally makes no difference to the mind's power to deal with them unconsciously. It clearly does make a difference and a valuable one.

Take as an example the effect of knowledge on appreciation. There are persons who decry any attempt to analyse a work of art as the proposal of a philistine; and we have all met students who were afraid that their delicate powers of appreciation and creation were being ruined by having to construe Virgil or study the technique of a Shakespeare play. Their view seems to be that there is no relation whatever, except one of hostility, between analysis and appreciation, that the only proper response to a work of art is one that is untarnished by the acids of intelligence, that the only true creation springs effortlessly out of a soul that has never been deadened by analysis. There is much nonsense in this. A mind with muscles so flabby that it sickens under a little gymnastics, is one whose creations we can afford to lose. And the fact seems to be that analysis, if not indulged to excess, is an aid, not a hindrance, to appreciation. A person who knows the difficulties of play-construction appreciates a good drama the more for his knowledge; the veteran music lover, who knows an opera in all its details and has heard it dozens of times, is a far better listener than the novice; everyone who has tried himself to master the violin or piano hears performances on his instrument with a fuller appreciation. There is something very unpersuasive in the view that as the *Causeries du Lundi* were written, or as Arnold's *Essays in Criticism* successively appeared, their authors' responsiveness must have been declining through the numbing effects of analysis. To be sure, those who protest against this view must be ready to hear strange theories ascribed to them; they are often accused of holding that absorption in a work of art is the same as analysis of it, that there is no such thing as an 'aesthetic' attitude, and that a work of art is really a second-rate work of thought, to be estimated by the ideas in it, and annotated and dissected by pedants. But this is nonsense again. We are not saying that the analytic and aesthetic attitudes are the same, nor even that they can coexist, but that the second will profit if it can draw upon the results of the first. The results of earlier knowledge may be as truly held in solution in our enjoyment of a poem as in our study of a steam engine, and the greatest poetry, while, of course, distinct in its end from philosophy or science, has been saturated with thought. The art that expresses nothing but sense and feeling cannot defend itself against the charge of emptiness by disclaiming interest in ideas. If it goes on polishing its expression, when it has nothing to express, it becomes in the end merely tiresome; and we should be spared much rubbish if criticism would insist on this.

18. When we see how readily perceptual thinking can draw on a complex past experience, we have the key to some forms of 'intuition'. Much of what passes as 'woman's intuition' is not intuition strictly, is not confined to women, and has no peculiar mystery. Of course, when someone after a few minutes' talk with another forms the firm idea that he is untrustworthy, or, in spite of an outward cheerfulness in a friend, perceives that he is in deep trouble, there may be instruments of knowledge at work of which we know nothing; the mind's knowledge of other minds is a province that has been imperfectly explored, and sweeping statements are not yet in order. But in principle, there is no more mystery in such thinking than in ordinary perceiving. There may be nothing more involved in it than that the observer is especially alert to particular kinds of data, and at the same time unusually averse from analysing things explicitly. Being deeply interested, for example, in personal differences, having observed them and mused upon them until their minutiae have grown significant for thought and feeling, he takes in at a glance many points that no more need explicit notice than the marks by which we recognize a friend, draws the perceptual inference from them, and being unable to assign the grounds of judgement, is thought to possess insight of some exceptional kind. It is not really exceptional, it is only more alert on the sensory and affective sides, and less analytic on the intellectual.

19. (3) We commonly find that, within the field of our special experience, such intuition can be drawn upon freely, while in other fields it deserts us. But we all possess in some degree, and some of us in high degree, the power of applying experience outside the field where it was gathered; and it is this that is meant by the 'flexibility' of perceptual thought. There are boys who, having taken to pieces a motor-car, and lovingly constructed a radio set, display a surprising competence about engines and electric devices generally; others who, on the strength of some knowledge of Latin or French, enter into the possession of further Romance languages as if into an inheritance. To other persons, every new type of machine and every new language requires that they start again relatively near the beginning.

Students of psychology and education have given much study to this matter of the 'transferability' of experience, since many questions of the educational curriculum turn upon it; but the results have been disappointingly various. Nor is it hard, on reflection, to see why. It is because the transferability depends not only on the subject-matters studied, but also on a special gift of the individual mind. Furthermore, this gift lies at the very heart of intelligence; it is a part of one's logical endowment; and hence the discussion of it is apt to take the psychologist outside the field of descriptive science. When Shakespeare makes Macbeth break out into an apostrophe to sleep:

> Sleep that knits up the ravell'd sleeve of care,
> The death of each day's life, sore labour's bath,
> Balm of hurt minds, great nature's second course,
> Chief nourisher in life's feast——

he was illustrating a power of prodigal transfer, inexhaustible in its analogies between different regions of experience, which appears in all Shakespeare's work. But it was power that belonged to the man, not to any special interconnection among his studies. If we should argue from the use he made of his 'little Latin and less Greek' to the utility of these studies generally, the argument would have small weight, for we must take into account, along with his modest knowledge, that power of seizing identities in the apparently diverse which is regarded by some writers as the defining point in intelligence. And so far as what operates through the mind is logical identity, or logical or aesthetic necessity, no purely descriptive psychology can hope to account for its behaviour.[1]

20. Thus the flexibility of perceptual thinking depends primarily on native logic. The intelligence that enables a clever boy to deal adroitly with a new engine or language after brief experience of these things seems at first a far remove from the intelligence that enabled Aristotle to produce his list of categories, but the two are in essence the same. If a boy applies his experience cleverly, it is because he is laying hold of the identities which, in spite of appearance, unite what he is confronting now with what he has confronted earlier. He has never seen the exact counterpart of the piston now before him, but the plunging action in a valve is something he has seen, and once he has seized the identity, he can attach to it what he has found to go with it in the past. It is not that he explicitly draws out the resemblance which supplies the ground of the transfer; he does this no more than the poet does in making sleep knit up the ravelled sleeve of care. But in both cases it is the grasp of an underlying identity that makes the transfer possible. And however different may be the interests it serves, this grasp of identity is itself identical wherever intelligence is employed. The logician with his table of categories and the philosopher who, after long reflection on man's history and nature, forms a concept of what man essentially is, are using a faculty at bottom the same as the poet's, who breaks into metaphor about life

[1] For the explanation and defence of this position, see Chap. XIII.

and sleep, and the boy's, who, having dismantled a Ford with effort, takes a Chevrolet to pieces with ease.

The further study of how identity works is best left till we can examine its part in the process of reflective invention.[1] But it will be clear even now, that with the emergence of conceptual thought, the grasp of identity must be enormously improved; indeed it is only in thought of this higher kind that identities *as such* can be grasped at all. When the hen returns to her nest and acts as if she were disturbed over the disappearance of some of her eggs, it is hard to suppose that she is simply blind to quantity; but it is equally hard to ascribe to her the notion of quantity as such. *We* do have this notion, and our having it adds greatly even to our perceptual thinking. When the thought of quantity or of any other abstraction is once explicitly formed, its dispositional use in perception becomes both easier and more exact. But it is noteworthy that even before conceptual thought has emerged, minds vary enormously in their power of construing the present through universals brought from the past.

21. Indeed, advance in this respect is one of the principal points in mental evolution, and it will repay us to get clear through specific cases what it means. The following cases form a series in which the flexibility grows continually greater; that is, the organism becomes more and more able to 'recognize' in what is before it identities with its past, and to make its response accordingly.[2] At the bottom of the scale lie organisms of which it is doubtful whether there is any carrying over of past experience, and indeed whether we are justified in speaking of experience at all. The paramecium that collides with an obstacle will back away and 'try' again at a slightly different angle, but there is doubt whether it tries the new angle because the old one failed, or for less interesting physical reasons.

[1] Chap. XXIII.
[2] For the examples in this paragraph I am indebted to Washburn's *The Animal Mind*, chiefly Chaps. X and XI.

Where, in order to apply past experience, the animal must run counter to instinct, there is a struggle. Bethe placed a crab in an aquarium where there was a dark corner, and in this corner placed a small cephalopod, a type of creature whose feeling for crabs is no friendly one. The crab, being of the sort that seeks dark places instinctively, made for the dark corner at once, and was seized by the lurking enemy. Six times Bethe took it out and gave it another chance, but it only fled into the arms of the enemy over again. Bethe concluded that this stupid species did not profit from experience at all; but this is too harsh a judgement, for it has been found that even a crab will rise on its dead self to better things if only it is given chances enough at something that instinct does not veto. When, in order to reach its aquarium, a crab had to choose the right path at two successive forks in the road, it went right fairly regularly after fifty trials. Perhaps this was a brilliant specimen, however, since a crayfish was found to need two hundred and fifty trials to learn perfectly a road with *one* fork in it. Spiders and ants do better. A spider, for example, that at first dropped promptly from its web at the sound of a large tuning fork, learned in about half a dozen trials to take it calmly. But the next day, the old panic recurred, and only after fifteen days did it learn for good that the sound was harmless. Ants that were greatly alarmed at first by a finger moved about near their nest, learned very quickly—in two or three trials—to let it go unheeded.

One expects more from the vertebrates, and is not generally disappointed; but there are some extraordinary dunces among them. Möbius's famous pike deserves mention here. He put this pike in one end of a tank, and in the other end a troop of minnows, which the pike contemplated hungrily through a glass partition. It cost the pike countless nasal collisions, which almost literally beat the conclusion into his head, to learn that the minnows were beyond reach; but he did master this in the end. However, he was only a sadder, not a wiser pike, for now the partition was removed and the minnows swam all round him in safety. Having got it fixed in his head that the minnows were not for him, he could hardly get it out again. A frog learned a two-choice route in about a hundred attempts. The superiority of the bird is shown in the fact that an English sparrow mastered without great difficulty a little maze rather like the model at Hampton Court. When we reach the level of most quadrupeds, we have taken another long step upward. Anyone who owns four-footed pets knows that, along with much stupidity, they show at times a genuine inventiveness; the dog will not always stay hopelessly at the door where his master vanishes, but will sometimes try another door; at times, in pursuit of a rabbit, he will cut a corner instead of going the long way round. But even his best is a poor thing if compared with the extraordinary cleverness of Köhler's apes. These had an almost inexhaustible repertory of devices for getting food that was beyond their reach—pulling it in with sticks, lassoing it with cords, swinging to it with ropes or trapezes, mounting to it on each other's shoulders, dragging up boxes and standing on them, even piling three or four boxes one upon another and scaling them to the summit.

22. Evidently on these last levels we have arrived at perceptual thinking of a different order from that of the earlier examples. A crayfish, faced with the *same* situation as before, may need hundreds of trials before it learns infallibly what will bring it to its end; a chimpanzee, faced with a situation which, as novel, is much harder, will often solve it ingeniously in one or two trials. Now the ape has no a priori insight into the connection between sticks and food; if its performance is so much better than that of lower animals, this is because its use of past experience in perception has a greater flexibility. And we have seen that this consists in applying to a new situation a meaning-mass drawn from the past, by reason of a more or less hidden identity. It consists in a better analysis and synthesis of the mnemic mass in the interest of an end.

Take the simplest of Köhler's experiments, in which he dropped a banana outside a chimpanzee's cage and just beyond

its reach. In this situation, an intelligent dog would be helpless;
why is the ape so much better? Partly, no doubt, because with
hands as well as feet, and with a tireless impulse to manipulate
things, he has been able to achieve a much richer experience of
possible tools. But it is not this that is his chief advantage.
However wide had been the dog's experience in worrying and
dragging sticks, it is unlikely that if confronted with this problem he would be able to do the right thing. The ape's advantage
lies in his power of implicit analysis, working directly upon
what is given him and indirectly upon his mnemic mass.
Whereas the dog would merely be aware, excitedly and indiscriminately, of food that he could not get, the ape is beginning
to be alive to further factors in the situation. We must suppose
that he is aware, however dimly, of the space he must cross as
a vital spot in the problem, that this singled-out element works
through identity to bring into play that part of his mnemic mass
concerned with such spaces and his dealings with them, and
that the space is thus perceived as 'a-gap-bridgeable-by-a-
stick'.[1] Not content with applying his mnemic mass in general
to the situation in general, he is beginning to respond differentially, which means that not only his attention to what is before
him, but also his evocation of 'traces', is more selective. The
elements of his mnemic mass are not all called upon equally;
the part concerned with the crucial element before him, the
space to be crossed, is specially active, bringing up the associated
suggestion, 'bridgeable-by-a-stick'. And again within this suggestion analysis is at work. Those qualities of the stick that
figure in the implicit idea are certainly not *all* its qualities;
they are those essential to the purpose in hand, those summed
up in 'something to poke or pull with'. If the ape were to see
a broom or a musket lying about, he would pounce upon it at

---

[1] That the ape is thus capable of fixing his attention on spatial
factors seems clear. 'At any time it may be observed that a chimpanzee,
before making a wide jump at a considerable height, looks carefully
to and fro across the intervening space. As an arboreal animal . . . he
must be able to measure distances. It would be quite unjustifiable to
object to the use of the term "measuring" in this connection.'—
Köhler, *The Mentality of Apes*, 46, note.

once as falling within the range of what he wanted. What we have at work here is thus the germ of the general idea.

'If we assert that the stick has now acquired a certain *functional or instrumental value* in relation to the field of action under certain conditions, and that this value is extended to all other objects that resemble the stick, however remotely, in *outline* and *consistency*—whatever their other qualities may be—then we have formed the only assumption that will account for the observed and recorded behaviour of these animals . . . almost every "movable object" becomes, in certain conditions, a stick.'[1]

23. Synthesis as well as analysis may occur in the mnemic mass. In a sense it occurs continually, for, as Semon emphasizes, a present perception may fuse the deposits of a great many different experiences, occurring at different times. But fusion is the word, rather than synthesis, for a union of this kind. The synthesis that marks a high level of perceptual intelligence is that in which the successive contributions are kept distinct, and yet combined in some sort of pattern. Suppose a dog or even an ape is taken around an octagonal field; can he, as he makes the journey, put together the sides, so that at the end he can view the circumscribed field as an octagonal area? Quite certainly not. Indeed, this power of turning the successive into coexistent parts of a pattern may be largely lacking even to primitive man. Galton writes of an African tribe:

'A Damara who knew the road perfectly from A to B, and again from B to C, would have no idea of a straight cut from A to C; he has no map of the country in his mind, but an infinity of local details. He recollects every stump or stone, and the more puerile the object the more strongly does he seem to recollect it. Thus, if you say, "I intend to sleep by the side of the great hill where the river-bed runs close under its foot", he would never recognize the place by description, but if you said, "under the tree, a little way on the other side of the place where the black and white ox lowed when the red ox was in front of him, and Koniati dropped his assegai", etc., etc., every savage

---

[1] Köhler, *op. cit.*, 36–7.

in the party would understand the exact locality. The Damaras
pick out their way step by step; they never dream of taking a
course and keeping to it.'[1]

The synthesis here referred to is one particular kind of synthesis, namely, spatial, and it is quite possible that a mind much
higher in the scale than a Damara should have a specific weakness for it.[2]

There are many further forms of synthesis, but we shall
select for mention only one, which is important at all levels,
that of means and end. Another of Köhler's experiments
illustrates this neatly; incidentally it served as a sort of simian
intelligence-test which only the best of his apes could pass. As
in the previous case, he would leave a short stick inside the
cage, and a little way outside it, would leave some fruit. This
made a simple enough problem for all his apes; they all without
exception would seize the stick, and try to rake in the fruit with
it. But he now complicated matters. He left the fruit too far
away to be reached with the stick at hand, but at the same time
left a stick that *was* long enough, lying a little distance off and
near enough to be reached with the shorter stick. The animals
would invariably begin by trying and failing with the short
stick, then pause and survey the scene; 'there are always in
the course of these tests some long pauses, during which the
animals scrutinize the whole visible area'.[3] When the eye of a
superior ape happened to light on the longer stick, the results
were impressive. He would immediately take the shorter stick,
run with it to the point where the larger one could be reached,
rake this in, and then with the help of this better tool capture
the fruit triumphantly. What goes on in his mind? We must

---

[1] Quoted in Stout, *Analytic Psychology*, II. 35.

[2] Carlyle's comments on Jeffrey would apply to many others: 'How
he found his way thither [to Carlyle's house] I know not (perhaps in
a cab, if quite lost in his azimuth); but I have more than once led him
back through Lincoln's Inn Fields, launched him safe in Long Acre
with nothing but Leicester Square and Piccadilly ahead; and he never
once could find his way; wandered about, and would discover at last
that he had got into Lincoln's Inn Fields *again*.'—*Reminiscences*,
II. 52.   [3] *Op. cit.*, 174.

suppose that as he contemplates the longer stick, it somehow presents itself to him in a new setting, with the short stick as a means to it, and it in turn as a means to the fruit. We need not say that there is any picture of this arrangement in his mind, or that there is anything at all in mind explicitly but the long stick that he sees; nor is it likely that without some part of the device actually before him, he ever manages to think of it. His thinking is undoubtedly thinking, but it is still anchored to sense; he cannot summon up and dismiss ideas independently of what the senses are pressing on him; his thought is *perceptual* thought.

Nevertheless, it has reached a level where it is on the very verge of breaking into free ideas. That the ape in some cases actually does cross the line and use such ideas, is virtually certain;[1] indeed, in the case last mentioned, if the ape, when he looked through the bars at the stick, formed a thought of the unseen fruit, and did not deal with it dispositionally through the fringe of perception, as we do with a pipe when we go for a match to light it, then he had already taken out his first papers in the republic of ideas. But though an ape does in moments attain to free ideas, his hold on them is tentative and wavering. Köhler found with some of his apes, that unless the stick fell within the same field of vision as the fruit, they were helpless; if they had to take their eyes off the fruit to look at the stick, or off the stick to look at the fruit, they could not keep the absent object in mind.[2] An ape, offered some fruit that was out of range, though accessible with the aid of a stick that hung on a neighbouring wall, would at once seize a box to stand on, and get the stick, but if he had to pass near the fruit on the way, his brave attempt would come to nothing; the immediate appeal of the fruit would drive the idea out of his mind.[3] To hold an idea fast is hard enough at all levels, and when we remember the efforts it has cost ourselves, we feel, in viewing these humble struggles, both a good deal of sympathy and a good deal of confidence that we understand.

[1] See particularly the experiments in *ibid.*, 279–82.
[2] *Ibid.*, 37–8.   [3] *Ibid.*, 180.

24. It will be plain from what has been said that the range of perceptual intelligence is enormous. Most animals spend all their lives, and all men most of their lives, upon its level. Upon this level, again, many of those faculties that imply a special fineness of judgement and cultivation of feeling have their characteristic play: not merely 'common sense', but also the sense of humour, the sense of honour, the sense of beauty, the moral sense, and the sense of justice. 'It seems absurd to say that a person who is distinguished for the justice of his conduct does not know what is just, and he might be rightly indignant if you denied that he knew the meaning of justice; yet he might easily be puzzled if asked to define it.'[1] What experience has demanded of him is not so much that he think about justice in the abstract, as that he be able to recognize it in the concrete, which is a different thing; and there may be an astonishing contrast between one's authority in recognition, and one's helplessness in explicit thought. Saints are seldom distinguished as moral philosophers, yet their sense of what to do in a concrete case is probably more unerring; excellent artists have not infrequently made themselves ludicrous when they have tried to talk about aesthetics. It has even been doubted whether, in view of what perceptual thought can achieve by itself, the mind has won any solid advantage in breaking loose from it. Is the power to look before and after worth the price of continual pining, worrying, and grieving for what is not? Would it not be better if our thinking were as little free as that of the ants, provided we could handle our practical problems as easily and as competently?

We must answer through a distinction. If the question is whether the escape from the perceptual level has tipped the beam in favour of happiness, this for our purpose is irrelevant; and fortunately, too, for without suggesting that Schopenhauer's answer is the right one, we must admit that since his day the answer has not seemed quite so obvious. But if the question is whether the escape has sped intelligence toward its goal in a completer intellectual grasp, then the answer is as easy for us

[1] Cook Wilson, *Statement and Inference*, I. 43.

as the question is important. The escape is very plainly a translation into a larger world. It is probably in the animal mind that perceptual thought is to be found at its purest, since here it is less complicated than in man with the results of higher processes. And if we examine such thought in the animal mind, we see that it labours under three enormous handicaps.

25. (1) As anchored to sensation, *it is dependent upon the chance offerings of the moment.* The animal mind, when not stimulated to thinking by an irritant from without, or pushed into it by an instinctive restlessness, does not and cannot think at all. If a cat sees a mouse wander into its field of vision, it can interpret what it sees as prey, and take action; or if it is hungry, it will go in search of food, though probably, like the wasp that stores provisions for its coming young, without explicit thought of its end. But unless prompted in one of these ways, it can think of nothing to do, and forthwith goes to sleep. If man's mind had been so constituted, his civilization would have been forfeit. For that is possible only through an elaborate taking thought of the remote, both in the sphere of practice, where the arts of controlling machines and men require constant reflection, and in the sphere of knowledge, where often the thought bears no relation to the immediate setting of the thinker. We still have our roots, as Aristotle saw, in the animal mind; but, as he likewise saw, all that is truly distinctive of human life comes of a thought that has been emancipated into a different kind of activity.

26. (2) *Perceptual thought cannot abstract.* To be sure, the defect here is not absolute. The specific attention which an animal sometimes gives to one aspect of what is before it, as when the dog singles out an odour for special notice, or an ape concentrates on distance, is certainly a step on the way to analysis and abstraction, and it seems so like what we do ourselves when we attend to the yellowness of a leaf that we may fail to see any difference. Nevertheless, the difference is great. How great is suggested by an extremely significant fact, namely, that there is no single kind of animal, not even the highest ape, that has anything approximating language. Exclamations it has in plenty, and imperatives and entreaties; but the amazing fact remains that it has no nouns. It is as totally lacking in names for trees and streams as it is in names for colour and distance.[1] The defect is not in speech organs, for many animals have a large range of vocal sounds. The only way to account for it is to suppose that the animals have no *ideas* of these things, or have them only in fugitive irrecoverable glimpses. If an animal as inventive as an ape could form the idea 'tree', it could easily find a symbol; and if it lacks the symbol, that can only be because it lacks the idea. Why is the idea so difficult? Largely, at any rate, because the animal cannot abstract. The thought behind common nouns is abstract already; to form the thought of tree is to grasp a class concept in which the abstraction of the essential from the inessential has already begun. This sort of abstraction is to man so easy that he does it at will; even when he is perceiving the yellowness of a leaf, he is isolating with the eye of the mind as well as with the eye of sense. Thus he can define with the greatest sharpness what he is attending to. From this invaluable access of power, of which language is the means and the symbol, the animal is cut off, as well as from that improved perception which, as we see, attends the power to abstract. In all those realms of experience that are opened by abstraction, the animal mind must be unimaginably grey and barren.

So would the human mind have been, except for its escape into free ideas. For perceptual thought there can be no science, for science depends on abstraction. Its laws do not state the relations between things as wholes, but between the abstracted properties of things. It says that the volume of a gas varies inversely with the pressure; it makes gravitational attraction a function of mass and distance. These are all characters got by

---

[1] Köhler says that it does not designate objects even by gestures.— *Op. cit.*, 305.

abstraction. With any particular solid or cloud of gas science has nothing to do. Its first step is to break things up into qualities, which it can then classify through their likeness and pursue into their connections. Because perceptual thought cannot do these things it falls short of science. The veteran weather prophet may 'feel' rightly that a storm is approaching; the expert in dyes whom we mentioned could tell accurately when he held enough powder in his hand for a given purpose; but their knowledge is not properly science until they can isolate the factors on which their results depend and state the connection as a law. It is true that for many purposes such abstract and explicit knowledge is needless. If the weather prophet's 'intuitions' about the weather work, he is willing to hand over to others the science of meteorology, and practical men have sometimes permitted themselves to be derisive about scientific knowledge as moving in a world of theory. This is a mistake. Such knowledge is the same in kind as their own, but with the terms and relations made more exact, explicit, and exceptionless. Thus scientific knowledge is always better than perceptual knowledge, even when it is a knowledge of the same things. Of course, the scientific expert often fails where the practical man succeeds. But that is no criticism of scientific knowledge as such. All it shows is that a particular scientist does not always succeed in dragging to light the various factors in a case, and that when this is true or the time is short, it may be allowable to fall back on the rough estimates of common sense. It does not show in the least that the explicit knowledge of relevant factors in which science consists is not vastly superior to any kind of intuition. Intuition, after all, is only science in a primitive form, and though it is sometimes a useful substitute in practice, it is always, and of its very nature, inferior as knowledge.

27. (3) *Perceptual thought is relatively helpless in dealing with what is new.* With what is old, its mnemic mass enables it to deal easily and even expertly. And if something new is offered that pretty closely resembles what is familiar, so that it can be dealt with by analogy, perceptual thought can sometimes rise to the emergency. If Köhler's apes lacked a pole, they would make a piece of board do; if he appeared with a toy animal, they would proceed at once on analogy and fly into a panic until the animal was proved lifeless. But this itself suggests how helpless is perceptual thought before the novel; it must depend on rough analogies, and, unable to analyse minutely, it is lost without these. A beaver or fox that is full of cunning in dealing with what instinct and experience have prepared it for, cannot make head or tail of an ordinary trap. A turnstile or a cage from which a stupid man would escape in a few minutes, will keep the cleverest of domestic animals confined for life. Thorndike has shown how quickly such animals learn the secret of escape if they get out through an aimless scratching and pawing, but to get out by accident is not to solve the problem, and it is here that the animal is helpless. It must deal with things as wholes; it cannot break the situation into parts, eliminate those that are irrelevant and confine itself to the others. Of course, stupidity the same in kind appears often enough among men; witness the child lost in the woods, the householder who arrives at home without his key, the bystander who is called on to help in case of accident, or the person who must unexpectedly deal with a drunken man or a burglar. In such cases, as in 'intelligence tests', thought may fail through mere excitement and apprehension, and its failure tells nothing whatever about intelligence. Where there is real stupidity, it consists in the same defect that makes the animal mind so helpless, the inability to break the situation into its parts, promptly isolating the novel and allowing this to develop its special suggestions. And thus this third defect of perceptual thought, its failure in dealing with the novel, is the outgrowth of the second, its failure in analytic abstraction.

But we have seen that at the top of the animal scale, perceptual thought is on the verge of a new flight. It is struggling after free ideas, and for brief moments it seems to achieve them. Their mastery in man carries him into a new world. To the means and the meaning of that mastery, we must now turn.

BOOK TWO

THE THEORY OF THE IDEA

CHAPTER VII

THE IDEA AS IMAGE

1. The attainment of free ideas marks our escape from the mind of the animal. We have seen that the animal mind does break through at times into thought of the absent, but this achievement is so uncontrollable, rare, and wavering, as hardly to affect the rule. The animal lives in a world of perception; its thought on the whole is sense-bound; it expressly recalls no past and expressly anticipates no future. Its senses may be refined in the extreme, and its emotions strong and various; its confinement to the perceptive world is quite compatible, as we have seen, with a kind of judgement, desire, and inference. Yet its constant preoccupation is with what is given at the moment in sense, and these processes are only a fringe to that. Even when a dog pines away in his master's absence, it is apparently the present absence rather than the absent presence that affects him. It is not churlishness that makes us say this, but merely the requirement of a consistent view of him, since if his mind could really play upon the absent, he would be able to scheme and plan in a way that he never does. We are forced to believe that his world is of far smaller dimensions than ours. Our thought, with all its weaknesses, can at least range afield in space and time; his thought remains tethered to sense.

With the coming of the free idea, then, we reach the upper air. What is meant by such an idea? If what is wanted here is examples, the question is easy. If what is wanted is a true account of the nature of such thought, the question is treacherous and difficult in the extreme; and unfortunately it is this last question that we have to face. But let us take the easier one first.

We are using a free idea whenever we think explicitly of what is not at the moment given us in sense. Merely to have a sensation is not to think. To perceive *is* to think, for it is to lay hold on truth or falsity. It is to grasp a sense quality *as* this rather than that, or as belonging to some thing. And plainly in such thinking there may be already a reference to what is absent. When I perceive a house, I take what I sense as continuous with what is beyond, and this reference to what is beyond belongs to the heart of the perception. But it is not a free idea, since it is, in the first place, tied to sense. It comes as the completion of what is given, and forms an unbroken whole with this, so that in perceiving a house I seem to be merely seeing it and not thinking at all. And secondly, the reference is commonly implicit. Though I certainly take the house to be more than the side I see, I do not think of the other sides explicitly. The status of this unexplicit reference we examined as best we could in studying perceptual meaning, reserving the study of explicit reference for Book II. Now it is just this explicit reference that we mean by a free idea. While the reference in perception is the reference of a divided mind, engaged partly with sensible quality and partly with its unpresented complement, in the free idea the reference to the absent is normally dominant and explicit. And it is no longer tied to sense. I can think of the house with my eyes shut or when I am miles away from it; and with the house standing there before me I can ignore it and think instead of Fujiyama or of an event long ago at Marathon. A free idea is an explicit thought which is independent of what is given at the time in sense.[1]

What is the nature of such thought? Since the answer we are to offer has been reached by a dialectic process, involving the consideration and rejection of important alternative views, we shall follow this procedure here. We shall take up, chapter by chapter, the theories that hold the field, accepting from each what we can and leaving the rest. And first for theories that make

[1] It would be wrong to say 'an explicit thought of what is not given in sense', for one can apparently perceive an object and at the same time think of it by means of a free idea. Here the object, or part of it, *is* given, but the idea is independent of its being given, in the sense that it could exist apart from the sensation, as perceptual meaning could not.

of the idea an image. There is a variety of these, but let us begin with the one that is nearest to common sense. This we must examine pretty fully, not because it is accepted as a whole by any present-day school of thinkers, but partly because, with common sense behind it, it exerts a strong continuous pressure on the thought of everyone, even the experts, and partly because it is important historically.

2. To common sense, an idea of anything is an *image that copies it*. Statements about what 'common sense' thinks, or 'science' thinks, or 'religion' or 'philosophy' thinks, are perhaps generally false, and certainly as a rule to be avoided; but here we are fairly safe. For common sense, the idea of anything is clearly not the thing itself, nor is it a bare, featureless act of mind. It is an ideal representation of the thing. And this representation is thought of as reproducing in a mental medium the features of the thing itself. Our natural terms in describing it are 'faithful' and 'accurate' or 'distorted', 'vivid' or 'faint', 'clear' or 'foggy', 'fragmentary' or 'full' and 'detailed'. Implicit in all these expressions is the notion of a copy and its original. And when this notion is dragged to light and made into a theory of the idea, it appeals at once to the plain man as the natural and sensible view. When the great exponent of common sense in philosophy, Locke, sought an account of the idea, it was this theory that he seized upon. If we look at the sun, he would say, we have sensations of various qualities; when we turn away and think of it, we are only experiencing these same qualities in the form of images, which are fainter copies of the qualities we sensed.[1] Berkeley and Hume laid down the

---

[1] 'The idea of the sun,—what is it but an aggregate of those several simple ideas, bright, hot, roundish, having a constant regular motion, at a certain distance from us, and perhaps some other; as he who thinks and discourses of the sun has been more or less accurate in observing those sensible qualities, ideas, or properties, which are in that thing which he calls the sun. For he has the perfectest idea of any of the particular sorts of substances, who has gathered, and put together, most of those simple ideas which do exist in it.' (*Essay*, II,

same theory as 'evident' in the first sentences of their chief
works. Ideas, said Berkeley, are 'formed by help of memory
and imagination—either compounding, dividing, or barely
representing those originally perceived directly';[1] 'by ideas',
said Hume, 'I mean the faint images' of 'impressions' gained
at first hand.[2] This is a simple and attractive view. As we go
about with eyes and ears open, things make impressions upon
our mind, or as we should probably say nowadays, supply us
with sense data. From them we form copies or images, and
then when we want to think of the things later, the images
are ready to hand. These images *are* our ideas. Is this not the
most reasonable account we can give?

Unfortunately it is all but worthless. In certain special
cases, as we shall see, the image does supply the stuff of thought,
but the theory that would identify them generally is riddled
with confusions and difficulties. We can only list rapidly a
few of the major objections. If the thought of a thing were the
image of it, the characters of the one should vary with the
characters of the other. But in fact their variations do not even
remotely correspond. (1) The thought often grows better as
the image dies away, and (2) when the image is most perfect,
the thought may be most inadequate. Both points are easy to
illustrate.

3. (1) That thought is not impaired by the dying away of
images may be shown either (i) by comparing different times

xxiii, 6–7.) It is clear that Locke is using the word 'idea' here in
different senses; it is for him a blanket term for 'whatever it is which
the mind can be employed about in thinking' (I, i. 8), and covers
equally what we should describe as sensed qualities, images, and
ideas. Hence, in stating his view of what we have called an idea, we
must go behind his own terminology.

[1] *Principles of Human Knowledge*, I, i.
[2] *Treatise*, I. i. No one of these writers held consistently to the copy
theory which they all began with; their variations on it would almost
fill a volume. I disregard these, since our main interest is not historical.
For a recent defence of the image theory, see Dickinson S. Miller,
Journal of Philosophy, Vol. 34, 701 ff. (1937).

in the history of the same man, or (ii) by comparing the thought of different men. (i) It often happens that the same man is in youth very free in his use of imagery while as years go on he resorts to it less and less. But if his thought is confined to imagining, then as he approaches maturity his thought grows thinner and poorer, and when he has reached the period when by every popular and scientific standard his mind is most mature and competent, it is all but empty of ideas. This is absurd. Dr. W. H. R. Rivers described himself as 'one of those persons whose normal waking life is almost wholly free from sensory imagery, either visual, auditory, tactile, or of any other kind. . . . It is clear to me that if it were not for my special knowledge and interest I should be wholly ignorant of its existence. . . (But) I have concluded, and I think I am justified in doing so, that before the age of five my visual imagery was far more definite than it became later. . . .'[1] Dr. Rivers was thus deficient in imagery of all kinds; he was, also, while thus deficient, a thinker of some distinction. If thought were imagery, these things could not both be true.

(ii) There are also enormous differences in imagery between one mind and another. This has been shown by many careful studies,[2] but never more strikingly than in the work which started the series, Francis Galton's *Inquiries*. His method was to send a letter to a great many different persons, many of them scientists of repute, asking each to call to mind his break-fast-table of that morning, and to answer some simple questions about the brightness, clearness, and colouring, of the image. 'The earliest results of my inquiry', he writes, 'amazed me. . . . I found that the great majority of the men of science to whom I first applied protested that mental imagery was unknown to them, and they looked on me as fanciful and fantastic in supposing that the words "mental imagery" really expressed what I believed everybody supposed them to mean. They had

[1] *Instinct and the Unconscious*, 11-12.
[2] E.g. Lay, *Mental Imagery*, Psych. Rev., Monograph Supplements, Vol. II, No. 7; Fernald, *Diagnosis of Mental Imagery, ibid.*, Vol. XIV, No. 58.

no more notion of its true nature than a colour-blind man, who has not discovered his defect, has of the nature of colour.' But there were also persons who reported images 'quite as bright as an actual scene' and 'all the objects well defined'. 'One statesman has assured me that a certain hesitation in utterance which he has at times is due to his being plagued by the image of his manuscript speech with its original erasures and corrections. He cannot lay the ghost, and he puzzles in trying to decipher it.'[1] Here were various minds, equally proficient in the use of ideas, some of which were profuse in imagery while others scarcely knew what imagery meant. Thought and imagery bore no relation to each other, or if there was one, it was vaguely negative; among philosophers whom he questioned Galton reported the visualizing faculty 'starved by disuse'! Here again, if thought is imagery, we should have something like self-contradiction.[2]

It may be said that this proves nothing. Galton was assuming that to use imagery was to use pictures. But later inquiries have brought to light a host of new kinds of imagery, of which one sort may be dominant in one mind, another in another, or which may be so united in the same mind that a 'subject who uses visual-object imagery almost wholly in one class of tests may be equally wedded to auditory-motor word imagery in another type'.[3] Hence Galton's scientists may have been as lacking in visual pictures as he believed, and still have carried on their thinking with the help of images of a different order. We must agree that this is true. Nevertheless, it is fatal to the contention it seeks to prove. Let us suppose that scientist A, having breakfasted with scientist B, tries to recall their breakfast menu, and does so through vivid pictures. Let us suppose

---

[1] *Inquiries into Human Faculty*, 58–67.

[2] 'Comparisons have now been made in many kinds of mental performances between the persons who are endowed with such images and those who are unendowed. In not one single kind of performance, so far, have the imageful persons shown any superiority over the imageless.'—Spearman, *Creative Mind*, 10.

[3] J. R. Angell, "Methods for Determination of Mental Imagery," *Psych. Rev. Mon*, Vol. 13 (1910), 81–2.

that B also recalls it, but through auditory-motor images connected with the use of words. Their images are as wide apart as two images can be. Their thoughts are of the same thing. If an idea must be an image that *copies* its object, the two thoughts could not possibly be of the same thing, whereas they obviously are.

4. (2) We have seen that thought may be improving while imagery is fading out. The converse is true; imagery is often at its best when thought is feeble. 'In general', wrote Macaulay, 'the development of the fancy is to the development of the judgement what the growth of a girl is to the growth of a boy. The fancy attains at an earlier period to the perfection of its beauty, its power, and its fruitfulness; and as it is first to ripen, it is also first to fade'.[1] Children may be far richer in vivid imagery than they ever are in later years. 'It seems to be a hard lesson', Galton remarks, 'for an imaginative child to distinguish between the real and visionary world.'[2] Are we therefore to say of these children that their thoughts also are then clearest and fullest? On the contrary, such imagery may stand in the way of thought proper.[3] One's thought of man, as distinct from animal, will remain poor and crippled so long as it is tied to the stake of imagery and can only revolve the circle of particular specimens. There have been many painters like Blake and Turner whose images of faces and scenes were such that they could paint from them almost as from life; and no doubt in the work of reproducing, this gave them an advantage. But one would feel it a paradox to say that their thought of nature or human nature was therefore at the acme of richness and clearness. At this rate the palm for mastery would have to be yielded to the insane.[4]

[1] *A propos* of Bacon, of whom he thought the opposite was true.— *Essays*, Oxford edition, 405.

[2] *Ibid.*, 127.   [3] *Ibid.*, 76.

[4] Some interesting cases are described in an old book, Wigan's *New View of Insanity*. A painter, for example, attained great popularity by

5. (3) Ideas are not to be reduced to images for the further reason that we can think of things of which no image or copy is possible. When I reflect, for example, that religious fears have often been the cause of unsettling the mind, I may call up certain images, but to say that I am thinking of nothing but what my images resemble is clearly mistaken, since there is no possible image of figures in flight, or ghosts walking, or hammers striking nails, that could cover what I mean by 'fears', 'mind', 'cause'. Indeed, in its dealings with the three kinds of idea involved here, (i) the general idea, (ii) the idea of non-sensible individuals, and (iii) the idea of relation, the combined ingenuity of Locke, Berkeley and Hume could not save the image theory from bankruptcy. These philosophers, like all philosophers, used such ideas constantly, but they felt uneasy about them, struggled to explain them away, and in spite of an acuteness which would have saved the theory if mere acuteness were enough, ended, all of them, in defeat. (i) As to general ideas, the most determined defence was Berkeley's. He saw that when we think of man as mortal, or of triangles as internally equal to two right angles, we are not thinking of any one man or any particular triangle. But he also saw that an image must have some particular character; it seemed ridiculous to say, as he understood Locke to say, that the image of a man need have no particular shape or colour, but could be at once straight and stooped, black, white, and yellow. But now if every image was particular, while some thoughts were clearly general, how was he to save the image theory? His solution was this: when we think of 'man' we do form an image, and this image is perfectly particular, but we take it as standing for any man and hence for all men. But this which seems at first so plausible

requiring one sitting only and then painting from his memory image. 'Gradually I began to lose the distinction between the imaginary figure and the real person, and sometimes disputed with sitters that they had been with me the day before. At last I was sure of it; and then—and then—'. 124. But Dr. Wigan puts one on one's guard by reporting that he 'restored to vigorous health' a man suffering from 'incipient moral insanity' by 'a large bleeding and a blister to the nape of the neck'!

was less a defence than a surrender. For he had to admit that
besides the image, we are aware of what it stands for, and that
without this grasp of its widespread reference the idea would
not be general at all. And this is really to admit that the image
by itself is not the idea, that what gives the thought its range
and sweep cannot be reduced to imaginal terms. Thus Berkeley
was in effect reducing the image to a convenience, which indeed
helps in carrying the reference, but may be made as sketchy
as one pleases so long as it performs this essential function of
carrying thought beyond it. If we take the image as standing for
all men, the *thought* is general, however particular may be
the image we call in aid. Thus in its handling of general ideas,
the image theory broke down.[1]

6. (ii) It broke down also in its account of our thought of
what is individual but non-sensible. Locke was as convinced
as were the Schoolmen, for example, that tables and chairs
were more than groups of sense qualities, that each thing was
an 'it', a bit of material substance which owned these qualities
while distinct from them. But it was only of sense qualities
that we could form images. What sort of idea was it, then,
that we had of this non-sensible something? Locke saw that
on his theory we ought to have no idea at all. And he frankly
says so: 'of substance we have no idea what it is, but only a
confused and obscure one of what it does';[2] we are like the
poor Indian who, being asked what supported the world said,
'a great elephant', and being pressed as to what supported the
elephant, said 'a broad-backed tortoise', and being pressed as
to what the tortoise stood on, could only say 'something, he
knew not what'.[3] We were therefore left in the undignified
position of talking about something continually with no idea

---

[1] For Berkeley's view, see his *Principles*, Introduction. He was
here attacking Locke, though Locke himself proposed essentially
the same solution: Essay, II, xi, 9, and III, iii, 11. It was accepted by
Hume as 'one of the greatest and most valuable discoveries that has
been made of late years in the republic of letters'.—*Treatise*, I, i, 7.
[2] First letter to Stillingfleet, *Works*, IV. 8.   [3] *Essays*, II, xxiii, 2.

of what we were talking about. Locke was sure that substance existed; he saw that he could not be thus sure without somehow thinking of it; yet on his own theory he ought not to be able to think of it. The image theory had broken down.

It broke down also with Berkeley, and at a similar point. Although of course Berkeley no longer believed in material substance, he believed as firmly as Locke did in substances of another kind, in himself, for example, and in God. But when he wrote his chief work, he was so intent on showing that we have no idea of material substance that he seems to have forgotten that the same arguments could be applied to our ideas of other substances as well. It would be interesting to know what passed in Berkeley's mind when, after the appearance of his book, this dawned on him; it marked his metaphysic for the destruction that soon fell on it. What happened in his mind we do not know, but we do know that in the second edition there appeared a brief note with this admission: 'We may be said to have some knowledge or notion of our own minds, of spirits and active beings, *whereof in a strict sense we have not ideas.*'[1] Again, and at a critical point, the image theory would not work. Berkeley saw, and rightly, that we can think of ourselves; he saw, and again rightly, that a self is not the sort of thing of which any conceivable image could be the copy. He thus came in full view of the conclusion that an idea and an image were not the same. And he did see it; though too late to do it justice. Although it should have altered his system profoundly, it remained as an unassimilated foreign substance.

7. (iii) No less signal was the collapse of the image theory in its attempt to deal with relations. This attempt was most notable in Hume, whose struggle to reconcile the view that perception is nothing but sensation, and thought nothing but imagery, with the fact that we somehow grasp the relations of identity and causality, is one of the decisive battles of philoso-

[1] *Principles*, Sec. 89, my italics. Hume pressed the difficulty home.

phic history. It is evident that when we see something move, we take it to be the same body as it was the moment before. Apparently, then, we do grasp the relation of sameness or identity. But is there any *sensation* or *image* of identity? Hume saw that there was not. But instead of revising his theory of knowledge to suit the fact, he denied the fact in order to save his theory of knowledge. He denied that there was any such thing as identity and held that our supposed thought of it was an illusion. When we take a moving body as the same, he said, what really happens is this: because our successive percepts are so like each other, we run them together and take many slightly different percepts for the percept of one thing. But there is no *one* thing or percept present, and the thought of it is an illusion. Unfortunately for Hume's theory, however, a thought that is an illusion is as much a thought as any other, and on his theory it should be impossible even to make such a mistake. If our ideas are images, and identity cannot be imaged, it is inexplicably perverse of us to have stumbled on such an idea, even in error, for it has no business there; and if, nevertheless, it *is* there, its presence should prove extremely upsetting. So it did.

And not less so the idea of causality, which Hume did his best to explain away. When we see a hammer about to descend on a nail, and say it will cause the nail to sink in, we seem to be thinking not merely of hammer and nail, but of something distinct from either, a peculiar connection between them. Hume saw with perfect clearness that if there were such a connection we could certainly form no image of it. But he was so confident that if we could not imagine it we could not think it, that he held we did not have the idea at all, but only a habit produced by experience of expecting one thing upon the occurrence of another. But no such device will serve. Even if we admit that in 'habit produced by experience' Hume is not using the forbidden idea, and that the thought of causality is a mere expectancy, which it is not, still in expecting one event to follow another we are referring to a relation that is even more troublesome than that of causality, the wholly unimaginable relation of time. No matter what stores of ingenuity Hume could bring to the business of explaining away, he could not get rid of either of these facts, that we do think of relations, and that we do not, because we cannot, form images of them. And when his successors made plain how important is the thought of relations for knowledge, it became clear that the image theory had not only failed, but failed at a cardinal point.

This result has been repeatedly confirmed experimentally.[1] One series of experiments which bears on the issue with special directness has been reported by Professor Woodworth in an essay on 'The Consciousness of Relation'. The method was to present someone with a problem that would require him to think of a certain relation, and then take his introspective report: for example, 'mice: cats :: worms :?' or 'a boy : a man :: a girl :?' 'In this form of exercise, the relation is suggested by means of two terms between which it holds, plus a third term which serves to indicate which of the possible relations between the first two terms is chosen. The relation must now be detached from the first pair of terms and transferred to another case.' The relevant results were as follows: sometimes a name or image occurred. 'Sometimes, however, and very often indeed, the transfer is accomplished without such a vehicle, though the relation remains in consciousness. The feeling of relation then appears as an "imageless thought" and seems as substantial a component of consciousness as are the feelings of the terms.'[2] Now it is needless for our purpose to raise at this point the controversial question whether the idea was really imageless, as Professor Woodworth believes. It is enough to point out that the relation was clearly and explicitly thought, and that if the thought were the same as the image, this too should be clear and explicit, but that it was so far from being so, as, in many cases, to elude introspection wholly. If the

---

[1] See the work of the Würzburg School.
[2] In *Essays in Honour of William James*, 492; this is even clearer where the relation grasped is extremely complex, and where the image, to correspond, must be equally so, yet is sketchy and elusive to the last degree. Cf. *ibid.*, 498–9.

thought of the object is clear and explicit while the image is neither, they are not the same.

8. (4) Even where the image is full and clear, it is often discrepant with what is thought of. (i) I recall that a moment ago, when a thought of religion came to mind, I had the image of a rose-window. But religion is a kind of experience, not a visible or tangible thing. A rose-window is precisely this kind of thing. One cannot copy the other. 'One has only to recall the complicated number-forms by means of which many persons accomplish their numerical computations to realize how utterly disparate content and function may be.'[1] (ii) Even when thought and image concern the same order of existence, they may differ in quality. 'Should we be asked, Are roses red? Has coal gas a foul smell? Is that white beast a horse? Is it true that he is dead? we should answer, Yes, our ideas are all true, and are attributed to the reality. But the idea of redness may have been that of a lobster, of a smell that of castor-oil, the imaged horse may have been a black horse, and death a withered flower.'[2] Here the sensible characters of what is imaged and what is thought of are in conflict. (iii) Sometimes there is conflict in degree. Professor Ward says that images do not vary in intensity, that our image of a loud sound, for example, is not strictly more intense than our image of a low one.[3] This seems to me questionable, but in any case the amount of truth it contains is more than can be dealt with by any image theory. When I think of a noise ten thousand times as loud as the tick of my watch, say the discharge of a gun, it is clear that the intensity of my image is not magnified ten thousand times when my thought shifts from one to the other. If, then, I succeed in thinking of the increased magnitude, it must be through other means than a copy. (iv) So independent are thought and image that the same image may be used by different thoughts and different images

---

[1] J. R. Angell, *Phil. Rev.*, VI. 650. [2] Bradley, *Logic*, I. 9.
[3] *Psychological Principles*, 171.

by the same thought. If I think of $2 + 2 = 4$, I may do so first with an auditory-motor image, then with an image of how it looks on a page;[1] and then later I may use either one of these images in the thought of mathematics generally. If so, thought and image cannot be the same.

9. (5) At the risk of seeming to pummel an unfortunate theory unduly, we may add one more set of objections which point to its weakness on the epistemological side. (i) It seems unable to distinguish imagination from memory. Images of the same kind may appear in both, but as a rule we can easily tell the difference between an act of memory and an act of free imagination. So far as the images used are alike, there must be something in memory besides the image which gives us our clue. But further, as an account of the way we know, the theory is inconsistent with itself and even with knowledge generally. Cook Wilson has put both points clearly. (ii) When we represent an idea as an image, he says, 'the chief fallacy' is that this 'assumes the very thing it is intended to explain. The image itself has still to be *apprehended* and the difficulty is only repeated. We still distinguish the image and the knowing, or perceiving, or apprehending of it.'[2] It seems to be admitted by the image theory that we lay hold of the image itself without any further image to help us; but if we can apprehend an object without the aid of imagery in one case, why should this be essential in other cases? (iii) The theory ends in scepticism. If our idea of an object is declared to be an image or copy of it,

> 'we naturally ask how we know that it is a copy; for it is not enough that the idea should be a copy; we must know that it is a copy or it would be of no use for the purpose. We can only know that a copy is a copy by comparing it with the original,

---

[1] Angell cites a case of thinking of an equation through the help of bodily strains, *op. cit.*, 650. T. V. Moore found, besides various other divergences, a difference in reaction-time between the apprehension of meaning and the formation of an image.—*Psych. Rev.*, XXII. 177 ff., 1915.   [2] *Statement and Inference*, II. 803.

and to do this we must apprehend the original itself. But *ex hypothesi*, it is the copy only which is before us in consciousness, and further, if the original were before us and apprehended, the copy would be superfluous. Again, the theory cannot guarantee that the supposed effect in our minds, the "idea" or "impression", is at all like the thing which is said to cause it; and worse than this, it cannot even account for our having the idea that there is any original.'[1]

The scepticism entailed by the theory is so profound as to be incompatible with any confidence in its own truth.

10. So far we have been assuming that if the idea is found in the image, this image copies the object. But ideas may be identified with images without any suggestion that copying is involved. This was the view of Professor Titchener, and it was supported, as his views usually were, by much careful introspection, both within and without the laboratory.

The theory appears most clearly when set in contrast with the views of other experimental inquirers whom he criticizes. The key to it is given in the attitude which, following von Aster and Dürr, he takes toward the work of Bühler. Bühler's method was to choose a number of subjects who were practised in introspection, put to them questions to which a Yes or No required some thought, and then ask them to describe as exactly as they could what took place in their minds. He found that his subjects continually described what took place in such language as this, 'The thought came to me that. . . ,' or 'It occurred to me that. . . ,' and he accepted this in all simplicity as a description of what went on. But von Aster and Dürr objected that in so describing their experience the subjects were not doing what they were told, and that Bühler had no business to accept it. For 'it is evident that to designate something as thought is not by any means to describe the nature of this thought'. 'The problem of the psychologist is to show the characteristics of all these acts of thought, not by reference

[1] *Statement and Inference*, I. 61.

to what is apprehended in them, but by demonstration of their proper nature.'[1] With this criticism Titchener agrees. To say what an idea is of, is not to report what happens in consciousness at all; 'for psychology of structure, that "of" which we have feeling is irrelevant. The psychological datum is the feeling itself, the feeling as felt';[2] the aim of true psychology is 'to describe the contents of consciousness not as they mean but as they are'.[3] If I think of Caesar landing in Britain, what I think of is no part of the process in me; strictly speaking, the psychologist should not even refer to it; his business is to say *how it feels* to think of Caesar landing in Britain.

Now if he confines himself to this programme, says Titchener, he will find that what is present in consciousness when he thinks is always something of the sensational type, that is, sensations or images. Titchener illustrates freely from his own experience; to exemplify his 'ideas of animals' he says:

> 'horse is, to me, a double curve and a rampant posture with a touch of mane about it; cow is a longish rectangle with a certain facial expression, a sort of exaggerated pout. . . . And what holds of triangles and horse and cow holds of all the "unpicturable notions of intelligence". No one of them is unpicturable, if you do but have the imaginal mind. "It is impossible", remarks a recent writer,[4] "to ideate a meaning; one can only know it." Impossible? But I have been ideating meanings all my life. And not only meanings, but meaning also. Meaning in general is represented in my consciousness by another of these impressionist pictures. I see meaning as the blue-grey tip of a kind of scoop, which has a bit of yellow above it (probably a part of the handle), and which is just digging into a dark mass of what appears to be plastic material.'[5]

Nor does the non-sensible character of what is thought of make the least difference to Titchener's conviction, since the idea need not be a copy. Hume's difficulties about relations do not touch him.

---

[1] *Am. Jour. of Psych.*, XX. 171–2 (1912); Dürr, quoted by Titchener. And cf. *Experimental Psychology of the Thought Processes*, 148–51.

[2] *Exp. Psych.*, etc., 255.   [3] *Ibid.*, 25.

[4] Bühler.   [5] *Ibid.*, 18–19.

'What do we experience when we have a "feeling of relation?"
What I myself experience depends upon circumstances. It was
my pleasure and duty, a little while ago, to sit on the platform
behind a somewhat emphatic lecturer, who made great use of
the monosyllable "but". My "feeling of but" has contained,
ever since, a flashing picture of a bald crown, with a fringe of
hair below, and a massive black shoulder, the whole passing
swiftly down the visual field from north-west to south-east.'[1]

11. If one complains that all this sounds a little grotesque, that
general ideas and the idea of relation must be something more
or other than these somewhat outlandish images, Titchener
would reply that to speak so merely implies the old confusion.
If we mean by 'idea' the logical meaning or what is meant,
we are speaking of what is psychologically irrelevant; if we
mean the idea that is actually in our minds, we shall find that
it always takes one or other of these imaginal forms. He would
not object to our saying that one of these images 'carries' a
further meaning or idea, but he would again insist that if we
are speaking of facts of consciousness, this meaning must
consist of sensations or images.

'I hold that, from the psychological or existential point of
view, meaning—so far as it finds representation in consciousness at all—is always context. An idea means another idea, is
psychologically the meaning of that other idea, if it is that
idea's context. And I understand by context simply the mental
process or complex of mental processes which accrues to the
original idea through the situation in which the organism finds
itself. . . . Meaning is, originally, kinaesthesis; the organism
faces the situation by some bodily attitude, and the characteristic
sensations which the attitude involves give meaning to the
process that stands at the conscious focus, are psychologically
the meaning of that process.'[2]

A prime example of such sensational context is words: 'words
themselves, let us remember, were at first motor attitudes,
gestures, kinaesthetic contexts. . . .' And thus 'The meaning
of the printed page may now consist in the auditory-kinaesthetic

[1] *Exp. Psych.*, etc., 185.   [2] *Ibid.*, 175–6.

accompaniment of internal speech; the word is the word's own meaning. . . .'[1]

Of course Titchener knew all the facts brought to light by Galton about 'imageless thought', and all the nuances with which the doctrine had been later advocated; he knew the whole literature as perhaps no one before or since has known it; and he remained unmoved. The apparently imageless thought, he believed, could be explained by one or other of two considerations: either that the observer was guilty of the confusion already remarked between 'statement of meaning' and 'description of process', or else was forgetting that thought may be indefinitely condensed or telescoped. The first point we need not return to.

The second gives Titchener's suggestion for explaining away some of the common forms of 'imageless thought'. When we are engaged in rapid reading, for example, there seem at times to be no images at all in consciousness, nor even the faintest sensations of subvocal speech, and yet we are undoubtedly apprehending the meaning of what we read. How can we identify ideas with what is sensational if nothing sensational is there? Titchener answers as follows: When we first think of a thing, our idea may consist of a full and detailed image. Through association with this image, however, its place may be taken by a certain form of words. As the idea is repeated, a more and more sketchy use of words suffices until all trace of verbal sensation may have vanished, to be replaced by a 'schematic kinaesthetic attitude'. Thus, 'I was not at all astonished to observe that the recognition of a grey might consist in a quiver of the stomach'.[2] And even this may have its substitute; 'there were instances in which the grey was "recognized" without words; without organic sensations, kinaesthetic or other; without the arousal of a mood; without anything of an appreciably conscious sort', through a mere

[1] *Exp. Pysch.*, etc., 177.
[2] *Ibid.*, 179; in rapid reading, 'sight and attitudinal feel do my skimming for me, with only occasional assistance from internal speech'. 208; and cf. 297.

act of the body. A critic of Titchener might seize on such a doctrine as admitting that after all we may be conscious without sensations or images, but he is expressly cut off by reading that consciousness and sensation die out together and that we must describe such a case as 'simply a "recognition" without consciousness'.[1]

Thus the theory consists in three propositions; that for a psychology of thinking (1) *what* we think of is irrelevant; (2) ideas and meanings consist in sensational material; and (3) the presence of this material is all we mean by being conscious.[2]

12. I do not believe any of these propositions to be true. But they are not of equal importance. It is really the first that gives the key to Titchener's position. If this proposition is granted, the others, though not necessary, become very much more plausible, while if it is false, the antecedent probability is strongly against them. What are we to say of this key proposition?

We must remark at once that it is extremely paradoxical, how much so can hardly have been realized by many who subscribe to it. If psychologists are to be forbidden to talk of 'logical meanings', if *what* we think of is to be counted irrelevant and ideas *of* are not to be mentioned, much of the importance of psychology has vanished. In its dealings with all the higher processes, the science will be confined to the marginal and irrelevant. Titchener admits or rather asserts that the images which are 'the vehicles of logical meaning' may be sketchy, irrelevant, and merely accessory,[3] and that there need be no relation between the definiteness of the image and that of the object it means.[4] He insists, nevertheless, that it is to these accessories that psychology is confined. Let us see what this

---

[1] *Exp. Psych.*, etc., 179.

[2] Affection (pleasure and 'displeasure') is here for convenience grouped with 'sensational material'.

[3] *Ibid.*, 13.   [4] *Ibid.*, 183–4.

leads to. Here are some of the conclusions that would follow from it: One might produce a biography of Euclid, psychologically satisfactory and complete, without any mention of geometry, and an exhaustive history of the consciousness of Gibbon without alluding anywhere to Rome. If the images through which Euclid thought of his theorems and Gibbon of his emperors bore as little relation to what they were thinking about as Professor Titchener's imaged scoop did to the nature of meaning, it will be admitted that the completest psychology might give scanty clues to what was engrossing their minds. It would still, in its own sense, be studying their. 'train of thought', but this train of thought would include nothing that they themselves, or indeed anyone but this special type of psychologist, would think important. Again, what is to be done with all the books that have appeared in recent years on 'The Psychology of Religious Belief', 'The Psychology of Reasoning', 'The Psychology of Beauty', 'The Psychology of the Crowd', 'The Psychology of Morals'? Such works try to show how our ways of thinking about certain types of object, or about objects generally, are developed and modified. If they are to be instructive, they must clearly have access to *what* we believe and the fluctuations in this. In Professor Titchener's psychology, the attempt to gain access is illegitimate. All such works, therefore, must confine themselves to the mere accessories of 'religious belief', of 'reasoning', etc., or else must be placed on the Index as psychologically uncanonical. And both these suggestions are paradoxes.

13. But the fact that such consequences are at first shocking does not, of course, disprove them, and Professor Titchener's abnegations on behalf of his science may still be necessary. However, it seems not difficult to show that from its own standpoint, as well as from that of common sense, such surrenders are unnecessary, impractical, and even inconsistent.

Suppose I am thinking of Caesar's landing in Britain. If I am to describe my thought scientifically, according to the

theory, I must omit mention of *what* I am thinking of, since
this does not belong to consciousness. Neither am I to speak
of an *act* of thinking of it, both because this would be describing
by means of the object again, and because no such referential
act is introspectively to be found. It looks to common sense
as if, with this, the thought had been eviscerated, as if both
the object and anything in my mind that could point to it had
been thrown out, and nothing left. But Professor Titchener
would say: No, there always remains a residue of imagery;
and the imagery of Caesar's landing, which serves to convey
the reference, is what, as psychologists, we must fix on. But
observe the straits in which the psychologist is thus placed.
If he says that we have imagery of Caesar's landing, which he
naturally tends to do, he is doing the very thing he is supposed
to avoid, namely describing a mental state through reference
to its object. If he is to keep to his programme of merely describing mental states, he must confine himself to the imagery itself
and disregard what it is *of*. But the unhappy fact is that this is
quite impossible. Granting that no precise copy of the object
is necessary, still the connection between the image and what
it is of is so close that to try to describe the image without
mention of its object is not only to fail in describing it, but
inevitably to misdescribe it. Professor Titchener seems to feel
this himself, for, with an instinct for exact description which
is sounder than his theory, he continually describes his own
mental states as images *of* horse, cow, meaning, and so on. Are
we to say that his description of these states is therefore the
less exact, that in describing his idea of a horse, he might
better not have spoken of a horse at all, but only of 'a double
curve and a rampant posture with a touch of mane about it'?
Indeed even this description contains references to the horse
which clearly should be excluded. If we do exclude them,
do we get a better description? On the contrary, we get one
that is less accurate. The image and the thought of its object
form so intimate a union, the one is so bathed in and permeated
with the atmosphere of the other, that when the image is dragged
from its element and set out alone, it proves to be a different

thing. The hard image now set before us by 'double curve, rampant posture and touch of mane' is not the flitting elusive wraith that carried our thought of horse, since this latter owes its character to being auxiliary in my particular mind to the thought of a special object. It is only as subserving that thought and playing its part in one whole with it that the image can be described with any sort of accuracy. Since it is only an aid to thought, it will be called into use only so far as the thought requires; and its true degree of prominence or shyness, of sketchiness or fullness, can be properly grasped only by entering into the thinker's whole state of mind. Professor Titchener knew that his image was of a horse, but for all he says of it by itself it might perfectly well have been that of a zebra or a lion; and as imagery is more and more dominated by thought, description becomes still more hazardous. Indeed in this very case, what definition the image has is gained chiefly by introducing (illicitly on the theory) a further reference to objects. Are not images of a curve, a rampant posture and a touch of mane, still images *of* things? To press such questions is to see that the theory before us is setting out on an impossible task. It tries to exclude the thought of objects that it may confine itself wholly to images, but it soon finds that it cannot describe the images without introducing what was to be excluded. Suppose it persists in the attempt at exclusion; what is it left with at the end? Pure sensations presumably, together with some images so far as these neither image any-thing nor mean anything. Here the science at last finds its province. It deals with experience so far as meaningless.

This is what such psychology comes to. The result was disguised from Professor Titchener because he did not carry his programme through with the ruthlessness required by con-sistency. What he proposed to do was to exclude logic from psychology by getting rid once for all of meaning in the logical sense. What he actually did, we have suggested, was to get rid of it in the major cases where its retention was important and to retain it in the minor cases where it was of comparatively little account, which was at once a compromise in principle and, so to speak, an error in strategy. If such compromises are to be avoided, we should realize, as students of psychology, that the science is here facing a dilemma, between whose horns there is no middle course. On the one hand is the proposal to admit logical meanings whole-heartedly; the science will then include in its province not merely the marginal images which 'carry' meanings, but the meanings themselves and all the conditions of their appearance and succession in consciousness. That psychology must include such things, and hence cannot be sharply divided from the philosophical study of mind, is a main contention of this work, to which we shall recur.[1] On the other hand is the proposal to banish logical meanings; and if this is to be done at all, it must be done with the thoroughness of a Sullan proscription. And we should be under no illusion as to what this involves. It involves that psychology has nothing to do with the mind as an apprehending agent, as an organ of knowledge or intelligence. It means that the history of consciousness is to be written without any note of the objects it is conscious of. It means that memories and beliefs, hopes and fears, desires and even imaginations are to be described in complete abstraction from anything remembered or believed, hoped or feared, imagined or desired. It means, if it is consistent, that the highest insight psychology can afford us into the working of the mind is to be gained by the study of nonsense syllables and their equivalent in images.

14. That, apart from what it implies about the importance of psychology, the view is really unworkable is indicated unawares in a remark that occurs repeatedly in the writings of Professor Titchener and those who follow him.[2] The images that serve as symbols of logical meanings, they say, are often *irrelevant* to those meanings. But they have apparently not reflected that there is nothing but a logical meaning that can be relevant or irrelevant to another meaning, and that in

---

[1] See Chaps. XIII, XXII, and XXIII below.
[2] Cf., e.g., Titchener, *op. cit.*, 13.

raising this point of relevancy they are again allowing images to cross the forbidden line into the territory of logic. If the image of a bald crown, which in Professor Titchener's mind symbolized the meaning of 'but', is irrelevant to that meaning, it is only so far as it is an image *of* something and thus not an image at all in the psychological sense, but a meaning as dealt with in logic. This lapse from consistency, small enough in itself, looms into something much larger when viewed reflectively. It is the hole in the dyke, through which the logic that was supposed to be kept out is bound sooner or later to come pouring in. To keep it out is impossible, no matter how narrowly one concentrates on the imaginal elements in mind. For whatever this degree of narrowness, psychology will retain in its programme at least the attempt to explain why these imaginal elements come and go as they do. And this it cannot explain if it leaves logical meanings out. Let us try to get this clear. The point can, I think, be proved, and the proof consists of two steps.

First, when accounting for the links in a chain of reflection, one cannot overlook the logical connection of each with the one before it, since the fact that what is asserted in one judgement entails what is asserted in another is often a part cause for that other's following. Since the evidence for this is set out below,[1] we shall here only refer to it and pass on to the second step, namely that the imagery used depends on the exigencies of thought or judgement in its logical sense.[2] If, to complete a syllogism, I must make a certain judgement, the imagery I use in making it will depend on the sort of help which that particular logical meaning needs to bring itself before the mind. If the conclusion required the thought of a horse, there would arise in Professor Titchener's mind the image of a double curve, etc. Why? Because the train of reflection required the thought of a horse, and the thought of

[1] See Chap. XII, Sec. 13; Chap. XIII, Sec. 10 ff.; Chap. XXII, Sec. 5 ff.; Chap. XXXII, Secs. 11–13.
[2] Cf. Clarke, 'Conscious Attitudes,' *Am. Jour. of Psych.*, XXII. 241.

a horse required this image as a support. There is no possible mode of explaining why this image occurred at this time and in this manner except by way of the meaning which used it as tool or instrument. Now to account for the images causally is just what sensationalist psychology means by explaining a course of thinking. To complete its own explanation, therefore, it must go beyond the image and hence also beyond its programme.[1] If this is true, the first of the three propositions to which we reduced Professor Titchener's theory is untenable. In the psychology of thinking, what we think of *is* relevant and indeed essential. And since, in Titchener's theory, this was the key proposition, we should ordinarily say but little of the other two, namely, that ideas, for psychology, consist of sensational material and that consciousness has no other meaning than the presence of such material. But we can hardly afford to pass them by, for they have been made essential parts in a theory of ideas that is far more startling than Titchener's, and is supported with more philosophical resource. Professor Titchener admitted that there were logical ideas, distinct from sensations, and images, though in excluding them from psychology he left them in a strange and dim limbo. Mr. Bertrand Russell has proposed a theory that would not even in logic allow them a separate status, but would reduce them, together with the mind itself and all that comes before it, to sensations and images. This theory is, like Titchener's, sensationalism in psychology, but it is something far more radical, sensationalism in philosophy too. We shall examine this view in the chapter that follows.

[1] It may be said that the explanation here pointed to is not causal, but teleological. The answer is that any explanation of a course of thinking must be both. See Chaps. XXII and XXIII.

CHAPTER VIII

MR. RUSSELL ON IDEAS

1. In his many writings, spread over many years, Mr. Russell has had much to say about the nature of ideas. It would hardly be fair to expect that contributions so widely scattered, and produced by so mobile and adventurous a mind, should fit into a quite coherent scheme. But on one occasion at least Mr. Russell set himself to deal with the matter in thorough and systematic fashion, namely, in his work on *The Analysis of Mind*. And since he could not deal with any subject in this manner without illuminating it, we shall find it worth while to study his theory in some detail.

It is perhaps not incorrect, and it is certainly helpful in understanding his unconventional views, to regard Mr. Russell's *Analysis of Mind* as governed by two motives. He wishes on the one hand to arrive at a view of mind that will give some hope of solving an ancient problem, the relation of mind and matter; and he wishes on the other hand to do justice to the new truth that he finds in behaviourism. As to the first point: why is it, he asks in effect, that we take mind and matter to be different? The natural answer is: because there are some features of mind, such as abstract ideas, emotions, beliefs and desires, which seem hopelessly irreducible to anything material; and there are certain features of matter, such as solidity and spatiality, which seem equally irreducible to anything mental. If such divisive elements could be resolved into the same sort of stuff, the problem would be solved. And the first step toward such a solution is to ask whether mind and matter have anything in common. Yes, Mr. Russell answers, they clearly do; *sensations* seem to belong by equal right to both realms. Looking first at the material side, is there anything in matter that cannot validly be reduced to sensations? Mr. Russell answers no: on this point he would accept the line of argument offered by Berkeley. But can the same be said of

mind? If it can, the problem of mind and matter will in principle be solved. And it is the main contention of *The Analysis
of Mind* that such an answer can be given, that ideas, beliefs,
emotions, and desires, all reduce to sensations or, what is at
bottom homogeneous with them, images. Thus matter and
mind are made of the same stuff. 'I believe that sensations
(including images) supply all the "stuff" of the mind, and
that everything else can be analysed into groups of sensations
related in various ways, or characteristics of sensations or
groups of sensations'.[1] And if psychology and physics remain
different sciences, it is because sensations, when grouped in
different ways, are found to obey somewhat different causal
laws, though even these may prove in the long run to be the
same. We shall more easily catch the point of Mr. Russell's
manipulations of the mind if we remember that he is trying
to construct a road to this metaphysical consummation.

The other leading motive that we mentioned, his desire to
assimilate the discoveries of behaviourism, fits perfectly with
the first. For so far as it can be shown that processes of thought
reduce, as the behaviourists contend, to reactions of the body,
just so far will his road be cleared of certain distinctively
mental features which have been supposed to make mind
irreducible. Mr. Russell is not a behaviourist; he is prevented
from going the whole way by the existence of images, which
he believes can be neither denied nor reduced to movements
of the body. But he does believe that all the supposed activities
of thought other than images and sensations can be resolved
away in the behaviourist manner. *The Analysis of Mind* ends in
the conclusion that there is probably nothing irreducibly
mental at all.

2. Bearing in mind these larger interests of Mr. Russell's,
let us now turn to his view of ideas. This appears most clearly
in his account of belief, and particularly in the sort of belief
involved in memory. I remember having toast and marmalade

[1] *Analysis of Mind*, 69.

at breakfast this morning, let us say. What form do the ideas
take in my mind? Mr. Russell answers that they may take
either of two forms, the form of images or the form of words.[1]
We must look at each of these.

In thinking of toast and marmalade, I may have the clearest
sort of images of how they looked on the table. And nothing
is more natural to common sense than to say these images
are ideas. But we saw in discussing Titchener's view that an
idea is always an idea *of* something, that it refers to or means
an object, and that this function of meaning is no fragment
of the image itself. Since this function goes beyond mere
sensory content, Titchener excluded it from psychology, but
Mr. Russell takes explicit account of it. He distinguishes what
confers meaning upon an image from what meaning is intrinsically. What confers meaning upon an image is belief, which
makes it feasible for us to say, when we have an image in our
mind, that something is being referred to. 'The memory-
belief confers upon the memory-image something which we
call "meaning", it makes us feel that the image points to an
object which existed in the past.'[2] What is the nature of this
belief? It is a *feeling*, says Mr. Russell, not easy to analyse,
but consisting undoubtedly of sensations.[3] If I have in mind
an image of raining, for example, this image is made into a
memory-idea, an idea of what is now happening, or an expectation, by the kind of feeling that accompanies it.[4]

An image is not an idea of anything, then, unless it is made
to mean something by this feeling of belief. But what does
'meaning something' itself mean? When we say that an image
means an object, Mr. Russell answers, we are saying one or
both of two things. One of these is that the image *resembles*
something else, which will therefore be its object. To be sure,
when I have a memory image of the toast and marmalade I
do not clearly distinguish image and object and say 'something
like my image occurred'; I have only the image and the feeling.
Nevertheless a little reflection shows that image and past

---

[1] *Analysis of Mind*, 241.   [2] *Ibid.*, 179.
[3] *Ibid.*, 250.   [4] *Ibid.*, 250.

event are clearly different and that the meaning of the first lies in its likeness to the second.[1] But meaning does not always consist in a direct likeness of this sort. Sometimes it consists in likeness of 'causal efficacy'. 'What is called an image "of" some definite object', say St. Paul's, 'has some of the effects which the object would have.' This applies especially to the effects that depend upon association. The emotional effects, also, are often similar: images may stimulate desire almost as strongly as do the objects they represent. When an image is vague and its meaning is hard to arrive at through likeness, this other method will often help. 'To arrive at the meaning of the image in such a case, we observe that there are certain respects, notably associations, in which the effects of images resemble those of their prototypes. If we find, in a given case, that our vague image, say of a nondescript dog, has those associative effects which all dogs would have, but not those belonging to any special dog or kind of dog, we may say that our image means "dog" in general. . . . The meaning of an image, according to this analysis, is constituted by a combination of likeness and association.'[2]

3. So much for the idea as identified with the image. But we have seen that according to Mr. Russell there is a second form in which ideas may appear, the form of words. By a word he means primarily an act of speech, 'a series of movements of the mouth'.[3] Words in this sense may mean objects just as images do, though there are certain differences to be noted. It is probable that the image is the original form of the idea, but 'by a telescoped process, words come in time to produce directly the effects which would have been produced by the images with which they were associated'.[4] So common has this substitution become that 'almost all higher intellectual activity is a matter of words, to the nearly total exclusion of everything else'.[5] Again, whereas an image can mean an

[1] *Analysis of Mind*, 179–80, 187.   [2] *Ibid.*, 209.
[3] *Ibid.*, 189.   [4] *Ibid.*, 206.   [5] *Ibid.*, 211; cf. 229.

object in two ways, a word can do so in only one. Words do not commonly resemble their objects; so 'the meaning of a word, unlike that of an image, is wholly constituted by mnemic causal laws. . . . The word "dog" bears no resemblance to a dog, but its effects, like those of an image of a dog, resemble the effects of an actual dog in certain respects. . . . A word, like an image, has the same associations as its meaning has. . . . If a word has the right associations with other objects, we shall be able to use it correctly, and understand its use by others, even if it evokes no image. The theoretical understanding of words involves only the power of associating them correctly with other words; the practical understanding involves associations with other bodily movements.'[1] And in the case of words, as in that of images, it is the feeling of belief that confers meaning upon the instrument.

Is the theory clear? Let us put it as concisely as possible, using the word 'proposition' as Mr. Russell does, to cover both images and word-groups. My thought about anything consists, then, in (a) a feeling of belief, directed upon (b) a proposition, which has (c) a meaning, consisting in either resemblance of proposition and object, or resemblance in their effects. What are we to say of the theory? It is to be feared that not much of it will survive scrutiny.

4. (I) The cardinal point in the theory is its doctrine as to the nature of meaning, for it is the possession of meaning that converts images and words into ideas *of* something. Now it is not difficult to show, I think, that meaning cannot be what Mr. Russell takes it to be, and even that in his statement of the view he has been compelled by the facts to desert it.

(1) Let us suppose that we are thinking of having had toast and marmalade for breakfast this morning, and that in doing so we employ an image. Toward this image, says Mr. Russell, we have a feeling of belief which could be expressed by 'this occurred'. 'This' in ordinary remembering is left

---

[1] *Analysis of Mind*, 210–11; cf. also 198.

vague; 'the image is not distinguished from the object which existed in the past'.[1] 'But when we become precise, our remembering becomes different from that of ordinary life',[2] in the sense that we distinguish the present image from the past fact; and our belief can only be expressed by 'something like this image occurred'. But clearly if this is the precise expression of our belief, then we have a thought of the past event that is other than the image; how else could the event be distinguished from the image and set down as something similar? How could we talk of a past event at all, as either like or unlike an image, if our thought of it is really identical with the image itself? This reference to the past event belongs, as Mr. Russell sees, to the very heart of memory; but where in his own scheme could it fall? It is not the image. It is not the meaning of the image, for that consists in the fact of similarity. It is not the belief directed upon the image, for that is a feeling, not the thought of an event. Though it is the cardinal point of memory, and indeed of ideas generally, yet the theory is such that it is either quite left out or else, if admitted, admitted illicitly. Nor could the theory be saved by saying that the thought which goes beyond the image to the object does so by means of another image. For if our memory is of the 'precise' kind, we shall again have to distinguish this image from the thought that goes beyond it, and so on indefinitely.[3]

5. (2) Thus the facts contain a kind of idea for which the theory does not provide. Unfortunately, what the theory does

[1] *Analysis of Mind*, 179.   [2] *Ibid.*, 180.

[3] Mr. Russell himself puts it clearly in another work (*Problems of Philosophy*, 180): 'We are certainly able to some extent to compare our image with the object remembered, so that we often know, within somewhat wide limits, how far the image is accurate; but this would be impossible unless the object, as opposed to the image, were in some way before the mind. Thus the essence of memory is not constituted by the image, but by having immediately before the mind an object which is recognized as past.' This comparison of present image with past object is either carried out through a further image or not. If it is, we have an infinite regress; if it is not, ideas need not be images.

provide seems to collide with the facts. We are told that an image means an object through being similar to it. Now, that when I think of something I may have an image that resembles it is of course admitted. But that the image's meaning the object is not the same as its likeness to it may be shown very readily. Suppose you have just seen an unlabelled picture of the Nawab of Pataudi and think of it by help of its image, while I think of the Nawab himself. It is quite clear that your image may be more like him than mine, but yours will not mean him at all while mine will. Your image happens by accident to be like some particular man of whose existence you have probably never heard. If meaning consists in likeness, your image should mean him more obviously than mine. But it cannot mean him, for you know of no such object to mean. If accidental resemblance is meaning, then in our everyday thoughts we are thinking of things and persons that we never heard of. This is absurd. Hence meaning does not consist in similarity.

6. (3) Many of the considerations that refuted the copy theory would here again be in order, but we will not repeat them. The reader may be surprised that such a writer as Mr. Russell should be unaware of such criticisms, or if aware, that he has not attempted to meet them. The fact is that he is aware of them, that he has tried to meet them, and that his writings in the days when he was occupied with these things indicate a gradual retreat. In a paper for the Aristotelian Society in 1919, Mr. Russell put the copy theory of meaning uncompromisingly: 'The "meaning" of images is the simplest kind of meaning because images resemble what they mean, whereas words, as a rule, do not', and 'thus the problem of the meaning of words is reduced to the problem of the meaning of images.'[1] This gives similarity a place of extreme importance. In the symposium on 'The Meaning of Meaning' at Oxford in 1920, when criticized by Dr. Schiller for his copyist predilec-

[1] 'On Propositions: What They Are and How They Mean', *Arist. Soc. Proc.*, Sup. Vol. II, 22.

tions he fell back wherever possible on the second view of meaning (likeness in causal efficacy).[1] In *The Analysis of Mind*, in which the Aristotelian Society paper is largely reproduced, such uncompromising sentences as the above have been omitted or toned down. The copy view is still clearly implied,[2] but there is so little desire to emphasize it that one almost has to hunt for it between the lines. Nor is his increasing shyness about this portion of his theory in the least surprising. How difficult it is even for a master fencer to defend it is shown in instructive fashion by his reply to Dr. Schiller at Oxford.

Against the resemblance theory of meaning, Dr. Schiller advanced three arguments. He contended (i) that if the image means the object through similarity, this 'incites to the inference that the more vivid the imagery, the clearer the meaning; but no such correlation can be observed. Meaning and image do not vary concomitantly, but rather inversely'. Mr. Russell has little difficulty in showing that this suggestion of an inverse variation carries the argument against him too far. 'Suppose you describe Niagara to two people who have never seen it, one a painter who translates all your words into images, the other a physicist whose thoughts are led by your description to geology and hydro-dynamical formulae. The above argument commits Dr. Schiller to the view that the physicist has a clearer apprehension of your meaning than the artist',[3] which appears untrue. This corrects an overstatement, but the thrust of Dr. Schiller's argument has still to be met. To develop this in our own way, we should say: if meaning were resemblance, then the clearer the image, the more evidently would it mean one particular object, whereas in fact it does not. If Mr. Russell replies that it does, he must also say some very strange things. He must say, for example, that when the artist thinks with full imagery of the falls of Zambesi, and the engineer with his

---

[1] *Mind*, XXIX. 398–404 (1920).

[2] As Bosanquet also interprets the theory. The intention is 'plain at once,' he thinks that in the chapter on memory 'the operative bond between content and object is similarity'.—*Three Chapters on the Nature of Mind*, 102. His discussion of 'The Russell Mind' has much of value.   [3] *Mind*, XXIX. 399 (1920).

meagre imagery thinks of Niagara, the artist's imagery means Niagara more clearly than the engineer's. But obviously it does not. The artist means the Zambesi, not Niagara; the engineer Niagara, not the Zambesi, and the thinness or fullness of their imagery cannot change this reference. Deny this, and you make intercourse impossible. For if one's image happens to be like the Zambesi more than like the Niagara, then for the time one cannot think of Niagara at all. One does not know what one means, and if one ever does, it is by accident. And that is absurd.

7. (4) Dr. Schiller advanced two other arguments, which may be taken together as showing that images vary independently of ideas, and hence cannot be as closely identified with them as Mr. Russell suggests. (ii) Mr. Russell's theory 'presupposes that all have mental images because they are essential to meaning, and no one can mean without them; yet it is admitted that empirically imagery is indiscoverable in many excellent reasoners, without damage or detriment to their meaning'.[1] Mr. Russell replies that originally images *were* necessary, but when they have been associated with words, those words can take their place in thinking. And when words do take their place, resemblance is no longer called for, since a word means its object through 'causal efficacy'. 'A word, through association, acquires the same causal efficacy as an image having the same meaning', and 'the essence of meaning lies in the causal efficacy of that which has meaning'.[2] To appraise this answer, we must know whether the second view of meaning, which here emerges, is sound or not. The same holds of the reply to Dr. Schiller's third argument.

(iii) The image theory 'would justify the deduction that the nature of the meaning must be profoundly affected by the nature of the imagery which conveys it; but no such influence can be traced. On the contrary, with the same meaning different

---

[1] *Mind*, XXIX. 393. For greater clarity I have changed the order in which the arguments are offered.   [2] *Mind*, XXIX. 398.

images may be conjoined, while different meanings may be conveyed by the same image'. Now so far as meaning consists in resemblance, which Mr. Russell says it often does, this reply is pertinent and indeed unanswerable. But a criticism that would be fatal to the view that images mean by resemblance would seem to lose its edge against the view that images mean through associates or effects. Mr. Russell accordingly falls back on this second view, with no further mention of resemblance. 'If the meaning of an image depends, as I maintain, upon its associations, it is clear that the meaning will be different to different people, or in one person at different times, if, as is to be presumed, the associations of the image are different on the two occasions.'[1] Undoubtedly, if the meaning of an image *does* depend wholly upon its associations. But we should not forget Mr. Russell's contention that sometimes it does not, but depends rather on resemblance;[2] and against this view of meaning Dr. Schiller's objections seem decisive.

8. (5) Both these views of the way in which images mean appear again in *The Analysis of Mind*. And irrespective of the truth of either, we may well ask whether it is likely that meaning consists in such extremely different things. I am thinking, let us suppose, of Niagara, and have in mind an image which is said to mean it. And of this meaning I can say that, however hard to catch and describe, it is a quite definite sort of thing, just as the reference to the past in memory and to the future in expectation are definite and definitely different, however hard it is to put the difference in words. With this in mind, we must meet these two proposals about the nature of meaning

---

[1] *Mind*, XXIX. 399.

[2] 'The meaning of words differs, as a rule, from that of images by depending upon association, not upon similarity.'—*Arist. Soc.* article, 19. When we have recalled accurately the looks of a room, 'for practical purposes we are justified in assuming that, in this case, our image resembled what the room was when we previously saw it. We may then say that our image "means" the room'.—*Ibid.*, 23.

as follows: Say if you will that meaning is resemblance. Or say if you will that it is the causal efficacy through which an image calls up the associations that an object would. But do not tell us that meaning is both, for the two are almost totally different. That the definite something I mean by meaning should *consist* now in one and now in the other of two relations that are as far apart as relations can be, is not really credible. One can hardly appeal to language, for the same word does at times stand for totally different things. The appeal is simply to what one means when one speaks of meaning something. And for my own part, though I find it extremely difficult to say what I do mean, I am clear that it is not *two* things as wide asunder as resemblance and causal efficacy. One or the other, possibly, but not both.

9. But does it really mean either? It is time we looked at Mr. Russell's second view, which is the one he stresses most. 'What is called an image "of" some definite object', say St. Paul's, 'has some of the effects which the object would have. This applies especially to the effects that depend upon association', but it applies also to effects in the way of feeling and outward behaviour. And this similarity in producing effects is what we mean by meaning. How will this serve?

Difficulties crowd in. (1) A moment ago, at Mr. Russell's suggestion, I did think of St. Paul's, but before the thought could sprout associates, it was cut off by my hearing footsteps outside my door. If meaning consists in giving rise to later associates, my image, so far as I can see, meant nothing. And this is incredible. When I mean something, does my image happen first, and its meaning arrive later? It seems to me quite clear that I can make a passing reference to St. Paul's, and that this reference is equally genuine whether it gives rise to a train of associates or not. Should I have meant St. Paul's more truly if I had gone on to think of Dean Inge, and then of his love of epigrams, and then, perhaps, of the epigrams of Martial? We may agree that my first image started off the train.

but surely not that it was meaningless until the train appeared. And how much of the train is needed? Would my image have meant St. Paul's more clearly if five steps rather than two were included within its 'causal efficacy'? These somewhat fantastic questions reflect their own character on the theory to which they are germane.

But that the image did not delay for its meaning until it had proved its causal efficacy can be shown by a consideration already used. We saw in discussing Professor Titchener's view that you cannot explain how one image calls up another if you take the first as quite meaningless. It is only because my image *already* meant St. Paul's that it could lead on to the thought of this cathedral's former Dean. If the image did not already mean St. Paul's, why should it call up the head of St. Paul's rather than the head of St. Peter's, or indeed anything rather than anything else? And if it did mean St. Paul's already, what becomes of the theory that meaning lies in causal efficacy? That efficacy is intelligible only if the theory is false.

10. (2) It is perfectly true, of course, that image and object often do give rise to similar thoughts and similar actions. But it is equally true that the image does not cease to mean the object when its effects begin to diverge from the object's effects. Sometimes that divergence is inevitable in the conditions under which the image appears. The effect upon a lover of his lass, one may perhaps assume, is gaiety, sprightliness and satisfaction. If he is where he can only think of her in absence, the effect of her image may well be melancholy and longing. Are we to say that because the image of her absent self produces such different effects it has so far ceased to mean her? On the contrary, it is because the lover's image continues to have the same meaning that his sighs are so frequent. Here the thought of the object, and the direct experience of it, produce effects that are very different, but the difference can be accounted for only if the object meant is the same.

11. (3) Let us suppose, however, that the two causal series are as like each other as possible. Would this resemblance make the image mean the object? To say yes is to go back to resemblance as the essential factor in meaning. And if meaning does not lie in the resemblance of image and object, we shall hardly expect to find it in a resemblance of what comes after them. For what it amounts to is this, that a train of associates resembles as a whole a certain train of outward occurrences, and hence the one train means the other. The sight of a dog arouses certain associates; the image of a dog arouses similar associates; the second series means the first through resembling it. But it is difficult to see how if resemblance falls short of meaning in a single image, it can suffice when applied to a succession. If resemblance is in principle an error, will not the second view share the fortunes of the first? Evidently it must. In defending his theory against Dr. Schiller, Mr. Russell held that criticisms which would be relevant against meaning as likeness were not relevant against meaning as causal efficacy. But if the doctrine of causal efficacy itself turns on likeness, as we now see that it does, this defence is no longer open. And the position is immensely weaker in consequence.

12. (4) But Mr. Russell has introduced in scattered passages some expressions that seem to modify his causal theory, and it may be said that if we take note of these, our difficulties will be lessened. For example, he raises the question what is meant by understanding a word, and answers, among other things, that you understand if, 'when you hear it you act *appropriately*' or 'associate' the word with another word (say in a different language) which has the *appropriate* effect on behaviour.[1] Little else is said on this matter of appropriateness,[2] but it is clear that if this idea is introduced into the theory of meaning, a new theory has replaced the old. For mere resemblance in effects will no longer constitute meaning; these effects must

---

[1] *Analysis*, 199–200; my italics.
[2] There are references to it on pp. 255, 259, 261, 278, 293.

be appropriate to the object, i.e., apparently they must fulfil some purpose or desire that we entertain in regard to it. Does this amendment help?

Unfortunately, no. Several of the defects that we have just found in the unamended form break out again in this one. We would point especially to the old *hysteron proteron* that dogs the heels of every causal and pragmatic theory of the idea. The word or image is to cause behaviour appropriate to some object; through causing this it means that object. But it does seem a little miraculous that a word or image which means nothing at all should have this special and gratifying result. Why my thought of something should help me to act appropriately toward it if it had no reference to this whatever before the behaviour supervened, is very hard to see. Surely, it is because I can think of it before I adjust myself that I succeed in adjusting myself at all; the thought conditions the adjustment, not the adjustment the thought. And the view has difficulties of its own which we can see to better advantage when we turn to the pragmatic theory of ideas, difficulties which chiefly arise from confusing such different processes as meaning an object and seeking a practical end. One remark here must suffice. When one grasps the meaning of the words 'St. Paul's', what is the 'appropriate behaviour' whose production is to form the meaning? I am thinking of St. Paul's at this moment, yet my behaviour, namely scribbling, does not seem remarkably appropriate. Suppose no discoverable behaviour at all is induced by words or image; would they then be meaningless? No. We are aware that there are many in these days who would resolve thought away into behaviour. But this reduction is far from obvious, far less obvious, for example, than the fact that men sometimes think in immobility and silence. And if they have ever succeeded in doing so, causing appropriate action is not the essence of meaning.

13. (II) It will be recalled that we distinguished three factors in thought as Mr. Russell conceives it, (*a*) a feeling of belief directed upon (b) a proposition, which (c) means its object through resemblance or causal efficacy. We have so far fixed our attention on the third element, or meaning, as the heart of the theory. What of the other two factors? Let us look first at 'propositions'.

A proposition as 'the content of a belief may consist of words only, or of images only, or of a mixture of the two, or of either or both together with one or more sensations';[1] what we believe is always a complex, of one or other of these types. The simplest of them is the image-proposition. If I think of a familiar room in which the window is to the left of the door, 'the image-memory consists of the image of the window to the left of the image of the door'.[2] And the resemblance between proposition and objective is 'the correspondence which constitutes truth';[3] 'we can say that true propositions actually resemble their objectives in a way in which false propositions do not'.[4] Propositions composed of words may be dealt with similarly. 'The meaning of a proposition (which apparently here means 'what is meant') is derivative from the meanings of the constituent words';[5] hence, 'for example, if the proposition is "Socrates preceded Plato" the objective which verifies it results from replacing the word "Socrates" by Socrates, and the word "Plato" by Plato, and the word "precedes" by the relation of preceding between Socrates and Plato. If the result of this process is fact, the proposition is true; if not, it is false. . . . More complicated propositions can be dealt with on the same lines.'[6] Such propositions are what we believe when the objective of the belief is something not given in sense. When the objective is so given, actual sensations, as well as words and images, may enter into the proposition. Thus 'when you hear a noise and say "tram", the noise enters into both the belief and its objective'.[7] Your proposition consists of a noise and a word, related in a certain way; the objective consists of the same noise and what the word means, namely the tram, related in a corresponding way. What you believe, however, is never,

[1] *Analysis*, 236.   [2] *Ibid.*, 274.   [3] *Ibid.*, 274.
[4] *Ibid.*, 273.   [5] *Ibid.*, 273.   [6] *Ibid.*, 278.   [7] *Ibid.*, 239.

as a whole, a fact; it is a proposition, whose correspondence with the fact is truth, and whose failure to correspond is falsehood.

Mr. Russell does not claim that the theory here imperfectly sketched is wholly adequate,[1] but considers it true so far as it goes. Even this, I think, is too favourable a judgement, for it is difficult to exhaust the ambiguities, conflicts with fact, and contradictions with itself, which seem to appear in it on reflection. Let me list rapidly some of the more striking of these.

14. (1) It is hard to credit that what we believe is ever a proposition as Mr. Russell defines it. The proposition 'Socrates precedes Plato' is said to consist of a set of words, and to the person who makes the assertion, a word is 'a series of movements of the mouth'. Thus what he believes is his own mouth-movements. I cannot persuade myself that there is any truth in this. If I were to express my belief in another language, the proposition as a set of vocalized words would be different, but will it not be admitted that what I believe is, or may be, the same? If so, what I believe is not a proposition. Nor is the matter much improved if the propositions are composed, not of words, but of images. Mr. Russell does not hesitate to use such expressions as 'I remember the content "eating my breakfast" ',[2] where the content means a set of images occurring at the present moment in my head. But if what I remember is only a set of present images, it is hard to see that I am remembering the past at all. To add that I have a feeling of pastness makes no difference in principle. One would have thought all this had been settled by the historic criticisms passed on Hume.

15. (2) The possession of meaning by images, we shall recall, was defined as a relation of resemblance to objects.

[1] *Analysis*, 278.   [2] *Ibid.*, 251.

Their *truth*, we now learn, is defined in precisely the same way. It follows that their truth and their meaning are the same thing; and from this it follows again that an image-proposition which is false must also be meaningless. But false beliefs have as much 'causal efficacy' as true ones, and so far they are declared to be meaningful. Thus false propositions both do and do not have meaning. The theory contradicts itself.

What is true or false, according to the theory, is always propositions,[1] which are complexes of terms.[2] The meaning of a proposition is to be derived from the meaning of its parts, which, in the case of an image-proposition, would consist of constituent images. These constituent images are not singly either true or false; it is only complexes of them that are so. Yet they are stated to have meaning; and this meaning is stated to consist in their resemblance to particular objects. But that is what truth consists in. The constituent images themselves therefore *are* true or false. What is true or false, then, is not only propositions. The theory contradicts itself again.

16. (3) The position of relations is left most obscure. The image-proposition consists of particular images related in a certain way; for example, 'in the image the window is to the left of the door'.[3] Such language implies that just as the imagined terms are distinct from their objectives and resemble them, so the imagined relation is distinct from the objective relation and resembles it. It is true that this gives rise to extraordinary difficulties which Mr. Russell does not touch. For whether there is actually in my head an image which could be broken up into parts, right and left, east and west, of each other, seems extremely questionable. Still, the theory pretty clearly involves it. Nevertheless, with this notion of subjective images and relations well in mind, we are met by the state-

---

[1] 'A proposition may be defined as: *What we believe when we believe truly or falsely.*' *Arist. Soc.*, Sup. Vol. II, p. 1.

[2] *Analysis*, 236.   [3] *Ibid.*, 274.

ment that when the above image-proposition is true, 'the very same relation relates the terms of the objective (namely, the window and the door) as relates the images which mean them'.[1] And when Mr. Russell says 'the very same' he presumably means it, since he has forcibly advocated the view that relations have no instances, that a given relation is simply self-identical wherever it appears.[2] The spatial relation in the image is thus not a copy of the outer relation but identical with it. It follows that if the window in reality is ten feet to the left of the door, then similarly in the image in my head the part that pictures the window is ten feet to the left of the part that pictures the door. On this point the most experienced judges are hatmakers, and it is to be doubted if they would assent.

In the case of word-propositions, this difficulty at first seems less acute. When I say 'Socrates precedes Plato', neither the temporal relation itself nor an image of it need be present; 'precedes' must mean this relation just as the two terms mean their own particular objectives. But when the word 'precedes' is said to mean relation, 'means' seems to have acquired a new significance. It does not mean 'directly resemble'; it must therefore mean 'resemble in causal efficacy'. Hence when we say that 'precedes' means the relation of preceding, we mean that the utterance of these syllables produces effects in the way of association or action similar to those produced by the actual relation of precedence that held between Socrates and Plato. And this makes nonsense. Otherwise the word 'means' is being used here in a sense for which the theory does not provide.

17. (4) This vacillation in the account of how words mean is paralleled in the account of *what* they mean. When we say 'Socrates precedes Plato', each word, we are told, means an objective in the real world. But remembering his doctrine that images are a more primitive kind of idea than words, for which

[1] *Analysis*, 274.   [2] *Principles of Mathematics*, Sec. 5.

words are only an acquired substitute, Mr. Russell, in his chapter on 'Words and Meaning', produces another theory. When a person 'is genuinely remembering, he has a picture of the past occurrence, and his words are chosen so as to describe the picture'; it is 'the possibility of a memory-image that makes the essence of the narrative "meaning" of words. In so far as this is absent the words are mere counters, capable of meaning, but not at the moment possessing it'.[1] This doctrine that what words mean in narrative is images, without which they have no meaning at all, seems clearly inconsistent with the doctrine just cited, that what they mean is objectives in the real world. Is the new one an improvement? The doctrine has been examined by Professor Joachim, who did not fail to draw the incredible but inevitable conclusion. 'When he says "Antony loved Cleopatra", he means—or at least the word-proposition means—that an Image loved an Image. It describes the unholy passion of one event inside his skin for another. . . It "means" that two "purely mental" entities were —or are—consumed with lust for one another.'[2] No further comment seems called for.

18. (5) Even, however, if this theory is regarded as (what it probably is) a mere aberration from the main doctrine, the way of arriving at what propositions mean is impracticable. To arrive at what is meant by 'Antony loved Cleopatra', Mr. Russell would apparently split up the proposition into words, find what each means in isolation, and take the resulting collection of facts as the objective of the proposition. Now most persons would say that if a foreigner wished to understand a sentence of Shakespeare, he would hardly arrive at what it means by substituting for the several words a collection of dictionary definitions. For such definitions taken in isolation

[1] *Analysis*, 201.

[2] *Mind*, N.S., XXIX. (1920), 412. For any such theory Professor Joachim's ten pages are charged with destruction. Most of his criticism of the Article still holds against the *Analysis*. To answer it, the theory would, I believe, have to be reconstructed from its foundations.

are rigid, unmodifiable blocks, whereas in actual thought what each word means is shaped and coloured by its context. The same is true of objectives and their parts. The relation meant by 'loved' in 'Antony loved Cleopatra' is not to be arrived at by defining 'love' in abstraction from the lovers who feel it, for the relation in this case takes its special character from the terms or persons it unites. It is not precisely the same relation that is meant in 'Darby loved Joan' or in 'Damon loved Pythias'. What is meant by a proposition is therefore not to be reached by regarding it as a collection of atomic particulars each standing by itself for a like particular. A proposition as a whole may stand for another whole; but neither of the one whole nor the other can it be safely assumed that the parts are little hard blocks which can enter unaffected into all manner of combinations. This is an old point and a good one; unfortunately to develop it fully would call for an examination of the atomic logic in general.

19. (6) The truth of a proposition is said to consist in correspondence with its objective. What does 'correspondence' mean? In the case of images we are told it means similiarity; what does it mean in the case of words? Since words ordinarily have not the slightest likeness to what they mean, truth must here mean correspondence of an extremely different kind. Now it is hard to believe that truth consists in extremely different things in extremely similar cases. It is hard to believe that if I think 'Antony loved Cleopatra' with the help of an image, and five minutes later without an image, the two assertions are true only in widely different senses. Should the person who accepted the first reserve judgement as to both the meaning and truth of the second until he knew whether I was using images, and having found that I was not, insist that my second assertion not only differed in meaning, but was true in a different sense? What the truth of a proposition consists in is of course no easy thing to discover; but whatever it is, we can scarcely believe that its nature is transmuted when we begin to talk rather faster, and hence lack time for the play of imagery.

20. (7) In view of these different notions of truth implied in his theory, one feels it very cheerful of Mr. Russell to say 'that the purely formal definition of truth and falsehood offers little difficulty'. This definition he proceeds to supply: 'a proposition is true when it points towards its objective, and false when it points away from it'.[1] But this is the language of metaphor. What does 'pointing' mean? In the case of images it means resembling; in the case of word-propositions, the relation by which words mean their objectives, which must be 'causal efficacy'. Both definitions lead at once to contradiction. If the truth of an image-proposition consists in resemblance to its objective, its untruth must consist in the absence of resemblance, i.e. in the absence of any fact which does resemble it. But the absence of such a fact means that the image has no objective, since such resemblance is what having an objective means. Yet Mr. Russell now defines an image as false when 'it points away from its objective', as if a false image had an objective to point away from. Thus the false proposition both has and has not an objective. Similarly of word-propositions. These are true if there is an 'objective which would verify our proposition',[2] false if there is not. Falsity apparently means having no objective, but it also means having an objective and pointing away from it, a phrase I will not attempt to construe.

21. (8) It is not only in false propositions that the absence of an objective leads to trouble, but also in every variety of imaginative discourse. When one forms the image of a character in fiction, there is nothing corresponding to it in that world of 'fact' which Mr. Russell's objectives inhabit. It therefore has no objective and cannot mean anything, not even if by 'meaning'

---

[1] *Analysis*, 273.　　　　　　　　　　　　　　　[2] *Ibid.*, 278.

you mean producing similar effects, since the objective has never existed to have effects. On this theory Bosanquet comments: 'Surely this is a fundamental error. . . Hamlet is an object of thought with his place in the universe, referred to by help of our infinitely varying mental images just as is Alexander the Great. Who thinks of Gurth as a mental image?'[1] It is certainly hard to believe that when we 'think of' Hamlet we are either not thinking of anything, or else thinking of an event going on in our heads. We seem to be remembering something distinct from our mental image in precisely the same way as when we mean an historical fact. Mr. Russell's theory does not account for this, for it requires him to say that, in this sense, we mean nothing at all.

Only a few of the more obvious criticisms have been mentioned, and it would not be difficult to continue. But perhaps enough has been said to show that the part played by propositions in Mr. Russell's theory of thought is a very questionable one.

22. (III) Over the third factor in Mr. Russell's analysis of an act of thought, namely the feeling of belief, we shall follow his example and spend little time. There is no attempt in his book to analyse it; he is not sure that it is capable of analysis. What he does think clear about it is that it is a 'feeling or complex of sensations',[2] that variations in this feeling, rather than any variations in content, are what distinguishes memory from assent and expectation,[3] and that it distinguishes all of them from mere imagination by making an image point to an objective beyond itself.[4]

I do not think it possible to arrive, on these lines, at anything like a satisfactory theory of belief. The reason may be given in a word; the theory makes belief too adventitious to its content. You have in mind, let us say, an image of the Statue of Liberty which at first is merely entertained; then,

---

[1] *Three Chapters on the Nature of Mind*, 132.
[2] *Analysis*, 250.   [3] *Ibid.*, 176, 250.   [4] *Ibid.*, 176, 179.

while this content remains precisely the same, you direct upon it a feeling of familiarity and pastness, and it becomes a memory; add to it a slightly different feeling and it becomes an expectation of seeing the statue. But belief is not something that can be tacked on and removed in this arbitrary fashion. Indeed there is part of this very account that implies as much. For if belief is really that which confers meaning upon a content, which makes it point to something as existing in the real world, then far from being a set of feelings that may be added to and subtracted from words and images, it is something vital to every variety of thought and virtually coextensive with mind itself. It is present in the animal mind from the first appearance of perception; for perception, as we have seen, implies judgement, and judgement is always a taking of something as belonging to the real world. Nor is it absent even in what is supposed to be bare contemplation or imagining, for here too there is a placing of something in reality. When we cease to believe in Hamlet as a historical character and think of him as belonging only in the world of fiction, does belief regarding him suddenly vanish, to be replaced by bare contemplation? or is not the truth rather this, that belief is still there unchanged, but that *what* we believe is altered? Our belief that he belonged to the world of physical fact is replaced by the belief that he belongs in the world of fiction; and this world too, however hard to place properly, falls somewhere within reality; if not, where else? History is not mere fantasy plus belief, for in fantasy belief is already present. Thus, if belief is really that which gives mind its reference to reality, it is no adventitious supplement to words and images but pervasive of the whole field where intelligence is at work.

23. One is reluctant to resolve a criticism of Mr. Russell's theory into a mere rejection *in toto*; that does not express (to borrow this much from him) one's 'belief-feeling' about it. Whatever Mr. Russell writes is notable, and of course much might be said in different vein about *The Analysis of Mind.*

It gives some examples of obedience to its own injunction, 'we must not falsify observation to avoid theoretical difficulties';[1] it is extraordinarily alive and generous to certain movements of thought, particularly of American thought, whose worth is too little known; its style, like J. S. Mill's, has that graceful lucidity that guarantees a wide hearing, even while it eases the task of criticism.[2] But if one may say so, this subject, if dealt with at all, should have been handled in far more guarded a fashion. In reading Mr. Russell's views on images and association, one has the sense that this sort of thing has been done before, and that if it is to appear so late in the day, it should show the results of intervening experience. If a philosopher proposes to restore large blocks of Locke and Hume, it should be with the amendments that later criticisms have rendered necessary. Such writers as Green and Bradley have subjected this type of psychology to exhaustive study; but, as Professor Joachim remarked, we are left quite in the dark as to how Mr. Russell would meet their criticisms. 'The criticisms, it is true, were published long ago; but the fact that they are familiar and even classical, and that nobody has ever succeeded in answering them, does not in the least diminish their force.'[3]

The fact is that in an inquiry about ideas, Mr. Russell's theory is better to start from than to end with, for it is pieced together from a great many theories, each of which, in the mind of another school, stands as a key to the theory of ideas. He makes words one of the two main instruments in thinking; the behaviourists leave out one of these and make ideas a matter of words exclusively. He suggests the view that thinking of an object means acting appropriately towards it, a view which carries us into the precincts of pragmatism. His theory of images, as we have seen, has strong affinities with the theories of Locke and Hume, and again, of Professor Titchener. The

---

[1] P. 164.

[2] If only Bosanquet had a trace of this! His elaborate criticism of Russell in *Three Chapters on the Nature of Mind* seems almost always right where one can be certain of its meaning, but it is handicapped from the outset by the painful contrast in clearness between itself and what it criticizes.   [3] Joachim, *Mind*, XXIX. 410.

view that meaning consists essentially in causality has been adopted as the central doctrine of Messrs. Ogden and Richards's work on *The Meaning of Meaning*. The theory that things and ideas are really of the same stuff, and that at least in perception acts of consciousness can be dispensed with, carries us to the 'radical empiricism' of James and the neo-realism of some of his followers. The theory that what the mind directly engages in thinking is not things but propositions takes us to the cardinal view of Brentano, Meinong, and Husserl, and by a slightly longer route, to the American critical realists. Again, in reducing things to sensations, and sensations to the stuff of which images are made, Mr. Russell moves, in this work, in the direction of idealism. His theory is thus an admirable link between old and new. In part it is a revival of Locke and Hume, but it is also an introduction to every theory of first importance now held regarding the nature of ideas. The main principles of these various schools are neither so numerous nor so unrelated as they at first appear, and if we confine ourselves to the single point of the nature of an idea, to review them is not, perhaps, impossible. At any rate this review will be attempted in the chapters that follow.

24. Before proceeding we should perhaps glance at a view just mentioned, which has certain marked affinities with Mr. Russell's theory, namely, that of Messrs. Ogden and Richards in *The Meaning of Meaning*. Their theory is not very fully elaborated; and as they are suspicious of philosophers and all their ways, and approach the problem through the study of language, they have neither expressed themselves nor guarded themselves as the true philosopher would desire. But their book is both ambitious and erudite.

They attempt to supply 'an account of thinking in purely causal terms',[1] to show that 'thinking or reference is reducible to causal relations'.[2] To use a favourite example of theirs,

---

[1] *Meaning of Meaning*, 50 (fourth edition, 1936).   [2] *Ibid.*, 73.

suppose I strike a match and expect a flame. To expect the flame explicitly is to think of it, and what does such thinking mean? They are clear that it does not mean having an image, since even if the image is present, the same problem breaks out again. The image means the object, and what we want to know is what 'meaning' or 'referring' is. The clue to our authors' answer lies in their notion of a 'context'. This notion plays in their psychology the part that an 'association cluster' did in the psychology of another day. According to this older psychology, ideas might become so associated that one invariably 'called up' the others of the group, and this stood for them, or 'meant' them. But Messrs. Ogden and Richards prefer to replace ideas by physical events, and 'clusters' by groups of these. 'To be directly apprehended is to cause certain happenings in the nerves, as to which at present neurologists go no further than to assert that they occur. Thus what is directly apprehended is a modification of a sense organ, and its apprehension is a further modification of the nervous system, about which we may expect information at some future date.'[1] Now the movements by which we strike a match, the hearing of the scrape, and the seeing of the flame, form a series of events which repeatedly happen together, and which have thus established connection in the nervous system. So that when we now start to strike a match, 'the excitation which results is different from what it would be had we never struck matches before. Past strikings have left, in our organization, engrams, residual traces, which help to determine what the mental process will be.'[2] It is the presence of these traces that lead us to expect the flame. And what is the expectation itself? 'The expectation is the excitation of part of an engram complex which is called up by a stimulus (the scrape) similar to a part only of the original stimulus-situation.'[3] And when we say that our expectation is 'directed to' the flame, 'directed to' stands for nothing more than 'similar *to what has been caused by*'. 'A thought is directed to flame when it is similar in certain respects to thoughts which have been caused by

[1] *Meaning of Meaning*, 81.   [2] *Ibid.*, 52.   [3] *Ibid.*

flame.'[1] Nor need there be any mystery about the meaning of cause. Two events are cause and effect when they are 'uniformly linked' so as to form a 'recurrent context', that is, when one regularly follows the other.

Now it is true that philosophers cut a sorry figure when critics collate and parade, as Messrs. Ogden and Richards do, the senses in which they have used the unfortunate word 'meaning'. But this is due, in part, to the fact that philosophers are dealing with a psychological and metaphysical problem of enormous difficulty; and they are perhaps not likely to be at once convinced by a theory which, in spite of our authors' depreciation of philosophy, is plainly another philosophical theory, less guardedly defended than some of its predecessors.

25. Let us look at the central doctrine. The expectation of a future event is defined as the excitation of a trace, an excitation similar to what such events have caused in the past. So far as this means that present thought depends upon past experience, that if nothing like a match or flame had ever acted upon us, we could not form the idea of it, we need not call it in question. Unless causes did work upon us, we should have no thought of these causes. Probably everyone will admit this. But to say that the thought of a thing is identical with its effect upon us, or is to be defined from its likeness to that effect, is to say something that is very different and very mistaken. I add a few reasons for thinking so.

(1) A thing's effects upon us may be many. Our usual reaction to the loud report of a gun may be to hear a sound, to start, turn pale, clench our fists, and do various other things. The present thought of the report is to consist of a reaction 'similar to what has been caused by' it. But *which* of its numerous effects is to be selected as essential? To say that our thought consists in all of them would be absurd, since we can obviously think of the gun's going off without behaving in all these ways. But if we make a selection from among them,

---

[1] *Meaning of Meaning*, 54.

we abandon the main principle. For it will not now be in virtue of being caused by the report that an event will be the thought of it, but in virtue of something else. And this something else will hold the essential difference.

26. (2) So far as our authors do specify the kind of effect they have in mind, the light we get is not refulgent. What is suggested is that if we saw the truth of the matter, we should perceive a thought to be 'a modification of the nervous system'.[1] Now whether it is plausible to hope that thinking can be reduced to nervous change we shall discuss in treating behaviourism, with which the present doctrine has something in common. But in the present stage of our knowledge, it is no help whatever to be told that thinking and nervous process are the same. A blow below the knee-cap may produce simultaneously a thought of the blow and the nervous process involved in a 'knee-jerk'. To say that these are fundamentally the same kind of thing is, for our present knowledge, like saying that red is fundamentally green. The statement is either nonsense, mysticism, or both. No one really means by his 'thought of an object' a nervous change. No one has the faintest notion of how such reduction could be effected. To our present knowledge, there are no two things in the world more radically disparate. Thus, to say that our thought of an object *is* an excitation of a nervous trace, if meant as a statement of present knowledge, is false, and if meant as what would seem to be true in the end, is at the best a pious wish. In neither case does it throw light upon what thinking distinctively is.

27. (3) When it is said that my thought of an object is a reaction similar to what has been caused by it before, the implication is that objects do in the first instance act on me

---

[1] The authors remark with regard to the nature of general ideas that 'much may be expected when the theory of the conditional reflex, due to Pavlov, has been further developed'. 66.

causally. And this can be maintained with some colour of truth so long as the objects meant are things that can collide with my organism, or cause some medium to do so. But the plausibility disappears when one considers objects that could not collide and could not conceivably be given in sense. Our authors have not, I think, adequately dealt with a point made long ago by Royce; 'It is hopeless, then, to persist in the hypothesis that the object of an idea is as such the cause of the idea. Were one to persist in such a view, what would he say about mathematical objects? Does the binomial theorem act as a seal, or any other sort of cause, impressing its image on the wax of the mathematician's mind? Do the properties of equations do anything to the mathematician when he thinks of them? Is not all the fresh creative activity in this case his own?'[1]

28. (4) But let us pass from the theory's emphasis on bodily reactions and assume that the thought of the object is taken as a physical event. Does being directed to an object mean 'nothing more than similar to what has been caused by it'? What has been caused by matches' bursting into flame is that we have had sensations of light and perhaps heat. Our present expectation or thought of the flame should therefore be like these sensations. Is it? If we hold that a thought is an image, we could maintain this with some plausibility, but our authors specifically deny that imagery need be present.[2] And if it is not present, their position becomes exceedingly obscure. For if the present thought is directed to the flame only so far as, without help from imagery, it resembles previous sensations of light and heat, it is difficult to see how it can mean flame at all. If there are no sensations of the flame present, if there are no images of it present, where is the resemblance on which the meaning turns?

[1] *The World and the Individual*, I. 316.
[2] *Meaning of Meaning*, 61.

29. (5) And similarity is a matter of degree while meaning is not. One thing is more or less like another, but how can I more or less mean a gunshot or a flame? A particular thought either means a certain object or does not. It cannot be said to mean the object more, or to be more directed to it, in the degree to which it resembles previous effects of this object. Yet this appears to be what the theory entails.

30. (6) If the theory is true, it would seem that the mental or nervous process should mean an object more specifically, the more simply and firmly the two are united by the causal tie. If, a thousand times in succession when the dinner bell rings, I have entered the dining-room and found food, the connection between bell and food will have become so close as to provide, on the theory, an almost perfect example of definite thought-reference.[1] A context has been formed in which the events are knit together with a maximum of firmness and a minimum of variation and irrelevance; the sound of the bell uniformly starts processes which end in the partaking of food. Can it be said that the processes aroused therefore *mean* the food more specifically? I do not think so. The more fixed the causal 'context' becomes, the more automatic it becomes, until explicit thought vanishes into habit. And again our authors appear to be in a dilemma. If they continue to hold that 'thinking or reference is reducible to causal relations', they should have in mere habit an example *par excellence* of the thought process—and such a conclusion is a paradox which must make seriously against them, unless indeed they mean frankly to embrace behaviourism. If, on the other hand, they say that thinking is not a matter of habitual response, but of mental reference, then I think the causal theory is doomed. For there is no reason whatever to believe that my mental reference depends upon recurrent association with its object. My thought of the food may be just as clear, unambiguous

---

[1] *Meaning of Meaning*, 56. I take as subject a man, not a dog as the authors do, to suit the needs of the argument.

and specific on the second occasion of hearing the bell as on the thousandth. Fixity in causal connection has little if anything to do with the relation of thought and its object.

Although we have been chiefly concerned in this chapter with theories of the idea as image, we have repeatedly been meeting suggestions that thinking may go on without images and in purely bodily terms. Both Mr. Russell and Messrs. Ogden and Richards hold language that shows strong sympathies with this theory; and even Professor Titchener has a passage in which he argues that 'the pointing-relation . . . is not uniquely an affair of mind' but has various physical analogues that approximate it closely.[1] It is time to inquire whether there is good reason for these sympathies, and to ask what light, if any, behaviourism has to throw upon the nature of thought.

[1] *Exp. Psych. of the Thought Processes*, 66–72.

CHAPTER IX

BEHAVIOURISM AND THOUGHT

1. Behaviourism is the theory that the mind may be adequately studied in the reactions of the body. It does not profess to be a metaphysic or a theory of knowledge; it commonly professes to eschew philosophical theories of every kind, and to offer only a method of psychological study. If therefore we are to criticize it from a philosophical point of view, as we propose to do, some justification seems called for.

The justification is this, that if an instrument for the study of mind is to be adequate, it must be adapted to what it studies; that behaviourism supplies an instrument adapted to bodily responses alone; that its claim to adequacy hence presupposes that mind *consists of* bodily responses; and that this, beyond any question, *is* a philosophical theory. One cannot settle the method of studying a thing without some notion of what the thing is, and a wrong notion may produce a wrong method. It is thus idle for behaviourism, or indeed any other form of psychology, to profess indifference to philosophy. What such professions commonly mean is not that philosophy is excluded, which is pretty clearly impossible, but that it is admitted unawares in large and dogmatic doses.

Our discussion will take the following order: First we shall try to get clear what behaviourism is, in the light of the factors that produced it. We shall then offer some criticisms of the doctrine in its most familiar psychological form. Finally we shall examine the speculative theory on which, however unwittingly, it rests.

2. Behaviourism sprang from two chief sources, a disillusionment with introspection as a means for studying the human mind, and the reassuring success of an opposite method of studying the animal mind.

The systems of psychology that held the field at the beginning of the century, the systems of Wundt, James, Titchener, Ward, and Stout, all used introspection as their chief instrument, though indeed not their only one. These men were all of them serious and capable investigators, who, conceiving psychology as a science, rather than as a branch of speculative philosophy, did their best to systematize the laws of mental phenomena. What was the result? According to the behaviourist, general failure, indeed mere wind and nothingness; nor, in view of their method, could it well be otherwise. 'In all other sciences the facts of observation are objective, verifiable, and can be reproduced and controlled by all trained observers.'[1] In psychology as the science of consciousness none of these features is to be found. Dealing with what cannot be seen or handled, weighed or measured, it becomes incapable of quantitative statement, and therefore of any exact laws. And even if some investigator were to find such a law, no one else could ever verify it, for one's consciousness remains inaccessible to all but oneself. 'As a result of this major assumption that there is such a thing as consciousness and that we can analyse it by introspection, we find as many analyses as there are individual psychologists. There is no way of experimentally attacking and solving psychological problems and standardizing methods'.[2] In such a science there is no 'community of data'; 'the psychology begun by Wundt has thus failed to become a science', and Dr. Watson goes on to say that it 'has still more deplorably failed in contributing anything of a scientifically usable kind. . . .'[3] To him the elaborate analyses of sensations so patiently carried out by Titchener, the endless dreary pages produced by the Würzburg school on imageless thought, and McDougall's long-continued effort to build a psychology on the basis of purpose rather than of mechanical law—to Dr. Watson these things were too arid and speculative to be longer

---

[1] J. B. Watson, *Psychology from the Standpoint of a Behaviourist*, third ed., 1929, 1.

[2] Watson, *Behaviourism* (1924), 6.

[3] *Psych. from St. of a Beh.*, 3.

endured. 'In 1912 the behaviourists reached the conclusion that they could no longer be content to work with intangibles and unapproachables. They decided either to give up psychology or else make it a natural science.'[1] But natural science studies what is public, physical, and quantitative; consciousness is apparently private, non-physical, and non-quantitative. To make their study truly a natural science they must therefore abandon consciousness as its subject-matter. But was such a step possible? Could there be a science of mind with consciousness left out?

3. As if to supply to this question a reassuring and timely answer, the second factor in the rise of behaviourism now appeared. This was the achievement of a surprising success in applying to the animal mind those methods of physical science which the behaviourists dreamed of applying to the human mind. Earlier animal psychology had been for the most part a collection of anecdotes, with very little experimentation and with loose standards of reporting. It had been assumed that the inaccessibility of the animal mind, far greater even than that of the human, made exact understanding impossible. But indirectly it proved a boon. For it forced students to exploit the more thoroughly the animal's outward behaviour; and this they did with great success. The most thorough student was Pavlov, but news of his St. Petersburg experiments reached this country pretty slowly, and apart from the one great debt of the 'conditioned reflex' method,[2] the American school seems to owe him little. More immediately telling was the work of Thorndike, whose experiments on animal learning began while he was a student under James. In his classic experiment of putting a hungry cat in a cage and studying its ways and means of escape, he gave up all attempt to read the cat's behaviour in terms of want or purpose. He assumed that for a physical response there was a physical stimulus, and he set out to discover how a given response could attach itself to new stimuli,

[1] *Behaviourism*, 6.   [2] *Psych. from St. of a Beh.*, xi.

and a stimulus to new responses, until he had elaborated a complete theory of how animals could acquire their complicated and apparently intelligent ways of acting. This theory he carried over and applied in his massive *Educational Psychology* to human learning as well. Thorndike, it is true, has never been a behaviourist. He has held that in order to explain the 'stamping in' of a certain response as a habit, and the dropping out of others, the *feelings* of pleasure and pain must be taken into account. Here Watson differed; he thought he could get on without these; frequency and recency would serve by themselves. With this conviction came the prospect of an animal psychology systematic and complete, yet with consciousness nowhere entering.

4. The behaviourism that came later is 'the direct outgrowth', its author says, 'of work on animal behaviour'.[1] Already in 1903, when he published an account of the learning process in rats, the idea was present that animal and human psychology might profitably follow the same lines. He began a lengthy series of experiments on the learning process in infants; these experiments seemed to the eager iconoclast to offer confirmation; and in 1913 appeared the first published statement of a new programme, an article on 'Psychology from the Standpoint of a Behaviourist' in the *Philosophical Review*. Six years later followed his chief work, bearing the same title. The preface announced that 'the reader will find no discussion of consciousness and no reference to such terms as sensation, perception, attention, will, image, and the like. . . . I have found that I can get along without them. . . .'[2]

Dr. Watson's view of consciousness has undergone a gradual change. He did not at first deny its existence; his view was the less radical one that since it could not be scientifically dealt with, it had best be disregarded. But his language soon became stronger. If the behaviourist disregards consciousness, he said, it is in the same way in which the chemist disregards alchemy

---

[1] *Psych. from St. of a Beh.*, xi.   [2] *Ibid.*, xii.

and the astronomer astrology. This sounded ominous. It sounded as if the traditional psychology were not merely unscientific, but a monger of mythologies. Dr. Watson was pressed to say more plainly if he meant this. And becoming confident with the accession of adherents, he said at last uncompromisingly that it was. The 'consciousness' that psychology has been studying has no distinct existence. 'If behaviourism is ever to stand for anything (even a distinct method) it must make a clean break with the whole concept of consciousness.' 'It has never been seen, touched, smelled, tasted, or moved. It is a plain assumption, just as unprovable as the old concept of the soul.'[1] 'The behaviourist cannot find consciousness in the test-tube of his science. He finds no evidence anywhere for a stream of consciousness, not even for one so convincing as that described by William James.'[2] 'We need nothing to explain behaviour but the ordinary laws of physics and chemistry.'[3]

5. It follows, of course, that thought, which is one form of consciousness, is also a product of myth-making. Ideas do not exist. Yet obviously when men have talked about thought, they have not been talking about nothing at all; there would seem to be some activity that differentiates a philosopher from a poet, or a philosopher awake from a philosopher asleep. This activity, if it is to be an object of natural science, must be a movement of physical organs. *What* movement is this? In the answer to this question behaviourism comes nearest to striking an original note. 'The behaviourist advances the view that what the psychologists have hitherto called thought is in short nothing but talking to ourselves';[4] 'thinking is merely talking, but talking with concealed musculature'.[5]

Dr. Watson usually defends this thesis by recalling how language habits arise. A child is handed a box, at the same time

[1] *The Battle of Behaviourism*, 15.   [2] *Ibid.*, 27-8.
[3] *Ibid.*, 27.   [4] *Behaviourism*, 191.
[5] *The Battle of Behaviourism*, 35.

hearing the word 'box' spoken. This is repeated until the sight of the box becomes a condition calling out the word 'box' from himself. But then 'there comes an occasion when the box can be seen but not reached. Action in the hand is blocked. He speaks "box" and may speak it persistently all over the house. . . . There has been a substitution of the language habit for a bodily habit. . . .'[1] Now if this language habit were exercised aloud whenever the child were so disposed, he would be a nuisance. He gradually learns therefore to inhibit talking aloud, and to speak sub-vocally or under his breath. But just as the talking aloud was a substitute for handling the object, so this silent speech is a substitute for talking aloud. In a great many persons, this process is still observable; when they are by themselves, or reading, their lips move, and a good lip reader can thus see them 'thinking' and even follow their train of 'ideas'. And if this cannot be done with most of us, it is merely because another substitution has taken place, which buries the movements deeper. For the more 'explicit' language habits we are substituting concealed or 'implicit' ones. Behind our closed lips there are still movements of tongue or larynx that could be registered and measured if one only had instruments fine enough. *And these purely physical movements constitute our thinking.* 'Thinking with us is sub-vocal talking';[2] 'thought is the action of language mechanisms.'[3] But Dr. Watson recognizes that a still further substitution is possible. Other physical reactions may come to stand for words or to replace them. Thus to the question whether all thinking goes on in words, he answers, 'Yes, or in *conditioned word substitutes*, such as the shrug of the shoulders or other bodily responses, found in the eyelids, the muscles of the eye or even the retina',[4] as well as in the finger movements of the deaf and dumb.[5] Each of these words or movements, it must be remembered, is a substitute for the direct reaction upon an object of the body as a whole;

---

[1] *Psych. from St. of a Beh.*, 352.   [2] *Behaviourism*, 194.
[3] *Psych. from St. of a Beh.*, 347.
[4] *Behaviourism*, 213; italics in original.
[5] *British Journal of Psychology*, Vol. II (1920), 89.

and since it is not likely that this reaction should be condensed, even by successive telescoping, into one corner of the body alone, it may even be said that 'we think and plan with the whole body'.[1]

This is the behaviourist theory of thought. Its importance for us lies, of course, in its being a clean-cut and radical theory of ideas, to the effect that there are no such things, and that what men have mistaken for them is the 'action of language mechanisms'. Dr. Watson's extension of this phrase to mean, in certain cases, any and every bodily response makes the doctrine somewhat ambiguous and elusive. But we shall try to deal with both sides of the ambiguity. First we shall discuss briefly the ordinary doctrine, that thought is sub-vocal speech. We shall then pass on to the claim that thought may consist of some other physical process which serves as a substitute for such speech.

6. The theory that thought 'is the action of language mechanisms' may easily be shown mistaken. It has one kind of defender, however, to whom the argument that follows is not addressed. If a man insists stolidly and unwaveringly that when he speaks of pleasure or pain, reflection or emotion, all he means by these words is certain bodily changes, and that he has not the slightest notion what is meant when anyone uses them in any other sense, argument becomes unprofitable. The only way to dislodge him is to show that he sometimes speaks and acts as if he meant something else than what he claims, but if he insists that he has meant one thing all along, there is nothing more to be done. It is not that he has won the argument; he would be equally beyond dislodging if he held consistently that whenever he spoke of the moon he meant a round of green cheese. You cannot persuade a person that he is confusing two things if he fails to see, or refuses to see, that there are two things to confuse. But to the mind of average keenness and candour who has felt leanings toward behaviourism, it can

[1] *Behaviourism*, 215.

easily be shown, I think, that the identification of thought with language mechanism runs flatly counter to his experience, and indeed is as strictly unthinkable as the identification of black with white.

In order to be as clear as may be, we shall set out the argument formally. We shall show briefly (1) that language may vary while thought remains the same; (2) that thought may vary while language remains the same; (3) that language may be present while thought is absent; (4) that thought may be present while language is absent. These considerations are not so much arguments as helps to the clarification of one's own meaning. They show that if behaviourism is true, we are all talking nonsense most of the time, and that if we really mean what we normally think we mean, then we cannot believe behaviourism, no matter how hard we try.

7. (1) First, then, language may vary while thought is the same. Suppose that an American, a German, and a Frenchman are all regarding a youthful and charming member of the opposite sex. 'Very pretty', comments the American. 'Sehr hübsch', remarks the German. 'Très jolie', exclaims the Frenchman. The three sounds they have uttered and the vocal reactions involved in them have been exceedingly different. If such reaction *is* the thought, the thought should have been different. But anyone who was not defending a theory at all costs would say what the plain man would say, that they all had the same thought, but were expressing it in different ways. And if this is true, speech and thought are not the same.[1]

8. (2) Thought may vary while speech remains the same. We may repeat an illustration from James. One writes the

---

[1] 'Let a man make to himself the idea of a figure with three angles, whereof one is a right one, and call it, if he pleases, *equilaterum* or *trapezium*, or anything else, the properties of and demonstrations about that idea will be the same as if he called it a "rectangular triangle".' Locke, *Essay*, Bk. IV, Chap. 4, sec. 9.

French words, *Pas de lieu Rhône que nous,* and asks a student to read them aloud. He says something like 'Paddle your own canoe', and then with a little shock of realization, 'Why, that's "paddle your own canoe!"' How is this shock to be accounted for on behaviourist principles? So far as the language mechanism is concerned, these two utterances are the same. There should not, therefore, be anything in the way of thought involved in the second that was not involved in the first. But there obviously is. It is precisely the fact that between the first utterance and the second the words have acquired a meaning that causes the surprise and amusement. One may of course explain that the two utterances have obscure connections, neural and muscular, which differ in the two cases, and that it is this difference in what is conditioned by the two expressions that constitutes the difference in meaning. But this is merely an abandonment of the view in question, that thought is to be identified with the process of speech. Whether it is an eligible retreat will be examined later.

9. (3) Language mechanisms may be at work where thought is not. The case last cited shows this also, but other examples are plentiful. Is the repetition of nonsense syllables thinking? It may be said that such repetition is not speech, but I do not know how the case would be made out except through insistence on a differentia of speech, namely meaningfulness, that would give the case away. Is the person who talks in his sleep thinking in precisely the same sense as when he is uttering the same words awake? When the servant girl mentioned by Coleridge repeated in delirium Hebrew passages, heard many years before in a rabbi's study and registered in her memory without ever being understood, was she *thinking* in precisely the same sense as the rabbi who originally uttered them? For that matter, cannot a parrot talk? It certainly has 'language mechanisms' that come into play with all degrees of 'implicitness' and 'explicitness'. Is it therefore thinking? But the view that since thinking *is* talking it is impossible to talk without thinking is so very odd and invites such unseemly pleasantries that it is perhaps better not to pursue the matter further.

10. (4) Thought may be present without speech. Since this point seems at once more questionable and more interesting than the last, it may be worth while to develop it a little more amply. It can be demonstrated in more ways than one. (i) We said long ago that we must be taken to think whenever we judge, i.e. whenever we accept or affirm anything as true or false. And it has been shown that such judgement is indubitably present in perception. But not even a behaviourist would say that whenever we recognize a road or building, or identify our own hat in a collection, the process consists of *sotto voce* speech. It is useless to insist that this might be proved by further experimentation. Experimentation will never prove that when I walk into a room and recognize at a glance three or four of my friends who are present, my vocal organs are naming them all simultaneously, or that when a lecturer in mid-course perceives an acquaintance in the crowd, his vocal mechanism can perform at once two incompatible tasks. Thus, even if it were true that all processes of explicit inference entailed the use of speech organs, it would still remain true that in perception there may be no trace of this. And since perception involves thought, thought may be present without language.

(ii) But is it true that explicit inference always does involve speech reactions? There is no good evidence for this whatever. Let us look at one of the commonest conditions under which inference is performed. A reader who follows understandingly any book on economics, philosophy, or law, is compelled to make numerous inferences; he is as truly performing an act of reasoning in following another's argument as if he had proceeded on his own initiative by a stumbling process of trial and error, though of course the process is easier. Now is it true that when I read an argument in print, I follow it invariably through sub-vocal speech? What we have seen already of the place of imagery in thinking would certainly not lead us to expect this. We saw that as we pass from mind to mind the types and amounts of imagery that serve to carry a meaning differ immensely, and that the sort of mind in which motor cues predominate, such as the sensation or image of vocal movement, is only one type among several.[1] It is possible, Galton showed, for a mind to use habitually a certain type of imagery at the start and gradually abandon it in favour of another type, or even in favour of thinking in which no imagery at all is introspectively discernible. Our present problem is very similar, though the question is not now whether the *image or sensation* of sub-vocal speech is always present when thinking occurs, but whether the act of speech itself is always so present; for if it is not, then speech and thought cannot be the same. This question is not to be settled by a priori considerations. Fortunately it has often been investigated, both through introspection and through instruments. Professor J. A. O'Brien, who has compiled a useful bibliography on the matter,[2] shows that while earlier investigators were inclined to think that all reading was attended by sub-vocal speech, later inquiry has brought to light many partial or complete exceptions. 'L'homme fait, qui lit silenceusement, accompagner chaque perception visuelle d'un mouvement secret d'articulation', wrote Ribot in 1879. Egger, two years later, writes, 'Lire, en effet, c'est traduire l'écriture en parole', and the German psychologist, Stricker, writing about the same time, agreed. Stumpf, Paulhan,

---

[1] Graham Wallas writes: 'Some of the most completely conscious and most rational thought may be carried on entirely by the use of wordless images. A very able and rapid financial thinker, who was trained as a mathematician, told me that even when his thought is most conscious and rational he thinks, like a chess-player, in terms of seen or felt wordless "situations". The wordless images of such a "situation" may be purely "kinetic", with little or no visual element. The chess correspondent of the *Observer* (February 8, 1925) writes that the great chess-player Alekine said that "he does not see the pieces in his mind, as pictures, but as *force symbols*; that is as near as one can put it in words".' *The Art of Thought*, 72.

[2] In his *Silent Reading*, 1925. I am indebted to this book for the historical facts in this paragraph.

and Baldwin, a few years later, 'agree with Stricker that abridged articulatory movements are usually present, but that they are necessary, or even, *de facto*, always present, they deny'.[1] Stricker had held that to think of a word, one must more or less sketchily pronounce it. Stumpf replied that if this were true, one would need to sing a note to recall it, whereas one could recall it without this; 'ohne lautes, leises oder stilles Singen kann ich verschiedene Tone vorstellen'. Baldwin went further and said that while imagining a note of a given pitch, he could vocalize another of a different pitch. Pintner, in 1915, reported a similar fact about speech. He asked certain subjects to read silently, and at the same time to count aloud a series of numbers, 13, 14, 15, 16, etc.; and this proved entirely possible. Now if, as the behaviourist says, thought is speech, one would suppose the only thought concerned lay in the reciting of the numbers. But it clearly did not, since the subjects were taking the meaning of the passages while their mechanisms of language were otherwise engaged.[2]

(iii) The behaviourist view becomes still less plausible when abnormal cases are considered. In cases of motor aphasia, the articulatory movements of speech are cut off through paralysis, though the patient may continue to read and follow the thought. How could he do this if the process of thought really lapsed with the process of speech?[3]

---

[1] *Silent Reading*, 104.

[2] 'We think, indeed, to a considerable extent, by means of names, but what we think of are the things called by these names; and there cannot be a greater error than to imagine that thought can be carried on with nothing in our mind but names, or that we can make the names think for us.'—J. S. Mill, *Logic*, Bk. II, Chap. 2, Sec. 2.

[3] Dr. Head, while doing careful justice to the value of words in thinking, makes it clear that his aphasic patients could still grasp a large range of ideas without them, through the aid of other symbols. Thus, 'No. 10 was able to recall spontaneously the shape and colour of his hives and to see the bees arriving at the entrance loaded with yellow pollen . . . when No. 2 attempted to give an account of a famous prize fight, he failed grossly so long as he relied on recalling what he had read. But my question, "Can you see it?" evoked so lively a series of visual images that he was able to describe many more details correctly; finally springing out of bed, he assumed the exact attitude

(iv) Another line of investigation that bears on this matter may be mentioned both for its theoretical and its practical interest. Some persons, as everyone knows, are able to read much faster than others. Macaulay remarked in his diary that he seemed to be able to read a book as fast as most men would skim it, and to skim it as fast as most men would turn the pages. 'A university friend', writes Huey, 'a mathematician, informs me that he has read the whole of a standard novel of 320 pages in two and one-fourth hours.'[1] Titchener remarks upon this statement, 'I should not have supposed that the rate of reading mentioned by Huey was exceptional; I certainly often read at the same or a higher speed.'[2] On the other hand, there are many persons who read little if any faster than if they were using the same words in talking. How account for this disparity? There are many causes for slow reading, from deficient ocular span to deficient general intelligence; but certainly one of the commonest causes is the habit of sub-vocal speech. The reader articulates to himself as he goes along, and hence his reading is retarded to about the speed of his speaking.[3] Now since the eye can take in words much faster than the tongue can pronounce them, it occurred to some investigators that by a change from speech reading to sight reading they might increase their rate. And this they did with marked success, both for themselves and for students whom they trained.

of the triumphant Carpentier gazing down on his vanquished opponent.' 'I was able to carry on lengthy conversations with one of my patients, aided by maps, pictures, and his use of a pencil, although his wife reduced him to incomprehensible jargon, and insisted he was out of his mind.'—*Aphasia and Kindred Disorders of Speech*, I. 520-1, 531. Of such cases McDougall remarks: 'Some patients can play such a game as chess, even though their cerebral speech-organs are so destroyed that, as well as finding it impossible to utter coherent speech, they cannot understand written or spoken language.'—*Battle of Behaviourism*, 71.

[1] *Psychology and Pedagogy of Reading*, 180.

[2] *Experimental Psychology of the Thought Processes*, 203.

[3] The person who belongs to this type will not find all writers equally easy. Wilfred Lay reports of one such: 'After reading to himself a few pages of Browning, his jaws became tired!'—*Psych. Rev. Mon. Sup.*, Vol. II. 24.

O'Brien assigned to six grades of school children a programme of daily exercises to decrease vocalization in reading, and in thirty-nine school days increased their rate of reading 56 per cent, an advance of 31 per cent over the increase of a similar set of pupils taken as controls. And the point of special interest is that along with this increase in speed went, not a decrease, but a slight improvement in the comprehension of what they read, an improvement that held both absolutely and by comparison with that of the controls.[1] This result forms a significant comment on the behaviourist theory. If a thought really consisted in the process of vocal or sub-vocal speech, is it likely that this process could be reduced almost or quite to the vanishing point while the comprehension actually increased?

11. But to all such attacks the behaviourist has ready a well-worn reply. The account of the orthodox psychologist, that what has happened is a transfer from motor to visual cues for carrying the meaning, he declines to accept. If sub-vocal processes are no longer in evidence, he insists that they are still there; they are only buried out of sight. The language mechanism is a very complicated and far-reaching system, and if the more conspicuous parts of it are not in play, the obscurer parts still may be. The principal organ of speech, the larynx, has been frequently removed altogether, and thought has still been possible. But this does not disturb Dr. Watson. He points out that 'so long as the air can pass from the lungs to the pharynx and mouth, faint whispered speech is possible'.[2] Suppose, however, that this passage of air is cut off, that below the larynx an opening is made in the trachea through which the patient is compelled to breathe; then, as he admits, all speech, even of the whispered kind, disappears. But he is still unmoved. For the

[1] *Op. cit.*, Chap. VIII. Cf. the conclusion drawn by Miss M. R. Fernald from her experimental work on imagery: 'Rapid reading produces in the majority of cases a reduction and slurring of the auditory-vocal-motor [processes of sensation and imagery], and in some cases a complete elimination of it.'—'Diagnosis of Mental Imagery,' *Psych. Rev. Mon. Sup.*, Vol. XIV. 48.

[2] *Psych. from St. of a Beh.*, 347.

upper organs of speech, the teeth, tongue, and lips, remain, and hence 'such individuals can and do still make all of the movements necessary for articulate speech. This is the answer to the criticisms which have been directed against the point of view that has been advocated throughout the text, namely that thought is the action of language mechanisms'.[1] But carry the assumption further. Suppose a radical motor aphasia were to paralyse those organs too. Or suppose, to take a less extreme instance, that one sits in silent meditation with no movements visible of the outward organs of speech, and suppose further (Bühler reports many such cases) that the subject, as a thought occurs, can detect no sensations of vocal movement from within; is the behaviourist troubled? Apparently not at all. He admits that such cases occur. But he insists that the thought consists in physical processes which are as yet beyond detection. 'The behaviourist's answer', says Dr. Watson, 'is that he can *at present* arrive at this conclusion only by making use of a logical inference. In those cases where the response to the stimulus is not immediate but where it finally occurs in some form of explicit verbal or manual behaviour, it is safe to say that something does go on, and that something is surely not different in essence from that which goes on when his behaviour is explicit.'[2] Now there is no catching the behaviourist while he plays this game. You no sooner show that thought is not to be identified with some particular physical process than you find him contending that it is some other and more obscure process which you, and perhaps everyone else, have as yet failed to detect, indeed that 'any and every bodily response may become a word substitute'.[3] Against such agility and elusiveness there is but one strategy that can avail. One must forsake the unending business of showing that this, that, and the other physical process is not to be identified with thought, and, attacking the matter in principle, show that in physical responses *as such* there is something that excludes this identification.

[1] *Psych. from St. of a Beh.*, 347. [2] *Ibid.*, 361.
[3] *Behaviourism*, 192.

12. The thesis, then, which we must examine is that a conscious process *is* the same thing as a process of physical change, and *which* physical process it shall be we may leave to the behaviourist's choice. For our contention about his proposal is this, that no matter what process of bodily change he may elect, to identify consciousness with it is strictly unthinkable.

Of course there are cases in plenty in which two things may quite legitimately be called the same. The actor on the stage and the same actor on the street present two very different appearances, but they are the same man. When I look first at the head and then at the tail of a coin, what I see is different, and yet I am seeing the same coin. And at first sight there would seem to be no more difficulty in saying that a conscious and bodily process may be the same, despite the difference of appearance, than to say so of a coin or of a man. Nevertheless, this would be a mistake. When we say that we are seeing the same coin, we do not mean that there is no difference at all between what appeared when we saw the head and what appeared when we saw the tail; we do not mean that the appearances themselves are the same, for that would be absurd; what is the same is not the appearances, but the thing that owns them. Similarly of the man. His two appearances are not the same, but he is the same in spite of their differences. Now is it open to the behaviourist to say in the same way that conscious and bodily processes are one? Clearly not. If he does say so, his programme loses its point; and if his programme is to retain any point, he is committed to an assertion of identity in the very sense which makes such an assertion nonsense. Let us get this clear.

If, when he says that mental and bodily process are the same, the behaviourist means that they are the same in the ordinary sense, the sense in which I say a man is the same or a coin is the same, what he means is that they are two aspects or appearances of something which owns both but is identical with neither. Just as the coin is not identical with one of its faces or the man with one of his appearances, so also that which is the same in bodily and mental process is not to be identified with either, but with something underlying them of which both are appearances. Is this the behaviourist's meaning? Obviously not, for it would amount to the proposal that metaphysics supersedes science, a consummation which he would most devoutly wish to avoid. It would imply that what science directly deals with is not the reality at all, but only the appearance of something else underlying it of which mind is one manifestation. This is of course a theory that has been held by respectable metaphysicians, but it is safe to say that no theory which thus exalts metaphysics at the expense of science can be what the behaviourist wishes to offer us.

What sort of identity is it, then, to which the behaviourist is committed? Unhappily it is precisely the sort which we saw in our analogies to be absurd. He is compelled to hold that the appearances themselves are identical, that a toothache *is* simply and solely a change in physical tissue, and the change in physical tissue is all we mean by a toothache. This is the only sort of identity that would leave any point in his programme. To say that mental and nervous processes are obverse sides of an underlying identity is, as we have just seen, out of the question. To reduce matter to mind by saying that the nervous process is at bottom an appearance presented by what is really mental would be the sort of thing that he describes as 'moonshine'. To reduce mind to matter in the same way, by saying that the ache is an illusion, something that is really a physical process which appears to us as mental, would be futile. For where are we to place the illusion? If it is a mistaken idea in my mind, then behaviourism is abandoned. If it is itself merely a nervous change, nothing is gained by introducing it, for it is just as difficult to see how an illusion that I am conscious can be a change in my nerves as to see this about consciousness itself. What is identical for the behaviourist is not some basic substance which is belied by one of its appearances; his programme requires him to say that the pain and the change in the nerve are literally and numerically the same, that when I speak of an ache or pain, the ache or pain I mean *is* nothing but a change in bodily tissue.

13. Now this view is silly. There would not be the least absurdity, although no doubt there are difficulties, in saying that the pain is *caused* by a physical change or that the two are differing *manifestations* of something that lies behind them; but to say that it *is* the pain is to say what no one can really think and what only a thoroughly muddled head could suppose he thought. If a great many otherwise sensible people do suppose that they think it, this can only be because they have confused it with some other theory of a similar sound, such as that there is an extremely close dependence of mind on body. But unfortunately, as Paulsen has pointed out, 'the absurd has this advantage in common with truth, that it cannot be refuted'. If a man insists that what he means when he speaks of having a toothache is that the molecules in nerve or brain are behaving in a certain way, I suppose he must be the final judge of what he means. But we have pointed out that there are ways of showing a candid mind that at times it does not really mean what it had supposed it meant. It is perfectly easy to be mistaken on this point. We would invite anyone who is inclined to take seriously either the present-day doctrine of behaviourism or the old-fashioned identity materialism, of which it is only the most recent form, to ask himself whether in the light of the considerations that follow such a position can really express what he means.

14. (1) We may note in the first place that the behaviourist's conclusion could never have been arrived at except through a process which proves it false. In lieu of each of the processes that used to be called mental he offers us a specific bodily reaction. Instead of the sensation of blue we have the visual reaction to light-waves possessing a determinate length; instead of a sensation of red, the reaction to waves of a different length; a train of thought is a series of movements in the vocal organs; an emotion a set of reactions in glands and viscera. How has the behaviourist been able to specify these processes so confidently and precisely? The difference between the nervous reaction which is to constitute one mental process and that which is to constitute another is often exceedingly fine. For example, the difference between the way my optic nerve behaves when stimulated by waves of 700 millionths and 400 millionths of a millimetre is so small that not only does it remain invisible to the naked eye, but after all attempts at instrumental observation, it remains for the most part a matter of conjecture. Why, then, the behaviourist's confidence that two different nervous processes are involved? Obviously because he has had two different sensations of the old-fashioned kind, the sensations of blue and red, and is convinced that for each there must be some physiological correlate. Is the difference between the two reactions of the optic nerve or even the difference between the auditory and the visual regions of the cerebrum so conspicuous of itself that one could mark them out from direct inspection as performing functions radically different? No one, I suppose, would say this, least of all anyone who has some acquaintance with the way in which discoveries have actually been made in the field of 'cerebral localization'.[1] The only way in which these discoveries could possibly have been made was for the observer to start with certain differences in consciousness as his cue, and then to search for their correlates in the nervous system and the brain. To explain these conscious differences was the motive of his search; without them he would have had no problem; and without checking their connection with physical processes through the ordinary inductive methods he would never have been able to tell when his correlation was achieved. The very process then, by which the behaviourist is enabled to identify conscious events with physical depends on the fact that they are different. If conscious differences had not been there to initiate the search and to check its conclusions,

---

[1] 'It (the method of introspection) has been applied in proper places by physiologists such as Johannes Müller, Helmholtz, Hering, and many others, men of the highest repute in their profession. We owe the most valuable results of sense-physiology to this method, without which the imposing and securely founded edifice of this science would never have been built.'—Semon, The Mneme, 41.

there would have been no problem at all. The history of behaviourism is thus its refutation.

15. (2) Not only has the conscious state, in distinction from the physical, been the indispensable clue to the latter; an elaborate knowledge of it was developed before the knowledge of its physical correlates came into existence. Now this is a very odd fact if bodily reactions are all there is to conscious life, since if this is true, anyone who was acquainted with conscious processes ought *ipso facto* to be acquainted with the bodily processes. But that the two kinds of acquaintance are not the same and do not involve each other can be illustrated almost endlessly. Since one would hesitate to charge a behaviourist like Dr. Watson with anything so frivolous, on his theory, as reading Plato, one may be permitted to point out that in the *Philebus* there is an elaborate and minute discussion of the kinds of pleasure, and the relation of pleasure to other elements of conscious life. If the behaviourist is right, Plato was either discussing the reactions of glands, viscera and the autonomic nervous system, or he was discussing nothing at all. But since Plato knew, and could have known, next to nothing about glands, viscera, and the autonomic nervous system, the inference is irresistible; he was thinking, i.e. vocalizing, 'moonshine'. This conclusion is more courageous than convincing. Once more, in the *Prior Analytics*, Aristotle dissected very minutely a common form of reasoning. The behaviourist points out that when such reasoning goes on there is a process of change in muscles, nerves and brain, and these physical events *are* the reasoning process. So far, therefore, as Aristotle analysed the reasoning process, he must have been speaking of these. The perverse logician has left his opinion on record, however, that this process, alone of all the psychical processes, had no physical basis whatever, and as for the brain, he believed its function to be the cooling of the blood. According to the behaviourist, therefore, Aristotle could not have been talking about the reasoning process at all, and was more ignorant of it

than a modern schoolboy; what he did discuss under that head
was an irrelevant mythology. Again I find this less than
convincing.

16. (3) Indeed there is more than one respect in which the
behaviourist might have profited from a perusal of the history
of logic. Logicians are the connoisseurs of certainty; and it is
therefore interesting to note that they have commonly found
it in the very realm which the behaviourist thinks an illusion.
Descartes may serve as the type of many. What gave certainty
to anything for Descartes was a kind of clearness and distinctness that could not be presented to eye or ear; and the one
thing he found himself unable to doubt was his own process
of conscious thinking. For example, he could not doubt that
he was doubting, for in so doubting he was doing the doubting
he doubted about. What would this argument come to if interpreted by a behaviourist? This, I suppose, that one cannot
engage in speech reaction of a certain type while simultaneously
engaging in another reaction of the same type toward the first.
This makes sense. But it misses altogether the cogency of the
Cartesian argument. If Descartes could not doubt that he
doubted, it was because there was an evident inconsistency
between the fact of his judging and what he judged; if one
cannot react through speech to a simultaneous reaction through
speech, it is merely because the organs are so constructed that
they cannot perform the two movements at once. What gave
force to the Cartesian argument was a relation of logical necessity holding between the meanings; it is only between such
non-sensible meanings that this relation can obtain; and both
such relations and such meanings are for the behaviourist non-
existent. But it is only in this realm of the non-sensible that the
relations of implication and consistency, or indeed any of the
relations of logic, can subsist; to say that two physical things,
two billiard balls or two boulders, implied each other or were
mutually inconsistent, would be nonsense. Such relations as
physical concomitance and collision, which the behaviourist

must offer as substitutes, are totally different things. Thus if he builds on the foundations he has laid, he has no title to a belief in logic or the use of it. Of course he does use it; everyone does and must. But the attempt to *prove* his case must proceed through an appeal to meanings and relations for which his theory has no room.[1]

17. (4) Such philosophers as we have mentioned—Plato, Aristotle, Descartes—who talked about conscious states were of course arch-dealers in mythology. Now it is instructive to consider how, on the behaviourist assumptions, all this mythology could have arisen. On these assumptions no one has ever observed an event of any kind except the movements of physical bodies; there is no other kind of event to observe. How, then, did the illusion that there were also pleasures, pains, and ideas ever grow up? Not from perceiving them in animals and other persons, for what we directly perceive in these cases is never conscious states, but only bodies reacting. Whence, then, the curious notion that there are such states? The answer one would ordinarily give is that we have known these states in ourselves, that when we have had them we have commonly acted in certain ways, and that when we have seen others acting in the same ways we assume that they feel as we do. But from this explanation the behaviourist is cut off. He cannot admit that even in ourselves we are aware of these conscious states. The result is that he is left without any explanation at all of the illusion that they exist. The illusion is universal; it is extremely strong; but it is wholly gratuitous. In spite of the fact that nothing exists but matter in motion, we have managed to conjure up a luxuriant jungle of mythology, in the way of sensations, pleasures and displeasures, emotions and

[1] 'The existence of universals is often denied; men are apt to imagine that if they exist one should be able to find them as one finds instances of them. Hence the remarks of Antisthenes—ἵππον μὲν ὁρῶ, ἱππότητα δὲ οὐχ ὁρῶ, "I see a horse, but not horseness"; to which Plato replied, that it was because, though he had eyes, he had no intelligence'.—Joseph, *Logic*, 27.

ideas, which has not the least foundation in anything that anyone has ever observed. The thing is as inexplicable as it is scandalous. The only course here open to the behaviourist is suggested by the remark that he is really the fundamentalist of the natural sciences. To account for such catholic human perversity, what he needs is a good robust doctrine of original sin.

18. (5) The great illusion is so troublesome that the behaviourist is moved at times to deny that the illusion itself exists. These sensations, images, and ideas that people talk of—they are words only: 'I frankly do not know what they mean', says Dr. Watson.[1] This statement, it may be remarked in passing, is somewhat puzzling. For according to the same writer, 'thinking is merely talking, but talking with concealed musculature'.[2] Persons, then, who are talking about sensations and ideas must be as truly thinking as anyone else. Dr. Watson is inclined to dismiss such thinking, however, as having no meaning. But to use meaning as the criterion for dividing the sheep from the goats is a surprising procedure. For meaning is one of the most objectionable of all the mythical entities of consciousness; and if the behaviourist is consistent (as he wants to be, though his scheme, as we have seen, has no place for such a relation) he cannot say that one way of thinking, i.e. talking, is more 'meaningful' than another. A clear physiological meaning of 'meaning' is called for, but missing. But this is only a passing remark. We were saying that the behaviourist sometimes denies that the illusion of consciousness exists. And it is worth seeing that while common sense is no great authority on scientific matters, it is quite adequate to refute a theory like this. If a dentist lays his instrument lightly alongside an exposed nerve, there happens what is ordinarily called a mild feeling of pain. If he plunges his buzzing file into the nerve and there turns and twists it, there happens what is called an excruciating

[1] *Psych. from St. of a Beh.*, xii.
[2] *The Battle of Behaviourism*, 34–5.

pain. According to the behaviourist there is no conscious difference between the one event and the other, since neither sensation nor any other form of consciousness exists. Nevertheless, even behaviourists have been known to prefer the one type of event to the other. Why? Because they have a passionate desire that one exchange of energy among molecules rather than some other should occur? Clearly not; the sorts of energy-exchange involved in different types of pain are far too little known to make definite preference possible. But even if they were known, why should a behaviourist be interested in one rather than another? He cannot say, 'because the one is more pleasant, or less painful, or more worth while, than the other'. Pleasure, pain, and value, are not particles in the physical world; they are not movements of such particles; they are not properties or relations of such particles; they do not exist there at all, as he has uneasily seen; in a world of mere matter in motion, no event is better or worse, more or less desirable, than any other. If, then, the behaviourist does desire one event rather than another, this can only be because it possesses, or seems to possess, some quality of pleasingness or worth that does not belong to it as a merely physical event. He cannot so much as seek to avoid a toothache without, by implication, forsaking his theory.

19. (6) That we really do mean something different by consciousness and bodily behaviour is made clear again by the different attributes that we assign to them.[1] We speak of an idea as clear or confused, as apposite or inapposite, as witty or dull. Are such terms intelligible when applied to those motions of electrons, atoms, molecules, or muscles, which for the behaviourist are all there is to consciousness? Can a motion be clear, or cogent, or witty? What exactly would a clear motion be like? What sort of thing is a germane or cogent reflex? Or a witty muscular reaction? These adjectives are perfectly in order when applied to ideas; they become at once absurd when

---

[1] Cf. Broad, *The Mind and Its Place in Nature*, 622–3.

applied to movements in muscle or nerve; and how account for this absurdity if we do not mean different things when we speak of ideas and movements?

On the other side, movements have attributes which are unthinkable as applied to ideas. Movements have velocity; but what is the average velocity of one's ideas on a protective tariff? Movements have direction; would there be any sense in talking of the north-easterly direction of one's thought on the morality of revenge? Finally Dr. Watson makes it plain that though there is much in the 'thinking activity' which is not yet visible to the eye, there is nothing in principle beyond the range of vision; the microscopic and concealed movements in the interior of the body need only sufficiently fine instruments to make them as apparent to the eye as gross muscular reactions.[1] Such confidence is hard to share. It means that a surgeon, if his technique were sufficiently advanced, could *see* my awareness of blue, or my opinion about behaviourism, or my headache, there in the tissues before him. This is surely nonsense. One can understand what it means to feel a headache, but to *see* a headache moving about in space is as unintelligible as to hear temperature or to smell the musical scale. Nor is it easy to see how such an absurdity could arise if the only difference between a headache and a handspring lay in gross physical magnitude.

20. (7) The arguments we have been using consist for the most part in mere appeal to common sense and have avoided those excursions into metaphysics which the behaviourist so much distrusts. The one further consideration we shall offer is of the same kind, though to him it may look at first suspicious. It is this, that if he is right, no judgement or idea can be either true or false; truth or falsity have no place in the behaviourist universe. This is a criticism of some moment, since even one who eschews metaphysics and conceives of science in the most

---

[1] *Psych. from St. of Beh.*, 360–4.

dogmatically fundamentalist manner values his position
because he thinks it in some sense true.

But how can a reflex be true? Is there any sense in saying
that the passage of air through the vocal cords, or the wagging
of the tongue, or the opening and closing of the lips, are themselves true or false? It is hard to conjecture what such assertions
could mean. To be sure, truth has been defined in various ways.
Sometimes it has been made to consist in correspondence, sometimes in coherence, sometimes in the production of good effects.
Could a bodily reaction be true in any of these senses? Not in
the sense of correspondence; for that would imply that when
I say 'New York has more than six million inhabitants', an
incident in my throat and mouth corresponds to the population
of a city; and that is meaningless. Not in the sense of coherence;
for, so far as one can see, any other incident in my body would
cohere equally well with the fact, and the incident that did
happen would cohere equally well with almost any other fact.
Nor in the sense of producing good effects; since an apoplectic
stroke, suffered immediately after judgement, might cut off all
good effects, while the judgement would still have been true.
The fact is that behaviourism has not offered, and cannot offer,
any intelligible account of truth. Mr. Russell, who has behaviourist leanings, was able to offer correspondence so far as he
identified ideas with images. But of course images have no
existence for a thorough-going behaviourism, and when we
tried to find from Mr. Russell how words could be true,
nothing was forthcoming that we could understand. And
without attempting to anticipate what the future epistemo-
logists of behaviourism may achieve, one may suspect that
where the greatest of their forerunners, Hobbes,[1] so signally
failed, they will not find success easy. For what they must
explain is such things as these: How a motion can be an error;
how the deflection of an air current through my throat can be
true, while the passage of a current through the pine trees
cannot; how, when questions are asked me and I go through
the motions of uttering the word yes, this motion may reflect

[1] He even says explicitly, at one point, '*ratio*, now, is but *oratio*'.

with equal faithfulness the characteristics of a thousand different situations. To carry behaviourism into the region of truth and falsity is to stir up a hornet's nest of paradoxes and absurdities, and all for one root reason, namely that 'it seems as non-sensical to call a movement true as a flavour purple or a sound avaricious'.[1]

21. We have dealt as elaborately with psychological be-haviourism as with some theories of the idea that have con-temporary names of weight behind them. This theory has no such names; it is a local cult which is in a minority at home, and has made few converts abroad. Our excuse for taking it seriously is not its intrinsic strength but the hold it has gained upon persons whose acquaintance with the history of thought has supplied no standards with which to evaluate it. Though its main principle could not conceivably be proved with test-tubes and microscopes, its flourishing of laboratory results has produced a widespread impression that it is something new, scientific, and demonstrable. In truth it is none of these. In principle, as Professor Broad has said, 'it is just old-fashioned materialism which has crossed the Atlantic under an *alias*',[2] and its devotees seem unaware that it has been discussed and dismissed repeatedly by some of the acutest of modern minds. Nor is it genuinely scientific. The 'logical necessity of affecting general anaesthesia'[3] makes it refuse to take account as facts of any data that do not fit a preconceived definition, and its main doctrine is a dogma laid down a priori. When the simplicity, amounting almost to *naïveté*, with which this doctrine is dis-cussed and accepted is compared with the acumen brought to its consideration by a long train of metaphysicians, from Descartes to Broad, who have weighed and rejected it, one is at a loss at first to account for its recent vogue among students of psychology, a vogue which, to be sure, has been rapidly

[1] H. W. B. Joseph, *Some Problems in Ethics*, 14.
[2] *The Mind and Its Place in Nature*, 617.
[3] Ogden and Richards, *Meaning of Meaning*, 23.

subsiding. But then one recalls that in America students of psychology are often permitted to become specialists in their science, to take doctorates in it, even to hold chairs in it, with an almost total ignorance of the history of reflection on the problems of body and mind. One would at least prefer this admission to accepting the gibe of Keyserling that behaviourism is the natural psychology of a people without inner life. But whatever the cause of its popularity, neither its intrinsic plausibility nor the quality of its advocacy inclines one to count it a serious danger in the long run.

CHAPTER X

PRAGMATISM AND THOUGHT

1. Pragmatism is a theory of truth which springs from a theory of thought. It holds that thought is an instrument to practical ends, and hence that truth is measured by success in reaching those ends. What has aroused most interest in pragmatism is no doubt its view of truth. But our theory of truth is commonly arrived at by way of a theory of thought. We know that it is the business of thought to seek what is true, and when we are asked what sense we attach to 'truth', we are likely to find our answer by looking into the activity of thinking and trying to make out what sort of satisfaction would bring it finally to rest. In puzzling out a problem, just when have we arrived at the truth of the matter? Presumably when our problem is solved. But when is the problem solved? No doubt when thought is satisfied. But when is thought satisfied? When it has got all the relevant facts into a system? When its suggestion has worked out in practice? Or when? One cannot answer this question from the outside. It can be answered only from within, through a disclosure by thought, in response to insistent inquiry, of the end it is really seeking. And to find that end is the business of the theory of thought.

Now the pragmatist theory of thought is a very remarkable one. It represents the reaction against, and the antithesis of, the rationalistic theory which held the field when it appeared. The main contrast may be put at once. The rationalist conceives of thought as an attempt to apprehend and understand the nature of things, and he considers himself to have achieved such understanding in the degree to which the matter apprehended exhibits logical necessity. The pragmatist, on the other hand, conceives of thought as *an instrument of behaviour, the producing and adopting of a plan of action,* and he considers the thought to have reached its end when the plan succeeds in practice. Let us take a simple case and analyse it in the pragmatic way.

2. I am walking across a field as darkness comes on. I am aware of my surroundings but not engaged in what would commonly be called reflection. Suddenly a dim shape looms up before me and brings me to an uneasy halt. I am uncertain what it is and do not know whether to proceed or to draw back. This, says the pragmatist, is typical of the way every problem arises; it grows out of a situation in which activity is blocked. Here a number of hypotheses dart into my mind: is the thing a stump, a rock, a bull? These hypotheses are 'ideas'; but what exactly are ideas? The pragmatist's answer gives the essence of his theory of thought. Ideas, he says, are plans of action. My real interest, when I think 'stump', is not in a theoretic identification of something as a member of the vegetable kingdom, but in getting safely by; the judgement 'that is a bull' is essentially a suggestion that I draw back or take to my heels. Suppose that in fact I judge 'that is a stump', and in accordance with this 'plan of action' proceed on my way. If the adoption of this plan takes me prosperously to the other side of the field, the judgement is verified and true, since that is the end for which thought was invoked. On the other hand, if there comes a snorting and pounding behind me and I am forthwith hoist by my own temerity, the plan has not worked; the judgement is erroneous. This simple case may be taken as a paradigm for thinking generally; and we may now look at the stages that the pragmatist would distinguish in it. In the main we shall follow Professor Dewey, since, of the analyses offered by pragmatists, his has gained the widest acceptance.

3. (I) *The occasion of thought.* It is important to note that by thought Dewey always means reflective thinking. The sort of thought that in our first book we found present in common perception in many degrees of complexity he would not recognize as thought at all. The reason is clear. If you conceive thought as a way of surmounting practical difficulty, it will naturally be absent where practical difficulty is absent; and in

the effortless, unpuzzled acceptance of tables as tables, and chairs as chairs, there is no sort of practical problem. On the other hand, if you conceive thought as that which is, or claims to be, a revelation of the real, it will be present wherever there is truth or error; and we held both to be clearly present in perception.[1] Our own study of thought has had, therefore, to begin at a lower level of experience than Dewey's. When he asks what is the occasion that gives rise to thought, he means How does *reflection* arise?

To that question he answers that it arises out of a conflict or tension that was present in experience before reflection began. Suppose the object dimly before me were perceived to be a cow that I have passed safely a hundred times; here there would be no tension, no problem and no judgement; I should merely go on my way mechanically in conformity to long habit. Suppose, again, that the object is neither familiar nor clearly seen, but that there is nothing about it to excite fear or curiosity. Here again there is perception of a kind, but nothing that would arouse thought. But suppose, finally, that the object is just familiar enough to tempt an advance, while at the same time strange and alarming enough to prompt me to take to my heels. Then there is tension; I am torn by promptings to do two incompatible things at once. It is precisely at this point and to provide a way of escape that judgement or thought arises. Of course the conflicts may vary infinitely in their character. I am hungry, but without food; how shall I get some? I am sailing when a storm arises; how shall I reach the shore? I have a taste for order, but my room is in a litter; something must be done. These are the kind of conflicts that forced thought into play in the first place, and still do so to-day; and they all exhibit the same pattern, a 'block-situation' in which an organic need is flouted by given fact. Where no such need is felt, as in sleep, thought has no occasion and does not appear; where the need can be met by habit or by instinct, as can most of the situations of common life, it

---

[1] James differs from Dewey here, holding a view of perception not unlike our own. See the chapter on Perception in his *Psychology*.

likewise does not appear; where habit and instinct prove insufficient and must be supplemented, the organism resorts to thought as an extra tool, which, though more efficient and flexible than these, is still an instrument to the same end. 'Men do not, in their natural estate, think when they have no troubles to cope with, no difficulties to overcome';[1] 'reflection appears as the dominant trait of a situation when there is something seriously the matter, some trouble, due to active discordance, dissentiency, conflict among the factors of a prior, non-intellectual experience; when . . . a situation becomes tensional'.[2]

4. (II) *The datum of thought.* The rise of reflection means the rise of this implicit conflict into explicit awareness. There the conflict manifests itself by splitting the field of experience into two regions. On the one hand there is crystallized out the element of brute fact, that which may be taken for granted because there is at present no question about it, the given, the datum. In the case before us the datum would be the misty shape in our path. Whatever it may mean, it is there; there is no question about that; the only question is what it means, i.e. what it calls for in the way of action. On the other hand, and over against this unquestioned datum, there is a region of uncertainty, of fluid and changing attitude, which is in course of development toward overt action. This is the region of *meaning*, of the ideal as opposed to the given, of what is felt as belonging to us rather than to objective fact. When this plastic mass takes form in a definite practical attitude, that is, in the adoption of one line of response to the exclusion of others, we are judging or thinking.

Let us look a little more closely at what the pragmatist calls the datum. Does he mean by this what is commonly

---

[1] Dewey, *Reconstruction in Philosophy*, 139.

[2] Dewey, *Essays in Experimental Logic*, 11; and cf. Chap. III. It is in these essays that Dewey gives his fullest and most technical account of the thought process, though his briefer, non-polemic *How We Think* is on some points clearer.

called a *sense* datum? Not at all; and he attaches weight to this denial; for he takes it as marking a significant difference from the older metaphysical logic. According to that logic, he says, the distinction between fact and meaning is an existential difference; the sense datum and its interpretation by thought are different orders of being. According to his own logic, the distinction is utilitarian; fact is what, *for our purpose*, is certain; meaning is what, *for our purpose*, is tentative. Hence the line between fact and meaning will vary with my situation and interest. If, as I crossed the field, it were daylight instead of dusk, what offered itself as fact would be extremely different; if I were a farmer hunting a cow that had just gone astray, I should draw the line differently again. But always, when we reflect, *some* datum is present. There is always a 'platform', something remaining 'untouched in the contention of incompatibles', a 'residuum of familiarity and certainty that cannot be eliminated'. And this is not a sense datum, but merely what for the present purpose remains unquestioned.[1]

It follows that some data are far richer than others. The expert geologist, for example, can take for granted a great deal that to the rest of us would offer problems. How have his data become so rich? The answer is, through *funded* meanings. After one has applied a meaning a few times and done so successfully, one no longer raises the old question; one incorporates the meaning in the fact and henceforth takes it for granted. Properly speaking a meaning so incorporated is a meaning no longer, since what made it a meaning was its function, and it is now functioning as fact; it is a sediment or deposit of meaning. It follows that we are literally constructing the world of fact as we go along. Knowing is the 'kind of action' that 'progressively and securely clothes natural existence with realized meanings'.[2] 'What was once the most

---

[1] 'Sensations are not parts of *any* knowledge, good or bad, superior or inferior, imperfect or complete. They are rather provocations, incitements, challenges to an act of inquiry, which is to *terminate* in knowledge.'—*Reconstruction in Philosophy*, 89.

[2] Dewey, *The Quest for Certainty*, 161.

vaporous hypothesis is consolidated into the hardest and most indubitable fact';[1] 'the world is constructed by experiment'.[2]

5. (III) *Ideas.* We have seen that the datum, for the pragmatist, is that part of the experienced field which is free from conflict and uncertainty. The meaning or idea is the other part, the region of hazard, adventure, and alternative possibilities. Given a situation in which some organic need is frustrated, experience quickly breaks up into unquestioned fact on the one hand, and, on the other, a proposal or set of proposals for dealing with this fact in such fashion as to satisfy the need. These are ideas. They are essentially bridges to span the gap between datum and purpose, tools with which to reshape the datum into what will answer the need. In our typical case, the need is obviously to get across the field; the datum is the misty shape before us; the idea is a proposal to deal with the datum—by standing still, by advancing, by running away—in such manner that the organism may reach its end. It is an instrument, an expedient, a practical device, a programme of behaviour. Since this view of the idea is the very essence of the pragmatist's theory, it will be well to have it in his own words, and in various forms:

> ' "Thought" is not a property of something termed intellect or reason apart from nature. It is a mode of directed overt action. Ideas are anticipatory plans and designs which take effect in concrete *re*constructions of antecedent conditions of existence.'[3]

> 'thought, our conceptions and ideas, are designations of operations to be performed or already performed. . . . The business of thought is not to conform to or reproduce the characters already possessed by objects, but to judge them as potentialities of what they may become through an indicated operation.' 'ideas are statements not of what is or has been, but of acts to be performed.'[4]

[1] Schiller, *Studies in Humanism*, 426.
[2] Schiller, *Personal Idealism*, 57.
[3] *Quest for Certainty*, 160.   [4] *Ibid.*, 132, 133.

'Now an idea or conception is a claim or injunction or plan to *act* in a certain way as the way to arrive at the clearing up of a specific situation. . . . Its active, dynamic function is the all-important thing about it, and in the quality of activity induced by it lies all its truth and falsity.'[1]

Dewey quotes James: 'It (the idea) appears less as a solution than as a programme for more work, and particularly as an indication of the ways in which existing realities may be changed. Theories thus become instruments. . . .'[2] And he adds: 'In other words, an idea is a draft drawn upon existing things, and intention to act so as to arrange them in a certain way.''[3]

Pragmatism was described by James as 'a new name for old ways of thinking'. He was too modest. We must do pragmatism the justice of recognizing that the theory stated above is both a radical and an original departure from earlier ways of conceiving thought.

6. (IV) *The Verification of Ideas.* The pragmatist's theory of verification follows directly from his theory of the idea. If an idea is in essence an instrument to a practical end, its success lies in reaching that end, and such success *is* truth. Similarly failure is falsity. Immediately after the passage last quoted Dewey adds:

'From which it follows that if the draft is honoured, if existences, following upon the action rearrange or readjust themselves in the way the idea intends, the idea is true.' Of ideas he says: 'They are tools. As in the case of all tools, their value resides not in themselves, but in their capacity to work shown in the consequences of their use.'[4]

Many persons have supposed that by 'consequences' the pragmatist meant implications, or whatever follows 'logically' from the proposition affirmed; and to use such consequences in verifying a theory has seemed natural enough; does not everybody do it? It is true that pragmatists have sometimes

---

[1] *Reconstruction in Philosophy*, 156. [2] *Pragmatism*, 53.
[3] *Essays in Experimental Logic*, 309, 310.
[4] *Reconstruction in Philosophy*, 145.

used 'consequences' in this sense. But it is of the first importance to understand that this is not their primary meaning, since if it were, pragmatism would have nothing new to say. What they mean by consequences is the actual physical changes that result from adopting some theory, that is, from putting it into practice.

> 'The reorganization, the modification, effected by thinking is, by this hypothesis, a physical one. Thinking ends in experiment, and experiment is an *actual* alteration of a physically antecedent situation in those details or respects which call for thought in order to do away with some evil.'[1]
> 'That all knowledge, as issuing from reflection, is experimental (in the literal physical sense of experimental) is then a constituent proposition of this doctrine.'[2] And again: '*If* ideas, meanings, conceptions, notions, theories, systems are instrumental to an active reorganization of the given environment . . . then the test of their validity and value lies in accomplishing this work.'

It should be noted that in the practical working of ideas lies not only the test of their truth, but their very truth itself. Again this follows from the pragmatist theory of thought. If thought is not an attempt to construe the character of what exists already, but an attempt to get something done, then it is meaningless to say that truth—the special end and aim of thought—consists in correspondence or internal coherence; that would commit one to saying that truth is something in which thought has no interest. If thought and truth are to be relevant to each other, truth must be reconceived. So long as the end of thought was taken to be the reflection of fact, truth was naturally conceived as fidelity to fact. Now that thought has been seen to have another aim entirely, namely, specific practical accomplishment, truth must be taken as success in reaching that aim. An idea is a plan of action; its truth is the success of that plan in practice. Thus the consequences that verify a judgement as true also *make* it true.

---

[1] *Essays in Experimental Logic*, 31.   [2] *Ibid.*, 13.

'. . . the true means the verified and means nothing else. . . .'[1] 'The hypothesis that works is the *true* one; and *truth* is an abstract noun applied to the collection of cases, actual, foreseen, and desired, that receive confirmation in their works and consequences.'[2] 'Truth for us', says James, 'is simply a collective name for verification-processes, just as health, wealth, strength, etc., are names for other processes connected with life, and also pursued because it pays to pursue them. Truth is *made*, just as health, wealth, and strength are made, in the course of experience.'[3]

'All "truths" must be verified to be properly true,' says Schiller; 'truths must be used to become true . . .'[4]

Here, then, is the pragmatic theory of thought. Thought is occasioned by a block to the activity of the organism, and it is essentially a process of overcoming that block. It proceeds through a placing on one side of that which can be accepted without question, and the generation of an idea, i.e. a plan of action, as to the way of escape. The adoption of this plan is judgement; its success is truth; its failure, falsity.

Of the four phases of this theory that have been distinguished, it is obviously the third that for us contains the heart of the matter, since it presents the pragmatist theory of the nature and end of thought. There is much that we should like to say of the other phases which only lack of space prevents our saying; without attempting a general appraisal of pragmatism, we shall here confine our criticism to this one head.

7. Ideas, we are told, are plans of action; they are 'statements not of what is or has been, but of acts to be performed'. They are, in their very essence, instruments with which to change our environment. This view is far less simple than it seems. A reflective analysis reveals that it challenges the received views in no less than five points: (1) As against the view that thought is primarily concerned to lay bare the fixed structure of things, it holds that thought is concerned

---

[1] Dewey, *Reconstruction*, 160.   [2] *Ibid.*, 156–7.
[3] *Pragmatism*, 218.   [4] *Studies in Humanism*, 8, 9.

invariably with what to do; (2) as against the view that thought
may at times explicitly concern itself with what happened in
the past, it holds of ideas generally that they are 'anticipations
of something still to come'; (3) as against the view that thought
may concern itself with what lies beyond experience, it holds
that thought is always intent upon changes within experience;
(4) as against the view that thought is mental, it holds, in at
least its Deweyan form, that thought is a function of physical
things; (5) as against the view that thought can achieve imper-
sonality, it holds that it is inevitably affected by instinct, desire
and feeling. Some of these contentions may be true and not
others; we shall therefore appraise the theory justly only if
we look separately at each.

8. (1) An idea is a 'plan of action'; 'knowing is itself a mode
of practical action';[1] 'the gist of scientific knowledge is control
of natural energies'.[2] What are we to say of this theory?

There can be no question, of course, that thought does have
practical utility, utility enormous and incalculable. It is a
commonplace that modern science, for example, has made
modern civilization possible. It is also beyond question that
scientific study has sometimes been, what the pragmatist
suggests it always is, an attempt to gain practical control of
nature. But these true and trite propositions are not what the
pragmatist is offering us, for no one would think of denying
them. The question is whether thought is invariably, because
essentially, a drive toward practice.

9. (i) If we turn to the history of science the evidence is
overwhelmingly negative. A distinguished student of scientific
thought writes as follows:

> 'The really profound changes in human life all have their
> ultimate origin in knowledge pursued for its own sake. The use
> of the compass was not introduced into Europe till the end of

[1] Dewey, *Quest*, 104.   [2] Dewey, *Reconstruction*, 42.

the twelfth century A.D., more than three thousand years after its first use in China. The importance which the science of electromagnetism has since assumed in every department of human life is due not to the superior practical bias of Europeans, but to the fact that in the West electrical and magnetic phenomena were studied by men who were dominated by abstract theoretic interests.'[1] 'Consider the early stage of mathematics. . . . About five hundred years before Christ, the Greeks initiated its theoretical development for the love of the theory.' At the beginning of the sixteenth century, 'the science had been studied for about two thousand years. It had been elaborated in great detail. But, allowing for some minor qualifications, nothing had come from it except the intrinsic interest of the study. Then as if a door had suddenly opened, Kepler produced the first important utilization of conic sections. . .'[2]

Henri Poincaré writes in the same vein:

'We have only to open our eyes to see that the conquests of industry which have enriched so many practical men would never have seen the light if these practical men had been the only ones to exist, and if they had not been preceded by disinterested madmen who died poor, who never thought of the useful, but who were nevertheless guided by something more than their own caprice.'[3]

To take but one more witness, Bertrand Russell:

'Almost all great advances have sprung originally from disinterested motives. Scientific discoveries have been made for their own sake and not for their utilization, and a race of men without a disinterested love of knowledge would never have achieved our present scientific technique. . . . Faraday, Maxwell, and Hertz, so far as can be discovered, never for a moment considered the possibility of any practical application of their investigations.'[4]

These writers, who here speak with special knowledge, seem to me in the right. Demonstration is hardly possible, for we cannot get inside the minds of Newton and Darwin, Gauss

[1] Whitehead, *Introduction to Mathematics*, 32–3.
[2] *The Function of Reason*, 58–9.
[3] I owe the quotation to Dean Inge, *Christian Ethics and Modern Problems*, 201.   [4] *The Scientific Outlook*, 153.

and Maxwell, to see what their motives were. But we know how little concern they displayed for the application of their theories in practice; we know that for many of those theories they could have found applications if they had tried; and it is incredible that, if the interest of their research was really to facilitate practical control, they should year after year have persisted in their work, regardless of whether it gave the least indication that it had, or ever would have, utility in practice. One may say, of course, that they were madmen, as Poincaré ironically suggests. Madness would then be an object of general admiration. But this view would hardly help the pragmatist; for thought is still thought, even if done by a madman, and ought not, in his account of it, to be thus impractical anywhere.

Pragmatists have sometimes replied that the practical interest that drives the mathematician and metaphysician, even if not an interest in applying theories immediately, is still practical in a larger sense. It is practical as the interest of the competitive sportsman is practical; that is, it is a bid for prestige in perhaps the only way that one's position and powers leave open. The aim of the runner is not simply to circle the track, but to outdistance all competitors, and if possible leap into a niche in the hall of fame by breaking previous records. The aim of the football player is not merely to carry the ball beyond the enemy goal-posts; if it were, he would steal out in the dark of the moon and put it there; his interest is in a feat where greatness is measured by the difficulties in his way; and his satisfaction is in the joy of surmounting them and getting the subsequent acclaim. So of the metaphysician. He is, as Matthew Arnold called him, an intellectual athlete. His interest is in gaining recognition, applause and security by carrying the ball of speculation farther, and through a more formidable field of subtleties, distinctions and intricacies, than for ordinary men is possible.

Such a theory is a healthy corrective to those, if there are such, who regard philosophers as disembodied intelligences with the single desire for more light. Some of the greatest virtuosi in thought as in art have frankly admitted that their motives were mixed; Hume confessed to having philosophized for fame, as Michelangelo confessed to having painted for money. But (a) the very mixture of motives here admitted makes it implausible to say that all our motives are of one type, the practical. The first impression that one gets in venturing into this twilight region of motivation is of the immense and bewildering complexity of men's interests, making one feel, regarding the pragmatist's exaltation of practical interest as the only one that ever drives us to think at all, that it is merely an attempt to force the facts into one of those a priori generalizations that he and his school had professed to abhor.

(b) The applause of others, still further, is not my act; even the enjoyment I get from the applause is not my act; it is difficult to see how ideas directed to such ends can be called 'intentions to act' at all. The pragmatist may reply that some specific action is still my immediate end, which is quite consistent with owning fame as my ultimate end. But it is precisely because it was so obvious that the immediate end of philosopher and scientist was *not* action that the doctrine of ultimate ends was invoked. One cannot fall back on ultimate ends because the immediate ones are non-practical, and then when the ultimate ends prove non-practical too, insist that the immediate ones are practical after all. To say that is not only contradictory; it is to render the whole argument pointless.

(c) In the analogy of the physical to the intellectual athlete, one important resemblance is slurred. The football player's success depends on conforming to the rules of the game. He wants to get the ball to the goal; he wants the applause of the crowd; but neither end is for him worth getting except through the scrupulous observance of regulations which are not of his own making. So it is with the thinker. He may pursue his speculation to gain an appointment, a livelihood, or applause; but the instant he allows these interests to override his concomitant interest in conforming to the exactions of logic, which are the rules of the game of thought, he is lost. Indeed in the long run his only chance of impressing his audience lies in forgetting the attempt to impress them while he follows his argument where it leads. The pragmatist error is like that of the hedonist. Pleasure is an actual and legitimate aim, but if anyone says that it is the only thing men are interested in, he invites the old and legitimate reply that much of the pleasure they actually get would have been impossible unless they had desired something else. If men have found pleasure in fox-hunting, it is only because for the time they could forget about hunting pleasure, and hunt foxes.

10. (ii) This leads us from the historical to the psychological difficulty in saying that thought is a means to practice. The view runs counter to the results of introspection. When we examine the motives of an act of thought, we normally find *two* motives, or sets of motives, which are sharply distinct from each other; and it is hard to resist the suggestion that the pragmatist has failed to distinguish them as clearly as he should. In every act of judging or thinking there is (*a*) the *outer* motive, the desire to accomplish something by the act— to confound or impress or entertain someone else, to advance or amuse oneself. Then there is also (*b*) the *inner* motive, the simple desire to see the facts. How completely distinct these are will be clear if we consider that they may vary independently of each other.

(*a*) Suppose I am left for an hour with a child, and have somehow to entertain him. Here is a practical problem. I strike upon the expedient of telling him stories about children in other lands, and proceed to run through my slender repertory. I tell him first about how children study, or used to study, in China, all shouting aloud at once; then about children skating to school on the canals of Holland; then about pupils and their *gurus* in India. Here the content of my *inner* motive, what I am seeking to single out, see truly, and report, varies constantly; my meaning glances from one fact to another as I go along. But my *outer* motive, the purpose that leads me to think, remains the same throughout, namely to amuse the child.

(b) Suppose that at intervals, while I am talking, two friends drop in. One is a veteran traveller; the other is the lady of my heart. Each asks me to repeat a story I have told to the child. It is obvious that if I comply, I may do so from very different *outer* motives. I know that to the traveller my story is stale and threadbare, and would not amuse him in the least; still I may repeat it to check its accuracy, or to tempt him into embroidering it. And if I tell the same tale to the lady, it may be in the interest of fortifying a favour that is too fluctuating. But throughout these variations of outer motive, my inner motive remains the same. I am meaning and reporting the same things. I may be using the story differently, but after all it is the same story that I tell. Can anything be clearer than that this interest in fact is distinct from the interest in achieving results? It is true that the two may never exist in separation, that all thought may have ulterior motives and all practice take account of fact. But this is neither here nor there. The point is that, separable or inseparable, these interests are *not* the same.

11. (iii) To these historical and psychological points we may add a logical one. What ideas intend, says the pragmatist, is 'certain changes in prior existing things'.[1] 'To judge that this object is sweet, that is, to refer the idea or meaning "sweet" to it without actually experiencing sweetness, is to predict that when it is tasted—that is, subjected to a specific operation—a certain consequence will ensue.'[2] Now it seems to me neither a fact nor even a logical possibility that such 'changes' or 'consequences' should constitute what I mean. When the plain man says that sugar is sweet, he is not asserting that something might *happen* to him if he engaged in certain actions; he is declaring that an attribute holds of the sugar now. It would be no answer to say that secondary qualities do not belong to things in nature; the issue is whether it is possible to *think* that they do; and of that the plain man's meaning is proof enough. But one does not need to rest one's case on the plain

---

[1] *Essays in Exp. Logic*, 304.   [2] *Quest for Certainty*, 137.

man. Not even the most sophisticated subjectivist really means by 'This lump is sweet' a hypothetical future event. To be sure, there *are* events that are of great importance to his judgement. If the event of tasting sugar had never occurred to him, he would probably not have made the judgement; if a like event, coming later, revealed that the sugar was not sweet, he would abandon his earlier belief, events are the indispensable vehicles by which qualities are laid hold of. But all this is quite irrelevant. The assertion of a quality remains one thing and the assertion of an event another. The thought of sugar as sweet is not the expectancy of a future change, but the assertion of a present attribute. That is attested unequivocally by an inspection of common meaning.

Here it is that the logical consideration enters. One can see that unless the meanings are accounted distinct, one arrives at nonsense in more than one way. 'That sugar is sweet'; 'if I taste that sugar, I shall have certain experiences of sweetness'; that these judgements express two truths rather than one is made clear, I think, by the fact that if the first were called in question, one would appeal to the truth of the second as an independent verification. If the two *meant* the same, there would be no virtue in such an appeal. Further, if the two meant the same, it would be nonsense that one should be true and the other false, whereas this is clearly possible. When a man says 'sugar is sweet', I may accept his judgement as true, even though I happen to know that his taste-bulbs have suddenly been paralysed, so that his prediction of what he would experience if he tasted the sugar no longer holds. The fact that such knowledge would serve to refute the second judgement but not the first is a further proof of their difference. Finally, it is impossible that meaning should be confined to change, for the thought of change without reference to anything that changes would, to say the least of it, be a feat of abstraction beyond normal powers. But it is idle to say that the thought of that which changes is itself the thought of change. And thus to say that all thought is concerned with change or with events cannot be true.

12. The pragmatist may reply that he does not need reminding of these platitudes, and is saying nothing opposed to them. Thus Professor Dewey, protesting against a critic's attributing to him the view that thought exists for action, writes:

> 'I have never taught that all needs were practical, but simply that no need could be satisfied without action. Our needs originate out of needs that at first were practical, but the development of intelligence transforms them so that there are now aesthetic, scientific, and moral needs.' Further, 'I have never said that thought exists for the sake of action. On the contrary, it exists for the sake of specific consequences, immediate values, etc. What I have insisted on is a quite different point, namely, that action is involved in thinking and existential knowing, as part of the function of reaching immediate non-practical consequences.'[1]

Many students must have read this with surprise. If they are familiar with Dewey's writings, passages will come crowding back that seem to bear a very different tenor. An idea is an 'intention to act so as to arrange them (things) in a certain way'.[2] 'Knowing is itself a mode of practical action';[3] 'ideas are statements not of what is or has been, but of acts to be performed';[4] 'an idea is a suggestion of something to be done or of a way of doing'.[5] And as if to enforce the idea that action is the ultimate as well as the immediate end: 'The end is no longer a terminus or limit to be reached. It is the active process of transforming the existent situation.'[6] In the light of these passages and a multitude like them, readers may perhaps be pardoned if they have supposed that, for the pragmatist, thought *did* exist for the sake of action. Yet Professor Dewey's denial is unequivocal, and, of course, for his own position

---

[1] Montague, *Ways of Knowing*, 135, note.
[2] *Essays in Exp. Logic*, 310.   [3] *Quest*, 104.
[4] *Ibid.*, 133.   [5] *Reconstruction*, 118.
[6] *Ibid.*, 177. Cf. James: 'And the tangible fact at the root of all our thought-distinctions, however subtle, is that there is no one of them so fine as to consist in anything but a possible difference of practice.' —*Pragmatism*, 46.

decisive. What can it mean? Apparently it means this, that while the *immediate* concern or preoccupation of thought is always with action, there may be an *ulterior* end to which this action is a means, and which itself is other than action. On this two comments are called for. In the first place, it does not meet the charge that according to pragmatism thought exists for action. For the central point of that charge is that the *immediate* preoccupation, the *direct* concern of thought need *not* be with action, that ideas generally cannot be called 'statements of acts to be performed', or 'suggestions of something to be done', that what I think of need not be 'a way of doing' of any kind. And to *that* contention the pragmatist has no answer, for this precisely *is* his untenable position. Nor can one make that position credible by adding that the action allegedly pointed to is itself instrumental to something else, for it is not this perfectly harmless contention, which most opponents of pragmatism would not dream of denying, that is under attack. That is a point that can only be settled independently.

But, secondly, suppose, since it has been raised, that it is settled as Professor Dewey above suggests. Surely the polemic of pragmatism will now have lost much of its force. The ends of thought need not now be practical; they are also 'aesthetic, scientific and moral'. To recognize distinctly 'scientific' needs is, I suppose, to recognize needs that are distinctively cognitive or theoretic; their satisfaction is now quite legitimate; and thought is free to enter their service. But why, if this is true, the sustained attack, in the *Reconstruction in Philosophy* and elsewhere, on the philosophers who seek such goods, and the demand that they return to something practical as alone worth while? Is it because Professor Dewey thinks their theoretic goods *comparatively* unimportant? Is it because they have miscalculated the value of action as a means to the goods of theory? But these are not differences of *principle* through which philosophy generally can be 'reconstructed', but only differences about the relative importance of certain ends and certain means.

13. (2) But the bias of thought for practice, while perhaps the most interesting, is not the only contention of the pragmatic theory of thought; the theory challenges accepted doctrine, as we have seen, in at least five points; and we must turn to the others.

Ideas are 'intentions to act'. We have looked at the 'act'; let us look at the 'intentions'. *Intentions*; that is, the reference is to the future rather than to the present or past. Dewey, expounding and accepting James on ideas, writes:

'what they, as ideas, ultimately intend is *prospective*—certain changes in prior existing things'.[1]

And presenting his own view:

'So far as ideas are not fancies, framed by emotionalized memory for escape and refuge, they are precisely anticipations of something still to come aroused by looking into the facts of a developing situation.'[2]

'Ideas are anticipatory plans and designs which take effect in concrete *r*econstructions of antecedent conditions of existence.'[3] In judgements about the past, 'the nature of the past event is subject-matter required in order to make a reasonable judgement about the present or future. The latter thus constitutes the object or genuine meaning of the judgement.'[4]

These passages seem clear enough. They appear to say that all thought has a future reference, and that no thought means or refers to the past. Such an interpretation fits naturally into the pragmatic view that ideas are instruments of action, means of escape from block-situations; for if ideas are really such instruments, they will be directed to the changes they may effect; and these of course lie in the future. The present writer must confess that in the light of such statements as the above, he for a time interpreted pragmatism as holding that thought of the past was impossible. This is a shocking doctrine, to be sure, but pragmatists are not notably averse to shocking people; and after all, there were these plain words. But he soon had a chastening experience of the perils of pragmatist philology.

[1] *Essays in Exp. Logic*, 304.   [2] *Reconstruction*, 143.
[3] *Quest for Certainty*, 160.   [4] *Journal of Philosophy*, XIX. 313.

He found that certain writers of repute had earlier extracted from these words the same meaning he had read in them, and, venturing to say so in print, had met with a denial from their author that he had meant anything of the kind.[1] And of course Professor Dewey does constantly use language that implies reference to the past, so that if he also held the view that such reference was impossible, the incoherence would be flagrant. But when charged with such incoherence, he replies that if we understand him, there is none; that one may hold with perfect consistency *both* that judgement may refer to the past *and* that every judgement refers to the present or future. His explanation is, in substance, as follows:

Judgement about a past event, like every other kind of judgement, is a process of settling a doubt, and may be conceived after the analogy of a trial at law. In each there are two elements that particularly require to be kept distinct. (1) In every trial there is a 'subject-matter', a great mass of accepted facts and considerations which are taken to be relevant and used as a basis for reaching a verdict, such as the evidence and the rules of law. (2) Then there is what may be called the 'reference', 'object', or 'meaning' of the process, which is the matter to be determined, for example the prisoner's guilt or innocence, and which gains expression in the verdict. It is in the former of these, the unquestioned, accepted subject-matter, that the retrospective reference lies. In attempting to determine the latter, the object of judgement, *what* the verdict shall be, which is after all the point of the process, our main concern is with the future. Let us now apply this distinction[2] to an ordinary judgement of the past. A biographer asserts that Swift married Stella. What is the subject-matter? It is the

---

[1] *Journal of Philosophy*, XXI. 197 ff. In Vols. XIX to XXI there is a valuable series of seven articles, three by Professor Dewey, three by Professor Lovejoy, and one by Professor Lamprecht, dealing chiefly with the point here at issue. See also Lovejoy's chapter in *Essays in Critical Realism*. Together with his three articles above mentioned, this forms a penetrating commentary on pragmatism, to which I am at several points indebted.

[2] I take it that this distinction is the same as that between 'content and 'reference' in *The Influence of Darwin*, 161.

mass of facts he takes as relevant and from which his decision springs, the testimony of Orrery, Delany, and Sheridan, significant passages in the *Journal to Stella*, various known facts about the conduct of Stella and Swift. What is the object or meaning of the judgement? With the main purpose of the distinction in mind, and in the light of various phrases, we should have expected Professor Dewey to say simply 'future consequences'. Ideas, we had read, are 'anticipations of something still to come'; it is 'the present or future' that 'constitutes the object or genuine meaning of judgement'. But Dewey here takes us by surprise. The object, he tells us, is more complicated; it is not the future change, but the entire continuum of events stretching from the event in the past—in this case the alleged marriage—to those of its present or future consequences which we should use if we wished to verify it.

> 'The object is some past event in its connection with present and future effects and consequences. The past by itself and the present by itself are both arbitrary selections which mutilate the complete object of judgement.' 'The object of knowledge in such cases is a temporal sequence or continuum including past-present-future.'[1] 'The object is a temporal continuum in which the past event is but one portion, a portion that becomes logically meaningless if it be isolated and made exhaustive.'[2]

Though this comes as a surprise, it is perhaps not hard to see why it should have commended itself. The pragmatists had taken the view that thought was always and essentially a means to future results; in these results, therefore, lay its meaning, its verification, its very truth. The recalcitrant judgement of retrospect now threatens to involve all this in ruin; its reference seems to be uncompromisingly to the past. Does it really ruin everything? No, there is one possibility. If it can be established that the concern of such judgement is not with the past alone, but the past *as continuous with and determining future consequences*, the situation is saved. Such an interpretation, by giving to the

---

[1] *Journal of Philosophy*, XIX (1922), 314, 351.
[2] *Ibid.*, XXI (1924), 201.

judgement of the past a public pragmatic baptism, would effectively silence those critics who charge that pragmatism does not provide for it.

14. The interpretation is ingenious, but the facts are against it. The intractable reference to the past, that skeleton in the pragmatic closet, is no sooner securely boarded up than it breaks out again to revive old scandals.

(i) Where exactly does it fall in the pragmatist's division of elements? Does the past event that is somehow referred to belong to the subject-matter or to the object? Unfortunately, he cannot assign it to *either* place. Suppose we assign it, as he sometimes urges, to the side of subject-matter.[1] This means that when I judge 'Swift married Stella', that event is to be put down among the 'accepted considerations' in which I acquiesce unquestioningly as a preliminary to the real business of judging. But surely my assertion of this event, far from being a preliminary or a side-show, is the very pith and point of my assertion. The main object of my concern is whether or not this event occurred, and to classify my assertion of it with my acceptance of unquestioned subject-matter is to leave the judgement gutted. It is in effect to deny that thought can ever explicitly concern itself with the occurrence of a past event, and to say that history in its entirety reduces to a 'subject-matter required in order to make a reasonable judgement about the present or future'. It would be interesting to know if Mr. James Harvey Robinson, who has accepted so much from pragmatism, would accept this also.

Unhappily, if the reference to the past is not part of our acceptance of subject-matter, neither is at home in the domain of meaning. We have seen that according to the pragmatist the judgement 'Swift married Stella', if it is to be capable of

---

[1] 'The nature of the past event is subject-matter required in order to make a reasonable judgment about the present or future. The latter thus constitutes the object or meaning of judgment.'—*Journal of Philosophy*, XIX. 313; cf. *The Influence of Darwin*, 141.

verification or truth, must mean, not only a past event, but that event as part of a chain of which some present or future link can be experienced. And with this he appears to think that the sting of the judgement of the past has somehow been drawn; if the object of such a judgement is the past, it is at least also the future; and thus we may say, after all, that judgements of the past do invariably have future reference. Professor Lovejoy's incisive comment on this can only be regarded, I think, as justified:

'Mr. Dewey seems to suppose that when it is shown that any valid and verified retrospective judgment contains at least an implicit reference to the present and future, we are thereby relieved of all logical concern about its primary reference to the past. It is as if an astronomer, observing in the spectrum of a star both red and yellow rays, should say to himself: "This red is evidently merely a red-in-connection-with-yellow; it will therefore suffice, in my study of the star, if I consider only the yellow, disregarding any problems which may have to do solely with the red." But, as Mr. Dewey's own expressions inevitably and repeatedly concede, the past reference still remains, an essential aspect of the present cognitive experience.'[1]

It may be asked, Why not allow the pragmatist his reference to the past? Why first reproach him for using language that seems to exclude such reference, and then continue to hound him when he seeks to admit it? The answer is that the exclusion of such reference is what his theory really requires and that his attempt to deal with it is a sort of afterthought which leaves it still unassimilated. In assertion about the past we have a type of judgement that is fundamentally inconsistent with the pragmatist's theory of thought, and in spite of his efforts and

[1] *Journal of Philosophy*, XIX. 507. Cf. the following from Professor Lamprecht: 'What we often seek to know is not the present and future which implicates a certain past, but the past which is implicated in the present and future. The object of knowledge is here neither the present and future nor the continuum of past-present-future, but the past which was once real and now is historical just because it is gone from us, the past which happens to be selected by us as a distinct item out of the more or less continuous history of nature and man.' —*Ibid.*, XX. 491–2.

protests he cannot accept it without either distorting its sense or disrupting his system. His chief contention about thought, the contention that has given his theory the names of instrumentalism and pragmatism, is that thought is the instrument of practice, a means of organic adjustment, of getting something done. But the thought that seeks to determine whether something happened in the past, however practical the end with which that judgement may be made, is palpably not, in its central assertion, concerned with action or control at all, or with any variety whatever of future consequences.

15. (ii) That the pragmatist has no place for judgements of the past is further attested by his way of dealing with casual reminiscence and with unverifiable historical belief. 'The development of reminiscence in old age', says Professor Dewey, 'is doubtless in part compensatory for withdrawal from the actual scene and its imminent problems, its urgencies for action.'[1] Doubtless; though not all elders, perhaps, would agree that surrender to the urgency of practice is the only way, or the best one, of knowing the real world. In any case, pragmatism takes a remarkable view of their thought. The old soldier who, in a mood of reminiscence, calls back the 'battles, sieges, fortunes' of his past, is apparently not thinking at all in any sense in which one can call his thoughts either true or false. Since thought is an instrument of action, summoned into use only by some block to practical response, and here both the block and the summons are absent, thought in the sense of judgement, the assertion of what is true or false, is likewise absent. But is not this very difficult doctrine? It is hard to see that the old man's recollections are a whit the less assertions, or one iota less true or false, because not aroused by some practical urgency. Such engrossment in the past seems to be taken by Professor Dewey as an indulgence in aesthetic fancy. But these memories may be accurate or wide of the mark, false or true; could that be said of aesthetic fancy? If the old

[1] *Journal o; Philosophy*, XIX. 312.

man, in idle reminiscence; says he was taken prisoner in the autumn of '63, when it was really the spring of '64, is he indulging himself in a day-dream? We are compelled, I think, on the contrary, to say that he has *judged* something to have occurred, and been mistaken.

There is a like difficulty about those judgements of history which, because asserted of the remote and trivial, are now incapable of verification.

> 'What did Brutus eat for his morning meal the day he assassinated Caesar? There are those who call a statement on such a matter a judgment or proposition in the logical sense. It seems to me that at most it is an aesthetic fancy such as may figure in the pages of a historic novelist who wishes to add realistic detail to his romance. Whence comes the intellectual estoppal? From the fact, I take it, that the things eaten for breakfast have left no consequences which are *now* observable. Continuity has been interrupted. Only when the past event which is judged *is a going concern having effects still directly observable are judgment and knowledge possible.*'[1]

That *knowledge* is here impossible may be conceded. If a past event is *spurlos versenkt*, gone without traces of any kind, whether witnesses, effects, or memories, the evidence needed for knowledge is clearly absent. But *judgement* about it impossible? Impossible in the proper sense even to *think* about such events? This doctrine, one suspects, will die of its own eccentricity, for it certainly involves very curious consequences. Suppose I guess or opine that Brutus did have breakfast on the morning of the assassination, and that it consisted of a little fruit and a dish of Roman oatmeal. This, says Mr. Dewey, is not really judgement or thought; it is 'at most an aesthetic fancy', and as such neither true nor false. But suppose a document comes to light, written by some Roman observer, which, by a happy accident, puts it beyond reasonable doubt that Brutus did breakfast in just that way. Does not that show that my opinion, whether I had a logical right to it or not, was in fact correct? But if correct, it was capable of truth or falsity;

---

[1] *Journal of Philosophy*, XIX. 311; italics here in original, as always unless otherwise noted.

and if thus capable, it was a judgement. And if it ever had this character at all, it must have had it *before* it was verified, since it is what I *then* thought that is verified now; the occurrence of the later event does not transform the nature of the earlier. Whether what I asserted shall be *known* to be true does depend upon the later event; nobody would doubt that. But it is either confusion or absurdity to say that the question whether I *meant* or *asserted* anything must wait for determination on what follows, and that a process that would otherwise have been mere aesthetic fancy is transmuted *post mortem* into judgement by the chance appearance of that which would confirm it. If it was not a judgement, there is nothing to verify; whereas verification clearly takes place. If it was a judgement, it must have been so when it occurred, independently of any prospect of verification. I do not wish to suggest that judgement may spring into existence with no grounds or evidence at all; and I do not wish to deny that there is a very important sense in which no one is properly thinking until what he grasps is grounded fully. But to say that precisely the same process is *not* judgement when the means of verifying it are still below the horizon, and *is* judgement when these means appear, is not only to confuse judgement with knowledge, but also to deny to many judgements of the past a meaning that they clearly possess.

16. (iii) One further comment. Suppose I make a certain judgement, and after a time experience the consequences that fulfil or verify it. By the time the consequences arrive, the judgement is of course a past event. How do I know that the consequences, when they arrive, are verifying or fulfilling anything? As Professor Dewey says, 'the fulfilling experience is not of itself knowledge'.[1] To know that the past judgement is verified is to look back from my present standing-ground and say, '*That* judgement yonder is being fulfilled in the events that are happening now'. Consider for a moment this

---

[1] *Influence of Darwin*, 87.

judgement of verification. Every judgement, we are told, has
a future reference, and until the consequences thus referred to
have unrolled themselves, it cannot be regarded as true. Very
well; suppose I affirm, as above, that the past judgement
receives verification in the present consequences. That judgement will itself have reference to *future* consequences, and
hence can be neither true nor known to be true till these consequences occur. But when they do occur, the judgement that
they verify the assertion pointing to them will itself have a
future reference upon whose fulfilment its own truth will in
turn depend. From which the odd conclusion follows not only
that no judgement is ever true at the time we make it, but
that no judgement whatever can at any time be known to be
true. It may indeed become true, but we can never *know* it to
be so. For the judgement that it is so always refers to *future*
consequences and will itself remain unverified till those
consequences appear. Thus we can never know that we
know anything.

Our conclusion about the judgement of the past is that its
essential meaning declines incorporation into the pragmatist's
theory of thought. It confronts him with the alternative of
either denying that it means what nevertheless it plainly does,
or admitting into his system a wine that is bound to break
the bottles.

17. (3) The next point in which the pragmatic theory of
thought runs counter to prevailing theories is closely connected
with the last, and is of the greatest importance for any such
theory. Most men believe that reflective thought can concern
itself with things that fall outside their own, or indeed anyone's
experience. This the pragmatist denies. He says that the thought
which does not lead on to differences in experience is not
thought at all, and that such differences exhaust the meaning
and truth of judgement. Pragmatism began, according to
James, with the insight of Peirce that the whole meaning of a
concept lay in the difference that would be made in experience

if the concept were true. Dewey, speaking for himself as well as Peirce, writes:

> 'In order to attribute meaning to concepts, one must be able to apply them to existence. . . . And the modification of existence which results from this application constitutes the true meaning of concepts.'[1] Again: '. . . the meaning of an idea is the changes it, as our attitude, effects in "objects." '[2] And again: ideas are 'indications of operations to be performed in order to effect a desired eventual rearrangement'.[3] In these rearrangements the meaning is fulfilled, i.e. the judgement is verified; 'final certitude can never be reached except experimentally— except by performing the operations indicated and discovering whether or no the intended meaning is fulfilled *in propria persona*'.[4]

These passages make it plain that a meaning or idea is a reference to changes which its own adoption is supposed to effect. But *what* changes? One would have thought that on so crucial a point the pragmatists would not fail to make themselves clear. But we have been unable to extract from their writings any clear answer to this question; or rather, we can extract so many inconsistent answers that the doctrine appears in the end a sort of hydra, which is almost beyond attack through the sheer multiplicity of its meanings. We shall comment briefly on what are perhaps the three most significant of these. The first would deny that reference beyond presented data was possible at all; the second would hold that it is possible, but is limited to individual experience; the third would extend the reference to the experience of others, but would deny that it could exceed this. Each of these doctrines seems to us clearly implied in pragmatist writings; each is inconsistent with both of the others; and each appears to be false in itself.

18. (i) The pragmatist may be surprised to hear that his theory confines him to the presentation of the moment, but it is easy to show that if he takes naturalism seriously, he is

[1] *Studies in the History of Ideas,* II. 355–6.
[2] *Essays in Exp. Logic,* 310. ·   [3] *Quest,* 143–4.
[4] *Influence of Darwin,* 103, note.

committed to nothing less. We may start from the unmistakable
fact that Professor Dewey distrusts and dislikes epistemology.
He does so because of his conviction that if one begins to play
its game, one is almost inevitably carried into epistemological
dualism, which in turn will very probably lead on to some
fantastic metaphysic of a dualist or idealist type, involving the
denial of naturalism. And as Santayana has said, it would be
hard to find a philosopher in whom naturalism was more
inveterate than in Dewey.[1] He holds that if you admit a world
of 'mental' experiences and ideas, distinct from the world of
tables and chairs, of bodies and their behaviour, you will never,
by any logical or metaphysical machinery, get them together
again.[2] There is no such thing as a distinctively mental content
which serves as the representative of something beyond it;
his theory, he says, is 'obviously inconsistent with presentative
dualism'.[3] Yet we have just seen that Professor Dewey seeks to
admit into his system the present reference to past events;
indeed he says unequivocally, 'I have not denied that practical
or instrumental knowledge involves a representation of non-
present existents by present data.'[4] This looks like a flat contradiction; knowledge both is and is not representative. But
Dewey is not unaware of the difficulty here, and he seeks to
meet it as follows. That which is immediately present and
carries the meaning is not an idea, and is nothing properly
mental at all; nor again is the process of meaning or referring
properly mental. Suppose a column of smoke on the horizon
suggests a camp-fire. Traditional psychologists would say
that the perception of the smoke gave rise to an *idea* of the fire,
and that it was through this mental vehicle that the absent
fire was presented. Dewey denies that any such vehicle exists.
What carries the reference, he says, is the smoke itself, which
is as truly physical an object as the fire. The only legitimate
sense in which it can be called mental is that it has a certain
function, the function of standing for something else.

[1] *Obiter Scripta*, 162.
[2] *Essays in Exp. Logic*, Chaps. IX and X.
[3] *Journal of Philosophy*, XIX. 359.   [4] *Ibid.*, XXI. 209.

'A thing which has or exercises the quality of being a surrogate of some absent thing is so distinctive, so unique, that it
needs a distinctive name. *As exercising the function we may call
it mental.* Neither the thing meant nor the thing signifying is
mental. Nor is meaning itself mental in any psychical, dualistic,
existential sense';[1] 'there must be some physical thing to
convey the meaning, if the latter is to be employed for intellectual manipulation and experimentation, or as an effective
hypothesis.'[2]

It is thus clear that *what* means, what carries the reference to
something else, is not an idea or a mental content, but a thing.
Now what exactly is intended by saying that this thing means
or signifies another thing? Dewey answers that this process
of meaning is as truly in the world of physical things and events
as either the thing meaning or the thing meant:

'This function, although embodying the logical relation, is itself
a natural and specifically detectable process among natural
things—it is not a non-natural or epistemological relation.'[3]
In what *sort* of physical process do these meanings consist?
'Of course upon my theory they are, existentially speaking, the
operations involved in any situation having cognitive reference.'[4]

The theory is now before us by which the contradiction about
transcendent reference is to be resolved. In every experience
of thinking there is something present that does refer beyond
itself, but since this representative is not 'existentially' mental,
epistemological dualism has been escaped.

19. (*a*) One can only say that, upon this theory, the pragmatist's escape from dualism is into something very much
worse. For if we take the above theory seriously, it means that
all meaning, thought, and reference are banished from the
world in every sense in which they transcend the directly
given. For physical things do not *mean* by themselves and in
their own right. The physical thing called smoke is as truly

---

[1] *Journal of Philosophy*, XIX. 358.   [2] *Ibid.*, 359.
[3] *Essays*, etc., 261.   [4] *Journal*, XIX. 358, note.

present to the man for whom it does not mean fire as to the man for whom it does; mere presence is not meaning. Because the letters carved on a Hittite rock are physically the same figures that they were to the men who carved them, are we to say that in seeing the figures we see the meaning? Obviously not. The *letters* do not mean. It was the Hittites who meant things *by* them; and it is precisely for that reason that the writing is so impenetrable to us; the Hittite *thoughts* upon seeing them had their being, not in the rock but in the Hittite mind; otherwise we could recover the meaning by mastering the physics of the rock.

(*b*) The pragmatist may point out in reply that though, in his theory, things mean, the meanings that they bear are not identical with the things themselves; they are *relations* or *functions* of these things. But this does not help. For these relations or functions, as we have seen, are themselves physical 'operations', and if there is anything clear about the function of meaning, it is that one can mean something by smoke *before* one has gone through the operations that would conduct one physically from smoke to fire. It may be true that in order to *verify* my meaning I should have to perform certain physical operations (though this does not seem to us true about thinking generally), but that is not here the point; the point is that the meaning, as opposed to its verification, may be present *before* the operations occur, and that hence to identify operations with meaning is impossible.

Where does this leave us? It leaves us absolutely imprisoned in the present datum. For there is nothing in the datum itself which could carry us beyond this, and the train of physical operations in which the function of meaning is said to consist has not yet unrolled. Thus the attempt to deal with thought in purely naturalistic terms merely drives it to suicide.

20. If Professor Dewey held to naturalism consistently, his theory of knowledge would be as bankrupt as naturalistic theories of knowledge commonly are. Fortunately he does not.

He frequently describes thought in ways that are beyond translation into naturalistic terms. Smoke 'is taken to mean something absent, say, fire. Yet it is not a case of sheer absence, such as total ignorance would imply. The fire is presented *as* absent, as intended.'[1] Professor Lovejoy has pointedly asked what is meant by saying that 'the fire is presented *as* absent'.[2] For there is certainly no such thing as this present-as-absent object in mere physical nature. When I look at the smoke and think of the fire, the *smoke* is not present-as-absent; it is merely present. The fire is not present-as-absent; physically it is just absent. Yet in some sense, the fire *is* present. What is this sense? In trying to avoid the obvious answer, namely, that it is present in consciousness, in thought or idea, pragmatic naturalists are ready to go to almost any extreme, to say that smoke *means*, to propose that chairs and tables look before and after, even to abandon their own principle that things are what they are known as, and deny that we are ever aware of having ideas at all. But too plainly we do have them. The only conceivable entity that could ever present anything as absent is an idea. How ideas do this is, of course, a nice problem, of which we shall have more to say later. What must here be insisted on is that if the reference to the absent is to be admitted at all—and the pragmatist, however inconsistently with his naturalism, does admit it—then the indispensable machinery of this reference must also be admitted; and that machinery, as he himself has just described it, could only be the idea. To talk about ideas as arbitrary figments of superstition, gratuitously dragged in by a timorous supernaturalism, is merely absurd; we are as familiar with ideas as we are with hands and feet. We cannot so much as think of a coming dinner without experiencing or meaning something that is neither absent as in total ignorance, nor present as in perception, but before us in that unique, though universally familiar, way that we call presence in idea.

Nothing less than such thought is implied in Professor Dewey's references to the present-as-absent. Hence he is an

[1] *Journal*, XIX. 354.   [2] *Ibid.*, XXI. 610.

epistemological dualist *malgré lui*. For he has admitted a present vehicle, other than the physical datum, which refers to, while clearly distinct from, the absent object. And if such a vehicle is admitted, it is difficult to see that pragmatism has any advantage over those philosophies that take the theory of knowledge seriously, and continue to struggle with the difficulties of the relation of thought to things.

21. (ii) The first theory implied in pragmatism regarding the reference of thought was a naturalistic theory, and this leads, as we have seen, to the imprisonment of thought in immediacy. But at times another view is implied, which we may call the individualist theory. It has its root in the notion that thought is a tool of the *organism*, an instrument of organic adjustment, a means to individual satisfaction. If such is the reference of thought, then, while I am no longer confined to the present, I am still confined to my own series of experiences. There are many passages in James and Schiller that point to this view, particularly if we bear in mind that for the prag-matist the reference of every idea is to those changes which at once confirm and comprise its truth. James, expressing the view of Schiller and himself, says that to be true 'means *for that individual* to work satisfactorily for him; and the working and the satisfaction, *since they vary from case to case*, admit of no universal description'.[1] Schiller ridicules the attempt to 'purchase exemption from the psychology of individual minds',[2] and holds that meaning and truth are so dependent on private purpose that 'the "same" predication may be "true" for me and "false" for you if our purposes are different'.[3] Dewey writes more cautiously; he nowhere says that meaning or truth is confined to individual experience, and indeed he does his best to deny it. And yet there is a great deal in his writing that without it is unintelligible. How does thought arise? Out of a

---

[1] *Meaning of Truth*, 243; italics mine.   [2] *Formal Logic*, 10.
[3] *Studies in Humanism*, 193.

block to activity. Whose activity? That of the individual
organism. What is the character of this thought? It is an
instrument of action. Whose action? That of the individual
organism. What is this action directed toward? Satisfaction.
What satisfaction? That which would satisfy the specific need
that the action was designed to meet. What need was this?
The need of adjustment, of restoring a divided experience to
harmony. Whose adjustment and whose experience? Those of
an individual organism. It is difficult to conceive whose else
they could possibly be. Dewey's naturalism with its behaviour-
istic leanings, his emphasis on biology and the influence of
Darwin on philosophy, his account of the origin of thought,
his conception of thinking as a way of acting, his stress on
specific needs and specific satisfactions, all this and a great
deal more are lost in mist if he is not talking of the behaviour
of individuals, of Smith, Jones, and Brown.

But if he *is* talking of these, how is he to escape the confinement of meaning to an individual stream of experience? The
tension that gives rise to thought is mine; the thought that
springs from it is simply an expedient of mine; the action to
which my thought is instrumental is my action; it takes its
character, we are tirelessly told, from the specific situation
in which my organism finds itself; certitude is achieved only
'by performing the operations indicated and discovering
whether the intended meaning is fulfilled *in propria persona*';
nothing whatever but these operations and their possible
fulfilment is either referred to by my thought or relevant to
its verification. A reader unversed in pragmatism might suppose
the charge unjust that it directs the reference of thought to
the verifying experiences themselves; belief in God, for
example, seems plainly to refer to God; could anyone really
identify the experiences that confirm a belief with the object
the belief refers to? Such a questioner has little conception of
how radical pragmatism is. It does quite literally say that what
I mean by God, the whole 'cash value' of that meaning, is
certain changes in human experience; and unless we take its
discussion of tensions, blocks, adjustments, satisfaction and

action in some Pickwickian sense, it is inevitable that for 'experience' we should read 'my experience'.

22. That the theory, so interpreted, is in conflict with the facts of reference need hardly be pointed out. As in the case of logical positivism, a very large part of philosophy, religion, and science would be instantly dropped as meaningless, since such concepts as that of God in the traditional sense, of reality as opposed to appearance, of an ultimate good, of the other side of the moon, of electrons and protons, of the physical universe generally outside the range of the 200-inch telescope, unquestionably claim a reference beyond the bounds of my own experience, either present or future. But the consequence is perhaps more disturbing that on this theory it could never refer to other selves. Certainly the aches and pains of other people, their pleasures, thoughts and purposes, are not given in my own experience; if the only ideas I can entertain are those whose 'intended meaning is (or may be) fulfilled *in propria persona*', I cannot think of them at all. Pragmatism is the victim here of another of those awkward alliances by which it has sought to strengthen its case, but which prove treacherous in the end. Its alliance with naturalism leads to a solipsism of the moment. Its alliance with radical empiricism, if taken seriously, can only end in destroying all reference beyond individual experience.

Pragmatists have protested vigorously against the finding of this implication in their theory. Their protests are variously based. (*a*) When Professor Pratt suggested the implication long ago, Dewey replied that the premises of the pragmatist had been misconceived. It had been assumed that the prag- matist, like his opponents, conceived of thought as a mental somewhat, inhabiting a private consciousness, and then *of course* the problem was urgent how thought could ever escape from this and make contact with a physical world. But the pragmatist, Dewey explained, begins with no such premise. The distinction between thought and things is for him a distinction of office or use. The mental does not differ from the physical in substance or kind; it *is* simply the physical conceived as performing a certain function, the function of standing for, or signifying, something else. Once understand that the pragmatist has avoided from the outset the old dualistic assumption, and the charge of confinement to his own experience will be seen to be baseless. This reply has sometimes been taken as decisive.[1] But whatever its value in the original controversy, it seems to us to ignore the true ground of the charge it seeks to meet. That ground is not at all that pragmatism assumes ideas conceived as mental, though we have seen that, however unwillingly, Dewey does admit these in effect; the ground is simply that, whether you take thought as mental or not, if you conceive it in the pragmatist way, as being in its nature and essence a means to successful behaviour on the part of an individual organism, the conditions you have yourself laid down for it prescribe inflexibly the limitations of which you are now so anxious to divest it. How they serve thus to limit it we have just seen.

(*b*) Sometimes, when confronted with the charge that he can mean only his own future, the pragmatist's reply is different again. He declares that thought is not an individual but a *social* affair.

> 'It is somehow born of a thoroughly social, objective world.' It remains 'all the while vitally and organically related to its matrix. *Not only in its origin, but in its continued development and operation must it always be a function of the whole social situation of which it is born.* However "private" or "individual" consciousness may be, it is never to be regarded as *wholly* or *merely* the function of an individual "mind" or "soul" or *of a single organism or brain.*'[2]

A. W. Moore, who wrote this, was surprised at the critics' failure to see that the pragmatists had meant this all along, and he seems to have thought the notion, once expressed, would

---

[1] As by A. W. Moore, *Pragmatism and Its Critics*, 225 ff. For the original papers, see Pratt, *Journal of Philosophy*, V (1908), 122 ff.; Dewey, *Ibid.*, 375 ff.; Pratt, *What is Pragmatism?* 123–6.

[2] Moore, *op. cit.*, 229, 230.

be found obvious. I confess that I do not find it so. I cannot imagine what is meant by calling a 'social situation' conscious, or saying that it can think. I find a clear sense in saying that we can think of the same things, that we can pursue the same end, that we can take account of each other's thoughts, that we often believe what we do because others do; but none of these things requires a 'social situation' that is conscious or thinks as a whole; and the one sense that might really help, that of the absolutists, according to which all things and all men are components of a single mind, is part of a metaphysic that pragmatists abhor. Nor do Moore's illustrations clear up the matter. He says that when I go to the dentist, 'his thinking is as literally a function of my organism as his own. *His* effort is *my* way of making *the* readjustment, which belongs equally to us both'.[1] If this means that the dentist and his work are agents that I use deliberately in reaching my end, it is true. If it means what it seems to say, that 'his thinking is literally a function of my organism' in the sense that my own thinking is, I confess I can make nothing of it. Of course words are defenceless things, and if I wish, I can define as a function of my organism whatever contributes in any degree to my reaching my end, from buses and dentists and forceps to the law of gravitation. But the unity I achieve by so doing is purely verbal. My own organism on the one hand and the things and persons I use or refer to on the other cannot be lumped together in one thinking and acting unit. However much these things and persons may do in forcing problems upon me, and in determining their nature, the unalterable fact remains that if thought is conceived as a biological instrument, then its generating need, the activity in which it consists, and the satisfaction it is designed to attain, are those of the individual organism.

23. (iii) Both the restrictions of reference with which we have so far dealt, though they seem to be clearly implied in

[1] *Op. cit.*, 232.

the pragmatist's writing, are generally disavowed by pragmatists themselves. The third restriction, to which we now turn,
is part of the orthodox interpretation of at least the Deweyan
type of pragmatism. James, on this as on many other major
points, is so full of contradictory statements that it is impossible
to extract from him any coherent theory. But Dewey's expostu-
lations with him served to mark out a more consistent pragmatism. James, in discussing certain religious ideas, points
out their practical value, and observes: 'Other than this practical
significance, the words God, free will, design, have none.
Yet dark though they be in themselves, or intellectualistically
taken, when we bear them on to life's thicket with us, the
darkness then grows light about us.'[1] James never quite settled
with himself whether beliefs of this kind had a reference
beyond experience, a meaning of their own, 'intellectualistically
taken', which was verified though not exhausted by later
consequences, or whether these experienced consequences
were *all* they meant. Dewey notes this irresolution and defines
his own view by contrast:

> 'Is it meant that when we take the intellectualistic notion
> and employ it, it gets value in the way of results, and hence has
> some value of its own; or is it meant that the intellectual content
> itself must be determined in terms of the changes effected in
> the ordering of life's thicket?'[2]

For himself he has 'no hesitation' in taking the latter view.
The ideas of God, design, etc., *mean* the experienced changes,
and these only. An idea which 'by its nature can never be
empirically verified, or cashed in any particular case' cannot,
for the pragmatist, have meaning at all. 'Reality must be
defined in terms of Experience';[3] and this experience, says
Dewey, is not yours or mine merely; the end of thought is
not 'some purely personal end, some profit upon which a
particular individual has set his heart'.[4] The meaning of an
idea, like the purpose and utility of a road, may lie in long-
continued service to an almost innumerable public.

[1] *Pragmatism*, 121.   [2] *Essays in Exp. Logic*, 316.
[3] Preface to *Studies in Logical Theory*.   [4] *Reconstruction*, 157.

24. In spite of the persuasive sound of this doctrine, it will not bear examination. (*a*) It distorts, and distorts violently, in the interests of a special theory, meanings of which I am far more certain than I can be of the theory itself. It tells me, for example, that to think of God in the sense in which people for many centuries have supposed they were thinking of Him is impossible; 'the pragmatic method would simply abolish the meaning of an antecedent power';[1] what people are really thinking of when they think of God is certain later experiences of myself and the race. Now it is certainly often difficult to say what one does mean by 'God'. But of one thing I am perfectly clear. I do *not* mean by 'God' a series of future experiences of myself and the race. Nor does it seem to me unduly assertive to say that I am in a better position to know about this than the person who questions it. To be sure, my meanings are sometimes so vague that another person could justly say to me, 'You really don't know what you mean'. But where the reference is moderately definite, gross confusion is hardly possible. If, so far as I can tell, I am thinking of my maiden aunt, I should be pretty confident that someone else would be wrong if he told me that this very same thought was a reference to the Codex Sinaiticus. And I do not think it would be much more plausible to tell St. Thomas, when he thought of God as existent but uncreated, that what he meant, though he did not know it, was a series of racial experiences that had not yet occurred. He took pains to be clear as to what he meant by God; he certainly knew what he meant by future experiences; and to say that to the end of his life he was confusing one with the other seems to me absurd.

We may be met here with the familiar reply that the absurdity lies only in our interpretation of pragmatism, that when it stresses the reference of thought to future experiences, all it means is that these must be forthcoming if the thought is to be verified. *If* God exists, as my thought intends, then experience will disclose some traces of His being. But this thoroughly conventional suggestion can hardly be what prag-

[1] *Essays in Exp. Logic*, 315.

matism means; indeed Dewey explicitly rejects it; it was one of those aberrations of James against which he felt obliged to protest. He holds it a mistake to say that 'the intellectualistic notion . . . has some value of its own', and insists that 'the intellectual content itself must be determined in terms of the changes effected'. That this latter construction is correct is confirmed by the polemic of *The Quest for Certainty*, which lays the sterility of modern philosophy very largely to the view 'that knowledge is concerned with disclosure of the characteristics of antecedent existences and essences', 'that the office of knowledge is to lay hold of existence which is prior to and apart from the operations of inquiry and their consequences'.[1] No, we must at least credit the pragmatist with saying something important. He is not repeating old saws to the effect that beliefs should be verified. He is not merely offering advice to the effect that philosophers should take thought for the morrow. He is proposing a revolution in the conception of meaning. He is contending that the reference of thought is always and solely to future perceptual consequences.[2]

25. (*b*) But there are further and, I think, insuperable difficulties in this doctrine. It implies that no general proposition can be so much as conceived. This implication has often been pointed out, and often protested against by pragmatists without, so far as I know, having ever been effectively answered. No series of particular experiences, even if that series were to include all the experiences in the history of the race, can exhaust the meaning of a universal proposition. And science would be impossible without such propositions. Every

---

[1] *Quest*, 71, 173.

[2] It may be said that this is inconsistent with Professor Dewey's admission that part, at any rate, of the object of thought in judgements of the past, is the past event, as opposed to future consequences. I fear it *is* inconsistent. But the above doctrine seems to be the prevailing one.

generalization in the physical sciences is dependent for its validity upon a law which pragmatism makes inconceivable. That the law of uniformity of nature is empirically unverifiable is notorious, and this implies that if taken in its received meaning, it would, for the pragmatist, be untrue. But he goes much farther. He is compelled to hold that the meaning it has always been supposed to have was never there to verify. What it has commonly been taken to assert is that causation is universal, that every event in nature, past, present, or future, observed or unobserved, follows from a cause. The pragmatist, if he is loyal to his prospective empiricism, must restrict this to 'all events that are yet to be experienced are caused'. But so to read the principle of uniformity is inconsistent with its use in science, and logically fatal. It is inconsistent with its use in science because the causal laws of science are conceived as holding equally in past and future, and because every inference from past to future asserts that law did hold in the past. It is logically fatal because every inference from one instance to another assumes the law of uniformity to be universal, and is invalid unless it is. But it is needless to take propositions as general as this. There is no law of any science that can be assigned, on pragmatic terms, the meaning that it bears in that science. It is idle to say that the physicist *means* by the law of gravitation only future experienced instances of it; if he did, they would not even be instances, for there would be no *law* that they exemplified; they would be chance resemblances only. That this view should be regarded as particularly close to science is curious, since it is compelled to reject the view of nature that most scientists accept, in which nature is infinitely greater than human experience of it and shot through with law. When the pragmatist thinks of the facts of nature, he is thinking, as Mr. Santayana says, of 'appearances integrally woven into a panorama entirely relative to human discourse. Naturalism could not be more romantic; nature here is not a world but a story'.[1]

[1] From a review of Dewey's *Experience and Nature*, *Obiter Scripta*, 171.

26. (*c*) Is the theory consistent with itself? There is good reason to suspect it is not. The answer depends on whether the pragmatist is offering the theory as itself a generalization. When he says that all thought refers to prospective experience, is he talking about future experiences of thought or about the character of thought as such? What his theory requires is the former. But if he does mean that, his doctrine loses much of its interest. It is not a philosophical doctrine at all, because it does not profess to hold of thought generally, but only of such experiences of thought as are yet to come. He may reply that to tax his doctrine with being unphilosophic is unjust, since, in the terms of his own theory, only this kind of philosophic doctrine is possible. But when he says *this*, is he putting forward only another particular proposition? It seems clear that he is not, that when he talks of what is and is not *possible* for thought, he is not talking merely of how thought may be expected to behave, but of what the nature of thought prescribes. And thus we are brought to the other sense in which his doctrine may be taken. It may be a genuinely philosophic assertion about the intrinsic character of thought. And there is every indication that this is what it is meant to be. When Dewey analyses the thought process, distinguishing its occasion, its data, its end, the process of verification, he certainly does not give the impression of seeking results or making predictions merely; he seems to be laying down a doctrine about the working of thought as such, a doctrine, therefore, which is as truly general as any law of physics, and which is as clearly meant to hold of thought as exercised in ancient Egypt or modern Patagonia as of the deliberations of to-morrow. This is plainly the sense in which most of his readers read him, and if they found that in this they were mistaken, that his doctrine neither held nor was meant to hold of thought as such, but only of the course of coming experience, their sense of its value would be very different. But if the analysis is, as it seems to be, offered as generic, then it is self-refuting. It is itself a judgement possessing that universality of meaning, that reference beyond the bounds of any possible verifying experience, which on pragmatic grounds should be impossible. Its own natural claim and sense are in open conflict with the view that 'the object of knowledge is prospective and eventual'.[1]

We have been studying the pragmatist view of transcendence, i.e. of whether ideas may refer beyond experience, and if so, in what sense. We have found three views, two implicit and one avowed. The first or naturalistic view, if taken seriously, would preclude transcendence wholly and confine thought to the immediate. The second or individualist view, which was implied by the pragmatist theory of the genesis of thought, and would limit reference to individual experience, is inconsistent with the belief in society. The third, or social view, would impose no restriction of reference except to future events in the experience of the race. But even this reference proves too narrow. For in numberless propositions, historical, theological, scientific, even in the main propositions of pragmatism itself, we are transcending the limit so imposed. On this matter of transcendence the only conclusion open to us is thus that pragmatism has still to evolve an acceptable theory.

27. (4) Fortunately, the other main points in which the pragmatist account of thought challenges accepted views may be dealt with more briefly.

Is Professor Dewey a behaviourist? He has answered the question in what looks like unequivocal terms:

> 'Instrumentalism means a behaviourist theory of thinking and knowing. It means that knowing is literally something which we do; that analysis is ultimately physical and active . . .'[2]
> 'More particularly, the pragmatist has insisted that experience is a matter of functions and habits, of active adjustments and readjustments, of co-ordinations and activities, rather than of states of consciousness.'[3] What used to be called 'states of consciousness' are really 'intra-organic events'; 'these events

---

[1] *Quest*, 173.   [2] *Essays in Exp. Logic*, 331-2.
[3] *Influence of Darwin*, 157.

> are continuous with extra-organic events . . . they serve as the
> means for the elaboration of a delayed but more adequate
> response . . .'[1]

Sense data are not in consciousness; 'from a strictly empirical
point of view, the smell which knows is no more merely mental
than is the rose known'.[2] Perception is not in consciousness;
'where, and in so far as, there are unquestioned objects, there
is no "unconsciousness". There are just things.'[3] Even ideas
are not in consciousness; they are 'intra-organic events,
adjustments within the organism'.[4] But if consciousness does
not appear in sensation, perception, or thought, it is safe to
say that it is not meant to appear anywhere. It is banished
from the pragmatist scheme of things.

Now our comments on the possibilities of behaviourism
as a theory of knowledge were given *in extenso* in the last
chapter. We saw that the attempt to identify the process of
thought with physical or organic changes was literally senseless;
it is about as intelligible to talk of a liquid solid or a snowy
blackness as to talk of a true or cogent or witty motion. But
we have covered this ground before, and shall only say that
if the above pragmatic statements are to be accepted at their
face value, the entire argument offered against the generalized
form of behaviourism is again applicable here.

I must confess quite simply to boredom with behaviourism,
and to a feeling that if it is not an almost incredible confusion,
it is a tiresome play on words. And if I believed Professor
Dewey to be really a member of this school, I should not have
paid him the sincere, if perhaps equivocal, compliment of
this extended criticism. But, as has already been more than
hinted, his philosophy bulges through the rickety crate of its
avowed behaviourism on every side. Its very essence is the
reality and power of reflective purpose, and where among
things do you find that? His pages are dotted with terms—
doubt, deliberation, inquiry, interest, inference, anticipation,
verification, truth—referring to objects that defy resolution

---

[1] *Essays*, etc., 227–8.   [2] *Influence of Darwin*, 104.
[3] *Essays*, etc., 225.   [4] *Ibid.*, 227.

into the movements of bodies. Even when he seeks with special care to exclude all reference to the mental as differing from the physical in kind, he still finds it necessary, as we have seen, to speak of the past and the remote as somehow 'present-as-absent', a kind of existence which, it is safe to say, no mere *thing* ever yet achieved.

What are we to say then as to whether pragmatism is also behaviourism? We must say, I think, that it is not really behaviourist, that it is far more responsible and sophisticated than that. Yet formally it disavows belief in any thought that is not a mode of behaviour in physical things. And this marks a conflict within itself. As Santayana has said, its naturalism is half-hearted. It wishes to have its cake and eat it, to make the best of both worlds, to use at will the apparatus of thought and purpose, and yet to get credit for the 'tough-mindedness' of the naturalist. But more than the word 'nature' is needed to bridge the chasm between these worlds, and we should suggest to the pragmatist that he make up his mind. If he means by nature what it means to the physical scientists whom he admires, then he can no longer continue to people it with anticipations, meanings and interests, which in nature as understood by the physicist would be as mythical as rocs and hippogryphs. On the other hand, if he means by it a sort of ultimate omnibus, in which meanings and verifications are somehow induced to sit companionably beside sticks and stones and organisms, then he should ask himself if he is not solving his problem with a word. For he is assigning to precisely that which is commonly meant by mind the *name* of nature, and concealing from himself the radical discrepancy under an identity of phrase.

28. (5) There is another and final point in the pragmatic theory of meaning that calls for comment. Philosophers have commonly assumed that it is possible to form concepts that are uncoloured by their own feeling, to follow their argument where an impersonal logic leads, and to reach conclusions dictated solely by the evidence, as opposed to their own biases and desires. This view is stigmatized by the pragmatists as 'intellectualism'. They do not believe that there is any such thing as a distinct faculty or function of intelligence which can go its own way uninfluenced by the rest of one's nature; thinking and knowing spring from every variety of need; they are activities of the man as a whole directed toward the satisfaction of this man as a whole, not to the satisfaction of any specialized logical sense. Hence the old ideal of the philosopher, 'passionless imperturbability, absolute detachment, complete subjection to a ready-made and finished reality', 'forswearing the reality of affection, and the gallantry of adventure',[1] must be abandoned for something more alive. And 'the moment the complicity of the personal factor in our philosophic valuations is recognized, is recognized fully, frankly, and generally, that moment a new era in philosophy will begin'.[2]

These statements by Mr. Dewey are forcible enough, but on this aspect of pragmatism he says comparatively little. While recognizing its importance, he seems to touch on it rather reluctantly; and though it would often permit and perhaps require his explanation of an opponent's error by the imputation of personal biases, his firm scrupulousness in controversy has forbidden its use.[3] Dr. Schiller's doctrine here was far more radical than Dewey's, and some critics, thinking that it had affected his polemical methods, avoided controversy with him. But it is certainly to Schiller that we must go for the clearest statements on this point.

> 'Whenever Logic, therefore, seeks to represent the actual nature of thinking, it can never treat of "the meaning" of propositions in the abstract. It must note that the meaning depends on the use, and the use on the user's purpose.'[4] 'Pure

---

[1] *Influence of Darwin*, 172.   [2] *Essays*, etc., 327.
[3] Though I think it has unconsciously influenced his account of the motives of rationalist philosophers, as offered in his *Reconstruction* and *Quest for Certainty*. I do not quite recognize in these likenesses the philosophers I thought I knew.   [4] *Studies in Humanism*, 82.

intellection is not a fact in nature; it is a logical fiction which will not really serve even the purposes of logic. In reality our knowing is driven and guided at every step by our subjective interests and preferences, our desires, our needs, and our ends.'[1] Hence the logician's approbation of 'the heroic self-sacrifice of his volitional preferences to "objective truth" which he "feels himself bound" to commit, is simply silly'.[2] 'Bias is and remains an ineradicable factor in all cognitive enterprises, and it is neither wise nor scientific to make believe that it has been eliminated.'[3] 'Actually every philosophy was the offspring, the legitimate offspring, of an idiosyncrasy, and the history and psychology of its author had far more to do with its development than *der Gang der Sache selbst*. . . .' 'A system of Philosophy is best regarded as a sort of poetry, and often of lyrical poetry at that!'[4]

Schiller's writing on pragmatism was full of assertions like these; and the central importance in his eyes of this entanglement of knowledge and thought with the rest of human nature is registered in the name of humanism, which he gave to his own theory.

This stress on the dependence of thought on non-rational pulls and pushes is less disturbing to-day than when Schiller gave it such provocative utterance; indeed Freud and his disciples have gone far toward making it a commonplace. And certainly at the lowest reckoning it contains much truth. Reflection supports the claims that meaning is affected vitally by its psychical setting, that thinking is most commonly prompted by non-theoretical interests, that it is capable of the craziest deflections and distortions under the influence of feeling and desire, that even when most rigorously controlled it never stays long in the groove of necessity, that no sharp line can be drawn between thought and feeling, that logical certainty carries with it psychological certitude, that logical necessity may enter as a contributing factor in the direction of psychical process and hence between the logic and psychology of thought there is again no absolute line, that the involvement

[1] *Humanism*, 9.   [2] *Studies in Humanism*, 92.
[3] *Mind*, XXXIX (1930), 486.
[4] *Must Philosophers Disagree?* 10, 11.

of thought with personality renders impossible complete mutual understanding, that probably no two persons, even in using identical words, ever mean wholly and exactly the same by them. These are very large admissions, and I think they must all be made to Schiller; indeed it is surely important, *humilitatis gratia*, that from time to time they should be repeated with emphasis and distinctness.

Does their significance go beyond this? Do they imply, as Schiller seems to suggest, that objective conclusions from objective evidence are impossible, and that even the thought of the most impartial minds is so deeply coloured with personal feeling, desire and prepossession that we must simply bow to the fact and content ourselves with living on personal islands, cut off from both objective truth and community of meaning? Such inferences seem to me to exaggerate beyond warrant the significance of the admitted facts.

29. (i) Granting that purposes and emotions do affect meanings, they affect some far less than others, the meanings of the mathematician, for example, than those of the artist. No doubt as the student of art works his way into his subject, the meaning of such a phrase as 'the art of Matisse' may change considerably; and when two artists use the phrase, it very probably does not mean for them quite the same thing; it has acquired rich overtones of value and emotion. Even so they can converse about it without seeming in Egyptian darkness as to each other's meaning. And when we turn to subject-matters with which feeling is less deeply engaged, our confidence that meanings are essentially the same may be complete. If two students of algebra see the same formula on the black-board, say $(a + b) \times (a + b) = a^2 + 2ab + b^2$, it is hardly plausible to say that their meanings are so perverted and permeated by subjective desire and emotion that they are not dealing with the same proposition. Nor are they wholly without check on this identity. If every relation and implication reported by the one appears to correspond to one reported

by the other, the likelihood that each is sunk in idiosyncrasy
may be reduced progressively to something like zero. One is
not totally unaware of the occasions and the extent of the
influence of feeling on thought, and can see, I think, quite
plainly that throughout most of the area of science, through
large reaches of logic and epistemology, and in many issues of
metaphysics, feeling is not deeply enough engaged to prevent
either substantial agreement between minds or substantial
fidelity to fact.

30. (ii) The admission that we can detect this influence is
itself significant, and in more than one way. It shows that
however strongly affected thought may be in fact by personal
desire and feeling, it is not so in intention or standard. If we
were really puppets of prejudice and incapable of anything
else, it would be senseless to condemn prejudice in ourselves
or others; yet that is what we do. The judge who reflects that
some statement in his charge to a jury was prompted by personal
dislike, or the scientist who realizes that it was vanity which
led him to withhold some negative evidence about his theory,
feels a shame that is irrational if loyalty to impersonal truth is
simply impossible. Schiller admits an ideal, but denies that
it is really impersonal. In our thinking

> 'we actually stop', he says, 'at the point at which we psycho-
> logically are satisfied,' 'but we can sometimes conceive ulterior
> purposes which would require further confirmation, and other
> minds that would be satisfied less easily. This engenders the
> ideal of a complete "logical" proof transcending that which is
> good enough for us, and capable of compelling the assent of
> all intelligences. But even if it could be attained, its certainty
> would still be psychological. . . .'[1]

There is nothing new in this attempt to explain logical
necessity through psychological fact. That it has failed and
must continue to fail has been shown, I think, often and
decisively, and an attempt will be made later to show this

[1] *Studies in Humanism,* 84.

again.[1] Here a remark or two must suffice. (*a*) The doctrine does not do justice to the radical difference between accepting something as fact and seeing that it could not be otherwise. There is an obvious and deep-going difference between 'grass is green' and 'at a given place and time grass cannot be both green and red', between '*x* is what men have always done' and '*x* ought to be done'. No succession of *is*'s will give a *must* or an *ought*, and descriptive psychology, which is an account of how men do think, feel and act, will always fall short of them. Nor can it explain their certainty as a mere feeling, for the feeling grows out of something belonging as truly in the content as anything else, a logically necessary nexus. (*b*) Any explanation of logical principles as having subjective validity only, presupposes such principles as objectively valid. Like every other theory, it involves argument from evidence; such argument is valid only if logical law is valid; and if this is admitted to be so valid, the conclusion of the argument is inconsistent with its own assumptions. For some such laws are assumed to be objectively valid in the very process of showing that none are so. (*c*) The significance of the theory would be destroyed by its own truth. For if thought is really controlled by bias, so also is the theory that it *is* so controlled. But why should I accept a theory that is itself admittedly the product of bias? If the theory is an *un*biased statement of truth, then it provides the exception which proves its own falsity. If it is itself an expression of bias, there is no more reason why I should accept it than I should some prejudice of my own which happens to be more pleasing.

31. (iii) The presence in the mind of an ideal of impersonal logic is significant in another way. Knowledge of bias may correct bias. One may allow for a prejudice consciously, and merely to see it as a prejudice tends to wither it away. If it is true, as it undoubtedly is, that no one has achieved the height

[1] Chap. XXVIII, and for the difference between association and inference, Chap. XXII.

(or depth) of the passionless sage, it is still surely undeniable that the effort to eliminate prejudice can largely succeed, that some men have succeeded more than others, and that their intellectual vision has been correspondingly cleared. One may even risk an example. I do not myself accept ethical hedonism, yet in my own mind, and I am sure in many others, one of the most persuasive considerations in its favour is the mere fact that it was accepted by Henry Sidgwick. Sidgwick's temper was so transparently judicial, 'prejudice against his own prejudices' was with him so habitual and ingrained an attitude, that when after the protracted weighing of pros and cons on an ethical problem he pronounced judgement upon it, the weight of the judgement was extraordinary. It is hard to see how anyone who had entered into the spirit of his fastidious and balanced discussions could feel it other than grotesque to apply to him the statement that our thought is 'driven and guided at every step by our subjective interests and preferences, our desires, our needs and our ends'. Nor do I think anyone likely to accept this view unless committed at the outset to gratuitous cynicism about human nature.

32. (iv) When thought is said to be driven by desire, it seems to be forgotten that the desire for impersonal truth is also a desire, and that it may drive with great insistence toward a satisfaction of its own. On this point we have already adduced testimony from distinguished men of science,[1] which there seems to be no reason to question. If the pragmatists wish to say that this interest in knowledge is an acquired taste, an off-shoot or by-product of other more important interests, they may do so, provided they add that the by-product is now independent, authentic, and powerful, that 'if man began to think in order that he might eat, he has evolved to the point where he eats in order that he may think'.[2] They would need to recognize, further, that the desire to know is in course of defining its end more clearly, that this end is not the end of

[1] Sec. 17.   [2] Montague, *Ways of Knowing*, 158.

human nature as a whole but a subordinate end within this, that it is so sharply distinct from the desire for power, or prestige, or security, or beauty, or wealth, that it may conflict with any or all of these, and that in rare cases it may mount to something like a passion, over-riding them and subjecting them to its service. It can furnish many excellent examples of what Chalmers called 'the expulsive power of a new affection'. That it need not be the servant of other passions, but may become in some degree their master has been the conclusion of some of the soberest and shrewdest students of human nature. 'To love truth for truth's sake', wrote John Locke in old age, 'is the principal part of human perfection in this world, and the seed-plot of all other virtues.' The same view was held by the thinker who is sometimes credited with introducing the pragmatic strain into modern thought. Bacon wrote: 'The inquiry of truth which is the love-making or wooing of it; the knowledge of truth, which is the presence of it; and the belief of truth, which is the enjoying of it, is the sovereign good of human nature.'[1]

33. We have now completed the review of the five leading points at which the pragmatist theory of meaning comes in conflict with accepted views: its instrumentalism, its futurism, its empiricism, its behaviourism, its humanism. We have confined ourselves to this side of the theory, partly because, as an account of the nature of thought, it is obviously the one that most concerns us, partly also because the other aspects, and above all that tempting target, the pragmatic theory of truth, has been so often and so adequately dealt with by other writers. In certain points of varying importance we have been able to agree with the theory. But on all the leading issues the

[1] According to W. E. Johnson, 'it is the presence of this purpose (the purpose of attaining truth) which distinguishes thought from other forms of mental activity. Thought may therefore be defined as mental activity controlled by a single purpose, the attainment of truth'.—*Logic*, I. xvii. That is also, of course, the doctrine of the present work.

tale has been a monotonous one of constantly repeated rejections. Whatever its merits in other respects, on this cardinal point of the nature, reference, and office of meaning in judgement, pragmatism seems to us about as uniformly in error as a theory could well be.

It is not a wholly pleasant business to deal in these unqualified negatives with so courageous and ambitious a theory, sponsored by honoured names. Hence it is the more satisfactory to be able to close this chapter of catholic dissent with an acceptance of the theory on one point of first importance. Thought *is* a means to an end; it is in its essence instrumental, it may be described not illegitimately as a kind of intention or purpose. Where the pragmatist is wrong is not in his insistence that thought is a means, but in what seems to us his perverse refusal to recognize that thought has an end of its own. Unfortunately this mistake is fundamental. For precisely to the extent in which thought is instrumental it is essential to conceive its end correctly. What is that end? The main task of the theory of thought is to supply the answer. In the chapters that follow, the outlines of our own answer will be seen emerging, and our final book will be devoted to making the picture, so far as possible, complete.

CHAPTER XI

REALISM: ACTS REPLACE IDEAS

1. We have now arrived at a number of conclusions as to what an idea is not. It is not an image. It is not a word, or that collection of words or images which is sometimes called a proposition. It cannot be defined, as by the authors of *The Meaning of Meaning*, as an effect of its object, or something like such effect. It is not a movement in larynx or brain. It need have no reference to, or bearing on, action.

To readers unfamiliar with that luxuriant jungle, the theory of knowledge, some of these suggestions will have seemed curious, particularly, perhaps, the behaviourist suggestion that ideas do not exist. As for behaviourism, however, the surprise will have partly disappeared upon the discovery that it is a new name for a very old way of thinking, namely, identity-materialism. It seems obvious enough that if you begin by wiping out consciousness, you will also wipe out ideas. But such a reader is probably satisfied that only a fanatic would wipe out consciousness, and that so long as consciousness remains, the existence of ideas is safe, however we may differ about their nature. But for this person there is now another surprise in store. For the theory we are about to consider does just the thing he supposes impossible. It does admit the existence of consciousness; it does not admit the existence of ideas. This is the conclusion of a thoroughgoing realism.

Shocking as this view is to common sense, it is based on a distinction that seems so simple and clear that once it is grasped the denial of ideas seems all but inevitable. So far as I know, the distinction was first drawn with full explicitness by Franz Brentano in 1874. In every cognitive experience, he said, two sides can be distinguished, on the one hand the *act* of laying hold, on the other *what* is laid hold of. The first of these, the act of apprehending, is obviously mental, and is proper matter or psychology. But the content or object laid hold of is not necessarily mental; indeed Brentano seems to have thought it never was. What belongs to psychology, he says, is 'not what is experienced, but the act of experiencing. Thus the hearing of a tone, the seeing of a coloured object, the feeling of warm or cold, and also the imagining of them, are examples of what I mean, as well as the thinking of a general idea, if indeed there is such a thing.' On the other hand, 'a colour, a figure, a landscape which I see; a chord which I hear; warmth, cold, odour, which I sense, and the pictures of these that appear in my imagination'—with all these psychology has nothing to do. They are 'physical phenomena.'[1]

2. It remained for Dr. G. E. Moore to take full philosophic advantage of this distinction. In his hands it was the small but very sharp stone with which he sought to slay the Goliath of idealism. He held that idealism had achieved an unmerited plausibility through confusing the things here distinguished. It had argued that knowledge is confined to what presents itself in experience, and that since experience is clearly mental, all we can know must be likewise mental. But the instant one realizes that 'experience' means two things, as far apart as two things can be, the argument is seen to prove nothing. Experience as my act of experiencing does indeed belong to mind; but this does not create the least presumption that experience, as *what* I experience, also belongs to mind; to suppose that it must is a gross confusion or a gross *non sequitur*. And Moore held, just as Brentano had held before him, that this distinction provides the best line of demarcation of psychology from other disciplines.[2] We could apply the same distinction to every kind of experience, to sensing and perceiving, to judging and inferring, to feeling and willing; we could find within each of these the familiar two components. Then, if we were psychologists, we could leave on one side all the *objects* sensed

---

[1] *Psychologie vom Empirischen Standpunkte*, 103–4.
[2] *Arist. Soc. Proc.*, 1909–10, 36–62.

or judged or willed; these are in general non-mental entities;[1] and we should concern ourselves altogether with our *acts and attitudes* toward these objects. For example, if I am first aware of a proposition, then doubt it, then judge it true, the proposition itself is something with which, as non-mental, the psychologist has nothing to do. His business is to fix his eye on what *is* mental, namely the varying acts, and to set forth as best he can their characteristics and differences. The ideas that he used to study have disappeared by a kind of fission. One half, the presented content, has joined the subject-matter of the other sciences. The remaining half, the act of engaging this content, still remains to him, but no one would call it an idea.

This is a clean-cut and intriguing view. How far Dr. Moore would still subscribe to it I do not know, but at any rate, its influence has been great, and the distinction on which it rests has been accepted, not only by realists generally, but also by certain experts in introspective psychology who have a special right to be heard, such as Ward, Witasek, and Messer. Indeed, the distinction is supported by so many names I respect, that I confess to some uneasiness in challenging it. Nevertheless, the result of an attempt to consider the matter soberly has been that this 'act' seems undiscoverable as a fact, unwarrantable as an inference, and unless further qualified, self-contradictory in implication.

3. What is to be said in its favour?

(1) It is held that we can directly observe it in introspection. Though 'I certainly never have been conscious of anybody else's thoughts or feelings or perceptions in that direct manner in which I am conscious of a colour when I actually see it . . .' says Dr. Moore, 'of my own mental acts, I am very often conscious in this direct manner'.[2] One expects to discover something that bears unmistakably on its face the look of an 'act', but it is all too probable that, like Hume and James when they

---

[1] An exception arises when, in introspection, we make an object of a mental act.   [2] *Arist. Soc. Proc.*, 1909–10, 43.

returned from the forlorn hunt for their own selves, one can only report odds and ends of sensory or conceptual content. For my own part, when I try to introspect my perception of a tree, or, taking a case which Alexander thinks better, since the act is there more conspicuous, when I try to introspect a desire, I can lay my finger on nothing that clearly answers to the description. The object that I desire is represented by some kind of experience-content which for the time may be left vague; and along with this I seem to catch faint stirrings of pleasure in the contemplation, and an unmistakable feeling of longing. But I cannot identify, as distinct from these, any *act* of desire. To be sure, introspection is a treacherous business, and I suspect that if I approached the facts with the expectation of finding an act, I should think I saw it. But when I reflect that there is nothing I would take as an act which someone approaching with a contrary expectation might not with equal right describe otherwise, I am forced to think that the discovery of acts is due less to impartial observing than to preformed expectations, and to exigencies in the theory of knowledge. Of course, one's failure may arise from being an insufficiently trained observer. But here one can take the appeal to others who cannot be so described, and who have also failed to find these acts. Among psychologists, there has been perhaps no better introspective observer than Titchener, but he could not find them. Among philosophers there has been no more acute psychological analyst than Bradley; he also could not find them. One might add other names of weight, but this is not an issue that can be settled by citing authorities. The doctors, even the best of them, disagree.

4. But it has been maintained that we are not confined to introspection for direct knowledge of these acts; we may make their acquaintance in another way. 'Direct acquaintance with cognitive acts', says Dr. Dawes Hicks, 'is, in any case, essentially different from introspection of them. We may be conscious of (or, more accurately, conscious in and through) mental acts, without making them objects of inner observation . . . we become aware of something mental in and through being aware at all.'[1] Dawes Hicks would not deny that we can discover such acts by introspection, but he would say that we *also* have this direct acquaintance with them. Alexander went farther. He held that this direct acquaintance is the *only* knowledge we can have of mental acts. These acts are extremely important, for they make the sum and substance of the mind; 'there is nothing in the mind . . . but acts';[2] but the mind, which is thus a set of acts toward objects, is not an object which can be looked at itself.[3] It is as true that we are aware of mental acts as it is that we are aware of outer objects, but we are aware of them in a different way. To the sort of awareness which we have of tables and chairs, Alexander gave the name of 'contemplation'; to our awareness of our own minds he gave the name of 'enjoyment'. And he held that whenever we are aware of outer objects we are at the same time aware of this awareness of them. It is to this second awareness that the name enjoyment applies. But when this has been made quite clear, Alexander added a remark which may be regarded as a complication or a simplification, according to taste. This second awareness, by which we become aware of the first awareness, is really the same thing. For to be aware of an object, not merely involves, but *is* to be aware of what we are doing. 'I am aware of my awareness as I strike a stroke or wave a farewell. My awareness and my being aware of it are identical.'[4] 'Every act of consciousness is then self-consciousness, not in the sense of containing reflection on itself, for this is just what is denied in calling it an enjoyment, but in the sense that whenever we know, we know that we know, or that knowing and knowing that we know are one and the same thing.'[5]

5. There are two contentions of interest here, (1) that we have an awareness of mental acts which is distinct from our

[1] *Arist. Soc. Proc.*, 1920–1, 159.
[2] *Space, Time, and Deity*, II. 118.   [3] *Ibid.*, I. 16–19.
[4] *Ibid.*, I. 12.   [5] *Ibid.*, II. 112.

awareness of things; (2) that to be aware of a thing, and to be aware that we are aware of it, are one and the same. On these we offer three remarks.

(i) How can both be maintained at once? Let us suppose that I am aware of a tree. Then, said Alexander, we must distinguish between my awareness of the tree (a contemplation) and my awareness of this awareness (enjoyment). But, if to be aware of anything means precisely the same as to be aware of this aware-ness, if 'knowing and knowing that we know are one and the same thing', Alexander has denied in the second proposition the very thing he affirmed in the first. For the things which in the first proposition he insists must be distinguished are the same things which in the second proposition he says must be identified.

(ii) Even if we take the second proposition apart from the first, it seems questionable as regards both fact and theory. Particularly on so latitudinarian a view of knowing as Alex-ander's, which makes it a mere compresence of mind and object, it seems doubtful if every animal that can be said to know has knowledge of its own knowing. And even if it does, the distinction in theory would remain. It seems at least conceivable that such an animal should be aware without being aware of its own awareness. If this is admitted to be conceivable, our point is made; for even if the two always happen together, the fact that they can be distinguished still shows that they are two.

(iii) But one may be sure that in a doctrine stressed by so acute and honest a mind as Alexander's, there lies a truth of importance. Here I take the truth to be this, that whenever we know, we are aware, as he said, of something that is not in the ordinary sense an object, but is as certainly there as objects themselves. My mind, when I am aware of a tree, is not ex-hausted in this awareness. The knowing by mind of its objects is not like the taking of a camera picture, where the details of a sharply delimited field are all recorded in equal light. For beyond or below the margin of explicit awareness, there are masses of vague sensations, fluctuating pleasures and pains, wellings of obscure emotion, which form a pulsing sense of life that is easier to recognize than describe. These are certainly present; our awareness of them is clearly different from our awareness of a tree; and they are bound up in a peculiarly intimate way with the sense of self. Nothing would be easier than to take this obscure, subjective, living, changing experience as an experience of the changing activities of the self. But it is not really such. This region of immediacy is, of course, an extremely shadowy one, so full of undefinable tensions, lifts and falls of mood, and flickerings in and out of half-formed images, that one can hardly say what is, or is not, there; and it is, no doubt, this elusiveness that has made possible such different accounts of it as are given for example by Bergson, Frederic Myers, and Bradley. Such elusiveness makes assertion about it easy, and verification extremely difficult. All one can say in the present case is that nothing definitely describable as an act of knowing seems to be discoverable in it.

6. (2) There are philosophers, however, who have held, as Ward did, that though acts of mind cannot be known directly, they can be known indirectly as a result of quite certain inferences. The acts themselves 'are by their very nature unpresentable'. 'We know of them mediately through their effects; we do not *know* them immediately in themselves.'[1] Let us turn then to the inferences which have been thought to make their existence certain.

Ward thought they could be inferred from 'their effects, by certain changes, i.e. which they bring about in the character and succession of our presentations'.[2] For example, perceptions and images are sometimes extremely dim. And so far as we can see, there is no accounting for this difference, except by supposing that there is an activity of attending which we are exerting more or less vigorously. A wound that in ordinary circumstances would cause intense pain, may pass wholly unregarded when, as we say quite accurately, attention is directed elsewhere. Conversely, details that would pass unnoticed are seen with the greatest readiness if we are actively looking for them. And when we wish

---

[1] *Psychological Principles*, 58.   [2] *Ibid.*

to, we can use attention like a searchlight, and sweep the field of presentation with its beam, bringing now this point, now another, into relief. How is all this possible, unless the self can shift its gaze at will, now granting and now withholding its attention?

7. Such instances do show, I think, that presence in the focus of attention does not depend upon intensity of stimulus alone. Some other element is often or always involved. But (i) do the instances show that this other element is a mental act, as opposed, for example, to elements of mental content? Take an instance in which the case for acts is strongest, the instance of 'voluntary attention'. Is it clear that this is inexplicable, except by appeal to acts which are 'by their very nature unpresentable'? Certainly other explanations have been offered which would seem to be equally plausible. Thus Mill and Bradley,[1] with all their differences, agreed that when I 'pull myself together' and concentrate deliberately on some matter in hand, what moves the concentration is not the fiat of an ego, but the idea of attending itself. There occurs to me suddenly the thought, 'No more idling about; I'd better be at this', and attention forthwith follows. The thought of attending draws the attention in its wake; there is no abrupt and inexplicable bolt from the non-phenomenal blue which arbitrarily lights up one thing rather than another. And when we consider all the other elements of mental content, such as impulses, obscure moods, and acquired interests, to say nothing of bodily factors, which may affect the prominence of objects in consciousness, to fall back on unpresentable acts seems a last resort.

8. (ii) But it may be replied: 'This resort cannot, in the end, be avoided. For suppose you did fall back, in the manner of

---

[1] Note by J. S. Mill to J. Mill, *Analysis of the Human Mind*, II. 372–7. For Bradley, *Mind*, O.S. XI (1886), 312: 'We make an effort and succeed, but where is the machinery? The machinery, I answer, consists of an idea which is able to dominate and so fixes an object connected with itself. This idea may be simply the idea of the presence of the idea required.' Cf. *Mind*, O.S. XII (1887), 67 ff. and 564 ff. for Ward's reply.

Mill and Bradley, on an idea of attending, or even on an idea of an idea of attending, to explain my attending voluntarily. This ultimate and determining idea itself is capable of moving to action only because it receives a measure of my attention. It is because, by an act of mine, I attend to it more rather than less, that it acquires the power it manifests.' This is not convincing. For (a) as we saw a moment ago, things may be brought to the focus of consciousness by factors to which voluntary attention is not given. And (b) even if this were untrue, one must still doubt whether reference to an unpresentable mental act really gives an explanation of anything. It is presumably an attempt to account for something as necessarily produced by a certain cause. Such explanation must always run: A is of such a character as to produce an effect of the character B, or B is of such a character as to be produced by a cause of the character A. If A produces B, it must do so in respect of some specific nature in virtue of which it acts in this way rather than that. Otherwise one could not specify the sort of cause from which anything followed, and causal laws would not exist. But in the present case we are offered, as explanations of known effects, causes which are declared to be 'unpresentable' and which, therefore, lack for us any traits which could mark them out as causes at all. I take it that the chief criticism of the old faculty psychology was that without knowing the causes independently, it inferred that they must exist from certain effects, and then said triumphantly, 'we can now explain these effects, for we have discovered that they are produced by such causes as necessarily produce such effects'. That, of course, was no explanation; it was merely a statement that one was called for. Is the present explanation better off?

9. (iii) How little it really helps may be inferred from the candid admission of one who has done much in behalf of such acts. Moore does not believe, as Ward did, that mental acts are 'unpresentable'. He agrees that they exist, and indeed no one has insisted more emphatically than he, that in every perception and thought, act is to be distinguished from object; but he has held, what Ward did not, that we can lay hold of such acts with the greatest certainty in introspection, and that their nature and varieties form the subject matter of psychology.[1] And yet he is impelled to make a strange admission about them. Having pointed out what a deadly blunder it is, not to distinguish act from object in our 'sensation' of blue, he continues:

> 'The term "blue" is easy enough to distinguish, but the other element which I have called consciousness—that which sensation of blue has in common with sensation of green—is extremely difficult to fix. That many people fail to distinguish it at all is sufficiently shown by the fact that there are materialists. And, in general, that which makes the sensation of blue a mental fact seems to escape us: it seems, if I may use a metaphor, to be transparent—we look through it and see nothing but the blue; we may be convinced that there *is* something, but *what* it is no philosopher, I think, has yet clearly recognized.'[2]

When the psychologist reads this, he is likely to become uneasy; he is offered an experience to study, but unfortunately the part of it which alone concerns him is 'transparent', and as indescribable as thin air. He begins to wonder whether he is supposed to make a profession out of describing the indescribable. It may occur to him, however, that what is hard to isolate in a single case may be brought into relief through many; perhaps as he runs through the colours of the spectrum, or turns from the experience of colour to that of odour, taste or sound, he will find something that varies in the series over and above the varying objects, something which he can identify as as act of perceiving. He can then study it independently. But from this hope he is cut off. For 'I am not sure', says Dr. Moore, 'that there is any such difference. I am not sure that, in any case whatever, two mental acts which differ in respect of the fact that one is a consciousness of one entity, and the other a consciousness of a different entity, need, for that reason, differ

---

[1] *Arist. Soc. Proc.*, 1909–10, 36 ff.
[2] *Mind*, XII (1903), 446; cf. also 450.

internally or qualitatively in any respect at all.'[1] Here the psychologist is no longer left in suspense about his fate; the language
may be merciful, but it is a sentence of expropriation from most
of his inherited domain. For what it tells him is this: 'You, as
a psychologist, are to study and describe mental acts. To you
the objects of these acts are nothing. Sensed colours and sounds,
perceived tables and chairs, conceived relations and attributes—
all these to you are irrelevant. Acts only matter. It is true that,
if you try to seize one of these, it proves transparent and eludes
you. It is true that if you try to describe how it resembles any
other, or differs from any other, you cannot do that either.
Still, as a psychologist, you *must* do it somehow. There is
nothing else for you to do.'

10 (3) We cannot suppose the psychologist would be jubilant
over this commission. At the same time, we must not exaggerate
the restrictions which the psychologist suffers at the hands of
Dr. Moore. He is not left quite as a man without a country or
an occupation. For, though acts of awareness seem to Moore in
quality indiscriminable, he thinks that there are other acts of
mind which *are* so discriminable. Thus one can distinguish
merely being aware of a thing from liking it, or liking it from
desiring it, or desiring again from willing and believing.[2] That
the difference lies in the acts and not in their objects is shown
by the fact that through a succession of varying experiences
our object may remain precisely the same. Since the object
remains the same while the experiences differ, what varies

---

[1] *Arist. Soc.*, Art., 48. Cf. again: 'It is impossible to verify by observation the existence of any internal qualitative difference between every
pair of acts which have different objects. When, for instance, I compare my direct consciousness of a particular blue colour, with my
direct consciousness of a particular red colour, or with my
direct consciousness of a particular musical note, I am unable to
detect by observation that these three acts have any difference at all
except that which consists in the fact that they have different objects.'
—*Mind*, XIX (1910), 403-4 (in a review of Messer). I repeat that Dr.
Moore's views have undergone change in certain particulars, and
perhaps in these points also.   [2] *Arist. Soc.*, Art., 49-50.

must be our own attitude toward that object. The point is put uncompromisingly by Professor Laird: 'It is plain, surely, that there may be very different cognitive attitudes towards precisely the same object. For example, we may at different times believe, doubt and reject precisely the same proposition. *Ex hypothesi*, these differences are not found in the object. For it is the same. These differences belong to the cognitive attitudes and we are acquainted with them as firmly, and as immediately, as with the differences between hoping and fearing, or between sour and loud. If this is mystical, let us all be mystics. It is better to be mystical than blind.'[1]

Now the differences of the non-cognitive attitudes among themselves I will not discuss, since it is with the cognitive attitudes alone that we are here concerned. The question is, then, Is it true that 'there may be very different cognitive attitudes towards precisely the same object?' In support of his answer, Professor Laird thinks it enough to say 'it is plain, surely'. But apparently I must plead guilty to blindness, since it is not plain to me. What is of more consequence, there must also be included among the blind, as Professor Laird of course knows, that distinguished group of logicians who, of all logicians, have perhaps known most about psychology.[2] Let us look at a case in point. Someone asks me, 'Have those transatlantic fliers arrived yet?' I answer, 'I don't know'. They may and they may not; my position is one of doubt. When, a little later, I have read a newspaper announcement, and go on to affirm that they have arrived, is the only change a change in my act? Has the object before my mind remained unaltered? If it has, my change in attitude is irrational and arbitrary, and since it has nothing to do with the content, might just as well have been a change to flat denial; it is the mere expression of whim or impulse, accepting or rejecting groundlessly. This is not the way in which sane minds work. The object before me,

[1] *Arist. Soc. Proc.*, 1920–21, 125–6.
[2] See, e.g., Bosanquet, *Knowledge and Reality*, 114–15; *Logic*, I. 33; Sigwart, *Logic* (Eng. tr.), I. 177. Bradley at first held that the same content could be doubted and affirmed, but later rejected this view. Cf. his *Logic*, I. 11 and note; *Appearance*, 366.

when I affirm, is not simply the same proposition that is before me when I doubt; it is the *proposition as grounded in the announcement*, and it is this change in the total object before me that forms the very essence of the change from doubt to belief. I find it hard to verify any other change at all. The movement from doubt to judgement is not a change in attitude, for doubt is already judgement; the change is a change in the judgement's content. To doubt as I did at first, is to judge: 'The fliers are somewhere in a certain region; I have no data that would indicate where.' When the announcement comes, these data are supplied. A total object in which a certain part, namely the location of the fliers, is indeterminate, is replaced by another total object in which new evidence has made that part determinate. The object is not the same here, nor is there any arbitrary inner shift. My mind, *qua* knowing, *is* a judgement whose only change is a change of content.[1]

11. (4) The writers who suggested this argument have offered others, which may to some persons be more convincing. They have pointed to certain everyday facts of which the only way to make sense is, they consider, to admit the existence of mental acts. (i) 'We all know that the sensation of blue differs from that of green. But it is plain that if both are *sensations*, they also have some point in common. What is it that they have in common?'[2] Not their sensory quality, answers Moore, for this differs. They must resemble each other in this, that in both the mind is addressing itself to an object; it is engaging it through consciousness or awareness. Acts must therefore exist to supply the common element in sensations whose objects differ. (ii) And consider the extraordinary consequences if one does not

---

[1] In holding that we never hold different attitudes toward precisely the same object, we are taking a view which Laird himself is inclined to take about feelings: 'It is far from certain that two different men can ever feel differently with regard to the same question. If we include in the question all the meaning it suggests to each of them, there will probably be a different question for each.'—*Problems of the Self*, 241.   [2] *Mind*, XII (1903), 444.

make such a distinction. Refuse to recognize that the quality blue belongs to the non-mental object, and you get the conclusion that your own awareness is coloured blue.[1] And to say that one's *mind* is blue or green is simply nonsense. 'A cathedral, as it is presented to the mind, is grey and made of stone. The mind is neither coloured nor stony.'[2] Thus again the same conclusion is required; act and object differ. Further (iii) 'I may judge today that the diameter and circumference of a circle are incommensurable, and I may judge it tomorrow. The acts of judgement are distinct because they occur at different times, but the object in each case is one and the same.'[3] Or again (iv) the act and object may occur at different points in time, or one may be temporal and the other not. 'It is clear, I think, that a man may apprehend things which are not contemporaneous with his process of apprehending. He may think, now, of his late unhappy soldiering, or of something which, like a geometrical truth, is, strictly speaking, timeless.'[4] Two things that thus differ enormously in duration are surely different and should be kept distinct.

This is true, but it is not exactly the point at issue. What these examples prove is that knowledge and its object are different; what they ought to prove is that the differentiating factor in knowledge is its being an *act*. Let us try to get clear what we admit, and what we are compelled to deny. We admit that 'I am aware of blue' is not the same as 'blue exists'; we admit that to describe a mental event as blue is an absurdity; we admit that many objects of knowledge are permanent, and that our knowledge of them is not. How far do these admissions carry us? Do they show anything more than this, that knowledge, in one of its aspects, is an event that happens in time? If I am to know that the diameter and circumference of a circle are incommensurable, that fact must not merely be; it must present itself to my mind; at some moment of time it must enter as a component part into my 'field of consciousness' or total experienced mass; it cannot hold forever aloof in its timeless

[1] *Mind*, XII (1903), 450.   [2] Laird, *Problems of the Self*, 19.
[3] *Ibid.*, 18.   [4] Laird, *Arist. Soc. Proc.*, 1920–21, 123.

status, but must condescend to appear in a context in which it is continuous with my momentary feeling. And with this recognition, we have all that is necessary to meet the difficulties just cited. Truth and reality are permanencies; granted. My knowing is not a permanency; granted also. But what follows from this is not that knowledge is an act, but solely that it is an event; and read in this light, the objections become harmless. The first argument becomes that what appears is not the same as the event of its appearing; the second becomes that such events are not blue or green; the third becomes that they occur at various times; the fourth becomes that the same object may appear repeatedly. And if the simple recognition that truth appears, that in one aspect it is an occurrence, is enough to meet these difficulties, why are acts needed? It is interesting to note in passing that even if these arguments are accepted, they prove too much. For, as has been pointed out by Broad,[1] if remembering is really an act by which I lay hold of the past, then it is incorrect to contrast my act as present with the event as past; if the event is really past and my act reaches it nevertheless, my act is not merely present, but past as well.[2]

12. (5) We turn now to another, and fifth, consideration of weight that has been offered for mental acts. Dr. Dawes Hicks has suggested an argument that reminds one of the argument of Lotze for the existence of a self.[3] There is more in a process like comparison, or in processes of inference generally, than the mere presence before the mind of objects, or of a procession marching past to be reviewed; it seems there must

---

[1] *Arist. Soc. Proc.*, 1920–21, 146.

[2] Mr. Russell once held the belief in mental acts, but long ago abandoned it. 'I have to confess that the theory which analyses a presentation into act and object no longer satisfies me. The act, or subject, is schematically convenient, but not empirically discoverable. I am at a loss to discover any actual phenomenon which could be called an "act" and could be regarded as a constituent of the presentation.'—*Arist. Soc. Proc., Sup. Vol.*, II, 1919, p. 25. Cf. also his *Analysis of Mind*, 17.   [3] *Metaphysics*, Sec. 240 ff.

be, presiding over the field and marshalling its figures, a self
which recognizes, compares, infers. 'Suppose it be said that
one idea is suggested by, and tends to combine with, another
which resembles it. Then, even though it be assumed that that
similarity is able to act as a force and to bring together two ideas
—an assumption I find it hopeless to try to understand—yet
the problem of how there comes to be *recognition* of similarity
or resemblance in what is in such a case apprehended, has not
been thereby so much as remotely touched.'[1]

Now the question 'how there comes to be such recognition',
assuming that it is answerable at all, does not seem to me
cleared up, or made appreciably easier, by the admission of
mental acts. In such processes as comparison and recognition,
they are not to be certified in introspection, nor do they really
help to explain. What happens in my mind when I am engaged
in comparing two things, say St. Peter's with St. Paul's, seems
to be something like this: first one object, then the other
appears at the focus of consciousness, and while one is dominant, the other retreats to the margin. As each object takes its
turn in the centre, those features in which it contrasts with the
other are specially dwelt on. There is a swift alternation of
contents, in which likeness emerges against a background of
difference, and difference against a background of likeness. And
when, after some hesitation, I recognize a friend in an apparent
stranger, there is present first the stranger, then the same
stranger transformed by an added meaning. That in both these
cases I am active in some sense, and that in each there is a
mental process, we may agree. But it is a process within the
content, not a process in which I station myself outside and
look at the content, as if the field of consciousness were a
tapestry hung on the wall, and knowing were the beam from a
lantern, which the operator concentrates arbitrarily, now on
one part, now on another. This image of the searchlight or
lantern has become so fixed in the minds of some of us that we
can hardly look at the facts without it. But when we try to look
independently, we see that it is only a metaphor, and what is

[1] *Arist. Soc. Proc.*, 1909–10, 282.

more, a metaphor that does not fit. The lantern, with an existence of its own apart from the screen, turns out to be merely
mythical; there is no space for its rays to travel through, nor
any time for them to spend travelling; and the rays themselves
seem required by the metaphor rather than the metaphor by
the facts. Dr. Dawes Hicks agrees that direct introspective
knowledge of mental acts is not to be had.[1] If this knowledge
is abandoned, the strongest remaining ground for accepting
such acts would appear to be their necessity in explanation. On
this necessity we have commented already, and will say here
only what Dr. Dawes Hicks says admirably in the same context
of faculty psychology: 'The faculty is only a repetition in a single
word, and in the very abstract notion of a "power", of the facts
that are being dealt with, and if these are not intelligible
in themselves, they certainly do not become intelligible by
being attributed to a faculty; the notion of the faculty is just
abstracted from the special facts which it is supposed to
render intelligible.'[2] For *faculty* here, read *act*.

13. (6) The reader may be inclined to protest: 'If the case for
acts is really so bad, if, as you suggest, there is no place for them
in either introspection or explanation, how did they ever become
so popular? Responsible philosophers would hardly set up a
scarecrow wantonly, and then insist that it was something
precious. If the mental act is an imposture, there must at least
be something about it that would lead men to take it otherwise,
but we are left at a loss to know what this is.' The protest is
justified. There *is* a reason why acts have become so popular,
and the reason is their supposed usefulness in the theory of
knowledge. It has been thought, as we have seen, that the
distinction between act and object disposes of idealism, and so
leaves the way free again for something that is more in con-

---

[1] *Arist. Soc. Proc.*, 1909–10, 273. A few pages later, however,
277–9, he seems to maintain, as against Moore, that different acts of
awareness are qualitatively distinguishable. If these differences in
quality are not knowable directly, it is hard to see how they are known
at all.   [2] *Ibid.*, 283.

sonance with science and common sense. Idealism held that objects were mental, because it confused the act, which really was mental, with the object, which was not, and once this confusion is exposed, its plausibility instantly vanishes. It is now open to us to hold that objects in every case are independent of knowing, that knowing never affects them, and hence that the form in which we know them is the form in which they exist apart from us. In knowing, we engage things directly and see them just as they are.

We do not propose to enter here into a discussion of realism generally. We are concerned in this chapter with one point only, whether there is any good reason for believing in the realistic substitute for ideas, namely mental acts. We have found no reasons of an empirical kind. Is there any good reason of an epistemological kind? *Does* realism gain an immense advantage through the distinction of act and object? *Are* common sense and science thus fortified against the paradox of idealism? I want to suggest two considerations that show the acceptance of such acts to be fatal to both science and common sense.

14. (i) The distinction is at first sight most attractive. The insistence that nature is not mental, that a sharp line must be drawn between what is mental and what is not, and that tables and chairs, rocks and rivers, lie on the farther side of the line, is welcomed as good sense by plain man and scientist alike. But, of course, a theory must be judged in the light of all its consequences, and as the remoter consequences begin to appear, these persons are bound to be shocked. If the distinction of act and content is valid of perception and conception, it is presumably also valid of pleasure and pain, dream and imagination, hallucination and memory. It is as easy to distinguish one's act of imagining or remembering from *what* is imagined or remembered, as one's act of perceiving from the thing perceived. But if this is true, the inferences are startling. First comes a shock to the scientists. For now, colours and sounds, hots and colds, will have their place in physical space along with electric particles and motions, which alone had been supposed to be there. If this is a shock to the scientist, however, it is so far received with equanimity by the plain man. But, as the following tale of consequences begins to unroll itself, we can only imagine both as scandalized together. First, my image of Mount Everest is in no way mental, but exists apart from me as truly as the mountain itself. And whether the space it exists in is taken as public, or private but independent of perception, extreme perplexities arise at once. Again, the contents of last night's dream are all somewhere existing now, for although my mind can, in a measure, select its objects, it can neither make nor destroy them. Once more, as we read a work of fiction, we are performing acts of imagination, but it is these alone that are rightly mental, not their objects; hence Hector and Priam, Quixote and Sancho, D'Artagnan and Dr. Jekyll and the Blessed Damozel are all permanent *dramatis personae* of the world, waiting for their 'creators' and spectators to come along. If the colour-blind man sees a red light as grey, it really is grey; if Dr. Broad's toper sees pink rats on the foot of his bed, the rats, or at least their parts, are there in their own right. And since, when we have a toothache, we can distinguish the quality of pain from our act of perceiving it, and the object does not depend on the act, we must regard the ache as an independent entity with which we have unhappily come in contact.

Now I am not here concerned to argue that these views are either absurd or false, and indeed there are persons of weight who would defend them.[1] I am merely suggesting that if a

----

[1] For example Alexander in *Space, Time, and Deity.* Illusory appearances, he held, 'are not the creation of the mind. What the mind does is to choose them from the world of reality. . . . The illusory object is as much non-mental as the real appearance.' In dreams we apprehend physical things. (II. 214–15.) 'Now sense perhaps you will admit to be public. But images, how can they be so? Are they not eminently private? The answer is no, except for the personal idiosyncrasy of the imager.' (228.) 'Many at least find it difficult not to think of hunger as a mental affection . . . but the localization of hunger in the body (however vague) is enough to dispel this misinterpretation. . . .' (172) Alexander did not consider all objects of hallucination

theory entailing such things is supposed to be of epistemological advantage, if it is supposed to bring the theory of knowledge into closer union with science and common sense, than, for example, objective idealism, it had better try again. To be sure, if the plain man is told that in perceiving tables and chairs we are only participating in the experiences of a divine being, he is startled, but I conceive that he is less startled than if told that Red Riding Hood and a toothache are physical objects out there in space.

15. (ii) Inconsistency with common sense and science, however, is a less serious criticism of a philosophical theory than inconsistency with itself. And so far as the theory holds that in knowing we directly engage by our act the physical thing itself, its consequences can be shown to be incoherent. Suppose I perceive a red ball. According to the theory, there is on the one hand a mental act, and on the other a red ball, and the one directly engages the other. Now suppose that from contemplating the red ball I turn to contemplating the conditions that lead me to perceive it. What I discover, of course, is that between the physical thing and my act of perceiving there is a long series of intermediate steps. It is needless to run through these in detail—the occurrence in the 'visual area' of my brain, the current in the optic nerve, the changes in rods and cones, the waves or 'wavicles' of light, the release of these by the physical thing. My act of perceiving the ball comes at the end of this series. But now note the incoherence. On the one hand my mental act is to take me directly to the physical thing, to pass without obstruction to the red ball out there in space and reveal it just as it is. On the other hand, if it does reveal things just as they are, it reveals among these things a long line of causal links which separate my act of perceiving from any physical thing it could perceive. If these links are

or illusion to exist in public space just as we see them; but their parts do, and the mistake consists in assembling them wrongly. 'The illusion is a transposition of materials.' (214.)

really there, then it is obvious that I *cannot* see directly the physical thing. Assume that the theory is true, develop it into its consequences, and it turns out that the theory is false.

16. We have seen in earlier chapters that the nature of ideas is extraordinarily hard to seize and define. But hard as this is, it seems still harder to dispense with ideas. We have had before us two attempts to do this, one made by the behaviourists, who would substitute for ideas a physical response, the other made by the thoroughgoing realist, who would substitute for ideas mental acts. In behaviourism we could find little more than elementary confusion. The belief in mental acts we have found supported by a very different sort of advocacy, both philo-sophical and psychological. Still, we cannot think it successful. We cannot accept the proposal to abolish ideas by breaking them up and dividing the spoils between acts and objects. Of some of the difficulties that would result on the side of objects we shall speak when we come in the following chapter to consider another kind of realism—critical realism with its doctrine of essences. For the present we have dealt with acts only, i.e. with the identification of ideas on their mental side with mental acts. We have seen that the introspective evidence for such acts is unsatisfactory, that the facts supposed to require them for explanation can be explained without them, and that the advantage they are supposed to confer in the theory of knowledge is more apparent than real.

We therefore reject these cognitive acts. But where does this leave us? Of course, we have still the objects that these acts were believed to engage. And if ideas are to be accepted at all, it would seem that the most natural course now open to us is to say quite brazenly that these objects themselves are ideas; that when we think of Julius Caesar, the real Caesar is present, not only *to* our mind, but *in* it and as a part of it. This idealist theory may have to be accepted, but, like the realism we have just examined, it is at violent odds with common sense and is to be accepted only from necessity. Is there any intermediate position? As it happens, there is. There has appeared comparatively recently a school of American thinkers who have elaborated a subtle compromise between the realism that would abolish ideas and the idealism that would assimilate the object to ideas. This is the school of Critical Realists. Their programme of compromise we shall examine in the next chapter.

CHAPTER XII

CRITICAL REALISM: ESSENCES REPLACE IDEAS

1. Critical realism is a compromise between views of the idea-object relation which it regards as extreme. On one side is a thoroughgoing realism which would abolish the idea by breaking it up into a mental act and non-mental object. On the other is idealism, which would abolish the non-mental object by assimilating it to the stuff of ideas. Critical realism begins by rejecting both the one and the other.[1]

Realism must be rejected because of its extravagant consequences. If everything in thought except the mental act is to be granted non-mental existence, then mirages and hobgoblins, pink rats and contradictory propositions, must all be actual existents like tables and chairs. So regarded, however, they are excrescences which the critical realist thinks should be removed by a judicious use of Occam's razor. But, having rejected realism, he also turns upon idealism. An object of thought, said Bosanquet, 'always and necessarily is in some degree a part of our psychical being, a particular mental state or occurrence, one with us in feeling and active in the total life of our mind'.[2] Against statements of this kind the critical realists, or at any rate the majority of them, protest as confused and undiscriminating. A physical thing is never really a 'mental state' or 'part of our psychical being'; mind and its physical object are two sharply divided existents, differing in time, in place, in causal context. If it is wrong to resolve ideas away into things, it is equally wrong to import physical existents into the mind.

Between these doctrines, says the critical realist, the best course is a *via media*. It is to recognize both mental states and independent things, to concede the gap between them, and then to show how, in knowing, we cross this gap. Cross it we un-

---

[1] See *Essays in Critical Realism*, Essay I (Drake).
[2] *Logic*, II. 297.

doubtedly do, for we do in fact have knowledge of stars and atoms, tables and chairs. When I look at a star, or think of it, I am contemplating something that is enormously far away and may even have ceased to exist at the time I contemplate it. Between the object and my thought of it there may intervene millions of miles of space and centuries of time. How does knowing bridge this gap? To import the star itself into the circle of my ideas, after the manner of the idealist, is impossible, for at the time I think of it there may be no star to import. To say that I am directly engaging the physical thing in space, after the manner of the realist, is precluded by the same fact. And yet how, by anything short of this, are we to gain knowledge at all? Knowing threatens to dissolve in paradox. If we are to grasp anything in knowledge what we grasp must be the thing itself, for to fall short of this is not to know *it*. But to grasp this thing itself is clearly impossible, for it is divided from our thought by impassable gulfs of space and time.

2. There is only one way, says the critical realist, in which this paradox can be solved. When it is said that the gulf *must* be crossed and yet *cannot* be crossed, both statements are true, but they are true in different senses. What we are said to reach when we succeed in crossing the gulf is not what we fall short of when we fail to cross it. What we reach is the *what* of a thing; what we fail to reach is its *that*. By the 'what' is meant the content or characters that make it the kind of thing it is, the set of qualities or attributes that give it a distinctive nature. Thus the 'what' of an orange consists of the colour, shape, juiciness, etc., which set it off as an orange from billiard-balls, stones, and apples, the set of features by which we should define it and describe it. This 'what' the critical realists refer to as an 'essence'. The 'that' on the other hand, is something totally different. It is not the character of the thing, but the *existence* of this character, its actual occurrence at some point in time and space, the fact of its happening, its embodiment as an actual thing or actual event. How different this element is may be

shown very readily. I may form an extremely full and vivid image of an orange, which may be almost exactly like the orange I saw a moment ago. Yet the two are a world apart. What is it that makes them so different? It is the fact that the orange actually exists at a point in space and time, while the image does not. The 'that' of a thing, its existence, is the element needed to make the imagined actual.

Let this distinction be grasped, says the critical realist, and the paradox of knowledge is solved. For it is now perfectly plain that, while we fail to reach the object in one sense, we do reach it in the other. When I think of the distant star, or when I look at it, it would be absurd to say that I am embracing its *existence* in my thought; the darting about of a comet in the depths of space is not an occurrence in my mind, which I can turn on or shut off at will. But it is equally clear that I do reach the star in another sense; I do grasp immediately its character of luminousness, since I directly see a point of light; and so far as the character of a thing *is* a thing, I may be said to grasp the thing itself. This is the solution of the problem. Knowing is at once direct and indirect. It is direct, since what I know, I know immediately; between my thinking and the content of my thought there is no possible intermediary. But it is also indirect, since I can know the existence of a thing only through its 'essence', its 'that' through its 'what'.

3. Now it is obvious that if my thought is to know directly the essence of something, that essence cannot be tied to the point in space and time where it is embodied. Even though the star no longer exists, its essence remains, for it is this that I now perceive. And since it does not cease to be when the object that embodies it dies, there is no reason for supposing it born when that object comes into existence. It is anchored to no single point in space or time, but may appear in any; that is, it is universal. Embodiment does not create it, nor dissolution destroy it; it has no place to call its own, it has no single life to live, yet it somehow *is*. It thus belongs to a realm of being sharply distinct from that realm of matter in which existences change and pass. It may appear in this latter realm, but is no more confined to it than the life of an actor is confined to his appearances on the stage. Since its alliance with the things that embody it is so little entangling, it may perfectly well be in different places successively or even at once. There is no reason why the character of the star may not associate itself both with an object remote in space and with my process of knowing here on earth, both with an object remote in time and with my conception at this moment. And this gives us the clue to the critical realist's definition of perception and judgement, two processes which, in his view, do not essentially differ. To perceive a thing is to take an essence presented immediately to my mind as the character of something existing in space and time.

For us, as students of the idea, everything turns on this essence'. It is the middle term between mind and things, the means by which we perceive them, the content through which we think them. Is it properly to be described as an idea? Is it a mental state, or is it a feature of the physical thing, or is it somehow both together? In order to appraise the theory, we must be clear on these points. But unfortunately this theory of essence varies considerably from writer to writer among the critical realists. On one main doctrine, indeed, all members of the school are united. But as soon as there is a division of labour to develop the doctrine, significant differences begin to appear.[1]

4. The main doctrine, on which all are agreed, is that 'when we "know" an object, we are assigning a certain "essence"—a character or group of characters—to some reality existing

[1] This chapter contains no study of Professor Lovejoy's remarkable book, *The Revolt Against Dualism*, owing to the mere accident of having been written abroad at a point where his work was not available. On referring to it, I felt that it should be dealt with either *in extenso* or not at all, and, space being limited, I have chosen the latter course, undoubtedly to the disadvantage of this study.

independently of the knowledge-process', and that 'truth is the identity of this essence with the actual character of the reality referred to. . . .'[1] Thought cannot seize the object as an existent; if it could, it could also generate and destroy this; but it can lay hold of the object as an essence or character. When we perceive, what we perceive is 'the logical essence of the real thing'.[2] When we think, what is present to our mind is 'the actual character of the object remembered or thought of'.[3] Such language makes it plain that critical realism is a genuine realism. What I think or perceive is not merely my idea nor does it depend on my apprehension. In perceiving, 'if we abstract from the seeing or givenness, the entire datum is physical (in the sense of essence, not of existence), or, to put it in the usual way, it is "objective" '.[4] That unless we do make contact with the actual character of things we are falling short of knowledge, is a platform on which the members stand in agreement.

Now what are the agencies by which we are brought in touch with this public reality? This is the question which, as students of the idea, must interest us most. Unfortunately it is also a question upon which critical realists find it impossible to agree among themselves. If the nature of things is to be revealed to us, it must be through some part (or the whole) of the content directly presented; but if we take the leading case of perception and ask whether the real object is presented through sense data, logical meanings, or subjective mental processes, we get affirmative answers to each. Now it would seem extremely doubtful whether these answers are consistent with each other, and still more so whether any one of them is consistent with that direct apprehension of the character of objects which is asserted in the main tenet of the school.

---

[1] *Essays in Critical Realism*, 117 (Rogers). The theory is in some ways strikingly similar to one offered by Bradley in 1883. 'Judgement proper', he writes, 'is the act which refers an ideal content [defined as a logical universal] to a reality beyond the act.'—*Logic*, I. 10.

[2] *Ibid.*, 223 (Strong).   [3] *Ibid.*, 25 (Drake).
[4] *Ibid.*, 229 (Strong).

5. Professor Strong is clear that the characters of sense data are themselves universals or essences, and hence fitted to present us with the nature of things. Their sensible vividness does not prevent their being universals; e.g. 'visual data as such are neither here nor there'.[1] They are not, to be sure, the only essences; when we think of virtue or a perfect square, the *what* before us is not to be exhausted by sense data.[2] Nevertheless, since the 'what' of anything is 'its entire concrete nature, including its sensible character',[3] and it is through sense data that its sensible character is initially presented, these data are an extremely important part of the essence; we depend on them for our knowledge of physical things. And there seems no reason to doubt that they give us such knowledge; when we see a face, says Professor Strong, 'the entire datum is physical', supplying us with 'the essence of a physical thing', though not, of course, its existence.[4] But then, having got it firmly fixed in mind, that sense data may reveal the real character of things, we are given an extremely effective set of arguments to show that these data cannot *be* the real things. The real thing has some stable character; sense data are endlessly variable. The real thing cannot be red *and* green, hot *and* cold, bent *and* straight; but the sense data of different perceivers may have all these qualities. 'As objects move farther and farther away from us, the data presenting them become smaller. Thus a human being becomes half and then quarter his normal size, and finally a mere speck on the horizon. We cannot suppose, consistently with physics or even with everyday sense, that the size of his body actually changes.'[5] These arguments seem to us, as they do to Professor Strong, to prove decisively that sense data in general *are* not physical things. Unfortunately they prove, to precisely the same extent, that these data cannot give the *character* of physical things. Indeed, all these arguments reach their end precisely by showing the incompatibility between the character we must attribute to real things and the character of the sense data. If this is accepted—and I do not

---

[1] *Essays in Critical Realism*, 232 (Strong).   [2] *Ibid.*, 231.
[3] *Ibid.*, 223.   [4] *Ibid.*, 229.   [5] *Ibid.*, 226.

see how it can be denied—we are left with conflicting doctrines: sense data do reveal to us the character of real things, so faith-fully, indeed, that 'the entire datum' of a face we see is 'physical', yet at the same time their divergence from this character is so great as to render identity incredible. Professor Strong even goes on to confirm our scepticism by a further line of argument. He emphasizes that sense data are directly dependent on the organism and vary with its condition. If so, it becomes still harder to believe that they give us in any case a literal coinci-dence with the character of the real.

It might be replied, of course, that nature has made some special provision for a coincident character in two events as differently conditioned as a perception and a falling star. But Professor Strong does not develop any such argument. It might be replied again that *some* of the characters presented in sense data—perhaps one in a hundred or a thousand—are beyond the reach of the fluctuation that affects the others, and hence can really belong to the logical essence of the thing. But again, and curiously enough, no such argument is developed. It might be replied, finally, that one can distinguish between the sense datum which is a sign, a mere carrier or instrument of meaning, and the datum that is affirmed as the character of the thing, and that the inconsistencies belong to the former, not to the latter. Professor Strong does make this distinction, but, apart from giving rise to many new difficulties,[1] it will not meet the present need. For it seems clear that the great majority of the

[1] E.g., (1) since Bradley's discussion of 'floating ideas', it has been hard to believe in content that appears in, or to, the mind without being affirmed as in any sense real; (2) it is hard to believe that the characters of the fleeting and distorted images which often serve to carry meaning subsist timelessly, just as they are, apart from our minds; (3) it is perhaps hardest of all to distinguish between such universal content and what Professor Strong would describe as 'states of our sensibility'. Thus 'cold' may be an essence ascribed to a physical object; or it may be 'a state of our sensibility', which serves as 'the vehicle of the givenness of this essence' (234), and as such it is a particular psychical existent. I cannot understand this. If cold is a character, then on Strong's assumption it is contradictory to call it an existent; if it is not, we are left in the dark as to what it is.

reds and greens, hots and colds, straights and crookeds, that we sense are not used simply as signs, but are taken as characters of the real.

In considering this account of essence, we find entering the thin edge of a very formidable wedge. The main doctrine, we saw, is this, that in knowing we apprehend an essence which, in favourable cases, is the nature or character of the real thing. According to Strong, sense data provide a part, and an important part, of this essence. But he has offered effective reasons himself for believing that, so far as the essence is composed of such data, it *cannot* be the character of the object. Just so far, therefore, the main doctrine becomes untenable.

6. But along with the foregoing doctrine, both in Strong's and other essays, goes a doctrine which, whether consistent with it or not, is worth distinguishing for its different emphasis. According to this new statement, we find the essences of things, not in sense data, but in what sense data mean or suggest. 'What is given is the meaning, and not the sensation.'[1] 'The visual, auditory, or tactile sensation' which serves as the 'vehicle' of the meaning is not an essence that is affirmed, but a 'state of my sensibility', 'a present particular existence'.[2] This doctrine has great advantages over the preceding one. As I walk around a table, the sense data presented are far too various and shifting, as we have seen, to allow any plausibility to the doctrine that they are its real character. But while the sense data vary, the shape perceived or judged remains the same. The shape I assign to the table, the shape I *mean*, the character read off from the sensory cue—this is something quite different from the sense datum, and it is this that provides us with the essence. Here we have the position chiefly stressed in the third essay. 'No two people seem to find the same group of images and sensations in their respective experiences, and yet all may agree in "meaning" the same thing. . . . This meaning is that which we find directly given to our thought . . . and I

---

[1] *Essays in Critical Realism*, 235 (Strong).   [2] 233, 234 (Strong).

shall therefore refer to it as the "datum" . . . it will almost invariably be seen to differ considerably from the group of revived and sensuous images which constitute the psychic state by means of which we conceive it.'[1] It is this meaning given to thought that provides our bridge to the real thing; it is this that is meant by essence; it is this that is ascribed in judgement; and it is this that, assuming the judgement to be a true one, presents us with the character of the thing itself.[2]

There is clearly a new emphasis here. Obviously Professor Pratt would not say, as does Professor Strong, that when we look at a face, 'the entire datum is physical'; indeed he says expressly, 'the quality group found in perception is not physical';[3] 'the characters meant and the characters sensed in perception are by no means identical'.[4] When Professor Strong wishes to provide illustrations of 'data', i.e. 'the logical essences of things', he most commonly chooses sense data— reds and greens, the cold of an ice-cake, the bent appearance of a stick. Professor Pratt reminds us that our sense data of the table are wildly various and that our real datum is the squareness ascribed in judgement. It is true that Pratt, in laying down this theory, says that the content affirmed may include the set of qualities immediately given to sense. But his emphasis is on the function of such 'quality groups' as 'a token or warning' rather than as a content actually affirmed.

We have seen that the first account of the vehicle by which essences are presented is hard to reconcile with the main position, namely, that the essence immediately grasped may give

---

[1] *Essays in Critical Realism,* 90 (Pratt).

[2] Cf. the following passages: 'When I think of the moon, I can distinguish (1) images of various sorts; (2) a meaning or datum not to be identified with my introspectively discovered images; and (3) a conscious outer reference of this datum (not of the images) to a point in space some thousands of miles distant from the earth.' (91). 'The characters meant and the characters sensed in perception are thus by no means identical. . . .' (91) 'Plainly a distinction must be made between the meaning which one entertains in conception and the particular images and sensations which introspection discovers in the process of conceiving.' (90.)

[3] 96.   [4] 91.

us the character of the real. Does this hold also of the second? I fear it does. To be sure, this second account provides a vehicle for the essence which is less variable and incoherent than sense data themselves; the *meanings* given to thought and affirmed in judgement are undoubtedly less capricious than such data; for example, the squareness of the table may be agreed upon by many minds, or continuously held by one, while the data presented to the eye are varying widely. Granted. But the conclusion hoped for is still distant. For if our judgements are more consistent than our sense data, they are still indefinitely less so than the character of the real world. If sense data vary with the organism, so do meanings. Indeed in any considerable period of individual or racial history, they vary more. As one grows from childhood to maturity, one's thought about things and persons changes profoundly, but there is probably no such change in the character of one's sense data, and certainly no such change in the real objects. As the race has advanced from the animal mind to savagery and then to science, the character it has ascribed to the stars, let us say, has undergone the most radical change, but hardly the character of the stars themselves. In estimating the claim of a judgement now made to reveal any fixed and final character in the nature of things, it is important to view it against the background, not of the changes of a day or a year, but of the history of thought as a whole; and so regarded, the validity of the claim appears very ill-founded indeed.

If it is on the wavering and changeable meanings affirmed in judgement that we must depend for the revelation of the real, all men have been steadily in error and will probably remain so. Mental evolution has not ceased with us. The objects in which our perception and belief have rested, like those of the men before us, will be broken up and carried down the stream of time. It may be said that there is nothing particularly heinous in such defect of certainty; it is the acknowledged position, for example, of absolute idealism. So it is. But a major claim of realism has been to deliver us from all this. We were supposed to get, here and now, a sight of the actual nature of things, a sight that was limited in its scope, but, within that scope, definitive. But we shall look in vain among the shifting clouds of meaning for the firmness and coherence of nature itself. There is not a single judgement we make whose meaning can be plausibly identified, just as it stands, with a piece of ultimate reality. The evidence for this view will be given later in detail.[1] Meanwhile, for those who accept it, that direct grasp of the ultimate nature of things which both realism and critical realism were supposed to give can only be an illusion.

7. The theory just considered is that the portion of the field of consciousness which must be identified with the essence is the logical meaning affirmed in judgement. At many points in the joint volume, this doctrine is struggling with another, which, in the sixth essay particularly, hovers always in the background and comes at times to unequivocal expression. It is a doctrine that has apparently been produced by the pressure of the facts upon the third theory. According to that theory, when I judge truly about an object, the character of the object itself is directly presented. If this is taken seriously, then when I *think* truly of certain features and contours as having belonged to Caesar's face, numerically the same features and contours that were embodied in ancient Rome are before me now. This direct apprehension of the character of objects absent and remote seems startlingly near to the neo-realism that our authors repudiate. Their discomfort about it varies, but the author of the sixth essay has felt this so keenly that he has in effect worked out a new theory to allay it. He does not appear, in the *Essays*, to regard this view as seriously heterodox, but when its implications are made explicit, it turns out to be a very different account from either of those just described. The theory is this, that what is presented to thought is not a timeless and independent universal, but a transient bit of mental content.

Consider the following language: 'The critical realist agrees

[1] Chaps. XXVII and XXXII.

with the idealist that the content is mental . . .'[1] '. . . both the content and the objectness are parts of the act of knowledge'.[2] Regarding memory, we must hold 'that the object of memory no longer exists, but that the claim and content are elements of the present act'.[3] The claim of naïve realism to apprehend the remote object itself is 'impossible because it would involve the leaping of spatial and temporal barriers in an unnatural fashion';[4] it is an 'illusion' to suppose that we 'handle mentally the very stuff of the physical existent'.[5] 'Knowledge is just the insight into the nature of the object, that is made possible by the contents which reflect it in consciousness.'[6] This can only mean that what we directly apprehend is not the actual nature or character of the object, as the other accounts suggest, but something else, a conscious content, which reflects this. Physical things undoubtedly exist apart from minds, 'but reflection has discovered that the content with which we automatically clothe these acknowledged realities is subjective',[7] and that 'the sensible characters' of things, which are 'so readily taken to be literal aspects, surfaces, and inherent qualities of physical things are subjective substitutes for the corresponding parts of the physical world'.[8] In perceiving, our attention does not 'leap across space to the thing'; 'the causal relation is from the thing to the organism',[9] and the content of perception, which is 'in the percipient himself',[10] 'must have the property of reproducing the character of the object in some measure'.[11]

Now is not all this clearly inconsistent with the accounts we have just considered? According to both of these, when we know a thing we come into contact with its character directly, whether through sense data or through logical meaning; according to the present doctrine, we never achieve such contact at all. To be sure, there are phrases that suggest a different reading; it is said, for example, that 'the physical world reveals itself in the data of observation',[12] and that between

---

[1] *Essays in Critical Realism*, 212 (Sellars).   [2] 215.   [3] 216.
[4] 200.   [5] 201.   [6] 200.   [7] 197.   [8] 191.
[9] 213.   [10] 196.   [11] 198.   [12] 202.

datum and object there is 'a logical identity'.[1] But these phrases do not show that the doctrine given in the quotations is not held also. They only show that the writer is bravely struggling to achieve the impossible task of equating his doctrine with the main theory of the volume.

8. The truth is that there are two different sets of facts to which critical realism has to do justice, but which seem to require diverging theories. One of these has been dominant in the mind of most of the authors, and has produced the view that what is apprehended directly is the non-mental essence. In the mind of Professor Sellars this dominance has been shared by another, which has produced a contrary view. On the one hand there are the facts of knowledge. We do somehow know things, and since what we lay hold upon in knowing is not their existence, it must be their character. And this is *literally* their character; it is no mere copy of it; critical realists insist that they are not offering us a return to Locke. If we cannot intuit, or know directly, what things are like, i.e. the characters that they have, then we cannot properly speak of knowing at all. Now since we do know, and since, in order to know, we must grasp directly the essence of things, it follows that we do so grasp them. Our thought is under the control of the essences that directly present themselves to us.

But then there is another set of facts to which justice must also be done, and which Professor Sellars' view seems specially designed to recognize. These are the facts of the dependence of mind on body. He holds that our thinking and perceiving are what they are, in respect to both act and content, as a result of physical causes. If the colour-blind man sees grey instead of red, and the insane man believes himself to be Caesar, their perceiving and thinking as they do result from peculiarities in the organism; and what is true of abnormal perceiving and thinking must be equally true of normal. If I think of Julius Caesar, my idea, both in act and content, is an event with a

---

[1] *Essays in Citical Realism*, 203 (Sellars).

cause in my cerebrum. And the effect, like its cause, is something local and transitory. It is an event that happens in me here and now, and is divided from the actual Julius Caesar by stretches of space and time. My thought is under the control of the organism.

9. Now these conclusions will not fit together. How can my thought of Julius Caesar be Caesar's actual character and also a subjective mental content, produced by changes in my organism? Yet Professor Sellars is compelled to say both. If he is to be a good critical realist he must say that the content we apprehend and affirm is objective, the essence or character of the real thing. But in justice to the second set of facts, he must also say that it is 'subjective' and 'in the percipient himself'. He must say, and he does say, that the very character of the objects reveals itself in the datum, and yet also that the object is separated from the datum by impassable barriers of space and time. He agrees that the content or essence belongs to the object, yet also holds that it is 'part of the act of knowledge'.. He is clear that critical realism has advanced beyond Locke and his theories of copying, and yet 'can see no objection to a critical copy-theory in the case of memory',[1] a case which in these matters is crucial. We grasp directly a complex of characters which have a 'logical identity' with those of the object itself, but this complex is also a mental content which 'reproduces' or is 'like' the nature of the object, and must therefore be different from it. We 'intuit' or seize immediately 'the actual character of the object', yet that which we seize immediately is a mental content separated from the object by a lengthy chain of causes.[2]

This criticism is not verbal. It is not to be met by any such easy expedient as saying that since the essence is universal, it

[1] *Essays in Critical Realism*, 216 (Sellars).

[2] If I select the essay of Professor Sellars for this special criticism, it is only because, writing with the mind-body relation more explicitly before him, he seems to me to reveal most candidly the difficulties which it entails for the theory of knowledge.

can be at once objective and subjective, here and now and yet also in remote places and times. The content, says Professor Sellars, is part of the present mental act and is caused by certain changes in my brain. Now if this content is, or contains a logical universal, identical with the character of the object, what are we to conclude? This, for example, that a momentary change in my brain is creating the expression that was worn by Caesar some twenty centuries ago, not a copy of it, but the expression itself; that the character of a star far distant and now extinct, is at this moment being generated by changes in my head; that when I look at a table, its own character, or part of this, while remaining in the table, is somehow transmitted without change along the links of a causal chain through ether, nerves, and brain, and appears in my mind in person. That such miracles as this are at every instant happening in the world I am unable to believe, nor do I suppose that Professor Sellars believes it either. Yet this is what his doctrine entails if the intuited content is to be at once an event organically caused *and* the character of the object. There is no way to hold both these views together. If one is taken, the other must be left. One may choose the main doctrine of the school, that what I intuit is literally the character of the object, and then to say that the content is mental, rather than non-mental, subjective rather than objective, that it is 'part of the act of knowledge', that it is organically caused, that it copies or corresponds to anything whatever, will all be false or misleading. Or one may say that the content *is* mental, part of the present organically caused act, etc., and then to say that we know directly the stable non-mental character of the actual object is really self-contradictory. And unfortunately if one elects the latter alternative and frankly abandons the attempt to combine it with the major tenet of critical realism, one's position is scarcely better. For no protestations can then disguise the fact that the position is virtually Locke's. The defects of such a position have been studied in Chap. VII.

It will be evident from what we have said that the critical realist doctrine about ideas is difficult to discover. It seems at times as if ideas had vanished as completely as from the most radical neo-realism, since it is held that the content of thought consists of timeless and non-mental universals. But always there hover in the background the mental images and mental states which serve as 'vehicles' for the essence, and Professor Sellars speaks quite simply of the essences themselves as ideas— naturally enough, since he 'agrees with the idealist that the content is mental'.[1] The different elements to which the term 'mental' is applied, and the obscure and various parts they are represented as playing, we have not space to explore. But it is evident that the main contribution of the school, and its substitute for the traditional notion of the idea, is its doctrine of essence. Upon this doctrine the members agree in concentrating their attention, and upon it we should concentrate also if critical realism is to be rightly appraised. What it means, we may repeat, is that in knowing we apprehend directly characters that in favourable cases are logically identical with the nature of the object itself. Apart from the special difficulties already noted in interpreting the doctrine, what are we to say of it?

10. (1) Let us take it at its simplest. If we strip from it the debatable claim that what we are commonly aware of are 'the logical essences of real things', there remains the less questionable proposition that what we are aware of is simply essences which may or may not be characters of anything that exists. An essence is universal and timeless, and essences are to be found wherever a 'what' is to be distinguished from a 'that'. Now it is not only in the sort of experience called cognitive that 'what' and 'that' can be distinguished; two sensations, affections, or emotions, may clearly differ from each other in character as well as in existence, and hence their 'what' and 'that' are not the same. And this leads us to a conclusion which Mr. Santayana indeed seems to recognize and accept, but which comes little to the fore in the joint volume and which is not

[1] *Essays in Critical Realism*, 212.

easy to adopt in its present form. This conclusion is that essences are 'the only data of experience',[1] that 'it is impossible that anything should appear which is not universal'.[2] When considered in examples, this doctrine is startling. Thus if I feel tired, what I feel has been in being from all eternity. If I am pleased with a new hat, everything which could distinguish the pleasure from a toothache subsisted before I was born. The content of every thought in precisely its state of vagueness, everything that I feel during a gust of anger or romance, whatever anyone experiences when he cuts his finger, or feels bored, or dreams, belongs to the eternal world where nothing comes to be and nothing passes. Not only all qualities that I am now experiencing but even that combination of them which marks my field of consciousness at the moment subsists without beginning or end. There is no such thing anywhere as the creation or origination of anything; there is only the embodiment of what subsisted already. Whether this doctrine is plausible I shall not undertake to say. I shall merely point out that when a doctrine with similar consequences is offered by Holt and Russell, we find it rejected by critical realists because it violates Occam's razor.[3] It is true that what they mean by this is multiplying *existences* beyond facts, whereas critical realism only multiplies *subsistences*. But it must be remembered that Holt and Russell, as neutral monists, did not multiply existences as opposed to subsistences; for they did not admit the distinction, and sought to reduce all things to universals. So far, therefore, as the objection is directed against the indefinite multiplication of logical entities, the case stands the same with critical realism as with Russell and Holt.

11. (2) Indeed, I think that in more than one respect the criticism brought against neo-realism is double-edged. We are told that the proposal to take secondary and tertiary qualities as actually belonging to objects is untenable. Why? Partly

[1] Santayana, *Scepticism and Animal Faith*, 89.
[2] *The Realm of Essence*, 38.   [3] *Critical Realism*, 16.

because a thing cannot have contradictory qualities (an argument that applies to all kinds of quality if to any); but partly, too, because the secondary and tertiary qualities so plainly depend on our organism. The differences between colours, for example, 'are differences produced primarily *in our organisms* by the same outward causes'. 'Neither at the origin-end of the ether-wave nor in our organisms is there so much selection as a passive causal process.'[1] How are we to interpret this? The secondary qualities, we have learned from Professor Strong, are as truly essences as the primary, and if so, all alike are independent of the organism and timeless. How can it be said also that they are dependent on the organism and effects in time?

It may be replied that the point of the argument has been mistaken. What depends on the organism is not the qualities, but only the occurrence or presentation of the qualities. When the colour-blind man sees grey instead of red, his organism has nothing to do with the character of his sense data, but only with enabling him to see them. Now such plausibility as this view may have, it derives from a latent and false analogy. We have really returned once more to the lantern and the screen. The world is a great and permanent tapestry; the brain is a sort of lantern which, through the turn of a screw, reveals one part rather than another of what is there outside us. Of course the lantern does not create the figures on the tapestry, and similarly the brain does not create the colours that we see. But the analogy does not hold. Lantern and tapestry are independent from the start, and it is clear that an event in one makes no difference to the other. But it can hardly be contended that a change in the brain produces a bare act of being alert or aware, which only happens to be an awareness of red because red comes sauntering by. Would it be maintained that what happens in my brain has nothing to do with making my sensation pleasurable or painful? If not, it is admitted that what happens in my body may be causally relevant to the *quality* appearing in consciousness; what happened there determined

[1] *Critical Realism*, 11 (Drake).

the appearance of *this* quality rather than *that*. If what happens in the organism is not connected *differentially* with the qualities experienced, it is meaningless to say that their 'differences are produced primarily in our organisms', nor is it possible to see how the organism could make them in particular appear. If there is such a connection, then the quality red itself is involved in the causal process, and to speak of essences as an order of inviolate vestals, holding no commerce with existence, admitting no influences and bearing no results, is false.

In sum, when we speak of one thing causing another, we imply that the character of the effect depends on the character of the cause; we never suppose that a characterless existence or event can produce something, or that a concrete cause can produce an appearance which is the appearance of nothing. Effects, like causes, are always concrete. If the appearance of essences is caused at all, they themselves cannot be wholly outside the process.

12. (3) And they are integral to causes as well as to effects. When I burn my hand, I quickly withdraw it. Before a sculptor sets his chisel to a block, he forms a notion of what is to emerge from it. Here the experience of an essence determines a course of bodily behaviour. Now the experience of an essence is an event, and it may be said that what caused the physical effect was the event and not the essence. But that is unintelligible. I repeat that an event is always compound; it is not an occurrence in which nothing occurs; it is always the occurrence *of* something. And *what* occurs is as important to the sequel as the occurrence of this 'what'. If this is denied, the only alternative is to introduce views of causality and inference which reduce both to complete contingency. Indeed, this is frankly done by the great writer who has given the metaphysics of critical realism its most attractive statement.

Essences, according to Mr. Santayana, never do anything. They subsist; they maintain their identity in their changeless realm of being; they are contemplated; some of them from time to time are incarnated or embodied. But even 'this descent or incarnation of essences cannot be their own doing, since all essences are inert and non-existent . . . Even the thinnest creations of spirit, therefore, are products of the realm of matter, and possible only within it. Incarnation is no voluntary emanation from above; it is a dire event, a budding torment, here below. A world of accidents, arbitrary and treacherous, first lends to the eternal a temporal existence and a place in the flux.'[1] And just as essences are not agents in their own embodiment, so they play no part in securing that others should be embodied. 'There is then no necessity in the relation between cause and effect, and no assurance that law is constant.'[2] Indeed Mr. Santayana's scepticism about causality is of the profoundest order. He not only denies all knowledge that event A must produce event B, but holds that no conceivable extension of knowledge could show that the character of A had anything to do with the production of B. For characters are everywhere inert essences. The executive order of nature lies below them and pushes them up like flowers in a garden, sometimes in patterns which we trace and find repeated; but since the only terms and patterns we can discover are themselves essences, the grounds alike of appearance and of succession must remain hidden from us. 'The mind cannot pursue the roots of things into the darkness; it cannot discover why they exist; it must be satisfied with noting their passing aspect, which is but an essence; and it must follow the chase, carried by its own galloping substance, to see what aspect they may wear next.'[3] 'No moment, no event, and no world can insure the existence or the character of anything beyond it.'[4]

If one is to hold to the complete inertness of essences, this is of course the conclusion one must draw. Mr. Santayana draws it courageously, but I do not think he keeps to it, or that anyone can keep to it. He appears ready to accept the maxim that what has happened will happen again 'wherever similar elements are in the same relations', though adding that

[1] *The Realm of Matter*, 84.   [2] *Ibid.*, 111.   [3] *Ibid.*, 103–4.
[4] *Ibid.*, 114, and cf. *The Realm of Essence*, 80–1.

this is 'only a postulate, which contingent, substantial and original facts may at any point disallow'.[1] So far as we know, however, they have not disallowed it yet, and continued concomitance with no connection is very like miracle. Indeed, that whenever event B has occurred, the character of its sole unvarying antecedent A has had nothing whatever to do with it, is a view quite at odds with that 'animal faith' which Mr. Santayana in other matters is disposed to respect.

And in fact he does respect it, even here, though his theory gives him small title to do so. 'For the material cause of anything . . .' he says, 'is a certain quantity of matter *already endowed with form*',[2] or 'the structure and movement of the substance at hand under those material circumstances';[3] and in expounding his naturalism he always proceeds as if variations in our mind or 'psyche' were induced by the changing character of our brains. It is not mere matter, then, but matter with form and structure, matter as embodying essences, matter as essence and existence in union, that acts as cause. And if so, essences are not inert after all. They are agents and combatants in the field of actuality. They co-operate decisively and momentously in the 'flux of existence'. The sharp separation which critical realism tries to establish between the 'realm of essence' and the 'realm of matter' cannot be maintained. In the very chapter in which Mr. Santayana condemns the Platonic idealists for 'fusing their physics with their visions', he describes matter as performing feats which would be unthinkable unless it were heavily charged with essence. And it is idle to say that essence is 'inert and non-existent' if it can acquire external relations and, through identifying itself with the nature of objects, move things and men and kingdoms to new issues.

13. (4) Causality is thus meaningless if essences really stand outside the process. So also is inference. We have seen that for

[1] *The Realm of Matter*, 109–10.   [2] *Ibid.*, 194; my italics.
[3] *Ibid.*, 195.

the critical realist my apprehension of an essence is an event with a physical cause; and for Mr. Santayana at least, the process of thought by which we grasp the affiliations of that essence is likewise physically caused at every stage. The essence revealed at one step has nothing whatever to do with determining what shall be revealed at the next. 'The intuition of the essence to be thought of next, even in the most obvious inference or deduction, must be generated by the movement of living discourse, and by the circumstances of some animal life. Essences are unsubstantial: the psyche, or matter elsewhere, is the substance at work.'[1] 'Dialectic, then, while ostensibly following ideal implications . . . secretly expresses a material life.'[2] 'The controlling force in reasoning is not reason, but instinct and circumstance';[3] 'the continuity is physical, not logical'.[4] On this head we shall have much to say later.[5] But it is perhaps apparent, even in advance of such discussion, that thought is not to be explained by abstracting from the content of each step and considering the whole as a train of characterless events. It is only if idea A has specific content, that is, presents a distinctive essence, that any warrant is afforded for B's succeeding rather than C's, precisely as in physical causality an existence or event without character would produce anything or nothing. Thinking, according to Mr. Santayana, is under the constraint of the organism. Thinking, according to Bradley, whose doctrine we are next to examine, *may* be under the constraint of the subject-matter. And it is perhaps enough to say that, unless this latter point is accepted, there is an end to any *explanation* of thinking, since there would be nothing discoverable in any step of the process which would offer the slightest suggestion as to *why* its successor followed. On such a hypothesis thinking, as Mr. Santayana frankly puts it, 'will never become anything but a perpetual genesis of the unwarrantable out of the contingent'.[6] I doubt if this statement in the end has any clear meaning, but the only satisfactory answer

[1] *The Realm of Essence*, 79.   [2] *Ibid.*, 99.   [3] *Ibid.*, 104.
[4] *Ibid.*, 103.   [5] See below, Chaps. XIII, XXIII, XXXII.
[6] *The Realm of Essence*, 81.

to it is to produce an account of thinking which shows that so far as it really is thinking, it never moves contingently, or generates without warrant. Such an account we shall try to supply.

To summarize: critical realism holds that the content of an idea is a set of timeless universals which may be contemplated or may be embodied, but which themselves neither suffer nor act in the field of existences. We have shown that they do both, that perception is unaccountable unless they suffer, that inference is unaccountable unless they act.

We have laboured this point because it is fundamental to a right understanding of the process of thought. If critical realism is correct about it, that process loses most of its significance. It becomes an irrelevant 'lyric cry in the midst of business', or a series of snapshots of an alien world produced by fortuitous changes in the brain. Stripped of the glamour with which a splendid prose has invested it, 'the life of reason' is a life of servitude to the irrational. Rationality becomes animal luck. Since the essences revealed to us are passive, the constraint exercised in inference is exclusively from below. If thought in a sense reveals the nature of things, it is neither the nature of things nor their connections that lays our thought under compulsion. There is no such thing as 'the self-development of an idea'; there is only an impulsive urgency to look at something else. And when we do look, the vital secrets are always withheld. 'Existence, not being included in any immediate datum, is always open to doubt';[1] what we intuit, being only inert essences, reveals nothing of the forces that control 'the dark engine of nature'. Reflection is a series of whimsical glances cast by an animal at the outward shows of things. We shall see later, if indeed we have not seen already, that this view does not comport with the facts. But even if it comported better with the facts than it does, one would wish to canvass more hopeful views before signing away so irretrievably the efficacy of one's mind.

[1] *Scepticism and Animal Faith*, 40.

14. (5) To turn now to further criticism: at first, it seems unambiguous to say that what we directly engage in knowing is 'the actual character of the object' or 'the logical essence of the real thing'. But as the explanations proceed, we grow puzzled. This does not mean, we are warned, that we directly know objects themselves; for there is a 'fundamental opposition between data and physical things';[1] the thing and its parts exist; essences as such do not exist; hence in apprehending them, we never lay hold of the existent. Now I suspect a confusion here between existence and existents. The existence of an object, we are told, cannot be included in the content of thought; if it could, the thought of a hundred dollars would coin them into fact. This we may grant. But having granted that we cannot intuit existence, we find ourselves called on to believe that we cannot intuit existents. But this is a totally different proposition. When I look at a coin, its existence is not part of the content immediately grasped, but if the characters I grasp are not existents, i.e. do not exist, what does exist? Can a coin exist with no character at all? That is meaningless. Can it exist with a non-existent character? Meaningless again. Hence its character must exist if it does. Its character is so integral a part of itself that if you removed from a coin its roundness, hardness, and other qualities, there would be no coin left. When we perceive the characters, we are perceiving something that exists, i.e. existents; and if so, we are directly acquainted with the object itself. Yet in critical realist writing, this seems to be constantly denied.

How are we to account for such a denial of the seemingly obvious? I have suggested that an illicit process from existence to existents has something to do with it. But fundamentally, it is the effect of making essence a weapon with which to do battle both before and behind, and finding that in the struggle one has to join alternately the ranks of one's enemies. In principle it is Professor Sellars' difficulty over again. While opposing Locke and the representationists, our authors are clear that unless we can know what actually exists, there is an end of

[1] *Critical Realism*, 225 (Strong).

knowledge altogether. While opposing idealism and neo-realism, it is clear to them that if what we know directly is what actually exists, we have all the horrid consequences about error that have made those doctrines notorious. Hence what we grasp directly is a *tertium quid*, itself neither mental nor physical, a neutral logical essence.

Now, the fate of *tertium quid* doctrines when applied to the problem of body and mind is very well known. The intermediate link is a limbo in which the differences that separate the sides are not so much reconciled as sunk and lost sight of. And since, as Professor Sellars has clearly seen, you cannot deal with the relation of mind and objects in complete abstraction from the problem of mind and body, the old difficulty returns to haunt you. The sides must be linked by a bridge of identity; yet when the link is produced and you scrutinize it, you see that the old 'either-or' breaks out again. What you directly engage is either identical with the object's nature, or it is not. If it is, the theory may as well throw in its lot with the objective idealists, for it holds, as they do, that the universals which from one point of view are my mind, are from another the object itself; and no attempt to avoid this conclusion by divorcing the object from its own nature can succeed. On the other hand, if the theory is to deny immediate contact with existents, holding that 'we know them *through* our percepts and ideas', and thus only 'know *about* them', then it must adhere to this and take the bitter with the sweet. It must admit that it is imprisoned as completely as Locke was in 'the iron ring of ideas', since all that it can directly grasp is its own mental content, which is denied identity with any existent. It cannot be neo-realist while attacking Locke, and Lockian while attacking neo-realism; we must insist that these positions are incompatible, and that it requires something more than essences to bridge the gap between them. The content I intuit is either the nature of the existent object or not. If it is, the theory in effect is objective idealism in disguise. If it is not, it is representationism in disguise.

15. (6) The doctrine of essence is supposed to apply equally to thoughts and perceptions. But it applies better, I think, to perceptions than to thoughts, and better to some perceptions than to others. It seems to have been designed to meet the cases where the characters meant are presented directly and explicitly, and it falls into embarrassment over the indirect and the marginal. According to critical realism, thinking of an object, like perceiving it, implies that some or all of its characters are directly presented. But suppose that I am listening to rapid conversation or engaging in rapid reading; I may clearly understand what I thus hear or read; but can it plausibly be suggested regarding everything I have thought of that its concrete character, or some piece of this, has been directly presented to my mind?

There are few difficulties in critical realism which Mr. Santayana, brooding over the position in an impressive row of volumes, has not felt and instructively dealt with. This particular difficulty has not escaped him. He has said, it is true, that 'any essence is a model of explicitness; it is all surface without substance. When it appears, it appears entire'.[1] But he realizes that there is more twilight about our thinking than such language would suggest, and that apparently we often think of things, without calling up their concrete character. To meet this fact he introduces what is described as an 'intent', that is, a reference through the use of a sign to an essence or fact that is not presented. To mean is not to intuit. 'The torments suffered by the souls in Dante's *Inferno*, for instance, are not intuited by the poet or the reader in their intended essence, for then he would be enduring these torments actually; yet he knows what he means by them; the words or images that suggest them are significant, and in proportion as they are well chosen, they converge upon the object, the unrealized essence of those torments, as they would be if actually felt.'[2]

It is clear that some such doctrine is necessary to cover the facts. Unfortunately, critical realism, if it is to retain what it counts as its chief advantage, is cut off from such a doctrine.

---

[1] *The Realm of Essence*, 81.   [2] *Ibid.*, 114.

Representationism is given up, and every true thought or perception is to lay hold immediately of the character of its object. It now appears that this is unnecessary. That character need not be presented at all. When I recall an object seen, what is immediately presented may be not characters of that object, but words or images which, perhaps, do not even resemble it and yet somehow mean it; and by such thinking I can attain to knowledge and truth. This is not the doctrine that was laid down by Professor Pratt. He did, it is true, insist that 'a distinction must be made between the meaning which one entertains in conception and the particular images and sensations which introspection discovers in the process of conceiving. These are the machinery of conception, so to speak—the "vehicle", as Strong expresses it, of our meaning. This meaning is that which we find directly given to our thought.'[1] This meaning is also, in whole or part, the character of the object. It is an obviously different doctrine that Mr. Santayana is laying down. He is saying that thought can make 'an essence an object of intent, when it is no longer, or not yet, an object of intuition'; we can think, through words or images, of characters that are *not* given. Now we have canvassed the difficulties of such language so laboriously when discussing Mr. Russell's teaching that we have no heart to raise them again. It must suffice to express surprise that this view should be taken by a critical realist. We had learned that to think of an object implies that some, at least, of its characters are directly apprehended. We now learn that we can think of an object, and think truly, when none of its characters are directly apprehended. But consider the consequences. If in some cases we can think of objects, and think truly, without intuiting their nature, why should this be necessary in any? If a falling short by direct apprehension of the nature of what is known is fatal to knowledge generally, how can it be consistent with knowledge here? If I can think of a thing truly though its essence does not appear in my content of thought, how can truth *be* identity of essence, between such content and the thing's character? Critical realism is again

[1] *Critical Realism*, 90.

forced to choose between its major doctrine and another
which, though a minor one, seems to be called for by the
facts. If the major doctrine is true, then to think of an unpresented essence appears impossible. But if this *is* possible,
how can it longer be maintained that in thinking of anything
truly I must intuit its logical essence?

16. It is time to turn from this appraisal. We applied to
critical realism to get light on the nature of the idea, and found
that what it offered was a substitute for the idea in the form of
an essence. When we think of an object the content before us
is that object—not its existence, indeed, which is beyond the
reach of direct apprehension, but its character, which, as
universal, can crop up in different places, times, and experiences. But in coming to closer quarters with the theory, we
found some differences of emphasis as to the region of experience in which these characters appeared, whether in sense
data or in the meanings affirmed in judgement. We then found
in one member of the school language which suggested that
the bold supplanting of ideas by essences had not been
carried through, and we paused to ask whether it really had
been. Dark secrets began to come out. If this member spoke
with halting accents, it was because with a tender intellectual
conscience he was carrying on his head the sins of many.
In spite of the group's insistence, in their main doctrine, that
the nature of things is given in the content of thought, they
were constrained to admit also that this content is dependent
on the organism, and separated by a causal chain from the
thing whose character it was said to be. Thus ideas reappear
on the scene and with them the old chasm between idea and
object. And for a chasm so formidable the bridge of essence
proved too frail a span. For even if essences could be active
in the field of existence, which at the cost of his theories of
causality and inference the critical realist denies, still the
mechanism of self-propagation by which an essence might
traverse the causal chain from thing to thought is unimaginable,

and such transition would be miracle or luck. Critical realism, in holding to an identity between experienced content and the nature of physical things, is making a bold attack on the paradox of knowledge, but in attempting to square its assertion with the admitted dependence of that content on bodily change, it falters, equivocates, and ends in unintelligibility.

Nevertheless, we consider it the most plausible and convincingly defended of all the theories we have so far considered. It has escaped from the *naïveté* of the copy theory, from Professor Titchener's distrust of metaphysics and the pragmatist's disbelief in it, from the behaviourist's metaphysical incompetence, from the *bizarrerie* of Mr. Russell's theory, from the neo-realist's notorious helplessness about error. If we are compelled to reject it, it is with very different feelings from those with which we have left most of the other theories behind; the amount of amendment with which we could accept it is relatively small. It has perhaps earned its name of Critical Realism. Nevertheless, it is not critical enough. With a theory that in essentials comes close, for example, to Bradley's, it does not show either his consciousness of difficulties or his thoroughness in meeting them. In regard to its central problem, namely how the character of objects can belong at once to the self and to the world, the metaphysicians of objective idealism had gone beyond critical realism before it was born. Some evidence of this may appear in the next chapter, where we shall study the views of one member of this school. Meanwhile, the position we have been considering is no halting-place. One may return from it into representationism, or go on from it into a revised idealism. But if one pitches one's camp in its territory, it is likely to breed strange humours in the brain. How otherwise can one account for that amazing, incongruous synthesis of naturalism and Plato that has been left as his maturest testament by the great artist of the school?

CHAPTER XIII

BRADLEY ON IDEAS IN LOGIC
AND IN PSYCHOLOGY

1. The last two chapters have been concerned with a single problem, which, in view of the failure of the theories reviewed to deal with it adequately, has now become acute. The problem springs from the obvious fact that when I think of anything my thought has two sides: on the one hand, something that goes on in me here and now; on the other hand, an object to which this event somehow points. The thoroughgoing realist is for keeping this plain distinction and avoiding complications; here is my mental act; there is the physical thing. The critical realist replies that complications cannot be kept out. When I think of Julius Caesar, there is of course the mental event, and there is, or was, Julius Caesar. But are these the only elements involved? If so, what are we to do with the *content* of thought? I think of Julius Caesar *as* this or that, as a general, a statesman, a writer; these attributes enter, in some sense, into my thought, else how could I assert them? They also belong to the object, for did not Julius Caesar possess them? You cannot take them as simply physical, says the critical realist, for then you must take such contents generally as physical, and that leads straight to nonsense; you cannot take them as simply mental, for then we shall be 'confined in the iron ring of our own ideas'. So he takes them as neither mental nor physical, but as neutral logical entities, which may appear to a mind or be embodied in a thing, but are exclusively tied to neither.

This is a marked advance over the simpler realism, but we have seen that one cannot stop here. And in looking around for a line of advance, our eye is bound to fall on a school which, of those not examined, stands easily first, and which, as it happens, has explored this matter more thoroughly than the critical realists themselves. It is true that objective idealists have been suspicious of psychology, and we shall see that in the province of thinking, this suspicion is not wholly unfounded. Some members of the school, however, have been peculiarly free from it, and pre-eminent among these is a thinker who not only revealed remarkable gifts in metaphysics, psychology, and logic, but, fortunately for us, turned the full power of those gifts upon the particular problem before us—F. H. Bradley. To this problem of the line to be drawn in thinking between what belongs to me and what to the object, Bradley returned again and again over a period of forty years, and in the numerous writings in which he touches upon it there are at least three distinguishable views. These views are of very different values, and they are not wholly consistent with each other. But in one of them we are brought nearer to the truth, I think, than in any view so far considered.

2. (1) Whenever we think, said the Bradley of early days, that is, whenever we judge or infer, there can be distinguished in our thought three aspects. 'In my idea of a "horse" we have (i) the existence of an image in my head, (ii) its whole content, and (iii) its meaning. In other words we may always distinguish (i) that it is, and (ii) what it is, and (iii) what it signifies. The two first of these aspects belong to it as a fact. The third is a universal which does not belong to it, but is thought of without a relation to its existence, and in actual judgement is referred away to some other subject.'[1] By the 'existence' of an idea Bradley means the fact of its occurrence in an individual mind at a particular time. By its 'content' he means 'the complex of qualities and relations it contains'.[2] His first proposal is to draw a line within this content, and to say that whatever is beyond that line falls to logic and the objective sciences, and that whatever is within it, together with the aspect of existence, falls to psychology. That he is right about so disposing of the idea as existence or event, there can hardly be reasonable question. Unfortunately, of his proposal to distinguish logical

---

[1] *Principles of Logic* (second ed.), I. 67.   [2] *Ibid.*, 3.

from psychological aspects within the content there can be no question either; for it is palpably wrong. But let us be sure the position is clear. Suppose that I am thinking of the quality of faithfulness, and the meaning is carried by the image, full or meagre, of a horse. It is obvious, says Mr. Bradley, that the meaning, in the sense of *what* I mean, is not merely my own idea. 'When I say "this horse is a mammal", it is surely absurd to suppose that I am harnessing my mental state to the beast between the shafts'; the 'contention that in judgement the idea is my own state as such, would be simply preposterous'.[1] When I think about faithfulness, I am thinking about a quality that appeared in countless cases before I was born and will appear in countless more, a genuine universal. This universal, as such, 'can not ever be an event, with a place in the series of time or space. It can be a fact no more inside our heads than it can outside them'; far from being my idea merely, it 'can live on strange soils, under other skies, and through changing seasons'.[2] But whereas, 'the idea does not happen, and it cannot possess a place in the series',[3] the image 'belongs to me and is an event in my history';[4] it is a 'hard particular' whose momentary existence is as truly to be referred to causes as any event in physical nature.

This looks like a clear-cut distinction. But of course both these elements, image and meaning, are before the mind together, and if they are really thus worlds apart, one is moved to ask Bradley how they are related. For this question he has a surprising answer. Having made it unmistakably plain that the image is a thing of the passing moment which 'belongs to me' and is 'in my head', and that the meaning 'can not ever be an event', inside our heads or outside, he now tells us that the permanent meaning is a *part* of this 'hard particular'. 'That connection of attributes we recognize as horse, is one part of the content of the unique horse-image, and this fragmentary part of the psychical event is all that in logic we know of or care for.'[5] 'The idea is the fact with its existence disre-

---

[1] *Logic*, I. 8.   [2] *Ibid.*, 7.   [3] *Ibid.*, II. 584.
[4] *Ibid.*, I. 8.   [5] *Ibid.*, 6.

garded, and its content mutilated. It is but a portion of the actual content cut off from its reality, and used with a reference to something else.'[1]

3. Now this view is untenable. (i) If the image is what Bradley says it is, a mere fact as opposed to meaning, 'a hard particular', 'an event in my history', how can a piece of it be eternal and a part of the physical world? This is like saying that a streak of lightning is a transient occurrence, though the upper half of it is eternal. Of course if the image, in respect to content, had been declared to be a meaning itself, the case would have been otherwise, but Bradley draws the sharpest contrast between image and meaning. Identify the horse thought of with a part of my mental event, regarded as a bare particular fact, and the conclusion seems to follow that horse and image must appear and die together; 'the beast between the shafts' is really my mental state, and in harnessing him, I am tying one such state to another—which is precisely what Bradley calls preposterous. (ii) He has told us himself that image and meaning may be different and incompatible. We think of a rose as red, but our actual image of redness 'may have been that of a lobster'. Yet he tells us in the same breath that 'what we really applied was that part of (its) content which our minds had fixed as the general meaning'.[2] But the peculiar redness which belongs to the rose and which I meant could not conceivably be *part* of the redness of the lobster because the two are discrepant. I might as well take a patch of white, and call a part of it black. (iii) The theory assumes that whenever we think, we are employing well-formed images. We have seen long ago that this is untrue. There are persons whose images are so faint and tenuous that they are unable, on introspection, to discover them at all; in other cases, the only imagery seems to be that of words. Now if the theory before us is sound, this absence of imagery should ruin the thought, and where the images are verbal, the meaning should be part of the words.

[1] *Logic*, I. 45–6.   [2] *Ibid.*, 9.

Neither conclusion can be accepted.[1] (iv) We have seen that
if the image is bare psychical fact, then the logical meaning
cannot be carved out of it. We may now emphasize the other
side: if meaning *can* be carved out of it, then the image is
already more than psychical fact. So far as it is an image *of*
something it is itself a meaning. If the image can be identified
as the image of a horse, then on Bradley's own showing it is
not merely an event in me; it carries already that logical content
which makes it more than a 'hard particular'. Bradley seems to
recognize this; yet he continues to speak of the image as if
it were merely psychical fact, with no logical interest at all.

4. (2) Here we have a convenient transition to a second view,
in which there are two marked advances upon the first. In this
second view he would freely admit what we have just contended, that the image of a horse has meaning, that it is already
the thought of an object; but he would so redefine the psychical
that such thought may be included in it. Secondly, he would
no longer say, what can hardly have been more than an unhappy
phrase, that logical meanings are abstracts from images.

> 'With every judgement there goes an element which is only
> personal and merely "subjective". There is surely something,
> when I judge, which you cannot take as belonging to the object.
> Certainly to this I agree, and to myself it seems even incon-
> testable. But what, I ask, do we mean by the "subjective"?
> For myself it is merely the irrelevant. It is that which does not
> count, it is that which falls outside of the matter here in hand,
> and does not now serve our purpose. . . . The merely personal
> is the irrelevant.'[2] 'Thus, in thinking, everything in my mind—
> all sensations, feelings, ideas which do not subserve the thought
> in question—is unessential; and, because it is self, it is therefore
> *mere* self.'[3]

According to this view, we may draw a line across the total
field of consciousness. On the farther side of this line will fall

---

[1] Cf. Hoernlé, *Mind*, 1907, 70–100, and Stout, *Arist. Soc. Proc.*,
1902–3; two excellent discussions. Bradley admitted later that images
were not always to be found.—*Logic*, I. 38.

[2] *Essays on Truth and Reality*, 329.   [3] *Appearance*, 100.

all the objects of explicit judgement or perception; on the nearer side will fall that mass of irrelevancy which, always present, is usually handled by such sensation, perception and judgement as are implicit or marginal. If we are to draw any line at all between subject and object, or self and the world, it is here within the field of consciousness that we must draw it, for Bradley tells us in his best Bluebeard manner that 'the Ego that pretends to be anything either before or beyond its concrete psychical filling, is a gross fiction and mere monster, and for no purpose admissible'.[1] The self or subject, then, consists of that mass of experience, or experienced matter, which remains unobjectified, such as obscure coenaesthetic sensations, peripheral pleasures and pains, moods and emotions, and those marginal ideas which are present without being affirmed explicitly.

5. Bradley has nowhere made a formal offer to psychology of this self or subject as its proper domain, but of course psychology deals with the psychical, and in this his favourite meaning for 'self' we also have one of the meanings Bradley gives to 'psychical'. It is natural to ask, then, whether this distinction will give us what we want. May we not surrender to logic and the objective sciences such concepts and relations as appear in explicit thought, and assign to psychology the region described as 'subjective'?

No; the apportionment is unworkable. It would assign exclusively to logic matter that belongs to psychology as well, and to psychology what only logic can deal with; indeed on its own premises such a division would be arbitrary. (i) If psychology were confined to the self or the subjective, and this were taken as the unobjectified or the marginal, think for a moment what would be denied it. In the first place, it would have to be silent as to the whole range of explicit awareness. What we commonly mean by sense perception, imagination,

---

[1] *Appearance*, 89.

and memory, every type of explicit idea and judgement and reasoning would fall outside its field. Similarly of explicit volition. Most wishes, hopes, desires, resolutions, choices, will be matter on which psychology has nothing to say. But it is just these things that in the past have provided the psychologists with a province, and to drive them from it would be to drive them from house and home. It is true that these processes are revelations of objects, and that these objects provide the matter of all the objective sciences; but such processes are also mental facts or events; if not, there is nothing mental. And if psychology is to study the mental, its access to them should clearly not be denied.

(ii) Neither is *logic* to be expropriated from the sphere of the *im*plicit. An idea may fall outside the interest of the moment and not be used in explicit judgement while still being affirmed implicitly. Mr. Bradley himself has said so. 'An ideal content can qualify and be attached to a subject apart from any predication in the proper sense or any explicit judgement.'[1] Now a judgement made implicitly is as capable of truth or falsehood as any other. If so, it is in the sphere of logic, whether relevant to those judgements that stand in the focus or not.

(iii) There is another implication in the theory which shows how impracticable it would be to confine psychology to the margin. We are told that the contents of self and not-self are for the most part interchangeable. What holds the focus at one moment may recede at the next to the periphery, and so become part of the content that belongs properly to the self; and similarly what is now apprehended implicitly may later be objectified, and thus shifted into the not-self. Now in view of this free trade in the commodities of the two regions, why should psychology be condemned to study them in the implicit region alone? The only reason would seem to be that what is grasped implicitly is altered in its nature when made an explicit object. But Bradley has elsewhere argued that in general 'attention' does not alter its object,[2] and hence that we may know explicitly the same things that we feel immediately. So

[1] *Essays on Truth and Reality*, 33.　　　　[2] *Ibid.*, 124.

far as this is true, it would be clearly arbitrary to confine psychology to the implicit.

6. (3) But neither of these two theories is Bradley's main proposal as to where we should draw the line. That proposal is implied in many passages, both old and new, in the *Logic*,[1] and appears again in *Essays on Truth and Reality*,[2] but it is set out most fully and clearly in a paper of 1900, called 'A Defence of Phenomenalism in Psychology'.[3] The proposal is here made that in partitioning logic from psychology, no line should be drawn at all through the contents of the mind. Psychology does not deal with part of those contents, set aside as 'psychical fact' or as 'subjective'; it deals with everything— image and meaning, self and its objects, sensations and emotions —that enters into experience. If he is asked, then, how the account of thought given in psychology differs from that given in logic, Bradley answers that it differs in point of view. For psychology the point of view is that of 'phenomenalism', and this means 'the confinement of one's attention to events with their laws of coexistence and sequence'.[4] How does this point of view differ from that of logic and metaphysics?

Whenever we think, says Bradley, we are, on the one side, laying hold of a world which is beyond our mere state of mind. To suppose that as I run through the multiplication table or gaze at a pyramid I am *making* the truth or reality of what is before me is absurd. 'Whatever else you can assert about truth, you must still be able to add that it was, and is, waiting there to be found, and that it is made by no man.'[5] 'The laws of the planets and stars, we believe, in part revealed themselves truly to Newton, but the revelation, if so, was something more than a mere personal event. . . There is for us no truth, we may say, save that which discovers itself to us.'[6] 'Every truth

---

[1] E.g. I. 38, 215; II. 449, 545–6, 549–50, 611–13.   [2] 326–7, 415.
[3] *Mind*, N.S. IX (1900), 26–45; reprinted in his *Collected Essays*, Vol. II.   [4] *Collected Essays*, II. 364.
[5] *E. T. R.*, 342.   [6] *Ibid.*, 85.

is eternal, even, for instance, such a truth as "I now have a headache". Truth qualifies that which is beyond mere succession, and it takes whatever it contains beyond the flux of mere events.'[1] No realist emphasizes more strongly than Bradley that meaning, in the sense of *what* I mean, is more than my private state and, with certain reservations as to form, is a solid permanent stone in the structure of reality. That is one side of the matter, the side that is of importance in logic and metaphysics. But there is another and complementary side, and this is the side of psychology. Granting that the logical idea is part of the real world, 'still every idea, I must assume, has an aspect of psychical event, and so is qualified as a particular existence'.[2] 'A truth, we may say, is no truth at all unless it happens in a soul and is thus an event which appears in time. As it there exists, and as by existing there it influences the future history of that soul, it is a matter for psychology. . . .'[3] 'If you confine your attention to the soul as a soul, then every possible experience is no more than that which happens in and to this soul. You have to do with psychical events which qualify the soul, and in the end these events, so far as you are true to your idea, are merely states of the soul.'[4]

7. This view is in some ways startlingly close to critical realism, so close that the reader may wonder why we should suppose it to have any advantage. Its central point is the same, namely that within an 'idea' one may distinguish a 'what' from a 'that', the content from the existence, and that this 'what' may be identified *both* with the content directly engaged and in some sense with the character of the independent reality. But it has at least two advantages. First, it has settled by a simple rule the controversy over mental states that tore critical realism in two. The majority party of that school held that the content asserted in judgement was a set of non-mental

[1] *Essays on Truth and Reality*, 340.
[2] *Logic*, I. 38 (new note 8).   [3] *Collected Essays*, II. 370.
[4] *E. T. R.*, 415.

universals; and then when they spoke of the mental state which served as the 'vehicle' for this content it was impossible to discover what they meant. On the other hand, we found Professor Sellars holding that the content *was* mental but resembled or reproduced the character of the object; and then this recurrent resemblance between independent series seemed miraculous. Bradley circumvents both difficulties. He gives character to mental states by granting them the 'what' of experience and saying that this 'what' is to be regarded as belonging to the stuff of my mind when taken in a particular context, namely the context of sensation, feeling and impulse which makes my field of consciousness distinctively mine. He avoids the difficulties about resemblance by denying that mind and the physical order are independent series between which correspondence must somehow be shown.

Secondly, he attaches to that 'identity of content' between idea and object which we have seen that realists of both varieties subscribe to, a widely different meaning. In reflecting on Professor Pratt's position, we saw that the content of judgement is in course of perpetual flux, of perpetual revision and expansion, and that there is no good reason anywhere to fix upon a special content as identical, just as it stands, with some fragment of ultimate reality. Bradley saw this clearly from the beginning. He saw that while in judgement we are always asserting of reality, this is not a reality of which our present ideas are the essence or the replica, but a reality that goes far beyond them. The real object that thought means is never exhausted by the fragmentary content which is all that appears to us; our reach exceeds our grasp. We do affirm of reality the content presented to us, but if we examine the meaning of reality implicit in all thought, we shall see that in that real world the fragments that are now presented to us cannot *as such* have any place. They belong indeed to reality, but not as a mirror of it, nor identical with it, but as a content which exhibits its character only in *degree*. They belong to reality, not as they stand, but only when so transformed that they can take their place coherently in an intelligible whole.

We do not suggest that this theory of Bradley's is in all respects satisfactory. But of the theories so far reviewed it seems to us the most keenly considered and responsibly advocated. But there are two problems immediately presented by it. What, more exactly, is the relation between the content of my idea and the reality to which it points? The language just employed is so redolent of a particular kind of metaphysics as to excite at once the gravest suspicions as to whether it has any clear meaning. Secondly, if it is soberly proposed to include within the idea as studied by psychology the content or 'what' that is presented, what sort of science will psychology be? How are the laws and relations of these contents, as studied by the psychologist, to be distinguished from their laws and relations as studied, for example, by the logician? The first question is the fundamental question of this section of our work; it will be resumed in the next chapter and will largely occupy us through the remainder of Book II. But as we go forward into dangerous territory, it may be well to guard our rear against sniping from the psychologists. The view we shall take of the nature of ideas is frankly metaphysical, and holds that psychology as commonly pursued is unable to deal with the problem. This view cannot fail to arouse psychological hostility. It will therefore be well to seize the opportunity afforded by Bradley's discussion of the matter, and through a few brief comments and criticisms to make our view explicit regarding the limitations of psychology in the study of thinking. We shall devote to this the remainder of the chapter.

8. Bradley tried to provide for psychology a point of view from which it could, like the other sciences, conduct its inquiries in peace, without suffering continual raids from the metaphysicians. If it is to be free from such raids, he thinks, it must perform an act of abjuration at the beginning. It is not the business of the psychologist any more than of other scientists, to set up as a hierophant of ultimate mysteries. We do not require of the psychologist or botanist that he should supply us views about the ultimate nature of life, or of the sociologist that he should write treatises on the metaphysics of freedom; such things are beyond his province; and 'when Phenomenalism loses its head, and, becoming blatant, steps forward as a theory of first principles, then it is really not respectable'.[1] What we do ask of any such science is 'to observe facts and to classify them, and then to seek to explain them— to explain, that is, not their ultimate nature, but their origin and the course which they take. It has to find so far as possible, the reason why they happen as they happen, and not the truth as to what they are'.[2] That also is what we should ask of the psychologist. What we should expect from his study of thinking is a causal explanation of why we think as we do. Is such an explanation possible without venturing beyond phenomena into logical and other necessities? Bradley implies that it is. I think we shall find good reasons why it is not.

Granting that explanation is to be in terms of causality, what does causality mean? Let us accept the definition actually used in the sciences generally. What they mean by the cause of a phenomenon is its sole unvarying antecedent. Any more intimate connection they do not ask. They do not ask, for example, that the connection be a self-evident one, enabling us to see not only that a certain effect does follow, but that in reason it *has* to follow. If it is found that, after an injection at a certain point of a certain amount of cocaine, a certain nerve is deadened, and the scientific worker can be sure that nothing else than cocaine has been added, he says without hesitation that the cocaine is the cause of the deadening.[3] To refuse to accept this as the cause until it can be demonstrated that the contact of cocaine with nervous tissues involves, by a self-evident logical process, just this result and no other, he would regard as absurd. 'Whether this result *must* follow the injection, so that you can deduce the one by logic from the other', he would say, 'I neither know nor care. If I can be assured that

---

[1] *Appearance and Reality*, 126.   [2] *Collected Essays*, II. 373.
[3] The difficulties in the method of difference do not affect the present point.

just this, and only this, invariably precedes the other, I know I have found a law, and for me that is enough.'

9. Can explanation of this kind account for the steps in a course of reasoning? Let us take, as a simple example, Thackeray's story of the Abbé and the nobleman. 'The Abbé, talking among friends, has just said, "Do you know, ladies, my first penitent was a murderer"; and a nobleman of the neighbourhood, entering the room at the moment, exclaims: "You there, Abbé? Why, ladies, I was the Abbé's first penitent, and I promise you, my confession astounded him." '[1] No doubt a course of reasoning completed itself with a gasp in the ladies present, and our question is, why did it complete itself in this particular way? If we give the type of answer just outlined, we shall say: One mental state causes another. We start with the mental state involved in thinking, 'his first penitent was a murderer'. This presumably leaves traces which, when combined with the mental state expressed by 'I was the first penitent', give rise to a third mental state, expressed by 'you are a murderer'. The case is parallel to other cases in natural science, the case of the cocaine, for instance, in which we have first a nerve, then an addition of cocaine, then a modified state of the nerve which is the result. And if the same conditions are repeated, we can be sure, in the one case as in the other, that the same result will recur. The laws that govern each are descriptive merely, presenting statements of antecedence and consequence. They are generalized descriptions of the behaviour of *genus homo*.

What shall we say of such explanation? Bradley writes at times as if it were as adequate to a course of thought as to a series of billiard-ball collisions. We must insist that this is not merely untrue, but the kind of blunder that cuts one off at the outset from any later understanding of the reflective process. The ladies' final state of mind was more than a result; it was a

---

[1] Bosanquet's version, *Implication and Linear Inference*, 26.

conclusion. In the scientific statement of antecedent and consequent, no matter how exactly put, the essential connection and the moving impulse are simply ignored. We shall try to get clear on this fundamental point by putting it variously.

(1) The true reason why the conclusion came into mind was an urgency to complete itself on the part of the thought preceding. However hard to describe, this inherent expansiveness of thought is something that is clearly present and that everyone knows. Given the premises, 'the first penitent was a murderer' and 'that first penitent was N', nothing more need be spoken; the circle of thought completes itself on the instant. And the point to be noted here is that this movement is governed by seen necessity. There is nothing remotely analogous to the addition of one bead to another on a string, or even to the propagation of movement along a row of billiard-balls. The conclusion is not merely a consequent in the scientific and temporal sense; it is equally a conclusion in the logical sense; and we know perfectly well that is why it appeared. It is useless to pretend that this is a case of mere antecedence and consequence. We have the best sort of evidence that it is not. We can watch our thought burgeoning; we can see that it develops as it does because it must, because it is being laid under compulsion by a necessity immanent in the matter before it. It is as truly the nature of thought to develop itself in accordance with such immanent laws, which are really *its* immanent laws, as of the seed to expand itself into the tree. And these laws are not mere rules of regular juxtaposition; they are the web of connections in which intelligibility consists; not laws of causal sequence but of logical or other necessity. No empirical or descriptive laws can explain what happens when we think. For thought is a teleological process in which a chief determining factor is, not a step in the series at all, but an end or value. The fragmentary matter before us, under constraint by an immanent ideal, is reforming and expanding itself in the direction of intelligibility. And because empirical science does not, and indeed cannot, recognize this

kind of constraint, its explanation of the process of thought cannot be complete.[1]

Thus, if 'science' has its ordinary meaning, a science of thought is impossible. Thought, looked at from the inside, is not a mechanical succession of ideas, but a cry for 'more light'. It is a restless seeking for a satisfaction of its own, and it is only when we stand inside it and see things through its own eyes that we begin to understand what business it is about. It is then apparent that the moving agent is as much the goal which thought is seeking as any event which came before to push it along, and that empirical explanation is bound to miss the point, as inevitably as popular attempts to capture the secret of genius by fixing one's eyes on the risings and goings to bed, the recreations and dietary, of some unfortunate hero. 'The vision and the faculty divine' is not in the habit of yielding its secrets to such probing. The reason is clear enough. Such explanation is purely external. It has not entered into the mind of its subject and caught the impulse and end that move him, and hence the springs of his life remain hidden from it. So it is with the study of thought. You cannot study it successfully taken as a series of states of mind, governed by laws of *de facto* succession. For thinking is not that sort of thing. It is self-development of ideal content under the control of an immanent end. And to see that end, you must look through the eyes of the thought itself.

10. (2) Does this mean that psychology, as descriptive science, has no business with the mind at all? Certainly not.

---

[1] I note that Professor Broad recognizes 'a type of causation to which there is nothing analogous either in matter or in the lower levels of mind. An essential factor in the cause is here the recognition by the mind at a certain moment of a timeless formal relation between two propositions. Thus a necessary condition of the occurrence of my belief in q is something which is neither an event nor a substance, nor a property of a substance, but a timeless relation between two propositions.'—*Indeterminacy and Indetermination, Arist. Soc. Proc.* Sup. Vol. X (1931), 154.

It does mean that psychology cannot explain a course of thinking; but the mind has other processes than thinking which call for investigation, and inadequacy in one region does not mean failure in all. For example, there seems to be such a fact as 'association of ideas',[1] and if so, it is a fact with which only psychology can deal. If there are two ideas connected by nothing but 'contiguity', and one regularly calls up the other; if, so far as we can see, there is nothing in the first thought which demands the others for its completion, then we have here a connection like that of cocaine and the nerve, where no necessity is discernible, but where there is behaviour according to law. Here, therefore, is matter for science, and for what science if not psychology? And this example is instructive, for it brings out clearly the difference between thinking proper, a process beyond the reach of science, and the association that is so often confused with it. Psychology, as a science of causal sequence, is bound to treat these processes alike. Associate X calls up associate Y which happens to have been contiguous with it in the past; just as thought A (of a triangle) calls up thought B (that its angles equal two right angles). But if the latter is thinking at all, the two processes are worlds apart. The movement in the first case has nothing logical about it; the movement in the second case is misconstrued *unless* it is seen as logical. For it is a movement by which the thought of a triangle, under the constraint of a logical system, works out into something it implies, and unless it is seen that this *is* an implication, the reason why thought took the line it did will be missed completely. To call this 'association', by contiguity or anything else, is to refuse to use one's eyes. It is that development of a conception according to the laws of its own nature, that struggle of an idea to achieve completeness as a system, which is the very essence of the activity of thinking, and marks it off from everything else. If we must have analogies, let us at least avoid the beads on a string and the billiard-balls in a row. When an amoeba puts forth a pseudopodium, its

---

[1] For evidence that a process of thought is more than a process of association see Chap. XXII below.

own substance is flowing out into its extension. When the sea throws arms up inlets, it is the same sea still in every remotest finger. And when, in a course of thinking, we pursue an idea into what it involves, what is really happening is not that we are tacking on a new idea which chance has conjoined with the first, but that the idea is expanding before us into a body organic with itself.

Nor is our conclusion different if, instead of starting with a premise and asking why it expanded, we start with the conclusion and ask why it appeared. Einstein concluded that, in passing the sun, a ray of light must be deflected from a straight course. This conclusion was preceded by a series of calculations, and on these calculations, it may be said, the conclusion causally depended. And so it did. If the calculation had not preceded, the conclusion would not have come. But then neither would the conclusion have come without something else, which psychological explanation cannot take into its reckoning. Plant the data given to Einstein in the mind of the ordinary man and, as that man will be the first to agree, you will not get the same result. They will lie there as lifeless and unprolific as a mass of dough. Why? In the last resort is there any reason but that he lacks Einstein's intelligence? The dough is there without the yeast. And intelligence is not, as the metaphor may suggest, one element in the efficient cause. It is no preceding mental state; it is no part of such state; it does not occur at one point only in time; it is chargeable with no special element in the result. It is the degree of advancement of an individual mind toward that rational order in experience which is the implicit end of thought as such. Hence it so permeates all one's ideas that, if we are to speak quite accurately, we cannot say that the data which Einstein dealt with ever entered the plain man's mind, or ever could. Now to neglect, in an account of thought, that which is so all-pervasive would seem preposterous, for without it the real explanation of thought's behaviour would be unattainable. But what else can psychology do? If intelligence is not part of the field of consciousness which can be isolated and studied by itself, if it is not an event which can be traced to causes or pursued into its effects, if it is not a relation of contiguity, causality, or succession, what purchase can be got upon it by any descriptive science? Of course it may be studied in its evolutionary development, and one may devise tests for its degree of advancement in individual minds. But the instant this is begun, the psychologist, wittingly or not, is a natural scientist no longer. To show this we shall put the point in one more form.

11. (3) The psychologist as a man of science is committed to the study of facts. As a man, standards or ideals, whether of truth or morals or beauty, of course concern him as much as anyone, but as a scientist, these are beyond him; his field is facts and their laws. And so far as he studies the understanding, his facts are those of actual thinking. Now if you set out to study the facts of actual thinking, you cannot arbitrarily choose some and reject others. The thinking of a genius, the thinking of an imbecile, the correct and mistaken thinking of the plain man, the thinking of the insane, are all equally facts. A complete psychology of thinking must take account of all of them. And there are apparently three ways in which it might endeavour to do this. It might attempt what Bacon recommended to the scientist, to report *all* the facts regarding his subject, and to interpret them only at the end. Again, it might study average thinking, omitting extreme variations. Finally, it might range the forms of thinking in accordance with their value, and confine itself to those which most repaid inquiry.

Unfortunately, to the psychologist, as psychologist, no one of these ways is open. To study all the facts would mean compiling unending cyclopaedias of promiscuous case-histories, describing the triumphs of geniuses, the maunderings of the unbalanced, and the gropings of half-wits. Even if this were practicable, which of course it is not, there would be little reason for calling it a psychology of *thinking*. The second proposal seems more promising. If one cannot study all the facts, perhaps by a sampling method one can elicit typical forms of thinking; and the task of the psychologist will be the description of these. But here he finds himself in a dilemma. If the range of facts to be studied is not restricted beforehand, the results will be worthless; the thinking exhibited in common by imbecile and genius would be about as interesting as the physiology possessed in common by man and amoeba. On the other hand, if the range is restricted, restriction must be made either arbitrarily or on principle. If arbitrarily, again there is no reason to call the science a science of thinking. If made on principle, this principle must be that thinking is more perfectly exemplified in some facts than in others. And this takes us to the third proposal. That proposal is that in different mental processes we can discern degrees of approximation to thinking that really is thinking, and that, so far as may be, the psychology of the process should confine itself to the pure type. But what is the test for the pure type? Once again, if this is arbitrary, the science may amount to anything or nothing. But if the test is not arbitrary, i.e. is not derived from external dictation, but is the one immanent in thought itself, then psychology is clearly no longer a descriptive science. It is not merely describing processes, it is evaluating them. It is saying that some processes are more truly thinking than others because in them the aim of thought is more fully realized, which means that they are cases of better or more perfect understanding. It pays more attention to the kind of thinking done by scientist or philosopher than to the kind done by imbecile or insane man because it believes that measured by this standard the former is more truly thinking than the latter. It appraises before it describes, in order that its description may not be wasted. Now such appraisal is necessary, we agree, if the study of thought is to be enlightening. But the point is that it is beyond the power of any science of fact. You cannot, as *facts*, rank genius above lunacy, because each is as much a fact as the other. Higher and lower, better and worse, value, worth, satisfactoriness—these are facts of no description whatever. If types of thinking, then, or forms of understanding, are to be distinguished as better or worse, the distinguishing must be done, not by any science which keeps exclusively to facts, but by one that can enter into the spirit of thought, and understand its end, and recognize in its flounderings struggles which, in this way and that, have fallen short of their aim.

We have laboured this antithesis between thinking as an ideal self-development dominated by its own peculiar aim, and thinking as a causal series of mental events, because it is the fact of this antithesis upon which everything turns. If such an antithesis can be drawn, then the programme for a psychology of thinking marked out by Bradley, which makes it a science of 'events with their laws of co-existence and sequence', becomes an impossible one. 'Why they happen as they happen' is what this science was to tell us. No science of fact can tell us that.

12. Readers who know their Bradley may say that all this was familiar to him, and that no one saw more clearly how inadequate were such doctrines as associationism to the real movement of thinking. This is true. His writings were a principal force in delivering the study of thought from the old mechanical empiricism. On the surface, therefore, he was inconsistent. But much that seems like inconsistency is in his case not really so, but rather a difference between levels of thought whose distinction he defended deliberately. Views that he justified in psychology he rejected in logic, and views that he accepted in logic were likely themselves to be rejected when they appeared at the bar of his metaphysics. His view of causal explanation is a case in point. (i) In his psychological essays he is willing to take causality quite simply as uniform sequence of phenomena, and to identify himself with the associationists. (ii) In the *Logic* he insists that cause and effect are not units conjoined by external juxtaposition, but elements linked by ideal and necessary connections. 'Causation is no mere phenomenal sequence. It implies a principle felt in the succession of the elements.' 'To say, This phenomenon B was the effect of A, implies the perception of an ideal connec-

tion between A and B. And this must be inference.'[1] (iii) In his metaphysics he maintains that even this relation must be abandoned, since under rigorous analysis it turns out unintelligible. Now these were not three inconsistent positions held unwittingly at the same time. They were conceptions whose differences, he thought, were justified by the working necessities of three different disciplines. Bradley, as himself a psychologist, knew that if the student of mental phenomena was to be allowed to lay down no formula till he could guarantee its metaphysical verity, he would lay down no formulas at all. Thus his limitation of psychology was part of his brief for its defence. Our criticism of his view is not that he was inconsistent, but that the programmes of the various levels cannot possibly be kept separate. The argument, in the one case that concerns us, has already been indicated. A psychology that kept to Bradley's programme would be so obviously inadequate to thinking that no psychologist who knew what he was about would commit himself to it. Either psychology must admit the operation of ends—logical, ethical, aesthetic—or it must drop thinking from its field.[2]

13. Suppose it soberly accepted this restriction and made no attempt to lay down the laws of thinking proper; does it follow that it would have to be silent about ideas? Not at all; it would still have to be relied on for much useful knowledge about them. If psychology cannot swallow up logic, neither can logic and the value sciences swallow up psychology. An idea, whether true or false, continues to have an aspect in which it is an occurrence in someone's mind, and there is a point of view from which even a pyramid is rightly regarded as a mental state. What is before me when I think of the pyramid may be said to belong at once to two universes of discourse. From one point of view it is continuous, in a sense to be later

[1] *Logic*, II. 538, 539–40.
[2] It is gratifying to find this admitted by the Gestalt psychologists: see Köhler's *The Place of Value in a World of Facts*.

defined, with a spatial world that owes nothing to my observing; from another it is continuous with that admiration or boredom, those pleasures and pains and irrelevant associations which, along with it, make up my state of mind. It is true that when you and I look at the pyramid, we habitually abstract from the background of personal feeling, and if we could not, it is hard to see how we could arrive at a common world. But to abstract so successfully as to be only 'pyramidally extant', as Sir Thomas Browne might say, to slough off this background wholly and subsist exclusively in the neutral and public, would be literally to gain the world at the cost of our own souls. In any case it is impossible. All objects come to us bathed in personal feeling and they are probably barnacled too with irrelevant ideas. Perhaps an ultimate metaphysic could show that in the chaos which forms my state of mind at the moment, just these elements had in reason to occur, and could only have occurred in this pattern. But this at least is certain, that if such a feat is ever accomplished, it will not be done without a knowledge of the facts. And the task of describing and mapping this jungle of the mind can be carried out by no science but psychology.

Let us conclude by saying more exactly what this means. If psychology elects to remain a descriptive science, what sort of light may we expect to derive from it on the process of thought?

14. (1) It can study pseudo-thinking. Strictly, a process of mind is thinking only so far as it realizes the end of thinking, which is always to understand, that is, to see things within a system which renders them necessary.[1] But most of what passes for thinking is far from this. To suppose that the thinking of the politician or the business man, even at its best, is a smooth triumphal march from ground to consequent, punctuated by no blanks and relieved by no truancies, has something comic about it. It would be described more

[1] For explanation, see below, Chaps. XVIII, XXIII, XXXII.

accurately as a painful muddling through a wilderness of irrelevancy to a goal dimly discerned and commonly missed. If all we knew about thinking came from logic, we should have sadly little insight into the way people actually 'think'. It may be retorted, what is the use of such insight if their minds work so irrationally? and the question has some point. Students of psychology, as of other sciences, would be saved from much futility if they realized more vividly that not all facts are on a level, indeed that there are many facts not worth knowing. It may be more profitable to study a mistake of Spinoza's than the highest intellectual flight of some Australian bushman. Still, it is the other side of the picture that now concerns us. No study of what thinking ought to be can be carried on in complete oblivion of what it is; for the logician depends as truly on actual thinking for discovering the forms of thought as the student of aesthetics does on the experience of beautiful things for suggesting the forms of beauty. The search is, in both cases, for what will satisfy a special impulse of the mind, and in practice it must proceed by comparing what satisfies more with what satisfies less. This requires an ample supply of cases. The relation of the psychologist to the logician is like the relation of the anthropologist or the sociologist to the student of ethics; he amasses information that is of interest to him in its own right, and to the student of values as fresh material on which to exercise his analysis.

15. (2) Any study of the *pathology* of thinking must lean heavily on psychology. Everyone knows that impulse, passion, and desire may work havoc with the attempt to think; and many subtle ways in which the distortion may be accomplished have been brought to light of late years by the psycho-analysts. Of course a purely descriptive psychology could not carry out in its own right a study of the pathology of thinking; you cannot study abnormality without using a standard of what is normal; and what is normal in thinking is not to be decided by counting heads. Still the services which psychology can render to such a pathology may be invaluable. There are few studies with a larger promise both of illumination and disillusionment than the study of how men's beliefs on every subject are affected by unrecognized impulses, feelings, and desires.

It is perhaps worth remarking that if the pathology of thinking does not belong to an empirical psychology, it does not strictly belong to logic either, but to a psychology informed by logic. Fallacies have always made an awkward subject for the logician. As cases of attempted thinking they interest him; as cases of failure to think logically, and, so far, to think at all, they seem to have no place in his science. Most first-rate modern logicians, Hegel, Sigwart, Wundt, Bradley, Bosanquet, Cook Wilson, Johnson, Whitehead and Russell, give them no space. Lotze grants them a brief discussion under the heading of 'applied logic'. Joseph relegates them to an appendix. Mill alone concedes them unstinted space in the body of his work. And Mill is the one great logician of the school which, following Hume, tried to rest logic upon psychology. He could hardly confine logic to the necessary, since for him there was no such thing. He could include reasoning that fell short of necessity, because for him all reasoning did. He was, I suppose, the only first-flight logician of modern times who would deny what we have been insisting on, namely that empirical science cannot give an adequate account of reasoning.

(3) We have just seen that feeling and desire may influence thought. The converse also holds; thought may transform feeling and desire. The psycho-analysts have too often forgotten this, assuming that thought is wholly at the mercy of impulse. There seems to be no good reason to believe this, however popular it may be with the kind of person who confuses sophistication with cynicism. And if there is not, if belief may profoundly affect the character of impulse, feeling, and will, then we have a further set of influences whose exploration must be assigned to psychology.

16. (4) To psychology will belong likewise the devices auxiliary to thinking, such as images and sub-vocal speech. These are no part of thought proper, but they are so closely connected with it as to be often mistaken for it; indeed their loss or injury may affect the power of thinking most seriously. The various ways in which they are used in thinking are the direct concern of the psychologist and of no one else.

17. (5) Psychology can describe the conditions of emergence of the various types of knowing in racial and individual life. Thus perception probably depends on earlier sensations; the formation of a general idea on the experience of objects that are much alike yet slightly different; the grasp of geometrical principle on the power to hold one's attention on the spatial aspect of things. The presence of these conditions does not explain what happens when we think, but thinking could not have happened without them.

18. (6) Finally psychology can perform a similar service for some particular act of thought. Insight does not come in unconditioned lightning flashes. It is usually achieved slowly and with effort through a series of steps that admit of description. There must be an initial impulse to understand; there must be some obstacle to this impulse; there must be the search for a hypothesis to meet the difficulty; a set of conditions that make the rise of a hypothesis possible; and so on. In his little book *How We Think*, Professor Dewey has furnished an admirable example of such a descriptive account of thinking. In our own Book III there is also much of this descriptive matter, and the term 'psychology of thinking' could not unjustly be applied to it. But it must be remembered that this psychology is one that has frankly abandoned the attempt to keep to 'facts' and insists that one will not make head or tail of thinking except as the working in and through the mind of an ideal of intelligibility. Such an account only, we hold, is realistic enough to explain what actually happens. But at every step in a course of thinking there are conditions, not part of the movement themselves, that immensely aid or retard it; and of these even a strictly empirical psychology can offer an account.

Now we are ready to pick up again the main thread of the argument. The question to which we have been seeking an answer is this: suppose we accept Bradley's contention that the idea, as considered by psychology, must include the 'what' or content; is any line then possible between psychology and logic? Bradley answered that there was, and he proceeded to what he described as 'a defence of phenomenalism in psychology'. But we have seen that thinking is not a process to which this or any empirical psychology is adequate. The processes falling short of thinking, the relations between thinking and other sides of our nature, the conditions and aids of thinking—on all these things such psychology can throw light. And that is much. Unfortunately, for our purpose it is not enough.

CHAPTER XIV

A THEORY OF THE IDEA

1. Our conclusions about the nature of ideas have thus far been chiefly negative. We have reviewed what appear to be the principal theories, and found none of them wholly satisfactory. But there is probably no such thing as a purely negative conclusion; when one denies that a thing is *x*, one always does so on the ground, explicit or not, that the thing has some positive character that excludes *x*. This is true of all the denials we have been making. Each successive rejection has been based on positive grounds, which have gradually been supplying a basis on which to construct a theory of our own. Furthermore, the rejection has in no case been complete. From every one of these doctrines there is something of importance that may be accepted and used.

There is an overwhelming amount of evidence that ideas are more than images, whether like their objects or different, and yet the image theory is more than a mere mistake. Galton's scientists could think of their breakfast table without any aid from imagery; to *define* idea as image is therefore impossible; but this does not show that where images *are* used they contribute nothing to thought. Indeed, the contrary is obvious. If a painter who uses visual imagery freely is suddenly deprived of it, he may discover in time some more or less tolerable substitute, but his thought is in the meantime ruined. Even if thought is not the same as imagery, it is deeply in debt to it; and both facts must be remembered by any theory pretending to adequacy.

So also of words. To say that we think in words, if words are taken to *be* thoughts or sufficient substitutes for them, is a mistake. Yet everyone knows that words, like images, aid greatly in the business of thinking, that there is an instant sense of the thought's being clarified when the words to express it have been found. This, too, must be remembered.

It is to be remembered again that the gap which the critical realists attempted to cross by the bridge of essence is a very real one, and supplies at once the most striking fact and the principal problem of knowledge. To say that my thought and its objects, myself and the world, are simply one and the same would not so much solve the problem of knowledge as deny that there was such a problem. As to the mode of bridging the gap, we could not satisfy ourselves that the critical realists had discovered the best means. But we can only agree with them in their insistence that the gap is there to be bridged. Thought cannot swallow its object.

The neo-realists we found less cautious. They would cut the knot rather than untie it, and would prefer to abolish ideas outright. But ideas have a stubborn reality of their own which, if it is not enough to swallow up objects, is at least enough to prevent objects from swallowing them. Neo-realism does scant justice to this reality. Nevertheless, its main principle can hardly be denied. If what is revealed to us in thought and perception is anything short of the object itself, how can we be said to know *it*? Critical realism insists that there is a gap to cross; neo-realism insists that we do cross it; both, so far, we must believe to be right.

Once more, behaviourism and the causal theory were clearly wrong in making the idea the physical effect of a physical stimulus. But the thesis they urge in common, that the shifts and changes of mental life have conditions in the body, is a fact of importance in epistemology as well as in common life. That a little strychnine or nitrous oxide or santonine should change the face of my experienced world is in itself enough to overthrow some theories of knowledge.

Finally, the suggestion of the pragmatists, that thought is an instrument of action, with no special purpose of its own, distorted the ends and the nature of thought. Everywhere and always, we should hold, thought does have an end of its own. Nevertheless the pragmatists are clearly right that thought is an end-seeking activity, whose goal, if we could but find it, would throw a flood of light on the processes of seeking it.

2. The idea is thus an *x* which must satisfy many conditions, positive and negative. What sort of thing must that be which refers to an object, yet is not the object; which calls words and images in aid, yet is itself neither word nor copy; which changes with bodily changes, but is more than any bodily change; which is always a means to an end, though not always to an end that is practical? That is the riddle we have to solve.

Now so far as I can discover, there is one way only of relating idea to object which offers any hope of meeting satisfactorily these various requirements at once. This is the relation of the potential to the actual, or (what is apparently a species of the same) of unrealized to realized purpose. The theory that will here be advocated, then, is in briefest compass this: Thought in its essence is an attempt to attain, in the sense of achieving identity with, a special end of its own. The relation between idea and object must be conceived teleologically, as the relation of that which is partially realized to the same thing more fully realized. When we say that an idea is *of* an object, we are saying that the idea is a purpose which the object alone would fulfil, that it is a potentiality which this object alone would actualize, a content informed by an impulse to become this object. Its nature is hence not fully intelligible except in the light of what it seeks to become. Mind, in taking thought, attempts to pass beyond its present experience to what it would be but is not yet, and so far as it has the thought of this end, it already *is* the end *in posse*. The idea is thus both identical with its object and different from it. It is identical in the sense in which anything that truly develops is identical with what it becomes. It is different in the sense in which any purpose partially realized is different from the same purpose realized wholly.

This theory will of course be far from commanding instant assent, and ought not to have this before its possibilities in dialectic and application are carefully explored. The natural apology for it would seem to be twofold. It would consist in part of a review of the difficulties which stand in the way of the more credible alternative theories; this part of the case we have completed already as best we could. The other part would consist in showing that it accords with what we know about the nature of mind and of knowledge, and with the empirical facts of thinking. A theory on a fundamental point can be appraised and properly understood only as its applications and implications are exhibited in detail. What follows is therefore as much explanation as defence. We shall try to show three things: first, that the theory just suggested stands in peculiarly close accord with what we know of the nature of mind; second, that it accords with the nature of knowing; third, that it accords with the empirical facts of thinking. The first two of these will occupy us in the present chapter, the third in the three chapters that follow. If we can establish such joint consonance with principles and with facts, we shall have as plausible a case for the theory as could reasonably be asked.

3. One's view of thinking and knowing is closely connected with one's view of the agent that does the knowing; so closely indeed that when an inquirer has adopted a theory on the latter head, he may find his views on the former all but determined for him. If he conceives the agent as the body, governed by those mechanical laws which hold sway, at the lowest reckoning, over the larger part of nature, then his theory of thought will hardly escape some form of behaviourism. Again, if he conceives of the mind as a congeries of images and sensations, after the manner of Mr. Russell, he will consider thought to consist of sensory content. Conversely, as one's theory of the mind goes far to determine one's theory of thought, so any theory of thought will entail much about the nature of the mind. When the relations between the two are so close, the truth about the nature of the mind is of great importance to us; for if our theory of ideas conflicts with this, the theory of course must go; while if it agrees, it has at least an important presumption in its favour. Is there any view of the nature of the mind so obviously required by the facts as to serve as a preliminary touchstone for the theory of ideas?

Theories about the nature of mind are too numerous even to be listed here. Nevertheless in their bearing on our present interest they break into two large camps, and as to these we must know where we stand, since if one of them rather than the other were elected, our theory would be ruled out at once. There are those, on the one hand, who think that mind is to be explained by resolving it into simpler elements, ascertaining the laws of these elements, and then compounding these laws to explain the behaviour of the whole. There are others who think it can be explained only through the end it is seeking to realize, and that the stages of its growth, either racial or individual, are to be understood as steps in a self-guided ascent. The one group holds, to speak in metaphor, that mind develops by being pushed from behind, the other, by being drawn from ahead. Both appeal in support of their views to the facts of evolution, but one group interprets evolution in mechanistic terms, the other in teleological. If the first group is right, our theory of ideas may as well be dismissed unread. If the second group is right, it may still be false, but since it will then be in close accord with what we know of the nature of mind, it will have acquired some antecedent probability.

4. The issue between these schools is clear cut. They agree that mind as we know it has in some sense evolved; they differ as to whether this evolution is to be explained by levelling up or levelling down. At the "top" of the scale, in the human mind, we have events that would seem very clearly to require purpose for their explanation; at the "bottom", in non-living matter, we have a causality that to all appearances is of an extremely different kind, excluding purpose altogether. Can one of these types of causality be reduced to the other? According to the mechanist we can level down. Mind, he says, has obviously evolved from matter; if we are to understand it, we must follow its generation in accordance with the laws of matter; and while in this process of generation there is much that remains obscure, such obscurity cannot hide the fact that matter *has* produced mind, nor even in general its way of doing this. For there is one kind of explanation which has succeeded over such an enormous range of facts that we can only suppose it again applicable here. It is a kind to which others are always reduced as soon as possible, and which nothing, so far, has conclusively resisted; indeed, to show in detail that anything is amenable to it has come to serve as the ideal of scientific explanation. Thus when we say that the mind is a proper subject for science at all, we are saying in effect that mechanistic explanation applies to it. Under what conditions will such explanation fully apply? Only when the following things are true: (*a*) all the different kinds of stuff of which the *explicandum* seems to consist are at bottom the same; e.g. organic and inorganic matter, hydrogen and oxygen, do not differ in the stuff or substance of their ultimate components; (*b*) this stuff is composed of indivisible particles (or at least of particles not divisible into others that behave differently); (*c*) all changes that particles undergo are reducible to one type, e.g. change of position; (*d*) every particle is governed in its interactions with every other by the same law; and (*e*) the laws of group behaviour are such as might be calculated from the laws of individual behaviour.[1] If we drive a billiard-ball into a group of others, it will scatter them in various directions. The directions, velocities, and distances attained by the balls might well baffle the calculations of every living physicist. But no one doubts, says the mechanist, that the behaviour of each ball is governed by law, that the law is the same for all, and that we need only an extension of the powers we actually have to make the dispersion calculable in every detail. Now the behaviour of human beings consists of events that are admittedly far more complex. But we have just seen that degree of complexity gives rise to no difference in principle; and if we know that this behaviour has arisen by continuous stages from that of inanimate matter, the conclusion is as good as demonstrated. Mind is essentially mechanical in its genesis, growth, and working.

This is the form in which the mechanistic ideal has been

---

[1] Cf. Broad, *The Mind and its Place in Nature*, 45.

traditionally conceived. The development of the new physics has shaken the confidence formerly felt in its applicability. Physicists talk little and reluctantly of stuff or substance; they prefer to think of their protons, neutrons, and electrons, as simply x's whose nature is sufficiently known through the laws of their behaviour. They are even uncertain whether the relations with each other of these minute components of matter are governed by causal law, and are coming to conceive of law itself as merely the statement of the probable behaviour of enormous aggregates of particles. These biologists who still call themselves mechanists often add a specific disclaimer of the older 'billiard-ball mechanism'. And certainly their modifications would require careful study in any review of the types of mechanism. But for our present purpose it will suffice to note: (1) that the mechanistic *ideal* of intelligibility remains as we have sketched it, the modifications being concessions made reluctantly and under compulsion to the seemingly irrational nature of things; and (2) that the difference between the various types of mechanism are insignificant when compared with the differences that divide all alike from any genuine teleology.

The mechanism that has abandoned atoms as little hard pellets and conceived laws as statistical formulae is a far more sophisticated affair than the older and simpler mechanism, but it seems to be as remote as its predecessor from purposive causation. In considering the issue, then, between the mechanical and teleological views of mind, it will perhaps entail no grave injustice, and it will certainly make for brevity, if, while noting that very various types of mechanism are currently held, we deal with them comprehensively under their simpler and ideal form. By mechanism, then, we shall mean the theory that would accept the ideal sketched above as applicable to nature and man. The considerations offered about it will hold, we believe, of the modified mechanism as well.

5. The teleological view of mind is at the opposite pole from mechanism. It holds that whatever may be true of inorganic matter or even of the matter of living bodies, mechanism breaks down utterly when it comes to the characteristic behaviour of mind. Take, for example, any instance of intelligent action. Suppose I wish to attend a concert, and go to the telephone to reserve a seat. I cross the room and pick up the receiver. Why? The mechanist would say that it was because my body, particularly my brain, was constituted thus and so, and had certain stimuli acting upon it; and that with a full knowledge of body and stimuli my behaviour could be predicted and explained. It will not do for the teleologist to reply merely that we do not actually have such knowledge. This any sensible mechanist admits. He adds, however, that one can no more show in this way that such behaviour escapes mechanical law than one can demonstrate a particular planet to escape the law of gravitation by showing that its orbit is not yet wholly accounted for. To refute the mechanistic theory, the teleologist must show not only that it fails in knowledge but that it is bound always to fail, that there is something in the nature of mind which stands permanently, because in principle, beyond the reach of such theory, no matter how far extended by future knowledge.

This the teleologist does seek to show. He holds that any extension of mechanism short of abandonment of it in principle would still miss the essential reason why I went to the telephone. That reason is that I *wanted* to attend the concert. And he insists that we shall never bring that want into the scope of a mechanical scheme by merely increasing the power of our microscopes, for it is not, like matter in motion, the sort of thing that an observer could observe, even if he were infinitely sharp-eyed. Our action has an inner aspect as real as the outer, and from the inner point of view, the action is essentially the pursuit of an end, a means to this end. Though my interest in the end and my decision to pursue it seem to have no possible place among moving particles, the teleologist is just as certain that they contribute to my behaviour as any mechanist could be that the motion of a colliding billiard ball has something to do with the motion of a second. And he would go on to say that whenever you find intelligence at work, you must explain in the same way.

6. Is it possible to find a middle ground between these violently opposing theories? Many believe it is, and have adopted as their middle position what is called 'emergent evolution'. This, too, has various forms, but in the most popular of these it differs from the older mechanism by giving up even the presumption that nature is predictable. It points out that one might have an exhaustive knowledge of the components of a compound taken separately and yet be helpless to predict how they would behave when put together. To use the stock example, one might learn all that it was theoretically possible to learn about hydrogen and oxygen, and their behaviour towards all substances except each other, and yet be unable to predict that when put together they would behave like water. A particle which obeys one set of laws when acting alone may obey a different set when it becomes a member of an aggregate. And according to many emergent evolutionists, this principle is enough in itself to bridge the interval between behaviour at the bottom of the scale and behaviour at the top. For just as a particle may behave otherwise when a member of an aggregate than when alone, so an aggregate may behave otherwise when a member of a larger aggregate than when a member of a smaller one. A particle may escape the laws of pure physics by entering into a chemical compound; this compound may escape purely chemical law when it enters into an organism; the organism may escape biological law when the cells combine to produce sentience, and so on up to the most complex forms of human or superhuman behaviour. And thus the chasm is spanned. The difference between the mechanical and the purposive is not a sheer antithesis but a difference in the structure and complexity of the wholes concerned.

But it is hard to see in this view any real compromise or conciliation. Mechanism is fully represented in it while true purposiveness is left out. One need not question the facts; it may quite well be true that at certain points in the scale there are eruptions of something quite unpredictable in terms of the older and simpler laws. What is questionable is the claim that we really have here a bridge between mechanism and teleology. What we rather have is a less simple kind of mechanism which is as remote as its predecessor from truly purposive behaviour. Old-fashioned mechanism said that you could deduce the behaviour of aggregates from the nature and laws of their components. Emergent evolutionism says that you cannot so deduce it because such behaviour is not the function of the individual elements either separately or in sum, but of a new pattern or structure that supervenes when these come together. For the teleologist, what is there to choose between these doctrines? He is persuaded that a certain behaviour is adopted because it is a means to an end. He is told that it occurs because the pattern of the organism has now become so complex as to make such reactions necessary. Is this purposiveness? He cannot see that it is. The mechanistic family resemblance is too strong. Hydrogen acts in a certain way because it possesses a certain nature; water acts in another way because it possesses a more complex nature; but in both the type of causality is the same. And while purposive causality does seem confined to patterns of some complexity, it is idle to say that this complexity explains it or makes it intelligible. Emergent evolutionism therefore does not reconcile the extremes. The chasm remains in principle unbridged.

Conciliation failing, the question recurs whether either type can extrude the other. Can we level down or level up? Can the domain of mechanism be extended to include the domain of mind and expel teleology from the province it claims; or can teleology be extended to cover events in nature generally and leave mechanism without a kingdom? The latter question need not be pressed, but the first demands an answer. I shall hold that the answer is No; that however successful in the outlying provinces mechanistic explanation may be, mind itself is irreducibly purposive and will elude the grasp of mechanism always. By way of evidence I shall mention three processes of mind whose nature, if closely observed, will place them, I think, beyond the reach of such explanation. These are the processes of (1) growth, (2) choice, and (3) inference.

7. (1) There is nothing in the movements of particles, or aggregates of particles, that corresponds to what we mean by development in a mind. Analogy begins only when, in the lower forms of life, such as the seed that becomes a plant, the adequacy of mechanism has already ceased to be obvious. For the mechanist, the growth or evolution of anything can only mean an addition to its particles, or a rearrangement of them, or both. The process is typified in the enlargement of a snowball as it rolls downhill or the formation of new patterns when the pieces in a kaleidoscope are redisposed. But such change is not growth or development. For *what* grows in such cases? The particles? They remain precisely the same as before; they are, at most, reordered. The aggregate of particles? But no physical aggregate can even increase in size, let alone truly grow or develop; the aggregate that forms the snowball at one moment has not enlarged at the next; it has merely had other particles disposed in a blanket around it.

'What then', an acute writer has asked, 'do we mean by "development", or do we mean anything? I think we do mean something, of which we recognize instances, but whose definition is at first sight so paradoxical that we might be inclined to question its occurrence if we were not confronted with instances. For it is a process in which what as yet in some sense is not brings *itself* into being. . . . A mind is not an aggregate whose components have been drawn from elsewhere. It does not develop at the expense of that on which it is said metaphorically to feed . . . there is a real coming to be of that which, in the sense in which it exists when it has come to be, did not exist before. And yet in another sense surely it must have existed; for else the mind has not developed. There is no process of development, unless what develops is all the time that which it comes to be. . . . This is not gratuitous paradox. . . . It seems paradoxical only so long as we take for examples of development what are not such, and try to assimilate

the evolution of species to that of atoms . . . in growth there is
a unity determining the continuous manifestation of a certain
form, but in aggregation not. . . . . But it is clear that it is nothing
physical—no physical unit, nor aggregate of physical units . . .
this unity is never sensibly manifested.' It is an immaterial
'subject which develops—which is one through a succession of
phases, and yet different in these phases'.[1]

This, I believe, is right, and would be generally recognized
as right if it were not for the inveterate habit of looking at
processes of life and mind through unrealized mechanical
analogy. This habit is perhaps the product of indolence; it is
easy to imagine things happening after the manner of moving
particles; it is difficult to follow a process that supplies no
material for such images. But we must do what we can to rid
ourselves of analogy and preconception, and to see the facts as
they are. And when we take growth or development where we
know it best, and try to describe accurately what happens
when, for example, we pass from a worse to a better understanding of something, or from feeble to full responsiveness to
a musical passage, it seems merely meaningless to say that
what is going on is a rearrangement of atoms or the enlargement
of an aggregate of these, even if the atoms, by some miracle,
have now become sensations or some other sort of mental entity.
What it does appear to be is a process in which the germinal
becomes the mature, the potential the actual; in which I
become what I had it in me to become; in which, as I review
it, I can see that what I am at present was there in embryo,
working itself out to completion, and laying the movement at
every step under constraint through the character of what was
to emerge. It is true that each stage conditions the next. But
why are these stages serial? Why does each as it arises move
on in a single direction? Because, as we can see at the end, the
same immanent purpose was working at each stage. *Where* the
movement was taking us at any step we could not say exactly,
but with the completion of the process it becomes clear that

[1] H. W. B. Joseph, *The Concept of Evolution* (Herbert Spencer
Lecture, Oxford, 1924), 12–16, 24, 22. I owe much to this admirable
lecture, and, I should like to add, to Mr. Joseph's writings generally.

the fulfilment we have reached, if new, is not wholly new, and differs from what went before only as a maturer form of the same; that this identical and continuous element has been working in darkness, freeing itself from irrelevancy, organizing its matter, enlarging its scope, until it is fully formed and ripe. We shall misconceive the process radically if we regard it as an adding or rearranging of units, for it is essentially a coming to be on the part of that which is not yet actual, in which the form of what emerges controls the course of its own emergence. This, to the mechanist, may be mysticism. If that is his verdict after examining the process we mean, we shall respect it. But if what he examines is, as is too likely, some utterly different process of nervous, muscular, or cerebral change, substituted by confusion for the process here meant, the verdict will be merely irrelevant.

8. (2) The teleological nature of mind is shown similarly in *choice*. Choice would most naturally be conceived by the mechanist as a conflict of physical forces, issuing in the predominance of one. It has often been maintained, both by mechanists and others, that something like this happens when a mind is torn between conflicting impulses. And there are no doubt cases of such conflict where the analogy is worth drawing. When one offers a squirrel a nut, the hesitant approaches and retreats suggest a quasi-physical tug-of-war between the impulses of fear and hunger. But this is not a case of choice. Choice proper begins when we are able to contemplate and compare two prospective experiences. Now comparison is rendered possible only by the possession of something in common by the things compared. In the case of ethical choice the common element is good or value, and choice involves the recognition that the good or value we seek will be realized more fully in one course than in another. This seeking after good or value is not one desire among others, which competes with them and in succeeding annuls them. It is something that is present in its degree in all desires, and must reach its end if at all by working through them. Similarly with the end itself. It is not a particular go od competing with other particular goods, but that whose presence in varying measure in all of them makes reasonable preference possible. Indeed choice is at bottom another kind of the same process we found in development, in which that which existed *in posse* actualizes itself in maturer form. Now the process of discerning an end to be realized more fully in one good than in another is certainly far removed from the process of being driven by the stronger impulse; and it is so plainly and radically different from any movement or collision of atoms or conflict of forces which can occur in the physical world that analogies between them are more likely to confuse than to clarify.

9. (3) *Inference* falls, even more clearly perhaps than develop-ment and choice, beyond the range of mechanism, but as we have said something about it earlier and must return to it later, we may here be brief.[1] The point may be put in either of two ways: either mechanism knows nothing of necessity while in-ference cannot do without it; or as the self-development of an idea, inference is another species of the process we have just been considering. Mechanism is content to take its laws as descriptions of fact rather than as statements of necessity. The law that A causes B, for example, is not a statement that A's nature necessitates B's; it does not pretend to say more than that A regularly *is* followed by B. This kind of mechanism has often been applied to mental process under the name of 'association'; and just as conflicting forces have a rough analogy with conflicting impulses, so the behaviour of units or particles that regularly go together is not wholly unlike what happens in consciousness, when, with guidance and tension relaxed, ideas gambol idly. But as an account of inference it is grossly false. For in all inference that is really such, if the

---

[1] See above, Chap. XIII, and below, Chaps. XXII, XXIII, XXXII, Sec. 11.

thought of B follows the thought of A, it is precisely because A and B are linked by the bond of necessity; A is felt as incomplete and not wholly intelligible unless its relation to B is perceived. Inference is no vaudeville stage where Act 1, the prestidigitator, may be followed with equal propriety by the performing seals or a song. If it were, there would, at bottom, be no distinction between Euclid and a day-dream. Inference is a process in which the nature of A, together with an immanent ideal of intelligible system, controls what shall emerge as B. A is recognized as a fragment, torn from a larger whole, and the mind in seeking this whole is compelled to develop A along some lines rather than others. This will be illustrated later on. Our point at present is that control by an immanent end (which we shall gradually come to recognize as the central character of mind), appears once more as the essence of inference. In ultimate principle, inference is one with growth and choice.

These instances show, I think, that when confronted by the distinctive activities of mind, mechanism is inadequate. Even in physical science the older mechanism is breaking down;[1] and its modifications, however much they may help it in physics, do not make it appreciably more relevant to the processes of mind. I do not believe that in dealing with those processes we can dispense with conceptions which, though unknown to mechanism, are as old as Aristotle, the notions of δύναμις and ἐνέργεια, of the potential that becomes the actual.[2] For mind develops, and nothing short of such conceptions will convey what development means.[3]

We may conclude that our provisional theory of the nature

[1] 'To-day there is widespread agreement, which on the physical side amounts almost to unanimity, that the stream of knowledge is heading toward a non-mechanical reality.'—Jeans, *The Mysterious Universe*, 148.　　　　　　　　　　　[2] *Metaphysics*, VIII.

[3] 'Rational purpose is, and will always in the end be, recognized as the distinctive feature in the activity of mind, and though it may fairly enough be maintained that the mind is more than its purposes, and that the purposes themselves grow and take definite shape in the very process of execution, this is only to contend that the mind, as we know it, is still imperfectly aware of its self and its own meanings.'—Hobhouse, *Development and Purpose*, xxx.

of ideas is in harmony with the general nature of mind, and entitled to such corroboration as this harmony implies. Indeed the agreement is so great as to be a little uncomfortable. We described an idea as a partially realized purpose, or rather a potentiality not fully actualized, and we have now seen that this general description applies likewise to mind itself, at least as revealed in some of its most characteristic processes. The line of distinction between mind and thought need not now concern us. But the harmony between our suggested theory of ideas and what we have seen of the general nature of mind is complete.

10. We turn now to the second point to be considered in this chapter. Does our conception of the idea accord with the nature of *knowing* as well as with the nature of mind? Of course if purposiveness belongs to mind generally, we should expect to find it manifested in the various functions of mind, and hence in the function of knowing. This expectation is amply confirmed.

By 'knowing' we mean knowing in its broadest sense, in which it includes all the activities of what is called the cognitive side of our nature, such as perceiving, judging, inferring, imagining, doubting, conjecturing, wondering. This is an old and familiar grouping which will probably be unquestioned, though it is not at first quite obvious what the principle of the grouping is. For if we take knowing in its ordinary sense of the certain apprehension of truth, these activities, as Cook Wilson has shown,[1] are not all of them species of it. To wonder, for example, although it would be counted unhesitatingly as a cognitive activity rather than one of feeling or willing, would just as unhesitatingly be excluded from knowing in the stricter sense just defined. By what right, then, are these various processes called 'knowing' activities? The answer points to the truth we wish to emphasize. They are united because they are all activities implying one end. When we guess or imagine or doubt or wonder we are not knowing in the full sense; if we

[1] *Statement and Inference*, I. 37–40.

were, we could doubt and wonder no longer; but though such processes have not yet attained to knowledge, they are all seeking or simulating it. Directly or indirectly, each points to knowledge as its goal.

Knowledge, then, is an end, and unless it is so taken the unity ascribed to the cognitive side of our nature will not hold. And when we go on to reflect upon this end, it seems clear that it is a state, not an activity or process. To be sure a process is necessary if we are to arrive at it; to attain knowledge is always to do so through some kind of mental activity, such as judgement or inference. But it will not do to *identify* knowledge with the processes of coming to know. We must distinguish knowing as the process *by* which knowledge is realized from knowledge itself as *that which* the process realizes in various degrees. This is a perfectly straightforward distinction with plenty of analogies. As I respond more fully to a thing of beauty, I appreciate its beauty more, but that does not make its beauty the same as my changing response. Just as beauty is something perceived in degree when I appreciate, so knowledge is something achieved in degree when I know.

Since knowing is a process that has knowledge as its end, to define it adequately would require a definition of that end. This, of course, would be no easy matter. We might indeed dismiss the question 'What is knowledge?' as an unreal one, since genuinely to ask a question presupposes that one can tell when it is answered; and if one knows enough already to know when 'What is knowledge'? is answered, one already knows what knowledge is.[1] This is not verbal trickery; there is substance in it; but the merely implicit knowledge of knowledge that it presupposes will unfortunately not serve our purpose. If the process of thought is a knowing activity, and knowing activities are definable only through the end they are attempting to realize, there can be no escape from the obligation to set out this end as explicitly and fully as possible. This obligation we shall assume in the proper place. But our interest for the moment falls short of this. We have suggested a theory of the idea, to

[1] Cf. Wilson, *ibid.*, 39; Lotze, *Logic*, Sec. 9.

the effect that it is its object *in posse*, and we want to be clear whether this theory comports or not with the facts about the process of knowing. It will here be maintained that it does. Indeed, we shall try to show that knowing is the sort of activity that even necessitates such a theory. This we shall try to establish through the following propositions: (1) the end of every knowing activity is to apprehend the nature of things, to see things as they are; (2) the end is equally to achieve a certain ideal set by the mind's own character; (3) in the long run these ends coincide; we must believe that thought discloses reality in the degree to which it achieves its own ideal.

11. (1) Our first proposition, that in knowing we aim at seeing things as they are, would probably be granted by all but the pragmatists, who interpret the aim of knowing in a way peculiar to themselves. We have weighed their claim and, for reasons that need not be rehearsed, have found it wanting. The above proposition, however, may be thought more applicable to some forms of knowing than to others. Doubtless in ordinary perceiving we are interested in discovering the features of an independent world, and most of us believe we are doing this successfully; but is this aim equally apparent in thinking of Julius Caesar, or in remembering yesterday's rain, or expecting rain to-morrow? I think it is, or at least becomes so with the slightest reflection. When we engage in any form of thinking, we are not playing with fancies merely, but on the contrary are trying to submit our thought to the control of something beyond it, in order that it may reveal the features of an outer world more fully and more exactly. This even holds in those relatively rare cases in which we are thinking of our own thoughts, for the idea we make our object seems always to be distinguishable from the idea through which we think of it. It is impossible to find an instance of thinking or knowing that does not go beyond its own machinery so far as to intend and claim the disclosure of an ulterior order to which it is in some sense adjusting itself. If this is realism, then all of us are realists.

12. (2) The truth of our second proposition seems almost equally obvious. If knowing aims at unbaring what is beyond itself, it also aims at a special kind of satisfaction. Its end (we do not like these terms, but they are useful) is at once immanent and transcendent. The transcendent end of knowing is the direct revelation in experience of what is also beyond it; this aim we have just described. The immanent end is to achieve a state of insight that will bring the theoretic impulse to rest. The desire to know is a desire for what will satisfy this impulse, and we accept as knowledge only what does so. The immanent goal of this impulse sets the direction in which knowledge develops and decides when the process shall be accounted complete. To seek to know is to put a question to the nature of things. How do we tell when that question is answered? Why do we accept one answer rather than another? The conditions are determined from within, but for us, not by us; what would satisfy the animal mind would not satisfy the human, and what would satisfy a poor intelligence would not satisfy a more exacting one. The character of the question asked and the quality of the answer accepted express and depend on the questioning mind. The mathematician goes on puzzling over his problem until he arrives at an insight that brings its elements into a certain order before him; then he stops and calls his problem solved. Why? Because he has found in this final order what satisfies the desire that moved him. His thinking has been a pursuit of this insight; it was the demand for it that drove him on from one step to another; it is only by the light of this immanent goal that he knows when he has reached his journey's end.

An immanent end is thus an ideal, which, because set by the mind's own nature, may guide and govern its activity in advance of any explicit desire. Once the seeking has reached what will satisfy it, we can see that it was in search of this all along, just as in feeling for the right word, though we cannot specify what we want beforehand, we can at once recognize it when it comes. The immanent end reveals itself only gradually. We must wait and see what satisfies us and compare what satisfies less with what satisfies more; we cannot plot the curve of our advance without reference to the path of our past successes. But every new step is a multiple gain. It clarifies the goal, marks the present level of achievement, and throws light backward along the line of march. But we never quite know our destination till we get there. The interest in beauty, for example, prompts to endless experiment; but in attaining one satisfaction it engenders a restlessness for another and subtler one, and thus it is never satisfied wholly. Who feels most keenly his defect of goodness? Proverbially, it is the saint.

This clearly holds of knowing. It is a process in which one side of our nature is progressively realized. And it is obviously controlled by an immanent end, an end which is as truly fixed by our nature as the sort of food and drink that will satisfy us. The end grows clearer as the impulse works itself out; but because the interest grows by what it feeds on, the end is forever receding, and knowledge that would satisfy wholly, like perfect goodness and perfect beauty, is at the rainbow's end. Why does an argument convince, or a system impose itself on us? Because it satisfies the demand of our nature at this level of development. But it is equally clear that what satisfies this nature at one stage may fail to do so at the next, and that the immanent ideal is revising, refining, reordering, expanding itself without ceasing.

13. (3) Thus knowing is doubly purposive. It aims at revealing the outside world; it aims equally at satisfying an inner demand. Now it might be maintained that neither of these ends is legitimate, since neither is attainable. This would be absolute scepticism. And I shall not argue against this position because I accept the traditional view of it as self-contradictory, and thus as not really a position at all. To say one knows that there is no knowledge is absurd. But if knowledge does occur, it must be admitted that both these aims and claims are in some degree realized in it. If it knew nothing beyond itself, it would have no object. If there were no demand for it to conform to, it would have no standard. It is obviously under double constraint. It is at once a revelation of the object and a realization of ourselves, an adjustment to outer supply and inner demand. And the question that presses for an answer is, How is this possible? How is it possible that what satisfies these two sets of conditions should be the same, that what is demanded by the theoretic impulse should be also what is thrust upon us by external reality?

There is one view of the relation of these factors that would render the problem insoluble, and this unfortunately is a view implicit in common thought. It is the view that the two factors, the immanent end to which knowledge must conform, and the object to which it must somehow also conform, are independent variables. For knowledge would then be either (i) miracle or (ii) fraud.

(i) Consider what would be implied. A logician demonstrates a theorem, and accepts the demonstration as convincing. Why does he accept it? All we can say is that his nature is so constituted that when a demonstration in accordance with the laws of identity, non-contradiction, etc., is offered, he finds it satisfactory; any question about the laws themselves would have to be answered in the same way. But he also finds that things themselves invariably conform to these laws. Qualities remain true to type; relations do not change their character overnight; he is so confident that things and events have fixed natures and laws that if a bit of chalk behaved differently to-day and yesterday, he would always assume, and with later justification, not that the thing changed its character but that he had failed to catch its true law. His thought thus reflects two things at once, the structure of the actual world and the nature of his own mind; and these two things are supposed to be independent. Now we must insist that to believe in coincidence of this kind is to put one's trust in miracle. If the immanent and transcendent ends of my knowledge are really independent of each other, then their coming together at any point is a matter of chance and their continuing to coincide is incredible. According to this, what happens in thinking is that, impelled by intellectual hunger, I formulate what will satisfy this, whereupon along comes Nature and pours at my feet great basketfuls of substantiated wishes. It may be objected that logic does not hold of the real world. But if not, there is no knowledge, and *cadit quaestio*. If this be thought too summary an answer to a position that has been taken seriously by logical positivism, the reader is referred to Chapter XXX below, where the matter is considered more fully in connection with the views of that school on necessity.[1] It may be objected from another side that though the coincidence does occur, there is nothing remarkable about it, since the forms that the mind finds satisfying are not brought by it to nature, but have been impressed upon it from without by incessant repetition. This is the traditional view of empiricism, which also will be discussed below.[2] For the present we need only point out that if logical law is merely the expression of frequency, it is not *necessary*, and that if it is not necessary, then the empiricist argument itself, which, like every other argument, relies upon such law, can only be called inconclusive.

(ii) For the believer in the independence of the two ends, the alternative to miracle is scarcely more inviting, for it amounts to the fraudulence of the knowledge claim, that is, to scepticism. We cannot now rely on chance coincidence; and there is nothing in the fact that a certain structure satisfies my knowing impulse to show that it coincides with anything beyond. The most rigid of demonstrations would leave us in doubt whether we had attained any sort or degree of correspondence with an outer world. Knowledge would be unrecognized good luck. Experience would be a sustained paranoia, which, even if it made occasional contacts with a world outside, would leave us uncertain what was dream and what fact. If the real world on the one hand and the immanent end of knowledge on the other are curves plotted on different bases, we could never count on their intersecting; and to suppose that by reaching the end of knowledge we should arrive at reality

[1] Esp. Secs. 12–17.
[2] Chap. XXVIII.

would seem about as reasonable as to suppose that the desire
of the moth creates the star.

14. Since the assumption that the two ends are independent
is thus disastrous, let us try the other alternative. What if they
are *not* independent?

This hypothesis can be narrowed. The denial of independence
may mean various things, but in virtue of earlier study there is
one suggestion that we can at once exclude, namely, that the
transcendent end, or object, can be identified with the immanent end so far as realized in present thought. To reduce the
transcendent end to the immanent end as now realized would
lead to solipsism; to reduce the immanent end, *qua* realized, to
the transcendent end would raise all the difficulties about error
that have been the bane of neo-realism. And either course would
bring us into collision with that curious but significant fact that
we found mentioned by Mr. Santayana—at some cost, we
thought, of consistency—the fact that I can think of a thing
without having either itself or any of its content present in
imagery. If idea and object cannot be wholly independent of
each other, neither can they be simply the same. This conclusion seems certain. Yet what are we doing when we accept
it? Did we not say a few moments ago that the natural claim of
knowing was to reveal the object itself, that this claim was valid,
and that unless it were so, there was an end of knowledge
generally? We must admit it; we did say this. Such a conclusion seemed then, and seems now, beyond escape. But let
us only think where it takes us. Our whole inquiry into the
nature of knowledge issues apparently in this, that idea and
object must be the same, yet cannot possibly be so. Is the
pursuit to die away in such a fiasco?

No. While this contradiction seems at first to reveal an insoluble paradox in knowing, it forces us, upon reflection,
toward an exit. All lines of escape but one seem to be cut off.
It is too late to declare for the independence from each other of
immanent and transcendent ends; we have abjured that course

with its attendant miracle or scepticism. It is too late to say that either of these is fully realized in experience as it is. What we can say is this, that any attempt on the part of thought to realize its immanent end, however feeble it may be, is also a partial realization of its transcendent end or object. Thought, if we may so put it, is a half-way house on the road to reality. Ideas are potential objects, entities whose nature and being lie in a germinal embodiment of that which they would become. To the apparently fatal demand that if knowledge is to be possible the idea must be at once the same as its object and not the same, we answer, that is precisely what it is. That such identity and difference are possible we have seen already in considering mental growth. The two may be the same, yet different, as a sapling that grows into an oak is the same tree, yet a different one. They may be the same as a man is the same when the infant becomes an adult, or as a purpose is the same when, in spite of deepening and broadening as it approaches its fulfilment, it is yet in strictest accuracy the same purpose it was at the start. *If thought can be seen as a stage on the way to its transcendent end or object, as that end itself in the course of becoming actual, the paradox of knowledge is in principle solved.* The idea can then be *both* the same as its object *and* different; the same because it *is* the object *in posse*; different because that object, which is its end, is as yet incompletely realized.

15. We have seen in earlier chapters the labyrinths of difficulty in which the chief alternative theories are lost. We venture to think that the theory here suggested, that the idea, and indeed knowledge generally, is partially realized purpose, might be found to do justice to the truth and to meet the main difficulties of all these views. Let us rapidly illustrate this in the leading cases.

The copy theory insisted that ideas must differ from their objects. We agree. It goes on to insist, further, that ideas must be like their objects. We agree again, but with a new notion of likeness which does justice to the facts, as the copy theory does not. Likeness for that theory meant the point-for-point resemblance that holds between subject and portrait. But we showed in discussing the theory that in many, indeed in most, cases no such resemblance was traceable in the idea. Yet one is reluctant to dismiss as merely absurd a theory of which every thinker feels the attraction who feels the pull of common sense at all. It is by no means wholly absurd. Ideas *are* like their objects but with a special kind of likeness. It is the likeness of what exists in potency to the same thing actualized; the likeness of a mind half grown to that same mind fully grown; of a purpose partly realized to the purpose fulfilled. Two of the chief contentions of the copy theory, the distinctness of the idea from the object and its resemblance to it, are thus admitted by our proposal but so reinterpreted as to conform to fact. On the other hand, the great weakness of the copy theory was its admission that the interval between idea and object was a chasm between different orders of existence, a chasm which, once admitted, could not be bridged by any machinery that the theory could devise. Its assertion of resemblance was thus left arbitrary and ungrounded. We have argued that no such chasm is there, or knowledge would be impossible. We can thus take over the truth in the copy theory without its attendant scandal.

Our proposal does similar justice to critical realism. The main contentions of that theory are that the *object* of knowledge transcends experience, but that the *character* of the object is presented in experience directly. Both these views we accept, but again by reinterpreting them. The object does fall beyond knowledge, but not in a way which precipitates us upon the unhappy dilemma between scepticism and animal faith. It falls beyond knowledge only in the sense in which an end that is unattained falls beyond a stage on the way to attaining it. For the critical realist every advance in knowledge leaves the object itself as remote as ever from the grasp of knowledge; for us every advance brings us closer to it. Thus we accept from critical realism, with a gloss of our own, the doctrine of the transcendence of the object. Similarly of the view that we apprehend the object's character. We do so apprehend it, but certainly not in such a way that the whole nature of the object, or even, with certain exceptions to be noted later, detached fragments or areas of this, appear literally in our minds. Such an account is too bold for the facts; it forgets the curious implicitness, indirectness, and shadowiness of our thinking, which has led the defenders of imageless thought to deny that any imagery of any kind need be presented. Their view is questionable. But their facts are of significance, and cannot, I think, be accounted for short of the view that what is actually in our minds is not the character of the object, nor normally a fragment of this character, but *that which if fully developed would* be the character. We agree that to think of the character is to have it present to us; but we must add that this presence is a matter of degree, and that it is entirely possible to think of the character with no part of its content directly present at all.

Thus freed of its special difficulties, the main positions of critical realism may be accepted. We shall see that the further difficulties about causality and inference can also be dealt with by the theory proposed. Both these processes are unintelligible if universals make no difference in the flux of events. In the critical realist theory they are cut off from such influence. On our theory they exert it continually.

Neo-realism also receives justice. What it is most concerned to insist on is that one knows things themselves, not substitutes or surrogates for them. We accept that position. But taken as the realist interprets it, it can be riddled with legitimate criticisms, both in its doctrine of the act, which was the point at which we attacked it, and in its doctrine of the object, where it falls foul of the theory of error. Even if it confines itself to perception, which it was specially designed to explain, its troubles are many; and when it is called on to explain how we can think of the absent, it is covered with confusion. The fact seems undeniable that we can think of and know the temporally and spatially remote. Realism would have us believe that in spite of being thus remote, such objects are directly presented. But how can they be both? Realism has no answer. The theory we are suggesting has. It is as fully persuaded as realism that what we know must be objects themselves, but it introduces the distinction required to save the thought of the absent from absurdity. Every attempt to know, it says, is an attempt to realize the mind's own nature; but since our thought falls for-ever short, we must distinguish what it is from what it aims at, the idea from the end or object which it seeks to be, but which, as mere idea, it has not attained. The real object is in both; it is present in person in our thought, even when we are thinking about the absent; but it is there, not in that flesh-and-blood actuality which would make thinking something monstrous, but in various stages of realization. With such a view, one may subscribe whole-heartedly to realism, while recognizing, as it does not, all the tenuousness and elusiveness in thought which psychological study discloses.

16. Just as we can find in the realist theories strong under-lying affinities with our view, so we can find them in the 'behaviour theories'. When behaviourism was in sore straits to discover the physical movements which in some cases of silent thinking were to be identified with the thought, it fell back, as may be recalled, on bodily 'sets' and attitudes. The device was desperate and for behaviourism really meant bankruptcy; but a sound instinct lay behind it. What the behaviourist would like is to take all thinking as overt bodily reaction to physical objects, and if allowed to select his own cases, he can usually find something like what he is looking for. But nothing is easier than to produce instances of thinking where neither object nor reaction is apparent. Then what to do? At this point we found the behaviourist resorting to the notion of 'motor sets', re-actions that are not yet really reactions, but the potentiality of such. And here he is closely skirting the truth. There is a sense, as we have seen, in which the thought of an object *is* the potentiality of it. Unfortunately, in the kind of world in which the behaviourist pitches his tent, these potentialities are non-sense. In a purely physical world, development, as we have described it, has no place. Such truth as does lie in his doctrine the behaviourist is cut off from seeing by his insistence on looking at the mind through mechanical analogies.

Pragmatism, in spite of its flirtations with behaviourism, is far nearer the truth. The purposive behaviour of mind and the instrumental function of ideas are the very foundations on which it builds. Nor is this the only element in pragmatism that we can gratefully take over. That ideas are in intimate dependence on our own nature, that all knowing is a process of seeking, that its true end is revealed only as the process advances, that ideas must in a broad sense be tested by their working, that our acceptances and rejections in thinking are determined in a sense by satisfaction, and that what shall satisfy us is somehow determined from within—all this we can accept. But there remains a flaw in the very base of the pragmatist theory, a flaw that makes its whole superstructure rickety and untenable. This is the position that thinking is a means to acting, and is to be tested by all the goods to which action itself may be a means. This doctrine was too much for us. We have seen that even when we are thinking in a practical interest, the purpose to know and the purpose to do are quite distinct. Knowing is purposive; this we admit and insist on; but we were compelled to add emphatically that knowing has an end of its own. We have thus rejected pragmatism, while still able to accept and use some of its most characteristic contentions.

17. It is perhaps not too much to say, then, that if our theory holds it will complete and combine these other theories and correct their special defects in a not unimpressive way. But before turning to detail, we must deal with an important point of principle. It is hardly possible that the explanation should have gone so far without suggesting the following objection: 'Your argument really denies the difference between thought and things; you are saying that if the immanent end of thought

were fully attained, it would be found identical with the
transcendent end, the object; which means that an idea, if
sufficiently developed and improved, would *be* a real thing.
But a physical thing, say a mountain, is a solid, brute existent,
as different from anyone's thought of it as a boulder from a
daydream. Are we to understand that my idea of the mountain
is the mountain itself in some vague unrealized state, and that
by completing itself it would *become* the actual mountain?
But this is the most fantastic view yet considered. For the
difference between an idea and a mountain is a difference in
kind, not in degree. A thing exists at some point in time and
space; it is unique; and from such uniqueness a mere meaning
is cut off by its very nature. Furthermore, if real things were
ends of ours and in some sense the fulfilment of our will, why
their notorious and stubborn nonconformity to that will? There
is no conceivable process of moulding or embellishing an idea,
of evolving or hardening or fattening it, that will turn it into
an actual thing'.

Everyone must feel the force of this objection. It has common
sense behind it and not a little philosophy. Unfortunately to
answer it as it deserves would almost require a system of metaphysics. Still, to pass it by would be to leave untouched what is
perhaps the most immediate and common objection that our
theory is likely to provoke.

The objection may mean either of two things. It may mean
merely that the being of nature is not exhausted in providing
ends for knowing; that mountains, for example, have a being of
their own regardless of the endeavours of your mind and mine
to know them. Or it may mean not only this but also that real
things could not possibly have potential being as idea, that
between idea and existence is a difference so fundamental
that no bridge can be built between them. The first of these
criticisms we shall leave for the present unanswered, partly
because it calls for excursions into ontology which we wish
here to avoid, partly because there is nothing obviously fatal
about it, if admitted. The second leaves the question open
whether things can exist apart from knowledge, and confines

itself to denying that objects can exist potentially in ideas or that ideas can be realized in objects. And on this something can be said. The criticism comes to this, that the relation between the idea and its real object cannot be the relation of potential to actual for three reasons, namely that physical existents are (1) different from anything mental in kind, (2) unique, and (3) not seldom at odds with our will. Now it is surprising how the substance vanishes from these reasons when they are placed under scrutiny.

18. (1) One who advances the first objection would probably take as characteristic the difference between sense data as typical existences and images as typically mental. It is easy to see, he would say, that the solid, extended physical things revealed to us in sensation are a world apart from our flickering images; the existent and the ideal are here different fundamentally and obviously. But is this so obvious? To be sure we do not, in our theory, identify the real object with anything that science or common sense has yet in its grasp, but even if we did it is by no means clear that this distinction would hold. Is not Mr. Russell right that 'images and sensations cannot always be distinguished by their intrinsic nature',[1] and indeed are essentially the same kind of stuff? Certainly their continuity suggests this. Sensations die away into images by a perfectly smooth transition; images frequently pass as sensations. Between what everyone would call a sensation and what everyone would call an image there is a series of intermediaries which partake of the nature of both. Thus there are 'positive after-images' which Ward describes as 'the original sensations in a state of evanescence'[2] and which Semon has elaborately studied as the 'akoluthic stage' of sensations. If any criterion of being an image is to be found in outlasting the external stimulus, then clearly these are images; yet they are so like sensations that Ward thought they should be roundly called such, and Titchener pointed out that 'many details may be

---

[1] *Analysis of Mind*, 151.   [2] *Psychological Principles*, 174.

observed in the after-image which escaped observation during the rapid glance at the real objects'.[1] There is again the 'negative after-image', with its complementary colour, which is so far like sensation that it appears itself bent or curved if projected on a bent or curved surface,[2] and is of course involuntary, yet is so far like the image that it follows the movements of one's head and may be affected even by changes in one's breathing.[3] Then there is the 'primary memory image', which 'in the case of vision, can always be obtained, and is obtained to most advantage by looking intently at some object and then closing the eyes or turning them away. The image of the object will appear for a moment very vividly and distinctly and can be so recovered several times in succession by an effort of attention'.[4] These are all cases in which imagery, to use Hobbes's phrase, is a sort of 'decaying sense'. And no doubt parallels in plenty would be found in which images are on the way to becoming sensations, as in the various stages of hypnotic suggestion and hallucination, if such cases were equally open to introspective study. Still further evidence that sense data are not alien in kind to the mental might be drawn from the continuity of sensation and affection. Psychologists commonly distinguish between the sensory qualities of a musical passage and the pleasure it arouses, between the pain and the 'displeasure' of an illness, but they find it so little possible to draw a sharp line between these that when they theorize they are prone to regard affection as a stage in the development of sensation.[5] Thus if it is argued against us that there is a radical difference in kind between that which we lay hold of when we apprehend physical objects, and such presumably mental things as affections and images, it may be replied that those who have considered the alleged difference most attentively have failed to find it.

19. (2) That ideas are germinal objects is not, then, a theory

---

[1] *Experimental Psychology, Instructor's Manual*, I. 47.
[2] Titchener, *ibid.*, 46.   [3] Helmholtz, cited by Titchener, *ibid.*, 43.
[4] Ward, *op. cit.*, 176.   [5] See, e.g., Titchener's *Text-book*, 260.

to be thrown aside because of insurmountable difference in content or kind. But it has been alleged that there is a further difference that *is* insurmountable, the difference between character and existence. When I say 'that mountain yonder', I specify and characterize the object by universals; I think of it through these. But these universals may be possessed by something else, while the thing I point to, the thing that owns them, is a unique, particular existent. As Bradley says, whatever character we ascribe in thinking 'is only a *general* character. It falls in the content and does not give the existence. It marks the sort but it misses the thing'. He puts the whole objection forcibly:

> 'When we say "It rained last Tuesday", we mean *this* last Tuesday, and not any other; but, if we keep to ideas, we do not utter our meaning. Nothing in the world that you can do to ideas, no possible torture will get out of them an assertion that is not universal. . . . The event you describe is a single occurrence, but what you say of it will do just as well for any number of events, imaginary or real.'[1]

Predicates are universals; the existing things of which they are asserted are unique particulars; and between these no bridge would seem to be possible. Is there any answer to this objection?

Bradley himself has suggested the answer.[2] What do we mean by a unique particular? Do we mean an existence different in kind from universals, or a uniqueness that universals themselves may confer? He answers that it is the latter. When we consider the uniqueness of the mountain, we find that, far from being hostile and repellent to thought, it can only be defined as a completion of that very set of universals with which it was so sharply contrasted. The argument for this is simple. It consists in showing how we should naturally go about it to define precisely what we mean when we say 'that mountain'. The natural and indeed the only way is to specify the object

---

[1] *Logic*, I. 63.

[2] *Logic*, II, terminal essays on 'Uniqueness' and 'This'; see also Royce, *The Conception of God*, 217 ff.

further by bringing before our mind more and more of its attributes and relations. It is 'the mountain on the horizon yonder' or 'the middle one of those three peaks' or 'the one with a shoulder on its right side and a cross-shaped scar near the summit'. As a rule when we thus specify, we do so for practical purposes, and for such purposes a little will go a long way. But in its demand for exactness of specification, the desire to know runs far beyond the simple requirements of action, and what we must therefore ask is how a mind prepared to press its demand to the limit would define what it means by 'that'. The answer remains the same, namely, by continued specification. For such a mind the sketchy descriptions used above would hardly serve as a beginning. For these few abstracted features might belong to any number of mountains, and even if in fact they did not, still they *might*, and so long as that remains true, one has fallen short of the particularity of the reference. By 'that' I mean something unique and wholly determinate, and to make this meaning explicit I should have to specify in such manner as to mark this mountain off from everything else, either actual or possible. I could not define it by its shape, for this shape is an abstract character which might be possessed by innumerable other things. Nor would it be enough to describe the geological features of the mountain, its flora and fauna, and its precise dimensions, for these are all still general characters which could conceivably appear elsewhere. Suppose that in addition to these I give the exact geographical location, specifying its relations to other things in space; would that carry me to the required definiteness? No, it would not. For that assumes that the space in which the mountain lies is itself unique, while it is clear, as we shall see, that other spaces can be conceived in which the internal relations of our own may be repeated.[1] We shall achieve a guaranteed uniqueness only when we shall have exceeded the bounds of all possible repetition, and exhausted the relations of the thing to everything else in the universe. This is the only uniqueness that the object possesses.

[1] Cf. Chap. XVII, Secs. 12-15.

To resume: we do undoubtedly refer to what is individual and unique. Undoubtedly also, if asked what we meant by this uniqueness or individuality, we should say it is that which makes a thing *this* thing, as opposed to everything else in the world. Well, what does make it this thing? To answer that question we proceed to enumerate its qualities and relations. But we find these indefinitely many. Any group selected as defining could in theory be repeated elsewhere, and so misses the uniqueness intended. What is it that passes judgement on these shortcomings? Obviously it is thought's own immanent demand. If there is a continuing sense of discrepancy between the generalities actually gained and the individual thing referred to, it is because complete individuality would require exhaustion of these generalities. Thought therefore persists in its attempt at definition. Is there any limit to such a search, any insight that would finally satisfy the demand of thought? Yes. In spite of the possibility that characters and groups of characters should be repeated in many instances, nobody can believe that there are many *universes*. Within the universe there may be solar and stellar universes and subordinate wholes innumerable, but they are all members of *the* universe, and to suppose this itself repeated would be senseless. If the reference of my thought, then, is to be released from ambiguity, I must pursue this defining course until, through fixing the relation of the 'what' before me to everything else, I have determined its place in the one real universe.

> 'In such a Whole each member would be characterized completely by its own place and function in the system. And clearly, taken so, each member would, if still finite, be none the less individual and unique. It would belong to a sort in respect to any one of its attributes, but of itself there could not possibly be ever more than one, and itself could never be made an instance or could appear as a member of and in a kind or class. . . . Hence such a finite being would be unique, unique relatively, and at the same time absolutely.'[1]

Fully to define what one means by this individual thing one must pursue its specification till thought attains its immanent

[1] Bradley, *Logic*, II. 656.

end. That end is attained when ambiguity is supplanted by full determinateness. Such determinateness can be arrived at only by travelling to its terminus the road of universals. And thus we find that uniqueness, individuality, far from being a foreign country, is itself the very goal of thought. It is the point at which the realization of the immanent end overtakes the transcendent end.

20. Such a theory offers on its surface a tempting butt for ridicule. 'You tell me I don't know what I really mean till I have related what is before me to everything else. I speak of a coal-scuttle, and you tell me I mean the universe. And I suppose that when I speak of a lamp-post, I mean the universe too. So that a lamp-post and a coal-scuttle are really the same thing. We all mean the same thing always. We can't disagree', etc. etc. Lest anyone should take such criticism seriously, we add two further comments. First, we are saying nothing so absurd as that people do not speak and think of lamp-posts and coal-scuttles; we are merely suggesting that if we reflect on our thought of the coal-scuttle, or of anything else, we shall see that the very impulse which led to our selecting and defining it will carry us out beyond it. We do not deny that one can mean the coal-scuttle; we do deny that in this or any limited object, that defining impulse which is the desire to know can find more than temporary rest. If we stop with the conception of the coal-scuttle, it is because, without our dominantly practical interests, there is no point in going farther; as we saw in the study of perception, the laying out of experience into things has followed utilitarian lines. But let the freer theoretic interest of physicist or philosopher play upon the same thing, and what seemed so simple becomes the hub of the universe, with relations of cause and effect, of likeness and difference, of implication, of temporal and spatial position, which link it to everything everywhere. We do not develop this context of relation, because we have other things to do than think, and because our indulgence of the theoretic impulse is guided and inhibited by more urgent need.

Secondly, if the theoretic impulse were given unrestricted play, we should see that the real object, the object that is fully determinate, the object of our ultimate meaning as opposed to our meaning when truncated by practice, is a very different thing from the object of common sense. The addition of so enormous a defining context would not leave the starting-point unaffected. The logic of this statement will be developed later when we discuss internal and external relations. Meanwhile an example will serve. Compare the way a newspaper probably presents itself to any of the higher animals with the way it appears to man. We cannot know what precisely goes on in the mind, say, of an ape; but after studies like Köhler's and others, we know that at least we have an illuminating glimpse. Now the light-rays stimulating perception are the same for the ape as for ourselves; his eyes and brain are similar to ours; it is not improbable that his sensations are likewise similar. Yet what he perceives must be startlingly different; so different that, if we use words accurately, there is no reason to say that the ape ever perceives a newspaper at all. Wherein lies the difference? Chiefly in this, that the ape cannot grasp the system of relations which for us make a newspaper what it is. The relations of this white rustling thing to public events, to the press that produced it, to the needs of readers and advertisers, the whole extensive context that is brought to bear effortlessly by human readers, is beyond the simian mind. The ape cannot grasp the real newspaper because the relations that so largely constitute it exceed his ken.

We believe, and not unreasonably, that the newspaper as defined in our own thought is nearer the fact than the newspaper grasped by the ape. We believe also that our perception exemplifies a mind more fully evolved, that is, a mind that more fully realizes the immanent end of mind as such. Is it not clear that these two series of changes tend to converge toward one goal? When should we arrive at that full determinateness which makes the object unique? When we arrive at that complete and integrated system which constitutes the immanent end of knowing. When would intelligence have evolved completely, that is, have become completely what it is seeking to become? When its object is fully known and determinate, when the content directly presented contains every character and relation involved in the transcendent end of knowing. Here the ends would coincide.

21. (3) The argument for the ultimate disparity of things and ideas had three counts. Two of these have now been dealt with in principle. The third was this, that if things as we now know them are the partial embodiments of any purpose or will of ours, they ought to show some conformity to our will, whereas, so far as we can see, they are utterly indifferent to it. The nature that we know is not actively hostile to our purposes any more than it embodies them; it is simply neutral, offering aids and obstacles impartially.

There is not much weight in this objection, if our position is understood. We may even concede all its claims. If you take our practical desires on the one hand, and on the other that common-sense order which represents the average level of our achievement in theory, and insist that the former reveals our real will and the latter ultimate reality, of course you will get a conflict, and on our theory it would be astonishing if you did not. But these provisos are not dictates of nature. We have insisted that the will to know, whose level of realization defines for us our present world, has an indefinite range of development beyond this; and the same holds of our practical wills. There is no more reason to say that our present wills, whimsical, irresponsible, and tentative as they commonly are, exhaust our real wills, i.e. wills for the good that would really satisfy us, than to say that the order of common sense is final reality. The line of answer is thus plain. If it is said that there is a conflict between present fact and present desire, we reply that that is true but irrelevant. If it is said that our practical and theoretical impulses would still collide when their ultimate issue had brought to light their ultimate ends, the answer is that this is a totally different position, which the evidence adduced does not prove.

These are some of the more obvious objections to our theory. Considering them has helped to clear up what the theory means. But plenty of difficulties remain; and there is perhaps no better way to say what must still be said in the way of principle than to anticipate the more awkward of these rapidly and with summary replies.

22. (4) 'According to you, the idea, if fully realized would *be* its object. The impulse to know something reappears as the impulse to *be* it. But surely I can refer to something or mean it without any such grotesque desire as to identify myself with it. For example, I am at this moment thinking of the great pyramid, but I certainly do not want to be the great pyramid; Heaven forbid'!

Of course not. Nor when you look appreciatively at a flower do you wish to convert yourself *in toto* into beauty. But does it follow from this that the attempt to appreciate is not an attempt to realize beauty, to get it as literally within your experience as a pleasure that may be sought for? And is not advance in appreciation a process of getting it there more completely? The aesthetic impulse surely *is* an attempt to realize beauty. Yet after all it is only one among many impulses, and it would be strange to say that our nature *generally* was transmuting itself into beauty as this one particular impulse realized its end. So of the impulse to know. Knowing is not all there is to human nature. The interest in solving a quadratic equation is not a desire that I personally and as a whole should become a solved equation. But is it, or is it not, an interest in getting the solution itself into my experience? Surely it is just that; I want to get a set of relations, partly now unknown, literally and actually within my experience, and anything short of this would be failure. The like holds of knowing everywhere. To the extent to which I know the great pyramid, it does enter into the content of my experience, and the impulse to know it could never be satisfied absolutely while any part of it was left out. But of course there is more of me than the impulse to know, and as before in the case of beauty, it would be absurd to say that because the end of this impulse is to realize its object, therefore this is the exclusive end of my nature as a whole. A *mere* mathematician or artist would be a pure abstraction, a naked cognitive or aesthetic interest somehow pulsating in a vacuum; in other words, not a man at all, but an impossible kind of monster.

23. (5) 'Are you not confusing thought with will? According to the theory, knowing is the self-realization of an idea. But then so is willing. You thus represent the two as the same.'

Formally, this objection is of course an undistributed middle, and this suggests its material defect. Probably it is true, as Spinoza thought, that thinking and willing are different forms of one *conatus*, different ways in which the same self realizes or actualizes itself. And they are so intimately connected that neither seems to occur without the other. As Professor Price says, 'there is no such thing as unintelligent action. *Das Thun ist auch Denken.* Further, even in the most purely theoretical activity we must attend, and attending seems to be a kind of willing'. He adds at once, however, the point that we must here insist on: 'But these facts, though important, do not have the faintest tendency to show that intellectual activity and practical activity are identical, or even alike.'[1] To say that they are not alike would no doubt go too far; indeed they are strikingly alike; and James, with his theory of ideo-motor action, which holds that the idea of an action tends inevitably to realize itself and that this tendency *is* will, came fairly near to conceiving of willing as we here conceive of knowing. Still the processes are plainly different. We are not called upon to define that difference precisely; all we need show is that on our theory there is a difference, or may be. And this seems no very

[1] *Perception*, 14-15.

severe demand. What will attempts to realize is, in the first instance, action; what thought attempts to realize may be anything whatever. Will is concerned with the future; thought is not restricted as to its object by any limitations of time. More essentially, will is a process of altering existence into conformity with present idea, while thought is a process of altering present idea into conformity with existence. These distinctions are not put forward as exhausting the difference between thought and will, but there is nothing inconsistent with our theory in making them; and if so, the charge that it is committed to identifying the two is unfounded.

24. (6) We may expect certain objections that have to do with truth and error. 'You say that the idea of an object may have little or no resemblance to it. Yet if the idea is to be true of its object, it must correspond to this faithfully. According to your theory, an idea that does not in the least correspond to an object may still be the thought of that object, and a *true* thought of it. Surely, that is absurd.'

Half of the answer to this objection lies in showing that the truth of an idea does not consist in resemblance, and the other half in showing that what it does consist in comports with our ideal theory. The first half has been supplied already. We saw when considering the idea as image that the notion that an idea must correspond to its object in the sense of resembling or copying it was indefensible. We may think of something in such a way that our thought is admittedly true of it, and yet have in our minds either no imagery at all, or at most a mere wrack or wraith, difficult for introspection to recover, and bearing, once it is recovered, no sort of resemblance to the object. Hence the notion implicit in the objection, viz. that a true idea must copy its object, is false. It may be replied that some correspondence there must be, since this is what truth means. Without denying this, we should ask leave to define correspondence in our own way, in which it would turn out to be something far removed from resemblance. What exactly we take to be meant by the truth of ideas will be explained in later chapters,[1] and to this account we must refer for the second half of the present answer. We shall see that the only sense of correspondence in which it is essential to truth is the sense in which the partial fulfilment of an end corresponds to the complete fulfilment.

25. (7) Next an objection regarding error. 'Suppose I think of the Persian victory over the Greeks at Plataea. According to the theory before us, the idea is the potentiality of the real thing referred to. Now in fact there never was such an event as a Persian victory over the Greeks at Plataea; though there was a Greek victory over the Persians. The fact that your idea refers to turns out to be non-existent; the potentiality is thus a potentiality of nothing, which means no potentiality at all.'

Royce confronted a similar objection to his own theory of ideas. He answered as follows: 'An error is an error about a specific object, only in case the purpose imperfectly defined by the vague idea at the instant when the error is made, is better defined, is, in fact, better fulfilled, by an object whose determinate character in some wise, although never absolutely, opposes the fragmentary efforts first made to define it.'[2] This, we hold, is the right answer, though perhaps it can be made clearer by restatement. The full character of what one refers to is never known at the time of reference. The discovery of this character, which is the discovery of what one really means, is a gradual process, in which premature attempts at explicitness and detail are bound to suffer later correction. In the case mentioned I clearly meant or referred to a certain battle; but as the character of that which was meant develops before me, I find that it excludes and rejects some of the attributes through which I conceived it. The development of my thought of the object into fuller concreteness, under the dominance of a logic pressing always for completeness and consistency, requires the

---

[1] XXVI and XXVII.
[2] *The World and the Individual*, I. 335.

continuous revising and rejecting of notions entertained along the way.

It may be said that these rejected ideas are still ideas, and, as such, must have their objects. So, in a sense, they must. Bradley's contention seems sound that there are no 'floating ideas', no predicates entertained by thought that are utterly homeless in reality; every distinguishable reference in the thought—to Greeks, to Persians, to a battle, a victory, etc.—is a reference which, if developed, would bring us to something in the real world. The error lies in supposing that these ideas, or any combination of them, tentative formulations as they are of a reality far exceeding our thought of it, would be ratified in their present form when we actually stood before the goal. In the case in question we can see that they would not; the concrete object does not embody all of the characters through which we think it; and this is what the error consists in. Generalizing: error is discrepancy between object and idea; to put it in our own terms, it is discrepancy between the end of thought and a premature formulation of that end, between what we really mean and what we take ourselves to mean; or perhaps better, between what we mean to mean, and what, in ignorance and precipitancy, we do mean.[1]

26. (8) 'You treat the relation between potential and actual as if it were the same as the relation between unrealized and realized purpose. But surely the first is far wider than the second. The seed is a potential flower, the acorn a potential oak, the embryo a potential man; but it would be absurd to hold that these things are unrealized *purposes* to do or be something. All purposes are potentialities, but not all potentialities are purposes. And the difference seems to lie in the addition of consciousness. Purposes are always conscious, while poten-

---

[1] Cf. Descartes's view that error arises from premature action of the will, i.e. from a judgement or assertion made before intelligence has completed its work. For the implications of our view regarding degrees of truth and falsity, see below, Chap. XXVII.

tialities are unconscious more often than not. To speak of thought as alternatively the potentiality of its object and a purpose or impulse to realize this is to describe it too ambiguously and therefore broadly to be of any use.'

If we have described thought broadly, it is because its range is in fact broad in the extreme, so broad that it is impossible to set any sharp boundary at either its upper or lower limit. The present charge is, in effect, that our theory fixes no boundary at the lower limit, and consequently that we allow thought to shade off into a state where there is no verifiable consciousness at all. The charge is true. We can only plead that the facts do not countenance abrupt beginnings. Anyone who would remain close to these facts is here confronted with an unpleasant dilemma: he must either admit that there is unconscious thought or assign the beginnings of consciousness to a lower stage than would be commonly approved. The writer's own inclination is towards the second of these views. But the theory, as here formulated, does not commit one exclusively to either; what it does do is to select as the essence of thought, not something that occurs only at the reflective level, after the manner of the pragmatists, but something capable of presence in appropriate degree far down the scale of life. We conceive the emergence of thought as a very long, slow process, whose beginnings, while the same in principle with what followed, would be unrecognizable as the same except in the light of this principle. There are large advantages in so taking it. We have found in dealing with perception that the structure and many changes of the conscious field were unaccountable without 'dispositions', which, if bodily arrangements, were so far from mechanical that they could co-operate actively with conscious purpose, and if mental, were inaccessible to introspection. We shall see later how the higher reflective processes are similarly aided and guided by influences from outside the focus of consciousness. To confine thought to processes that were definitely and fully conscious would exclude the whole range of these twilight functions. And we have felt them too important to exclude.

Our theory would say that wherever there is true teleological determination, that is, wherever the process of development is determined by that which is coming to be, we have at least the rudiments of a thought process. This does not involve panpsychism, for the panpsychist would ascribe consciousness even to outwardly mechanical processes. But it does involve following the roots of thought far deeper into its biological soil than students of its higher manifestations are prone to go. If they are reluctant to go so far, they can perhaps still make our theory acceptable by a slight revision. They might confine their study to what we should call the potential as it appears in explicit consciousness; and if they were content to conceive of thought in this way, identifying it with the potential *qua* conscious, they would at least have gone far with us. They would have a theory that would relieve them of what they regard as the awkward baggage of subconscious or unconscious ideas, and would still distinguish the thought element in consciousness from others such as sensation, affection, emotion, and volition.[1] By far the larger part of our own study is devoted to thought of this fully conscious and explicit order. But we have deliberately preferred to define the function in such a way that, while inevitably involving difficulties of continuity, it still recognizes that continuity as a fact and en-bles us to deal, not with explicit thought alone, but also with the matrix in which it lives, a matrix of subconscious or quasi-conscious elements without whose co-operation we are convinced that its course is not intelligible.

27. (9) 'But both the relation of potential to actual and the relation of purpose to fulfilment are *temporal* relations, while that of an idea to its object is not. The purpose comes *before* its fulfilment, and by its very nature can only look forward. The acorn must *precede* the oak of which it is the potentiality. But thought need not precede its object. It refers as certainly, easily, and naturally to what is past or present as to the future.'

[1] Though volition involves thought.

We have already seen that against one form of the purposive theory this objection is conclusive. The pragmatist,
conceiving of the idea as an intention in the straightforward
sense, was all at sea when called upon to deal with other
objects than future experiences, such as past events, or timeless
relations;[1] he had either to deny the fact of the reference, or
reconstrue it into a reference to something else, either course
being fatal. Now it must be admitted and emphasized that such
terms as 'purpose' and 'teleology', 'fulfilment', 'end', even
'potential', do carry in ordinary use a reference to time; that
when we apply them, as we have done so freely, to the relation
of idea and object, the suggestion is therefore natural that we
conceive it as a temporal relation; and yet that so to conceive
it is plain nonsense. We have said this unequivocally in dealing
with pragmatism, and we should deserve no sort of sympathy
if we now withdrew it in our own interest. Nor do we have
the slightest intention of withdrawing it. We prefer to take it
as a touchstone of fact with which our theory must be made
consistent if it is to stand.

Now it will clearly not be thus consistent so long as the
terms above cited are taken in their ordinary, i.e. their temporal, connotation. The question therefore is whether they retain
the meaning required when this connotation is stripped off. I
think they do. Indeed one can see on reflection both that the
temporal aspect of the relation is not the essential part of it,
and why it has mistakenly come to be thought so.

Suppose a mathematician is working on a problem. He is
given the general conditions of the solution and he bends his
thoughts to filling the blank in his knowledge. Let us say that
after an effort, long or short, he reaches his end. Here is a
clear enough case of fulfilment of purpose. It is also clear that
the process of fulfilment was a temporal process in which the
end, in the sense of goal, presented itself only at the end, in the
sense of terminus, of a series of steps or approximations. When
the thinker reaches his goal and has the solution in detail before
him, he sees for the first time just what it was that he was

[1] Chap. X, Secs. 21-25.

seeking, and he may see also that unless he had been willing to go through those steps, with their gradual approximation to the goal, he would never have reached it. And of course time was the condition of his advance, without which the movement from stage to stage would have been impossible; the realization of his end was a gradual change, and time is the form of change. But it would be absurd to say that the conditions framing the solution and constituting, in our language, the transcendent meaning of the idea, were themselves merely a stage in this process, whose only being lay in their emergence in the thinker's mind. They were 'there' all along. And plainly at every stage of the process there was a relation between such thought as the thinker had then achieved and this as-yet-unrealized end. *That* relation is *not* a temporal relation. The reason why it is supposed to be is that the only way we have of coming to know the related terms is by passing in time from the one to the other; the temporal passage is so invariably the vehicle through which the relation is presented that we come to think of it as itself belonging to the relation, so that when the nexus of potential and actual, of unrealized and realized purpose is referred to, it always suggests this temporal transition. But if we are to take every relation presented to us in this serial fashion as itself a relation of before and after, or as meaningless without this form, we shall be assigning to the temporal aspect of things, important as this admittedly is, a place it does not deserve. The stages in the evolution of a flower, whether a single specimen or a species, may be considered as the more or less adequate forms of an identity quite independently of their order in time.

Unfortunately we lack names for this relation. As we have seen, the terms most naturally used are impregnated with suggestions of time, and thus ambiguous—'rudimentary', 'advanced', 'growth', 'development', 'purpose', 'realization', 'fulfilment', 'seeking'. Possibly it would be better to manufacture terms *ad hoc*. But even if we had no prejudices about usage—which we have—a great advantage would thereby be forfeited; for after all, it is precisely in these temporal sequences that the relation we have in mind is most commonly and clearly presented. The well-known terms are therefore deliberately adhered to, in spite of their ambiguity. We shall only warn the reader again that when we speak of the relation between idea and object as that of unrealized to realized purpose, we are speaking of what may be called the essential or logical aspect of that relation, *not* of the temporal lapse or process through which we come to know it.[1]

We have now canvassed what are perhaps the most probable objections to our theory. Of course it may be said that our whole explanation is of the *obscurum per obscurius* order, and that what is now called for is an explanation of 'actualizing the potential' and 'realizing an end'. But the meaning we attach to these terms will be best brought out in the course of applying the theory to the various types of idea and to the movement of reflection. Certainly, the path of clarity does not lie through speculations on the meaning of self-development as this appears on the lower levels of life. If there is any truth in our theory, it would reverse the right order of approach to try to construe explicit thought through phenomena at the bottom of the scale. For those phenomena themselves are intelligible only with reference to what they may become. In dealing with thought the right order of procedure is from end to beginning rather than from beginning to end. Hence the way to understand the nature of ideas and the course of the thought process is to study them in those forms where their end is most clearly apparent, indeed to study that end itself if we can get at it. We shall not ignore the more elementary types of idea, but our main concern in the two books that follow will be with the course of explicit reflection and its goal. The study of the higher processes should reflect light upon the earlier; and this should be found particularly true of the study, later attempted, of intellectual and artistic invention.

'Creative or rather plastic mind is that which moves towards ends which are worth reaching, and because they are worth

[1] For the difference between temporal and non-temporal teleology see Bosanquet, 'The Meaning of Teleology', *Proc. of Brit. Acad.*, 1906.

reaching. It gets a better view of them as it advances, not so much because they are nearer as because its own nature as mind is being all along developed by its own activity and its experience, and this development means precisely that its purposes are clearer, more harmonious, and more comprehensive.'[1]

28. For readers not at home among theories of thought, it should perhaps be added that the theory here offered is not new. For a time I ignorantly supposed it was. When I first worked it out in my own mind, I was not aware of following anyone. But as I went on to seek confirmation of it, I saw that something very like it was the common property of metaphysicians of the Platonic turn of mind from the father of the great succession down to Bradley, Bosanquet, and Royce. I hope that the satisfaction derived from this somewhat overwhelming access of support outweighed any passing pricks to the vanity of authorship. And not wishing to presume on endorsements so august, I would not claim more from them than a general expression of sympathy. But there is one of these thinkers whose agreement may be claimed more confidently and in more detail. This is Royce. The theory here advocated is stated in its essential outlines under the heading 'The Internal and the External Meaning of Ideas' in *The World and the Individual*; indeed it is central to his metaphysical system. His development of it is very different from the present one, to be sure; he never applied it, apparently, to the types of idea or the movement of reasoning, and used it only as a step in metaphysical construction. But a few sentences from his work will show how unfounded would be any claim of ours to originality and how firm a support may be derived from him:

'In seeking its object, any idea whatever seeks absolutely nothing but its own explicit, and, in the end, complete, determination as this conscious purpose, embodied in this one way. The complete content of the idea's own purpose is the only object of which the idea can ever take note. This alone is the

[1] Hobhouse, *Development and Purpose*, xxxi.

Other that is sought.' 'The idea is a will seeking its own determination. It is nothing else.' 'To say, "My idea has reference to
a real Being", is to say, "My idea imperfectly expresses, in my
present consciousness, an intention, a meaning, a purpose; and
just this specific meaning is carried out, is fulfilled, is expressed,
by my object".' 'The object is for us simply the completely
embodied will of the idea.'[1]

29. Let us now summarize. This chapter began with a
statement of the conditions, formulated by previous study,
which a theory of the idea should fulfil. It was suggested that
to conceive the idea as a partially realized purpose or as the
object itself *in posse*, might satisfy these conditions. We asked,
first, whether such a view would harmonize with what is
known about the general nature of mind. There was no agreement, we discovered, as to how this nature was to be conceived, but the main issue lay between two principles for
explaining it, the teleological and the mechanical. By examining
certain central activities of mind, we saw that teleology was as
clearly necessary as mechanism was inadequate, nor was there
any compromise between them that would cover the ground.
So far, then, the general nature of mind appeared to be in
harmony with our theory. We then asked whether a similar
harmony was to be discovered with the nature of knowledge.
We found that in every act of knowledge a double aim was discernible, the aim at satisfying a special impulse, and the aim at
apprehending independent reality. In some degree, every instance
of knowledge realizes both ends coincidently. How explain such
coincidence? To suppose it the product of chance or miracle
would be to abandon the inquiry. The account we offered was
that any fulfilment we may attain of the immanent end is also
a partial realization of the transcendent end, and that what
satisfied the intellect *was* so far the real. This account we found
to agree with what was most acceptable, and to clear up what
seemed least acceptable, in the accounts examined earlier.
Nor did the most obvious difficulties of the theory seem, on

[1] *The World and the Individual*, Vol. I. 329, 332, 353, 355.

consideration, decisive. The disparities between idea and object in quality, in uniqueness, and in harmony with desire, turned out to be less than ultimate disparities. The theory did not commit us, as it seemed to do at first, to saying that mind as a whole seeks identification with objects, or that intelligence may be reduced to will. Instead of colliding with our conceptions of truth and error, the theory seemed to accord with these rather strikingly. It did lead us to look for the roots of thought at a surprisingly low level, but this, with its admitted difficulties, was in any case inevitable. And the final difficulty, that idea and object were not connected temporally, disappeared when it was seen that a non-temporal teleology was a perfectly clear notion.

There are many who will feel that the true test of such a theory, however, lies less in its success in running the gauntlet of speculative objections than in its power to apply itself illuminatingly to the various types of idea. In the chapters that immediately follow the main types of idea are considered. We believe that the theory will be fortified by such a review. Nevertheless we shall try to study these varieties of idea for their own sake.

CHAPTER XV

THE ELEMENTARY TYPES OF IDEA

1. We have proposed to reconceive the relation of an idea to its object in terms of the relation of a purpose to its end. When we say that an idea is *of* an object, we mean that it is the sort of experience which, if its immanent end were attained, would *be* that object. The relation is not one of mere identity, nor of copy and original, nor of effect and cause, nor of means and end; it is rather the relation of potential and actual, of something partially realized to the same thing fully realized.

Now if this suggestion is sound, ideas might be justly classified according to any one of several principles. They might be classified, in the first place, according to the objects in which they would be realized if fulfilled; and such a classification would probably end in the sort of attempt that Aristotle made in the listing of the categories, the attempt to enumerate the ultimately different kinds of thing that it is possible for us to think of. Or secondly, ideas might be classified, not according to their ends or objects, but according to the degree of their development, that is, according to the degree in which, given the same end, they afforded knowledge of that end. Or thirdly, they might be classified according to the order of their appearance in either racial or individual growth. The first of these ways would too easily make us forget the tentative and developing things that ideas are now in a discussion of their ultimate or penultimate objects. The second and the third both fall within our interest, for we have seen that thought involves in its very essence a kind of conation, in which something imperfectly developed becomes more fully itself as it succeeds. So we shall have to combine in some fashion both these methods. It is impossible to do so strictly, for the historical order is not always the same as the order of increasing grasp. Nevertheless the history of individual growth, to which for convenience we shall chiefly confine ourselves, displays a fairly continuous development in grasp; with however many exceptions in individual cases, the two orders in the main coincide.

In discussing the types of idea, then, we shall begin with (I) the idea that is involved implicitly in perception, examining at the same time its way of breaking loose from sense and establishing itself as an idea in its own right. We shall then look at (II) the nature of our first free ideas; then at (III) the true place of the image in thinking; and finally, in the chapters that follow, at those two ideas that are of most importance in the higher reaches of mind, (IV) the abstract idea and (V) the general idea.

2. (I) If the mind grows in the way intimated in the last chapter we should expect no immense leaps forward and no sharply marked stages, but a smooth continuous ripening. This expectation is fulfilled. We saw that between sensation and perception no hard line can be drawn; nor is there any such line between perception and conception. When the mind is ready to pick the fruit of free ideas, it finds that they have already so ripened within the atmosphere of perception that they fall of their own accord. If we look closely at those of our ideas that still hang to the perceptual tree, we can distinguish three more or less clearly marked species.

(1) First there are the ideas arrived at through what was called, after some debate, 'implicit inference'. We do not as a rule think expressly of the other side of an apple or the inside of a box, or the under side of a table; we form no explicit ideas of the weight of an orange; we do not spend time speculating whether the chair, if we choose to sit in it, will hold us up; whether water will wet and fire burn. Yet our grasp of what *is* presented to us, and our behaviour toward it, is as if these other aspects were before us sensibly. What is sensed is grasped as belonging to a whole, even though the outlying parts of this whole are not sensed themselves. But though these outlying parts are not sensed, neither do they remain for us mere nothings. The thought or 'acceptance' of them falls somewhere in

the extensive limbo of the implicit, a limbo admitting of all degrees between total oblivion and the clear explicitness of focal attention.

3. (2) Secondly, there are features that resemble those just mentioned in being grasped implicitly, but differ from them in falling within the field where discrimination would be possible. 'A child in trundling his hoop has an explicit or an implicit thought of it at will; and the explicit thought includes implicit thoughts of the circle, of velocity, and acceleration; but it is with difficulty that the child is gradually brought to an explicit thought of these.'[1] It would be easy to say that in perceiving his rolling hoop, the child must have ideas of these features, since if they were removed from the object before him, it would lose its character and fall away into something nameless. In a sense this is true; indeed the highest intelligence also remains rooted in perception. The abstractest ideas that enter a mind like Newton's are ideas and attributes and relations belonging to objects perceived hourly—number, equality, motion, rate of motion. And to scorn closeness to sense perception, as not quite compatible with acuteness or depth in thinking, is a mark less of depth than of the misunderstanding of what is the proper material for thought. Nevertheless, it is at best only an implicit idea of such features that is attained on the perceptual level.

'When an infant stares at four lights in a row, and sees them blown out one by one, it may have no thought of time, number, position, or cause, though these are all before its eyes.'[2] The categories, in both the Aristotelian and the Kantian senses, are there in perception from the beginning, though we repeat that what is first in order of nature may be last in the order of explicit knowledge. Thus the conception of time is one of the most elusive and difficult conceptions that metaphysicians are called upon to handle, yet in its perceptual form every child

[1] Mitchell, *Structure and Growth of the Mind*, 252.
[2] *Ibid.*, 234.

uses it daily. The chief characteristic of that form is that the idea is still bound up with a perceived whole undistinguishably; the pure time that the metaphysician isolates, or seeks to isolate, is still immersed in matter, giving indeed, a structure to this matter, as the skeleton does to the flesh, but so intimately enmeshed in this that the mind cannot penetrate to its hard and clean-cut outline. We shall see the means by which this penetration is achieved when we come to examine abstract and general ideas. Meanwhile we must admit that a child is already using the thought of time when at a certain hour he expects the dinner bell, when he tries to prevent the mention of bed-time, even when he cuts a corner in play. If he comes later, as is the lot of a few, to reflect on the nature of time itself, his effort will be directed to making explicit, and freeing from irrelevancy, precisely that thought of time which he has used implicitly from the beginning.

So of the thought of space. We suggested long ago that the attempt to derive the idea of space from the experience of what is spaceless is futile; our experience of space is as old as we are. But space as it first appears to us is so inextricably one with what fills it that the clear distinction of the two comes only with development and effort. Birds have a marvellous sense of direction and distance, but one would hardly find in their little heads abstract ideas of space. Higher apes, in their measuring of distance, give more sign, as we have seen, of selective attention to the spatial aspects of things, but probably their grasp of it is purely perceptual, a grasp of this visible and traversible expanse, not of spatial relations as such. Indeed it was probably long after geometrical devices had been used for laying out and dividing land that the notion ever suggested itself of abstracting and studying these for their own sake. And here the history of the individual mind recapitulates in broad fashion the history of the race. Triangles at first appearance are probably nothing more than particular bits of white paper cut out idly with the scissors for their diverse and amusing looks. Even for the schoolboy, the chalk-lines on the blackboard invade the triangle's essence. When he has seen that these are irrelevant, and has risen to the thought of space and its relations as such, he probably still habitually thinks of it as a stretch or expanse *of* something, if only blue sky or darkness, and must make an effort to realize that this filling too is adventitious, and that space is simply a relation of systematized outsideness, by itself neither sensible nor imaginable. Of course, most minds never come near such a conception, as indeed for all ordinary purposes it is unnecessary that they should. We think space before we think *of* it, and we think of it in a matrix of irrelevancy long before we think of it pure. And if the first of these stages is enough, with its merely implicit grasp, to guide a swallow in its perchings and swoopings, if it will serve for the most delicate flickerings and caromings of a billiard player, it is small wonder if, with most of us and for the most part, space remains to the end in the charge of implicit thought.

Time and space are only examples taken arbitrarily. What has been said about them could be said of all manner of qualities and relations present in perception, but grasped only implicitly.

4. (3) The third species of perceptual idea may be thought by some to be a mere illusion. It is not concerned with the sensible complement of the given, like the first type, nor with an undiscriminated feature of the given, like the second, but with the setting or background of what is given. In first meeting a stranger, one may be struck at once with certain oddities of feature and manner that seem eccentric or even comic. Suppose that in time the eccentric stranger becomes an intimate friend. Does our perception of the irregular face, queer nose, and big ears remain unaffected by what in years we have come to learn of him? Surely not. Consciousness does not grow by juxtaposing new blocks to unaffected old ones, but by inner transformations and total suffusions. Even the look of things is affected by increasing knowledge and altered feeling, and as we recall our first impression of the familiar face, we may be surprised and amused at the difference. The present impression is what it is because it is imbedded in the funded knowledge of years, and obscurely flooded with habitual feeling. But, of course, all that knowledge and feeling are not now explicitly present. Hence the paradox: focal experience is what it is because of a great fringe of retained experience, but the retained experience, when we come to look for it, is conspicuously not there. It was in part this paradox which forced us long ago into a theory of dispositions.[1] The considerations that drove us to that theory need not be rehearsed. Suffice it to say that we had to conclude a scholar's funded capital to be an effective part of himself, even when he was not recalling it. We must thus admit a third kind of perceptual idea, an idea that is present only in the form of a disposition.

5. Dispositions are treacherous things. But it is gratifying to see how a theory we were earlier driven to by the independent study of perception can now be assimilated and illuminated by our theory of ideas, indeed how all three types of perceptual idea fall readily into place if that theory is accepted. The theory, as we have seen, is a reflection in the field of ideas of a special conception of mind and knowledge. According to that conception, every act of mind, and therefore every act of knowing, is an act of will, in the sense that it is a movement of expansion or self-realization of that which before was only potential. What it really is that thus expresses itself we can tell only by what it becomes, by watching it move toward its immanent end. And while we have not as yet sketched that end with any fullness, it is easy enough to see the general direction in which the quest of knowledge is moving. The impulse to know is an impulse at once to widen and to order the field of experience, to give it that special completeness and coherence which will satisfy theoretic desire. To attain a thorough knowledge of anything is at least to gather all its factors into a single whole in which their relations are clearly grasped. Now, perceiving is one of the forms in which the impulse to know expresses itself.

[1] Chap. IV, Sec. 16 ff.

Hence it shows the same nisus of the mind toward completeness and order which this impulse shows everywhere. But for reasons that will perhaps remain beyond our grasp, the energy of the impulse is limited and its path severely hedged by conditions. One of these conditions, we saw long ago, is a law of parsimony. The mind's focus is small. However much, in bursts of energy, it may drive back its margins, they remain contracted at the best. But we have now seen that the impulse to development is of the essence of mind, and hence that mind is never exhausted by what at any moment it has explicitly become. Below the narrow crater of explicitness are volumes of potentialities pressing toward actualization in consciousness, and approximating it in many degrees. If now we keep all these facts before us—the struggle for expansion and order, the law of economy, the mind's complex capacities, and the probability that each of these is realized in degree—the structure of perception becomes more intelligible. From the very beginning, when attention lights upon the nucleus of qualities, the mind seeks to invest it with a context and develop it into a whole. Nor is this development ever capricious, any more than an acorn is capricious when it imposes upon the matter supplied to it a characteristic form. The expansion of the given remains relevant to the immanent end of the movement, theoretic, aesthetic, or practical; it is notorious, for example, that strategist and artist make different things of the same landscape. But by the law of economy, perhaps we should say by the very conditions of finititude, all that the mind seeks to be cannot come at once to explicit realization. What would complete the fragmentary given into the whole that is sought for must remain in the region of unrealized or half-realized potentialities. When we look at a friend, the very perception of him as a friend means that the nisus toward completion has been at work, for what we see, taken by itself (an impracticable proviso, by the way), would be a meaningless fragment. The needed complement of this fragment is really part of the mind of the moment, pressing toward explicitness; as are also in their degree those ideas of our friend's special traits, and of his place in the animate world, which in this case would form our second and third types of perceptual idea. Thus all the characteristically perceptual ideas fall into their places if viewed as factors in an attempt by the mind, made under limiting conditions, to affirm itself in a whole of explicit knowledge.

6. These ideas are all sense-bound and they are shared by the human with the animal mind. They are not part of what is given, but they are so integral with it and dependent on it, that once the given is removed they are unable to stand alone, and vanish with it. But what we commonly mean by ideas is something different, namely the thought of an object when that object is not given, and when the thought is independent of what does chance to be given. We must now ask, How do such ideas break loose from perception? What is it that leads us to think explicitly of the absent? How do we come to distinguish between what is actually given and what exists for us only in ideas? One answer will serve for all three questions: What liberates ideas is conflict. When there is a conflict between an implicit idea and what is given in fact, the idea tends to force itself into explicitness and into recognition *as* an idea. This conflict may be of various kinds, of which by far the most important are two, the conflicts (1) between fact and perceptual expectation, and (2) between fact and need.

(1) A child has found again and again in caressing his puppy that a wagging tail shows good humour. As yet he has not thought separately of the sign and the signified; he simply sees the puppy as pleased. Let us suppose, now, that he transfers his attentions to the cat, and, seeing a wagging tail, takes the cat also as pleased. The return he now gets for his caresses is the shock of a scratch. What will be in his mind when he approaches the cat later? In the light of his experience, it is not hard to conjecture. By reason of his dealings with the puppy, the wagging tail would naturally carry with it the perceptual idea of the animal as pleased. But the shock received from the cat leaves him uncertain. He hesitates, and with his hesitation

begin reflection and wisdom. He cannot take the cat as pleased, for so taking it is inhibited by the counter tendency left by the scratch. He cannot take it as ill-disposed, for the long line of welcomed caresses have left their witness against that suggestion. Thus the difference is forced upon him between what is actually presented in sense and what offers itself only tentatively and against protest. This latter is set aside as a region of unrealized possibilities, of mere ideas as opposed to facts. Henceforth the inquiry must be more discerning; within the perceived 'animal-wagging-tail', he must discriminate different features to which the rival ideas may be respectively attached. The defeat of perceptual expectation, with the demand that results from it for a nicer accommodation between the given and the ideal, is one of the two main springs of reflection.

Of course, the power to weigh ideas against each other in the light of fact implies that an idea can be held in mind after the fact has rejected it. Here lies a chief distinction between the animal mind and the human. In the human mind, the theoretic impulse has reached a far greater strength, and instead of merely discarding an idea when this is repulsed by fact, retains it and seeks a place for it elsewhere. The intelligent child who is scratched does not simply abandon the thought of his pet as pleased, but according to his degree of interest, keeps it and ponders what it is in the fact which would make it truly apply.

'If we descend in the scale no further than to dogs', says Bradley, 'we are struck by the absence of theoretical curiosity. Let them see an appearance to be not what it seemed, and instantly it becomes a nonentity. An idea, we may say, is the shadow of an object; and that to a savage is another kind of object, but to the dog it is the thing or just nothing at all. The dog has not entered on that process of reflection which perhaps has not led to any very sure result. When his heart, like ours, is baffled and oppressed, and gives matter to his brain it has no strength to cope with, he can neither send his hopes into another world than this, nor repeat like a charm, and dream that he believes, that appearances may be nothing to a soul which feels them. I do not know the formula which would prove to his mind a satisfactory solution of his practical troubles; but his system of logic, if he had one, would be simple; for it would begin, I am sure, and would end with this axiom, "What is smells, and what does not smell is nothing".'[1]

7. (2) The conflict between fact and expectation is not the only conflict that may liberate ideas; they may be freed also by the conflict between what is given and what is needed. Hunger as a rule passes on to quench itself in actual satisfaction. But let us suppose the impulse blocked; what will happen? It will tend to realize itself in idea, though there will remain a painful discrepancy between this merely ideal satisfaction and the stubborn facts of want. Similarly anger and sex jealousy tend to pass into abortive ideal satisfactions which are flouted by facts insubordinate to our wills. Again the violence of the contrast forces upon us the distinction between two realms, and again our advantage over the animal mind is signal. When an animal seeks restlessly to satisfy the promptings of hunger or sex, there is no reason to suppose that it knows what it is looking for. It is so made that these feelings prompt it to act in a certain way until the restlessness is quelled; if it was able to hold the absent end before it, it could also develop this ideally into various means of attainment, and its behaviour would be less random and groping. But that ideal satisfaction which in the animal mind is either never attained at all, or on collision with fact is dropped instantly, can be retained and developed by man even to the point of disease. And the contrast between fact and ideal, besides being a principal source of reflection, is also the source of explicit will. It is because man can retain his idea of an absent good, and construct ideal bridges between it and his present state, that he is able to convert his life from a continued anxious adventure into something like an ordered march.

8. II. What are our first free ideas like? It is very hard to say; we have long been using such ideas before we begin to

---

[1] *Logic*, I. 31; cf. also pp. 29–30, and *Mind*, XII (1887), 373; Ward, *Psych. Princ.*, 187–8.

examine them for their own sakes, and then they have lost
their first innocence. It is even hard to tell when a free idea
has really appeared. The distinction between free and tied
ideas, like other distinctions in mental growth, is one of degree.
A child and a dog, let us suppose, fare forth together to a
certain corner of the yard, where a strange dog suddenly
appears, and there is a dog-fight. When the companions return
to the same spot later, what goes on in their respective minds?
The dog may sniff, and look about suspiciously, and bristle at
a sound; it seems as though he were remembering the invader;
is he? If this means entertaining an explicit idea of the
earlier incident, there is no good reason to think he is, for his
behaviour may be explained without it. As a result of his past
experience, this corner has a new quality for him; he perceives
it as a dangerous spot; and perhaps his perception specifies the
danger as a canine one, though to turn his expectation into
words is bound to give it too great a sharpness. What about
the child's experience? It *may* be of the same kind. He may
have established a connection between this corner and being
terrified, such that when he goes there he finds it merely a
terrifying place. Indeed he may even fall short of this, and
simply feel unaccountably afraid when he is in this spot, without
any perceptual connection of the spot and the terror. But again
he may, and, of course, eventually does, go far beyond his
companion in the retention of the earlier experience. Superiority here means that what he experienced earlier presents
itself with (1) greater explicitness, (2) greater definiteness, and
(3) greater independence of what is now given.

(1) By being more explicit we mean that it is brought nearer
to the focus of attention. One of the chief defects of a merely
perceptual intelligence, we have said, is that it cannot analyse;
it cannot isolate from the place itself its character of fearsome-
ness, and concentrating on this, attach it to its proper subject.
This isolating and making explicit occurs when any type of
perceptual idea is converted into a free idea. And greater
explicitness is connected (2) with greater definiteness, though
of course the two are not the same thing. This definiteness

may be present in any degree. The child's first thought of the invading dog may be of nothing more specific than a dangerous something connected somehow with this spot; if he is a little further advanced, it will be of a dangerous animal, or of a black and dangerous animal, or of a black dangerous long-haired dog, until in time he commands a memory which would supply him effortlessly with a pretty complete description of the invader. We have seen that if animals ever do break through into free ideas, these certainly remain very vague; those of a human mind may rapidly reach a high degree of definition.

Along with the greater explicitness and definiteness of the free idea, goes (3) its greater independence which, once more, is a matter of degree. The child, like the animal, is at first dependent on sensory cues. If he thinks about food, it is because he is hungry; if he thinks about the dog, it is because he comes to the same place again, or because seeing another dog reminds him. With mental advance, his dependence on sensory cues grows less and less, and a very slight resemblance between what is given and what went before will summon the past event into memory. The amount of resemblance needed depends on native stupidity. There are some minds that find it difficult, their lives through, to break out of the perceptual circle, to remember what they did the day before yesterday, to plan what they will do to-morrow, or to grasp without effort anything that is not either directly before them or immediately connected with this. There are others, certain poets for example, to whom experiences that would to most persons be relatively meaningless are rich in suggestion through remote and subtle analogies. There are others again, such as philosophers at their professional task, who have no need of perception except to provide ultimate raw material; their train of ideas is so largely independent of sense that it seems to move in a different world from the region around them. Socrates, standing fixed in thought through a bitter night while his companions in arms camped about him to watch the performance out;[1] Archimedes, lost in his circles on the floor, until the Roman

---

[1] *Symposium*, 220.

besiegers broke in and cut him finally off from them; Hegel, finishing the *Phänomenologie* with the guns of Jena in his ears[1]— these tales have no doubt been improved in the re-telling, but their verisimilitude is enough.[2]

Once an entrance has been effected into the world of ideas, the power to move about in it is partly a matter of knowledge and practice. But the original power to enter it is a matter of native differences between man and man, and man and animal, whose results can be easily enough described, but whose causes are buried as deep as those of intelligence itself. In the end we have not the slightest notion why it is that the child at a certain age bursts out into free ideas, while the dog who has been growing along with him must remain a prisoner within perception. In the minds of both of them alike expectation and fact are in conflict, but in one of them the conflict gives release and in the other only frustration. Nevertheless, we can see pretty clearly what the agencies are which, once the free idea has appeared, serve to fix it in independence. Of these, three are of especial importance.

9. (1) The first of these gives what may be called the 'final cause' of the retention and development of free ideas. This is the interest in knowing. Now the interest in knowing is an interest in increasing and ordering our experience. It is thus suggested that the interest which seizes and holds the first free idea does so, not for the sake of the idea itself, but for the sake of the part it may play in inference; and this suggestion we accept as sound. But it seems doubly paradoxical, for we ordinarily suppose that practical interests precede theoretical,

---

[1] Rosenkranz, *Hegels Leben*, 228, tries to appraise the story.

[2] Sometimes as a result of disease the grasp of something through free ideas is destroyed, while the grasp through tied ideas remains. Stout cites a case from Charcot, of a patient who could no longer imagine colours, but could still sort wools, and from Bateman of a patient who had lost his memory for the names of things, but could at once recognize these names when offered.—*Analytic Psychology*, II. 5.

and that single ideas precede inference. These views are by no means mere mistakes. The truth here is tangled enough to require some effort if it is to be followed clearly.

The use of missiles, shelters, and rafts was probably in the first instance accidental, but their continued employment was not so; it implied a rude power of taking thought. Unquestionably the main stimulus to such thought was practical need. The deliberate use of missiles, for example, would be for food or for self-protection; of shelters, for comfort and safety; of rafts, for help in pursuit or escape. Take the use of missiles. Early men presumably threw things at each other in play much as apes do now, and it is not unlikely that the missiles occasionally took disastrous effect. Let us suppose that the pressure of hunger later drove the same men to the thought of prey. Such a thought of itself would be entirely useless, and for this reason was probably dropped habitually for a long time after it first put in an appearance. It first became of value when instead of lying dead it came alive, and began to spawn and proliferate, when the thought of the prostrate prey, for instance, developed, through its identity with the prostrate victim of the missile, into the thought of using a missile as a means. This is what we have in mind when we say that the free idea is retained for the part it may play in inference.

But it may be said that, granting this, our aim in inferring at all is purely practical; it is merely to construct a bridge by which a present want, in this instance hunger, may pass to its satisfaction. But this does not put the case adequately. It may be admitted at once that the dominant want *is* practical, and that to rank the primitive desire to know as equally strong with the desire for food would be absurd. Nevertheless we have seen that the only way to understand the aims and capacities of a growing mind is to read them in the light of what they may become. And it is clear that the interest in knowing does grow into the sort of interest that develops an idea into a system for the sake of this system itself, that is, for the sake of the insight supplied in it. This mature theoretical interest does not, of course, spring full-fledged into existence; it must develop for a long period under the wing of the far more intense and insistent interests of the life of action. But the fact that it is subordinate is no reason for denying that it is distinct. And what is suggested here is that this germinating theoretical interest, which is able to use the idea as a key to unlock a system, is a principal ground of difference between brute and human. That difference does not lie in the intensity with which the same practical end is sought; the starving man is as much interested in food as the starving brute. The true difference is rather this, that while the brute must proceed by endless trial and error, man can divert some of the stream of energy into the employment of theory; he conquers by dividing *himself*. The caged animal can only claw his bars fruitlessly. The caged man spends less energy in violence and more in taking thought, and is sooner out.

This difference in method continually shows itself even in advanced human life. To surrender wholly to one's desire for anything is usually a bad way to get it. The persons, who when lost in the woods or caught in a theatre fire, are notoriously unlikely to come out, are the ones who 'lose their heads' and surrender madly to the impulse to escape. Distinguished baseball players, when a crisis grows particularly tense, often 'fan out' abjectly; anxiety to convert another often robs us of the arguments by which we might succeed; discretion is the better part of valour. In all these cases, the dominant interest is practical; but this interest, if it is to be successful, must admit a concomitant minor interest in the facts. And this minor interest, awaking spontaneously within the circle of the practical, fixes the free idea in its independence by making it a factor in inference.

10 (2) Once the idea has emerged, it is further fixed by a co-operative process in which success, repetition, and forgetting play the chief parts. These factors should be kept distinct. If an idea has been used successfully, then when a crisis like that which produced it occurs again, the idea itself will probably occur again; and this repetition of an idea 'stamps it in', or puts it more fully within our command. And it may thus appear that success and repetition really reduce to a single factor, that success has to work through repetition. But this would be a mistake. Sometimes they even compete against each other, and it is worth noting that when they do, success usually succeeds. When we are finding our way through a city, which turn is more likely to be chosen, one that has been repeatedly taken with bad results or another that has been taken only once but with good results? Undoubtedly the latter. This familiar little fact has not been enough reflected on. It goes very deep into human nature, and is inexplicable, I think, on any sort of mechanist or behaviourist principle. For it means that our selection of ideas or reactions is governed not merely by association, or by the wearing of nervous channels, but also by their relevance to an end, in short that no process of learning can be accounted for if the control of purpose is left out. Thus a free idea that has actually helped us to the end, theoretical or practical, that it was called into being to secure, has taken one step on the way to making itself a permanent tool.

But though success tends to fix a free idea apart from repetition, repetition greatly helps. The laws of habit as statements of tendency apply of course to the mind as well as to the body, though so far as intelligence is genuinely at work, habit may at any moment be overridden. Learning to use free ideas is rather like learning to ride a bicycle, in which, if one can manage the first hundred yards, one can go on for miles. It is hard for us to realize, now that the use of ideas has become so easy and constant, what a feat it is for a child to form any clear notion of an event that happened six months ago. Facility comes with practice, here as elsewhere. If the city boy seems to use ideas with more ease and variety than the country boy, the difference may lie not at all in his native intelligence, but solely in what a more varied environment has exacted from him.

The material for free ideas is supplied by past experience, and theoretically anything that we have experienced may be thought of again. But the fact is that relatively few of the events that have happened to us are ever thought of later, and that much of the matter they supply to us is never again explicitly used. What determines the selection? The main factor is practical need. But this is supplemented by a combined process of repeating and forgetting. Suppose that to-day I have a series of experiences, A, B, C, D, gained in a visit to a cathedral. If to-morrow something recalls the cathedral, I shall find that many of the details are already gone, even if I make an effort to rehearse the visit. If on the day following I again think of the cathedral, I shall find that my thought is once more a selection, working this time upon the matter thought of the day before, which had been 'stamped in' by that process of recall. It is thus a selection within a selection. Time puts the stuff of experience through a series of sieves. And the point of interest here is that what passes the sieves, namely those objects and events of our past which we can now think of, and the matter we now use in thinking of anything, is largely determined by chance repetitions. Unable to spend the present in rehearsing the past, we leave the selection to accident. On my visit to the cathedral I see for the first time a clerestory. If something challenges me to think of it next week, it can probably still present itself in idea, and a very few repetitions will place it permanently at call. But if it is not again called up for years, it is probably lost. What parts of our experience shall provide the matter for free ideas thus depends largely on which are reinforced by fortuitous repetitions, and which are allowed to fall into oblivion through neglect.

11. (3) The third great agency in fixing free ideas is language, which calls for a more circumstantial mention. By 'language' here is meant not lang age generally, but the use of names. The stage of development at which names are given to things comes after a long evolution in which language expresses without designating. Most of the higher animals have a variety, some of them an immense variety, of sounds that could be used to designate things if only they had the power to think of them. Since they lack this power, their language expresses rather feelings than ideas. It is made up of interjections, complaints, warnings, and entreaties. Thus a dog has a great gamut of expressions for the various degrees of rage, pain, and eagerness, and yet strictly he never speaks a word. How words or names develop out of this stage of mere expression, whether the 'bow-wow' theory is right about it, or the 'pooh-pooh' theory, or the 'goo-goo' theory or the 'ding-dong' theory, or whether, as seems more probable, they all hold, though of different elements in language, it is happily needless to discuss. The one important fact for us is that somewhere in the dimly lit period between higher animal and lower man, sounds made merely from impulse came to be associated with things experienced at the time, and hence to be used as signs of them. With the achievement of this use, the mind gained an immense and manifold aid in its struggle after the mastery of ideas. This aid took various forms.

12. (i) 'The spoken word', says Stout, 'shows in a high degree the reproductive efficacy characteristic of a percept.'[1] When we perceive an orange or a table, the implicit ideas involved in the percept are tied so closely to what we see that we take them along with the sensations and without an effort. The vividness and steadiness of the sensations communicate themselves to the idea. Now words do for the free idea what sensations do for the tied idea; they give it an anchorage in the sensible which prevents its immediately drifting off. We are all more at home among percepts than we are among ideas, and even those who are most practised in the business of thinking find words necessary if their thought is to have its fullest clearness and steadiness. Anyone may prove this of his own thought by a simple experiment. Let him try to think of something, particularly of something abstract, without using the regular word for it, and then let him note the change when that word comes. Let him think of what Darwin stands for, or

---

[1] *Analytic Psychology*, II. 195.

of Lincoln's attitude toward his critics, or of the peculiar
qualities of Bunyan's or Johnson's style, and then note the
stronger and steadier grasp when he can pass to 'the evolution
theory', 'magnanimity', 'simplicity', 'ponderousness'. The
coming of these words somehow precipitates the mist, turns
flimsy and floating mental paper into hard coin. It 'gives to
airy nothings a local habitation and a name'. Not that it gives
sensible body to the ideas themselves, for in these cases neither
the things thought of, nor the thought of them, can take wholly
sensible form. But it does so virtually by bringing ideas within
the perceptual sphere of influence. By infection from the word,
which is as sensible as a stone, the idea catches the word's
vividness and fixity.[1]

13. There is a danger here. It is true that a word is commonly
learned by association with its object, and hence it may be
supposed that when we now use words in thinking, we first
form the thought of the object and this calls up the word
associated with it. But the connection is far more intimate; the
word and the definite meaning come together, just as sensation
and meaning come together when we perceive. The same holds
of words and feeling.

'It would be truer to say that the expression *is* the completed
feeling; for the feeling is not fully felt till it is expressed, and
in being expressed it is still felt, but in a different way. What
the act of expression does is to fix and distinguish it finally;
it then, and then only, becomes *a* determinate feeling. In the
same way the consciousness which we express when we have
found the "right word" is not the same as our consciousness
before we found it; so that it is not strictly correct to call the
word the expression of what we meant before we found it. This
remains true of more developed forms of expression; and

---

[1] 'Ruskin, in his *Fors Clavigera*, relates that the sight of the word
"crocodile" used to frighten him when a child so much that he could
not feel at ease again till he had turned over the page on which it
occurred.'—Ward, *Psych. Prin.*, 296, note.

following it out, we may say that what is absolutely unexpressed and inexpressible is nothing.'[1]

'When in grief, or joy, or love, one reads or recalls the work of a great master, and says, "That is just what I feel", the words have made a difference, have they not?'[2] 'The poem is not the translation of the poet's state of mind, for he does not know till he has said it either what he wants to say or how he shall say it.'[3] 'The little girl had the making of a poet in her who, on being told to be sure of her meaning before she spoke, said, "How can I know what I think till I see what I say?"'[4] This is not to hold, in the manner of some behaviourists, that the thought *is* the word, a suggestion that is wrecked upon the simple consequence that we should then have totally different thoughts when we speak German and say 'sollen' and when we speak English and say 'ought'. But it does imply that a thought unexpressed remains as truncated or abortive as the plan of a painter that does not reach the canvas. What Croce has made a commonplace about the artistic idea holds of all ideas, that we do not fully know what our idea is till we express it, and hence that idea and expression are indivisible.

14. (ii) Along with the greater vividness and fixity that are bestowed on ideas by words, there goes a greater *distinctness*. We have seen in discussing the second type of perceptual idea that in ordinary perceiving we use many ideas, of space, time, number, and so on, which are not as yet singled out from each other. If they are to be converted into free ideas, this singling out must be achieved. And to achieve it is practically impossible without associating the different ideas with names that are

---

[1] R. L. Nettleship, *Philosophical Lectures*, I. 130. The language of p. 138 puts, in a general way, our own view of thinking: 'all thinking proper is the consciousness of the coming of the self to itself; the self *expresses* itself.'

[2] Mitchell, *Structure and Growth of the Mind*, 373.

[3] Alexander, *Beauty and Other Forms of Value*, 59.

[4] Wallas, *The Art of Thought*, 106.

sensibly distinct. Here again name and idea are not the same, and for a given idea, broadly speaking, it is unimportant what word is chosen. What is important is that the differences in the ideas, which at first we find it hard to grasp, should correspond to plain differences in sensation, which we find it easy to grasp. A child who would find the difference between three and four quite beyond him, if called on to think them apart from instances, finds the distinction easy enough if it is presented through coloured balls. Primitive tribes are reported who are able to handle numbers as far as their fingers will go, but are lost when these digits fail them. Now words, like fingers, give a quasi-sensible discreteness to ideas which, without them, the feeble powers of the early mind could not distinguish. They differ in length, sound, and formation, and even if alike in these, they may differ in pitch, like Chinese words. And once a fresh idea has had plainly affixed to it one of these sensible tags, it has been really won for the first time.

> 'To give a name', says Bosanquet, 'is for civilized thought the first step in knowledge.' 'The limitations of popular nomenclature form the limitations of popular observation. When we are brought face to face with a scientific classification and the terminology it involves, we are astounded at the blindness in which we had contentedly been living. Every yellow ranunculus we called a buttercup, every myosotis a forget-me-not, every large umbellifer a hemlock; not merely as an epithet, but because we really saw no difference.' 'To give names that endure is with few exceptions the prerogative of genius. The number of terms which we inherit from Plato and Aristotle is among the most striking proofs of the immense advance which they won for the human intellect. These two great minds mapped out the world of knowledge in its essential features much as we have it before us now, and gave its main divisions the names which they still retain.'[1]

15. (iii) Now distinction, as an intellectual process, never occurs alone. The truth is, that any account of the advance of thought which represents mental processes or kinds of idea as

[1] *Logic*, I. 7–9.

emerging successively, like segments added to a line, is bound
to be false. That may be the way a pavement is laid, but it is
not the way a tree grows, or a mind. If a mechanical analogy
is wanted, we might better say that the rise of thought is like
the rise of a gas-tank, in which all the parts of an extended
structure rise together, and not from non-existence, but from
submergence. There is a sense, as we have seen, in which the
very highest mental process, inference, is present in the
beginnings of perception. We have made no attempt to distinguish between an earlier use of ideas and the later making
of judgement, for there really is no distinction; to have an
idea *is* to judge from the very first, not explicitly or determin-
ately, perhaps, but still to judge.[1] And so here in naming
something, we do not merely distinguish it from something
else, and then later discover a likeness between it and what is
distinguished from it, and then later still classify the two
things as different kinds of the same. Distinction, identification,
and classification all occur together; they are indeed, the same
process looked at from different points of view; and they are
all present in a more or less germinal way in the first use of
language. The growth of mind consists less in an addition of
faculties and processes than in a fuller and more explicit
functioning of processes that are at work already. And what is
suggested here is that when the child first intelligently applies
to his pet the word 'dog', he is grasping a double identity in
difference which, however vaguely, fixes the dog's place in a
scale of classification. This may appear an alarming framework
to saddle on the helpless mind of a child. But it is simpler than
it seems.

Suppose that, with the help of a word, a child has formed
a free idea. He remembers the dog that frightened him at the
end of the garden, or he notes that the local Santa Claus is
dressed in bright red. In thinking 'dog' or 'red', we are suggest-

[1] Thus in distinguishing types of idea we are not contrasting these
as ideas with later judgements, for judgement is present throughout.
On this point the errors of ordinary logic books, and of some extraordinary ones, like Mill's and Lotze's, have been perhaps enough
exposed.

ing, he is using a double identity-in-difference. If we take the red as our example, the first of these identities is one that is higher than red in the scale of generality, one of which red forms a 'difference'; the second is red itself, with differences of its own within it. Let us get these clear. We saw that to name is to distinguish. In naming red, then, we distinguish it from something else. From what? From other possible colours; if things were uniformly red, we should never distinguish it at all. Now to distinguish red from other colours, involves perceiving it as the species of a kind, a kind of which they are other forms. If you distinguish red from yellow, or any other colour, you do so within the genus colour, which reveals itself in each, though in different ways. And unless you did have in mind this genus or identity,[1] you could not make the distinction, for the only difference between colours lies in their different ways of being *colour*, as anyone may readily see by trying to find their difference elsewhere.

To name, then, is to distinguish, and to distinguish is to discern what is distinguished as one among the possible forms in which an identity may be realized. This is the first of the two identities-in-difference which we said that naming implies. The second is suggested by the familiar saying that language always generalizes. To name a thing is not only to add fixity or steadiness to our thought of it, but to establish it as a thing we may come back to at will, and which is open to others' thought as well as our own. A thing or event with a name is public and in a sense enduring, for anyone may have access to it at any time. To name and think of red, therefore, is literally to identify or recognize it, to find in it that which, while remaining itself, may be presented again and again. Such an identity is always a type that may in theory have various instances, and it is usually, like red, a genus with not only instances, but species. Reds are many, but all are kinds or forms of red. Hence red is itself an identity with differences falling under it, and without being grasped as such an identity it could never have received a name.

[1] For the nature of identity see Chap. XVI.

It will now be clear what was meant by saying that when we name we classify through double identity. The thing distinguished by being named is grasped as identical with what is above it, or more general, through being one form of a genus; it is grasped as identical with what is below it, or less general, through being itself a genus which may take alternative forms. But to grasp anything in this manner is what classifying means.[1]

It would be easy to object here on the score of 'the psychologist's fallacy'. We may be charged with doing what old painters of the Nativity did, and writing preternatural years and penetration on childish faces. But this objection, even if true, would have less weight than it seems to have. If growth were simply the addition of the novel, it would indeed have weight for then the ascription to one level of what emerged only at the next would be merely false. But where the only way to define something is in terms of what it becomes, the refusal to anticipate may be itself an error. 'Characteristics which attract general notice only when full-grown, are traceable far back when we come to look for them; and further, they are frequently implied by the nature of an individual long before any scrutiny can detect them. It is a cheap and false accuracy to express such a growth in successive stages according to the definite emergence of obvious features, without scrutinizing the continuous identity which is present from beginning to end.'[2] If we are to describe the facts of primitive thought, we must bear the later stages also in mind as we do so, for we must so describe it as to allow of its becoming what it eventually does become. Now we can see that a full consciousness of what we are doing in naming something would show that we are classify-

---

[1] Nettleship puts it in a sentence or two: 'All classification is a development of the elementary art of distinction, and every name is the germ of a classification. For all classification is arranging experiences according as they exhibit a certain identity in various ways; and to name it is to ident. y.'—*Phil. Lect.*, I. 134.

[2] Bosanquet, *op. cit.*, I. 15. In accordance with this conviction Bosanquet, in his discussion of the implications of naming (pp. 7–28), finds in it already the rudiments of the 'concrete universal' which provides the key to his logical system and to the 'principle of individuality and value'.

ing in the way described. It would be absurd, we agree, to say that such consciousness is there from the beginning. But we must certainly say this, that from the first employment of names, we are thinking in such a way that, when this maturer consciousness comes, it comes not as something merely new, but as what has been present all along, in the sense that it is what our thought has been continually trying, more or less successfully, to be. To recognize by name the familiar flower in a crannied wall is not to grasp its place in the ultimate scheme of things; agreed. But it is to start on the road toward nothing less. For it is to commence a process of identifying and distinguishing, and therefore of relating to what is above and below, which, short of this consummation, can only arbitrarily be brought to a halt.

Language, then, consolidates the conquest of free ideas by imprisoning them in a fixed order of classification.

16. (iv) We saw that the mastery of ideas is promoted by whatever facilitates our repeating them. Language does this preeminently. It does so partly through creating more occasions for reflection, partly by easing recall when the occasions come.

The service of the word to the free idea we have compared with the service of sensation to the tied idea. Now although the tied idea is called up only by sensation that is involuntarily aroused, the free idea may be called up either by this or by a word. The range of occasion for free ideas is thus immensely increased by language. Our first distinctions are frequently made when, in the presence of an object, someone points out to us a special feature and gives it a name. The reappearance of this object gives us an opportunity, and perhaps a stimulus, to repeat the distinction; for example, a prism, once its way of diffracting light has been pointed out to a child, may always suggest this property when it appears later. But so may the *word* 'diffraction' suggest it; and thus whenever the child comes upon this word in his reading, or hears it in conversation, he is called upon to form the idea again. The occasions for strengthening one's grasp of an idea may thus be multiplied many times through mastering the spoken and written word for it.

And the mastery of the word renders unprecedentedly easy the mastery of the idea, that is, its ready and complete recall. If, whenever a child found difficulty in thinking of the properties of a prism, he could conjure the thing itself before him, and think with the aid of perception, his earlier difficulties would be much smaller. Now the striking fact about thought through words is precisely that it is a kind of perception at a higher level, in which the sensory element is controlled, not by an external stimulus, but by ourselves. It possesses, as we have seen, much of the perceptual vividness, fixity and distinctness; but it also confers upon us a power which in perception would be sheer magic, the power to summon and dismiss the sensory nucleus itself. And as in the one kind of thinking, so also in the other, the amount of nuclear sensation needed is reduced by practice. If a person is barely known to us, we need a fairly full view of him to be sure of our identification; when we know him well, a much slighter glimpse will suffice. So when ideas are still growing in a young mind, their roots must be heavily earthed in sense or they will be blown away as soon as planted. The child roots them more firmly by repeating their names aloud, savouring these over and over, and fixing their feel and sound. But soon speaking aloud becomes unnecessary; speaking to himself will do as well. Then internal speech grows sketchier, until in the end, he can think with fullness and speed by the help of nothing better, so far as introspection reveals, than mere shreds and tag-ends of subvocal speech, if indeed even these are present. Nor need there be the least loss to thought in this economy of sensation. There are those who prefer reading a tragedy to hearing it on the boards; their own faint elocution carries the meaning more richly and unambiguously than the voiced words of the actors. So there are musicians who would rather read a score at home than hear it performed, at least unless superbly done. This suggests, and quite truly, that the same rule of economy that applies to language spoken or heard, applies to language read or written. In following the thought of another, by means of print, we have at first to spell the words out laboriously, and probably aloud. Reading later becomes a talking to ourselves, until in time we find, unless bad habits have ensnared us, that we can read immensely faster than we can talk. The next step, which many persons never take, is to abandon the spoken accompaniment altogether and to depend on the visual cue alone. And even this can be economized so that the mind may take the meaning of a phrase or sentence from the mere shapes of words or word groups, and catch the sense as well as if each syllable had been enunciated. Short of this method, the great readers could never have done what they did. We have already quoted Macaulay's remark that he could read a book as fast as most people could skim it, and skim it as fast as most others would turn the leaves.[1]

Now the facts that through a word we can capture an idea, and that to form a word is not much harder than to wink, imply a luxurious ease of mastery when we have subdued words to our service. Nor is the new advantage wholly a matter of ease. If we compare words with images, for example, we find them at once more precise and more variously efficient. As a rule, the fuller an image is, the more ballasted it is with irrelevancy, and hence the more dangerous to the true flight of thought. We shall illustrate the point in a moment when we come to look more closely at the place of imagery in thinking. From this burden of irrelevant suggestion, the word is free. It has occurred again and again with different forms of the same idea until its only settled connection is with what is essential in this idea. Hence the use of words is a chief agent, not only in

[1] 'I finished the *Iliad* to-day. . . . I could not tear myself away. I read the last five books at a stretch during my walk to-day. . . .' He was of course reading the Greek. Trevelyan's *Life*, 491. I am not suggesting that the purely visual reader does not lose much of the sensuous side of style. I think he does, and that since this side may be profoundly expressive of a writer's mind, such a reader may lose heavily. No purely visual reader would catch the full sense of Browne or De Quincey. There is therefore literary ground for the counsel which Faguet gives as the leading maxim of his *L'Art de Lire*: 'lire lentement'.

the fixing of free ideas, but also in the development of these into general ideas. As our reliance on imagery grows less and our reliance on words greater, our use of explicit generality becomes easier and more habitual. This in itself would go far to explain the displacement of images by words in our maturer thinking. But the displacement is furthered by another important circumstance. Words are owned in common in a way that images are not. If I think of friendship through an image of Damon and Pythias, the image is my private property, and my having it does nothing to plant it in your head. But the spoken word not only expresses and thus clarifies my own thought; it also arouses the thought in you. Thus the use of language, with its tendency to fix, distinguish, and repeat ideas, enlists in its support the enormous power of our desire to know and be known by others.

17. (v) This fact that the word is a link between minds, is worth noting separately. There is an early and strong desire in each of us to imitate others, to feel with them, and to get them to feel with us. Now feeling is usually, many psychologists would say always, *about* something; it is interest *in* something, antipathy *to* something, fondness *for* something; and so on. And it is a significant rule of human nature—significant because it shows how intimately men are members one of another—that pleasurable emotion shared is intensified and painful emotion shared is lightened. Hence the impulse to get others to share what we feel applies to the whole gamut of human feeling. And so far as it is true that feeling must be feeling toward something, the way to arouse in others the feelings we have ourselves is to make them share our objects. In simple cases, this may be done by a gesture, as when one points out a rainbow or a ship at sea. But the moment one passes beyond such cases, words are indispensable. How could I make another share my feeling about the mathematical trueness of the rainbow's arc, for example, or about somebody's cruelty to a dog yesterday, or about the League of Nations, without words?

I may indeed fail in any case, but such hope as I have must rest on words almost wholly. As men ascend from the perceptual level and their solidarity lies more and more in the world of ideas, they depend increasingly on words for maintaining the common scene. How effectively words may do this is evident in any lecture-room where a speaker is addressing an audience, a scene which to an animal, an angel, or a behaviourist, could hardly be intelligible. Here, in virtue of one organism emitting noises and others hearing them, we have a collection of minds sustaining an identical world of feelings and ideas. The sustaining pillars are words. We communicate feelings by thoughts, and thoughts by language.[1] And so far as in our intercourse with others we succeed in transmitting feeling, that very success, in such social beings as we are, strengthens the feeling and, by intensifying the interest, intensifies the thought. Thus language works complexly and cumulatively for the liberation of ideas. It places in the hands of each of us the key to a wide realm of common ideas, and thus tempts into action the whole strength of our social impulse; then as the impulse rushes to take possession of that realm, it adds impetus to the intellectual seizure through the exhilaration of the joint enterprise.

18. We have now seen the character of the first free ideas, and the agencies which, after their achievement, aid in consolidating the conquest. It may have been noticed that, although we have pointed out that the first free ideas are germs from which later thought develops, we have not considered these ideas in the light of our special theory. This has been deliberate. It is a pity to keep halting an orderly march to raise controversial themes, and if there are readers who cannot go all the way with us, we want them to go as far as they can. But while our aim in this chapter is primarily to study the types of

[1] Not that this is the only way to communicate feeling. Verse, on its sensuous side, and music are other means. But it is by far the most important way.

ideas, it is secondarily to show that they may all be interpreted
by a single theory of what a thought or idea is, and we must
now ask whether the simple free ideas that we have been concerned with are amenable to that theory. Our ruefully thoughtful child, it will be remembered, was forced by a shock from
the cat to think of the cat's feeling. It will be instructive to
press home the analysis of this case, since it may be thought
to involve, on our own theory, a discrediting paradox. What
could be meant, on that theory, by the thought of a feeling?
The answer is that it is an experience which points to the feeling
in the sense of actually containing the feeling in an undeveloped
form; it means the feeling in the sense that if it completed itself
and achieved its immanent aim, it would *be* the feeling itself.

I have just seen Othello, let us say, and 'I cannot get out of
my head' the Moor's overpowering despair upon discovering,
too late, his mistake. What exactly does my thought of despair
consist in? It is not an image or copy of it; we are beyond such
suggestions now. It is not a set of words, if only because we
can think of the despair without words. It is not a bit of physical
behaviour; it is not a pragmatic attempt to do something; it
is not, as a neo-realist might suggest, the very despair of Othello
himself, or my own indescribable mental act; it is not, as a
critical realist would say, the quality or character of that despair
divorced from its existence in Othello or his creator, and now
presenting itself to my mind. We have weighed these proposals
laboriously and found them wanting. In their place is offered
this, that the thought of the passion is the mind's effort to
realize that passion, and that it becomes adequate to its object
just so far as this effort succeeds. Such an account implies
that there is no sharp line between thought and feeling, or
between thought and any other type of experience. To think
of anything is in some degree to participate in the nature of
what is thought of, whatever that may be. It is hence a mistake
in principle to co-ordinate thought with other types of experience; thought *is* experience of any kind so far as this shows an
impulsion to self-fulfilment.

I think casually of Othello's despair. I proceed to dwell on it till my thought of it becomes full and vivid. What makes my second thought better than my first? Or to ask the same question, what is it that makes Shakespeare's thought so very much better than either? The answer commonly given is that his thought is a better thought because it comes nearer to being a reliving of the very feeling itself; and we are so bold as to suggest that this common answer is the right one. Shakespeare 'was nothing in himself', says Hazlitt, 'but he was all the others were or that they could become'. That is our point; if he *thought* so adequately about others, it was because he almost *was* what they were. When he wrote about despair and jealousy, he wrote from the inside; it does not seem to be *thought about* them that is expressing itself at all, but despair and jealousy themselves. How far thought is encouraged to go in its attempt at realization depends on the dominant purpose of the moment. A casual reference to Othello's feeling demands a minimum of such realization. The work of a dramatist demands almost a maximum. When a true dramatist is at his best, he never gives the impression of having arrived by a process of thought at how his characters should act; he has so sunk himself in the stuff and substance of their minds that he has become all but one with them; his thought of them is virtually a living of their life. His thought's aim, as Mr. Bradley contends, is the aim of all thought, is to commit suicide in its own character and become one with the very reality.[1]

19. Of course, objections occur at once. 'This is merely realism over again. Realism is to be rejected because it holds that the idea *is* the object; you are now saying yourself that the idea is the object—with the trifling addition that it is the object in an undeveloped or partially realized state.' But the 'trifling' addition makes all the difference. It is one thing to say that in thinking about Othello's feeling, what is in my mind is the actual feeling of an actual Moor. It is quite another thing to

---

[1] *Appearance and Reality*, 168, 179.

say that it is a more or less distant approximation to what such feeling would actually be. The first position leads to the confounding of thought with reality, and makes fragmentary Othellos, hippogriffs, and fairies consort unintelligibly with the embodied things and persons around us. The second position admits the distinction between thought and things while defining their connection. However far the dramatist goes toward creating another mind, there remains an enormous uncrossed interval, for even thought the most full and vivid falls short of the infinite detail of reality. Thus ideal and real remain distinct, but definitely related.

20. 'But the relation is far from definite. You say that the thought of Othello's feeling is an attempted but imperfect realization of that feeling. But suppose that, by reason of some catastrophe or other, I experience an actual despair instead of merely the thought of it. This is, no doubt, less intense than some other experience of the same feeling that I might have had instead; it is therefore an approximation to it, and may be called a partial realization of it. Is it therefore an *idea* of this feeling? You are apparently obliged to say so; yet that is absurd.' The answer seems clear enough. Between despair on its own account and the thought of Othello's despair, there is evidently a difference which our theory must allow for. Now it not only does allow for it; it makes plain the nature of the difference. Is not the difference this, that in my thought of Othello's feeling there is a sense of incompleteness, of unfulfilment, of reaching beyond itself, of being a surrogate for something at once fuller than itself and yet an expansion of itself, which is never present in any feeling taken barely as such? In mere naked sensation or emotion, if such existed, there would be none of this sense of incompleteness, since they would be barely immediate, and such immediacy excludes self-transcendence. But self-transcendence of this sort is precisely what ideality means. There is thus no need and no excuse for confusing thought with feeling.

21. 'Ah, yes', may come the reply, 'the theory begins to be clear. A feeling like despair is not, as such, the thought of anything. Only it is a necessary accompaniment of the thought. When I think of someone else's despair, what happens is this, that I have the feeling in some degree, and along with this the idea that someone else is having a similar feeling. This is an intelligible notion. But in the first place, it is absurd to say that the present feeling is part of the thought, for the two are sharply distinguishable. And if this is true, if my present thought is a purely intellectual affair, with no admixture of feeling, then it is meaningless to say that it is a "partial realization" of the feeling to which it refers.'

Such an attitude is natural and perhaps common, but we must repudiate it expressly. The naturalness is due to an extremely easy confusion in analysing processes which, like poetic composition, seem to involve 'emotion recollected in tranquillity'. Let us say that a writer has had a very moving experience to which he later wishes to give expression. What he does, it is said, is to call up in recollection the scene that aroused his feelings; this recollection in turn induces the feeling itself in a mild form; such mildness, unlike the original violence, makes it possible to turn upon it an introspective eye; and it may thus be contemplated and expressed in relative tranquillity. We are not concerned to deny that this process occurs. What we do wish to deny is that the process of recollecting a past emotion is the same as the process of introspecting a present one. The process just described is not the recalling of a particular emotion at all, but the recalling of objects calculated to arouse a particular emotion. Of course, the present experience of an emotion similar to a past one may for practical purposes be as good as the thought of a past one itself; so the two processes are easily confused. If we are to be clear, however, we must keep them distinct. What we contend is that the thought of an emotion, whether that emotion is past, present, or future, is not merely a thought of the original stimulus combined with an emotion aroused by that thought; it is a partial realization of the very emotion thought of. And if this implies that an absolute line between thought and feeling cannot be drawn, that is precisely what we have already suggested.

22. III. The relation of idea and feeling offers a useful clue to the relation of idea and image. There have been distinguished writers, as we know, who have taken the position that the idea *is* the image and is never anything else. That position we have examined in discussing the copy theory. The evidence against it was overwhelming. Thought may improve as imagery vanishes; it may lay hold on relations and essences of which images are impossible; and even where images are possible and are used, they may bear little if any relation to the accompanying thought. To say that whenever we think, our thought *consists* of imagery is out of the question. Yet no one can believe that with this mere negation we have told the whole truth about the value of imagery. For according to this account it has no value for thinking at all, and is a mere execresence; and this runs counter to a general and not unreasonable conviction. Is it likely that so many persons should have held that ideas and images are identical, and that most special students of the matter should hold that in a course of thought 'accurate introspection always reveals the image, explicit or implicit',[1] if the two are unconnected? This is hard to believe. Even though imaging cannot be generally identified with thinking, it does provide an important support to it.

Imagery supports thinking much as words do, and much as sensation supports perceiving.[2] Thought sets out in the beginning from the shore of immediacy, and is reluctant to lose its anchorage there. In the firmness and vividness of sensation, in the definite movements of the spoken word, in the image, whose sensible quality is so like that of the actual thing, there

[1] J. R. Angell, *Psych. Rev.*, VI. 651.

[2] 'Thus the inside of a known house is much better realized when we are looking at its outside than when we are away from it, and some chess-players have told me that it is easier for them to play a game from memory when they have a blank board before them than when they have not.'—Galton, *Inquiries*, 75.

is something secure to tie to. For most persons, to call up an image of the Capitol at Washington and to maintain it for a time before the mind is very easy. To maintain the idea of government with the same steadfastness is very much more difficult. But if thought can be linked to imagery, the fugitive and elusive ideas gain by contact something of the stability of the image. Thus in most thinking the work of the image is the same as the work of words. The image is not the idea, yet it is far too useful an aid to be thrown away.

23. Is this the whole sum of the image's function? Is it simply a crutch, external to the thought itself and perhaps dispensable without loss when the mind comes of age? This seems to have been the view of the image most frequently expressed by Bradley. 'The idea in judgement is the universal meaning; it is not ever the occasional imagery . . .'[1] 'The common view, which identifies image and idea, is fundamentally in error. For an image is a fact, just as real as any sensation; it is merely a fact of another kind and not a whit more ideal.'[2] And he points out, as we have seen, that between thought and image there may be gross discrepancy. Bosanquet writes similarly. 'The psychical images that pass through our minds might be compared to a store of signal flags. Not only is it indifferent whether your signal flag of to-day is the same bit of cloth that you hoisted yesterday, but also, no one knows or cares whether it is clean or dirty, thick or thin, frayed or smooth, so long as it is distinctly legible as an element of the signal code.'[3] Now for most of our thinking this account of the image's function may be accepted. The image, far from being the thought, does seem, as Bosanquet says, to be commonly indifferent to it. But is this true always? I cannot think so. Indeed there are cases in which the image, in whole or part, seems to be identical with the idea itself.

Take one of Mr. Bradley's cases: when I attempt to form

[1] *Principles of Logic*, I. 10.   [2] *Appearance and Reality*, 163.
[3] *Logic*, I. 68–9.

an idea of the colour of a rose, I find that I use a rose-image whose colour I catch distinctly. Now does the image of the colour fall quite apart from the idea? Is it nothing but a pair of psychological stilts supporting a logical meaning from the outside? The evidence is against this.

'We *use* these images', says Bosanquet, 'make them starting-points of thought, treat them as containing approximations to what we mean; we direct ourselves to omit parts of them, or to note that they require weakening or intensification. "Not quite sky blue, but a little darker"; "Between pleasure and pain"; "A baritone is in quality something like a tenor, though with points of resemblance to a bass." '[1] Now is it only when the quality of an image *approximates* to the quality thought of, when quality meant and quality thought of are diverse, that the image is thus made use of? Surely, when I think of the red of a rose, the colour I mean may be *precisely* the colour of the image. I summon up the image of a deep red rose, and say in effect that the colour I mean is *that*. And it is hard to believe that the imagined colour is something belonging only to a contrivance 'in my head', as Bradley would say, or, as Bosanquet would say, to the 'signal flag'. One could swear by Occam's razor that the fact is simpler. The image of the colour is more than an external aid; it provides the very stuff of the idea; it *is* the idea itself.

Indeed both Bradley and Bosanquet will be found, I think, really to have meant this. In some passages already examined, Bradley explicitly maintains that the idea consists of part of the image cut off and fixed as a meaning.[2] This seems clearly inconsistent to be sure, with the passages just quoted, in which he insists that the 'idea is not ever occasional imagery'. How is so apparent an inconsistency to be explained in so coherent a writer? One may hazard that, when Bradley talked of the image, he was thinking at different times of different things, and that these different things corresponded roughly to the two sides of his chief distinction within experience, the 'that' and the

---

[1] *Logic*, I. 40.
[2] *Ibid.*, I. 4, 9; see above, Chap. XIII, Secs. 2, 3.

'what'. Sometimes he meant by 'image' 'psychical event', thought in its aspect of fleeting occurrence, a mental happening, that which enables one to say *that* an idea has occurred, irrespective of *what* is contained in it. At other times he was thinking of the image as a 'what', a set of presented qualities falling for the most part, though perhaps not wholly, outside the dominant thought of the moment.[1] With this distinction in mind, we can see that his thinking on the matter was more coherent than it seems. When he denied that the image could be the thought, he was denying that the universal colour for example, which is before my mind when I think of it, is exhausted by a momentary occurrence 'in my head' or elsewhere. In this he was surely right. When, again, he said that part of the image's content could be used as idea, he meant the image as a 'what', not a 'that'; and here also we should hold he was right. On the main point then, our view of the image is Bradley's view. As a rule, and for the most part, the imagery in our minds will be found irrelevant to the dominant idea. When this is true, the image is employed for the same reason that language is, namely that it gives external support. But occasionally it is not true, and at least part of the image serves as the idea itself.

One cause of Bradley's vacillation about the image we have already found to be a source of weakness in Titchener's theory. When leaning to his first view of the image Bradley was apt to describe it as 'a hard particular', from whose nature universality was excluded; and this was substantially Titchener's view also. But it cannot be held consistently. The instant we come to describe the image we find that in its very essence it is an image *of* something and so contains the self-transcending meaning which Titchener would exclude from psychology. It is as idle to put the image wholly outside of thought, or beneath it, as to put perception there. To perceive a house is certainly not to sink ourselves in the mere sensation of it; thought, as we have seen, enters variously; and it does so equally

---

[1] The first meaning appears to be used in the chapter on 'Thought and Reality' in *Appearance*; the second, though not quite consistently, in the early pages of the *Logic*.

in imagination. When this is clearly realized, the absolute division between logical meaning and imagery which Bradley and Titchener at times insisted on becomes untenable.

24. This view that the image is in most cases merely the signal flag for thought, while at times its content supplies the idea itself, seems in accord with the empirical facts about the use of images. Thus it is quite true, as Bradley points out, that there may be a conspicuous discrepancy between the image and what it means. We have used this fact as evidence to show that idea and image are not simply to be identified. Nevertheless, it seems clear that if I am thinking of the colour of a rose, the image of a lobster would be a less useful image than that of a rose itself, indeed that it would stand in the way of any vividly realized thought of the rose. The most natural interpretation of such facts is this, that just as a signal flag which in itself has nothing to do with what it means may nevertheless stand for it, so an image may serve to 'carry' an irrelevant meaning; while at the same time the image has the immense advantage of being able at times to supply the stuff of thought itself.

25. Our theory is, again, supported by the facts about the variation of imagery. Such variation occurs from age to age, from situation to situation and from man to man. As to variation with age, the general rule is apparently this, that imagery is less resorted to as age advances. The rule is exceptionally well exemplified in certain professions; Galton found that 'scientific men, as a class, have feeble powers of visual representation. There is no doubt whatever on the latter point, however it may be accounted for.'[1] On the other hand, certain classes provide exceptions. 'It is undoubtedly the fact', continues the same writer, 'that mechanicians, engineers and architects, usually possess the faculty of seeing mental images with

[1] *Inquiries*, 60.

remarkable clearness and precision.'[1] The simple explanation he suggested for these facts, seems to cover both the rule and the exceptions, and our theory accords with it reassuringly. Some things are capable of being imaged and some are not; where the interest remains fresh in things that are imaginable, such as colour and form, images are naturally used; and use gives facility. On the other hand, there are things that cannot be imaged at all, or else only in inadequate fashion; and where this is true, imagery is little resorted to, and is enfeebled through disuse. Hence the frequent barrenness in imagery of philosophic and scientific minds.

> 'From this point of view', says another writer,[2] "we may say that the more we know about a thing, the less we are able to represent it adequately as a mental picture.' 'For the zoologist, the "animal kingdom" is a general conception, embracing in a single system a vast variety of determinations, which are also general. It includes, besides the abstract characters which might be formulated in a definition of the term "animal", the universal modes of variation, through which these characters are specified in the graduated system of genera and species. This vast multiplicity of highly general characters cannot be brought before consciousness in a mental picture, or even in a series of mental pictures.'

Thus our theory that in favourable instances image and idea may 'overlap' seems to accord with the facts both of increasing use and of increasing disuse of imagery as age advances.

Just as one's use of imagery may vary from age to age, so it may vary, at the same age, from one situation to another. 'Individuals are rarely, or never, so circumscribed as regards their available imagery that they cannot at need fall back upon some variety not regularly used . . .'[3] One of the questions Dr. Lay asked of a large number of artists was, 'When a violin

---

[1] *Inquiries*, 74–5. That visual imagery *need* not be profuse or vivid even here, however, is shown by Lay's study of the use of images by 125 New York painters and sculptors.—*Psych. Rev. Mon. Supp.*, Vol. II. 7.

[2] Stout, *Analytic Psychology*, II. 208, 210.

[3] J. R. Angell, *Psych. Rev. Mon. Supp.*, Vol. XIII. 74.

is suggested, do you first think of the appearance of the instrument, or the sounds made when it is played?' One respondent answered unhesitatingly 'the appearance', but went on to add what would, no doubt, apply to most others, 'the word *violin* would have an entirely different effect on me if used in a sentence dealing with a piece of music. Then I should think of (which from the context means imagine) its nasal singing'.[1] Now if some type of imagery is dominant, we should expect this not to be abandoned unless some special advantage accrued, the most obvious advantage being the power to seize, through the image, the precise features of the object thought of. This is apparently just what takes place. Thus once more, the view suggested of the relation of idea and image comports with the facts.

Imagery, finally, varies from man to man. 'In some individuals', wrote James, 'the habitual "thought-stuff", if one may so call it, is visual; in others it is auditory, articulatory, or motor; in most, perhaps, it is evenly mixed.'[2] It is true that pure types, persons for example, who use auditory imagery only, are very rare; Meumann reported that he found no one who, in thinking, used *heard* words only. Miss M. R. Fernald concluded that 'the most common type involves a combination of visual images for objects, and auditory-motor for words, though many variations appear in this general scheme' and 'an individual's type can be adequately indicated only by an extended statement'.[3] Nevertheless it remains true that in many persons, if not in most, one type of imagery is dominant. Now, · so far as this dominance results from the advantage found in using imagery, and this advantage is the result of the image's providing the idea itself, we should expect the loss of such imagery to produce, not merely an inconvenience, but a very considerable loss of power even to think of what had formerly been dealt with by images. And this is apparently the fact.

[1] *Op. cit.*, 20. Cf. Pear, *Remembering and Forgetting*, 22.
[2] *Psychology*, II. 58.
[3] *Diagnosis of Mental Imagery, Psych. Rev. Mon. Supp.*, Vol. XIV. 131.

Illustrative cases are naturally rare, but a good instance in point is fully reported by James, from Charcot.[1]

> Mr. X., a merchant born in Vienna, 'enjoyed an exceptional *visual* memory. He no sooner thought of persons or things, but features, forms, and colours arose with the same clearness, sharpness, and accuracy as if the objects stood before him. When he tried to recall a fact or a figure in his voluminous polyglot correspondence, the letters themselves appeared before him with their entire content, irregularities, erasures, and all. . . . He could never think of a passage in a play without the entire scene, stage, actors, and audience appearing to him. He had been a great traveller. Being a good draughtsman, he used to sketch views that pleased him; and his memory always brought back the entire landscape exactly. . . . His auditory memory was always deficient, or at least secondary.' Then, after a period of over-strain, came a serious mental breakdown, which, however, was reported to entail 'no other disturbances but the loss of visual images'. But this loss went appallingly deep into the patient's power to think. 'When asked to describe the principal public place of the town, he answered, "I know that it is there, but it is impossible to imagine it, and I can tell you nothing about it". He has often drawn the port of A. To-day he vainly tries to trace its principal outlines. Asked to draw a minaret, he reflects, says it is a square tower, and draws, rudely, four lines, one for ground, one for top, and two for sides. . . . Similarly, he drew a shapeless scribble for a tree. . . . He complains of his loss of feeling for colours. "My wife has black hair, this I know; but I can no more recall its colour than I can her person or features." '

It is hard to read such an account, and still believe that images provide nothing more than an external framework for thinking. To eradicate them completely meant, in this case, to abolish all free or vivid thought of the matter to which they specially belonged. That this *proves* the identity of thought and image in such conditions is, of course, not maintained here; there remains the alternative interpretation that the use of a particular tool had become so habitual that the patient was helpless without it. But although, in the case cited, we learn that auditory-motor imagery did partly replace the visual in the handling of

[1] *Psychology*, II. 58–60.

words and figures, there is no suggestion that they fully restored the power to think of form and colour. The most natural interpretation is that the loss of imagery affected thought, not only indirectly, through the removal of one of its tools, but directly, through the destruction of its substance.

26. There are three points in our theory of the image: first, that the image commonly serves as an aid to the idea, like sensation in perception and words in thinking; secondly, that in some cases the image itself, in whole or part, *is* the idea; thirdly, that when the image does function, it is the imperfectly realized object itself. The first two of these points are perhaps now sufficiently clear, and we turn to the last.

I am thinking again, let us say, of the colour of a certain rose, and in doing so, I form an image of the rose. Our contention is not only that the image of the rose's colour is the thought of that colour, but that it is a thought which is essentially a purpose, a purpose to realize fully an experience that at the moment is imperfect. To get evidence on this, one should ask oneself whether, in calling up a colour, one is not making some kind of effort to bring the real colour before the mind, and whether, as one gets 'more of an idea' of this, it does not become more vivid and distinct. We have given our own answer already. The idea of the colour is a half-way house on the way to the full experience of it. The attempt to know, the attempt to think, is really an attempt to be. Thought, like mind generally, is a movement of self-expansion and self-fulfilment, a movement that can attain its aim only as the immanent end approximates the transcendent end and thus brings thought to rest in the object itself.

This theory does not seem at first to apply equally to all cases. It may be said that the imagining of a colour is a privileged instance, and that the theory looks less attractive when applied to thinking by means of words. When I make a casual reference in speech to the colour red, my meaning is plain enough, but surely I am making no sort of attempt at a 'realization' of colour.

The answer to this objection strengthens our case, for it makes clear how on our theory the two kinds of thought may be not only discriminated but related and appraised. If ideas are attempts of mind at self-fulfilment they will show varying degrees of adequacy. The sort of idea of colour that is involved in a passing verbal reference is an idea, to be sure. But then there are ideas and ideas; and is this the most adequate idea of the object that I can form? Plainly not. Very well, what step does thought naturally take to render itself more adequate? It proceeds to develop the idea that was rudimentary and embryonic into an idea that is definite and complete. It turns from word to image, and then goes on to bring into clearest definition the parts of the image that are relevant.[1] And this movement is not felt as a replacement of one idea by another. The idea is the same throughout, while yet passing through a series of changes. Does this series show any direction? Surely it does. Looked at from without, the idea is seen to be approximating to its object; looked at from within, it is seen to be evolving toward definition and concreteness. And the two ends lie in line. To become more concretely defined *is* to be approximate to the object, here and everywhere. The aim of thought is to fulfil itself in the reality.

Indeed, as we have noticed, this aim seems particularly clear in our thought of such things and qualities as are naturally presented in images. When we get inside of the thought, when we ask ourselves what we are really trying to do in thinking of the rose's colour, the answer that we are making a picture of it, or making a noise or motion about it with our mouths, or anything whatever except that we are trying to realize in our own experience that very colour itself, seems foreign and artificial. It seems still more so when we think of the familiar example of the man born blind. We ordinarily say, and rightly, that such a man can form no idea of colour. But he can certainly refer to it or mean it in some sense, since he is perfectly well

---

[1] Language 'is a substitute for imagining, as imagining is a substitute for the use of our senses'.—Mitchell, *Structure and Growth of the Mind*, 367.

aware that others are having an experience that, in him, is absent. When he refers to what is missing, his thought is not concerned with just nothing; he *is* thinking of colour after all; he does have some idea of it. And yet this was said a moment ago to be impossible. Now on our theory this paradox is no paradox at all, but something eminently natural. Allow that the idea is a partial realization of its object, and again the two ideas fall into place as differing stages in one endeavour. To form the thought of a colour which is at all adequate to its object, a mind must own the imaginal stuff that makes approximation possible; and since one congenitally blind is without this, no concrete idea is open to him. But while concrete realization is denied him, an abstract realization is not. And we are to see shortly that the abstract idea is a concrete idea in germ. He knows that what he is missing is a kind of sensory experience; this character, however general, does belong to the thing itself; and to this extent he is actually entering into the character of his object. That this extent is very small is, of course, just what the facts require. It is thus made clear how, for the man who sees and the man who does not see, the thought reference may be the same while the thoughts themselves differ profoundly.

27. It has been remarked by Bosanquet that 'there is no meaning in setting up the mere existence of images as a phase of mental development at all'.[1] Certainly their presence is not the mark of any particular level of development; being, as a rule, adventitious to thought, they may be present either sparsely or in profusion at almost any level. Even the confident generalization of Galton that they prevail particularly among children and savages is not now accepted without doubt.

'Indeed, it may be questioned', write Messrs. Ogden and Richards, 'whether mimetic imagery is not really a late, sporadic product in mental development. We are so accustomed to beginning psychology with images that we tend to think that minds must have begun with them too. . . . They have certain

[1] *Three Chapters on the Nature of Mind*, 98.

oddly limited uses as economizing effort in certain restricted
fields. The artist, the chess-player, the mathematician find
them convenient. But these are hardly primitive mental occupa-
tions. Hunger rarely excites taste images, the salivary flow
occurs without them. Route-finding in pathless wilds or metro-
politan suburbs is best done by sense of direction and perception
alone. On the whole, a mimetic sign is not the kind of thing that
a primitive mind would be able to make much use of.'[1]

This is a warning that may well be heeded. Still, the probability
is on the other side. That probability is that where the mind
remains preoccupied, as is the mind of child and savage, with
the sensible aspects of things, the mental device that is specially
appropriate should be especially relied upon. If this is the fact,
it has this as its other side, that images are less and less used
as thought develops.

The reason is three-fold. For most thinking, imagery is
inadequate, irrelevant, and uneconomical. That it is inadequate
may be seen by considering some of the commonest objects
of thought. Whenever we use 'and' or 'but' or 'if', whenever
we use a number, whenever we compare things as better and
worse, or before and after, or cause and effect, our thought is
employed upon objects which no imagery can picture, and to
which not even Hume could make it seem adequate.

And because it is thus inadequate, it is also irrelevant. If I
think of the President of the United States, I may do so by
help of an image which reproduces his features faithfully and
in detail. But the President I am thinking of is not a set of
facial features, but a person, who is not only incapable of being
given in sense, or all at once, but unites in himself a mass of
functions of literally unimaginable complexity. And since it is
of the person and his functions that I am thinking, rather than
of the mere look of his face, the more detailed my image is,
the more irrelevance it drags in. Galton, in his admirable old
chapter, puts this point too. 'My own conclusion is that an
over-ready perception of sharp mental pictures is antagonistic
to the acquirement of habits of highly-generalized and abstract
thought.'[2] The tendency of the image is to divert the thought

---

[1] *The Meaning of Meaning*, 61.   [2] *Inquiries*, 60.

from essences, relations and functions to the sensible appearance of things, and, except in special cases, this is not our major
interest in them.

Because the image gets in the way of the idea, it is, in the
third place, uneconomical. Unless we are thinking of sensible
aspects, a word will carry our ideas as well as an image; further,
it is quicker, and easier to form, and far more communicable.
To cling to images in such circumstances would merely waste
energy. Hence they are let fall into disuse; more than this,
they are actively huddled out of sight. 'There is evidence that
the ordinary dearth of visual images in us, and their extreme
faintness as a rule, are largely due to their being inhibited or
controlled.'[1] The mind on active service is averse to super-
numeraries on its roll.

28. We are now ready to move forward from the simpler
types of idea. We have been engaged primarily in this chapter
with three types of these: the tied ideas that form an integral
part of perception; the earlier free ideas; and images. We have
attempted to trace the process by which tied ideas break loose
from perception, and the means by which their freedom is
consolidated. Of these means the most significant are those
involved in the use of language. As for images, we found that
as a rule they are not to be identified with ideas at all, and are
largely irrelevant to them; yet in certain special cases we were
compelled to say that idea and image were coincident. Having
stated the more obvious facts about each of these types, we
raised the question whether the theory of the idea sketched in
the previous chapter comported with these facts. It apparently
did so in each case.

But these are elementary types of idea. We must now turn
to those more advanced types that are chiefly relied on by scientific and philosophical knowledge. The going will not be easy.
But at least, as thought rises in the scale, there is a corresponding
increase in the rewards of studying it.

[1] Mitchell, *Structure and Growth of the Mind*, 305.

CHAPTER XVI

THE FALSE OR ABSTRACT UNIVERSAL

1. When we turn from the image to the concept we return from a byway to the highroad of mental development. Images have been discussed in some detail because their relation to thought is so intimate that they have often been identified with thought itself. But the thinking that uses images stands at no one level in the growth of thought, nor can it even be called one kind of thinking; to call it so would be to classify thinking by what is extrinsic to it. And so long as the image provides the idea with only an external support, there is no reason to regard it as either a part or a species of thought.

The case is otherwise with the concept or general idea. It lies, beyond any doubt, in the main stream of thought, and it seems to represent a distinct stage of mental achievement. A class, that is, a set of objects united by likeness or identity, would seem to lie beyond the reach of the tied ideas of perception or those first thoughts of persons and things that come when ideas have broken their anchorage in sense. Yet there is nothing clearly marked or abrupt in the coming of the general idea. Mental growth, we may repeat, is not an affair of hard separations and fast barriers; it is the sort of change in which something becomes what it had in it to become already, and thus becomes more fully itself. This suggests that there are really no *types* of idea at all, but only stages in the development of a single function. And that indeed is the truth of the matter. Ideas are not a set of alternative tools, like a range of surgical forceps, between which we may choose in laying hold of an object. If we want to think of something there is only one way to do it.

We have found that generality is already present in the earliest free ideas, and very obviously so in the first intentional use of words. To call something a dog is to classify it, to grasp it as a kind or type, to recognize it as an instance of a character or a set of characters that may go beyond it and be exemplified elsewhere. Not that the child could set out the common traits explicitly; that is a later achievement; but unless they are grasped implicitly his identification of a dog as a dog rather than as a deer or a door-post becomes unintelligible. If one common noun rather than another is applied to an object this is because the name has a felt propriety, and what could this propriety rest on except the possession by the object of the qualities to which the name is attached already? Thus in the use of a common noun we are already grasping a universal, that is, a character that may not be exhausted in this instance, but has, or may have, other embodiments. But this is not the first appearance of the universal. It will be recalled that even to perceive anything is to perceive it *as* something. And to perceive it as something is once again to use a universal. From the beginning of its traceable history, thought works through identity in difference, and every type of it we have studied has exhibited this same form.[1]

So long as a form of thought is used implicitly, however, it almost defies analysis. Only when it arrives at explicitness can its structure be clearly seen. But once it has reached the light, the path it has followed underground is relatively easy to trace, since a mind and its ideas are to be understood only through what they are seeking to become. What exactly this is may prove beyond us. But at least the general idea is the most highly evolved type of idea that thought has attained, and hence more light on the nature of thought may be gained from its study than from that of any preceding level.

2. Before analysing the general idea, it will be well to do what we did in the case of the earliest free idea, and ask what are the conditions under which it arises. One condition often mentioned may be dismissed at once. It has been suggested

[1] What is said here and in the following pages about universals is subject to interpretation by the special theory of universals offered later.

that a general idea is really an aggregate of particular impressions; and it has been supposed that experience begins with the grasp of determinate individual things, that little by little we gather the impressions of these things together into groups, and that a general idea *is* such an aggregate. My first experience of a dog, for example, is something quite particular and leaves a particular impression behind; but when my second and third experiences, also of particulars, have come and left their impressions, I have a little collection of similar images, and this is my general idea. The only reason for mentioning this theory is that it illustrates a tendency as wrong as it is natural. It assumes that what experience begins with is individual things, whereas in both personal and racial history this grasp is a gradual achievement. In the race, it probably did not emerge for some millions of years. 'Not until the level of higher vertebrates is reached have we any clear evidence that one individual is recognized as distinct from another— as ewes and their lambs, for example, recognize each other in a flock.'[1] And we may again recall the remark of Aristotle that the infant calls all men father. The source of the error lies in the 'psychologist's fallacy' of imputing to the early mind what is easy and natural to it now.

But in seeking to avoid this fallacy, it is only too easy to fall into an opposite one. Having seen that we do not reach universals by putting together particulars, one may conclude that we reach particulars by analysing universals, that 'knowledge is a process from the more abstract to the more concrete, not the reverse, as is commonly supposed'.[2] But this also will not do. It is too likely to suggest that an infant falls from the clouds upon the topmost twig of the tree of Porphyry, and only releases his grasp of pure being as he feels his footing secure on the thicker branches below. The truth lies in neither of

---

[1] Ward, *Psychological Principles*, 288, note. He continues: 'Strictly speaking, everything that truly is at all, is individual; yet, as Leibniz long ago remarked, "paradox though it appear, it is never possible for us to know exactly the individuality of anything, for individuality involves infinity".'

[2] Green, *Introduction to Hume*, Sec. 40.

these extremes. The advance of thought is not alone a synthesis of particulars nor alone an analysis of universals; it is both together, operating upon an experience in which both elements are present but undistinguished. 'All that is in consciousness seems to present both difference and identity',[1] and neither could have come to light before the other.

3. The question then is, What is it that forces us on to the explicit use of universals? To this the general answer is, any process whatever that prompts us to identify what we took as different, or to differentiate what we took as one. Psychologically, both these activities turn upon the power to direct attention to one element rather than another within a whole. The ultimate conditions of identification and differentiation would thus be the original conditions of attention. We have mentioned the most important of these already in treating of discrimination in perception, for example strength and repetition of stimulus, and initial affective 'meaning'. But they operate also at higher levels. For example, the child who has suffered repeated, intense, and various attacks of illness will have a general idea of ill health which is far in advance of the child who 'does not know what illness means'. Again, the interest in food, leading through sheer native intensity to an insistent singling out of things good to eat, carries us very rapidly to the general idea of food, while of things that are equally common but fail to attract such interest—for example time, extension, and matter—such ideas come far later.

They come toward the higher end of a process that runs through all degrees of explicitness. If we are to see this process at its lower end, where the general idea is just breaking loose from the early free idea, we may well look at what is expressed by a proper name. When a child refers to his sister by name, he certainly need not be thinking of her appearance in some one dress, or her behaviour at some one moment. On the other hand he is not thinking merely of a set of abstract common

[1] Bosanquet, *Logic*, I. 26; cf. Ward, *op. cit.*, 304.

properties exemplified in her looks and actions. He is thinking, to put it formally, of an identity which is not confined to any appearance, and yet is not distinguished in his thought from the various appearances it has displayed. The universal is restless for escape, and in a maturer mind, would rise easily into the light of an explicit thought which would set the more distinctive personal traits in clearer definition. We have here the correction of a very common mistake about the way general ideas are achieved. It is often said that we reach such ideas by 'abstracting from particular things what they have in common'. But we have seen that these 'particular things' are from the beginning more than particulars, that even to perceive a thing is to perceive it *as* something, and hence to use the very generality supposed to be reached by later abstraction. 'To form a concept by abstraction in this way is to look for the spectacles we are wearing by the aid of the spectacles themselves.'[1]

Our question then still is, What is it that pushes the universal up into explicitness? And the answer is the same as before: Whatever promotes the processes of identification and distinction. But here there are factors accelerating these processes which were not at work while discrimination remained in the perceptual sphere. These new moving forces are *acquired interests* and their chief tool, *language*.

4. The child who refers to his sister by name is not, so far, using a general idea. But 'any personal or practical interest in the results to be obtained by distinguishing, makes one's wits amazingly sharp to detect differences'.[2] Suppose, for example, that the child with a normal interest in the sympathy of others likes his sister better than someone else, and wants to convey this fact. How is he to go about it? He can say, 'I like X, and I don't like Y', and at times, no doubt, the process stops there. But this by itself is a lame way of making

[1] Sigwart, *Logic*, I. 249 (Eng. trans.), 'the concept as a work of art must always be preceded by the idea as a natural development'.—*Ibid.*
[2] James, *Psychology*, I. 509.

another understand. To be sure of success in conveying his feeling, he must make that other see what it is that he finds attractive about X and what makes Y unattractive. Thus the mere natural wish for sympathy may push one into comparison. And comparison is here no longer the implicit process that it is in the infant who, offered a red ball and grey one, unreflectingly chooses the red. The mind is now moving in the larger region of free ideas, and it has gained the command of language. Hence comparison is not the tame business of pointing to differences in the little circle of perception. The mind has begun the analysis of its objects of thought. And once more it is *words* that serve as the chief external implement. Words that were attached to distinct features in their presence are now used to fix them in their absence. A word is like a shaft which in a childish hand can be used as a spear to pin down what is near and palpable, and then when greater strength has been attained, can be fitted to the bow of thought as a far-flying arrow to bring down what is elusive and remote.

5. Now comparison is in principle everywhere the same. It is a process of bringing to light differences against a background of identity or of identity against a background of differences; and in both cases it is a process that forces universals into light. Interest may centre on either side. In the case just mentioned it centres in the differences. Only by making clear, first to himself and then to others, what was likeable in X and unlikeable in Y could the child get understanding or support. To make this clear means to isolate within X and Y certain characters or traits, which, as not themselves at the moment perceived, call for the use of free ideas, and, as more than merely particular, call for ideas that are general. When one thinks of the unkindness of Y and the kindness of X, one is grasping attributes *as* attributes and has crossed the line into explicit generality.

One is also grasping an identity of which the attributes

are differences. To contrast X's kindness with Y's unkindness is to compare two persons with respect to something common, namely, disposition or character, and in recognizing the contrast we help ourselves to seize the likeness. Indeed to distinguish and to identify are two sides of one operation. Whenever we compare things together they are in some degree alike to start with, or comparison would never occur to us. Of course we can assert in words a difference that seems to imply no common character at all; we may announce, for example, that a symphony is not a salamander. But then nobody thinks in this fashion. Nobody compares things felt to be utterly diverse. When we actually do compare things, it is because some likeness has suggested it; we have the initial sense that somehow they are alike and yet somehow also different; and our interest, so far as intellectual, is to make this 'somehow' clearer and more precise. Thus we may feel it profitable to compare the points of two horses; the comparison is enlightening, not only because it awakens us to fresh facts, but also because these facts reflect light backward, revealing themselves as alternative forms that may be taken by a common nature. Our understanding of the horse generally and our orderly grasp of detail are simultaneously increased. Or we compare a horse with a giraffe, since the comparison brings to light instructive diversities within a common animal nature. Or, once more, we may compare an animal with a plant, since here again a common character, that of the living organism, is revealing distinguishable forms of itself. But unless moved by some out-of-the-way interest, humorous or technical, one would not compare a salamander with a symphony, or a horse with the north pole. Thus, just as comparison forces us to isolate the characters that make things different, so at the same time it forces into light the characters owned in common. Clearness about likeness and clearness about difference subserve each other.

6. Is there any limit to the process of making new distinctions? None. Our first vague identities have no sooner split themselves

up than each of the differences shows signs of a further fission, and so on down as far as practical or theoretical interest may drive us. It takes some time, as we saw, to break up an initial world into things and persons. But then as one person after another presents himself to us, our recognition of human nature grows more instant and certain; and at the same time differentiations appear within it, between man and woman for example. Then these differentiations turn out themselves to be identities, calling for further internal distinction. Men are not all alike; we begin to see that while they are all of them men, there are almost endless varieties of men, good and bad, old and young, gruff and gentle. But can we rest in these distinctions? Plainly not. Though each at the moment may have seemed final, we find what they give us is again universals with species below them; gentleness, for instance, may be that of affection, training, policy, or weakness. And these distinctions, once achieved, are only signals to carry the process still further. Nor is there any end to the process. How far we actually go depends in part on how far our practical interests make it worth while to go, in part on how able we are to carry a complex structure in mind.

It was suggested at the beginning of this chapter that the general idea supplied the best key to the nature of thought. We can now see more clearly what this means. It means that in this idea we have a type that is repeated at every level of the activity of mind. Such an insight makes clear in turn what is meant by some common statements which seem at first scarcely consistent. It is said on the one hand that 'the sense of sameness is the very keel and backbone of our thinking',[1] and on the other that the measure of a man's mind is his power to make distinctions. Both statements are true, though each needs the other as a supplement. The eye that penetrates through surface differences to the common nature or law would be either diseased or superhuman if it went directly to identities without having to strip off differences, and logically

---

[1] James, *Psychology* I. 459; cf. Ribot, *L'Évolution des Idées Générales*, 10

speaking, saw all men as skeletons walking. And power of discrimination does not mean mere subtlety of sense, so that a creature combining the dog's nose with the eagle's eye must have a better mind than ours. It means not only the power to see differences, but also the power to subordinate these, and thus to unify them through their places in a hierarchy. Toward such a hierarchy thought moves inevitably. And its mode of building is always the same. Whether working implicitly or explicitly, whether it is laying its foundations in the relative darkness of common perception or working in the lofty stories that have been added by speculation, if it is using an idea it is always doing the same thing. It is bringing to light the unities that run through experienced differences, ordering the many through the one. And now that, in the general idea, this method has reached explicitness, it is time we gave it something of the analysis it deserves.

7. The general idea presents at first glance an impenetrable thicket of problems. It was already offering difficulty in the fifth century B.C.; it provided the most celebrated of the disputes of the scholastics; it exercised and divided the school of experience, provided the Hegelians the weapon for a philosophical revolution, and gave Huxley the opportunity to clear the whole matter up with the aid of photography! If such treacherous ground could be avoided we should make a wide circuit rather than go near it. But it lies directly in our path.

Happily, as one comes nearer, the problem breaks up into well-defined subordinate ones. First, there is the question what is actually in one's mind when one thinks a class idea. It was this question on which Berkeley differed so sharply from Locke, and which gave rise to the doctrine of the generic image and to James's notion of a psychic fringe. Secondly, there is the question what is the object of the idea; is it a universal separable from particulars, or a universal that is resident in the particulars, or just the particulars themselves? This is the question (or the main point of it) that divided the schoolmen, and produced the doctrines of *universalia ante rem, in re,* and *post rem.* Thirdly, if there is any such thing as a universal, what sort of thing is it? Is it an element that remains precisely the same through all its instances, an element that, like a Ford part, can be removed from one context and used in another without the slightest modification? Or is it something with a connection more intimate and pervasive, like that of one bodily organ with others? It is this final question that divides the defenders of the abstract and the concrete universal, the formal from the philosophical logicians; and we shall find it at once the most difficult and most important of the three.

We have already intimated, either directly or indirectly, the sort of answer we should give to the first two questions. The question what is in our minds when we use a general idea has been met by reviewing the principal theories about the nature of ideas—that they are images, that they are words, that they are mental acts, and so on. The only plausible answer, we found, was that ideas *are* their objects undeveloped or partially realized. With this discussion behind us of the mental content of ideas generally we can deal in summary fashion with special theories about the mental content of the general idea.

8. We know at once what to say, for example, if it is suggested that a general idea is a generic image. To those who hold that an idea is only a fainter copy of a percept no theory could be more natural; and when Mr. Huxley, carrying Hume farther, pointed to the perfect mechanical analogy offered by Galton in his new method of compounding photographs, the suggestion seemed so simple as to be inevitable. The suggestion is this: Every fresh perception of a thing modifies the image left by earlier perceptions; so far as it repeats the earlier ones, it fortifies and makes vivid the repeated elements within it, while so far as it fails to coincide, the new elements conflict with the old and cancel each other out. Thus what remains is a nucleus of constant elements surrounded by a fringe of misty uncertainty. The mind works like a camera plate in which a series of quick impressions have been made one upon another.

'This mental operation may be rendered comprehensible by considering what takes place in the formation of compound photographs—when the images of the faces of six sitters, for example, are each received on the same photographic plate, for a sixth of the time required to take one portrait. The final result is that all those points in which the six faces agree are brought out strongly, while all those in which they differ are left vague; and thus what may be termed a *generic* portrait of the six, in contradistinction to a *specific* portrait of any one, is produced.'[1]

But this theory is false in principle, as we have seen long ago. It assumes that ideas *copy* their objects, that the more general an idea is the thinner is its object, and that it conforms itself to this object by trimming its own edges. But, based upon the notion that an idea is a picture, the theory collapses when this base is removed. And of no sort of thought is it more obvious than of the general idea that ideas are not pictures. For example, if we think of horses as faithful animals, it would be ridiculous to say that our object is the blurred and shadowy shape which is all a composite picture could offer us. We are thinking of flesh-and-blood horses, past, present and to come, not of some thin extract which by no possibility could exist or be faithful to anyone. And to this object that we are actually thinking of no image could be adequate. For one thing, its parts would be incompatible, as was shown once for all in Berkeley's comments on Locke. It is perfectly possible, Berkeley said, to refer to many things at once, for example to triangles generally, as when we say that *any* such figure has angles equal to two right angles; but an image that is at once isosceles, scalene, and right-angled would be an impossible monster.[2]

---

[1] Huxley, *Hume*, III. Ribot thinks that the general idea in this form, which he admits, however, to be 'une forme inférieure de l'abstraction', is already used by children four or five months old. —*L'Évolution, etc.*, 28. Ward also thinks such images are in very common use.—*Psychology Applied to Education*, 78-9.

[2] *Principles*, Introduction, Sec. 13.

This surely is sense. Similarly we can make judgements about horses such that if a black horse and a white horse were marshalled before us, we should recognize at once that both were included in what we meant. But if our idea is to be a generic image, what will be its colour? If it is the colour of either horse, it will so far fail to mean the other; if a blend, it will mean neither.

And apart from the error of taking an idea as a copy, the theory makes the further blunder of confusing the general with the individual pared down, of suggesting that the difference between the thought of a particular horse and the thought of horses generally is the difference between a detailed image and the same image when some of the detail is whittled away. 'But in itself', as James remarks, 'a blurred thing is just as particular as a sharp thing; and the generic character of either sharp image or blurred image depends on its being felt *with its representative function*.'[1]

9. Berkeley saw this, and his theory, in consequence, was really in advance of Huxley's. To combine in a single image all that the general idea referred to, he saw to be impossible; but, still clinging to the Hobbesian notion that ideas were 'decaying sense', he thought that the general idea was the image of a particular thing *taken as standing for* its class. But in saying this he was abandoning the image theory. For now the thought lay not in the image, but in the way it was taken, in the meaning or reference that went along with it.[2] James, as we have just seen, put his finger on the difficulty, but in the act of doing so, he fell into an almost identical error, an error he shared with Professor Titchener and other psychologists who try to keep clear of metaphysics. But James's substitute for the idea, in the form of a 'psychic fringe', is both so interesting and so illustrative of the strength and weakness of the introspective account of thinking, that we are tempted to quote the gist of it.

[1] *Psychology*, I. 478.   [2] See above, Chap. VII, Sec. 5.

'What must be admitted is that the definite images of traditional psychology form but the smallest part of our minds as they actually live. . . . Every definite image in the mind is steeped and dyed in the free water that flows round it. With it goes the sense of its relations, near and remote, the dying echo of whence it came to us, the dawning sense of whither it is to lead. The significance, the value, of the image, is all in this halo or penumbra that surrounds and escorts it. . . .' 'One may admit that a good third of our psychic life consists in these rapid premonitory perspective views of schemes of thought not yet articulate.' 'Again, when we use a common noun, such as *man*, in a universal sense, as signifying all possible men, we are fully aware of this intention on our part, and distinguish it carefully from our intention when we mean a certain group of men, or a solitary individual before us.' 'And what is it exactly that is in our mind when we have such an intention? It is not an image, but a feeling.' 'If there be such things as feelings at all, *then so surely as relations between objects exist* in rerum natura, *so surely, and more surely, do feelings exist to which these relations are known.* . . . We ought to say a feeling of *and*, a feeling of *if*, a feeling of *but*, and a feeling of *by*, quite as readily as we say a feeling of *blue* or a feeling of cold.'[1]

Now on our own theory of the idea, there is legitimate meaning in speaking of a feeling of blue or a feeling of cold. But neither on our theory, nor on James's, nor on any other, can it be intelligible to talk of a feeling of *and* or a feeling of *man*. James himself gives the reason. When pointing out the mistake in taking the generic image as idea, he shows that what makes an image general is not its sensible quality, but the performance of a function, the function of carrying thought out and away beyond the symbol. Now precisely the same comment is to be made on the theory of the idea as a fringe of feeling. That such feeling does accompany thought, suffusing and fringing it as he says, is no doubt true; and James's genius as a psychologist is never brighter than when he is turning its light on these gossamer fringes. But if an image cannot be an idea without a 'representative function', how can a feeling be?

[1] *Psychology*, I. 245–56; italics in original. Various excerpts have been joined and the order transposed.

If it is this function, and this alone, that gives generality to the image, how can the feeling dispense with it? And if it cannot dispense with this, then is it not clear that the fringe of feeling *is* not the thought or meaning at all, but, like the image, merely an aid and abettor? There is always something self-transcendent about an idea; about mere feeling there never is. In this self-transcendence lies the mystery of the idea and also its very essence; and we have argued that if one refuses to see this, if one glues one's eye to the mental event and ignores the purpose to go out to an object, if one forgets that thoughts are not merely events but the apprehension of what is beyond them, if one thus distils from 'scientific psychology' all traces of metaphysic, one gets purity, it is true, but purity at a price. Ideas will be so purified that they will not be ideas *of* anything, and hence they will not be ideas at all. Distil 'meaning' out of psychology and what is left is in very truth meaningless.

These two theories of what is present in mind when we use a general idea, the theory that it is a generic image and the theory that it is a fringe of feeling, are mentioned here only as examples. They have been instanced to show how our conclusions about ideas generally may give guidance in treating of special forms of idea. But though they are not the only theories on this head, they are at least typical and conspicuous; and there are no others that we know which cannot be dealt with in the same fashion, by applying our conclusions about ideas generally.

10. Now just as prior discussion has anticipated our answer to the first question about the general idea, so also it determines our attitude on the second, the question whether the object of an idea really contains a universal, or whether it is nothing but a set of particulars. Indeed the answer to this question follows from the mere assumption that knowledge is possible, and this assumption we have made throughout. Unless there are universals there are no identities; and unless there are such identities a false report must be rendered by every perception, judgement and inference. Every perception: since to perceive anything is to perceive it *as* something, that is, as an instance of a universal which might be exemplified otherwise. Every judgement: for the thought of S and P is the thought of something that maintains identity in spite of being diversely characterized. Every inference: for if the subject that enters our premises is not the same that accepts our conclusion, the inference is broken-backed. 'The unity, reality and identity of the universal in the particulars is presupposed in every sentence that we utter.'[1]

11. But what sort of entity is this universal? This is the third of the chief questions about the general idea, and the one which concerns us most. If it is true, as we have argued, that the idea *is* its object partially realized, the nature of the general idea can be seen only through what it apprehends. Now to the question what the universal is which the idea apprehends, there are two chief answers. The first is the product of a long and distinguished tradition, which in the main is still widely accepted; and it has the advantage of being very easy to understand. But we are compelled to hold it false. The second, while also the product of an ancient tradition, has had in comparison few defenders or expositors, and it is exceedingly hard to get clear. But we shall see that it is nearer the truth.

12. The first answer comes from the traditional formal logic. Since this logic has been one of the most potent factors in the moulding of western thought, and since, on this point, its influence has been all but decisive, we must look at its position with some care. Its view of the general idea is as follows: Such an idea is the thought of a class, and a class is a set of objects with one or more attributes in common. To think the idea 'horse' is to refer at once to the set of attributes in virtue of which we identify an animal as a horse, and to all the Dobbins,

[1] Cook Wilson, *Statement and Inference*, I. 344.

Black Beautys, and Man-o'-Wars that possess those attributes. The set of common attributes is called the *intension* of the class name, the individuals in which they occur its *extension*. Of these two sides of the idea's meaning, the intension is more interesting. For it is the intension that gives what is distinctive and characteristic; when we think of anything whatever, we do so through thinking of its character. Now what is the character we think of when we use a general idea? Formal logic answers with its doctrine of the 'abstract universal'. It answers that what is before us is the logical intension, that when we think of horses in general, we refer, so far as we refer to character at all, merely to the set of attributes which all horses possess in common. It follows that as thought grows more general, including more and more individuals in its range, there will be less and less in common, so that increasing generality really brings increasing emptiness. Let us get this quite clear.

I am observing, let us say, a blackboard covered with figures. I observe a number of these more closely and notice that they are triangles. I am thus using a general idea, the idea of triangles, and I have formed it by leaving out all points in which the figures differ—the right-angled character of one and the obtuse-angled character of another—and thinking only of the points in which they agree. On looking further, however, I find other types of figure, four-sided, five-sided, many-sided. These differ, of course, from the triangles; still, I notice that all are alike in being rectilinear figures. In rectilinear figure-hood I have thus reached another general idea, which is also a wider one, since it extends over more varieties.[1] And I have reached it in precisely the same way as before, by leaving out,

---

[1] There is, of course, inconsistency here. In the preceding paragraph, extension, the range of differences from which the common qualities were abstracted, was said to consist of individuals; here it is taken as species. But this is an inconsistency in the tradition of formal logic itself. When defining extension as opposed to intension, that tradition usually identifies it with individuals, not species; but its doctrine of inverse variation is nonsense unless extension means species, not individuals. The more modern formal logic distinguishes explicitly between the inclusion of one class within another, and an individual's membership in a class (Peano's 'epsilon relation').

once again, all that was peculiar to each variety and keeping only what they had in common. Suppose now I take another step forward. I compare rectilinear figures with curvilinear figures, and of course discover that though they differ in the form of their bounding lines, they are all alike in being figures. Here is a new and still wider universal, gained, as before, by dropping out the differences and fastening upon what is the same. And of course I can go further still. I can compare figures with volumes, and show that, in spite of their differences, they are both spatial forms; and then go on to compare spatial with other forms of being, till I arrive at that which everything has in common with everything else, mere *being* itself. The process is sometimes illustrated with letters:[1]

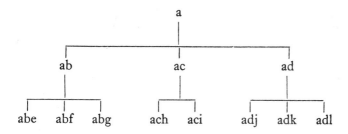

Here it is evident that if I start at the bottom, I reach the top by leaving some elements out, and if I start at the top, I move downward by adding elements on. To move up the scale of generality means to grasp universals containing less and less; to go down it is to grasp universals containing more and more. Hence the most general idea is the emptiest.

13. In spite of its attractive simplicity, this view of the universal is false. Bosanquet is perhaps right in saying that 'nothing has been more fatal to the truth and vitality of ideas than this prejudice'.[2] Its error lies in misconceiving the relation

---

[1] Joseph, *Logic*, 138. This view of the relation of genus and species is not Mr. Joseph's own.   [2] *Logic*, I. 61.

between the universal and what falls under it, in supposing that genus and species are so externally related that, in thought if not in fact, they may be cut apart without damage to either. The truth is quite the contrary.

(1) Consider any link in the classification above, the link for example between the genus 'figure' and the species 'rectilinear figure'. According to the theory before us, the genus 'figure' is reached by omitting the differences of the species and retaining only what is common. The species in this case are two, rectilinear figure and curvilinear figure. Hence to reach the genus 'figure' we must leave out what makes these different. The 'figure' then which we reach as genus will be neither 'straight-line figure' nor 'curved-line figure' but just 'figure'. Now no such figure can either exist or be conceived. 'Figure composed of lines that are neither straight nor curved' are words without a meaning. Figure is figure at all only as it is made of lines; and lines are lines at all only when they have some form. Hence if you take form away, you abolish figure with it. The universal, far from being a separable element, is thus so sunk in its differentiations that without them it would be nothing. The converse relation is, if anything, clearer still. Take away from the various figures what makes them figures and nothing remains. It may be said that lines might still exist, even if they did not enter into figures. But such lines would not be *these* lines, for these *are* the sides of a figure, and if figure went, they too would go. Thus, just as figure has being only in its differentiations, so these have being only as differentiations of it.

This point has been variously illustrated by Cook Wilson.[1] He asks us to

'take, for example, redness and blueness, which we naturally call species of colour. If we eliminate all that is meant by colour, nothing whatever is left, or, if we suppose some differentiating element left, it would have to be something different from colour. Thus the difference between red and blue would not be one of colour, whereas it is colour in which they agree. and

[1] *Statement and Inference*, I. 358–9.

colour in which they differ.'[1] Again, 'the sphere is not a determination of the general notion of space by something else not
space which makes it a sphere and not space in general. On the
contrary, space cannot be differentiated by anything else than
what is spatial. Space is not a genus forming part of the being
of the whole sphere: on the contrary, the whole being of the
sphere is spatial. Again, odd and even numbers are said to be
species of number, but we cannot eliminate number from
them and leave something non-numerical; for odd is intelligible
only as meaning odd number.'

Thus an individual or a species is not a mere aggregate of
characters, nor is the genus such an aggregate with some of
its parts subtracted. In the construction of genus and species,
the notions of addition and subtraction do not apply.

14. (2) This becomes clearer as the attempt to apply them
is followed out to its results. Suppose that the object of my
general idea is an abstract universal in the sense defined; to
reach the thought of its species, I shall then keep this as a
nucleus and add features from the outside. 'From the outside'
is important. For the species are not now conceived as forms
that the genus must take in order to be at all. The relation is
purely casual; you may add to the nucleus any characters
whatever, provided only they are not incompatible, and get
a species of the genus. It follows that in developing the genus
triangle, for example, I need no longer keep to right-angled,
obtuse-angled, and acute-angled; I can branch out at will
into triangles that are red and blue, regular and rakish, big
and little. But rightly seen, this is only a freedom to deny the
nature of things and to pay the inevitable price in confusion.
It would place on a level characters that it is impossible to conceive so. The least reflection shows that 'right-angled' and 'red'
bear utterly different relations to the triangle that is called

---

[1] Colour offers a challenging instance of the genus-species relation,
since the relation is so clearly present, while yet so difficult to analyse.
Cf. Lotze, *Logic*, Sec. 15; James, *Psychology*, I. 493; Kemp Smith,
Mind, 1927, 397 ff.; W. E. Johnson, *Logic*, I. 176.

their genus. To be right-angled is a way of being a triangle; to be red is not. Take the character of being right-angled away from a right-angled triangle and you have nothing definite left. Take redness away and nothing essential is touched. The one is integral to the structure it belongs to; the other is no more integral than a tender is to a steamship; it is a foreign object towed into proximity and moored alongside. Yet, according to the traditional logic, this foreign character, redness, has just as much right to be called the genus of which this triangle is a species as triangle itself. Since it is a character that the triangle possesses in common with other red things, 'red thing' is as truly a genus of which triangle is a species as triangle is a genus of which red ones are species. But both statements are plainly false. We may call a figure a species of coloured object, just as we may call colour the distinguishing mark between kinds of figure; but, try as we will, we cannot think in this fashion. For a species is a genus's way of being; triangularity and redness are not ways of being each other. Thus, according to the traditional logic, when I think a general idea, my object, the class intension, may have nothing to do with the essential nature of anything that falls under it. Any of an object's qualities, no matter how accidental, will do equally well to provide us a genus under which to think it, so that—to take a last example—the object that I am writing on is described with equal right as 'a desk', 'a brown something', and 'something with an inkspot on it'. And this is absurd. The first character covers its nature far more fully than the second or third, which in comparison are but lightly tangent to it. In sum, then, the abstract universal leads to the meaningless result that a universal may be embodied in characters that have nothing to do with it.

15. (3) If the universal is an abstraction, then the wider the class it is abstracted from, the fewer and leaner should be its features; this, as we saw, is the traditional doctrine. It will be argued shortly that it is a crude bit of logic, but as psychology it is worse, for 'it ignores in the most absolute and unmeaning way everything which gives substance and character to thought'.[1] A small boy, let us suppose, is keenly interested in sailing toy ships in a pond. His toy ships are in some sense ships, and so far his idea of ships, though very slender, will not be merely blank. He then goes to the seaside and makes the acquaintance for the first time of steamers. Common sense would be inclined to say that what answered to the word 'ship' would now become fuller for him. But no: the formal doctrine has it that his concept must become poorer, since all that differentiates his toy ships from the steamship is dropped out—such as the sails and wooden bodies of the one, and the elaborate propelling machinery of the other. And as his experience widens, the concept contracts toward the vanishing point, all the more certainly, of course, if he takes to the sea as his profession and lives among ships. As he makes the acquaintance of yachts and schooners, brigs and brigantines, rotor-ships, smacks, and battleships, each new type that he comes to know reduces the content of his concept, since only what is common to all can be retained in it. Thus when the man who has spent his life on the sea talks about ships, his concept is a poorer thing than yours and mine, who have been landlubbers all our days. And this is nonsense.

16. (4) That it really is nonsense is shown further by the way in which the general idea develops itself in inference. This is a large topic which will concern us later; but take only a single point, the way in which such an idea maintains itself against attack. When a false generalization is made, which is the man whose thought of the class will most readily give refutatory instances, the man with broad experience or the man with little? Someone remarks to an old sailor that sailing ships have two masts with a triangular sail on each. If our concepts become thinner as experience widens, it would be precisely the old sailor whose general idea would leave him

[1] Lotze, *Logic*, Sec. 33.

most helpless before such a suggestion. Since these characters
are absent from numerous sailing ships, he would long ago
have dropped them from his thought of the class. In his mind
there would be a meagre abstract which would enable him
only to say this, that he did *not* find there the characters named.
The very breadth of his experience would have made his idea
more barren; the more general it became, the fewer would
be the points of attachment through which it might call up
associates; yet the only way he could proceed would be by
counting over the associates in search of an exception. Is this
the way an expert's mind works? Plainly not. Far from being
thin and barren, his general idea is extraordinarily rich and
prolific. Suggest to the old salt two-mastedness and triangular
sails as characteristics of sailing ships, and his thought specifies
itself at once in contradiction. Two masts? Certainly not!
There are smacks in plenty with only one. Triangular sails? No
again; brigs are sailing ships that are square-rigged. The point
is that a genuine grasp of the universal carries a grasp of the
species with it. Where such a grasp is really present, the bringing to light of the species is not a random running over of
attributes with which the nuclear ones have been associated.
That is not what it seems like in the doing, and not what it is.
It is rather the making explicit and detailed of what was
germinally present already, the evolution of the undeveloped,
not the enumeration of associates. Nothing short of this will
explain the control over instances that generic thinking gives.[1]

17. (5) To name but one more difficulty, the abstract
universal does not allow for blanks in the constitution of its
species, and such allowance is essential. Suppose we are using
the general idea 'man'; the only features before us, according

---

[1] 'No definition will really be worth much to anyone who cannot
realize how different the thing defined would be in different circumstances. Thus a definition of democracy means most to him whose
mind is most fully stored with a knowledge of history and of insti-
tutions and of human life; he can realize what government of the
people by the people for the people (if that were our definition)
really involves.'—Joseph, *Logic*, 106.

to the formal tradition, would be those possessed in common by all the individuals to whom we gave the name. What are these features? They are such as 'rationality', 'two-leggedness', 'the sense of right and wrong', 'the sense of humour'. But it is perfectly easy to adduce instances to which the name would be given unhesitatingly, but in which a character thought distinctive and requisite is not there. If it is a mark of man to be rational, do we cease to be men when extreme age robs us of our faculty? On the theory in question, we must say yes; we are then a non-human species of animal. Is two-leggedness a mark of man? Then there is many a man, or rather, many an animal who once rightfully bore the name of man, that has lost its humanity through a surgical operation. Or is moral sense, or the sense of humour taken as a mark? Then an infant or a melancholiac will fall under the ban. Now it is surely evident that these exclusions are artificial; to any one of these instances the name of man would be given without hesitation. But this forces upon the formal logician a dilemma. He must exclude from his universal every major characteristic that distinguishes man from animals generally, and then the artificiality of his scheme stands exposed; or else he must admit to the universal characters *not* common to the species, and then his scheme is abandoned. It is the latter view that we hold correct. The truth seems to be, as Lotze maintained,[1] that a universal of this kind is a scheme in which the normal characters, rationality, physical form, etc., are indeed represented, but by a 'determinable' which leaves their amount unsettled and can remain a part of the concept even when that amount, as in exceptional species, falls to zero. If this view is not adopted, then the success of thought in dealing with the materials given it is beyond understanding. For not only those species of a genus in which a character is at zero quantity, but also every variation of attribute, would be unmanageable. If rationality is taken as a common character in man, only that degree of it could be retained which was repeated in every man, and the slightest variation above or below would have to be excluded.

[1] *Logic*, Sec. 23; and cf. Cassirer, *Substance and Function*, 21–3.

Needless to say, no such fixed degree is discoverable. And if not, we are in our familiar position again. The universal is not an extract from its species. It is the undeveloped schema of its species, which is neither their lowest common denominator nor their explicitly set out sum, but that which contains them within itself as its alternative possibilities.

18. 'What is the point', it may be asked, 'of belabouring at such length the relic of an archaic logic?' The answer is that however ancient this logic may be, it is still very much alive. The logic about which most has been heard in recent years, the logic variously described as modern, mathematical, and symbolic, is still formal logic, however much it may have extended the older system; and it still believes in the abstract universal. Nor is this doctrine an unimportant technicality. As one's attitude toward it varies, one will not merely adopt different views of the nature of thought, but will turn one's face toward different systems of logic and metaphysics. And the more clearly its defenders realize its strategic importance, the more stubborn grows the defence.

One of the commoner modes of defence is to accuse the critics of the abstract universal of confusing their logic with their psychology. They peer into their minds, it is said, to find what is there when they are using a general idea, and if they fail to find a class intension, they insist that they are not thinking of it. But this is to confuse two different things. When one speaks of a class intension or extension, one is speaking of the *object* of a general idea, what it refers to; when one speaks of the idea itself, one is speaking of some bit of consciousness which serves to carry the reference. This last is proper matter for psychology, while it is the object only that is of interest to logic; the two are neither the same nor need they be even remotely alike; and to confuse them would be to muddy logic hopelessly through an infusion of psychology.

It would indeed. The accusation, to be sure, might carry greater force if it came from another quarter. For never do the defenders of the abstract universal appear so ill at ease as when they are treating of psychology, nor can they well be said to have made any serious study of how the two sciences are connected. On the other hand, the chief critics of the abstract universal, for example Hegel and Lotze, Bradley and Stout, have been conspicuous both for being deeply versed in psychology and for having made its relation to logic the subject of thorough study. What they would answer to the present charge we shall not attempt to say. But if brought against the theory sketched above of how idea and object are related, the charge of being immersed in psychology seems peculiarly inept. We have held that an idea is the presence in the mind of an object partially realized. Hence to study ideas profitably we must study the objects they are seeking to be. To study the general idea, therefore, we must study the object of that idea, which is apparently a universal. What we are thus committed to examine, by the very terms of our theory, is the universal as it exists in nature. And when we contend that the abstract universal is a fiction, we are not asserting merely that introspection fails to find such a thing among the contents of the mind. To be sure we do say that, and have illustrated it in passing. But we say also, that there is no such thing *in rerum natura*. Colour that is not this colour or that, number that is not odd or even, an animality neither human nor bestial, these and all such objects are myths, and if a logic is so made as to require them, then so much the worse for the logic.

Indeed the case against the abstract universal when considered objectively is so strong as to suggest a confusion among its adherents of the very type they attribute to their critics. One suspects they have reasoned as follows: As our thought ascends the scale of generality, it becomes vaguer and vaguer. If we are thinking of a particular thing, we can realize its nature pretty fully, but this is increasingly difficult as the objects referred to become more numerous and diverse. The reference becomes more indefinite. Probably the imagery becomes more indefinite too. Thus the thought of Bernard Shaw may carry with it much special detail, the thought of Caucasians less, of man less still, while as we go on to 'animal' and 'organism', imagery may almost vanish. 'So, because in the term of wider, as compared with that of narrower extension there is often little definite, we are apt to suppose instead that there is a definite little'.[1] This 'definite little' is then taken as what the idea apprehends, and we have the abstract universal. But there is a double confusion here. The argument confuses indefiniteness with narrowness, as Mr. Joseph's statement suggests. It then goes on, by a second confusion, to assign to the object of my thought the narrowness of content which, with the help of its earlier confusion, it had assigned to the thought itself. Thus it is the acceptance of the abstract universal, rather than of the concrete, that injects an irrelevant psychology into the counsels of logic.

19. The abstract universal may be accepted, however, without such confusion. It has defenders who are quite aware of the dangers here, who are clear that what they are speaking of is the object, not the idea, and who would insist that the abstract universal actually exists in nature. 'If this seems hard to believe', they would say, 'it is because you are confusing distinctness with separate existence. We deny as firmly as you do that there are creatures at large in nature such as number without oddness or evenness, or triangularity without shape. But such monsters are in no way necessary. What we maintain is not that triangularity is a *separate* object, but only that it is a *distinct* object, i.e. that within the nature of any triangle you can distinguish the public and common characters shared by all triangles alike from those that belong to some special types. The common characters cannot secede from a given triangle and scuttle off in a grotesque group of their own; admitted. But being quite distinct from the others, they can be thought of in their distinctness, and that is all we are maintaining. And that they are in fact so thought of can be proved by a very simple consideration. Constantly when we have to

---

[1] Joseph, *Logic*, 140.

draw inferences, we use the generic qualities to the exclusion of the specific, and this would be impossible if we could not grasp them by themselves. Thus when we draw an isosceles triangle and prove from it that its angles equal two right angles, we can see that its being isosceles has nothing to do with the matter, and that the conclusion follows solely from its being a plane figure bounded by three straight lines. But this is all we mean by triangularity. Thus we plainly succeed in using triangularity in the abstract. And using it here means thinking it.'

20. This is a telling defence. We are told that to think the abstract universal is to mark off or delimit in thought the characters possessed in common. When we hold that this is impossible, what exactly are we saying? Are we saying that the same shades of blue cannot appear on two canvases? Are we saying that threeness must be different as it appears in three apples and three pears? No. To be sure, we shall see that even in these cases ultimate refinements may leave qualms, but the refinements would have different grounds from those now in mind. Our contention is simply that in all cases where there is a genuine relation of genus and species, the genus cannot be grasped in isolation, that is, without reference to its species. Blue is not a genus of canvases or threeness of fruits. Triangle *is* a genus of isosceles triangle, and colour of blue. Now if genus and species are related as the doctrine before us suggests, they must be so everywhere, and mere inspection will show that they are not. This is easier to see in some cases than in others. Take colour. That we do think of colours as belonging to the same genus will probably be admitted. We should, then, be able to mark off in thought the area they have in common. But it will probably also be admitted that this is beyond us; we cannot break up the colour blue into components, one of which belongs only to itself, while the other turns up also in red, yellow, and green. And if we cannot make this abstraction, what does the abstract universal consist of? Professor Kemp Smith does not think this difficulty insuperable. 'How have the diverse colours come to be referred to the same class, and therefore to be included under the same general term, if they have no character in common, save only that of belonging to the class?' 'It is only by direct observation of the various colours, and by observing how each, in contrast with some other, *is capable of defining outline*, that we are justified in concluding that in virtue of this common characteristic they can all be ascribed to a single class'.[1]

Now to say that this is what makes us class them together as colours is to say that this is what we *mean* by colour, and that seems to me untrue. It is to take a property for an essence. It is like saying that, because whenever we feel hot the hotness must have some degree, hotness and having a degree are the same thing.[2] Sigwart thought the only common element we could single out in colours lay in their relations to the eye; but that this is equivalent to failure he recognized by adding that 'these relations are not elements of the ideas themselves'.[3] A more recent writer, who would be counted, I think, a defender of abstract universals, Mr. W. E. Johnson, admits that no common element can be abstracted from colours, and offers the following subtle substitute: 'the several colours are put into the same group and given the same name colour, *not* on the ground of any partial agreement, but on the ground of the special kind of difference which distinguishes one colour from another; whereas no such difference exists between a colour and a shape'.[4] But this does not help us. For one thing, it seems defective logically. The way in which the species of a genus differ from one another depends itself upon the character of the genus. If two tones differ from each other in a manner other than that in which two figures differ,

---

[1] *Mind*, 1927, 399, 401; my italics.

[2] This property of defining outline against each other does not even seem a necessary means of distinguishing colours. If my visual world were first all green and then all yellow, etc., would there not be distinction of colour without marking of outline?

[3] *Logic*, (Eng. trans.) I. 263.   [4] *Logic*, I. 176.

it is surely because tone, being what it is, differentiates itself in one way, and figure, being what it is, differentiates itself in another. To condition the identification upon the mode of difference is thus to argue circularly, since the mode of difference is conditioned upon the identity, and could not be grasped apart from it. And even if we dispensed with the universal 'colour', it would only be to introduce another universal, with the original difficulties increased. For if colours are classed together by reason of an identical mode of difference, then that identical mode of difference becomes their genus, or, as Mr. Johnson would say, their 'determinable'. And to say that a colour is a way of differing from other colours is meaningless. But apart from that, there is this further and decisive difficulty: The abstract universal colour was rejected because no such common element could be discovered; but unfortunately the way in which colours differ is just as incapable of isolation as the way in which they agree. The new abstraction is thus as useless as the old.[1]

[1] Professor Kemp Smith's three excellent articles (*Mind*, 1927) on 'The Nature of Universals' conclude with a theory of his own. The theory, in essence, may be stated thus: Suppose we take A_1, A_2, and A_3, particular instances of precisely the same shade of red. What we directly apprehend, when we look at one of these, is a *particular character* which is unique and never recurs. But this character is also apprehended as being of a *type*, and this type is identical in all the particulars that have it. 'The type of universal, A, as such, is a predicate not a character; but A_1, A_2, A_3, etc., being what they are, it is truly predicable of them. Hence, when we say, "This flower is red", what we are asserting is "This flower has a character which is of the type, 'being red' ".' (413-14.)

(1) Professor Smith's distinction here between 'character' and 'type' seems to me a distinction without a difference. When he speaks of the purely particular 'character', he is speaking of some 'what', some qualitative nature, or not. If he is not, there is surely nothing that could have or embody the type. But one gathers that he is, since he says, 'A_1, A_2, A_3, etc., being what they are, it [the type] is truly predicable of them.' The words I have italicized seem necessary, but seem also to surrender the case. If the 'what' in 'being what they are' refers only to an aggregate of particulars so far lacking a common nature, then there is nothing in virtue of which identity of type could be predicated. Professor Smith seeks to make the distinction clearer by adding that a chief respect in which 'being a character' differs from

Now what holds of colour holds of all other genuine genera. The same difficulty breaks out, for example, in placing any sense quality whatever within its genus, and recurs continually as we go up the scale. To illustrate in the present case: we class colour and taste together as kinds of sense quality; what is it that they have in common? If one is a behaviourist, the answer will no doubt be ready; both are nervous reactions. We will not argue this, since anyone capable of believing it will have closed this book long ago. But if this simple faith has been denied one, the difficulty will be serious. Nor does it become less serious as one goes up the scale. Assuming that we have found the qualitative identity that binds taste, colour, etc., together under the head of 'sense quality', what is the bond of identity between this on the one hand and affection (pleasure and displeasure) on the other? And when this identity has been found, what is the simpler identity it shares with such very different contents as we experience in inference and desire? The puzzle is the same throughout. We class certain things together unhesitatingly and with complete agreement, even

'being a type' is that in apprehending a type we consider other instances, whereas in apprehending a character we do not. I cannot think this relevant. Universals do not wait for existence upon our recognition. Whether a character is, in his sense, universal or not depends, I should suppose, on whether it *does* or *can* have other instances, not on whether we happen to think of them.

(2) So far of Professor Smith's view of universal and particular. His view of genus and species is really the same, for the genus is realized only in particulars, in all of which it is identical. Species are not alternative forms of the genus, for the genus, being unalterable, has no such forms; 'the variety of the sub-types . . . so far as type is concerned [is] really irrelevant. . . . What tends to conceal this from view is that the subtypes are always more than simple embodiments of the more general type, and therefore involve for their apprehension the recognition of further types' (415). Such a view seems to me to deny that there is a genus-species relation at all. You start with colour, e.g., as an abstraction identical in the species of colour; what differentiates red, I understand, is its embodiment of a 'further type', which is different from the type 'being a colour'. But this implies that red is a compound of elements conjoined. I see nothing in such a view to make 'red' and 'colour' more closely related than 'red' and 'sour'. And since they are so, this view is inadequate to the nature of thought.

where no common element can be isolated. But according to the doctrine of the abstract universal it must have been isolated, since this is what generalization means.

21. In spite of the commonness of such classes, the defenders of the abstract universal may reply that we are making far too much of them. For even if we cannot isolate a common element, what this proves, they may suggest, is not that the common element is missing, but only that we have not grasped it distinctly and explicitly. If someone said that he noticed a likeness between two brothers, but on being questioned could not say where it lay, we should not necessarily put him down as deluded. For we know that we may perceive an identity long before we can define it explicitly. If this is used as a universal, it will then no doubt be lacking in sharpness of outline, but that is no sufficient reason for denying that it is there at all. Unfortunately, however, this sort of apologetic does not apply here. It is true, as we have admitted and urged, that a universal may be used in perception before it is made explicit. But in the kind of thought we are discussing explicitness is of the essence. No one doubts, I suppose, that we do have an explicit idea of colour. Now according to the doctrine of the abstract universal, the common element in colours is the dominant reference of that idea; it is therefore explicitly before us if anything is. And it must also be isolated or demarcated for such isolation from varying context is, as we have said, precisely what generalization means here. When therefore the doctrine says that in thinking certain general ideas we have a set of isolated characters in the focus of our attention, and a painstaking analysis indicates that such isolation neither is nor can be achieved, is it not time to reconsider the doctrine?

Nor is any defence to be found in saying that the difficulties with the abstract universal arise only from the mistaken attempt to *imagine* it instead of conceiving it. If one holds that conceiving *is* only imagining, as Berkeley did, one is bound to reject such universals; as he saw, one cannot imagine a triangle that is of no species, or a colouredness that is no colour in particular. But our troubles do not disappear when we have rejected Berkeley's view of conception. Is it really easier to conceive or abstract colour than to imagine it? What exactly are you *conceiving* when you think of the abstract essence of colour which is present in all colours but uncontaminated by any of them? The difficulty is not escaped by shifting the problem from imagination to conception. Indeed it is in the conceptual field that our argument has been conducted throughout.

22. It may be said, however, that the abstract universal may be present in some genera without being present in all, and the adducing of certain out-of-the-way cases does not disprove the actual and extensive use of such a universal. Even in such cases as spatial figure, where genus and species may be admitted inseparable, this universal does appear to be used. And genus and species *must* be distinguishable here, since the universal is constantly used in its naked abstraction in the drawing of general conclusions. Indeed there are many who would say roundly that with the abstract universal science itself stands or falls. For what does science mean? It means, first, the endeavour to single out by analysis the attributes of things, and secondly, the endeavour to connect these attributes according to law. And the possibility of either step seems to turn on the abstract universal. 'Science . . . is the detection of identity, and classification is the placing together, either in thought or in actual proximity of space, those objects between which identity has been detected. Accordingly the value of classification is co-extensive with the value of science and general reasoning.'[1] When a physician diagnoses a case, what he is doing is trying literally to *identify* the disease, to find symptoms which will prove it an instance of a type and capable, therefore, of being

---

[1] Jevons, *Principles of Science*, 673–4. Why Jevons should say that 'placing together in actual proximity of space' is classification is not clear. The operation is logical, not physical.

dealt with in familiar ways. And allowing for the difference between a priori and empirical sciences, this is also what the geometer does in analysing figures. The analysis is present already in the bare recognition of an equilateral triangle, for even in recognizing he is classing by genus and species, and so beginning the dissection. And the purpose of the analysis is still the same. It is to bring to light identities, to the end that if the figure, for example, displays triangularity, he can go on at once to ascribe to it whatever this attribute entails. Now is it not clear in all these cases that unless we can reach precise identities, we shall, as scientists, have failed? What is the use of singling out the character of triangularity if, once we have caught it, we find it changing in our hands and never bearing the same features twice? How would medicine or chemistry be possible if no element and no disease remained true to type? Thus to deny the abstract universal looks like a denial of law itself. A law is a statement that things of the same kind will behave in the same way. And to deny the abstract universal seems equivalent to a denial that any precise identities exist or that two things ever do behave in quite the same way.

This defence is not likely to be underestimated; it wears its importance upon its face. The likelihood nowadays is rather that, upon any threat to science, we should rush to defend Gibraltar with tin swords. If we are really faced with an ultimatum—either accept the abstract universal or abandon science—of course there would be no choice. But happily that is not the alternative. What we shall give up if we reject the abstract universal is not science, but one theory about science. The truth is that the nature of universals is not a scientific question. It concerns, to be sure, the object of every scientific operation alike, but just for that reason it makes no special difference to any. Mathematicians, doctors, and chemists do not wait on the metaphysicians' doorsteps for the approval of their technique or the blessing of their particular results. On the other hand, to argue that because it makes no special difference, the work of the metaphysician is idle, is to take a contracted view of things. There are plenty of legitimate questions that science, as such, does not and cannot answer. Physics discusses the laws of motion; it would be exceeding its special task if it were to initiate discussions on the nature of law. Chemistry analyses substances, but should we expect it also to analyse analysis or to theorize about the concept of substance? Science in every department consists of a process of thought, but the validity of the laws of thought is no part of its province. Thus the questions what essentially science is doing, and how significant is its enterprise in the light of what reflection reveals to us about the nature of thought and reality, are matters for metaphysics rather than for science itself. And whatever answers to these questions the metaphysician may see fit to give, science may rightly proceed upon its own course. It is amply justified of its fruits.[1]

23. We may thus return to the issue feeling free. Science does not commit us to any theory of the universal, beyond saying that since different things have in some sense the same properties and obey in some sense the same laws, universals or identities in some sense must exist. What that sense is remains to be discovered. And we are now in a better position to see what precisely the issue is between abstract and concrete universals. It is twofold. First, does there exist in nature any generic quality which runs with unvarying identity through all the species of a genus? Secondly, whether such an identity *exists* or not, can we *form the idea* of it and use this idea to advantage? As regards the first point, the defenders of the concrete universal would, I think, deny unanimously that such an identity exists. As regards the second, their position is more uncertain, some holding and some denying that such abstractions can actually be thought. Our own position is at least uncompromising. We hold that such identities *neither* exist, *nor* can be thought.

The issue on the first point may be put thus. The defenders of the abstract universal would say that just as there is an

[1] For fuller discussion of the problem, see Chap. XXXI, Sec. 19 ff.

abstract triangularity which remains identically the same in all triangles, so there is an abstract identity which remains the same in all colours, or tastes, or sounds. Their opponents would reply that just as there is obviously *no* abstract identity which remains unvaried in all colours, so there is none in triangles, or diseases, or men.

'If triangularity be defined as the type "three-sided rectilinear figure" ', writes Professor Kemp Smith, 'then through all variations of type the number, straightness and closedness of the sides remain unvaried. In these respects the type is absolutely uniform and identical in all triangles, however otherwise they may vary.'[1] That puts the abstract view with all possible clearness. Take now a statement of the opposite view. Mr. Joseph is discussing the question whether such an entity as rectilinear figurehood exists unvaried in all its species. He answers No; 'it is not quite the same thing in the square or pentagon as it is in the triangle. So intimately one are the differentia and the genus, that though we may refer different species to the same genus, yet the genus is not quite the same in each; it is only by abstraction, by ignoring their differences, that we can call it the same . . . the genus as it were fuses with the differentia, so that each infects the other through and through'.[2]

It is the latter view that is here accepted. We hold that the triangularity itself varies as one passes from an equilateral triangle to an isosceles, and from that to a scalene. We shall no doubt be told that if it is defined quite clearly, so as to identify it with threeness, straightness, and closedness of sides, then, since each of these remains the same, triangularity also remains the same. But if this is meant as an argument, it is not an impressively good one. It begins by taking for granted that these characters *are* the same in their various embodiments; they may be or they may not; if they should turn out to be true genera as opposed to specific universals,[3] we should hold that they are not; and to assume otherwise would beg the question.

[1] *Mind*, 1927, 416. [2] *Logic*, 83.
[3] See below, Chap XVII, Sec. 6 *ad fin.*

But even if we admit their perfect identity, the argument still is wanting. It says that when identity is established for each component of triangularity, it is established for triangularity itself. Now if triangularity consisted simply of threeness *plus* straightness *plus* closedness, there would be force in this; but it does not. It consists in a combination of these things, an arrangement which in no two species of triangle is the same. What sort of arrangement is this? We can define it verbally; and for most purposes there is no harm in saying that we can think it clearly in its abstraction. Such idea as we form of it can be converted so readily into the thought of the various species of triangle that it does not occur to us that our grasp of the genus is less perfect than our grasp of the species; the difference between an undeveloped schema and an identical essence is not of practical moment. But once we raise the question explicitly whether in the equiangular, the isosceles, and the scalene triangle there is a nuclear and identical triangularity unaffected by its various embodiments in the species, we can only answer No. To repeat: if we try to make triangularity out of a mere aggregate of attributes, we shall not get it at all; while if we combine them in such a way as to give its essence, we find this so implicated with the species that it has nothing quite distinct to call its own. It is not their nucleus; it is something cloudy, amorphous, and germinal, which achieves distinctness only as it is developed into its species.

Thus what is true of colours is true of triangles. And we should hold that it is likewise true of all other genera, from animals to diseases. To insist on an abstract animality, running like a golden thread through snakes and pigs and Socrates, is to read into the nature of things what is only a useful convention. Let one take any or all of the defining characters of animality, say, learning by experience, and ask oneself whether the process of learning by experience as it occurs in Socrates is identical with what we call by the same name in the pig or the reptile. The answer will again be No. To this the abstractionist may reply that the extreme differences in context have led us confusedly to foist these differences into the nucleus of identity itself. We answer, Put it so if you wish, but please accept our assurance that we do this with open eyes. Please do not believe that if the process of learning by experience *were* one in the snake and Socrates, we should drowsily think it two because it was somehow bound up in the one case with two-leggedness and in the other not. We are awake enough to perceive these confusions for what they are; and standing in full view of them, we say it is the abstractionists that are deceived, not we. It seems to us a lazy logic that would allow language and mechanical analogies to impose upon it this type of universal. Such a logic supposes that animality is a little movable block which may be put with one set of blocks to make leoninity, and with another to make humanity; and that the little pile labeled 'humanity' may then itself be shifted about, making with one collection, Mongolianity, and with another Caucasianity. If anyone, after reflection, thinks that this is the way genus and species are actually related in things, we do not know how to argue further. There are no analogies we can usefully bring to bear; the relation is unique; and the uncritical attempt to construe it through spatial analogies is largely what has caused the trouble. All we can say to such a person is that if he will take off the glasses of analogy and look at the matter directly, he will see that animality is *not* an unmodifiable flint core that picks up different kinds of accretion; indeed it is nothing actual at all; it is something that becomes actual only in its developments and differentiations—in, for example, its Socratic and its reptilian forms.

24. Unhappily, the influence of language and analogy being what it is, to remain at this point of view is all but impossible. The summit is scarcely attained before it is deserted even by many of its best defenders. None of these is more effective, for example, than Cook Wilson, yet Wilson contradicts himself on successive pages when trying to get the distinction clear. In the background of his mind the traditional conception of logic is working so potently that at times it pushes the abstract

view into unequivocal statement: 'The genus is identical in all its determinations, but not identical with them.'[1] How could it be, he argues, if the species implies the genus; implier and implied cannot be one. Then with this sharp cleavage in mind we read that 'the species have not only got something identical in them but that whatever else they have somehow belongs to this identical something. Redness, in fact, agrees with blueness in that in which it differs from blueness. . . . Colourness inevitably covers the whole nature of redness and of blueness'.[2] And here we are lost. The two statements are inconsistent. The first says that the genus does not comprise its differentiations; the second says it does. (Indeed, the second is self-contradictory even when taken alone. To say that 'redness agrees with blueness in that in which it differs from blueness' is to say that the two both do, and do not, agree.) Wilson apparently feels the strain between these views of the universal, for he lays down an imperfectly developed distinction between its 'identical being' and its 'complete' or 'variable' being. 'In this identical being is included its quality of having the series of phases of variable being; so that, in this sense, the whole of its variable being is comprised in the identical being', though he adds that it is 'not a part or constituent element of the identical being'.[3] But this is a case of *obscurum per obscurius*. What we want to know is how a genus that is the same in its species can yet comprise their differences, and the solution is that the genus includes the *quality of having* these. But the words 'having these' contain the whole problem. And in addition to solving nothing the statement is false. On no consistent theory could an invariant genus include, besides the common qualities, the quality of having others not common. For then part of its nature, as appearing in X, would be to have the

[1] *Statement and Inference*, II. 671–2; cf. 675.

[2] *Ibid.*, II. 672–3; 'there is nothing in the specific universals except the being of the genus' (676).

[3] *Ibid.*, II. 674. On the next page part of what is meant by 'comprising' the species is said to be 'necessitating' them. I should add that in spite of these criticisms I owe much to Cook Wilson's discussions of this problem.

qualities of Y, and vice versa; hence X and Y would coincide. But in spite of such wavering, what we regard as the difficult truth struggles clearly to light in some of Cook Wilson's writing. The movable block theory of the universal will not do. He sees and says plainly that it does violence to the nature of things, and while disliking talk of a 'concrete universal', he describes and accepts something very like it. 'The universal as genus is not something in the specific universal with the differentia added to it as something outside it. . . .'[1] 'The genus includes all there is in the species, there is nothing left over. The differentia cannot be separated from the genus as something added on to it, it comes from within it. The species is a necessary development of the genus; even and odd are not outside number, but necessitated by its nature as number.' 'The individual is the fully realized universal, the realization of the species, as the species is of the genus.' 'The genus is less than any one of its species only when represented in our subjective and incomplete abstraction.'[2] It must be admitted that this view is full of difficulties and that precisely in the form here expressed it will not stand. But so far as concerns the first issue about the abstract universal, whether it really exists in the nature of things, I believe we have here the answer. It does not.

25. The final sentence from Cook Wilson raises the second issue. He suggests that though the abstract universal does not exist, yet something of the sort may be represented 'in our subjective and incomplete abstraction'. This is a very common view even among those who hold that the generic properties of things are neither separable nor invariant. To mention but three names, all weighty however, this seems to be the position taken by Nettleship, Joseph, and Bosanquet. 'The fact of triangularity', writes Nettleship, 'is not, and cannot be, separ-

---

[1] *Statement and Inference*, I. 335.   [2] *Ibid.*, I. 359, 360.

ated from the various forms of isosceles, scalene, etc.; it is *in* them, just as life cannot be apart from, but is *in* the various forms of life. We may, however, give a meaning to the distinction in the following way. We may, for convenience' sake, mentally hold apart a certain fraction of the fact; for instance, the minimum of meaning which justifies us in using the word "triangularity". We may call this the generic triangle, and distinguish it from particular forms of triangle.'[1] 'Can we not and do we not', Mr. Joseph asks, 'conceive a rectilinear triangle with regard to those points in which equilateral, isosceles, and scalene agree, and without regard to those in which they differ? and may not this notion be perfectly precise and definite? . . . We must admit that this is possible.'[2] Finally Bosanquet writes so frequently as if such abstraction were practicable that he has been taken severely to task for it as an admission inconsistent with his main position in logic.[3]

There is force in this criticism, and I do not think the writers quoted can be wholly acquitted of inconsistency. We are explicitly told that the genus, e.g. triangularity, varies from species to species.[4] There is, therefore, no identity of this name which remains precisely and definitely the same. We are nevertheless told that we *can* single out such an identity, and gain a notion of it that is 'perfectly precise and definite'. This is puzzling. The very reason these writers insist that there cannot be an abstract universal, identical in its various species, is that we cannot so *conceive* it. Their present admission, then, is equivalent to saying that we can form a 'perfectly precise and definite notion' of the inconceivable. We have an abstract but definite idea of that which, in this abstractness and definiteness, can neither be nor be conceived.[5]

---

[1] *Philosophical Remains*, I. 218; see also 155. [2] *Logic*, 142.
[3] Kemp Smith, *Mind*, 1927, 154–6. [4] Joseph, *Ibid.*, 83.
[5] One gathers from more recent writings of Mr. Joseph that he would bridge the gap between these two positions by saying that generic identity is a matter of degree. 'Generic identity, it would seem, may show its differentiations with more or less suppression, if one may so put it, of the identity. Vertebrate structure is so one in vertebrates of different kinds that one may indicate the identity diagrammatically. Colour is not so one in different colours that the

If our contention here is correct, it is clear that we must go the whole way in opposition to the abstract universal. We must not only deny that it is separable in fact from its differentiations; that is no more than would be said by many of its defenders. Nor must we merely deny that, while inseparable from its species it remains identical in them, though this denial is fully warranted. We must declare a whole-hearted, root-and-branch war against it, and deny that such a universal is even thinkable. Just that we hereby do.

But retribution is instant. For the plain fact rises up to mock us that we do use general ideas, and that such use would be impossible unless somehow we found identity in variety. It is all very well to reject as unthinkable the idea of such an identity, but to do so seriously seems worse than trifling; it seems a downright impossibility. For if the species of one genus have no identity running through them, how could the genus be one, or, therefore, a genus at all? and what would be the sense in species that were not species *of* anything? On the other hand when we come to hunt for such an identity, it is nowhere to be found. The case seems hopeless.

But we have been in 'hopeless' situations before. Indeed we were in one not long ago whose features were rather like the present one. An idea *had* to be different from its object; otherwise why call it an idea? Yet it *could* not be different, for then in grasping the idea we should not be grasping the object at all. This difficulty seemed insoluble until it occurred to us to read the relation in terms of teleology. Was not thought, in its very essence, an attempt on the part of the mind to realize, to be, its object? and itself, so far as merely ideal, the same as that object realized partially? If we could say this, both of the seemingly contradictory demands would be satisfied.

identity can be visually indicated. The completest differentiation is that of being, in being a substance, being a quality, being a quantity, etc.; so that Aristotle said being is not a genus. Good, if it is in all the categories, is almost as profoundly differentiated as being, and cannot be called by the name of one of them, a quality.'—*Arist. Soc. Proc.*, Sup. Vol. XI (1932), 143. This is a difficult view to grasp or expound, but in the end perhaps equally difficult to avoid.

Thought must be the same with its object; well, it is. It must be different from its object; it also is. What if this equally formidable antinomy of the universal and its embodiments were soluble in the same way? We shall develop this promising suggestion in the next chapter.

CHAPTER XVII

UNIVERSALS, GENERIC AND SPECIFIC

1. We have seen that the abstract universal, though a very useful fiction, is a fiction none the less. There is no abstract colouredness, or triangularity, or animality, that maintains itself in absolute identity throughout a range of species, and is converted into a species by the process of tacking on further characters from without. The relation of genus to species is more intimate. In isolation from its species a genus can neither be nor be clearly conceived; its only way of being real is to find embodiment in them. On the other hand, it seems clearly distinguishable from its species; it can neither be simply resolved into them nor pronounced a mere nonentity and blank. Is there any solution of the riddle?

The more one digs around the roots of this ancient problem, the more insistently do two theses press for belief. The first is that the generic universal *is* the partial realization of its more specific forms. The second is that it exists only as the *thought* of these.

(1) For the first of these theses we have been more or less prepared by the bankruptcy of its alternatives. The chief of these are (a) to make the universal an abstract from its species or particulars, (b) to make it co-extensive with them, (c) to combine these views. By the first course a wooden tradition, helping itself out through mechanical analogies, has foisted itself upon logic disastrously. The second is, if anything, worse; for, professing in words the distinction between genus and species, it really does away with this. As for the prestidigitating attempt to keep both balls in the air at once, it is perhaps safe to say that if Cook Wilson could not do this, it is unlikely that anyone could. These views must all be rejected. Yet there is an important and obvious truth in each of them, which any alternative theory must retain. Granting that animality is not present in every horse and species of horse as a miraculously detachable

block, it is still plainly in some sense there. Again, it reaches out to all its species and has its existence in and through them, so in a sense it is true to say that it is one with their totality. Both rejected positions, thus interpreted, are true; and if true, they can be combined.

What we want is a theory that will reject the two falsities and retain the two truths. Is there such? We contend that the key is again provided by the relation between purpose and realization. When an inventor makes a model or a poet a lyric the purpose and product are obviously different, and yet are one. They are one in the sense that the product is the *development* of the purpose, the purpose matured or realized. The inventor recognizes in the model the specification of his earlier thought; and if the poet did not find in the finished lyric what his mind had been 'feeling after', he could not regard it as his own doing. The preliminary rough draft, the first dim conception, is there in the product. But it is certainly not there detachedly. It is not present as one Chinese box is present inside another, any more than the boy is so present in the man or the acorn in the oak. And yet to conceive the relation in this way is just what the abstract universal tries to do. Failing to see that the little word 'in' is big enough to contain a metaphor, it takes the primitive meaning in all dull seriousness, and then blinks and grows stubborn when the plain facts are pointed out. But those facts are still more stubborn. They are these: first, that the differences of a universal, whether species or individuals, do have something in common, and second, that if we examine the object of the ordinary general idea this common essence fails to appear. We have a right to insist that any theory of the universal should give an account of these facts. It is idle to go on saying that in the thought of 'animal' the abstract intension is there before us; too palpably it is not. It is equally idle to lament that if this abstract identity is given up, all identity goes with it. For we are offering another identity which does not lend itself to either actual or ideal excision, and yet must be admitted as perfectly genuine by everybody. And the large claim is here made for it that it avoids the

absurdities while retaining the truth of its rivals. It accepts
from the abstractionists that the universal is both something
less than its varieties and *in* them, but it insists that it is in them
not adventitiously but vitally, as the purpose is in the poem.
On the other hand, with the theory that would make the genus
the totality of the species, it agrees that the universal is not
fully itself until it finds in them its realization; but it is not
merely lost in them; it remains something different. The universal is thus *in* its differentiations; it is *identical* with them;
it is *distinct* from them. Call that paradox if you will; but take
it with its commentary and the paradox is merely verbal.

2. (2) If we can agree that the universal is thus related to
its species as potential to actual, we shall be readier to take
the next step and say that it is always ideal. We have seen that
thought, and indeed mind generally, is a striving for self-
realization, a process in which something comes to be that
which it has it in it to be. The general idea is no exception. It
is a process that moves to its end through a differentiation
directed from within; and the process is a living one which
belongs to the nature of mind. Now it is just this sort of vital
relation that links the universal to its embodying forms. Once
we have seen that this relation declines to be fitted into any
spatial or mechanical frame, that it is not even vaguely like
juxtaposition, that it does not imply a mental round-up of
similars, that it is not a relation of container to contained, nor
of whole to part, but a relation between stages in one development, the ineptitude of mechanical analogies becomes apparent.
For it is only in the domain of life that development in this
sense occurs.

'Do you mean to say, then, that the universal does not exist
in nature at all, and is a fiction of our own making?' That
depends on what is meant by 'nature'. If it means the reality
we should arrive at if the ideal of thought were achieved, the
answer is Yes, for in such a reality there would be nothing
merely potential. If it means the order of things and persons

dealt with by common sense, No. For anything in that order is itself not more than a half-way house between the ideal and the fully real. The question makes the old assumption that between thought and thing there is a clear cleavage, and that you can set up the idea on one side and its object on the other. We have explored this assumption in all its principal forms, and have discovered no form of it that does not crumble on exposure to light. The truth turned out to be this, that the idea *is* the object on the way to its realization. We are now proposing to take the universal and its varieties in the same way, to regard it as the thought of these. In thus taking the universal as ideal, are we saying that it is subjective merely? We must answer as before. The black-and-white dilemma implied in the question, 'Is the idea the same as the object, Yes or No?', must be rejected. To be sure the object is always present in the idea, but in the sense of being realized more or less. It is not a matter of 'either-or'; it is a matter of degree.

Here is a theory of the nature and object of the general idea. No doubt it is full of difficulties; all such theories are. For they must manage to satisfy at once the logician, the metaphysician, and the psychologist; and there is no safety short of a huge fortress of theory, presenting in complete detail the relation of mind and the world. Such an account is not here possible. The next most convincing course would be to select the more obvious difficulties that arise from these three sides and show that the theory can meet them. This is what will be attempted in the small space at our disposal. But our purpose is not argumentative merely. We shall defend by trying to explain, on the principle that the best defence of any theory is to show that it fits the facts. And let us turn to psychology first.

3. Does this theory of the universal as the potentiality of its differentiations accord with the way in which knowledge arises and grows? At first glance it does not. What we should perhaps expect, on such a theory, is that we should begin with the most general ideas and that mental growth should lie in the progressive differentiation of these ideas. And do we not in fact, arrive at general ideas in the reverse order, building them up by abstraction from particular things? No, this is not the fact, as we have seen already.[1] The perfectly specific things we are supposed to begin with do not exist for us at the start. The process of achieving them has been likened to 'the steady increase in clearness and distinctness of a landscape as morning breaks. At first sight the child may still confuse M with W, the cowslip with the primrose, and the cat with the rabbit: only on closer scrutiny do the differences "emerge".'[2] And when the differences do emerge, it is always as differences *of* a universal. 'There is no absolutely immediate apprehension'; 'every definite content of consciousness is experienced as a modification of something else.'[3] Acquisition is at every stage a specification of the general. To appropriate means, at the least, to identify, and to identify means to find in something the embodiment of a universal. Suppose, for example, that I come across a piece of obsidian. If I am an expert geologist, I shall identify it at once as a kind of volcanic rock; if I am not, my thought must still proceed in the same way. A universal specifies itself before me, though of course the specification cannot go so far; it stops with the recognition that this is a kind of mineral, or perhaps only a kind of physical thing. But if the thing did not present itself as the specification of any universal whatever, if it were a thing of no kind at all, I could not so much as perceive it. In all knowledge universals are being realized. And to grow in knowledge is to exchange

[1] Chap. XVI, Sec. 2.

[2] Ward, *Psychological Principles*, 191; 'we find genera recognized before species, and the species obtained by adding on differences, not the genus by abstracting them' (p. 304). We have seen the danger in the phrase 'adding on'.

[3] Nettleship, *Philosophical Lectures*, I. 171, 212. In a little-read part of T. H. Green there occurs what looks like a suggestion of the very theory of thought and its development that is defended here; he speaks of 'the progressive specification of the general idea (which is the true process of knowledge, corresponding to evolution in nature). . . .'—*Works*, II. 160.

a more generic grasp for a more specific. It is a movement in which the indefinite defines itself, the potential realizes itself, the relatively formless gains body and outline.

There is an obvious danger here in confusing an advance from the general to the specific with an advance from the vague to the definite. According to Ribot what we are describing is an advance of the latter kind. 'The one applicable formula', he writes, 'is this: *Mind moves from the indefinite to the definite*. If one makes indefinite and general synonymous, one may say, no doubt, that what appears at the beginning is not the particular. But no more is it the general, in the exact sense of the term; it is the vague.'[1] This is so evidently sensible as to call for some statement of how we stand toward it. We should hold that there are two senses in which the general, as distinct from the vague, is prior to its specifications, one of these a temporal sense, the other a logical. It has sometimes been suggested that all progression in knowledge is a spinning out of what was latent in the individual mind, that ideally experience could be dispensed with and the whole complex order of things hatched a priori from within. We are of course not proposing this, but we may well follow Leibniz in holding that there is an important element of truth in it. The advance of knowledge is not a process without control or direction; it is a drive toward the realization in experience of a certain pattern which is not assigned to the mind from without but supplied by its own nature, a pattern that governs, if not the material offered it, at least the way in which this material is ordered and assimilated. What this pattern is will concern us later. But we have seen already that mind *is* a potentiality of that which it is not yet but is seeking to become. In this sense the potential precedes its realizations. In a second sense, however, and one that we are more immediately concerned with here, the general is prior to its specifications logically, though the two come to light together. One does not start with the idea of animal, and by means of it recognize cows and horses; nor does one start with individual animals and work up from

[1] *L'Évolution des Idées Générales*, 39.

them, since without the idea of animal they would not be perceived as animals. What happens with widening experience is, on the one hand, that the universal gets more richly embodied, and, on the other, that things get more precisely defined and related as they are perceived to embody the same universal.

There are at least two senses, then, in which the general is prior to the specific in the growth of knowledge. Our proposal to take the general as the potential accords with both.

4. Does it accord also with the way in which general ideas, once we are in command of them, are actually used?

It would be easy to parade the better-known psychological facts about the general idea, and compare the way in which our theory meets them with that of its better-known rivals, such as the 'sample' theory of Berkeley, Huxley's 'generic image', and James's theory of the 'psychic fringe'. We will not undertake this tiresome business. In large part, it has been done already, and further comparison may be left to the curious. We turn to a more interesting test. General ideas, as actually used, provide very different degrees of mastery. Does our theory allow for these degrees or do anything to explain them?

A few phrases from common speech will make clear the sort of differences we have in mind. We often hear it said of someone that his grasp of a subject is 'merely academic', that it is 'too abstract to be of any use', or that he 'indulges in mere generalities'. Yet praise of the opposite kind of grasp is expressed in terms that are oddly similar: 'X has such a remarkable grasp of principle'; 'he always penetrates through to the law of the case'; 'he knows the theory of his subject and not merely the details'. In the one set of phrases generality seems to be deprecated, in the other praised. Both attitudes are justified, for beneath the apparent similarity there is a profound difference in the thought. The first type of generality is that of the doctrinaire; and 'the doctrinaire is an idealist, who refuses to see that though ideas may be right in the abstract yet the nature of the circumstances under which and of the objects to which they are to be applied must limit not only their practicability but even their binding force'.[1] He is exemplified by the politician who 'knows' democratic govern-ment is the only kind that will work and is for imposing it on every sort of community; by the botanist who is running over with book knowledge, but cannot tell a daisy from a marigold; by the medical graduate whose head is full of names and formulae, but if called on to deal with some simple malady is all at sea. The other type, where generality is admired and envied, is that of the expert in his own field. It is that of the accomplished judge, for example, who sees instantly how this case is to be classified and what in particular the law implies for it, and could adduce precedents *ad libitum* if needed. It is the mastery so readily recognized in the talk of anyone who is at home in his subject. The true expert is not given to 'sweeping generalizations'; he is too much alive to differences for that; he prefers to confine himself to what, on demand, he could convert into cash. The two types are familiar enough. What precisely the difference consists in is harder to say.

But it is interesting how much easier it is to put this differ-ence in terms of our own theory than it is in the terms of most others. Indeed, upon the ordinary theories the difference is a mystery. Since the thought is supposed to be the thought of a class, and to think of a class is in some sense to think of its members, the most obvious way to distinguish is to say that in the better thought these members are explicitly represented, while in the inferior type they are not. But this only brings out the curious fact that they are not so represented in either. To say thereupon that the thoughts of the various members are 'associates' which in the one case have never been formed and in the other case stand ready to be called up, is to miss the part that these 'associates' play. The point about them is that though they are not explicitly present, neither are they mere outsiders waiting to be called in; they have continued to be present so effectively that they actually control the thought and make it veer in the closest conformity with them. It is this

[1] Lotze, *Logic*, Sec. 243.

presence of invisible resources, this easy and mysterious intimated mastery of supporting troops lying outside, which would spring into action at a sign from him, that makes us listen to the expert as one having authority. And on our theory the relation of his thought to these hidden reserves can be simply stated. The *explicit* thought *contains* them, in the sense that at a moment's notice it could resolve itself into them; it is itself their partial realization; or, as we have put it earlier, it is the very purpose to become these, arrested short of its end. It *means* them; the relation we have just described is what we mean in such contexts by meaning. The general thinking we praise is that which in this sense involves its instances in itself. The general thinking we deprecate is that which does not.

This is why 'the more abstract is always the better grasp if adequately taken'.[1] How much is explicitly present makes no difference. 'If my perception of the ink bottle before me need not include a thought of the bottom of it, so far more highly organized conceptions do not contain, but take for granted, the particular thoughts into which they can be resolved.'[2] 'Into which they can be resolved'; note how the facts have forced the language into a mould that one can hardly suppose its author would literally accept. Note again the following: 'What are usually called "general" ideas (often in a disparaging way) are just not true generalities. They will not hold or apply in particular instances, just because they are not the generals *of* the particulars. If a man acts upon his "general idea" of motion, in this sense, he may find that it is not true, but the reason is that it is not the true general idea of motion, for that carries with it the consciousness of its possible modifications . . . it is not the generality of a general idea that makes it vicious, but its imperfect generality, which is also its imperfect particularity.'[3] Every word of this we can assent to except the phrase, 'carries

---

[1] Mitchell, *Structure and Growth of the Mind*, 341.   [2] *Ibid.*, 342.

[3] Nettleship, *Philosophical Lectures*, I. 223–4; cf. 158, and also this: 'the better we understand anything, the less we need instances; and, the less we understand anything, the more we need them.' 223. See, further, some suggestive remarks in Ruskin, *Modern Painters*, Vol. I, Pt. II, Sec. I, Chap. 3.

with it the consciousness of its possible modifications'. The general idea does not really do that; it only behaves as if it did.[1]

5. From these psychological matters we turn to some questions that are sure to be asked from the side of logic.

'How do you propose to distinguish between the general and the abstract?'

In common speech this distinction hardly exists. It is the distinction illustrated in the thought of Caucasian on the one hand, and on the other, in that of whiteness taken as the characteristic of Caucasians. To either of these we could apply both 'abstract' and 'general' without any sense of strain. And this is not the mere inertia that will not discriminate until it has to; it is supported by good authority. Bradley, for example, writes that 'there is no real difference between the "general" and the "abstract"; for, taken in comparison with the particular thing, the general idea is a mere abstraction'.[2]

We agree with the point implied here that the distinction is ultimately one of degree. But we agree also with Bosanquet's

---

[1] Since we have discussed the thought of the doctrinaire, perhaps we should mention his counterpart, the provincial. The doctrinaire deals in generalities that are bogus certificates because he has no cash into which to convert them; the provincial carries in his pocket a few sound coins, and on the strength of them issues bills of every denomination. The doctrinaire 'must have cold and selfish Scots, crafty Italians, vulgar Americans, and Frenchmen, half-tiger, half-monkey . . . like the symbolical characters in some of Shakespeare's plays, "a Tapster", or "a Lord Mayor", or in the stage direction "Enter two murderers".' (Newman, *Grammar of Assent*, 33.) The provincial 'talks of the relations of Church and State, when all he is thinking of is increasing the church-rate to raise the parish beadle a suit of gold lace'. (Ward, *Psychology Applied to Education*, 83.) From his knowledge of his village he generalizes about the world. But the two errors are in principle the same. They lie in the failure to see that any genuine universal must be the universal *of* its instances, and is answerable to them in detail. The doctrinaire tries to use the universal without the instances; the provincial calls in from the outside a universal that will not fit them. Cf. Lotze, *op. cit.*, and Newman's account of 'notional' and 'real' apprehension, *Grammar of Assent*.

[2] *Logic*, I. 81–2.

remark that all distinctions in logic are in the end distinctions of degree, and here degree may mean much. Contrast, for example the thought of man and the thought of whiteness. There is a clear and conspicuous gulf between them; in the first the 'differences' of the universal are individuals: in the second they are characters or qualities. This disparity it is well to mark by differing names: as we have called the first the *generic* universal, let us call the second the *qualitative* universal. Is the distinction between the two kinds of objects, between individuals and qualities, quite ultimate and plain? This question has often occupied logicians. Mill's answer, which was based on an ancient tradition, may be taken as typical. When we refer to whiteness we are referring to a definite and easily distinguished feature of some concrete whole; when we refer to men, we are referring to the concrete wholes themselves. Now the attributes, even the common attributes, of human beings, or any set of members of what he called a 'real kind', are inexhaustible. To think of such a class is to think, not of any particular property, but of 'an indeterminate multitude of properties', 'an infinite series of differences' which mark off this class from others.[1] The truth in this theory we shall underscore in a moment; meanwhile it is hard to see that on Mill's assumptions it can stand. If thought is to copy perception, and we have never experienced this 'infinite series', how can we think of it? And how could we know about a class that it had such an infinite series except by exhausting the series, which we never can do? In Mill's account generic thinking remains something of a mystery.

Cook Wilson undertakes to correct this account. He follows Mill in distinguishing, as different kinds of universal, what we should describe as the qualitative and the generic. 'Whiteness' stands for a kind of attribute, 'man' for the 'whole nature' of men. 'Such universals of individual things', he goes on, 'are of a problematic nature: they contain this infinity [the infinity Mill speaks of] as the thought of a potentiality which may be developed without limit. They do not in fact express the nature

[1] *System of Logic*, I. 7, Sec. 4.

of a thing; they are rather the idea that there is a particular thing and that it has within it this infinitely developable nature.'[1] This comes very near to the account which the reader will probably anticipate as our own. But it is not altogether clear. It can hardly mean that whenever we think of man, we make an explicit judgement that the men we are thinking of have 'an infinitely developable nature'; certainly no such judgement is there. Nevertheless it is plain that our reference runs far beyond anything that is at the moment explicitly realized, and the question remains how we are to construe this reference. How can we refer to qualities that we may never have experienced, whose nature is unknown to us and perhaps beyond our power to know? We are told that the qualities which unite to form the individual are infinite. But how can a thought aimed at infinity have so definite a direction?

Our answer in outline is as follows, and it begins with a denial. (a) When we think of man, there is not before us, explicitly or implicitly, any set of invariable qualities shared by all men in common; such a set of qualities neither exists nor can be clearly conceived; and here Cook Wilson, at least at times, is with us. (b) The universal we do grasp is one which, developed to the full, would *be* the various individual men; and here again Wilson is apparently with us. (c) This indeterminate universal, which is a potentiality only, does not exist in the real world independently of mind; its only being is in thought. And here we part company with Wilson. He would say, presumably, that this potentiality, this indeterminate universal, exists independently in the nature of things. To be sure his language is not unambiguous, and might be construed to support our position. He says, as we have seen, 'Such universals . . . contain this infinity as the *thought* of a potentiality', etc. This certainly sounds as if the universal might consist of my own thought. But in general he insists so strongly that 'the universal is not a mere thought of ours', but 'something we ascribe to reality itself',[2] presumably with justice, that we can only suppose this a slip. So we must go our own

---

[1] *Statement and Inference*, I. 376.   [2] *Ibid.*, I. 335.

way. We hold that the fully real is never indeterminate and never potential. These adjectives belong to thought. It is the very essence of that thought to seek fulfilment in a reality that *is* fully determinate. Thought never wholly fails, though neither does it ever wholly succeed, in compassing its end.

6. Thus may be explained at one stroke the indeterminateness of my mental content and the curious power that it retains to direct the reference. The fact of this indeterminacy we may now perhaps take for granted, and with it a final riddance to a pair of twin fictions: one the fiction of certain logicians that what is in my mind is a clean-cut logical intension, or its copy, the other the fiction of certain psychologists that it is a generic image. Instead we have a theory that at least comports with the indefiniteness which the psychologist has actually found, and found so puzzling.[1] The reason for this indeterminacy in my mental content is that the universal is itself indeterminate; indeed, the two indeterminacies are the same. On the other hand, the way in which this indeterminate content carries the reference to what is beyond it is also explained. Mill was right in holding that we do in fact refer to an 'inexhaustible series' of attributes, even though, on his theory, our thought of them would have to be put down as a 'final inexplicability'. We should agree also with Cook Wilson in holding that the universal is a potentiality which contains this series within itself. But it can hardly be right to say, as he at least implies, that this potentiality is itself what we are thinking of when we think of men. Flesh and blood men are more than such potentialities. If so, the paradox remains. These real men, we are told, lie at the end of an inexhaustible series of attributes, very largely unknown. How is it, then, when we are travelling in the dark and do not know where we are going, that we can still talk so familiarly about our unknown destination? The answer can only be that our thought involves it, contains it, points to

---

[1] It is natural to think here of the Würzburg school.

it, in that peculiar way in which anything undeveloped points to its completion. If the reference is vague, that is precisely what we should expect of an undeveloped idea. Take anything genuinely capable of development—a seed, for example, or a plant—and the less developed it is, the harder we find it to tell what it *really* is, which means here what it *would* be if it became fully itself. So of the idea. When we are thinking of anything profoundly real or important, we never know exactly and in detail what we mean. We are a little like the artist in *Don Quixote* who, when asked what he was painting, said, 'That is as it may turn out'; and just as the artist is often surprised at the final issue of his effort, so we shall often be astonished to find what that is in reality at which our thought is feebly aiming. Yet between the thought and thing there is an unmistakable continuity, revealed when the process has reached its term. To come back to our example, what we mean when we speak of man we do not wholly know. But set the strangest Terra del Fuegian or Andaman Islander before us, and we shall at once admit that we meant him among the rest. Why? Because, though we may never have heard of him or his kind, we see that if our thought had been fully developed and specified, it must have included him.

It will now be clear how our theory would distinguish between the abstract and the general. The difference is only one of degree, and corresponds to the difference between the qualitative and the generic universal. An idea is called general if, at a given level of development, its immediate end is relatively remote; it is abstract, if at the same level, the end is relatively near. When we think of a genus whose members are individuals, we are aiming at something that exceeds the present compass of our thought by a distance virtually infinite. In thinking of whiteness we choose a very much nearer mark. The thought still fails to reach and realize its object, as every idea fails, but the amount of the object that it leaves out, if we may speak so, is very much smaller. Our thought of whiteness is obviously more adequate than our thought of man; Why? Chiefly because it is so much less ambitious. It is content to aim at an attribute of things rather than at the things themselves.[1]

This distinction throws light beyond itself. It suggests, for example, that the theory of the abstract universal is due in part to a confusion between abstractness, as above defined, and generality. Logicians have sometimes forgotten that in thinking of men we are thinking of *men*, and not of certain attributes men are supposed to have in common. Because the distinction is one of degree, it serves, again, to suggest that a qualitative as well as generic universal may be realized in various species. It is often said that in abstracting we single out some feature or relation of a thing and fix attention upon it exclusively, and it is commonly implied that the object of abstraction is completely specific. But clearly it need not be. Whiteness, for example, is certainly abstract, but it is also a genus with species under it, namely the various shades of whiteness.

But may not *one* of these shades of whiteness be repeated in another context? And if so is it not clear that our account of the generic and of the qualitative universal will not apply to it? Either one of these universals, we have suggested, is best conceived as the potentiality or partial realization of its species; there is no such real thing as colour that is no special colour, or whiteness that is no shade of whiteness. But once we have arrived at the fully specific in some definite shade of colour, may not *that* be given elsewhere, and does it not conform to the traditional notion of the universal as that which may be the same in different contexts?

It must be agreed that there are such universals. Their acceptance must be qualified by certain conditions that we shall have to consider when we speak of internal relations;[2] and we shall soon see that some philosophers would prefer to say that it is not literally the same shade that exists in two different

---

[1] 'Abstract', as here contrasted with 'general', has a more specific meaning than it has in the phrase 'abstract universal'. This phrase is commonly used to refer to both generic and qualitative universals.

[2] Chap. XXXI, Sec. 19 ff.

patches, but only instances of that shade. But pending discussion of these points, it seems clear that such universals exist and are common. The 'same' note may be sounded twice over, the 'same' darting pain experienced; a basin of water is felt to be as hot as a moment ago. It is obvious that we cannot deal with a quite specific quality of this kind as we should with universals like horse or colour. It is not a meaning that seeks specification beyond itself; it is quite specific already. It is what we call the *specific* universal (omitting at times the adjective when it is clear from the context what sort of universal is meant). What is the test when we are dealing with a generic universal like *man* or *colour* and when with a specific universal like *this yellow* or *threeness*? The test is specificity or definiteness of content. When we try to find in that which is common to all men or to all colours something completely definite, we are baffled, and are compelled in our search for it to go on to their specific embodiments. When we arrive at *this yellow* or at *three* we seem to have reached as specific a content as experience can yield.

Let us note the senses in which the term universal has now been used. The abstract universal, as discussed in the last chapter, is the common character of a genus, conceived as identical in all the species of that genus; this universal, we have held, cannot be clearly thought, nor does anything in the real correspond to it. Secondly, there is the generic universal, which we have held to be legitimate, but to exist only in idea; it is a potentiality partially realized, which, if realized fully, would *be* its alternative species. Thirdly, there is the qualitative universal such as whiteness or sweetness, which, as just explained, differs only in degree from the generic universal. Fourthly, there is the specific universal, such as a completely specific colour or odour or taste, which may be identical with itself in various contexts.[1]

---

[1] Complete self-identity in various contexts implies complete independence of some contexts, or at least of some elements in them. We shall see later (Chap. XXXI and XXXII) that *in the end* such independence is nowhere to be found. But obviously the believer in internal relations would not get far if at every stage he tried to say only what was true in the end.

7. But we must return to the point of a moment ago. We said that a qualitative universal was not essentially different from a generic one; and this will probably be objected to on the ground that the generic universal refers to individuals and the qualitative universal to attributes or relations. Can it be meant, we may be asked, that between these two there is no ultimate difference at all? The answer is Yes; there is no ultimate difference. We should hold that the individual things in which the generic universal would be realized may themselves be resolved away into specific universals. We saw in studying perception that when we attempt to go beyond the attributes of a thing to an 'it' which has them we are defeated, and that the unity and distinctness of the thing, which to common sense appear so final and self-evident, result less from any natural necessity than from our carving the joints of nature along lines marked out by practical need. The distinction between attributes and things is not a distinction between attributes on the one hand and some occult and featureless substratum on the other; it is a difference between characters taken severally and the same characters grouped together for special causes or ends. That the plain man *supposes* there is more to thinghood than this is no doubt true, but the substance he does believe in dissolves on analysis.

A further objection is likely. A generic universal refers to a plurality; yet our account of it would apply about equally well to the thought of an individual thing. Are we really denying that between these modes of thought there is any essential difference? In a sense we must plead guilty to this charge. The thought of a class and the thought of an individual both proceed through the use of universals. Each uses the universal to point beyond itself to the wholly determinate. Each, in order to reach the wholly determinate, would have to supplement itself indefinitely.[1] To follow a generic universal in its radiations through many species and individuals would perhaps be a more difficult task than to follow the thought of an individual

[1] For this process in the thought of an individual, see Chap. XIV, Secs. 19–20.

into its own complete determination. But the task is not different in kind. It differs only in degree, and in a degree so difficult to define as not to be worth using as a basis of ultimate distinction. In this essential they are alike, that they call for a specification of our idea to a point indefinitely beyond its present form. It is, of course, admitted that a distinction does exist here which is of extreme importance to common sense and its logic. Those logicians who think logic should conform to common sense and keep clear of metaphysics may be not a little shocked when the distinction is called in question between reference to an individual thing and reference to the members of a genus. And of course we shall not dream of denying either the fact that this distinction is used nor the contention that for science and common sense that use is indispensable. But it is important to look away occasionally from these established distinctions to the ultimate end that thought is seeking. And that end, we are coming to see (and shall see much more clearly in our final book), is the pursuit of the universal into full determinateness or concreteness. To this farther pursuit we are prompted by the thought of individual and of class alike, unless for practical or other purposes the expansion of meaning is arrested. And what we wish to suggest is that in the course of this pursuit the boundaries that separate things as we know them will be obliterated, and hence that in the end generic ideas can have no place. It must be admitted as undeniable that the immediate reference of the general idea is to individuals. But undeniably also the ultimate end of thought is to apprehend the true and real, and the test of truth and reality (again the defence must be offered later) is satisfaction of the demand of thought for coherence within a system. The question, then, whether the general idea as we now use it is an ultimate form of thought is the question whether the individuals it refers to will satisfy that demand, or whether on inspection they dissolve. The position we shall advocate is that they do so dissolve. Indeed, we shall be compelled to hold of both the individuals forming the scope of the generic universal and the instances or particulars that form the 'differences' of the specific universal that they will not stand in the end. We may expect vigorous protests from the partisans of both. Let us deal first, and very briefly, with individuals, and then look more carefully at 'particulars', since the acceptance of particulars would probably form for both parties the last line of defence.

8. By 'individuals' here we mean the individual things and persons of common sense—Jones and Smith, dogs and cats, watches and pins. And the question is whether these are hard and exclusive units, or whether, on reflection, their separateness gives way. Common sense, as we saw a moment ago, is untroubled by any doubts. It would say that no matter how much alike two pins might be, they were obviously two different pins. But when urged to say precisely what it is in one pin that makes it different from another, common sense has nothing intelligible to answer. If it says that what makes them different is the differing matter in them, the question at once arises, what makes the matter in this pin different from the matter in that? To reply, certain qualities possessed by the one and not by the other, is to invite the obvious answer that the qualities— hardness, heaviness, colour, shape, any others we might mention —are all of them universal, that they might be repeated together as well as singly, and hence that they cannot serve to make *this* lump of matter the unique thing that it is. To reply, again, that the relations of the two are different, that A is to the left of B while B is to the right of A, or that the relations of A to the surrounding objects are different from B's, is to fall once more into the same difficulty. For relations are as truly universal as qualities; and unless we hold to an absolute space, unrepeatable even ideally, a doctrine that to us seems untenable, we must admit that no finite set of relations confers uniqueness. In short, we face a dilemma. If we take what individuates to be a set of relations or qualities, we get what is still universal, and thus fail of our end. On the other hand, if we give up universals and try to burrow below them, if we resort, like Locke and

Aristotle, to a characterless ὕλη or substance which, diverse from characters, still somehow supports them, we find ourselves chasing shadows. In either case, the hard exclusiveness of individuals breaks down.

9. There are many writers to-day who would agree so far, but would draw back from the conclusion to which we feel compelled to go on. They would agree that in the *nature* of an individual there is nothing but qualities and relations, and that these are all universals. But they would deny that the individual can therefore be dissolved away into universals. If asked to say what it is in which a match differs from a pin, they would point first to differences in quality, structure, and use. But if we said, on the strength of this, 'you agree, then, do you, that the only difference between one thing and another lies in these features?', they would have an emphatic and, at first glance, effective answer: 'No, certainly not.' For even if two sets of qualities, or, for simplicity's sake, two single presented qualities, were absolutely alike, they would still not be the same. Precisely the same character may be presented in both cases; the colour of this pin may be precisely the same as the colour of that pin, but what you have before you will still be two and not one. For a *specific universal may have instances.* The particulars may vary while the universal is the same. The same 'what' may have different 'thats'. And once this is seen, the plausibility of your theory goes. That theory is based upon the assumption that the only differentiations of a universal are species or kinds. With such an assumption, to say that the differentiations of a universal are developments of it has an air of plausibility. There does seem to be something in triangularity which dictates and limits the forms of its specification. But the plausibility vanishes when it is realized that besides generic there are specific universals, and that the differentiations of the specific universal are particular instances. These are in no sense 'developments' of the universal; they are mere brute differences, forced on us unintelligibly from without. Granted, if you wish, that all colours and kinds of triangle are specifications or developments of colour and triangularity, it is preposterous to say that what distinguishes two instances of precisely the same shade, or two examples of an isosceles triangle, is itself an outgrowth of triangularity or colour. Nothing in the nature of these universals will throw the least light on whether their particulars shall be a thousand, or a dozen, or none at all, or how, if some do appear, they will differ from each other. We agree that so far as individuals are complexes of qualities in relation, you can break through the lines that separate them; the same quality and the same relation may appear elsewhere. But a quality or relation or complex of these may also be considered as something *occurring or existing*. So considered it is a particular. And what makes it particular is neither a universal nor any specification of a universal, but the mere brute fact of existing at a certain point in time and space. Your theory of the universal as the potentiality of its differences is therefore wrecked on the fact of particulars.

I suspect that most philosophers of the present day would support this criticism. It would certainly receive the support of a school whose influence to-day is great, the school of mathematical logicians. Their doctrine is built upon 'the fact that mathematics (and with it, logic) is concerned with extensions rather than intensions'.[1] The theory of classes forms an integral and essential, even if not fundamental, part of their teaching.[2] Unfortunately it is not easy to extract from the classic of this school, *Principia Mathematica*, any clear notion of what a class means. In certain passages, it appears as 'a symbolic or linguistic convenience', 'an incomplete symbol';[3] elsewhere we read that 'a *class* (which is the same as a *manifold* or *aggregate*) is all the

---

[1] Whitehead and Russell, *Principia Mathematica*, second ed., I. 22.

[2] The fundamental part is the theory of propositions, but this is held to imply the theory of propositional functions, and this in turn the theory of classes. It is thus worth noting that if the latter theory should prove untenable, it would follow by 'the principle of transposition' (the rule of the consequent) that something must be wrong with the foundations.

[3] *Ibid.*, I. 72, 81, etc.

objects satisfying some propositional function'.[1] Sometimes, as in the case of qualities, the class is held to consist of the instances of the quality; though in the case of relations, of which there are also classes, it consists, not of the instances of the relation, since a relation apparently has no instances, but oddly enough, of the couples, triads, etc., which the relation unites.[2] The mathematical logicians would agree that 'the class *men* is not the same as its defining function, "x is human" '[3] but is rather 'x(ϕx), the x's for which the function ϕ is true';[4] and one naturally concludes from this that if there were no such x's, there could be no such class. But this, one gathers, would be deplorably wrong-headed. The class of present inhabitants of the moon,[5] the class of Chinese popes,[6] the class of knighted scavengers and even of squared circles,[7] are as good classes as any other, though they happen to have no members. Whether any consistent doctrine of classes is to be extracted from such statements, we shall not inquire.[8] One point, however, is abundantly clear. In spite of the null class, in spite of the disavowal by *Principia Mathematica* of any assumption that classes exist,[9] in spite of the free admission that intension is necessary to a class, it is left unmistakably plain that without extension a class is nothing. And by extension is meant the particulars or instances, the occurrences or embodiments in which a universal displays itself, taken as themselves irreducible to anything universal.

What are we to say here? Are we to say that while the universal may cover the whole nature of its species, there is something in particulars that is irreclaimably beyond it? We suggest that there is no good reason whatever for saying so.

---

[1] Whitehead and Russell *Principia Mathmatica* second ed., I. 23.

[2] *Ibid.*, 200. 'Thus, the relation of "husband of" in a strictly monogamous country would have as its extension all the *pairs* of husbands and wives.'—Eaton, *General Logic*, 256, note.

[3] Eaton, 414.   [4] *Ibid.*, 411.   [5] *Ibid.*, 421.

[6] Stebbing, *Modern Introduction to Logic*, 148.   [7] *Ibid.*, 184.

[8] Some of the difficulties are discussed by Dr. Paul Weiss, 'The Metaphysics and Logic of Classes', *Monist*, January 1932.

[9] I. 72.

Our position in this ancient controversy may be put simply: There are no particulars. For what gives apparent particularity to any character or complex is itself always universal. The belief that there are particulars radically different from universals can be adequately explained as the result of a twofold confusion.

These confusions we shall turn to in a moment, but first let us consider a case: I have before me two patches of white which are indistinguishable in their shade. Are there two whitenesses before me or one? Common speech would say that we have, or at least might have, 'the same shade' in both patches; and this we accept. It is true that persons who say it may easily begin to doubt, and may then amend it to the effect that what we really have is two shades exactly similar. But this is meaningless. If the shades are exactly similar, then so far as their *quality* is concerned, they are one. If they are not one, where do they differ? To point to some difference other than one of shade would be irrelevant, for it is only shade that is in question. And if we keep to shade, it is admitted that no difference is there. Either, then, the shade is literally one, or we are contradicting ourselves. To admit that in respect to shade there is no difference, and to say at the same time that the shades are two and merely similar, is to talk incoherently. The position that identities in the form of specific universals do exist is thus exceedingly strong.

10. Many critics would, so far, no doubt agree. But the question at issue is not whether there are universals, but whether there is not also something other than universals. The arguments, or as we have just called them, the confusions, that make most people think there is, appear to be two; first, that particulars are directly apprehended in sense, and second, that they are required by difference of position in space and time. To appraise these arguments adequately is no short or easy task, but it can hardly be avoided.

So difficult is it to estimate the first of them, namely that particulars are directly given, that the same thinker in different moods may take opposite views about it. Thus when Bradley was writing his *Logic*, the idea that particular things could be dissolved into universals was so repugnant that even the consideration that such particulars would introduce into the world a surd and opaque element, unmanageable by reason, left him unmoved. He confesses that 'to the arguments urged by reason, and which demonstrate that an element which is not intelligible is nothing, I possibly might not find an intelligible reply'. But 'an obstinate instinct', a 'lingering scruple', the product, perhaps of a 'weakness of the flesh', makes the view intolerable to him that the world of real existence is a 'spectral woof of abstractions, or unearthly ballet of bloodless categories'.[1] But this was the younger Bradley whose metaphysic, as he admitted, was not thought out.[2] In the ten years that followed the writing of this passage, he reflected much and acutely on the matter, and the result shows a significant change. There is now no particularity in things that is alien to thought and unassimilable by it, nothing that resists inclusion in that intelligible system of universals at which thought aims. To be sure, thought in reaching this aim would pass over into reality and commit suicide *as* thought. Still 'there is nothing foreign that thought wants in desiring to be a whole';[3] its end is a system of universals, not an aggregate of particulars. In short, it is required by the nature of thought, and not interdicted by the nature of things, that thought should go on to bridge the interval between itself and its object, and, by compassing both 'what' and 'that' within one whole, should override their difference.[4]

[1] *Logic*, II. 591. The passage is perhaps the best-known in Bradley's writings. It is in line with his earlier discussion of the 'this'. I. 65.

[2] *Ibid.*, I. x–xi; II. 591, note.

[3] *Appearance and Reality*, 181, second ed.

[4] 'In any something the distinction of "that" from "what" is not absolute but only relative. . . . All appearance in the end is but content and character. . . .'—*Appearance*, second ed., appendix, 586. The true position was held unwaveringly by Bosanquet. 'Individuality cannot possibly rest on designation'; 'in principle, uniqueness depends on completeness of explicit conditions and not on designation, and thus we are intensifying and not enfeebling it as we tend to complete

This, we hold, is right. The impression that particular and universal are ultimate disparates is an illusion. It is commonly believed that, granting a state of whiteness, i.e. a specific universal, to be the same in various instances, still what keeps these instances apart is something non-universal. But what can this something be? Not, of course, something in the whiteness itself; if we said that, we should not only contradict ourselves in the manner described above, but we should also have admitted that the difference lies not in particulars, but in characters or universals. Does the difference lie, then, in the greater intensity or vividness or arrestingness of one patch? But these are universals still. Is it in the special combination of these characters, and perhaps of others, in a pattern felt in each case to be unique? But we see on reflection that the pattern in which attributes are combined is as truly universal as the attributes themselves; so the uniqueness that turns on it must vanish with the rest. Does the difference lie, then, in a difference of relation to surrounding objects or to the self? This is to fall back on the second argument, and we shall turn to that in a moment.

11. But now if there is nothing in so-called particulars except what turns out to be universal, how has common sense come by its conclusion that there are unique particulars? Various factors have probably contributed. We saw long ago that in dealing with the qualities of physical things, common sense accepts vaguely an 'it' that owns these qualities, though not itself a quality. We were able to see in this insistence only the survival of a kind of primitive anthropomorphism. The belief in 'hard particulars' comes to much the same thing, and so far can be similarly explained. Still this by itself will not

the organization of experience through ideas'. 'It is altogether perverse to find it in the character of the datum of mere contact.'—*Logic*, II. 260, 261, note. Cf. Bradley's Terminal Essays in the *Logic* on 'Uniqueness' and 'The This'; also his *Essays on Truth and Reality*, 264–5.

suffice, for even when it is seen and allowed for, the feeling persists of a great gulf fixed between particulars and universals. Can this persistence be explained short of the admission that there are particulars? We believe it can if the following factors are added to the account.

First, there is the vague assumption that what is universal is always dim and shadowy and bloodless, and that what is particular is always forcible and vivid. On this assumption, a vivid colour, or an intense tooth-ache would be irreducible to anything universal. But why a quality should cease to be universal by becoming vivid is not evident. The quality of an intense red or an intense pain is surely as repeatable in various contexts as a quality that is less intense. Secondly, we vaguely associate the particular with what is given or forced upon us, and the universal with the product of our own reflection; and, so thinking, we take sight and sounds and odours as of a radically different order from universals. But again we are starting from a false assumption. The multiplication table is as truly forced upon us as the colour of this rose, yet the entities and their relations are all plainly universals. Thirdly, there is the vague assumption that particulars are what we perceive and universals what we conceive, and that there must be a difference of object corresponding to the difference of function. But apart from the difficulty of drawing sharp lines between these functions, we should find that the difference in mental acts is itself an inference from the difference in their objects, and hence an argument from this latter difference would be circular. Finally there is the vague conviction that in what is particular there is a multiplicity of aspects and attributes which our thought has failed to reach and might never be able to exhaust, while a universal character like equality or threeness is relatively definite, transparent, and exhaustible.

Now this is true. It is the first of this series of common-sense convictions about particulars that has been true; and we suggest that it is sufficient by itself to cover all that is valid in the common-sense position. The particular white is to be distinguished from the universal white by the fact that it is taken *in situ*; it is thought of implicitly as a focus of radiating relations. When the white is conceived as a universal, it is divested of these relations artificially; but when it is thought of as this particular white, it is taken as the centre of an inexhaustible web of them, linking it to objects innumerable. This is all that particularity means. And of course if we took this white in its relations to everything else in the universe, we should have something unique and unrepeatable. But no 'particular' ever is so grasped. The narrow complex of relations in which it presents itself and which confers particularity upon it is always theoretically repeatable, and is therefore itself universal. But if what confers particularity is itself universal, there is no essential difference between particulars and universals. The common-sense conviction is thus untenable.

12. We have just said that the complex of relations which serves in fact to make things particular, is itself universal. This will be disputed vigorously. Indeed, the denial of it constitutes the second principal argument against the reducibility of particulars. This argument appears in different forms. Sometimes it is a direct appeal to the reader's insight to recognize that a particular is uniquely defined by certain of its relations; sometimes the further argument is pressed that unless one admits such uniqueness, one must end in self-contradiction. The first form of the contention has been advanced with great persuasiveness by Professor Montague. He writes:

'The given elements of experience are complexes of universals, each complex being associated with a particular position in the space and time series. It is this latter factor of position which constitutes particularity and makes each individual numerically different from each other individual. . . . *In short, a particular is nothing but a complex of universals endowed with a position in space and time.*'[1]

[1] *Ways of Knowing*, 77. Italics in original; this holds of later citations except where a note says otherwise.

Mr. Montague is emphatic that 'the time and space factors of
position' are not to be regarded, as they are by extreme rational-
ists, as 'additional universals':

> 'The additional something that differentiates the particular
> from the universal is position in space and time . . . existence
> is not a new *quality*, which when added to the other qualities
> of a possible object makes it actual. It is rather a thing's *relation*
> of interaction or spatio-temporal connection with the totality
> of other things.'[1]

This is an invitingly simple and straightforward view. On
reflection, however, difficulties begin to appear.

(1) On one interpretation of the theory, which in the light of
the language used is a natural one, the view is hardly consistent
with itself. A thing, we read, is a complex of qualities and relations, and it is the relations, above all the temporal and spatial
relations, that prevent its evaporating into a mere complex of
universals. We are also told that to arrive at a universal 'it is
necessary only to fix the attention upon the quality or relation
as it exists *in situ*, and to affix a name to that part of the complex
which has been thus discriminated'.[2] Now are the temporal and
spatial relations of a thing among the universals that we can
thus single out? Mr. Montague replies that they are. Thus
if the individual is a horse, '*the time at which the horse was seen*,
the place where he was, his qualities, generic and individual,
may become in turn the exclusive object of my thoughts'.[3] So
attended to, each is a universal. Spatial and temporal relations
are thus themselves universals. And so what is added to a
complex of qualities to take it out of the realm of universals
turns out to be nothing but further universals.

In making such criticism are we offering anything better
than an undistributed middle? Universals are reached by
abstraction; spatial and temporal relations as such are also
reached by abstraction; therefore spatial and temporal relations
are universal. If this is our argument, it is, of course, formally
worthless. It would have weight only if being taken in abstrac-

[1] *Ways of Knowing*, 110, 111.   [2] *Ibid.*, 76.
[3] *Ibid.*, 72; italics mine.

tion were regarded, not as an adventitious character which happened to belong alike to universals and spatio-temporal relations, but as something *constitutive* of universality. On this assumption, the fact that relations of space and time may be apprehended in abstraction *would* show that they are universal. Does Mr. Montague make this assumption? I can hardly suppose he does. But it sounds at times as if he were saying: What makes a thing particular *is* its involvement in a web of relations; what makes it universal *is* its disengagement from this web in thought; which disengagement *is* abstraction. And it is worth seeing that if this is maintained, it will not stand. If such disengagement renders a quality universal, it will also render a relation universal, or any set of relations to which it can be applied. Where A is lighter than B and darker than C, I can abstract these relations from the concrete situation as readily as I can the qualities; and therefore if either is universal, both will be. But it is precisely such relations as these that form a term's 'denotation' and make it particular. The relations supposed to particularize are themselves all universals.

13. (2) Some philosophers would, no doubt, reply that though this holds of some relations, it does not hold of spatio-temporal relations. These are a class apart, and can particularize where others cannot. But it is hard to find adequate grounds for this. To be sure, a thing's relations to other things in the way of worth, for example, or degree, are less distinct and easy to apprehend, and thus in the work of designation are less useful; but it is not clear why this should diminish their value in principle as determinants of uniqueness. The only ground I can see for thinking so is that, while the other relations of a thing are capable in theory of being repeated, its relations in space and time are not. On this one can make no better comment than was made by Bradley more than fifty years ago:

> 'We must get rid of the erroneous notion (if we have it) that space and time are "principles of individuation", in the sense that a temporal or spatial exclusion will confer uniqueness upon any content. It is an illusion to suppose that, by speaking of

"events", we get down to real and solid particulars, and leave
the airy region of universal adjectives. For the question arises,
What space and time do we really mean? . . . it is clear that
exclusion within a given series does not carry with it an absolute uniqueness. There is nothing whatever in the idea of a
series to hint that there may not be any number of series,
internally all indistinguishable from the first. . . . If we simply
attend to the series itself, and, declining to look outside, confine
ourselves to the consideration of its character, then all that it
contains might be the common property of innumerable
subjects, existing and enjoyed in the world of each, a general
possession appropriated by none. . . . Such particularity in space
and time, such an exclusive nature, after all, is only a *general*
character. It falls in the content and does not give the existence.
It marks the sort, but it misses the thing.'[1]

This gives the principle clearly. Sets of spatial or temporal
relations, taken in abstraction, may be many; hence position
in one of them will not by itself confer uniqueness. If anyone
doubts whether such plurality is thinkable, perhaps an illustration will help. Suppose we were so made that we spent half
of each day in dream and the other half 'awake', and that all
the things and events in one half duplicated the things and
events of the other; which world would be the real one? The
question is not new, and the answer, I suppose, is pretty well
established; the two orders would have equal title to real
existence. But note that there would be no spatial uniqueness,
not even if the orders were extended to infinity; for however
far the determination of a thing were carried in one order, it
could be paralleled in the other.

14. (3) It may be replied that particulars may be saved if
we give up the view that what particularizes is merely relations
in space and time, and include other relations as well. Anyone
who depends on relations to particularize is under a constant
inward pressure to enlarge the area and multiply the kinds of
these relations. If he selects a certain set of relations in space,
he soon sees that this set might ideally be repeated, so he ex-

[1] Bradley, *Logic*, I. 65–6; cf. also I. 290.

tends it to include all space. Since, again, a plurality of spaces seems conceivable, he goes on to include within his particularizing complex the temporal as well as spatial relations of his term. Then, reflecting that there is no cogent reason for selecting these rather than other sets of relations, he goes on to include still further sets of relations, such as the logical and the causal, and ends by saying that one never gets what is fully particular until one has specified its relations of every kind to everything else in the universe. I understand that this is Professor Montague's own position.[1] He holds that there are 'any number' of relational systems besides those of space and time that contribute to particularity. The inevitable end of such reflections seems to me clear. So long as one remains within a limited field of relations one is always confronted with the theoretic possibility (and nothing more is required) that this complex should be repeated, and just so long one is tarrying within the land of universals. If this domain is to be escaped, it can only be by carrying the widening circles of relations on all their planes to completeness. When that completeness has been achieved, then, and only then, will one have attained particularity. But surely this conclusion is disastrous for those who believe in particulars in the ordinary sense. For all that we commonly call particulars, pots and pans, mountains and rivers, are now seen to be universals. The only true particular is the absolute.

15. (4) We add another comment for which a remark of Cook Wilson's has provided the cue. He points out that if we get the true universal of any given particular, we have something that covers the whole nature of that particular. This is sometimes forgotten, even by logicians. They offer as particulars of blueness particular blue flowers. But this clearly is a mistake. To be sure, a flower may be as truly a particular as anything can; a given hyacinth is a case of 'hyacinthness'; but 'in the

[1] *Ways of Knowing*, 81, 339-40, 355-7.

sentence "this flower is blue", "this flower" is not a particular of "blueness", since blueness does not cover its whole nature: the true particular of blueness is the *colour* of the flower, not the flower itself'.[1]

If we take this simple point seriously, we may save ourselves more than one confusion. It will be less easy to talk loosely, as mathematical logicians are inclined to do, about different propositional functions determining the same class. We read that 'the range of possible determinations of two variables may be the same';[2] and that 'a single (self-identical) thing may participate in many different universals; a single class of things may, therefore, be defined by many different propositional functions'.[3] 'Thus the class *men* is determined both by the defining property *rational animal*, and by the defining property *being two-legged and featherless*. "It is", as Mr. Russell points out, "this fact that a defining characteristic is never unique which makes classes useful." '[4] No doubt common sense and some science do deal with classes in this rough and approximate way. Since, to paraphrase the language used, a single lump of sugar may participate in the universals whiteness and sweetness, it will serve as an instance of both. But surely this is deplorable logic. Since the lump includes *both* whiteness and sweetness, to regard the lump as a whole as an instance of whiteness, is to include within the instance of whiteness that which is not whiteness at all. And that is nonsense. So far as the lump is sweet, it is not an instance of whiteness; and so far as it is white, it is not an instance of sweetness. Hence Mr. Russell's explanation of the usefulness of classes, that their defining characteristic is never unique, misses its mark. How, if one speaks strictly, a 'defining characteristic' that does not define uniquely can *define* at all is a puzzle; but let that pass. The fact Mr. Russell is pointing to, is apparently such as this: that when we look over our instances of the character 'having a specific gravity of

---

[1] *Statement and Inference*, I. 349.   [2] *Principia Mathematica*, 5. .
[3] Eaton, *General Logic*, 418.
[4] Stebbing, *Modern Introduction to Logic*, 148. The quotation is from Russell's *Introduction to Mathematical Philosophy*, 14.

19.27', we find these uniformly accompanied by instances of the character 'soluble in aqua regia'; hence one defining characteristic of a class can be used as an index to the other. But surely what we have here is not two universals whose 'particulars' are the same, a quite unthinkable notion, but something very different and very simple, namely two universals whose 'particulars' *accompany* each other. Thus if a class is taken as the instances of a universal, it is bound to lack that usefulness that Mr. Russell ascribes to it, while if it does possess this, it is thereby shown to be not a class.

Whether Professor Montague would agree with us here against the mathematical logicians I do not know; but I hope and believe he would. If he did, it would be fair to press the inference that, even upon his own theory of particulars, particulars cannot strictly differ from universals. In the colour of a blue flower we recognize, he would say, a particular whose universal is some shade of blueness. What is it that distinguishes this particular from its universal? Professor Montague would reply, I suppose: The particular is the universal *related* in this way and that to *a, b, c,* etc. But to say that the universal is particularized *in* these relations would be to say that the universal can be particularized in an alien or foreign content; and this we have seen to be meaningless. So far as a particular is a particular of whiteness, it cannot include within itself its own relations in space. Hence we are confronted with a dilemma. If we take as the particular of a universal the whole complex of the universal-*in-situ*, our particular is not *of* the universal at all, since it errs by gross excess. On the other hand, if we omit from the particular what is alien and irrelevant, the difference vanishes; particular and universal are the same. This, we urge, is the right conclusion. It is perfectly true, of course, that between the universal taken by itself and the universal *in situ*, there is an important practical difference; and this difference is what the current distinction really comes to. There is even a marked theoretical difference, and we shall later find it necessary to go beyond Professor Montague himself in maintaining the importance to the universal of the

context in which it appears.[1] But just as we have argued that
what is 'added' to a universal to make it particular is still universal, so we should here insist that the core added to is not something mysteriously different from the universal, not the universal
plus existence or givenness or contact or something else; it is
just the universal itself.[2]

16. We have been considering an argument for particulars
which would distinguish them from universals through their
position in relational systems. We must look now at a special
and telling form of this argument. In this form, it would go
on to maintain that what owns such relations *must* be particulars,
since the assumption that it is universals would lead to
contradiction or absurdity. Mr. Russell puts the argument as
follows: Take two patches of white which, in respect to colour,
are indistinguishable, but which are in different places in
space.

> 'It is this spatial plurality which makes the difficulty of the
> theory that denies particulars.' In virtue of the properties of
> space, 'the numerical diversity of the two patches of white is
> self-evident. They have the relation of being outside each other,
> and this requires that they should be two, not one.' '. . . for
> example, if *x* is above *y*, *x* and *y* must be different entities'.
> 'Thus the fact that it is logically possible for precisely similar
> things to co-exist in two different places, but that things in

---

[1] See the discussions in Chaps. XXVII, XXXI, and XXXII on
coherence and internal relations.

[2] There is a further serious difficulty with the view that position in
space and time confers particularity. My present toothache would
seem clearly enough to be particular. But what is its spatial position?
Mr. Montague would probably meet this by reference to his own
theory of consciousness as potential energy in the brain. But for one
who holds the above view of particulars, while unable to believe that
conscious events are in space, there is bound to be trouble. Mr. R. B.
Braithwaite, holding this view of particulars, but naturally hesitating
to apply it to mental events, is driven to propose that the universal-
particular distinction be abandoned altogether in the mental realm.
(*Arist. Soc. Proc.*, Sup. Vol. VI, 1926, 35.) It would be more plausible, I think, to give up his theory of the distinction.

different places at the same time cannot be numerically identical, forces us to admit that it is particulars, *i.e. instances* of
universals that exist in places, and not universals themselves.'[1]

Thus, to say that the whiteness which appears in the two
patches is literally and numerically the same whiteness would
be to say that something can, at the same time, be above and
below, to the right and the left of itself. And that is absurd.
This sounds decisive, since the axiom that a thing cannot be
in two places at once would seem beyond question.

17. (1) But it is doubtful whether any course we could take
here would avoid violence to the axiomatic. At any rate, I do
not see that the course just described avoids it. What we find
in each of the patches is, we are told, not a universal which is
numerically the same in both; that would put the universal
in two places at once. What each has is only an *instance* of this
universal. But then, what is it that makes each an instance?
Surely it must be the presence in it of the universal in question.
And so the absurdity, if it is such, of a universal in two places
at once, is not escaped after all. You avoid saying that the same
whiteness is in two places by saying 'No, not numerically the
same whiteness; only instances of the same'. But these can be
instances of the same only if the same is possessed or exemplified
by both; that is the lowest price at which the privilege of being
an instance can be purchased. And thus you admit what you
were trying to avoid. It is true that this conclusion can be
escaped, but the alternatives would seem to be worse. One
might say, for example, of the instance, as of the patch, that
what is present in it is not the universal whiteness, but only an
instance of this. What would make anything an instance would
thus be the presence in it of an instance of an instance, which,
of course, would be but an instance of another instance, and
so on without end. This will convince nobody; by such a
process, one would never reach the universal at all; and failing

[1] *Arist. Soc. Proc.*, N.S., Vol. 12, 1911–12; I have pieced together
passages from pp. 10, 17, 11, in this order.

this, the instance would not be an instance of anything. Or
again, one might make valour one's discretion, and say boldly
that the two patches have nothing in common whatever.
This would be equivalent to the denial that there is any such
thing as identity. But one cannot even present such a position
self-consistently. For in doing so one at least assumes the
identity of what one is putting forward and what someone else
is supposed to believe; and universals are again admitted.

18. (2) Thus the argument we are examining lacks coherence.
In order to dispose of a universal which is in different places
but self-identical, it must introduce this again surreptitiously.
And if we look at the argument in its larger context, we discover
further incoherence. Mr. Russell, who appears here as the
defender of particulars, has also advocated the view that
relations have no particulars.[1] He would say that in '3 is greater
than 2' and '5 is greater than 4', we do not have two instances
of the relation 'greater than'; we have only one relation connecting two different pairs of terms. If Antony is bound to
Cleopatra by the relation of loving, and Othello is also bound
to Desdemona by the relation of loving, then the binding tie
in the two cases is numerically the same.

On this two comments suggest themselves. In the first
place it seems impossible that the sharp line here proposed
between qualities and relations, as between entities that have
instances and others that lack them, can be maintained. To say
that when we judge 'Antony was amatory' we *are* pointing to
an instance of love, and when we judge 'Antony was amatory
toward Cleopatra' we are *not* pointing to an instance of loving,
seems incredible. We may say that on examination both the
apparent instances are themselves sets of universals, as I think
we must eventually; or we may try to resolve both into particulars, as some of Mr. Russell's followers have done.[2] But to

---

[1] *Principles of Mathematics*, Sec. 55.

[2] F. P. Ramsey, for example; see *Mind*, N.S., Vol. 24, October
1925; *Arist. Soc. Proc.*, Vol. 6, 1926, 17 ff. It is perhaps needless to
add that I see no hope along these lines.

say that in the one case we have a particular, though not in
the other, is to force a distinction upon the facts which those
facts are quite incapable of bearing. In the second place, the
distinction tempts to a reply *ad hominem*. To admit it is to
involve oneself in the same kind of paradox that Mr. Russell
considered a barrier to qualitative identity in the two patches;
and we should urge that if this barrier can be surmounted here,
it can there also. If we suppose that between Antony's loving
Cleopatra and Othello's loving Desdemona (let us assume for
convenience that the latter pair once lived) some sixteen
centuries intervened, and if we suppose further that the
relation of loving was the same, do we not find this same relation appearing both before and after itself? And is this less
paradoxical than saying a thing can be to the right and left
of itself? It may be maintained, of course, and I think Mr.
Russell does maintain, that such relations are not in time any
more than they are in space. But to deny that Antony and
Othello loved at any time seems equivalent to denying that they
ever loved at all. Our conclusion, then, must be this: one who
holds that relations *can* dispense with instances is hardly in a
position to hold that qualities *cannot* dispense with them. If one
can surmount the paradoxes in the first case, there is no reason
why one should not surmount the very similar ones in the
second.

19. (3) The difficulty of accepting particulars may be brought
out in another way. If there are such things at all, they must
present themselves either as something that is asserted, or as
something that is asserted about. There are writers who maintain that frequently, if not always, they figure as predicates;
others who hold that they figure only as subjects. Thus Mr.
Joseph holds that our predicate, when we attribute wisdom to
Socrates, is not wisdom, the universal, but a particular instance
of it. 'As I understand the issue', he writes, 'no universal is ever
predicated of a particular (I would rather have said of an
individual). If Socrates was wise, it was because an instance of

wisdom dwelt within him . . .'[1] Mr. Russell, on the other hand, writes that 'if predication is an ultimate relation [as he thinks it is], the best definition of particulars is that they are entities which can only be subjects of predicates or terms of relations, *i.e.*, that they are (in the logical sense) substances'.[2] Now I do not see that particulars can perform either of these functions, nor therefore that they have any function at all.

Of the first position, that particulars figure as what is asserted, a telling criticism was offered by Mr. Ramsey,[3] and we shall not go beyond it. He points out that what we assert cannot be instances, for the reason that it would then be impossible to assert falsely. Assume that when we say something of Socrates, we are asserting an instance or a particular; and assume further that we are saying something false, such as 'Socrates is foolish'. If the proposition really is false, there will be no such particular at all as a Socrates who is foolish. But if there is no such particular, it cannot be used in assertion; and hence, on the theory before us, the assertion cannot be made. But since we know that it is made, the theory that would compel us to deny this must be mistaken.

Let us turn to the other alternative. If particulars cannot stand as predicates and be asserted, can they serve as the subjects to which universals are ascribed? This view is no more plausible than the other. For what *is* the particular of which, on this theory, the universal is asserted? We have seen that to take a whole individual as the particular of all the universals that meet in it is a logical error; so far as the 'particular' is anything that does not exemplify its own universal, it is not the particular of *that* universal at all. Hence if the subject of 'this is white' is to be truly the particular of the universal predicated, that subject can only be 'this white'. But 'this white' is just the specific quality presented to us; and as this is also what we are asserting, the difference between subject and predicate disappears. Our predicate and our supposed subject are both universal, and the *same* universal. If it is insisted that there is

[1] *Arist. Soc. Proc., ibid.*, 8.   [2] *Ibid.*, N.S. Vol. 12, 23.
[3] *Ibid.*, Sup. Vol. 6, 18.

something more in the subject, we would ask that it be pointed out. We cannot anticipate the answer, but we may offer a dilemma on the horns of which any answer will probably fall. If this 'something more' goes beyond the nature of the universal asserted, offering as subject, for example, some temporal segment or spatial area, then the subject is not a particular of *that* universal, and to insist that it is, would mean logical chaos. On the other hand, if the particular contains nothing beyond its universal, then it is idle to say that they are different. And if it is objected that in thus identifying predicate and apparent subject with one universal and so with each other, we are setting the judgement adrift with no subject whatever, we can only say, as on another point earlier, that the answer has been given long ago. It is a mere mistake to take the grammatical, or even the logical subject of judgement as necessarily the true subject. These are as genuinely universals as the grammatical or logical predicate. What is asserted is the universal, or complex of universals represented by both together; and as for the subject, 'the true subject of judgement is, not this or that finite person or thing, but the ultimate reality'.[1]

20. (4) All this may be thought a beating about the bush. Mr. Russell's point was simple and definite, namely that if we did away with particulars, we should have to say, for example, that the same universal was both to the left and to the right of itself. We have been arguing that our opponents themselves have not got rid of paradoxes, but we shall hardly remove the beam from our own eye by pointing to the mote in someone else's. Mr. Russell's criticism has still to be met.

Dr. G. E. Moore has met it by drawing a distinction which we would gladly adopt if we could. In replying to a defence of particulars by Stout, he writes:

> Professor Stout's whole point seems to me to rest on supposing that there is no distinction between the sense in which two *concrete things* can be said to be "locally separate", and that in

[1] Bradley, *Logic*, I. 181, and almost *passim*.

which two *characters* can be said to be so. . . . I admit . . . that it is impossible for one and the same concrete thing to be in two different places at the same time. But when we speak of two qualities as "locally separate" we seem to me to be using the phrase in an entirely different sense. All that we mean, or can mean, by it, is, I think, that the first belongs to a concrete thing which is locally separate (in our first sense) from a concrete thing to which the second belongs. And with *this* sense of "locally separate", it seems to me perfectly obvious that a quality can be "locally separate" from itself: one and the same quality can be in two different places at the same time.'[1]

I have not succeeded in following this. It seems by no means clear that when we speak of two qualities as in different places, our sense is 'entirely different' from what it is when we say this of things. On the contrary, when the plain man speaks of the colour or shape of a leaf, it seems to me that he thinks of this as where the leaf is, and as locally separate from the qualities of another leaf in precisely the same sense as is one leaf from another. Nor does there seem to be any good reason for gainsaying him here. When we were studying 'things' we found nothing in them but qualities in relation. Hence if a thing is in a certain place, its qualities must be there; if these are not there, what is? To say, then, that by a quality's being in two places at once, and by a thing's being so, we mean something 'entirely different' is not an available line of escape.

Our reply must be more radical, for the objection goes very deep; indeed it points to nothing less than a conflict between categories, between identity on the one hand and spatial and temporal relation on the other; nor does there seem to be any way of meeting it except to decide for one of the parties. And this is a very grave responsibility, for both are accepted with absolute confidence by science and common sense. That identity is so accepted scarcely needs showing. No one doubts, in the ordinary course of things, that the same tree or person may persist, or that the sums of two columns of figures may be the same. To be sure, as we have seen in the preceding chapter, abstract identities are not always discoverable where they are

[1] *Proc. Arist. Soc.*, Sup. Vol. 3, 1923, 105-6.

supposed to be. But to abandon identity generally would be to abjure all reasoning, since inference moves through identity; indeed this alternative is not intelligible. And it is useless to offer a substitute 'just as good' in the form of the 'exactly similar'. For the substitute is really nothing but the old identity reappearing under an *alias*.[1] Identity is indispensable. But then, on the other hand, spatio-temporal difference seems indispensable too. Few axioms are more compelling, as we have seen, than that a thing cannot at once be in two places. And since, if a thing is spatial, some at least of its qualities must be spatial too, it would seem that the axiom holds also of these qualities; they too, are cut off from being in two places at once. If you say they can be, you end in the quicksand Mr. Russell warns of, the conclusion that precisely the same entity is to the right and left of itself. And that again is nonsense. We are thus in an extraordinary position. Identity and spatio-temporal difference are both indispensable. Yet if we take identity seriously, we land in spatio-temporal absurdity; and if the exclusiveness of space and time is taken seriously, we end by denying identity. What are we to do?

So far as I can see, there is but one way out, and that a most disagreeable way. One or other of the two things described as indispensable must somehow be surrendered. And if compelled to abandon one, we can hardly hesitate to say which. It is, no doubt, a shock to common sense to hear that spatio-temporal arrangement cannot be real just as it appears, but at least this is not nonsense or inconsistent with itself. On the other hand, a general denial of identity would be both.

No one will accuse us of blind partisanship for identity, for we have devoted the last chapter to an attack on the most popular form of it. The set of explicit and conspicuous qualities that are supposed to be identical in all triangles and all colours we could not find. And when we come to consider internal

---

[1] 'What in principle is the objection to this use of "exact likeness"? The objection is that resemblance, if and so far as you make it "exact" by removing all internal difference, has so far ceased to be mere resemblance, and has become identity.'—Bradley, *Appearance*, second ed., 595; cf. his *Logic*, I. 286–7, 377–8, and above, Sec. 9.

relations (Chaps. XXXI and XXXII), we shall see that there are difficulties even about what we have called specific universals—threeness, this shade of white—which will incline us to say that identity is a matter of degree, attaining here its maximum, rather than that it is anywhere absolute. But in attacking the abstract universal, we were not seeking to destroy identity; we were seeking to find its true residence; and unless it is granted a residence somewhere, we do not believe that either scientific generalization, or indeed thought of any kind, can be made intelligible. Compelled, then, to choose between identity on the one hand and spatio-temporal arrangement on the other, we can only choose identity. *Choice*, indeed, is hardly the word; we 'can no other'.[1]

Where the stakes are so tremendous, one must be clear about the issue. What we assert is that if you take identity seriously, you cannot also take the space and time order to be real, just as it comes to us. And since to reject the reality of this order is a violent expedient, there are, no doubt, those who will say: 'I would rather take my stand with particulars, and the space and time that go with them, than vote for identities at so prohibitive a cost.' But we must repeat that this course is not open. You cannot give up identity even if you want to. And, to put as a second point what is partly the same, the issue is not a bare alternative between the following: on the one hand, identity plus the belief that there is nothing but universals; and on the other, space and time plus the belief that there is nothing but particulars. You do not get rid of universals merely by believing in space and time, for they crop out again everywhere within these orders themselves. Every relation in space—to the left of, above, east, west—is a universal; and a body's extension seems just as plainly universal as its colour or its weight. Thirdly, though taking all attributes as universals does force

---

[1] Mr. Russell, in the article quoted, appears to save both categories by saying that what is identical is universals only, and what is locally separate is particulars only; hence no conflict arises. But this turns on the assumption that a universal can be particularized at a point in space or time without being there itself, and this we have found unthinkable.

us to call in question the space-time order as we know it, the mere acceptance of that order does not prove that particulars exist. For particularity, properly conceived, is the uniqueness achieved by *exhausting* a thing's relations; and thus mere loyalty to space and time will not rescue their contents from universality. It is an illusion to suppose you can save a plurality of particulars by standing up boldly for space, time, and common sense. For none of these, either singly or in their unity, will really serve to particularize.

It is impossible here to run out all the momentous consequences of preferring identity to the space-time order. Our point has been simply to meet what looked like a decisive argument for particulars, namely that to deny them entailed the nonsense of saying that what is the same could be in two places at once, or to the right or left of itself. We have replied that to ordinary thought this is indeed nonsense, but that the belief in spatio-temporal particulars leads in the end to worse nonsense still, since it involves the denial of identity. And because there was some hope of escaping the nonsense about space and time, if we could suppose these to be other than they seemed, while there was no hope whatever if we gave up identity, we threw in our lot with the latter.

21. Perhaps the most obvious objections to our theory of the general idea on its logical side have now been dealt with. To the objection that it failed to distinguish the general from the abstract idea, we answered that it does distinguish these, though by a difference of degree only. To the objection that it failed to allow for the plurality of its objects, we answered that this plurality might be of two sorts, of individuals or of particulars. If the first was meant, our reply was that an individual was a synthesis of characters, and these being universal, their synthesis was, or might be, universal also. If the second was meant, we found a more elaborate analysis necessary. The existence of particulars was usually supported either by an appeal to common sense, or by arguments drawn from position in space and time.

The common-sense conviction, we pointed out, rested on obvious confusions. The argument from spatio-temporal position was more formidable; but having examined the main forms of it as presented by two prominent advocates, we were compelled to dismiss it too. Apparently our position still stands.

According to that position, if we may repeat for clarity's sake, the universal triangle or man or colour is not as such real. There is no abstract triangle or triangularity existing in all triangles as a little hard nucleus unaffected by the mode of its realization; there is no abstract humanity that is quite identical in all men; there is no colour that is colour in general. The generic universal lies not in the reality thought about, but in our thought about that reality. And this thought is in essence a purpose, seeking to define and fulfil itself in its object. Hence to get enlightenment about it, we must address ourselves to its end; and in the course of our discussion this end has become clearer. It was natural to suppose that the end in which the thought of man would find fulfilment was individual men. But an individual revealed, on closer scrutiny, nothing but a synthesis of characters and relations which were themselves universals in the traditional sense. Could we say, then, that the differences between individuals were illusory? At first glance, No; for even if individuals were wholly made of universals, these universals still differed in their instances, which themselves seemed irreducible. Thus it looked as if we should have to amend our theory and say that the general idea was fulfilled, not in a range of individuals but in a range of particulars. So to particulars we turned our attention, only to find them vanishing before our eyes. The particular, like the individual thing, turned out to be an aggregate of specific universals. Would it do, then, to say that what a general idea referred to, was a range of aggregates of this kind? For all purposes of common thought, for all purposes of scientific correlation, Yes; in any ultimate sense, No. For if thought, on one side, lives and moves among these aggregates, it means, on the other, to assert of the real; and between that real and these loose aggregates there is a great gulf fixed. The real which thought seeks and means is an intelligible real. And these loose congeries of characters that concern it immediately are *not* intelligible if taken as they come. Their linkage within and without is accidental; and against such mere conjunctions thought always in the end rebels. At a certain level, and for purposes other than its own, it may acquiesce in them. But since its central and driving impulse is the hunger for necessity, it cannot be put off with them indefinitely; its demand is for something better.

By 'better' can only be meant what is more satisfactory to this impulse to understand. And such satisfaction can only be achieved when the loose aggregates that now present themselves as 'things' are seen to be bound, both within and without, by bonds that are intelligible. We say that a rose is red and sweet. If *and* were an intelligible relation, it would be pointless to ask why, in this case, redness came linked to sweetness rather than something else; but the question is clearly meaningful. It may be, of course, that between these qualities there is no relation that in the end is intelligible, that their association would still seem an accident even to one who knew all about them. But certainly no reason for believing this is to be drawn from our present ignorance, and if thought cannot assume that to its questions there are intelligible answers, it will die from lack of motive. It can only hold its goal to be legitimate until this is proved to be illegitimate. Again, just as we must assume that the qualities of one thing are intelligibly connected, so we must assume that the things themselves are linked intelligibly in a system that includes them. We say that a triangle has three angles. But *three* belongs to the system of number, and to grasp its nature and implications would carry us to the farthest limits of that system. *Angle* belongs to geometric space, and if we were to develop all that is implicit in the concept, perhaps nothing in geometry would be left out. So of all the other characters of anything; each lies in a web or plane extending far beyond itself; and what we call the thing is an intersection of these planes. Thus thought cannot rest in the thing. It finds itself carried out along each of these planes and then seduced by the suggestion that the planes must be further

related to each other. The generic universal, triangle, can specify
its meaning only in the alternative species of triangle. These
species, as the thought develops, resolve themselves into sub-
species, and these again into 'particulars' which, as we have
seen, are properly aggregates of specific universals. But neither
can thought rest with these; it must introduce a system among
them, and then, if possible, a wider system. And once launched
on this process of expansion, where are we to halt? Are we to
say that every thought is the start of a pilgrimage which, if
pressed, would take us *everywhere* else? We shall find this hard
to gainsay. We may arbitrarily cut off the enterprise at any
point, and, of course, we do so constantly. But it seems clear
that, left to itself, the theoretic impulse cannot rest while anything in the universe is outside the web of necessity. Thought
is the movement of experience toward a special type of completeness; it is the pursuit of intellectual integrity; and so long as
the field of experience remains a litter of *disjecta membra*, such
integrity is still to be achieved.

But here we are anticipating. With such reflections we are
leaving the field of ideas and entering that of inference; and
we must now turn to the modes by which thought expands and
connects its ideas. To be sure there is no clear line at which
idea passes into reasoning, and we have insisted upon the
restlessness of that impulse which would expand every thought
into system, and necessary system. Two very large questions
remain: What are the steps by which that expansion is effected?
How are we to conceive of the necessity in which thought can
ultimately rest? The first of these questions will be dealt with
in Book III, which follows; the second in Book IV.

GEORGE ALLEN & UNWIN LTD

Head Office:
London: 40 Museum Street, W.C.1

Trade orders and enquiries:
Park Lane, Hemel Hempstead, Herts

Auckland: P.O. Box 36013, Northcote Central, N.4
Barbados: P.O. Box 222, Bridgetown
Beirut: Deeb Building, Jeanne d'Arc Street
Bombay: 15 Graham Road, Ballard Estate, Bombay 1
Buenos Aires: Escritorio 454–459, Florida 165
Calcutta: 17 Chittaranjan Avenue, Calcutta 13
Cape Town: 68 Shortmarket Street
Hong Kong: 105 Wing On Mansion, 26 Hancow Road, Kowloon
Ibadan: P.O. Box 62
Karachi: Karachi Chambers, McLeod Road
Madras: Mohan Mansions, 38c Mount Road, Madras 6
Mexico: Villalongin 23, Mexico 5, D.F.
Nairobi: P.O. Box 30583
New Delhi: 13–14 Asaf Ali Road, New Delhi 1
Toronto: 81 Curlew Drive, Don Mills
Philippines: P.O. Box 157, Quezon City D–502
Rio de Janeiro: Caixa Postal 2537–Zc–00
Singapore: 36c Prinsep Street, Singapore 7
Sydney, N.S.W.: Bradbury House, 55 York Street
Tokyo: P.O. Box 26, Kamata

Language and Reality

THE PHILOSOPHY OF LANGUAGE AND THE PRINCIPLES OF SYMBOLISM

by Wilbur Marshall Urban
Author of *Valuation: The Theory of Value, The Intelligible World*, etc.

Language and Reality deals with the problems of language and symbolism which have been in the forefront of philosophical discussion in recent years. It includes two parts, entitled the Philosophy of Language and the Principles of Symbolism. In the solution of the problems, the bearing of linguistic science on debatable points has been studied and the role of Symbolism in the various fields of science, art and religion examined. An attempt is made to formulate a general theory of Symbolism.

The central thesis of the book is that problems of knowledge and truth are inseparable from problems of language. The main argument thus resolves about the treatment of two themes: the notions of communication and intelligibility. All knowledge, including what we know as science, is, in the last analysis, discourse, and the conditions of intelligible communication thus become the basal problem of any philosophy. The relations of these two notions, together with that of verification, have been worked out on new lines, and an attempt has been made towards a solution of the problem.

The author holds that an adequate philosophy of language is the necessary prolegomena to any metaphysics. A study of the language and symbolism of metaphysics, from this standpoint, justifies, he believes, the claim of metaphysics to be a valid form of knowledge. The book may, therefore, be viewed as a contribution to metaphysics.

Some Main Problems of Philosophy

by G. E. Moore

'An important book . . . we find in it the most salutary spectacle of a writer determined to make himself absolutely clear, to claim no solution where none is reached, and to be distracted by nothing whatever from the pursuit of literal truth, good sense, and plain language.'—*Listener*.

The Discipline of the Cave

by J. N. Findlay

Identity and Reality

by Emile Meyerson

The Modern Predicament

A STUDY IN THE PHILOSOPHY OF RELIGION

by H. J. Paton

Professor Paton's Gifford Lectures, delivered in St. Andrews in 1950 and 1951, are not directed primarily to professional philosophers: they are intended for all thoughtful men who are affected by modern discontents. Free from the paraphernalia of footnotes and appendices and written without the austerity of continual qualifications, they attempt to discuss, as simply and dispassionately as possible, the predicament of men, and especially religious men, living in an age of scientific scepticism and in a world wholly different from that in which religion had its birth and growth.

Belief

by H. H. Price

These two volumes are based on the Gifford Lectures delivered at the University of Aberdeen in 1959–60, though a good deal of new material has been added since.

Kant's First Critique

by H. W. Cassirer

This book is one of the few published in this country which deal fully with the whole of Kant's *Critique of Pure Reason*. The author engages in a detailed investigation of the text of the Aesthetic and Analytic, and pays the same close attention to the Dialectic which seeks to establish the fallaciousness of all arguments purporting to lead us beyond sense-experience. The work is throughout both expository and critical in character. It is written in simple and straightforward language, all matters which could be of interest only to Kantian specialists have been rigorously excluded.

Nature, Mind and Modern Science

by Errol E. Harris

The author of this book asserts that the prevailing fashion of Empiricism is a return to an obsolete and outdated type of philosophy which is not in harmony with the scientific temper of the modern age. He argues that it is a doctrine appropriate to a stage of scientific advance that has long been superseded.

Clarity Is Not Enough

ESSAYS IN CRITICISM OF LINGUISTIC PHILOSOPHY

by H. D. Lewis

This book provides samples of such criticisms, ranging from the work of fairly traditionalist thinkers to second thoughts about linguistic philosophy on the part of writers who, without having been strictly linguistic philosophers themselves, have been much influenced by this movement and know it well from within. A very rough chronological order is followed. It is hoped in this way to help the layman as well as the professional philosopher to view the course of recent philosophy in a truer perspective. A further expectation is that this venture will help the cautious return to metaphysics which seems to be on its way. For if the lessons of empiricism and linguistic philosophy (and, as Professor Price shows in the opening chapter of this book, these are considerable) are to be put effectively in the service of more venturesome constructive philosophy, the errors and limitations of linguistic philosophy, as well as its achievements, must be well understood. There will also be found in this book some hints of the constructive work which philosophers may best undertake today.

The Commonplace Book, 1919-1953

by G. E. Moore

Edited by Casimir Lewy

Few men have influenced more the thought (and, in some ways, as Keynes has well shown, the practice) of his time than Moore. He was the close associate of some of the ablest men of our day, Russell, Wittgenstein, Keynes, and several others; and among the most gifted philosophers writing now are many who acknowledge a great debt to Moore's example and to his careful, if severe, tutelage.

In the course of his life Moore filled several notebooks with carefully worded reflections, and those who did not have the benefit of close contact with him when alive may come very near to it in the selections which Dr. Lewy, himself one of Moore's pupils, has made for the present volume. The selections range from very short suggestive comments, sometimes repudiated with typical candour later, to close philosophical analysis in Moore's best vein. They cover a wide variety of topics and they reflect not only what Broad described in an obituary notice as Moore's 'immense analytic power' but also those qualities which made him, in the words of the same eminent writer, 'so exceptional and lovable a personality'. For these reasons this book should have much of interest for the layman as well as for the professional philosopher.

LONDON: GEORGE ALLEN & UNWIN LTD
NEW YORK: HUMANITIES PRESS INC